Mikal Gilmore has covered and criticized rock and roll and its related issues and culture for many national publications including the *Los Angeles Times*, *L. A. Weekly* and *Rolling Stone*. He was music editor for *L. A. Weekly* and has worked on the staff of *Rolling Stone* for twenty years, where he has profiled many cultural figures. His first book, *Shot in the Heart*, won the Los Angeles Times Book Prize, The National Book Critic Circle Award, was shortlisted for the Esquire Prize for Non-Fiction and was a New York Times Notable Book of the Year. He lives and works in Los Angeles.

night beat

A SHADOW HISTORY
OF ROCK & ROLL

Collected writings by

mikal gilmore

PICADOR

First published 1997 by Doubleday
a division of Bantam Doubleday Dell Publishing Group Inc.
1540 Broadway, New York, New York 10036

This edition first published in Great Britain 1998 by Picador
This edition published 1999 by Picador
an imprint of Macmillan Publishers Ltd
25 Eccleston Place, London SW1W 9NF
and Basingstoke

Associated companies throughout the world

ISBN 0 330 36891 5

1 3 5 7 9 8 6 4 2

A CIP catalogue record for this book is available
from the British Library.

Printed and bound in Great Britain by
Mackays of Chatham plc, Chatham, Kent

contents

contents

contents

With a daytime of sin and a nighttime of hell
Everybody's going to look for a bell to ring . . .
All through the night

LOU REED,
"ALL THROUGH THE NIGHT"

night beat

introduction

i guess I could say what many people of my age—or people who are
younger or even older—might be able to say: I grew up with popular
music encompassing my life. It played as a soundtrack for my youth. It
enhanced (sometimes created) my memories. It articulated losses, angers,
and horrible (as in *unattainable*) hopes, and it emboldened me in many,
many dark hours. It also, as much as anything else in my life, defined my
convictions and my experience of what it meant (and still means) to be an
American, and it gave me a moral (and of course immoral) guidance that
nothing else in my life ever matched, short of dreams of sheer generous love
or of sheer ruthless rapacity or destruction.

I can remember my mother playing piano, singing to me her much-
loved songs of Patsy Cline and Hank Williams, or singing an old-timey
Carter Family dirge, accompanying herself on harmonica. As I remember it,
she wasn't half-bad, though of course I'm forming that judgment through a
haze of long-ago memories and idealized longings.

It was my older brothers, though, who brought music into my house—
and into my life—in the ways that would begin to matter most. I was the
youngest of four boys; my oldest brother, Frank, was eleven years older than
I, Gary was ten years older, and Gaylen, six years older. As a result, by the
time I was four or five in the mid-1950s, my brothers were already (more or
less) teenagers—which means that they were caught in the early thrall and
explosion of rock & roll. As far back as I remember hearing anything, I
remember hearing (either on one of the house's many radios, or on my
brothers' portable phonographs) early songs by Bill Haley & His Comets,
Carl Perkins, Johnny Cash, Fats Domino, the Platters, Buddy Knox, Chuck
Berry, the Everly Brothers, Sam Cooke, and Ricky Nelson, among others. But
the biggest voice that hit my brothers' lives—the biggest voice that hit the
nation—was, of course, Elvis Presley's. In the mid-1950s, every time Presley
performed on nationwide TV (on the Milton Berle, Steve Allen, or Ed Sulli-

van shows) was an occasion for a family gathering—among the few times my family ever collected for any purpose other than to fight. Those times we sat watching Presley on our old Zenith were, in fact, among our few occasions of real shared joy. For some reason, the appearance I remember most was Elvis's 1956 performance on the Dorsey Brothers' "Stage Show" (which was also the singer's national debut, and was followed by six consecutive appearances). I remember sitting tucked next to my father in his big oversize brown leather chair. My father was not a man who was fond of youthful impudence or revolt (in fact, he was downright brutal in his efforts to shut down my brothers' rebellions). At the same time, my father *was* a man who had spent the better part of his own youth working in show business, in films and onstage and in vaudeville and the circus, and something about rock & roll's early outlandishness appealed to his show-biz biases (though his own musical tastes leaned strongly to opera and Broadway musicals). After watching Presley on that first Dorsey show, my father said: "That young man's got real talent. He's going to be around for a long time. He's the real thing." I know how cliché those remarks sound. Just to be sure my memory wasn't making it all up for me, I asked my oldest brother, Frank (who has the best memory of anybody I've ever known), if he remembered what was said after we'd watched Presley on that occasion. He repeated my father's declaration, pretty much word for word. I guess my father had a little more in common with Colonel Tom Parker than I'd like to admit, but then, like Parker, my father had also once been a hustler and bunco man.

So rock & roll as popular entertainment was welcomed into our home. Rock & roll as a model for revolt was another matter. When my brothers began to wear ducktails and leather motorcycle jackets, when they began to turn up their collars and talk flip and insolently, likely as not they got the shit beat out of them. I guess my father recognized that rock & roll, when brought into one's heart and *real* home, could breed a dislike or refusal of authority—and like so many adults and parents before and since, he could not stand that possibility without feeling shaken to the rageful and frightened core of his being.

I NEVER GOT TO HAVE my own period of rock & roll conflict with my father. He died in mid-1962, when I was eleven, when "The Twist" and "Duke of Earl" were my picks to click. Hardly songs or trends worth whipping a child until he bled.

A little over a year later, President John Kennedy was shot to death in

Dallas, Texas. It was a startling event, and it froze the nation in shock, grief, and a lingering depression. Winter nights were long that season—long, and maybe darker than usual. I was just twelve, but I remember that sense of loss that was not merely my own—a loss that seemed to fill the room of the present and the space of the future. By this time, my brothers were hardly ever home. Gary and Gaylen were either out at night on criminal, drunken, carnal activity, or in jail. My mother had the habit of going to bed early, so I stayed up late watching old horror movies, talk shows, anything I could find. I remember—in January 1964—watching Jack Paar's late night show, when he began talking about a new sensation that was sweeping England: a strange pop group called the Beatles. He showed a clip of the group that night—the first time they had been seen in America. It's a ghostly memory to me now. I don't remember what I saw in the clip's moments, but I remember I was transfixed. Weeks later, the Beatles made their first official live U.S. television appearance, on February 9, 1964, on the "Ed Sullivan Show." The date happened also to be my thirteenth birthday, and I don't think I could ever have received a better, more meaningful, more transforming gift. I won't say much here about what that appearance did to us—as a people, a nation, an emerging generation—because I'll say something about it in the pages ahead, but I'll say this: As romantic as it may sound, I knew I was seeing something very big on that night, and I felt something in my life change. In fact, I was witnessing an opening up of endless possibilities. I have a video tape of those Sullivan appearances. I watch it often and show it to others—some who have never seen those appearances before, because those shows have never been rebroadcast or reissued in their entirety (there isn't much more than a glimpse of them in *The Beatles Anthology* video series). To this day, they remain remarkable. You watch those moments and you see history opening up, from the simple (but not so simple) act of men playing their instruments and singing, and sharing a discovery with their audience of a new, youthful eminence. The long, dark Kennedy-death nights were over. There would be darker nights, for sure, to come, and rock & roll would be a part of that as well. But on *that* night, a nightmare was momentarily broken, and a new world born. Its implications have never ended, even if they no longer mean exactly what they meant in that first season.

It was obviously a great time, though it would soon become (just as obviously) a complex and scary time. It was a time when almost every new song was shared, discussed, and sorted through for everything it might hold or deliver—every secret thrill or code, every new joyous twist of sonic texture. "The House of the Rising Sun." "Stop! In the Name Of Love." "Help Me Rhonda." "Mr. Tambourine Man." "(I Can't Get No) Satisfaction." "Positively 4th Street." "Help!" "California Dreamin'." "Good Lovin'."

"When a Man Loves a Woman." "Summer in the City." "Sunshine Super-
man." "I Want You." "96 Tears." "Paint It, Black." "Over Under Sideways
Down." "Respect." "Ode to Billy Joe." "Good Vibrations." "The Letter." It
was also a time of many leaders or would-be leaders—some liberating, some
deadly. Mario Savio. Lyndon Johnson. Robert Kennedy. Julian Bond. Richard
Nixon. George Lincoln Rockwell. George Wallace. Martin Luther King, Jr.
Malcolm X. Hubert Humphrey. Eldridge Cleaver. Shirley Chisolm. Jerry
Rubin. Tom Hayden. Gloria Steinem. Abbie Hoffman. There were also the
other leaders—some who led without desire or design, but who led as surely
(and sometimes as liberatingly or as foolishly) as the political figures. The
Beatles. Bob Dylan. Mick Jagger, Brian Jones, and Keith Richards. Timothy
Leary. Jimi Hendrix. Jane Fonda. The Jefferson Airplane. Aretha Franklin.
James Brown. Marvin Gaye. Sly Stone. Jim Morrison. Charles Manson.

As you can tell from those lists, the 1960s' ideals, events, and moods
grew darker—and they did so earlier than many people would like to acknowledge. In the middle of 1967—the same season that bred what became
known as the Summer of Love in San Francisco's Haight-Ashbury, and the
same period when the Beatles summarized and apotheosized psychedelia
with *Sgt. Pepper's Lonely Hearts Club Band*—I came across an album I really
loved (still perhaps my favorite of all time): *The Velvet Underground and Nico*.
It was a record full of songs about bad losses, cold hearts, hard narcotics, and
rough, degrading sex. I took to it like a dog to water (or whatever dogs take
to). It was the first subject—in a long list—of arguments that I would enter
into with friends about rock & roll. In fact, it was my first rock & roll choice
that actually cost me some fraternity. When I was a senior in high school, I
was part of a Folk Song after-school group. We'd get together, under a
teacher's auspices, and sing our favorite folk songs—everything from "Kum
Ba Yah," "Michael Row the Boat Ashore" and "We Shall Overcome" to
"Blowin' in the Wind" and (gulp) "Puff the Magic Dragon." At one meeting,
each of us was invited to sing his or her favorite folk song. I sang Lou Reed's
"Heroin." I was never welcome back in the group.

A YEAR LATER I was out of high school, into college, not doing well. I
was going through one of my periodic funks, following one of my periodic
failed love affairs (the woman of this occasion became a born-again Christian
and married the man who impregnated her; later, she became one of the
most wildly game sexual people I've ever known or enjoyed, but that *is*

another story). In this period—the late winter of 1969 and the early winter of 1970—I was taking a lot of drugs, learning how to drink, and staying up all night until the sun rose, then I'd hit the bed (actually, the floor, which *was* my bed at the time), and finally find sleep. (Interestingly, at least to me, I returned to this pattern—the staying-up-until-sunrise-then-running-to-hide part—for the entire month in which I wrote and revised this current volume.)

By this same period, something called the "rock press" had developed: magazines like *Cheetah*, *Crawdaddy!*, and *Rolling Stone*, where one could read passionate and informed opinions and arguments about current music and, better yet, could also learn about earlier musicians who had helped make the late 1960s' and early 1970s' innovations possible—everyone from Robert Johnson, Louis Armstrong, Bessie Smith, Billie Holiday, and Duke Ellington to the Carter Family, Lotte Lenya, Miles Davis, Charles Mingus, Thelonious Monk, and Ornette Coleman (some of whom were still alive, making vital music) and countless more. As a result, the journalism (that is, the essays, rants, profiles, interviews and historical perspectives) of such writers as Ralph Gleason, Paul Williams, Greil Marcus, Jon Landau, Dave Marsh, Langdon Winner, Jonathan Cott, Lester Bangs, Paul Nelson, Nick Tosches, Robert Christgau, and Ellen Willis came to seem as exciting and meaningful to me as much of the music they were writing about—though too damn few of them for my liking were willing to stand up for the Velvet Underground and Lou Reed (Willis, Nelson, and Christgau being notable and important exceptions).

It was not until 1974 that I began writing about popular music. What made this possible was Bob Dylan's "comeback" tour (his first such American trek in eight years) with the Band. This was also a time, I should note, when I spent my days working as a counselor at a Portland, Oregon, drug abuse clinic and my nights smoking as much marijuana as I could find—a contradictory (probably hypocritical) turn of affairs, but hardly an uninteresting one. Then I saw Dylan in early 1974 (again, on the occasion of my birthday, ten years after the Beatles' debut on Ed Sullivan), and an old girlfriend suggested I write about the event for a local underground newspaper. After doing so, I never looked back. The piece, of course, was awful (at least to my eyes today), but that hardly mattered. I'd managed to put together my two greatest dreams and pleasures: writing (as a result of a love of reading) and music criticism (as a result of listening to music). When I finished that article, I knew what I wanted to do: I wanted to write about popular music—it was pretty much all I cared about as a vocation. Within a season I had quit my drug counseling job (also had cut way back on my drug intake—a connection?), and started writing for a number of local publications. I also began writing jazz reviews for *Down Beat* (jazz, by this time, had come to mean as much to me as rock & roll—a passion that isn't evident enough in this present volume), and along with the help of some good friends, I was soon editing a Portland-based magazine, *Musical Notes.* A few dreams were now active in my life.

Then those dreams turned to nightmare, to the worst horror I could imagine. I am sorry if you have already heard this story—perhaps you have—but there is no way I can finish this introduction without being honest about this particular passage in my life.

In 1976, when I was twenty-five, I began writing for *Rolling Stone.* When the magazine came along in 1967, it announced itself as a voice that might prove as fervent and intelligent as the brave new music that it dared to champion. From the time I began reading the magazine, I held a dream of someday writing for its pages. To me, that would be a way of participating in the development of the music I had come to love so much.

In the autumn of 1976, I learned that *Rolling Stone* had accepted an article of mine for publication. I was elated. Then, about a week later I learned something horrible, something that killed my elation: My older brother, Gary Gilmore, was going to be put to death by a firing squad in Utah. It didn't look like there was much that could stop it—and I didn't know if I could live with it.

A few months before, in April 1976, Gary—ten years my senior—had been paroled from the U.S. Penitentiary at Marion, Illinois, to Provo, Utah, following a fifteen-year period of often brutal incarceration, largely at Oregon State Prison. Unfortunately, Gary's new life as a free man shortly grew troubled and violent, and on a hot and desperate July night, my brother crossed a line that no one should ever come to cross: in a moment born from a life of anger and ruin, Gary murdered an innocent man—a young Mormon named Max Jensen—during a service station robbery. The next night, he murdered another innocent man—another young Mormon, Ben Bushnell, who was working as a Provo motel manager—during a second robbery. Within hours, Gary was arrested, and within days he had confessed to his crimes. The trial that followed was pretty much an open-and-shut affair: Gary was convicted of first degree murder in the shooting of Ben Bushnell, and he was sentenced to death. Given the choice of being hung or shot, Gary elected to be shot.

All this had happened before I began writing for *Rolling Stone,* and a few months later, when I *did* begin working for the magazine, I never mentioned anything about my brother or his crimes to any of my editors or fellow journalists. Only a handful of my friends knew about my strained relationship with my troubled brother. The truth is, I had put myself at a distance from the realities of Gary's life for many years; I told myself that I feared him, that I resented his violent and self-ruinous choices, that he and I did not really share the same bloodline. After Gary's killings and his subsequent death sentence, I felt grief and rage over his acts, and I also felt deep and painful humiliation: I could not believe that my brother had left his family with so much horror and shame to live with, and I could not forgive him for what he had done to the families of Max Jensen and Ben Bushnell. But in a way, the whole episode seemed more like a culmination of horror rather than its new beginning. That's because part of me believed that Gary would *never* be executed—after all, there had not been any executions in America in a decade—and that he instead would simply rot away the rest of his life in the bitter nothingness of a Utah prison. At the same time, I think another, deeper part of me always understood that Gary had been born (or at least raised) to die the death he would die.

Any hope for serenity in my life had been destroyed. Shortly after I heard about Gary's wish to be executed, I told my editor at *Rolling Stone,* Ben Fong-Torres, about my relationship with Gary. By this time, Gary Gilmore was a daily name in nationwide headlines, and I felt that the magazine had a right to know that I was his brother. Fong-Torres, who had lost a brother of his own through violence, was extremely sympathetic and supportive during the period that followed, and eventually he gave me the opportunity to write about my experience of Gary's execution for the magazine. To be honest, not everybody at *Rolling Stone* back in early 1977 thought it was such a great idea to run that article ("A Death in the Family," March 10, 1977), and I could understand their misgivings: After all, what would be the point of publishing what might appear to be one man's apology for his murderous and suicidal brother? Still, following the turmoil of Gary's death, I needed to find a way to express the devastation that I had just gone through, or else I might never be able to climb out of that devastation. With the help of Fong-Torres and fellow editors Barbara Downey and Sarah Lazin, a fairly decent and honest piece of first-person journalism was created, and in the process a significant portion of my sanity and hope were salvaged. More important, perhaps the people who read it got a glimpse into the reality of living at the center of an unstoppable national nightmare.

In the season that followed Gary's death, I went to work for *Rolling Stone* full-time in Los Angeles. It wasn't an easy period for me—I felt displaced, and (once again) was drinking too much and taking too many pills—but the magazine gave me plenty of slack; maybe more than I deserved. As time went along, I began to find some of my strength and purpose again as a music writer, and *Rolling Stone* gave me the opportunity to meet and write about some of the people whose music and words had mattered most in my life. It was also a season in which I spent many nights lost in the dark and brilliant splendor of punk. I liked the way the music confronted its listeners with the reality of our merciless age. Punk, as much as anything, saved my soul in those years, and gave me cause for hope—which is perhaps a funny thing to say about a movement (or experiment) that's first premise was: there are no simple hopes that are not false or at least suspect.

I WROTE FOR *Rolling Stone* from 1976 until the present—sometimes as a staff writer, sometimes as a contributor. In the years after 1979, I also wrote for *Musician* and the *Los Angeles Times* briefly, and in the early 1980s I was (for a year or so) the music editor at the *L.A. Weekly*. In the autumn of 1982, I became the pop music critic of the (now defunct) *Los Angeles Herald Examiner*, where I worked until 1987. For the first two or three years, the *Herald* was a sublime place to write; it was a paper that allowed writers to find and exercise their own voice, sometimes at great length (I'm afraid I became a bit long-winded during that period, but brevity has rarely been my strong suit). Then, sometime in 1985, a new managing editor came in to the paper—a self-described "neo-conservative." I've never shared much affinity with conservatives of any variety (I'm pretty much an American leftist and have not been shy nor apologetic about that leaning). In August 1985, I reviewed a live performance by Sting for the *Herald*. Sting wasn't a performer or songwriter I liked much—that was plain from my review—but I admired two things about his music at that time: his willingness to attempt adventurous, swing-inflected pop with a band that included saxophonist Branford Marsalis, and his acuity about the realities of mid-1980s, Margaret Thatcher-defined British politics. I was particularly taken by his performance of a song called "We Work the Black Seams," and I wrote the following about it:

> "We Work the Black Seams" . . . was perhaps Sting's only
> serious statement that wasn't saved solely by the prowess of his
> band, as well as the only one that didn't need saving. In part,
> that's because with its lulling arpeggios and mellifluent chorus it
> is the one song in Sting's new batch that is most like his Police
> material. But there's more to it than that: It is also the one song

uttered from outside Sting's usual above-it-all perspective—a song
told from the view of a British coal miner faced with the uncaring
determinism of his government. In order to tell his tale . . .
Sting climbs down deep inside the place and conditions where the
character lives: He is aware that the fate of the miner's
professions—and therefore the future economy of his class—has
already been irrevocably shut off, and so he sings his account in a
tired and resigned voice, but also with a dark, deadly, righteous
sense of pain and anger: "Our blood has stained the coal/We
tunneled deep inside the nation's soul/We matter more than
pounds and pence/Your economic theory makes no sense."

The *Herald*'s new editor was not pleased to read such sentiments in his
paper. He sent a message to me via another editor: "Rock & roll is music
about and for teenagers. Write about it from *that* point of view." I ignored the
warning—in fact, I stepped up my politics—which meant that soon my life
at the *Herald* was hell. I wasn't alone. I watched the paper's managerial
structure drive some of its best writers out of the company. The managers
believed, I was later told, that it was perhaps the writers' affections for style
and point of view that was costing the paper its readers (and hell, maybe they
were even right).

I left the *Herald Examiner* in 1987, but by that time I was badly disillusioned. Plus I was going through another of my end-of-the-world romantic
aftermaths. I wasn't sure I wanted to remain a writer—but what else did I
know how to do? A sympathetic friend and editor at *Rolling Stone*, James
Henke, gave me a series of assignments. I remember *hating* writing each of
them. All I wanted to do was sulk and drink and hate some more. Still, I had
bills to pay. Looking back, I see how those assignments helped save me and
also taught me some invaluable lessons: one, that summoning the will to
write—even at the worst points in my life—meant I had an inner strength
that was invaluable and that I should trust; two, that I had not yet lost my
love for popular music and its meanings and how it mattered to its audiences. Plus, I realized it still mattered to *me*—that is, it still helped me.
Popular music, all said and done, was among the best friends—and one of
the few real confidants—I'd ever known in my life. Whereas you could talk
to and confide and hope and trust in a lover, that lover might still leave
or betray you. A great song, by contrast, would talk *to you*—and its
truths would *never* betray you. At 3 A.M., outside of the greatest and most
sinful sex, there was nothing that could mean as much as a pop song
that told you secrets about your own fucked-up and yearning
heart.

A FEW YEARS AGO, after the publication of *Shot in the Heart* (a story about my family's generational history of violence), I received several letters from readers asking me to compile some of my earlier writings for publication. I didn't much like the idea. I thought my pop writing was too disjointed and had covered too much musical stylistic terrain to work in any cohesive volume. Also, I'd just finished a book about looking back at my past. I wasn't anxious to start another—especially since reading my old writings always made my skin crawl. Instead, I preferred to write my own original history about rock & roll's epic patterns of disruption, but that idea didn't excite most of the people I talked to. After all, it was a season when pundits like Allan Bloom and William Bennett could write depthless and malicious indictments of popular culture and achieve fame and success for doing so. A history (and defense) of rock's agitation did not prove an appealing idea to some people.

Then, following an article I wrote for *Rolling Stone* in 1996 about the death of Timothy Leary, I again received requests for a collection of writings. I felt a little more receptive to the idea by that time, because I knew I had a handful of articles I'd like to have enjoy a second (if only brief) life. At first, though, the process of selecting those articles was not fun. I'm a big believer that one should *never* read too much of one's own writing; you begin to see all the repetitions, all the flaws. A week into the project, I felt like bailing out. Also, I'd written so much about some subjects—such as Bob Dylan, Lou Reed, punk, and Bruce Springsteen—that I wasn't sure which piece (or pieces) to pick as the most representative.

Then one morning, about 2 A.M. (my favorite hour—that is, next to 3 A.M.), I came to understand something that should have been apparent all along: Without realizing it, I had been writing my own version of a rock & roll history for over a generation. I began to see how I could collect some of my preferred (at least to my tastes) writings, yet also refashion them to construct an outline, a shadow, of rock & roll history—and that is what I have tried to do here. This is not, of course, a proper history of rock & roll; there is far too much that is not addressed in this book as widely as it should be (including blues, punk, jazz, and hip-hop—all of which have been great adventures that have made rock & roll count for even more). Instead, I've tried to construct a volume out of a mix of personal touchstones (Bob Dylan, John Lydon, Lou Reed, and others), interview encounters (such as the Clash, Sinéad O'Connor, Miles Davis, and Keith Jarrett), and a sampling of critical indulgences (Feargal Sharkey and Marianne Faithfull's "Trouble in Mind," among the latter). Some of these pieces are printed here pretty close to their original published form, but most have been revised, reassembled, rewritten, or newly thought out. The Bob Dylan chapter, for example, includes elements from over twenty-three years of articles I've written about Dylan, plus many new passages.

I've tried to put it all together in an orderly way that might make for a story arc of sorts, from Elvis Presley's invention and weird fame to Kurt Cobain, and the horrible costs of *his* inventions and weird fame. "A STARTING PLACE: A JULY AFTERNOON," is about Elvis, where it all begins—or at least where it began in my own life. "Setting Out for the Territories" is about the people who took Elvis's possibilities and expanded them—the obvious folks: the Beatles, Bob Dylan, and the Rolling Stones; in this section, the story moves from the 1950s to the 1960s. "Remaking the Territories" is more or less about what happened in the 1970s (with the exception of disco, which is addressed in the following section). These are stories about people who began to expand and remake rock—sometimes with wonderful and sometimes horrible results. "Dreams and Wars" is largely about what happened in the 1980s, as rock (again) took on the powers that be—or actually, the other way around: the powers that be took on rock & roll, in big, bold, ugly ways. This section forms the story (in my mind) of some of what rock means in America and what it has said about the nation, its promises, betrayals, and politics; what Americans think of rock & roll in return; how dance music and heavy metal and rap work and *matter* for their audiences; and how moralists have tried to shut the whole thing down. There's also a Michael Jackson chapter in this section, because it's the best place for it and after a while, Jackson too became part of the problem. "Lone Voices" is a section about people (some well known, some obscure) who made lone and brave choices and music in the 1980s and 1990s. Finally, "Endings" is exactly what its title proclaims: stories about how some people lived and died, in both their music and their lives.

IT IS NOW 1997, as I write this. I am a forty-six-year-old man. I still spend far too many post-midnights listening to new and old loved music. (And far too often hear from my girlfriend: "Could you *please* turn that down *just a little*? And *when* are you coming to bed?") I still love popular music—from Robert Johnson, Billie Holiday, Louis Armstrong, and Frank

Sinatra to Nine Inch Nails, Marilyn Manson, Tupac Shakur, and (still and always) Bob Dylan—above all other twentieth-century popular culture forms.

And yet there is something about today's music that bothers me terribly—or to be more accurate, about today's music business. I am troubled by the way the music industry (and not just major corporate labels, but also numerous independent outfits) sign or record artists for what these labels see as a certain sound, quirk, style, nuance, niche, or whatever—and are loathe to allow those artists to expand or develop much beyond that one *thing*. That is partly why we see so many one-hit wonders—or one moment wonders— whether it's Green Day, Cowboy Junkies, the Offspring, Faith No More, or (I'm willing to bet, though maybe I'm being unkind) Alanis Morissette. These artists are milked, drained, toured, and discarded before they even have a shot at a second round. It's a new kind of pop hegemony—a blockbuster hegemony, not at all unlike the blockbuster mentality that has made so much modern film tiresome, predictable and limited. As much as I'm not a real fan of U2, R.E.M., or Pearl Jam, I admire the way they resist being stratified, directed, or contained.

Still, I don't want to sound like a grumbler or somebody who has lost faith. Pop music hegemony is nothing new. The industry loves it, seeks it— that is, until somebody *shatters* the security of that dominance: somebody like Elvis Presley, the Beatles, the Sex Pistols, Nirvana, N.W.A. Then, the industry goes off in search of artists who can parlay all the new dissidence and invention into yet *another* newer, hipper, profitable version of dominance. It's maddening, but it's also fine—sometimes, in fact, it's great fun. That's the way things work. Somebody makes a moment or career out of sundering the known order and sound, and then the industry and culture try to make that act of sundering into a model for mass commodity. I'm not sure it's entirely bad—if only because it guarantees that, come tomorrow, somebody else, somebody new and wonderful and daring and deadly, will have something to disrupt and displace, to the pleasure and outrage of many.

Besides, for all the inevitable corporate appropriation that goes on in popular music, rock & roll and hip-hop still face much more serious problems and enemies: All those folks like William Bennett, C. DeLores Tucker, Newt Gingrich, Bob Dole, and (I hate to admit it since I voted for the fuckers twice) Bill Clinton and Al Gore, who *still* blame rock & roll for social problems, and who still refuse to acknowledge their own hand in lining the "bridge to the twenty-first century" with some deadly potholes. I am glad that popular music continues to seem like a risk and threat to those people, and I am glad it still seems like an opportunity and voice for liberation (and offense) for others. I am also immensely thankful that I was allowed to come of age in an historical moment—that is, to "grow up"—when rock & roll made some bold and upsetting advances, and I am thrilled with the realization that I will "grow old" with music that will continue to do the same.

That's why, today and tomorrow, I'll look to artists like Trent Reznor, Marilyn Manson, Wu-Tang Clan, Tricky, Prodigy, Bikini Kill, Fluffy, and Sleater-Kinney, as well as Bob Dylan (and Jakob Dylan, for that matter) and Lou Reed, for the kind of courage, insight, and beautiful violation that have made rock & roll such a great adventure and such a great disturbance in our culture, our arts, and our values. Without these artists, and others like them, the future won't count for as much as the past—and all tomorrow's nighttimes of sin might not be as illuminating.

MIKAL GILMORE
MARCH 17, 1997
LOS ANGELES

PART 1

a

starting

place:

a july

afternoon

elvis presley's

leap

for freedom

It was a typically heat-thick July day in 1954 in Memphis—a city steeped in raw blues and country traditions. Sam Phillips—a local producer who recorded such bluesmen as Howlin' Wolf, Bobby "Blue" Bland, B. B. King, and Walter Horton at the beginning of their careers for Chess Records, and had started his own fledgling hillbilly label, Sun—had been working steadily for months with a nineteen-year-old, long-haired, bop-wise kid, both of them groping for some uncertain mingling of black credibility and white style. Phillips and the kid—Elvis Presley, who had a startling musical aptitude and a first-hand flair for the blues—understood that hillbilly and black music forms were on the verge of a pop-mainstream breakthrough. Both men were ambitious enough to dream of spearheading that change; one was daring enough to turn his ambition into a hook for generational rebellion, though he probably saw it as little more than an act of impulsive swagger.

What happened that afternoon was both hoped for and totally unexpected, and comes as close to a real myth-producing event as pop culture has yielded since the unreal flight of Huckleberry Finn. By all accounts it was a casual occurrence. Presley was in the Sun studio with guitarist Scotty Moore and bassist Bill Black, working up some country numbers for the heck of it, trying to get a feel for throwing a song on tape with enough life to bounce back. The impromptu band took a break and Presley impulsively began playing the fool—the most acceptable guise for his inventive verve. He fell into an Arthur "Big Boy" Crudup song, "That's All Right," and the rest of the band fell in behind. Elvis turned the moment's frolic into a vaulting exercise in rhythm and unconstraint, and Phillips, working in a nearby room, recognized that it was something to be captured. He had the band reenact the moment, and under that impetus, Presley turned his performance into a grasp for freedom, quite unlike anything else in American pop history.

The record of that performance—with a hepped-up version of the bluegrass standard, "Blue Moon of Kentucky," on the flipside—made Presley an immediate local hillbilly star, though many listeners reacted to the music with immediate shock and anger. (By September he was playing the Grand Ole Opry, where he was ridiculed.) No matter. A year later, Presley was on the national charts, still being slotted as a hillbilly cat. Six months after that he was the most famous and controversial figure in America—an unstoppable force who served to reshape the pop mainstream (making black and hillbilly music not just imminent but dominant), and who almost single-handedly redefined what it meant to be an American visionary, an American artist, in a fierce new time. No other modern legend was to be so widely damned at first as a threat or joke, only later to be understood as one of our purest, most commonly acclaimed heroes.

NOW, THESE MANY YEARS later, it is almost impossible to consider the subject of Elvis Presley without giving ground to the demands of myth and hyperbole. Perhaps that's the way it should be. Presley is one of the few American post–World War II heroes who remains largely undisclosed by the particulars of his "real" life—he seems no more knowable for all that has been learned about his private reality. Was Presley, as writer Albert Goldman charged in his lurid anti-Southern, anti-indigent, anti-rock biography of the singer, a vile womanizer and overgorged drug abuser, a crass rube unworthy of his fans? The answer—at least in part—might well be yes. Does this knowledge somehow diminish the value of the singer's influence or the verity of his importance? The answer, this time, resoundingly, is no. As Presley biographer and critic Dave Marsh has commented, "You don't need to be a great man to be a great artist," an acknowledgment that, in the passage from untidy truth to exalted myth, certain artists and celebrities earn their shot at transfiguring our culture, and maybe our lives to boot, regardless of their character lapses.

Of course, there's an equally unnerving truth to be faced here: Simply, that great art isn't exactly the vindication for a life or career poorly lived—that great art, in fact, doesn't necessarily exonerate the person behind the art or bring us any closer to the real experience of that person's life. Thus, after a point, after his impact was enough to change the course—indeed, the meaning and reach—of popular culture, Presley's art no longer stood for or belonged solely to him: It also became whatever we made (and remade) of it. That is why his effect remains so overpowering forty-four years after his initial explosion of fame, and a generation after his pitiable death.

And yet the irony of all this is that Presley himself—possibly the one figure more people in contemporary American pop history have agreed on than any other (have lovingly elected as hero, leader, saint, cynosure)—stays as elusive as he is enticing. Some of us delve in to his sexual and religious preoccupations as a way of comprehending or "knowing" him; others pore over the minutiae of his music. It's as if we expect something to fall into place one of these days, expect to learn whether this young iconoclast turned fallen nighthawk and wretched glutton was really a bunco man, fool, traitor, conqueror, or simply one of our greatest involuntary democrats. The true object, though, of this delving is always our wayward selves: Somewhere along the line, some of us feel, we mislaid something by loving Presley—that when he lost touch with his own sublime fire, some shared joy dropped into the darkness and was never fully recovered. By looking for Presley, we are hunting after the terrible mystery of how many of us lose our dreams yet keep our power. Consequently, we may want—or need—more from the singer now than we did that July afternoon over forty years ago when Elvis Presley made a unique reach for fame and liberation that had the effect of making rock & roll a transformative—no doubt unstoppable—national fact.

WITH THE IMPORTANT exception of Martin Luther King, Jr., no other activist or popular hero has better defined the meaning, potential, and shortcomings of the modern American birthright—no other figure has mixed the ambitions and risks of American myth so promisingly—as Elvis Presley. He defined revolt, aspiration, opulence, humility, pettiness, generosity, frivolity, significance, prodigy, waste, renewal, corruption, dissolution, and a kind posthumous transcendence. He did it all without design, with little more than intuition and nerve, and interestingly, he accomplished it with only the assertive mix of his own raw talent and provoking personality. He did not perform as a "creative" force *per se*—a songwriter or pop philosopher—but as a man of deeds, action, and experience.

This may not seem so much when compared with the work of such musical figures as Louis Armstrong, Robert Johnson, Billie Holiday, Duke

Ellington, Charlie Parker, Hank Williams, Miles Davis, Ornette Coleman, Bob Dylan, Jerry Garcia, Duane Allman, Sly Stone, Marvin Gaye, Randy Newman, or Bruce Springsteen. One could claim that all of these artists made lasting legacies out of personal vision and defined themselves as much by their thought and work—their creative invention—as their personality. In a certain way, perhaps all are greater artists than Presley. That is, they are all folks who wrestled with the meaning of their place in American society with uncommon self-awareness, who expressed their discoveries, doubts, and inventions with exceptional (if only sometimes instinctive) understandings of the state of the culture around them, who could apply a full-fledged sense of history and tradition to modern styles and predicaments—which is something that Presley only managed occasionally. For that matter, one might infer that whatever sense of culture, history and politics the singer did possess was, as often as not, depressingly uninformed—and one might even be right.

And yet Elvis opened more doors, bounded into the unknown with a greater will to adventure than those other artists, and that is why, all these years later, we still remember him with a special thrill. Without Presley as an exemplar, rock & roll may have proved less of a lasting force because it may also have proved less alluring: It was the idea that any of us could grow up to be like Presley—rather than we could grow up to be like James Dean, Marlon Brando, J. D. Salinger, Norman Mailer, John F. Kennedy, Ronald Reagan, a soldier or an astronaut—that made rock the most vital of our national assets this last near-half century. Better than anybody but Martin Luther King, Jr., Presley personified and stylized the modern American quest for freedom, experience, and opportunity. Chances are, we will be enjoying (or recoiling from) the aftereffect of his exploits for many years to come.

If one accepts Elvis Presley as the definitional American modernizer, and rock & roll as the primary postwar art form, then it is interesting to examine rock (and not just American rock) for how well its successors have made good on Presley's promise: That is, after the call to freedom has been sounded, what's next? How does one raise the stakes, expand the territory? In some ways, that is the main question that the rest of this book will try to explore, though no volume can yet be close to providing final answers.

PART 2

setting

out

for the

territories

beatles

then,

beatles

now

In the 1950s, rock & roll meant disruption: It was the clamor of young people, kicking hard against the Eisenhower era's public ethos of vapid repression. By the outset of the 1960s, that spirit had been largely tamed, or simply impeded by numerous misfortunes, including Elvis Presley's film and army careers; the death of Buddy Holly; the blacklisting of Jerry Lee Lewis and Chuck Berry; and the persecution of D.J. Alan Freed, who had been stigmatized on payola charges by Tin Pan Alley interests and politicians, angered by his championing of R&B and rock & roll. To be sure, pop still had its share of rousing voices and trends—among them musicians like Ray Charles and James Brown, who were rapidly transforming R&B into a more aggressive and soulful form—but clearly, there had been a tilt: In 1960, the music of Frankie Avalon, Paul Anka, Connie Francis, and Mitch Miller (an avowed enemy of rock & roll) ruled the airwaves and the record charts, giving some observers the notion that decency and order had returned to the popular mainstream. But within a few years, rock would regain its disruptive power with a joyful vengeance, until by the decade's end it would be seen as a genuine force of cultural and political consequence. For a remarkable season, it was a widely held truism—or threat, depending on your point of view— that rock & roll could (and *should*) make a difference: that it was eloquent and inspiring and principled enough to change the world—maybe even save it.

How did such a dramatic development take place? How did rock & roll come to be seen as such a potent voice for cultural revolution?

In part, of course, it was simply a confluence of auspicious conditions and ambitious prodigies that would break things open. Or, if you prefer a more romantic or mythic view, you could simply say that rock & roll had set something loose in the 1950s—a spirit of cultural abandon—that could not be stopped or refused, and you might even be right. Certainly, rock & roll had demonstrated that it was capable of inspiring massive generational and social ferment, and that its rise could even have far-reaching political consequences. That is, admiring and buying the music of Elvis Presley not only raised issues of sex and age and helped stylize new customs of youth revolt, but also inevitably advanced the cause of racial tolerance, if not social equality. This isn't to say that to enjoy Presley or rock & roll was the same as subscribing to liberal politics, nor is it to suggest that the heroism of R&B and rock musicians was equal to that of civil rights campaigners like Martin Luther King, Jr., Medgar Evers, or Rosa Parks, who paid through pain, humiliation, and blood for their courage. But rock & roll *did* present black musical forms—and consequently black sensibilities and black causes—to a wider (and whiter) audience than ever before, and as a result, it drove a fierce, threatening wedge into the heart of the American musical mainstream.

By the 1960s, though, as the sapless Eisenhower years were ending and the brief, lusty Kennedy era was forming, a new generation was coming of age. The parents of this generation had worked and fought for ideals of peace, security, and affluence, and they expected their children not merely to appreciate or benefit from this bequest, but also to affirm and extend their prosperous new world. But the older generation was also passing on legacies of fear and some unfinished obligations—anxieties of nuclear obliteration and ideological difference, and sins of racial violence—and in the rush to stability, priceless ideals of equality and justice had been compromised, even lost. Consequently, the children of this age—who would forever be dubbed the "baby boom generation"—were beginning to question the morality and politics of postwar America, and some of their musical tastes began to reflect this unrest. In particular, folk music—led by Peter, Paul, and Mary; Joan Baez; and, in particular, Bob Dylan—was gaining a new credibility and popularity, as well as an important moral authority. It spoke for a world that *should be*, and it was stirring many young people to commit themselves to social activism, especially regarding the cause of civil rights. But for all its egalitarian ideals, folk was a music of past and largely spent traditions. As such, it was also the medium for an alliance of politicos and intelligentsia that viewed a teen-rooted, mass entertainment form like rock & roll with derision. The new generation had not yet found a style or standard-bearer that could tap the temper of the times in the same way that Presley and rockabilly had accomplished in the 1950s.

WHEN ROCK & ROLL'S rejuvenation came, it was from a place small and unlikely, and far away. Indeed, in the early 1960s, Liverpool, England, was a fading port town that had slid from grandeur to dilapidation during the postwar ear, and it had come to be viewed by snobbish Londoners as a demeaned place of outsiders—in a class-conscious land that was itself increasingly an outsider in modern political affairs and popular culture. But one thing Liverpool had was a brimming pop scene, made up of bands playing tough and exuberant blues- and R&B-informed rock & roll.

One Saturday morning back in 1961, a young customer entered a record store called NEMS, "The Finest Record Store in Liverpool," on Whitechapel, a busy road in the heart of the city's stately commercial district. The young man asked store manager Brian Epstein for a new single, "My Bonnie," by the Beatles. Epstein replied that he had never heard of the record—indeed, had never heard of the group, which he took to be an obscure, foreign pop group. The customer, Raymond Jones, pointed out the front window, across Whitechapel, where Stanley Street juts into a murky-looking alley area. Around that corner, he told Epstein, on a smirched lane known as Mathew Street, the Beatles—perhaps the most popular of Liverpudlian rock & roll groups—performed afternoons at a cellar club, the Cavern. A few days later, prompted by more requests, Epstein made that journey around Stanley onto Mathew and down the dank steps into the Cavern. With that odd trudge, modern pop culture turned its most eventful corner. By October 1962, Brian Epstein was the Beatles' manager, and the four-piece ensemble had broken into Britain's Top 20 with a folkish rock song, "Love Me Do." There was little about the single that heralded greatness—the group's leaders, John Lennon and Paul McCartney, weren't yet distinguished songwriters—but nonetheless the song began a momentum that would forever shatter the American grip on the U.K. pop charts.

In many ways, Britain was as ripe for a pop cataclysm as America had been for Presley during the ennui after world war. In England—catching the reverberations of not just Presley, but the jazz milieu of Miles Davis and Jack Kerouac—the youth scene had acquired the status of a mammoth subcultural class: the by-product of a postwar population, top-heavy with people under the age of eighteen. For those people, pop music denoted more than preferred entertainment or even stylistic rebellion: It signified the idea of autonomous society. British teenagers weren't just rejecting their parents' values—they were superseding them, though they were also acting out their eminence in American terms—in the music of Presley and rockabilly; in blues and jazz tradition.

When Brian Epstein first saw the Beatles at the Cavern, he saw not only a band who delivered their American obsessions with infectious verve but also reflected British youth's joyful sense of being cultural outsiders, ready to seize everything new, and everything that their surrounding society tried to prohibit them. What's more, Epstein figured that the British pop scene would recognize and seize on this kinship. As the group's manager, Epstein cleaned up the Beatles' punkness considerably, but he didn't deny the group its spirit or musical instincts, and in a markedly short time, his faith paid off. A year after "Love Me Do" peaked at number 17 in the *New Musical Express* charts, the Beatles had six singles active in the Top 20 in the same week, including the top three positions—an unprecedented and still unduplicated feat. In the process, Lennon and McCartney had grown enormously as writers—in fact, they were already one of the best composing teams in pop history—and the group itself had upended the local pop scene, establishing a hierarchy of long-haired male ensembles, playing a popwise but hard-bashing update of '50s-style rock & roll. But there was more to it than mere pop success: The Beatles were simply the biggest explosion England had witnessed in modern history, short of war. In less than a year, they had transformed British pop culture—had redefined not only its intensities and possibilities, but had turned it into a matter of nationalistic impetus.

Then, on February 9, 1964, following close on the frenzied breakthrough of "I Saw Her Standing There" and "I Want to Hold Your Hand," TV variety-show kingpin Ed Sullivan presented the Beatles for the first time to a mass American audience, and it proved to be an epochal moment. The Sullivan appearance drew over 70 million viewers—the largest TV audience ever, at that time—an event that cut across divisions of style and region, and drew new divisions of era and age; an event that, like Presley, made rock & roll seem an irrefutable opportunity. Within days it was apparent that not just pop style but a whole dimension of youth society had been recast—that a genuine upheaval was under way, offering a frenetic distraction to the dread that had set into America after the assassination of President John F. Kennedy, and a renewal of the brutally wounded ideal that youthfulness carried our national hope. Elvis Presley had shown us how rebellion could be fashioned into eye-opening style; the Beatles were showing us how style could take on the impact of cultural revelation—or at least how a pop vision might be forged into an unimpeachable consensus. Virtually overnight, the Beatles' arrival in the American consciousness announced that not only the music and times were changing, but that *we* were changing as well. Everything about the band—its look, sound, style, and abandon—made plain that we were entering a different age, that young people were free to redefine themselves in completely new terms.

All of which raises an interesting question: Would the decade's pop and youth scenes have been substantially different without the Beatles? Or were the conditions such that, given the right catalyst, an ongoing pop explosion was inevitable? Certainly other bands (including the Shadows, the Dave Clark Five, the Searchers, the Zombies, Gerry and the Pacemakers, and Manfred Mann) contributed to the sense of an emerging scene, and yet others (among them the Kinks, the Who, the Animals, the Rolling Stones, and—especially—Bob Dylan) would make music just as vital, and more aggressive (and sometimes smarter and more revealing) than that of the Beatles. Yet the Beatles had a singular gift that transcended even their malleable sense of style, or John Lennon and Paul McCartney's genius as songwriters and arrangers, or Brian Epstein and producer George Martin's unerring stewardship as devoted mentors. Namely, the Beatles possessed an almost impeccable flair for rising to the occasion of their own moment in history, for honoring the promise of their own talents—and this knack turned out to be the essence, the heart, of their artistry. The thrill and momentum wouldn't fade for several years; the music remained a constant surprise and delight, the band, continually transfixing and influential, as both their work and presence intensified our lives. In the end, only their own conceits, conflicts, ambitions, and talents served as decisive boundaries.

In short, the Beatles were a rupture—they changed modern history—and no less a visionary than Bob Dylan understood the meaning of their advent. "They were doing things nobody else was doing. . . . ," he later told biographer Anthony Scaduto. "But I just kept it to myself that I really dug them. Everybody else thought they were just for the teenyboppers, that they were gonna pass right away. But it was obvious to me that they had staying power. I knew they were pointing the direction that music had to go. . . . It seemed to me a definite line was being drawn. This was something that never happened before."

THE BEATLES, of course, were hardly alone in transforming the 1960s' pop soundscape. Bob Dylan—inspired by the Beatles' creativity, freedom, and impact—moved on to electric music in 1965, to the outrage of the folk community though also to an incalculable benefit for rock & roll. The Rolling Stones—whose pop careers the Beatles helped make possible (in fact, Lennon and McCartney wrote the band's first hit single, "I Wanna Be Your Man")—were already impressing nervous adults as being a bit repellent for the obvious sexual implications of a song like "(I Can't Get No) Satisfaction." And there was much more: Some of the most pleasurable and enduring music of the 1960s was being made by the monumental black-run Detroit label, Motown—which had scored over two dozen Top 10 hits by 1965 alone, by such artists as Smokey Robinson and the Miracles, the Supremes, Marvin Gaye, Stevie Wonder, the Temptations, Martha and the Vandellas, Mary Wells, and the Four Tops. By contrast, a grittier brand of the new soul sensibility was being defined by Memphis-based Volt, Stax, and Atlantic artists like Sam and Dave, Booker T. and the MGs, Wilson Pickett, Carla and Rufus Thomas, Johnnie Taylor, Eddie Floyd, James Carr and William Bell, and most memorably, Otis Redding. In other words, black forms remained vital to rock and pop's growth (in fact, R&B's codes, styles, and spirit had long served as models for white pop and teen rebellion—especially for the young Beatles and Rolling Stones), and as racial struggles continued through the decade, soul—as well as the best jazz from artists like Miles Davis, John Coltrane, Eric Dolphy, Ornette Coleman, Archie Shepp, Cecil Taylor, and Sonny Rollins—increasingly expressed black culture's developing views of pride, identity, history, and power. By 1967, when Aretha Franklin scored with a massive hit cover of Otis Redding's "Respect," black pop was capable of signifying ideals of racial pride and feminist valor that would have been unthinkable a decade earlier.

Yet perhaps the greatest triumph of the time was simply that, for a long and glorious season, *all* these riches—white invention and black genius— played alongside one another in a radio marketplace that was more open than it had ever been before (or would ever be again), for a shared audience that revered it all. Just how heady and diverse the scene was came across powerfully in the 1965 film *The T.A.M.I. Show*—a greatest-hits pop revue that, in its stylistic and racial broadmindedness, anticipated the would-be catholic spirit that later characterized the Monterey Pop and Woodstock festivals. For those few hours, as artists like the Supremes, Beach Boys, Chuck Berry, Smokey Robinson and the Miracles, Marvin Gaye, Jan and Dean,

James Brown, and the Rolling Stones stood alongside one another onstage at the Santa Monica Civic Auditorium, rock & roll looked and felt like a dizzying, rich, complex, and joyous community, in which any celebration or redemption was possible.

IN ONE WAY or another, this longing for community—the dream of self-willed equity and harmony, or at least tolerant pluralism in a world where familiar notions of family and accord were breaking down—would haunt rock's most meaningful moments for the remainder of the decade. Unfortunately, the same forces that would deepen and expand the music's social-mindedness—that would make rock the most publicly felt or consumed part of an actively self-defining counterculture—were also the forces that would contribute to the dissolution of that dream. In 1965, after waging the most successful "peace" campaign in America's electoral history, President Lyndon B. Johnson began actively committing American troops to a highly controversial and deadly military action in Vietnam, and it quickly became apparent that it was the young who would pay the bloodiest costs for this horrible war effort. Sixties rock had given young people a sense that they possessed not just a new identity but also a new empowerment. Now, Vietnam began to teach that same audience that it was at *risk,* that its government and parents would willingly sacrifice young lives for old fears and distant threats—and would even use war as a means of diffusing youth's new sovereignty. The contrast between those two realizations—between power and peril, between joy and fear—became the central tension that defined late '60s youth culture, and as rock reflected that tension more, it also began forming oppositions to the jeopardy.

Consequently, the music started losing its "innocence." The Beatles still managed to maintain a facade of effervescence in the sounds of albums like *Beatles for Sale, Help,* and even *Rubber Soul,* but the content of the songs had turned more troubled. It was as if the group had lost a certain mooring. Lennon was singing more frequently about alienation and apprehension, McCartney about the unreliability of love—and whereas their earlier music had fulfilled the familiar structures of 1950s rock, their newer music was moving into unaccustomed areas and incorporating strange textures. Primarily, though, the band was growing fatigued from a relentless schedule of touring, writing, and recording. Following the imbroglio that resulted from Lennon's assertion that the Beatles were more popular than Jesus, and after one last dispirited 1966 swing through America (in which they were unable to play their more adventurous new material), the Beatles called a formal quits to live performances. Also, it was becoming evident that youth culture (especially its "leaders": pop stars) were starting to come under fire for flouting conventional tastes and morals. Mick Jagger, Keith Richards, and Brian Jones of the Rolling Stones were arrested for drug possession in a series of 1967 busts in London, and were pilloried by the British press and legal system. "I'm not concerned with your petty morals which are illegitimate," Richards bravely (or perhaps foolishly) told a court official at his trial—and it was plain that generational tensions were heating up into a full-fledged cultural war.

Maybe these developments should have been received as harbingers of dissolution, but the vision of rock as a unifying and liberating force had become too exciting, too deep-seated, to be denied. By this time rock & roll was plainly youth style, and youth was forming alternative communities and political movements throughout Europe and America. In the Haight-Ashbury district of San Francisco, something approaching utopia seemed to be happening. Bands like the Jefferson Airplane, Grateful Dead, Quicksilver Messenger Service, Big Brother and the Holding Company, and the Charlatans were forming social bonds with the same audiences they were playing for, and were trying to build a working communal ethos (and social redemption) from a swirling mix of music, drugs, sex, metaphysics, and idealistic love.

In mid 1967, after a year-long hiatus, the Beatles helped raise this worldview from the margins to worldwide possibility with the release of *Sgt. Pepper's Lonely Hearts Club Band*—a cohesive, arty, and brilliant work that tapped perfectly the collective generational mood of the times, and that reestablished the foursome's centrality to rock's power structure. It wasn't that the Beatles had invented the psychedelic or avant-garde aesthetic that their new music epitomized—in fact, its spacey codes and florid textures and arrangements had been clearly derived from the music of numerous innovative San Francisco and British bands. But with *Sgt. Pepper*, they managed to refine what these other groups had been groping for, and they did so in a way that unerringly manifested the sense of independence and iconoclasm that now seized youth culture. At the album's end, John Lennon sang "A Day in the Life"—the loveliest-sounding song about alienation that pop had ever yielded—and then all four Beatles hit the same loud, lingering, portentous chord on four separate pianos. As that chord lingered and then faded, it bound up an entire culture in its mysteries, its implications, its sense of power and hope. In some ways, it was the most magical moment that culture would ever share, and the last gesture of genuine unity that we would ever hear from the Beatles.

Sgt. Pepper was an era-defining and form-busting work. To many, it certified that rock was now art and that art was, more than ever, a mass medium. It also established the primacy of the album as pop's main format—as a vehicle for fully-formed conceptual ventures and as the main means by which rock artists communicated their truths (or pretensions) to their audience, and by which they conjoined and enlightened that audience. Rock was filled now with not only ideals of defiance, but dreams of love, community, and spirituality. Even the Rolling Stones—who always sang about much darker concerns, would start recording songs about love and altruism (that is, for a week or two). "For a brief while," wrote critic Langdon Winner of the *Sgt. Pepper* era, "the irreparably fragmented consciousness of the West was unified, at least in the minds of the young."

But that blithe center couldn't forever hold. By the time *Sgt. Pepper* was on the streets, San Francisco's Haight-Ashbury was already turning into a scary and ugly place, riddled with corruption and hard drugs, and overpopulated with bikers, rapists, thieves, and foolish shamans. In addition, a public backlash was forming. Many Americans were afraid they had lost their young to irredeemable allures and ideologies, and in California, Ronald Reagan had already won a gubernatorial campaign that was largely predicated on anti-youth sentiment. It was a time for media panic, for generational recrimination and political separatism, for opposing views of America's worth and future. It was an intoxicating time but also a frightening one. Known certainties were slipping away, or being abandoned. More and more, it looked as if there were no turning back, and as if *everything* were at stake.

I<small>N</small> FACT, more was at stake than anybody realized. The Beatles would make more great music, but their collective fate was twisting out of their control. In August 1967, Brian Epstein died alone in his London home of a sleeping pill overdose. Epstein had made many business and personal errors, but he had remained steadfast in his belief in (and love for) the Beatles, and without him, the group was soon rudderless. In May 1968, John Lennon began an affair with Yoko Ono—a respected avant-garde artist who had been part of New York's Fluxus movement. Soon after, he left and divorced his wife, Cynthia Powell, and his resulting inseparable closeness with Ono caused much tension within the Beatles' world. Paul McCartney, meantime, tried to keep the band on course (sometimes disastrously, as with *Magical Mystery Tour;* sometimes splendidly, as with *Abbey Road*), but the other group members began to resent and distrust what they saw as the bassist's egoistic bossiness. There were other trying matters: the drug busts of Lennon and Harrison, plus the arrival and bullying manner of new manager, Allen Klein (despised by McCartney, entrusted by the others, and eventually sued by all). But the decisive rift in the Beatles occurred in the relationship between McCartney and Lennon. *Theirs* was the real romance and unbelievably creative partnership that made the Beatles' popularity grow and span the world, and when that mutual affection and cooperation was over—like the dissolution of any major passion—there was no turning back. The Beatles went on to record *The Beatles* (better known as the White Album); they also made *Let It Be;* then they made *Abbey Road.* But regardless of the merits of any of those works, it was difficult for those four men to remain comfortably in the same room for long.

The Beatles ended in April 1970, at almost the same moment that *Let It Be* became their fourteenth number 1 album. Maybe the end was none too soon, but it was clear that, as they finished their union, the Beatles also finished a great adventure and a worthy dream.

In the documentary film *Let It Be* (and even more memorably in the book *Get Back,* which accompanied the British release of the film's soundtrack), McCartney, Lennon, and Harrison argued endlessly among each other over the most artful way of making what was originally intended as artless music, while also trying to make the hapless event of the film seem like a natural document of their musical communion. The group had been marked by the emerging cynicism of the era that was to follow. They were already regarding one another as creations of undeserved hype. For everything they had once been—lively, novel, and uplifting—the Beatles ended as bitter, mutually unbelieving strangers.

I T I S N O S E C R E T that for the better part of the next two decades, the former Beatles preferred to have little to do with each other or their momentous history. Something about being the Beatles—an adventure which, for the most part, had been so marvelous to observe—left the four men at the heart of the experience seeming wounded, haunted, even bitter. "We were just a band who made it very, very, big," John Lennon told *Rolling Stone's* Jann Wenner in December 1970. "That's all."

And then, to stick his point, in one of the best songs from the outset of his solo career, Lennon declared: "I don't believe in Beatles. . . . /The dream is over." It was a brave thing to say; no doubt painful as well. But what about the legions of admirers who *had* believed that dream, who had come of age with the Beatles, whose world and lives had been transformed in part by the band's growth? "It's only a rock group that split up," said Lennon. "It's nothing important. You know, you have all their records there, if you want to reminisce." George Harrison added: "All things must pass," before embarking on a solo career that, far too often, indicated that among those things that are truly perishable are passion, vision, and purpose.

Even when some of the more grievous injuries began to heal between the former bandmates—in particular, the rift between Lennon and Paul McCartney, the songwriting team who had enjoyed the closest relationship within the group, but whose parting was especially caustic—the four men and their former commonwealth remained entangled in complex lawsuits. (At one time or another, the ex-Beatles were involved in litigation—or prospects of litigation—with the band's onetime manager, Allen Klein; the band's major label distributor, EMI; Lennon and McCartney's music publishers; and, of course, with each other. The imbroglios lasted until 1989.) No chance, in the midst of such sustained disagreements, for the mythic reunion that so many fans, journalists, and concert promoters kept hoping for. ("Saturday Night Live"'s Lorne Michaels parodied this mania by offering the foursome *one thousand dollars* for a one-time appearance. According to one delightful rumor, the band came damn close to taking him up on the offer.) Indeed, for some music devotees, the idea of a reunited Beatles became something like a pop culture version of the quest for the Holy Grail: If the group would *just* get back together, the thinking went, perhaps some of the 1960s' lost ideals of unity and hopefulness might be regained. The former Beatles wanted no part of such a delusion; it would've been a work of fake community. Besides, theirs was a done history. Time to move on, to face their new destinies as four grown men. Separately.

Then, in December 1980, an unhinged Beatles fan shot John Lennon to death outside Lennon's Manhattan apartment building, just a few weeks after the former Beatle had released his first new music in four years. A fucking awful payoff: six bullets for a man who had enriched the lives of millions, and who had helped transfigure an entire culture. The Beatles' dream—and any chance it might be reanimated—was finally, irrevocably, over. In 1989, when asked again if the band might still get back together, George Harrison stated: "As far as I'm concerned, there won't be a Beatles reunion as long as John Lennon remains dead."

Well, not so fast. In the mid-1990s, the Beatles were back, with two "new" Beatles songs: "Free as a Bird" and "Real Love," written and sung by, of all people, John Lennon. The surviving Beatles—McCartney, Harrison, Ringo Starr—regrouped in the studio again, singing and playing along with Lennon's tape-recorded voice (from demos of unfinished late 1970s songs, given to McCartney by Yoko Ono), and working cooperatively to shape a collective biography of the band. In addition, the group produced nearly seven hours of previously unreleased Beatles recordings (comprising three full-length double CD sets, and two shorter CDs—the latter featuring the "Free as a Bird" and "Real Love" singles and other tracks). Plus, there was a ten-hour, multimedia video history of the band, *The Beatles Anthology*, narrated for the most part by the Beatles themselves (McCartney, Harrison, and Starr contributed original interviews for the project; Lennon was heard posthumously, from earlier taped statements). In effect, we got what we were never supposed to get: a Beatles reunion. Or at least its 1990s equivalent—a virtual reality–style mix of disembodied dead voices and polished up-to-the-minute ambitions.

The only question was: How much did all this new product contribute to our appreciation of the Beatles' music, or our understanding of their history? A fair amount, it turns out, though perhaps not always in ways that the Beatles intended.

THE MUSICAL component of the *Anthology* series—the three double CDs and two CD single sets—are a rich if problematic trove. Combined, the eight CDs offer over 140 recordings—including unreleased masters, outtakes, live sessions, demo recordings, cover versions, rehearsals, and improvised performances—all of which have been unavailable in any form on authorized Beatles albums and collections until 1995 and 1996. As history, as a means of showing how the Beatles developed the textures, arrangements, and contents of their songs, and also how they rejected or renovated their mistakes, much of it is fascinating. In particular, the three versions of "Strawberry Fields Forever" on *Anthology 2* (which covers the 1965–68 period in which the Beatles went through such matchless experimental growth) show how a simple, sad-toned folk song grew into an orchestrated, style-shattering elegy to lost certainties. On the same album, there is also a quartet version of "A Day in the Life" which is perhaps even more affecting than the original, if that's possible.

But as wondrous as some of the tracks are on the first two *Anthology* sets, neither collection really plays through as a truly satisfying or moving listening experience. *Anthology 1* is unfairly bogged down with speech excerpts that deprive the rock & roll sequencing of much of its momentum. *Anthology 2*—which should have been the most monumental of these packages—lacks real cohesion; it moves from simple, wonderful, primal rock to baroque psychedelia too quickly, too inexplicably. Also, two versions of "Fool on the Hill"—let's admit it—are two too many. (Though the set also includes a fierce, punklike version of the "Sgt. Pepper" reprise, with McCartney affecting a Bob Dylan–inflected yowl, that burns the original version to the ground.)

It is surprising, then, that *Anthology 3* not only works as the best of this series, but is also perhaps the most revealing album in the Beatles' entire catalog. This set covers 1968 to 1970: the Beatles' fateful period. These were the years when friction set in between the band members, when John Lennon met Yoko Ono and embarked on making avant-garde art and dabbling in radical conceptual politics, and it was the period when Apple Records (the Beatles' own label) was established and then quickly spun out of control. The music on the albums from this time proved wildly uneven. The two record set *The Beatles* (better known as the White Album) was brilliant yet disjointed—as if it had been made by four independent men rather than fashioned by a true band—whereas *Abbey Road* came across as a unified masterstroke from start to finish. *Let It Be* (recorded before *Abbey Road*, but released later) began as an album and film project called *Get Back*, and was to present the Beatles playing live, uncluttered by studio artifice (in keeping with late 1960s' pop's return-to-the-roots rage, inspired by Bob Dylan's acoustic rock & roll gem, *John Wesley Harding*). The Beatles lost interest in *Get Back* and put it on hold. By the time the album was released—as *Let It Be*—the band had broken up and John Lennon had recruited producer Phil Spector to remix and orchestrate some of the tracks (sort of John's revenge on Paul—maybe on all the Beatles). Coming as the Beatles' final album, *Let It Be* felt indifferent and haphazard—by far the lowest moment of the band's output. After hearing it, it was a bit easier to let the Beatles go.

Anthology 3 changes the way one hears this period's music—in a way that I've never heard another pop retrospective accomplish. The set's alternate tracks play pretty much in the order the music happened, and what emerges redeems some of what had once seemed abject. Many of the versions of the White Album tracks included here are from solo acoustic demos recorded by the various songwriters (Beatles Unplugged!), while others are rough sketches with different configurations of the band playing together. Either way, these alternate White Album tracks are mesmerizing—like ghostly survivors that divulge the music's real, long-ago secrets. Paul McCartney, not usually regarded as the Beatles' hard-tempered personality, turns in a lengthy, ominous reading of "Helter Skelter" that feels scarier than the frenetic original. He also takes the one-trick "Why Don't We Do It in the Road," and imbues it with a weirdly wonderful, deranged passion. There is much, much more on *Anthology 3* that is transfixing—especially George

Harrison's acoustic solo version of "While My Guitar Gently Weeps" and John Lennon's spooky "Come Together"—but the set's real value is in what it tells us about the Beatles' relationship during this period. Clearly, this was bottom-of-the-soul time. Many of this collection's songs are brimming with desolation, aloneness, and fear, and yet from that came some inspired and enduring songwriting. More important, while you can hear the tension between group members in some of the tracks (John mocking Paul at various points in "Let It Be" and "Teddy Boy"), you can also hear the real pleasure and affinity that took place within this band. Listen to John and Paul's lovely harmony singing on "Two of Us": These men were already on the way out of each other's lives, and yet they could still bring out the best in one another, and could still revel and take pride in that realization. *Anthology 3* is a wonderful story of lost and found and lost-again community. It is the Beatles' equivalent to Bob Dylan's *Basement Tapes*, perhaps even darker. Hard to believe that, in 1996, we could receive a new Beatles album that is so moving.

The video half of the *Anthology* series—which purports to be the Beatles' sole true autobiography—is an elaborate expansion of the three-part TV special of the same title, first broadcast in November 1995, to mixed reviews. This extended edition is a vast improvement, and is generally worth the ten hours required to sit through it. In particular, there is some amazing black & white footage in its early parts (from a film by Albert and David Maysles) of February 7, 1964—the day the Beatles first arrived in America. Following a hilarious press conference, we view the band members in the back of a limousine, entering Manhattan for the first time. We see their looks of nervousness—then astonishment—as they listen to live radio's coverage of their coming. When they pull in front of the Ed Sullivan Theater, from inside the limousine you see the swarm of screaming young women that engulfs the car, stopping it. The limousine slowly draws away from the crowd, and is flanked by policemen on galloping horses. There are several other great moments throughout *Anthology*—including concert scenes in the United Kingdom; Sweden; Washington, D.C.; and Los Angeles, and the recording session for "A Day in the Life"—but there is nothing that matches the impact of the Beatles' arrival in Manhattan. It is a moment of pure, true, meaningful history—the Beatles' entry into the modern mind—and after that day so much would be different.

Unfortunately, as *Anthology* progresses, the Beatles (or at least Harrison, Starr, and McCartney) tend to gloss over some of the rougher milestones of the band's story. There is no reference, for example, to the Beatles' tense parting with the Maharishi Mahesh Yogi in 1968, nor is there any mention of John Lennon's sudden separation from his first wife, Cynthia, for whom the divorce was especially hurtful. It's as if Yoko Ono simply material-ized at an ideal time in Lennon's life, and filled him with new purpose. For that matter, there's precious little of Yoko Ono in *Anthology* at all (though when she makes her appearance, it's accompanied by a somewhat sinister song fragment: "She's not a girl who misses much . . . ," from "Happiness Is a Warm Gun"), and there is no admission of the resentment she met with. Indeed, the Beatles fairly idealize the whole last period of their association, making it seem as if their break were simply a logical development. They had done enough together, and it was time to go their severed ways. In truth, the Beatles' ending was ugly and nasty. There were rancorous fights between McCartney and the others over accepting Allen Klein as the band's new manager (Paul wanted Lee Eastman, his father-in-law), and there was real aversion and blame leveled at Ono by some of the people in the Beatles' circle. Most obviously, there was the bitter rift between Lennon and McCart-ney, which effectively finished the group. None of this is admitted here, though after so many years of legal suits and other strains, it's understand-able that today's Beatles wouldn't want to go back to those moments.

Even so, *Anthology* makes it plain that there was a great deal of pain involved in being the Beatles, and that pain started much earlier than many of us might have realized. Ringo Starr tells a harrowing story about how a plainclothes policeman accompanied him onstage at a Canadian appearance, after Starr had received a death threat for being Jewish ("One major fault is I'm not Jewish," says Ringo), and George relates how, during a tense appear-ance in Japan, every time an unexpected loud sound occurred, the band members would look around to see which of them had been shot. Harrison also discloses his anger about the Beatles not being able to control their own schedules or movements during their hectic tours, and also tells how, in 1964, he finally balked and insisted that the Beatles not participate in a ticker tape parade planned for a San Francisco appearance. "It was only . . . a year," he says, "since they had assassinated Kennedy. . . . I could just imag-ine how mad it is in America."

The Beatles were at the eye of a tremendous storm of public feeling, and though Harrison claims they were the sanest people in that scenario, it's also clear that their fame had isolated them from some of the meaning and pleasure of their experience. As you watch *Anthology,* it becomes plain that the Beatles—or at least some of them—may not have really loved their audience, at least after a certain point. In the Beatles' minds, it appears, that audience became an enclosing and demanding reality, always wanting, often threatening, rarely understanding enough. Harrison, in particular, has the most to say on this point. "They used us as an excuse to go mad, the world did," he states, "and then they blamed it on us." Later, he tells a story about visiting the Haight-Ashbury—the San Francisco district identified with the hippie movement—at the height of its fame, and shares his disgust at the constituency he saw there. "Grotty people," he labels them, with clear disdain. And in *Anthology*'s closing section, Harrison says: "They [the Beatles' audience] gave their money and they gave their screams, but the Beatles kind of gave their nervous systems, which is a much more different thing to give."

This distaste for the public's clamor is possibly the single greatest revelation to be found in *Anthology*. But there is another side to the story— namely, that this same public also gave the Beatles something tremendous, something more than money and screams. That audience gave the Beatles an inspiration to get better, an opportunity to grow, and a willingness to grow along with them. Without the context of that audience, it doesn't seem likely that the group could have made such a form-stretching work as *Revolver* or such a culture-defining statement as *Sgt. Pepper's Lonely Hearts Club Band*, because the pop audience of that time, as much as any of the era's musicians, was also raising the stakes on what was allowable and what was necessary, and was also delivering judgment on the caliber of what was being offered. The Beatles' record sales were, as much as anything, a sign of love and appreciation for the band—a mass of *go-ahead* votes. Without that support, the Beatles would have mattered a lot less, and probably would have accomplished a lot less as well.

And yet, in *Anthology*'s insularity, there is never any acknowledgment of that debt. The audience that loved this band was perhaps never seen as real or worthy partners in the group's journey. The Beatles had only each other and their work for solace, and in time, they didn't even have that.

WHATEVER ITS FLAWS or merits, *The Beatles Anthology* proved fairly eventful in 1996—at least in a certain way. When *Anthology* first aired in America in 1995, the program drew over 50 million viewers during its three nights of broadcast—something smaller than the record-breaking audience of 70 million who tuned into the group's first "Ed Sullivan Show" broadcast in 1964, but still, no other popular music figures have ever been granted a six-hour prime-time television special. In the show's wake, much of the Beatles' extant catalog (the thirteen original albums, and five collections, including the 1994 *Live at the BBC*) returned to *Billboard*'s charts, and sold dramatically. In addition, the three double CD *Anthology* packages, released over the course of the year following the broadcast, also did well—selling over 5 million units to date. Once again, the Beatles loomed as a big and competitive force in the pop world. In fact, according to SoundScan—the company that monitors music sales—the group has sold 27 million CDs since 1991. All this sales activity prompted the *London Observer* to remark: "In 1996 the Beatles have achieved what every group since them has failed to do: become bigger than the Beatles."

It's a clever comment, but it also begs a few other comments. In the 1960s, the Beatles being "big" meant something—a great deal, in fact. It meant that not just the Beatles, but whole new styles and values had become big, and were upsetting prior styles and values. It meant that an increasingly bold and empowered generation had elected its own aesthetics, its own ideology, its own leaders—and that such pop artists as the Beatles (or Bob Dylan, or the Rolling Stones, or Aretha Franklin, Jimi Hendrix, or Janis Joplin) were the exemplars of this movement. In this context, to become "bigger than the Beatles" would have meant signifying a greater consensus. It would have meant to be not just more popular, but also more embodying, more centralizing, for an entire generation. Today, such a possibility no longer seems practical or desirable. Indeed, the notion of gigantism as consensus, as a sign of unifying agreement in the pop world, has now collapsed, for better or worse. In the years since the Beatles' disunion, the Rolling Stones, Fleetwood Mac, Peter Frampton, Donna Summer, the Bee Gees, Michael Jackson, Prince, Bruce Springsteen, Lionel Richie, Madonna, the Grateful Dead, Whitney Houston, Nirvana, U2, Garth Brooks, Hootie and the Blowfish, and Alanis Morissette (among others) have all been "bigger than the Beatles"—that is, they have all sold more individual albums or played to greater numbers of people. But as often as not, the size of these artists' successes has meant nothing more than just the triumph of size itself—or at least has meant nothing more outside the artist's particular audience. Bruce Springsteen's fans will attest to the meaning and worth of his music and popularity, but Prince's audience (or Michael Jackson's, or Madonna's) might not agree—and whatever their merits, few if any of the performers mentioned in this sentence appeal to today's younger progressive audience.

The point is: There is no longer a center to popular music, no longer any one single, real mainstream. Instead, there are many diverse mainstreams and excluding factions, each representing its own perspective, its own concurrence. Snoop Doggy Dogg may reign over one mainstream, Whitney Houston or Hootie and the Blowfish over another, R.E.M., U2, Pearl Jam, and Smashing Pumpkins over yet others. But nothing unifies popular music's broadest possible audience in the way that Elvis Presley or the Beatles once managed. Not even the idea of "popular" music binds that many of us—and maybe that's not a bad thing. In any event, about the only thing today's pop world might agree on is *not* to agree on too many shared tastes or tenets.

The Beatles are still big—no question. They still sell millions of albums, and their legend probably remains unrivaled. But the Beatles—at least today's Beatles—are not really "bigger" than the Beatles, because today's Beatles can no longer change the world the way yesterday's Beatles did.

So the *final* real question is: What is it, then, that the Beatles can possibly say or mean to modern times?

IF ONE IS TO judge that question solely by the band's two new songs, the answer would be: Probably not that much.

Never mind all the criticism that there's something false or shameful about the surviving Beatles modifying the late John Lennon's unfinished music. Harrison, McCartney, and Starr did not embarrass themselves or the Beatles' reputation with these efforts. The final results sound as if everybody involved worked sincerely and meticulously, and with "Free as a Bird" in particular, they even created something rather moving. At one point, McCartney asks: Whatever happened to the time and life that the band once shared? How did they go on without one another? The song isn't a statement about nostalgia, but rather a commentary on all the chances and hopes, all the immeasurable possibilities, that are lost when people who once loved each other cut themselves off from that communion. Not a bad or imprecise coda for what the Beatles did to themselves, and to their own history (and to their audience) with their dissolution. The only problem is, neither "Free as a Bird" nor "Real Love" imparts any real urgency, or aims to capture a mood or moment—which is something the old Beatles accomplished so well in albums like *Revolver* and the White Album, and in songs like "Revolution," "Hey Jude," "Get Back," and even "Let It Be," with the latter song's yearning for serenity as the outside world turned troubling and uncertain. The modern Beatles sound . . . *careful,* maybe even a bit removed from the world around them.

But that only makes sense. The world around them has changed considerably since these men last gathered together to make music. These are harder times, both in terms of style and content, and the sensibilities that the Beatles once stood for are not as dominant now. In today's cutting-edge popular music, one doesn't hear the residue of the Beatles so much as you hear, say, the long-shadow influence of the Velvet Underground (whose primal drive and dissonant textures have had great bearing on the music of David Bowie, Patti Smith, Talking Heads, U2, and R.E.M., among others), or the sway of James Brown (whose sharp, tense style of funk propulsion had tremendous rhythmic impact on numerous diverse artists, including George Clinton, electric-era Miles Davis, funk and disco bands like Ohio Players and Chic, and many of today's hip-hop performers and producers). Moreover, the Beatles' most oft-cited thematic concerns—their reflections on love, concord, and spirituality—may seem quaint in comparison to the concerns of artists like Nirvana, Pearl Jam, Hole, or Tupac Shakur, who sang vital, rageful songs about vulnerability and self-destruction, loneliness and malevolence. It isn't that the Beatles didn't allow darkness into their music. There was a frequent mean streak in some of John Lennon's earlier songs—such as "Run for Your Life" and "Norwegian Wood"—later replaced by the existential dread of "She Said She Said" and "A Day in the Life." In addition, as the bulk of *Anthology 3* makes plain, much of the Beatles' concluding music was rife with images of chaos, isolation, anger, panic, and drug-steeped sadness. Even so, many commentators tend to remember the Beatles for their blithe sentiments about love as a major work of will, and courage and redemption. Fine ideals, to be sure, and in the setting of their time, even somewhat inspiring and comforting. But in the *real* end, you likely need a lot more than love to make it through this world or redeem your losses. Sometimes darkness is irrefutable, and sometimes love and understanding can't save a troubled heart or a soul in harm's way. Just ask Kurt Cobain or Tupac Shakur— or for that matter John Lennon. That is, if you could ask them anything today.

But if today's Beatles can't speak to today's realities, it's also hard to imagine that today's popular music could speak with such weight and force without yesterday's Beatles. Let's put it another way: Imagine no Beatles. Imagine they had never happened, had never participated in modern history. Their accomplishments, as I mentioned earlier, were many: from signifying not only that the most massive population of youth in history was about to find new dreams, new purposes, new identity—and in time, new causes and beliefs—to helping establish that rock & roll was now a protean and important art form. This isn't to say that the Beatles were the first people who proved that popular music forms could be "art" (Louis Armstrong, Robert Johnson, Billie Holiday, Frank Sinatra, Hank Williams, and Elvis Presley had already proved that point long before), nor is it to say that they raised rock to new sophisticated levels that transcended what it had once been (some people believed this, maybe even some Beatles believed it, but to their credit, the latter moved past that fallacy fast). Instead, it is to say that the Beatles' growth—in union with Bob Dylan's innovations—made plain that pop was a field willing to extend its own aesthetic by incorporating modifications from other disciplines, and that a rock & roll song was capable of expressing truths as complex and consequential as anything to be found in contemporary literature or film. And it was the Beatles who as the 1960s rose and fell, inevitably epitomized that era's longing for ideal community. Later, when the band fell apart in such messy fashion, the Beatles also served as a metaphor for the disintegration of that dream.

But perhaps the single most important thing the Beatles accomplished was to follow through on a trend that had been started years earlier by jazz, country-western, and rhythm & blues artists, and carried farther by early rock & rollers like Elvis Presley and Chuck Berry. The music these people made had one quality in common: It was the sound of those who had been shut out of the American dream and denied entry into the "respected" arts. In the 1940s and 1950s, it was easier to keep these people out—in fact, in the 1950s, many of the early rock & roll heroes met with systematic and continuous attempts to resist the disruptions they were bringing into mainstream culture. The Beatles never met with the same sort of hindrance because they were seen, at first, as eccentric in charming and wholesome ways that helped offset the horror that had settled on America in the aftermath of John Kennedy's murder. We needed something different—something outside ourselves, our culture and history, and our own pain. By the time adult moral and political reaction began turning against the group—in the late 1960s, when Lennon declared the band "more popular than Jesus," and when the group members began to experiment with drugs and to speak out against the U.S. involvement in Vietnam—it was too late to undo what the Beatles had enabled. The Beatles had not just entered but had also transmuted the mainstream; in doing so, they made it open to countless other outsiders and insurgents. There are forces still reeling from that turbulence. Such critics as former drug-war czar William Bennett, House Speaker Newt Gingrich, former presidential candidate Bob Dole, and the late author Allan Bloom have all railed against the cultural convulsions of the 1960s, and have announced it is time to roll back its influence. But all the protesting and moralizing in the world will never be able to undo the glorious rupture that the Beatles—and their many compatriots—effected in modern arts and modern times.

The Beatles are history—as in: *past,* out of here, gone, yesterday. The Beatles are also history in the sense of having helped remodel a time and its people, and in the sense of opening up so many conceivabilities. Imagine that this *hadn't* happened. Subtract everything from today that resulted from how this band exploded that epoch. Chances are, most of the artists' stories that follow in this volume may never have developed in quite the same way that they did, or may not have meant as much. Chances are—because the Beatles reclaimed the promise that pop songs could work as both disruption and epiphany—you might not even hear rock & roll as the force of revolution *and* revelation that it has been heard as for these last few decades. And you know that would be an awful hole in our history. Don't you?

subterranean:

bob dylan's

passages

Something about that movie, though, that I just can't get it
out of my head
But I can't remember why I was in it, or what part I was
supposed to play
All I remember about it was, is Gregory Peck and the way
that people moved
And a lot of them, they seemed to be looking my way.

BOB DYLAN
"BROWNSVILLE GIRL"

It was one of the odder moments in the history of televised rock &
roll.

Bob Dylan had been invited to play at the 1991 Grammy Awards ceremony, on the occasion of receiving the National Association of Recording
Arts and Sciences Lifetime Achievement Award. In theory, these prizes are
bestowed to acknowledge a performer's invaluable contribution to the modern history of popular music. In Dylan's case, though, it was a ludicrously
belated recognition: Though he had affected both folk and popular music
more than almost any other figure in American culture, Dylan hadn't been
honored—by NARAS, nor most of the established music industry for that
matter—during the period of his greatest innovations, a quarter-century
before. Indeed, in 1965—the year that Dylan released "Like a Rolling Stone"

and transfigured rock & roll—the Grammy for Record of the Year was awarded to "A Taste of Honey," by Herb Alpert & the Tijuana Brass. Dylan himself would not receive a Grammy until 1979, for "Gotta Serve Somebody."

Maybe Dylan was thinking about this when he took the stage that night. Or maybe he had other matters on his mind. In any event, on this occasion, Bob Dylan proceeded to behave precisely like Bob Dylan. Accompanied by a motley rock & roll outfit, he delivered a snarled, throttled version of his most embittered anti-war song, "Masters of War," and did so during the peak season of America's adamant support for the Bush Administration's Persian Gulf War. It was a transfixingly weird performance: Dylan sang the song in a flat, rushed voice—as if he realized that no matter how passionately or frequently he sang these words, it would never be enough to thwart the world's appetite for war—while the band behind him blazed like hellfire. For days after, critics would debate whether the performance had been brilliant or embarrassing (why bother to protest a war, some asked, when the song's lyrics couldn't even be deciphered?), but this much was plain: Dylan's appearance was also the only moment of genuine rock & roll abandon that the Grammy Awards had witnessed in years.

Moments later, a deliriously amused Jack Nicholson presented Dylan with his Lifetime Achievement Award. Dylan, dressed in a lopsided dark suit, stood by, fumbling with his gray curl-brim fedora and occasionally applauding himself. When Nicholson passed the plaque to him, Dylan looked confused. "Well, uh, all right," he said, fumbling some more with his hat. "Yeah. Well, my daddy, he didn't leave me too much. You know, he was a very simple man. But what he told me was this: He did say, 'Son . . .'" And then Dylan paused, rubbing his mouth while silently reading what was written on the plaque, and then he shook his head. "He said so many things, you know?" he said, and the audience tittered. "He said, 'Son, it's possible to become so defiled in this world that your own mother and father will abandon you. And if that happens, God will always believe in your own ability to mend your ways.'"

After that, nobody was laughing much. Dylan gave a final tip of his hat, spun on his heels, and was gone. One more time, Bob Dylan had met America, and America didn't really know what to make of him.

THE FIRST TIME I met Bob Dylan was in the autumn of 1985—the day he showed up at my front door. He looked like I hoped and feared he would:

That is, he looked like Bob Dylan—the keen, fierce man who once tore apart known views of the world with every new song he delivered.

What brought Dylan to my door was simply that we had an interview to do, and since he had to come to Hollywood anyway that day, he figured we may as well do it at my place. While this certainly made the meeting more thrilling for me, it also made it a bit scarier. More than twenty years of image preceded Dylan on that day. This was a man who could be tense, capricious, and baffling, and who was capable of wielding his image—and temper—at a moment's notice in a way that could stupefy and intimidate not only interviewers, but sometimes friends as well.

What I found instead was a man who didn't seem too concerned with brandishing his image, even for a moment. He offered his hand, flashed a slightly bashful smile, then walked over to my stereo, kneeled down, and started to flip through a stack of some records on the floor—mostly music by older jazz, pop, and country singers. He commented on most of what he came across. "The Delmore Brothers—God, I really love them. I think they've influenced every harmony I've ever tried to sing. . . . This Hank Williams thing with just him and guitar—man, that's something, isn't it? I used to sing those songs way back, a long time ago, even before I played rock & roll as a teenager. . . . Sinatra, Peggy Lee, yeah, I love all these people, but I tell you who I've really been listening to a lot lately—in fact, I'm thinking about recording one of his earlier songs—is Bing Crosby. I don't think you can find better phrasing anywhere."

That's pretty much how Dylan was that afternoon: good-humored and gracious, but also thoughtful in his remarks. And sometimes—when talking about his Minnesota youth, or his early days in the folk scene under the enthrallment of Woody Guthrie—his voice grew softer and more deliberate, as if he were striving to pick just the right words to convey the exact detail of his memory. During these moments he lapsed sometimes into silence, but behind the sunglasses (which he never removed), his eyes stayed active with thought, flickering back and forth, as if reading a distant memory.

For the most part, though, sipping a Corona beer and smoking cigarettes, he seemed surprisingly relaxed as we talked that afternoon. He grew most animated when he talked about a video shoot that he had done a short time before to promote his most recent album at that time, *Empire Burlesque*. At Dylan's request, the shoot had been done under the direction of Dave Stewart, who was then a member of Eurythmics. "His stuff had a spontaneous look to it," said Dylan, "and somehow I just figured he would understand what I was doing. And he did: He put together a great band for this lip-sync video and sets us up with equipment on this little stage in a church somewhere in West L.A. So between all the time they took setting up camera shots and lights and all that stuff, we could just play live for this little crowd that we had gathered there.

"I can't even express how good that felt—in fact, I was trying to remember the last time I'd felt that kind of direct connection, and finally I realized it must have been back in the 1950s, when I was fourteen or fifteen years old, playing with four-piece rock & roll bands back in Minnesota. Back in those days there weren't any sound systems or anything that you had to bother with. You'd set up your amplifiers and turn them up to where you wanted to turn them. That just doesn't happen anymore. Now there are just so many things that get in the way of that kind of feeling, that simple directness. For some reason, making this video just made me realize how far everything has come these last several years—and how far I'd come."

SEVERAL MONTHS LATER, in late spring 1986, my conversations with Dylan continue.

It is just past midnight, and Dylan is standing in the middle of a crowded, smoke-laden recording studio tucked deep into the remote reaches of Topanga Canyon, outside Los Angeles. He is wearing brown-tinted sunglasses, a sleeveless white T-shirt, black vest, black jeans, frayed black motorcycle gloves, and he puffs hard at a Kool while bobbing his head rhythmically to the colossal blues shuffle that is thundering from the speakers above his head.

"Subterranean," he mutters, smiling delightedly.

Sitting on a sofa a few feet away, also nodding their heads in rapt pleasure, are T-Bone Burnett and Al Kooper—old friends and occasional sidemen of Dylan. Several other musicians—including Los Lobos guitarist Cesar Rosas, R&B saxophonist Steve Douglas, and bassist James Jamerson, Jr., the son of the legendary Motown bass player—fill out the edges of the room. Like everyone else, they are smiling at this music: romping, bawdy, jolting rock & roll—the sort of indomitable music a man might conjure if he were about to lay claim to something big.

The guitars crackle, the horns honk and wail, the drums and bass rumble and clamor wildly, and then the room returns to silence. T-Bone Burnett, turning to Kooper, seems to voice a collective sentiment. "Man," he says, "that *gets* it."

"Yeah," says Kooper. "So *dirty*."

Everyone watches Dylan expectantly. For a moment, he appears to be in some distant, private place. "Subterranean," is all he says, still smiling. "Positively subterranean," he adds, running his hand through his mazy brown hair, chuckling. Then he walks into an adjoining room, straps on his weatherworn Fender guitar, tears off a quick, bristling blues lick and says, "Okay, who wants to play lead on this? I broke a string."

Dylan has been like this all week, turning out spur-of-the-moment, blues-infused rock & roll with a startling force and imagination, piling up instrumental tracks so fast that the dazed, bleary-eyed engineers who are monitoring the sessions are having trouble cataloging all the various takes— so far, well over twenty songs, including gritty R&B, Chicago-steeped blues, rambunctious gospel, and raw-toned hillbilly forms. In part, Dylan is working fast merely as a practical matter: Rehearsals for his American tour with Tom Petty and the Heartbreakers start in only a couple of weeks, and though it hardly seems possible in this overmeticulous, high-tech recording era, he figures he can write, record, mix, and package a new studio LP in that allotted term. "You see, I spend too much time working out the *sound* of my records these days," he had told me earlier. "And if the records I'm making only sell a certain amount anyway, then why should I take so long putting them together? . . . I've got a lot of different records inside me, and it's time just to start getting them *out.*"

Apparently, this is not idle talk. Dylan has started perusing songs for a possible collection of new and standard folk songs and has also begun work on a set of Tin Pan Alley covers—which, it seems safe to predict, will be something to hear. At the moment, though, as Dylan leads the assembled band through yet another roadhouse-style blues number, a different ambition seems to possess him. This is Bob Dylan the rock & roller, and despite all the vagaries of his career, it is still an impressive thing to witness. He leans lustily into the songs's momentum at the same instant that he invents its structure, pumping his rhythm guitar with tough, unexpected accents, much like Chuck Berry or Keith Richards, and in the process, prodding his other guitarists, Kooper and Rosas, to tangle and burn, like good-natured rivals. It isn't until moments later, as everybody gathers back into the booth to listen to the playback, that it's clear that this music sounds surprisingly like the riotous, dense music of *Highway 61 Revisited*—music that seems as menacing as it does joyful, and that, in any event, seems to erupt from an ungovernable imagination. Subterranean, indeed.

I F THERE WAS any central message to Bob Dylan's early music, perhaps it was that it isn't easy for a bright, scrupulous person to live in a society that honors the inversion of its own best values, that increasingly turns from the notions of community and democracy to the twisted politics of death and abundance. To live through such times with conscience and intelligence intact, Dylan said in his music, one had to hold a brave and mean mirror up to the face of cultural corruption.

These days, of course, the politics of corruption and death are doing just fine, and are fairly immune to any single pop star's acts of sedition. But back in the fevered momentum of the 1960s, when he first asserted himself, Dylan had a colossal impact on the changing face of American culture. In that decade's early years, folk music (which had been driven underground in the 1950s by conservative forces) was enjoying a popular resurgence, inspired by the (on the surface) wholesome success of the Kingston Trio (though there was nothing wholesome about their 1958 number 1 single, "Tom Dooley"— a century-old song recounting the true story of a man hanged for knifing his girlfriend). Under the influence of Joan Baez and Peter, Paul, and Mary, folk was turning more politically explicit, and was also becoming increasingly identified with civil rights and pacifism, among other causes. But it was with the young nasal-toned, rail-thin Bob Dylan—who had moved from Minnesota to New York to assume the legacy of folk's greatest hero, Woody Guthrie—that 1960s' folk would find its greatest hope: a remarkably prolific songwriter who was giving a forceful and articulate voice to the apprehensions and ideals of the emerging restless generation. With "Blowin' in the Wind" and "A Hard Rain's a-Gonna Fall," Dylan penned songs about racial suffering and the threat of nuclear apocalypse that acquired the status of immediate anthems, and with "The Times They Are a-Changin'," he wrote an apt and chilling decree of the rising tensions of the coming era. "Come mothers and fathers/Throughout the land," he sang, in a voice young with anger and old with knowledge, "And don't criticize/What you can't understand/Your sons and your daughters are beyond your command/Your old road is/Rapidly agin'/Please get out of the new one/If you can't lend your hand/For the times they are a-changin'."

In those first few years, Dylan was already beginning to transform the possibilities of popular songwriting—opening up the entire form to new themes and a new vernacular that were derived as much from the ambitions of literature and poetry as from the traditions of folk music. (In 1963, Peter, Paul, and Mary had two Top 10 hit singles written by Dylan, "Blowin' in the Wind" and "Don't Think Twice, It's All Right.") But Dylan would soon go on to change *all* of what popular music might do. Inspired by both the popularity and the inventive song structures of the Beatles—who had exploded on America's rock scene in early 1964—Dylan was feeling confined by the limited interests of the folk audience, and by the narrow stylistic range of folk music itself. After witnessing the Beatles' breakthrough, and after hearing the rawer blues-based rock being made by the Animals and Rolling Stones, Dylan realized it was possible to transform and enliven his music, and to connect with a broader and more vital audience in the process. (When the Byrds scored a June 1965 number 1 hit with their chiming folk-rock cover of Dylan's "Mr. Tambourine Man," it only further convinced him.)

On July 25, 1965, Dylan took the stage at the Newport Folk Festival with the Paul Butterfield Blues Band and played a brief howling set of the new electric music he had been recording—and shocked folk purists howled back at him in rage. And for fair reason: The fleet, hard-tempered music that Dylan began making on albums like *Bringing It All Back Home* and *Highway 61 Revisited*—music unlike any reinvention of folk or pop that we had heard before—effectively killed off any remaining notions that folk was the imperative new art form of American youth, and conferred on rock a greater sense of consequence and a deeper expressiveness. Clearly, it was music worth the killing of old conceits and older ways. In particular, with "Like a Rolling Stone" (the singer's biggest hit, and the decade's most liberating, form-stretching single), Dylan framed perfectly the spirit of an emerging generation that was trying to live by its own rules and integrity, and that was feeling increasingly cut off from the conventions and privileges of the dominant mainstream culture. In the same manner that he had once given voice to a new rising political consciousness, Dylan seemed to be speaking our deepest-felt fears and hopes—to be speaking for *us*. "How does it *fee-eel*," he brayed at his brave new audience, "To be without a *home*/Like a complete *unknown*/Like a *ROO-olling STONE?*"

How *did* it feel? It felt scary; it felt exhilarating; and suddenly it felt *exactly* like rock & roll.

WITH BOTH HIS early folk writing and his mid-1960s switch to electric music, Dylan gave voice to the rising anger of a bold new generation. In the process, he recast rock & roll as an art form that could now mock an entire society's values and politics, and might even, in the end, help redeem (or at least affront) that society. Also, Dylan proved to be a natural star. He cultivated an impeccable gaunt-and-broody look and a remarkably charismatic arrogance. He was razor-witted, audacious, and dangerous, and he was helping to change the language and aspirations of popular music with his every work and gesture. In addition, Dylan's interplay with the Beatles had seismic effect on popular music and youth culture. Combined, the two forces changed the soundscape of rock & roll in thorough and irrevocable ways that, a third of a century later, still carry tremendous influence. The two forces also had a sizable impact on each other. The Beatles opened up new possibilities in style and consensus; without their headway, Dylan likely would never have conceived "Like a Rolling Stone," much less enjoyed a smash hit with it. But if the Beatles opened up a new audience, Dylan determined what could be done with that consensus, what could be *said* to that audience. His mid-60s work reinvented pop's known rules of language and meaning, and revealed that rock & roll's familiar structures could accommodate new unfamiliar themes, that a pop song could be about *any* subject that a writer was smart or daring enough to tackle. Without this crucial assertion, it is inconceivable that the Beatles would have gone on to write "Nowhere Man," "Eleanor Rigby," "Paperback Writer," "Strawberry Fields Forever," or "A Day in the Life," or even that the Rolling Stones would have written the decade's toughest riff and most taunting and libidinous declaration, "(I Can't Get No) Satisfaction."

Dylan also bore influence on the Beatles in two other important respects. For one thing, he was reportedly the person who introduced them to drugs (marijuana, specifically), during his 1964 tour of England. This brand of experimentation would gradually affect not only the Beatles' musical and lyrical perspectives, but also the perspectives of an entire generation. Indeed, in the mid-1960s, drug use became increasingly popular with young people and increasingly identified with rock culture—though it certainly wasn't the first time drugs had been extolled as recreation or sacrament, or exploited for artistic inspiration. Many jazz and blues musicians (and, truth be known, numerous country-western artists) had been using marijuana and narcotics to enhance their improvisational bents for several decades, and in the '50s, the Beats had brandished dope as another badge of nonconformism. But with '60s rock, as drugs crossed over from the hip underground (and from research laboratories), stoney references became more overt and more mainstream than ever before. Getting high became seen as a way of understanding deeper truths, and sometimes as a way of deciphering coded pop songs (or simply enjoying the palpable aural sensations of the music). Just as important, getting stoned was a way of participating in private, forbidden experiences—as a means of staking out a consciousness apart from that of the "straight world." Along with music and politics, drugs—which at this point largely meant marijuana, but would later incorporate psychedelics, amphetamines, barbiturates, opiates, and cocaine—were seen as an agency for a better world, or at least a short-cut to enlightenment or transcendence. And though the Beatles would stay demure on the subject for another year or two, by 1965, hip kids and angry authorities were already citing such songs as Dylan's "Rainy Day Women #12 and 35" for their "druggy" meanings.

The other thing Dylan did for the Beatles was to help politicize them (in fact, he helped politicize a vast segment of rock culture), inspiring the group to accept their popularity as an opportunity to define and address a vital youth constituency. Following Dylan's example, Lennon and McCartney came to see that they were not only speaking for a young audience, but for a generation that was increasingly under fire. More and more, their music— and rock at large—became a medium for addressing the issues and events that affected that generation.

As a result of all this influence, Bob Dylan was—next to Elvis Presley—the clearest shot at an individual cultural hero that rock & roll ever produced, and though he certainly pursued the occasion of his own moment in history, he would also pay a considerable cost for his ambition. You can see the payment already beginning in *Don't Look Back*, D. A. Pennebaker's documentary of Dylan's 1965 solo tour of England. At every step of the tour, the young Dylan is met with rapt seriousness and testy curiosity, but also with the kind of pop-minded idolatry he had yet rarely enjoyed in America. And quickly enough, Dylan gets the better of it all—or at least seems to. He subverts an interview with a stuffy *Time* magazine correspondent into a stinging dismissal of the media, and how it bowdlerizes art, life, and truth. "I'm not gonna read any of these magazines . . . ," says Dylan, " 'cause they just got too much to lose by printing the truth, you know that."

"What kind of truths do they leave out?" asks the interviewer.

"On anything!" answers Dylan. "Even on a worldwide basis. They'd just go off the stands in a day if they printed really the truth."

"What is really the truth?"

"Really the truth is just a plain picture," says Dylan.

"Of what?" asks the interviewer. "Particularly."

"Of, you know," says Dylan, "a plain picture of, let's say, a tramp vomiting, man, into the sewer. You know, and next door to the picture, you know, Mr. Rockefeller, you know, or Mr. C. W. Jones, you know, on the subway going to work, you know. . . ."

Another time in the film, Dylan rails viciously and proudly against a drunken party-goer ("Listen, you're Bobby Dylan," slurs the drunk. "You're a big international noise." Snaps back Dylan: "I know it, man, I know I'm a big noise. But I'm a bigger noise than you, man.") And in one particularly funny but cruel scene, Dylan calculatedly picks apart a painfully unassured science student. ("When you meet somebody," asks the student, "what is your attitude toward them?" Dylan doesn't pause a beat. "I don't like them," he says.)

In each of these encounters, Dylan acquires new and startling traits of self-certainty, and they're all manifest in the quick, cocky expressiveness of his face. It's a sharply handsome, mutable-looking face, as vain and brooding as Presley's, as veiled and vulnerable as James Dean's. Yet at other times it registers exhaustion, fear, and the demands that come with fame and irrevocable knowledge. Sitting on a train bound for Manchester, his features looking wan and pinched, hands shielding his eyes, you get the sense Dylan probably wanted to crawl out of many of his own best moments. The pressure was under way, and it ate at him quickly. Compare the cover portraits from *Highway 61 Revisited* (1965) and *Blonde on Blonde* (1966) and you can find visible evidence of the singer's increasing strain. In the *Highway 61* picture, Dylan looks exactly like what he was: a smart, self-assured street- and pop-wise twenty-four-year-old poet-prodigy, willing to stare down the world with a defiant gaze. By the time of the *Blonde on Blonde* photo—shot maybe six months later—he looked wasted and wary. In less than a year, Dylan had seemed to pass from youthful assurance to a haunted and dissolute weariness. What you heard on *Blonde on Blonde* was a wizardly greatness; what you saw on its cover was the visage of a man being consumed by that greatness. It was a bit like coming across a picture of what Robert Johnson might have looked like, just before the end.

In July 1966, shortly after the *Blonde on Blonde* sessions—and immediately following a tumultuous concert tour of the United Kingdom with his backing group the Hawks (later renamed the Band)—Dylan was riding his motorcycle one morning nearby his home in Woodstock, New York, when the back wheel locked and he was hurtled over his handlebar. He was taken to Middletown Hospital, with a concussion and broken vertebrae of the neck. An impending sixty-date concert tour of America was canceled and so were all future recording sessions. He retreated to his home in Woodstock, with his wife and children, and spent months holed up with his friends in the Band. According to some rumors, Dylan was not as seriously hurt as was widely believed, and had decided to use the time off to immerse himself in his new family life. According to others, Dylan also used the sabbatical to recover from the intense psychological turbulence and rumored drug-and-alcohol bents of his short-but-titanic season as the king of rock & roll.

During that layoff period—in that same season that became known as the Season of Love—Dylan sat around at his Woodstock home and in the basement of a nearby house rented by members of the Band, and in essence reevaluated not just his music, but his political and spiritual tempers as well. All together in that time, Dylan and the Band recorded something over one hundred tracks—many of them new songs (most improvised on the spot) and several others that were covers of old folk, country, and rock & roll songs. What resulted was a set of recordings that many fans and critics regard as Dylan's most haunting and arcane body of work (author and critic Greil Marcus has written an entire terrific volume on the subject, *Invisible Republic*, published in 1997). Interestingly, Dylan himself would only rerecord two or three of those songs for release on his own later albums (though several tracks appeared on subsequent collections of his unreleased material, and many of the songs—most notably "I Shall Be Released," "Tears of Rage," "You Ain't Goin' Nowhere," and "Too Much of Nothing," were soon covered by such artists as Peter, Paul, and Mary, the Byrds, and the Band). Finally, in 1975—eight years after those sessions—Dylan authorized an official release of some of those recordings, *The Basement Tapes* (though if you look hard enough, you can find a five-CD set called *The Original Basement Tapes* that pretty much documents the entire affair; it's well worth the search and the expense).

As Marcus and others have noted, the basement recordings are full of strange parables, biblical references, half-finished tales of humor, flight, death, and abandonment. It is all roughhewn, primitively recorded—as if a ghost were taking it all down in its impalpable memory. And yet there is something about those songs that seems timeless, as if all the tumult going on in the world outside (a tumult that Dylan helped make possible with his earlier mind-challenging style of rock & roll) was simply far removed. At the same time, you *do* hear America—its joys, its losses, its fears, and betrayals— in those basement recordings as you hear it nowhere else in Dylan's music, not even in his early, more explicitly political anthems. What remains interesting, though, is how distant Dylan has sometimes seemed from what he and the Band created during that long season.

There is a spooky, unforgettable bootleg video of a visit between Dylan and John Lennon, as they sit in the back of a limousine, winding their way through London in post-dawn hours. It was shot in 1966 (for the singer's *still*-unreleased, astonishing film, *Eat the Document*), during Dylan's wild and dangerous U.K. tour with the Hawks, and in the roughly twenty minutes that the episode lasts, you can see that Dylan was a man clearly close to some sort of breakdown. At first he and Lennon are funny and acerbic—not to mention competitive—in their exchanges, though it also seems apparent that Dylan has been up the entire night, maybe drinking; maybe taking drugs. Suddenly, he starts to come undone. He is sick of having a camera in front of him at every moment, and more than that, he is *literally* sick. He turns pale and begs the driver to get him back to the hotel as quickly as possible. Lennon, meantime, is cautious, trying to stay clever, though he looks clearly horrified at what he is witnessing. Had Dylan kept up that pace—that pace of indulgence, that pace of making music that challenged almost every aspect of the world, music that outraged his old fans and caused his new fans to want him to push even *harder*—he might well have been dead within a season or two. The psychic costs of that sort of artistry, of that force of invention, can be unimaginable. It was as if Dylan danced extremely close to the lip of an abyss. *We* wanted to know what he saw there—we wanted to know so that we could have that knowledge without running the ungodly risk of facing that abyss ourselves. Dylan probably got as close to that edge as one can and still remain alive, and finally he decided that the glimpse alone was not worth his obliteration. Dylan, it seems, saw too much too fast, and was afraid of ever getting that close again to chaos.

At least, that's one way I have sometimes thought about what informed Dylan's retreat into Woodstock and into the fraternity of the Band and their music-making. It was a way of finding what could be recovered after one had learned too much about the meanness of not just the world outside, but also about the dark, troubled depths of one's own heart. Still, periods of retreat can sometimes be as painful to recall as whatever led to the retreat in the first place, and for whatever reason, Dylan has only occasionally incorporated the basement material into his active repertoire. Years after that time, Dylan would tell biographer Robert Shelton: "Woodstock was a daily excursion to nothingness." The Band's guitarist Robbie Robertson, in a conversation with Greil Marcus for the purpose of Marcus's *Invisible Republic,* seemed to confirm Dylan's comment: "A lot of stuff, Bob would say, 'We should *destroy* this.' " In that nothingness, though, Dylan made some of his best music, and—not for the last time—reinvented himself.

EIGHTEEN MONTHS after his 1966 accident—and at the peak of rock & roll's psychedelic era—Dylan returned to the pop world with *John Wesley Harding:* an acoustic-guitar and country rhythm–section album, featuring a man who was now singing in a startlingly mellifluent voice. Along with the basement sessions, *John Wesley Harding* was music that set out to find what could be salvaged in the American spirit—what values of family and history might endure or help heal in a time of intense generational division and political rancor. It was as if Dylan were trying to work against the era's context of rebellion and refusal, a context that he, as much as anybody, had helped make prevalent. (Indeed, almost every work Dylan made subsequently would run against the grain and temper of the predominant rock & roll sensibility.) Or perhaps he had simply lost his affection for a cultural momentum that, in his rush to fame and invention, had almost cost him his life and sanity.

But Dylan had changed rock & roll too much to undo or stop its drift, or to be released from the promises of his earlier visions. *John Wesley Harding* was simply further proof: The album's stripped-down sound and bare-bones style set in motion a wide-ranging reevaluation—and reaffirmation—of rock & roll root values and had a tremendous impact on everyone from the Beatles and Rolling Stones to the Byrds and Grateful Dead. In effect, *John Wesley Harding* flattened the visions and ambitions of psychedelia. After hearing *John Wesley Harding*, the Beatles made "Get Back," the Stones revivified their blues sensibility with *Beggar's Banquet,* the Grateful Dead made their countryish masterpieces, *Workingman's Dead* and *American Beauty,* and the Byrds (who had now acquired the remarkable Gram Parson) became an unabashed, fully-formed country-western band with *Sweetheart of the Rodeo.*

This trend began to disturb some critics a year later when, in 1969, Dylan recorded his own full LP of lovely and pure country songs, *Nashville Skyline,* that included a raggedy duet with C&W star Johnny Cash. The immediate effect of this offbeat turn was to complicate the myth of Dylan's personality, and the meanings of his music. It made him appear more enigmatic, mysterious, and abstruse, and raised questions not only about the validity of his musical departure, but about our political responses to it. Since country music was widely viewed as the music of a working-class sensibility, and since it represented a conservative audience that was seen as stalwart supporters of the war in Vietnam, did this mean that Dylan had now turned political sides? Or had he simply lost faith in political solutions altogether? ("Dylan's calm sounded smug, tranquilized," wrote historian Todd Gitlin in *The Sixties.* "To settle his quarrel with the world, he had filed away his passions.") Could music this refined and seemingly apolitical have any real meaning for a young audience still under the shadow of the Vietnam War? After all, rock & roll was supposed to be *for* a young audience, and in the climate of the late 1960s, that audience was politically concerned—in fact, mortally threatened. How could a rock figure of Dylan's caliber make music that failed to respond to those concerns? Like Elvis Presley before him, Bob Dylan changed the course of a nation, and then, it seems, attempted to remove himself from the ramifications of such an act.

Typically, Dylan was rarely helpful when it came to discussing such matters. In a 1968 *Sing Out!* interview (perhaps the most intriguing Dylan has ever given), Dylan's friend Happy Traum told the singer that Dylan's latest songs weren't as "socially or politically applicable as they were earlier." Dylan replied: "Probably that is because no one cares to see it the way I'm seeing it now, whereas before, I saw it the way they saw it. . . . Anyway, how do you know that I'm not, as you say, for the war?"

Some detractors accused Dylan of misreading the times, of refusing to commit himself on demanding issues, and perhaps they were right. But all the critical scrutiny only managed to obscure the truth that much of Dylan's post–*Blonde on Blonde* music was still wondrous. *John Wesley Harding, Nashville Skyline, New Morning, Pat Garrett & Billy the Kid,* and *Planet Waves* comprise a lovely, daring body of work. And even such broadly reviled works as *Self Portrait* and *Street Legal* are graced with more affecting music than most critics still care to admit. (If you need proof, play *Self Portrait*'s "Copper Kettle" some late night, when you have both a dismal—at least melancholy— mood and a strong drink at hand.) If much of Dylan's early 1970s work would no longer transform pop music or youth style, it was partly because the pop world didn't much want a Dylan it couldn't own or define—a Dylan unwilling to make obvious, assuring gestures—and perhaps Dylan didn't much want that audience.

For a brief period in the mid-1970s, this all changed. In 1974, Dylan mounted his first tour in eight years (again, with the Band), resulting in the raucous *Before the Flood.* At its time, it proved the most successful rock tour to date. Then, Dylan recorded what many critics still view as his single finest work, *Blood on the Tracks.* All the singer-songwriter's old wit and fire were back in fine form—but there was also a new, more aching depth, which many observers attributed to rumors that Dylan's marriage with Sara Lowndes was beginning to pull apart. In 1976, another fine album, *Desire.* Then, another major tour: Dylan barnstorming across America with the Rolling Thunder Revue, putting on some of the most fanciful and tantalizing shows of the decade, singing and writing like a man newly possessed.

Perhaps, then, it should have come as no surprise that, after this extraordinary season of renewed popularity, Dylan would make his boldest bid at disengaging himself from pop concerns. This time out, he turned his perspective to making "born again" Christian moralist music that had little lasting favor among most rock critics and pop faddists. Indeed, the cut-and-dried piety and matter-of-fact singing in Dylan's Christian music caused many of us to wonder whether his early greatness had simply been a fluke, or something that had now evaporated. Indeed, some of that music *was* pretty trying—just about all of *Slow Train Coming*—but parts of *Saved* and *Shot of Love* were plain bracing, especially the former's "Solid Rock," which sounded like the Sex Pistols proclaiming the might and wrath of early Christianity's world-shattering vision (which, come to think of it, really isn't that much different than punk's early world-shattering vision).

After the Christian venture (which, in some ways, I think never really ended for Dylan), it seemed to many fans that Dylan had now lost not just a certain vital sense of commitment, but also much of his relevance. Though Dylan would go on to make much lovely and resourceful music, he would never again produce work that would change or redefine America and its music or culture ("Like a Rolling Stone," as much as in any work in pop's history, *made* the times—in fact, the song didn't attract an audience so much as simply ran it over with the impact of the inevitable). Dylan's surpassing moment—among the brightest and most influential moments in modern American culture—had come and then, more quickly than any admirers ever expected, it had passed, and with much of his subsequent music he simply tried to outdistance the claims of his own past. Consequently, Bob Dylan found himself in a dilemma shared by no other rock figure of his era: He had been sidestepped by the pop world he helped transform. For the last thirty years or so, he has had to cope with that knowledge—and he has also had to cope with the knowledge that an increasingly capricious pop world has never really forgiven him for having lost the momentum of his frenzied, world-breaking vision.

BACK AGAIN to 1986—when I speak with Dylan during his recording sessions for what would become, in part, his *Knocked Out Loaded* and *Down in the Groove* albums. At that time, Dylan is in the midst of a period of high activity. For one thing, there's been his participation in the pop world's increased spate of political and social activism, including his involvement in the USA for Africa and Artists United Against Apartheid projects and his appearance at the Live Aid and Farm Aid programs (the latter, an event inspired by an off-the-cuff remark Dylan had made at Live Aid). More important, there were intriguing indications in 1983's *Infidels* and 1985's *Empire Burlesque* that the singer seemed interested in working his way back into the concerns of the real-life modern world. The latter album, in particular, plays as an artful attempt at adapting his music to recent advancements in pop sound, style, and technology. Yet the album's most affecting song, "Dark Eyes," is also Dylan's simplest, most ancient-sounding track in years. "Dark Eyes" is a statement of conscience, emotional distance, and moral divergence, and Dylan plays it straight from the heart—just his own voice, guitar, and harmony carrying the reverie, as if it were a dark madrigal. Over wistful staccato chords, and in a lovely high voice, Dylan looks back and ahead at the same time, and directly into the specter of unforgettable memories that seem indivisible from an uncertain future. "I live in another world," he sings, "where life and death are memorized . . . /Oh time is short and the days are sweet and passion rules the arrow that flies/A million faces at my feet but all I see are dark eyes." In the mid-1980s, "Dark Eyes" sounds to me like the music Bob Dylan might yet make, when he again cares enough to forget the vagaries and vogues of the modern pop scene.

Of course, Dylan has his own views about all this talk of decline and renewal. A little later in the evening at the Topanga studio, while various musicians are working on overdubs, he sits in a quiet office, fiddling with one of his ever-present cigarettes and taking occasional sips from a plastic cup filled with white wine. We are discussing a column that appeared in the April issue of *Artforum,* by critic Greil Marcus. Marcus has covered Dylan frequently over the years, but in 1986 he is less than compelled by the artist's recent output. Commenting on Dylan's career, and about a recent five-LP retrospective of Dylan's music, *Biograph,* Marcus wrote: "Dylan actually did something between 1963 and 1968, and . . . what he did then created a standard against which everything he has putatively done since can be measured. . . . The fact that the 1964 'It Ain't Me, Babe' can be placed on an album next to the 1974 'You Angel You' is a denial of everyone's best hopes."

Dylan seems intrigued by Marcus's comments, but also amused. "Well, he's right and he's wrong," he says. "I did that accidentally. That was all accidental, as every age is. You're doing something, you don't know what it is, you're just doing it. And later on you'll look at it and . . ." His words trail off, then he begins again. "To me, I don't have a 'career.' . . . A career is something you can look back on, and I'm not ready to look back. Time doesn't really exist for me in those kinds of terms. I don't really remember in any monumental way 'what I have done.' This isn't my career; this is my life, and it's still vital to me.

"Then again, I never really dwell on myself too much in terms of what I've *done.* For one thing, so much of it went by in such a flash, it's hard for me to focus on. I was once offered a great deal of money for an autobiography, and I thought about it for a minute, then I decided I wasn't ready. I have to be sat down and have this stuff drawn out of me, because on my own I wouldn't think about these things. You just go ahead and you live your life and you move on to the next thing, and when it's all said and done, the historians can figure it out. That's the way I look at it."

He removes his sunglasses and rubs at his eyes. "I feel like I really don't want to prove any points," he continues. "I just want to do whatever it is I do. These lyrical things that come off in a unique or a desolate sort of way, I don't know, I don't feel I have to put that out anymore to please anybody. Besides, anything you want to do for posterity's sake, you can just sing into a tape recorder and give it to your mother, you know?"

Dylan laughs at his last remark. "See," he says, "somebody once told me—and I don't remember who it was or even where it was—but they said, 'Never give a hundred percent.' My thing has always been just getting by on whatever I've been getting by on. That applies to that time, too, that time in the sixties. It never really occurred to me that I had to do it for any kind of motive except that I just felt like I wanted to do it. As things worked, I mean, I could never have predicted it."

I tell him it's hard to believe he wasn't giving a hundred percent on *Highway 61 Revisited* or *Blonde on Blonde.*

He flashes a shy grin and shrugs. "Well, maybe I was. But there's something at the back of your mind that says, 'I'm not giving you a hundred percent. I'm not giving *anybody* a hundred percent. I'm gonna give you this much, and this much is gonna have to do. I'm good at what I do. I can afford to give you this much and still be as good as, if not better than, the guy over across the street.' I'm not gonna give it all—I'm not Judy Garland, who's gonna die onstage in front of a thousand clowns. If we've learned anything, we should have learned that."

A moment later an engineer is standing in the doorway, telling Dylan the overdubs are done. "This is all gonna pass," Dylan says before getting up to go back into the studio. "All these people who say whatever it is I'm supposed to be doing—that's all gonna pass, because, obviously, I'm not gonna be around forever. That day's gonna come when there aren't gonna be any more records, and then people won't be able to say, 'Well *this* one's not as good as the last one.' They're gonna have to look at it all. And I don't know what the picture will be, what people's judgment will be at that time. I can't help you in that area."

TWO WEEKS LATER, Bob Dylan sits on a dog-eared sofa in the Van Nuys studio where Tom Petty is working, sipping at a plastic cup full of whiskey and water. He blows a curt puff of smoke and broods over it. His weary air reminds me of something he'd said earlier: "Man, sometimes it seems I've spent half my life in a recording studio. . . . It's like living in a coal mine."

Dylan and Petty have been holed up in this room the better part of the night, working on a track called "Got My Mind Made Up," which they have co-written for Dylan's album. By all appearances, it's been a productive session: The tune is a walloping, Bo Diddley–like raveup with Delta blues–style slide guitar, and Dylan has been hurling himself into the vocal with a genuinely staggering force. Yet there's also a note of tension about the evening. The pressure of completing the album has reportedly been wearing on Dylan, and his mood is said to have been rather dour and unpredictable these last several days. In fact, somewhere along the line he has decided to put aside most of the rock & roll tracks he had been working on in Topanga, and is apparently now assembling the album from various sessions that have accrued over the last year. "It's all sorts of stuff," he says. "It doesn't really have a theme or a purpose."

While waiting for his backup singers to arrive, Dylan tries to warm up to the task of the evening's interview. But in contrast to his manner in our earlier conversations, he seems somewhat distracted, almost edgy, and many questions don't seem to engender much response. After a bit, I ask him if he can tell me something about the lyrical tenor of the songs. "Got My Mind Made Up," for example, includes a reference to Libya. Will this be a record that has something to say about our national mood?

He considers the subject. "The kinds of stuff I write now come out over all the years I've lived," he says, "so I can't say anything is really that current. There may be one line that's current. . . . But you have to go on. You can't keep doing the same old thing all the time."

I try a couple more questions about political matters—about whether he feels any kinship with the new activism in pop music—but he looks exhausted at the possibility of seriously discussing the topic. "I'm opposed to whatever oppresses people's intelligence," he says. "We all have to be against that sort of thing, or else we have nowhere to go. But that's not a fight for one man, that's everybody's fight."

Over the course of our interviews, I've learned you can't budge him on a subject if he's not in the mood, so I move on. We chat a while, but nothing much seems to engage him until I ask if he's pleased by the way the American public is responding to the upcoming tour. Demand has been so intense that the itinerary has been increased from twenty-six to forty shows, with more dates likely. In the end, it's estimated that he'll play to a million people.

"People forget it," he says, "but since 1974, I've never stopped working. I've been out on tours where there hasn't been *any* publicity. So for me, I'm not getting caught up in all this excitement of a big tour. I've played big tours and I've played small tours. I mean, what's such a big deal about this one?"

Well, it *is* his first cross-country tour of America in eight years.

"Yeah, but to me, an audience is an audience, no matter where they are. I'm not particularly into this *American* thing, this Bruce Springsteen–John

Cougar–'America first' thing. I feel just as strongly about the American principles as those guys do, but I personally feel that what's important is more eternal things. This American pride thing, that don't mean nothing to me. I'm more locked into what's real forever."

Quickly, Dylan seems animated. He douses one cigarette, lights another, and begins speaking at a faster clip. "Listen," he says, "I'm not saying anything bad about these guys, because I think Bruce has done a tremendous amount for real gutbucket rock & roll—and folk music, in his own way. And John Cougar's great, though the best thing on his record, I thought, was his grandmother singing. That knocked me out. But that ain't what music's about. Subjects like 'How come we don't have our jobs?' Then you're getting political. And if you want to get political, you ought to go as far out as you can."

But certainly he understands, I say, that Springsteen and Mellencamp aren't exactly trying to fan the flames of American pride. Instead, they're trying to say that if the nation loses sight of certain principles, it also forfeits its claim to greatness.

"Yeah? What are those principles? Are they biblical principles? The only principles you can find are the principles in the Bible. I mean, Proverbs has got them all."

They are such principles, I say, as justice and equality.

"Yeah, but . . ." Dylan pauses. As we've been talking, others—including Petty, guitarist Mike Campbell, the sound engineers, and the backup singers—have entered the room. Dylan stands up and starts pacing back and forth, smiling. It's hard to tell whether he is truly irked or merely spouting provocatively for the fun of it. After a moment, he continues. "To me, America means the Indians. They were here and this is their country, and *all* the white men are just trespassing. We've devastated the natural resources of this country, for no particular reason except to make money and buy houses and send our kids to college and shit like that. To me, America is the Indians, period. I just don't go for nothing more. Unions, movies, Greta Garbo, Wall Street, Tin Pan Alley, or Dodgers baseball games." He laughs. "It don't mean shit. What we did to the Indians is disgraceful. I think America, to get right, has got to start there first."

I reply that a more realistic way of getting right might be to follow the warning of one of his own songs, "Clean Cut Kid," and not send our young people off to fight in another wasteful war.

"Who sends the young people out to war?" says Dylan. "Their parents do."

But it isn't the parents who suited them up and put them on the planes and sent them off to die in Vietnam.

"Look, the parents could have said, 'Hey, we'll talk about it.' But parents aren't into that. They don't know how to deal with what they should do or shouldn't do. So they leave it to the government."

Suddenly, loudly, music blares up in the room. Perhaps somebody—maybe Petty—figures the conversation is getting a little too tense. Dylan smiles and shrugs, then pats me on the shoulder. "We can talk a little more later," he says.

For the next couple of hours, Dylan and Petty attend to detail work on the track—getting the right accent on a ride cymbal and overdubbing the gospel-derived harmonies of the four female singers who have just arrived. As always, it is fascinating to observe how acutely musical Dylan is. In one particularly inspired offhand moment, he leads the four singers—Queen Esther Morrow, Elisecia Wright, Madelyn Quebec, and Carol Dennis—through a lovely a cappella version of "White Christmas," then moves into a haunting reading of an old gospel standard, "Evening Sun." Petty and the rest of us just stare, stunned. "Man," says Petty frantically, "we've *got* to get this on tape."

Afterward, Dylan leads me out into a lounge area to talk some more. He leans on top of a pinball machine, a cigarette nipped between his teeth. He seems calmer, happy with the night's work. He also seems willing to finish the conversation we were having earlier, so we pick up where we left off. What would he do, I ask, if his own sons were drafted?

Dylan looks almost sad as he considers the question. After several moments, he says: "They could do what their conscience tells them to do, and I would support them. But it also depends on what the government wants your children to do. I mean, if the government wants your children to go down and raid Central American countries, there would be no moral value in that. I also don't think we should have bombed those people in Libya." Then he flashes one of those utterly guileless, disarming smiles of his. "But what I want to know," he says, "is, what's all this got to do with folk music and rock & roll?"

Quite a bit, since he, more than any other artist, raised the possibility that folk music and rock & roll could have political impact. "Right," says Dylan, "and I'm proud of that."

And the reason questions like these keep coming up is because many of us aren't so sure where he stands these days—in fact, some critics have charged that, with songs like "Slow Train" and "Union Sundown," he's even moved a bit to the right.

Dylan muses over the remark in silence for a moment. "Well, for me," he begins, "there is no right and there is no left. There's truth and there's untruth, y'know? There's honesty and there's hypocrisy. Look in the Bible:

You don't see nothing about right or left. Other people might have other ideas about things, but I don't, because I'm not that smart. I hate to keep beating people over the head with the Bible, but that's the only instrument I know, the only thing that stays true."

Does it disturb him that there seem to be so many preachers these days who claim that to be a good Christian one must also be a political conservative?

"Conservative? Well, don't forget, Jesus said that it's harder for a rich man to enter the kingdom of heaven than it is for a camel to enter the eye of a needle. I mean, is *that* conservative? I don't know, I've heard a lot of preachers say how God wants everybody to be wealthy and healthy. Well, it doesn't say that in the Bible. You can twist anybody's words, but that's only for fools and people who follow fools. If you're entangled in the snares of this world, which everybody is . . ."

Petty comes into the room and asks Dylan to come hear the final overdubs. Dylan likes what he hears, then decides to take one more pass at the lead vocal. This time, apparently, he nails it. "Don't ever try to change me/I been in this thing too long/There's nothing you can say or do/To make me think I'm wrong," he snarls at the song's outset, and while it is hardly the most inviting line one has ever heard him sing, tonight he seems to render it with a fitting passion.

AGAIN, 1986. Another midnight in Hollywood, and Bob Dylan, Tom Petty, and the Heartbreakers are clustered in a cavernous room at the old Zoetrope Studios, working out a harmonica part to "License to Kill," when Dylan suddenly begins playing a different, oddly haunting piece of music. Gradually, the random tones he is blowing begin to take a familiar shape, and it becomes evident that he's playing a plaintive, bluesy variation of "I Dreamed I Saw St. Augustine." Keyboardist Benmont Tench is the first to recognize the melody, and quickly embellishes it with a graceful piano part; Petty catches the drift and underscores Dylan's harmonica with some strong, sharp chord strokes. Soon, the entire band, which tonight includes guitarist Al Kooper, is seizing Dylan's urge and transforming the song into a full and passionate performance. Dylan never sings the lyrics himself but instead signals a backup singer to take the lead, and immediately "I Dreamed I Saw St. Augustine" becomes a full-fledged, driving spiritual.

Five minutes later, the moment has passed. According to Petty and Tench, Dylan's rehearsals are often like this: inventive versions of wondrous songs come and go and are never heard again, except in those rare times when they may be conjured onstage. In a way, an instance like this leaves one wishing that every show in the True Confessions Tour were simply another rehearsal: Dylan's impulses are so sure-handed and imaginative, they're practically matchless.

Trying to get Dylan to talk about where such moments come from—or trying to persuade him to take them to the stage—is, as one might expect, not that easy. "I'm not sure if people really want to hear that sort of thing from me," he says, smiling ingenuously. Then he perches himself on an equipment case and puts his hands into his pockets, looking momentarily uncomfortable. Quickly, his face brightens. "Hey," he says, pulling a tape from his pocket, "wanna hear the best album of the year?" He holds a cassette of *AKA Grafitti Man*, an album by poet John Trudell and guitarist Jesse Ed Davis. "Only people like Lou Reed and John Doe can dream about doing work like this. Most don't have enough talent."

Dylan has his sound engineer cue the tape to a song about Elvis Presley. It is a long, stirring track about the threat that so many originally perceived in Presley's manner and the promise so many others discovered in his music. "We heard Elvis's song for the first time/Then we made up our own mind," recites Trudell at one point, followed by a lovely, blue guitar solo from Davis that quotes "Love Me Tender." Dylan grins at the line, then shakes his head with delight. "Man," he says, "that's about all anybody ever needs to say about Elvis Presley."

I wonder if Dylan realizes that the line could also have been written about him—that millions of us heard his songs, and that those songs not only inspired our own but, in some deep-felt place, almost seemed to *be* our own. But before there is even time to raise the question, Dylan has put on his coat and is on his way across the room.

IT IS NOW eleven years later, 1997, and Bob Dylan—presently in his late fifties—is still an active figure in rock & roll. Over the last several years he has been busier than at any time since the mid-1960s, releasing several collections of new recordings—even at one point writing and singing with the first major group he has ever joined (the Traveling Wilburys, including George Harrison, Tom Petty, and the late Roy Orbison).

Yet despite this renascence, and despite the enduring influence of his 1960s work, the modern pop world has lost much of its fascination with Dylan. In the last several years, artists like Bruce Springsteen, Prince, Madonna, Public Enemy, Metallica, Snoop Doggy Dogg, Nine Inch Nails, Kurt Cobain, Beck, Pearl Jam, U2, and Courtney Love have all produced (more or less) vital work that has transformed what popular music is about and what it might accomplish, and some of that work has affected the culture at large, fueling ongoing social and political debate. Dylan hasn't made music to equal that effect for many years, nor has he really tried to. At best, he has tried occasionally to render work that taps into pop's commercial and technological vogues (such as *Empire Burlesque* and 1989's *Oh Mercy*), or has mounted tours designed to interact with the massive audiences that his backing bands attract (such as his 1980s ventures with the Grateful Dead and Tom Petty and the Heartbreakers). More typically, he has produced records that many observers regard as haphazard and uncommitted (like *Knocked Out Loaded, Down in the Groove,* and 1990's *Under the Red Sky*—though to my tastes, they are among his best latter-day records and hold up wonderfully). In the early 1990s, he also released a mesmerizing set recorded for MTV, *Bob Dylan Unplugged,* plus two all-acoustic albums of folk material by other artists, *Good as I Been to You* and the exceptional *World Gone Wrong.* The latter two records feature some of the most deeply felt, spectral singing of Dylan's entire career—the equal of his best vocals on *Blonde on Blonde, The Basement Tapes, John Wesley Harding, Pat Garrett & Billy the Kid,* and *Blood on the Tracks.* (They also feature his all-time best liner notes. "STACK A LEE," he writes "is Frank Hutchinson's version. what does the song say exactly? it says no man gains immortality through public acclaim." Later he writes: "LONE PILGRIM is from an old Doc Watson record. what attracts me to the song is how the lunacy of trying to fool the self is set aside at some given point. salvation & the needs of mankind are prominent & hegemony takes a breathing spell.")

Good as I Been to You and World Gone Wrong remind me of something Dylan told me during our first conversation, back in 1985. We had been talking about the music of Bruce Springsteen and Dylan said: "Bruce knows where he comes from—he has taken what everybody else has done and made his own thing out of it—and that's great. But somebody will come along after Bruce, say ten or twenty years from now, and maybe they'll be looking to Bruce as their primary model and somehow miss the fact that his music came from Elvis Presley and Woody Guthrie. In other words, all they're gonna get is Bruce; they're not gonna get what Bruce got.

"If you copy somebody—and there's nothing wrong with that—the top rule should be to go back and copy the guy that was there first. It's like all the people who copied me over the years, too many of them just got me, they didn't get what I got." Over thirty years after Bob Dylan's first album (which was also a testament to his folk sources), *Good as I Been to You* and *World*

Gone Wrong are reminders of what the singer "got"—and *still* gets—from American folk music's timeless mysteries and depths.

In addition, Dylan has been touring almost incessantly for over a generation now. Beyond his stylistic, political, philosophical, and personal changes, beyond the sheer weight of his legend, Dylan continues to play music simply because, in any season, on almost any given night, it is what he would prefer to be doing; it *isn't* just a career, but instead, a necessary way of living. It's as if Dylan were committed once again to the restless troubadour life that he effectively renounced following his motorcycle accident, and as if he is now more invested in music's sustaining power than ever before.

In short, there remains much that is illuminating and beautiful—and also profoundly unsettling—to be found in Dylan's ongoing work. On his best nights onstage, for example, he might take a song like "Stuck Inside of Mobile with the Memphis Blues Again" or "Desolation Row," and turn it upside down, filling it with new wit and craziness. Moments later, he may turn around and deliver a folk ballad like "One Too Many Mornings" with a heart-stopping grace, in a voice as sweet as the voice with which he first recorded it, over thirty years ago, or he can take "John Brown" (for my money, his best anti-war song) and render it with a force that is truly breathtaking. In addition, Dylan's best post-1970s songs—including "The Groom's Still Waiting at the Altar," "Man in the Long Black Coat," "Under the Red Sky," "Dark Eyes," "Every Grain of Sand," "Death Is Not the End," "Blind Willie McTell," and "Dignity"—aren't that much of a departure from such earlier touchstones as "Like a Rolling Stone" and "I Shall Be Released." That is, they are the testaments of a man who isn't aiming to change the world so much as he's simply trying to find a way to abide all the heartbreaks and disillusion that result from living in a morally centerless time. In the end, that stance may be no less courageous than the fiery iconoclasm that Dylan once proudly brandished.

IT IS TEMPTING, of course, to read some of Dylan's recent music as a key to his current life and sensibility—but then that has long been the case. That's because, in the aftermath of his motorcycle accident, Dylan became an intensely private man. He did not divulge much about the details of his life or the changing nature of his beliefs, and so when he made records like *Nashville Skyline, Self Portrait,* and *New Morning*—records that extolled the value of marriage and family as the redemptive meaning of life, and that countless critics cited as Dylan's withdrawal from "significance"—many fans assumed that these works also signified the truths of Dylan's own private life. Later, in the mid-1970s, when Dylan's marriage began to come apart, and he made *Blood on the Tracks* and *Desire*—with those records' accounts of romantic loss and disenchantment—his songs seemed to be confessions of his suffering, and the pain appeared to suit his artistic talents better than domestic bliss had. Well, maybe . . . but also maybe not. The truth is, there is still virtually nothing that is publicly known about the history of Bob Dylan's marriage to Sara Lowndes—how it came together, how it survived for a time, or how and why it ultimately failed.

Since that period, there is even less that is known about Dylan, beyond a few simple facts: namely, that he has never remarried (and has apparently never found a love to take the place of his wife, except, perhaps, his love for God), and he reportedly maintains an attentive and close relationship with his children. Past that, Dylan's personal life pretty much remains hidden; in fact, it is one of the best-guarded private lives that any famous celebrity has ever managed to achieve. Dylan's friends do not disclose much about his secrets—except, that is, when they leak his unreleased recordings—and Dylan himself likes discussing these matters even less than he likes discussing the meanings of his songs.

Which only causes one to wonder: Are Dylan's songs truly the key to Dylan? Does his life still pour into his work? And is he a happy man—or have his history and vision instead robbed him of the chance for peace and happiness forever?

There are, of course, no definitive answers to questions like these, and maybe they aren't even the right questions to be asking. Then again, with Dylan it isn't always easy to know just what *are* the right questions to ask. During those recording sessions for *Knocked Out Loaded*, back in 1986, I once or twice tried broaching some of these topics with him. One night, at about 2 A.M., Dylan was leaning in a hallway in an L.A. recording studio, talking about 1965, when he toured England and made the film *Don't Look Back*. Though it was a peak period in his popularity and creativity, it was also a time of intense pressure and unhappiness—a time not long prior to his bizarre, early-morning limousine ride with John Lennon. "That was before I got married and had kids of my own," he told me. "Having children: That's the great equalizer, you know? Because you don't care so much about yourself anymore. I know that's been true in my case. I'm not sure I'd always been that good to people before that time, or that good to myself."

I asked him: Did he think he was a happier man these days than twenty years before?

"Oh man, I've never even thought about that," Dylan said, laughing.

"Happiness is *not* on my list of priorities. I just deal with day-to-day things. If I'm happy, I'm happy—and if I'm not, I don't know the difference."

He fell silent for a few moments, and stared at his hands. "You know," he said, "these are yuppie words, *happiness* and *unhappiness*. It's not happiness or unhappiness, it's either blessed or unblessed. As the Bible says, 'Blessed is the man who walketh not in the counsel of the ungodly.' Now, *that* must be a happy man. Knowing that you are the person you were put on this earth to be—that's much more important than just being happy.

"Anyway, happiness is just a balloon—it's just temporary stuff. Anybody can be happy, and if you're not happy, they got a lot of drugs that can *make* you happy. But trust me: Life is *not* a bowl of cherries."

I asked him if, in that case, he felt he was a blessed man.

"Oh yeah," he said, nodding his head and smiling broadly. "Yeah, I do. But not because I'm a big rock & roll star." And then he laughed, and excused himself to go back to his recording session.

That was about as far as we got with that line of questioning.

A couple of nights later, I saw Dylan during another post-midnight visit. "I'm thinking about calling this album *Knocked Out Loaded,*" Dylan said. He repeated the phrase once, then laughed. "Is that any good, you think, *Knocked Out Loaded?*"

Dylan was in that album's final stages, and he wanted to play me the tape of a song called "Brownsville Girl," that he had co-written with playwright Sam Shepard and had just finished recording. It was a long, storylike song, and it opened with the singer intoning a half-talked, half-sung remembrance about the time he saw the film *The Gunfighter,* starring Gregory Peck: the tale of a fast-gun outlaw trying to forsake his glorious, on-the-run life when another fast-gun kid comes along and shoots him in the back. The man singing the song sits in a dark theater, watching the gunslinger's death over and over. As he watches it, he is thinking about how the dying cowboy briefly found a better meaning of life to aspire to—a life of family and love and peace—but in the end, couldn't escape his past. And then the singer begins thinking about all the love he has held in his own life, and all the hope he has lost, all the ideals and lovers he gave up for his own life on the run—and by the time the song is over, the singer can't tell if he *is* the man he is watching in the movie, or if he is simply stuck in his own memory. It was hard to tell where Dylan ends and Shepard begins in the lyrics, but when "Brownsville Girl" came crashing to its end, it was quite easy to hear whom the song really belongs to. I've only known of one man who could put across a performance that exhilarating, and he was sitting there right in front of me, concentrating hard on the tale, as if he too were hearing the song's wondrous involutions for the first time—as if it were the first time Bob Dylan was hearing about the life he has led and can never leave behind.

I didn't really know what to say, so I said nothing. Dylan lit a cigarette and took a seat on a nearby sofa and started talking. "You know, sometimes I think about people like T-Bone Walker, John Lee Hooker, Muddy Waters— these people who played into their sixties. If I'm here at eighty, I'll be doing the same thing I'm doing now. This is all I want to do—it's all I *can* do. . . . I think I've always aimed my songs at people who I imagined, maybe falsely so, had the same experiences that I've had, who have kind of been through what I'd been through. But I guess a lot of people just haven't."

He watched his cigarette burn for a moment, and then offered a smile. "See," he said, "I've always been just about being an individual, with an individual point of view. If I've been about anything, it's probably that, and to let some people know that it's possible to do the impossible.

"And that's really all. If I've ever had anything to tell anybody, it's that: You can do the impossible. *Any*thing is possible. And that's it. No more."

On that night, as on so many nights before and since, I realized that it has indeed been something special to be around during a time when Bob Dylan has been one of our foremost American artists. I thought back to my youth and how Dylan's music had helped inspire my values and also helped nurture my spirit through several seasons of difficult and exciting changes. I was not alone in these responses, of course. Dylan managed to speak to and for the best visions and boldest ideals of an entire emerging generation, and he also spoke to our sense of scary and liberating isolation: the sense that we were now living on our own, with "no direction home," and that we would have to devise our own rules and our own integrity to make it through all the change. In the process, Dylan not only heroically defined the moment, he also invented rock & roll's future: He staked out a voice and style that countless other budding visionaries, including Bruce Springsteen, Patti Smith, Elvis Costello, Sinéad O'Connor, and Beck would later seek to emulate and make their own. And because he did this so affectingly, it became easy to take him and his work personally, to believe that he was still tied to our dreams and our hopes for pronouncements that might yet deliver us. Tom Petty's drummer, Stan Lynch, once told me: "I saw many people who were genuinely moved by Dylan, who felt they had to make some connection with him, that this was an important thing in their life. They wanted to be near him and tell him they're all right, because they probably feel that Bob was telling them that it was going to be all right when they *weren't* all right, as if Bob knew they weren't doing so well at the time.

"They forget one important thing: Bob doesn't know them; they just know him. But that's all right. That's not shortsightedness on their part.

That's just the essence of what people do when you talk to them at a vulnerable time in their lives. It doesn't matter that he was talking to them by way of a record; he was still talking to them."

Or, as Bruce Springsteen once noted, in some remarks directed to Dylan on the occasion of Dylan's induction into the Rock & Roll Hall of Fame, "When I was fifteen and I heard 'Like a Rolling Stone' for the first time, I heard a guy like I've never heard before or since. A guy that had the guts to take on the whole world and made me feel like I had 'em too. . . . To steal a line from one of your songs, whether you like it or not, 'You was the brother that I never had.' "

It's an understandable sentiment; to some of us, the epiphanies of youth count as deeply as the bonds of family. But as Dylan himself once told an interviewer: "People come up to me on the street all the time, acting like I'm some long-lost brother—like they *know* me. Well, I'm not their brother, and I think I can prove that."

It may be the only thing that he has left to prove—that he is not, after all, his brother's keeper—though in a sense, it hardly matters. The truth is, Dylan is still attempting to sort out the confusion of the day in the most honest and committed way that he knows. That is probably about as much as you can ask of somebody who has already done a tremendous amount to deepen our consciousness and our time. In the end, Bob Dylan remains a vital American artist—and one who we should be proud to claim as our own.

the

rolling stones'

journey

into fear

It may seem hard to fathom these days—watching Mick Jagger and Keith Richards' aged incarnations of their former terror-bringing selves—but there was a time when the Rolling Stones seemed the unmistakable apotheosis of rock & roll: superlative purveyors of blues and rhythm & blues who dramatized first the pop rebelliousness, then the moral disdain and political uncertainty, of an entire social movement. Later, when that uncertainty turned into frustration, and the frustration into malignancy, the Rolling Stones also mirrored the dissolution of their generation.

Maybe a better way of putting this is to state that the Rolling Stones said as much about the shared social condition of our lives as anyone else in rock & roll; in fact, they may have been pop's last *real* unifying force. By that I mean the Stones became a focal point for rock at a critical juncture: The Beatles had disintegrated in pain, Bob Dylan had seemingly traded his world-altering iconoclasm for family security, and the late 1960s psychedelic rock movement had turned hollow, even harmful. Then: There were the Rolling Stones again, back from a fitful term of drugs and death (actually, that term wasn't *quite* yet over for the band), singing songs boasting collusion in evil and revolt, touting themselves as "The World's Greatest Rock & Roll Band," and providing the music and performances to support either claim. Nobody since then has won such widespread assent, or seemed to define for so many what rock & roll should mean and look and feel like. This isn't to say that other artists didn't have as much impact on rock & roll (certainly the Sex Pistols and Nirvana—plus many rap artists—transformed rock's meanings, and large parts of its audience as well). Nor is it to say that other artists didn't prove better sellers than the Stones. Still, the Rolling Stones were perhaps the *last* thing that the rock & roll world at large seemed to agree on, and all the disagreements since then either amount to what one believes we've gained or what we've lost.

Which is to say that, in certain respects, the last twenty years or so haven't really proved that favorable for the Stones—or at least for their place in that later span of history. Following the 1960s, the group hit a long, limp stride, relying on their reputation to buoy them when their music couldn't. More important, the reference points of rock changed ineradicably: Punk bands like the Sex Pistols and the Clash had stolen the moment and sought to indict the Stones as an outmoded fetish, as well as symbols of inflated privilege and decadence. The charge wasn't far off the mark: The Rolling Stones had backed off from every notion of rebellion save an arrogant conviction in their own rank—a belief that allowed them not to flout authority so much as *own* it. The punks hit the Stones hard—alongside such songs as "Anarchy in the U.K." and "Guns on the Roof," the Stones' "Street Fighting Man" sounded like an anthem of equivocation—and though the group hit back a little with 1978's *Some Girls,* it wasn't enough to regain their cutting edge. The group still sold, still carried the weight of myth and sensation, but that's all that can be said of their story now for far too many years.

Still, the journey that brought the Stones to their own dissolution was rich, remarkable, and genuinely brave (though perhaps also mean and foolhardy). Along the way, the band became a measure of when rock music and its culture succeeded most and then failed bitterly; indeed, at that time, the Rolling Stones were the best definition rock & roll had of a center—a center that could not hold. In the years that followed, that center became scattered—as if hit by a shotgun blast. Other times, it seemed replaced by a void. Either way, it may be that nobody can ever define it again in quite the same way as the Rolling Stones once did, long ago, in frightened, ecstatic, and audacious times.

IN THE EARLY and mid-1960s, the Rolling Stones earned what was likely the most important designation of their career: Simply, they were a great white blues and rhythm & blues band. Unlike Elvis Presley, the Stones didn't help reinvent or transmogrify black music. Instead, with *The Rolling Stones, Now!, Out of Our Heads, 12 × 5,* and *December's Children,* they sought to assimilate or adopt Chicago blues and Chuck Berry–style rock & roll—which isn't, as some detractors suggested, the same as purloining or exploiting that music. For the most part, the Rolling Stones were upwardly mobile young men, enamored with black music's emotional artistry, though not so much the music's emotions—at least not the deep-rooted agony and fear (and *release* from agony and fear) that permeated American blues. (For the Stones, that deepening would come later.) In the mid-1960s, the Rolling Stones came closer to stylizing their own feelings in brittle, tense, keen-edged rock & roll singles like "19th Nervous Breakdown," "Have You Seen Your Mother, Baby, Standing in the Shadows," "Get Off of My Cloud," "The Last Time," and "(I Can't Get No) Satisfaction"—the latter among the 1960s' most defining pop songs. Not surprisingly, the emotions conveyed in these songs were those of disdain and rancor, arrogance and ennui.

My best remembrances of seeing the band—that is, except in the film *Gimme Shelter*—are from this period, during their 1965 U.S. tour, at an appearance in Portland, Oregon. I recall Brian Jones, squatting on his haunches, playing dulcimer embellishments on "Lady Jane," then picking up a teardrop-shaped guitar, clutching it high and tight to his chest during "The Last Time," standing insanely close to the stage's edge, inviting more real danger than even Mick Jagger did. I remember Jagger in an off-white suit, a bright blue ruffled shirt, barefoot and messy-haired, pulled up into a mock-toreador's stance, coaxing the audience with the shimmies of his tambourine, getting upbraided by a policeman down front who had to hold off the rushing kids, then kicking trash in the cop's startled face, waving him off with a scornful flick of the wrist, as if to dismiss, forever, any last threats of authority. I'd never seen anything that flirted so wildly and ably with mass chaos, and I'd never seen anything so magnificent. Later, I read something by critic Jon Landau that explained that show: "Violence. The Rolling Stones are violence. Their music penetrates the raw nerve endings of their listeners and finds its way into the groove marked 'release of frustration.' Their violence has always been a surrogate for the larger violence their audience is so capable of."

By 1966 and 1967, the Rolling Stones had come into their own. With *Aftermath, Between the Buttons,* and *Flowers,* the band made some of their most inventive music: part blues-based, part surreal pop, frequently eloquent, occasionally drug-steeped, and always best when it cut between affectations with the fleet, fiery glint of rock & roll. The band's 1967 work, *Their Satanic Majesties Request,* was at one extreme an overblown response to the

Beatles' *Sgt. Pepper's Lonely Hearts Club Band* and the pervasive pop psychedelia of that season. In another way, *Satanic Majesties* was a work that tapped or mocked the effete creative sensibility of that period as effectively as *The Velvet Underground and Nico*. At the time—and especially in the years that followed—*Satanic Majesties* was dismissed as an ambitious mess. Today, to my ears, it plays wonderfully, and beneath its occasional concessions to that season's notions of simple altruism, beats a dark, dark heart.

But it was with *Beggar's Banquet* (1968) and *Let It Bleed* (1969)— albums more or less of a piece—that the Rolling Stones made their most intelligent, committed, and forcible music. These were, in large measure, records about social disorder and moral vacillation, and more than before or since, the band seemed to say something about the moods and idealism coming apart all around them. The timing couldn't have been better. By 1968—a year in which Robert Kennedy was murdered in Los Angeles; Dr. Martin Luther King, Jr., was shot to death in Memphis; and the broken hopes of millions of people erupted in costly, long-term violence (climaxing at the Chicago Democratic National Convention, at which police brutally bludgeoned American youth)—rock & roll had become a field of hard options and opposing arguments. The Beatles seemed dazed and wary by their role as youth leaders. On one hand, they recorded two versions of "Revolution," in which they opted in, and then out, of the notion of violent revolt; then, on the flip side, they issued "Hey Jude," their greatest anthem of community and forbearance. By contrast, the Stones faced the contradictions of their position more directly. In "Salt of the Earth" (from *Beggar's Banquet*), Jagger extolled the working-class masses only to admit his hopeless distance from any real involvement with such people ("When I search a faceless crowd/A swirling mass of gray and black and white/They don't look real to me/In fact they look so strange"), and in "Street Fighting Man" (banned in several U.S. cities for fear that it might incite further political riots), the Stones admitted to both a desire for violent confrontation and a longing for equivocation ("Hey! Think the *time* is *right* for a *palace* rev-OH-*loo*-tion/But *where* I *live* the *game* to *play* is *compromise* SO-loo-tion"). For that matter, the Rolling Stones were asking some of the toughest questions around ("I shouted out, 'Who killed the Kennedys?' " sang Jagger in "Sympathy for the Devil"), and they didn't hesitate to deliver hard answers ("Well after all, it was you and me"). In addition, the group had suffered its own loss when Brian Jones left the band in June 1969, and was found dead in his swimming pool a month later.

The passion and persuasion of that music carried over to the Rolling Stones' historic 1969 U.S. tour, but so did the risk, culminating in the Altamont debacle that left four people dead, including one black man, Meredith Hunter, stabbed to death in front of the stage by Hells Angels while the group played an uneasy set.

LET'S STOP the story there, because in a way, that's where the story *does* stop. The Rolling Stones would go on to make some good-to-great work, including *Exile on Main Street* (a 1972 album of dense, brutal music that worked beyond rebellion, or more accurately, worked *against* rebellion in the sense that it cultivated dissipation); *Some Girls*, in 1978 (as R&B-informed as their early records, as prideful as *Aftermath*); and 1981's *Tattoo You*, with the band's last great single, "Start Me Up." I'd even be willing to add *Dirty Work* (1986) to the list—if only because, for once, the group's music was revolving around notions of anger, emptiness, and rejection that seemed candidly self-derived and mutual-directed—plus 1995's live album *Stripped*, because it features some of the best singing of Jagger's career: He finally sounds like an aged blues-jazz-pop pro, as mean, witty, and weathered as latter-day Frank Sinatra. (It really makes you wish Sinatra had covered Bob Dylan's "Like a Rolling Stone," or Jagger and Richards' own "The Spider and the Fly"; like Jagger, Sinatra would have torn the songs open anew.)

But after *Exile on Main Street*, the Rolling Stones would never again make music that defined our times, that helped us or even hurt us. They would never again make music that mattered much outside the needs and contexts of their own career—and even then it's hard to imagine that records as inconsiderable as *Goat's Head Soup*, *It's Only Rock 'n' Roll*, *Black and Blue*, and *Emotional Rescue* mattered even to the Stones.

SO, WHAT HAPPENED? What flattened one of the smartest, most fear-some bands that rock & roll has ever known? For a chance at an answer, let's consider what two different kinds of historians have to say. The first histori-ans to consider is a pair of authors, Stanley Booth and Philip Norman, each of whom in 1984 published essential books about the band. Both books—Booth's *Dance with the Devil* (later retitled *The True Adventures of the Rolling Stones*) and Norman's *Symphony for the Devil*—managed to rehabilitate the spirit of the Stones' peak period better than even a replaying of the group's music might, which is no small accomplishment. On the surface, such works of remembrance might seem superfluous at best. Rock & roll, after all, is an art-and-entertainment form bound in immediacy and performance, and it isn't easy for a retrospect to add much to our understanding of that music's impact or meaning. (Which is to say that no work of criticism or biography can possibly replace—or perhaps even truly deepen—the experience of first hearing "Sympathy for the Devil," "Street Fighting Man," "Gimme Shelter," "Midnight Rambler," "Brown Sugar," and "Casino Boogie" and understanding that well-defined visions of murder, revolt, chaos, rape, racism, and profligacy had just become notions to dance to.)

Still, Booth and Norman's narratives succeeded because the authors understood not merely the Stones' token tough-guys stance, but because they comprehended the quite real nihilism that consumed the band's ideals and creativity (and, at times, their physical health), and how the journey into that nihilism mirrored the dissipation of pop culture at large. In both books, it is the disintegration and death of the group's founding member, guitarist Brian Jones, in July of 1969, and the debacle a few months later of the Altamont free concert, that spells the effective end of the Stones' journey.

Of the two works, Stanley Booth's does the more impassioned job of putting across the Rolling Stones' remarkable rise to deterioration. A powerfully adept stylist with a seemingly inborn comprehension of blues music and blues sensibility (he also wrote about Elvis Presley, Bukka White, Howlin' Wolf, and B. B. King, among others), Booth attached himself as a journalist to the Rolling Stones' odyssey in England, during one of Brian Jones' starcrossed drug-possession trials, and then finagled his way onto the group's epochal (and fateful) 1969 tour to compose this book.

Some years later, resolved to overcome some of the emotional and drug problems which had derived, in no small part, from his association with the band, Booth finally pulled free of the Stones' sway to tell his tale—a tale that is as big and funny and bitter and shattering as the failure of an entire generation. True to his original intent, Booth's account sticks to the time frame of that single tour, interspersed with chapters detailing early band history. While one can't help but feel Booth has a much larger, probably more incriminating tale he could reveal, his implicit dismissal of everything in the Rolling Stones' history after the horror of Altamont is perhaps the most truthful and succinct summation possible of the consequence of the band's last twenty-eight years of touring and record-making: Simply, they are of little consequence whatsoever.

More important, of course, Booth's narrow focus on the Stones' late-1960s epic lends his insider's view a certain grim effect. He recounts the story of the band's trek to Altamont in parallel motion with a chronicle of their early ascent and its sad climax—the decay, dismissal, and subsequent death of Brian Jones—until by the book's end, there seems a certain inevitable connection between the two events, as if whims, ambitions, insights, and indulgences such as the Stones' couldn't help but demand human cost.

But Booth never draws his characters as mere exploiters or spoilers. He insists, and rightly, that at their best the Rolling Stones aimed to meet, understand, provoke, and rattle the spirit of their times with more inquiring intelligence than most of their contemporaries. "The Stones and their audience," Booth writes at one point, "were following decent impulses toward a wilderness where are no laws, toward the rough beast that knows no gentle night, nor aught obeys but his foul appetite."

In Jagger, particularly, we find a disdainful and intelligent blues fancier who meant to confront the moral and political questions of the late 1960s without forfeiting his taste for pop privilege. It is a contradictory approach, of course—one that cannot work. But to Jagger's eternal credit, with such overpowering, nondoctrinaire, and darkly compassionate songs as "Salt of the Earth" and "Gimme Shelter," he raised political pop to a summit that wouldn't be equaled (or topped) until the music of the Sex Pistols and the Clash. At the same time, with "Sympathy for the Devil," Jagger questioned the nature of personal and social evil with such flair that many listeners bought the song's surface allure of infamy and missed its underlying plaint. At Altamont, Jagger came face to face with the fatal outcome of his labors, and his music, manner, and singing were never the same after. Helping provide the context for murder can do that for you.

By the end of his tale, Booth has found his voice and momentum with a pitch and passion I've rarely seen equaled in pop journalism. He pulls us into the mad, deadly center of Altamont with the awful, compelling tone of someone who understood *exactly* the meaning of what he saw there on that day—on that occasion which was the worst in rock's public history, which helped kill off whatever thin idealism that 1960s youth might still have claimed. "You felt," writes Booth, "that in the next seconds or minutes you could die, and there was nothing you could do to prevent it, to improve the odds for survival. A bad dream, but we were all in it." Compared to Booth's account, all other recapitulations of Altamont—even the Maysles Brothers' excellent documentary, *Gimme Shelter*—seem secondary. Reading Booth's narrative, you can hardly wonder that it took him nearly fifteen years to face the task of remembering. I, too, would try to defer reiterating such fear and slaughter, even if it meant deferring my craft.

Compared to Booth's work, Philip Norman's *Symphony for the Devil* reads simply like a scrupulous history—which is exactly what it is. Indeed,

Norman—who wrote *Shout!,* the beautifully factual account of the Beatles' career which somehow seemed to miss altogether the spirit of that band's music—does an immensely more able job of recounting the Rolling Stones' familial and sociological origins and detailing the resounding impact the band had on the British pop scene. In addition, such necessary extras as early producer-manager Andrew Loog Oldham and Jagger's protégé-paramour, Marianne Faithfull, receive a full-fleshed, good-humored treatment here, while the always fascinating, perpetually heartbreaking Brian Jones undergoes a more critical (though no less compassionate) examination.

Both books finally reach much the same deduction: that the Rolling Stones came as close to the truth about pop's real sociopolitical effect—and spiritual cost—as anybody during that naive-but-dread-filled term of 1969, and that such insights probably stunned the band into a long season of grandiose irrelevance. So Mick Jagger became a sometimes silly peacock, and Keith Richards became a rather pampered excuse for an outlaw; so Bill Wyman was, for a time, an irreclaimable womanizer, and Charlie Watts remained the finest and kindest drummer in rock & roll; so guitarist Mick Taylor saw death coming down the same long slide that claimed Brian Jones and stepped out of the band, and his replacement, Ron Wood, seemed merely a spirited prop, meant to assure Jagger and Richards that the band still had a hard-tempered, exciting presence onstage. Why, then, do the Rolling Stones keep going—when loving fans like Booth and Norman figured out that their real dream died that one cold day twenty-eight years ago, knifed to death before their eyes, as they pondered the meaning and freedom of responsibility, and the connections between ideals of loving community and violent revolt?

Norman more or less says the Rolling Stones keep on because their image is too immunizing—from a brutal world that promised to shove a knife right down their throats just for asking the right questions at the right time—ever to let go of. Booth doesn't pretend to say why, because he realizes it means turning the questions on ourselves, on the terrible corrosion of our own beliefs about what rock & roll might accomplish, and about everything it failed to change. He comes to this resigned but hardly uncaring place with the knowledge of one who once stared into the passageway to hell and finally found a way to move beyond the terror of that vision, and for that reason his book outdistances anything the Stones have wrought since *Let It Bleed.* Also for that reason, Booth's is clearly the work to choose between the two volumes—that is, if you only have so much taste for tales of generational decline. Because Booth brings us closer to all the Rolling Stones' failures and deaths, he ultimately makes us feel more alive—and hopefully, more frightened.

OUR NEXT HISTORIAN is Mick Jagger himself. After all, it's only fair.

I've been reluctant to include any question-and-answer format interviews in this volume, since, to be truthful, when that form of writing succeeds it is as much the work of the person being interviewed as it is of the person asking the questions. That is, the interviewee more or less makes the article succeed or fail by the nature of his or her own thoughtfulness and articulation. Jagger's interview is the one exception I'm happy to make, but because, believe me, getting Mick Jagger to talk at length about the Rolling Stones' history was neither an easy or fun endeavor. I spoke to him on three occasions in London in the summer of 1987, for *Rolling Stone*'s twentieth anniversary issue. We talked once in a pub, once in a large Indian restaurant that Jagger had reserved for just the two of us (he was clearly delighted when I offered to pick up the tab), and once at the Rolling Stones' offices near King's Row. After each conversation, I genuinely had a painful headache. Jagger was certainly gracious, but the man had been interviewed for over a generation by that time, and he was quite practiced at the art of evasion. Sometimes I had to pose questions in several forms—or try to back into them—before he would divulge much. Later, when I transcribed and edited the interview, I was startled to see how much he *did* have to say about some matters, and not surprised to see how much he held back in other areas. Along with Lou Reed, Joe Strummer, Bob Dylan, Leonard Cohen, and only a few others, Jagger is among the smartest people I've had the chance to interview, though more than any of the others, Mick cost me a small fortune in Tylenol.

This interview originally appeared—in greater length—in *Rolling Stone*, November 5, 1987, and appears in this collection by kind permission of Straight Arrow Press.

We hear a great deal of talk these days about how inventive and magical and bold the sixties were. In fact, it's not uncommon to hear people speak of those times as if they were somehow better than any time that has come since. Do you share that perspective?

Every time is special, surely, unto itself. But to actually say it was better in 1964 or '65—I find that a bit strange. I mean, maybe it *was* a bit better, because you were, like, twenty years old back then, and you looked better, and you didn't have any responsibilities. You splashed around the beach and didn't have a mortgage and five children to look after. Given all that, it might appear better, though the truth may be that you were having a hard time back then, because you were strung out on too many acid trips or something. You forget about all that. I'm not talking about my own personal experience. I'm talking about people that actually, um, nostalgize. Is that a verb? It should be.

But yes, things were very different then than they are now. And they're never going to be the same.

I mean, there are two views of the sixties: one, that it was just a big hype; the other, that it was a wonderful—I hate to use the horrible word *renaissance,* but I suppose I can't think of a better one—that it was a wonderful renaissance of artistic endeavor and thought. But the underside to it all, of course, was the war in Vietnam and various other colonial-type wars. Also, all the political unrest of the times, particularly in Europe. I realize that most people tend to think that all the political unrest took place in America, but I really think it was on a much smaller scale there than you realize. To be honest, I don't think *real* political change ever took place at all in the United States. I mean, there were all the protest movements and so on, and I suppose there was some philosophical change, but in terms of deep political change, I don't think it ever really happened.

That's one of the ironies about all the current nostalgia for the sixties: Although we seem to believe that those times awakened our best ideals, I'm not convinced that we've carried them over to the present day with any lasting practical political or social impact.

Nor am I. On the other hand, one can't ignore all the social undercurrents of the time—how people became more tolerant of certain kinds of ideas and looks, and how that tended to influence general social thought. For example, look at the changes in civil rights. It's just tolerance of other people's ideas and the way they look and think. Perhaps that was the one political change in the United States that really took hold. It may not be perfect, but in the area of different minority groups achieving the political weight they deserve—or in the acceptance of feminist thought—at least there's been some improvement. But perhaps none of that alters the political power structure.

Looking back at the early and mid-sixties, the political climate in both the United States and Britain seemed relatively liberal—at least, compared with the political climate in both countries today. Do you think that atmosphere helped contribute to the sort of cultural explosion that rock & roll became during that decade?

No, I don't really think so. By the time the Labour party came into power in Britain in 1964, youth culture was already a *fait accompli*. That is, youth had already benefited from the prosperous inflationary period of the early sixties—that whole period of teenage consumerism that Colin MacInnes wrote about in books like *Absolute Beginners*. I mean, in the early sixties the cult of youth was already well on its way. In Britain, youth was already largely economically independent, and it just got more that way as things went on. So when the Labour government came in, they had no choice but to run with youth culture as an idea, because they couldn't afford to put it down. They wanted to be seen as trendy—*all* socialist governments want to be seen as trendy. They want to be seen as the friend of the young, because the young are the ones that are going to vote for them. You know, [former prime minister]Harold Wilson used to invite black singers to 10 Downing Street to try to look trendy.

Meanwhile, the government's policy *really* was to stop all this going on, because youth culture was entrepreneurial—not really socialist at all. Also, much of what was going on in youth culture wasn't really considered the nice thing to do.

At the time, it seemed that if there were any real leaders, they were artists like the Beatles and the Rolling Stones. Did you ever feel that you and the Beatles were helping to break the culture open?

It was more a sense of sharing a joke that these people were taking it all so seriously.

To be honest, we never set out to make cultural changes, though as they were coming, one was dealing with them on a natural basis. We *were* making certain statements and so on, but I don't recall actually intellectualizing those things—at least early on. Initially, I think the driving force was just to be famous, get lots of girls, and earn a lot of money. That, and the idea of just getting our music across as best we could.

And I think that's perhaps where that attitude of defiance really came from: those times when you'd come up against somebody who would say, "No, you can't do that. You can't go on television, you can't do this." But that had all been done before, really, back with Elvis on the "Ed Sullivan Show" and all that. What was happening with us wasn't anything new.

But nobody had really talked about the idea of Elvis Presley wielding political power. By the mid-sixties people were talking about artists like the Stones, Beatles, and Bob Dylan as having genuine political and cultural consequence.

What I'm saying is, I don't think any of us set out with a political conscience. I mean, I exclude Dylan, because he *definitely* had a political consciousness. And there *might* have been a seminal conscience in both our groups, but I think it really only applied itself to the actual mass culture at hand. You know, questions like "What do you think of people wearing their hair long?" or "What do you think about your clothes—aren't they a bit scruffy?" That was the real thrust of it all at the beginning. I think it was more social than it was political. You know, you'd go into a restaurant without a tie and get thrown out. It was really pathetic.

But wasn't there something implicitly defiant or contemptuous about the band's stance? For example, that famous incident in which the band got arrested for pissing against a garage.

I didn't take that as a social event. It was just bullshit, really. And I bet Andrew Loog Oldham [the Stones' manager in the sixties] paid ten quid to the garage man to ring the police [*laughs*]. That was the level it was on.

Yet with songs like "Satisfaction," "Mother's Little Helper," and "19th Nervous Breakdown," it certainly seemed that the Rolling Stones had something of their own to say—something a bit tougher and more questioning than one was accustomed to hearing in typical songs of teenage love and unrest.

As you got older during that time, you know, you got a bit more mature. Still, you've got to remember that for every one song that took some serious social view—like, say, "Mother's Little Helper"—there were loads of others that were just teenage bullshit. From the Stones, from the Beatles, from everyone. I mean, perhaps what we did in this period was to enlarge the subject material of popular music to include topics outside the typical "moon in June/I've got a new motorbike" teenage genre. We said you can write a song about anything you want. And that was really a big thing—it's certainly one of the big legacies in the songwriting area that we left, along with other artists.

I guess what I'm saying is that very early on, the Stones—more than the Beatles, more than Dylan, more than anybody—were viewed as something akin to social outlaws. One manifestation of that image was the way in which the Stones were seen as adherents of illicit drugs.

Aldous Huxley and Timothy Leary were the real proselytizers of that. I don't recall ever being a proselytizer myself. I don't ever recall saying, "This is what *I* do, and *you* should do it, too." I'm not saying I didn't privately think it, but I never was one who went out and actively said anything about it. Actually, you kind of kept quiet about it, because it was like hip peer-group behavior that musicians and other artists had indulged in for decades. It wasn't something that you wanted to spread outside. Just the opposite, because it was *your* little thing, and *your* little group of people did it. That was what made your group different, really, from the rest. You didn't like the idea of everyone else doing it. It was just this thing for creative artists.

Still, your audience was certainly hip enough to know what was going on. Weren't you concerned about the influence you might have on them?

It was all in the open before you could even think about it. You found yourself defending it without meaning to. Still, I don't recall defending it as a thing that anyone else should do. I might have said something like "Well, it's up to me what I want to do," but that's different. I *still* consider that different. It's the freedom of choosing your own personal experience, and these questions of freedom—whether you wanted to take LSD or *not* go to Vietnam—were sort of major legal and philosophical points of the time. It still seems absurd to me now that anybody can actually be put in jail for smoking marijuana or even selling it. It's absurd. Certainly this became one of the major arguments of the time: "This is my body, and you can't legislate what I do with it." Which is true: You *can't*. You can't just pass laws and enforce them, as far as drugs are concerned. It doesn't work. It didn't work during Prohibition, and it doesn't work with cocaine.

Looking back, are you unhappy that the Stones became identified by so many people as standing for drug use?

Yeah, I think it's very bad. As I say, I don't remember ever proselytizing for it myself, though, of course, you were sort of put on the spot to defend what you did. And you didn't want to say, "Oh, well, I'll never do it again," because that was absurd. So you were seen as defying authority, and in a way, that was the only stance to be taken. I didn't see any other stance to take. What were we going to do? Community service? You know, they weren't offering community service—they were offering *jail*. So, yeah, you got identified with the drug thing and with being an outlaw.

But I think it became a tremendous bore to everyone in the Rolling Stones who ever got either arrested or involved with drugs. In Brian Jones' case it probably contributed to his death. So it was tremendously regrettable—especially the damage it did by persuading people how glamorous it all was. In reality, it was also detrimental to the work the band was doing. And it went on and on and on.

Did it ever feel as if the Rolling Stones might not survive that particular passage?

Oh, yeah. Several times. Because you had to spend so much time defending yourself. In a way it was like being Lenny Bruce: He was a wonderful comedian, but he spent so much time defending himself every time he said "fuck" that he was never funny anymore.

You might get different answers from different people in the band, but if I remember right, it was not the intention of the Rolling Stones to become drug-user outlaws. It was a real drawback as far as creativity went. And it went on until 1977, with Keith's bust in Toronto.

All those things affected the band and gave us this image of being like a real bunch of outlaw dope fiends—which was to a certain extent, I suppose, true. But it was also imposed, somewhat. Because I think the original intent was just to do what one did and not make an issue of it.

There were other ways, though, in which the Stones came to be seen as advocates of evil. One of the more famous examples is your song "Sympathy for the Devil," which some fans saw as a delightful outright alliance with Satan and all that he represents. I wondered, though, if you actually intended the song more as a comment on the nature of personal evil—you know, the idea that if there's any devil in this world, it's the devil that lives inside each of us. In other words, it isn't Satan who ruins the world, but you and me.

Well, I don't want to start explaining my old songs, because I think it's much more pleasurable for people to have their own interpretation of a song or novel or film or so on. I don't think authors want to go around pointing out what people have taken wrong, so I'm not going to do any explaining, except to say that your point of view seems a pretty valid one to me [*laughs*].

You've obviously been thinking about "Sympathy for the Devil," and you got it right. More or less. But if some people want to take these things literally—I mean, if they only want to look at them on one level—well, that's fine, you know. It's just schoolmarmy for *me* to say you've got to look underneath the surface. If people want to take it literally, they take it literally.

But was it ever troubling that some people saw the Stones as some sort of devil worshipers?

I thought it was a really odd thing, because it was only one song, after all. It wasn't like it was a whole album, with lots of signs on the back—you know, sort of occult signs. It *was* only one song, and people seemed to very much embrace the image so readily, which has carried all the way over to heavy-metal bands today. There's a huge following for all these hocus-pocus bands, so obviously the subject has a vast commercial potential. But I should say here, we did *not* set out to make such a commercially exploitable thing out of the idea.

Perhaps what made the topic so potent is that it hadn't been addressed that way in popular music before. Also, you didn't treat the idea as if it were hocus-pocus. You seemed to take your subject seriously.

Well, for the duration of the song. That's what those things are about. It's like acting in a movie: You try to act out the scene as believably as possible, whether you believe it or not. That's called *good acting.* You have to remember, when somebody writes a song, it's not entirely autobiographical. I suppose it's a natural assumption that when somebody sees a songwriter like, say, Lou Reed or myself talking directly to an audience, that we're somehow relating a personal experience or view. And while I think that personal experience is a wonderful thing to build a song on, I also like to embellish personal experience with imagination. Like most writers do. The thing is, people *want* to believe. If they believe it, then great. If you are writing a novel, and somebody believes that you *know* the subject, then it's all the better for you. Because that's what you're trying to achieve.

What if what they believe is something troubling—something that could have a damaging influence?

Well, you've got to be careful. If you're doing a song that says heroin is great . . . I can't remember what Lou Reed's "Heroin" is about, to be honest.

The song doesn't proselytize for heroin—it simply depicts what the drug is like. It's certainly not a celebration.

But you know what I mean. People don't listen to that. They go, "Yeah, heroin—*great!*" But "Sympathy for the Devil" was pretty . . . ah, well, it's just one song, as I said. Hell, you know, I never really did the subject to death. But I *did* have to back off a little, because I could see what was happening. It's an easily exploitable image, and people really went for it in a big way. And I backed off, because I didn't want to go down that way—you know, have people thinking that was my thing. I wanted to have other subjects and other roles, and you get typecast in there if you don't watch it. I mean, the Rolling Stones were very typecast from early on in a way, with all the things we've talked about. Myself, I was *always* typecast as rebellious and so on. It was very difficult to come out with any other image, or when you did, you were ignored by the media.

Another song that seemed to find the Stones siding with transgressors was "Street Fighting Man." In a period when bands like the Beatles were carefully aligning themselves with the nonviolent factions of the anti-war movement, the Stones seemed more inclined to consider the notion of violent revolution.

Just the opposite. I don't think violence is necessary in this society to bring about political change. I was never supportive of the Weathermen or anything like that. I *never* believed that the violent course was necessary for our society. For other societies perhaps, but in ours, it's totally unnecessary. It's just morally reprehensible. And that's what I'm saying in that song, really. However romantic the notion of manning the barricades may seem . . . I mean, that romantic ideal actually brought down a government very close to here—the de Gaulle government in France. And in America, you had the rioting at the Democratic convention in the same year. So there was a lot of street violence going on, for very ill-defined reasons. I'm not quite sure what all that was really about, when you think about it now. I mean, the Vietnam War was somewhat a part of it, but was that the reason for the Paris riots? It's very hard to put your finger on what it was all about. It was a violent period. It didn't seem to have a lot of point to it. There was no great *cause* that was felt.

Well, as you say, in America we had the Vietnam War to oppose.

You had the war. But there were other things to revolt against, weren't there? When you actually look back on it, it's very hard to pin down what these causes were. Now maybe you'll get a lot of letters saying, "Mick Jagger doesn't remember. We were fighting for a lot of things—for the rights of minorities, to end poverty, and so on." And that's all certainly worth fighting for. But it's got to be said: There were a lot of people who wanted violence for its own sake. And in every crowd, these people tended to be the most loud-mouthed. You have to remember violence is the most exciting thing that ever happened to some people.

But this whole issue of violence seems indivisible from the Rolling Stones' image. In fact, to some people, it was synonymous with the band. You said it yourself, that violence is exciting for some people. Was it ever troubling to you that this was the image that many people had of the Stones? Or did it help energize your performances?

It's a . . . it's a *very* difficult question. I mean, I don't know what to say. [*Pauses.*] The best rock & roll music encapsulates a certain high energy— an angriness—whether on record or onstage. That is, rock & roll is only rock & roll if it's not safe. You know, one of the things I hate is what rock & roll has become in a lot of people's hands: a safe, viable vehicle for pop. Oh, it's inevitable, I suppose, but I don't like that sort of music. It's like, rock & roll—the best kind, that is, the real thing—is always brash. That's the reason for punk. I mean, what was punk about? Violence and energy—and *that's* really what rock & roll's all about.

And so it's inevitable that the audience is stirred by the anger they feel. That's probably one of the ideas. Now, if that anger spills out into the street, that's not funny for people. But if it's contained within a theater and a few chairs get broken, my opinion at the time—and my opinion now—is, well, so what?

But the truth is, I don't like to see people getting hurt. At early concerts we did, the police used to . . . I remember vividly the first time we played Memphis. Little girls would be standing up taking pictures, and the police would come down front and *bang*—these girls would get hit over the head with a billy club. And the same happened in Europe, in Germany and Holland—this gratuitous violence from the police or the bouncers or whoever they were, the people there with the muscle. And the audiences were often provoked by that *more*—that the authorities were creating these confrontations. Because otherwise, nothing much really happens at rock shows. I mean, you get a few kids onstage. But when they start to put huge flanks of police or private security in there, with the sole idea of showing how butch they are—the classic case being Altamont—then there's trouble.

Anyway, it's never been my intention to encourage people to get hurt. In fact, we used to always stop in the middle of a number if we saw someone getting hurt. I remember doing that many times. And yes, sometimes it got out of hand.

Well, it doesn't really happen anymore.

Perhaps the most famous instance of it getting out of hand, as you mentioned, was at Altamont. Over the years many people have asserted that the violence that occurred on that day was somehow a consequence of the dark imagery the band had been flirting with all along. Looking back, does that seem like a fair accusation?

It's not fair. It's ridiculous. I mean, to me that is the most *ridiculous* journalistic contrivance I ever heard. I disagreed with Jann Wenner at the time. I *still* disagree with him. I *don't* think he was at the concert. I don't think any of the writers who wrote about it so fully were ever there. Everyone who lived in San Francisco—including a lot of those people who wrote about Altamont—knew that a lot of concerts had gone on with all these same organizers, with the Hell's Angels. It had simply happened a lot in San Francisco. And it may sound like an excuse, but we believed—however naively—that this show could be organized by those San Francisco people who'd had experience with this sort of thing. It was just an established ritual, this concert-giving thing in the Bay Area. And just because it got out of hand, we got the blame. Well, I think that was passing the buck, because those writers who were there *knew* we didn't organize the concert. I mean, *we did not organize it.* Perhaps we should have—that's another question. In fact, that was one of the lessons well learned.

But at the time, I naively thought that these people in San Francisco were the most organized people, because at that time they had a lot going for them, a lot of respect. And I went along with it. If I'd known it was going to be what it was, obviously I wouldn't have done it. It was foolish of me to be so naive, but we were still living at the end of the "everyone's together and lovable" era, and San Francisco was supposed to be the center of it all. That's one of the reasons we did the concert there.

So I don't buy all that other bullshit. I mean, that's an excuse made by the people in San Francisco. And I don't like when they completely put the blame on us. *Some* of it, yeah. But not all of it.

In their recent books about the Rolling Stones, Philip Norman and Stanley Booth—

God bless them both.

Both authors have claimed that after Altamont, the Rolling Stones were never quite the same—that the group was never quite as willing to invoke violence in its music, or even face tough issues, except in largely superficial ways.

I don't know. I mean, it sounds really good in a book, you know, to have, like, this great claim: "And that was the end of the era." It's all so wonderfully convenient.

But, you know, it *did* teach me a lesson. The lesson is that you can't do a large show without, um, control.

But as to violence and so on . . . well, we did a song on the last album that's quite violent ["One Hit to the Body"], and I don't think . . . well, *maybe.* I mean, you can postulate all you want about what happened on that day. I don't know. I felt very upset. And I was very sad about the violence, the guy that died and the Hell's Angels behaving the way they did. It was *awful.* It was a horrible thing to go through. I hated it. And the audience had a hard time. It was a lesson that we all learned. It was a horrible experience—not so much for me as for the people that suffered. *I* had a pretty easy ride, you know—I was lucky. There's no doubt that it did leave . . . a regret. And it left things at a very low ebb at the end of what was otherwise a very successful tour—in fact, the first major arena tour.

So, I don't know—I'm not the one to make the judgment, except to say I think it's a bit convenient when you're writing a book. I mean, this notion of "the end of the sixties"—it's just too good to be true. I mean, things aren't quite as simple as that. But it was . . . it was . . . an *experience.*

Let's move ahead a couple of years, to the time that you recorded Exile on Main Street—*an album that many critics now regard as the Rolling Stones' finest work.*

I don't.

You don't?

No. It's a wonderful record, but I wouldn't consider it the finest of the Rolling Stones' work. I think that *Beggars Banquet* and *Let It Bleed* were better records. They're more compressed. You know, when you put a double album out, there's always going to be something that could have been left off and would have made it maybe better.

But, you know, *Exile* . . . its reputation just seems bigger now than it was back then. I remember it didn't really sell well at the time, and there was only one single off it. And we were still in this phase where we weren't really commercially minded; we weren't trying to exploit or wring dry the record like one would do now, with a lot of singles. I mean, we weren't really looking at the financial and commercial aspects of it.

But the truth is, it wasn't a huge success at the time. It wasn't even critically well received. I think if you go back and look at the reviews, you'll see I'm right. It mostly got very indifferent reviews. And I love it now when all these critics say it was the most wonderful thing, because it's a lot of those same guys who, at the time, said it was crap! Anyway, I think *Exile* lacked a bit of definition. I'm being supercritical, I know, but the record lacks a little focus.

But that's part of what seems to lend the record its force. It seems like a work of world-weariness—the work that results from a time of disillusion. In that sense, it also seems a bit of a definitive seventies work.

Is it? I don't know what the seventies is really all about. Spandex trousers, isn't it? And, you know, funny clothes? I think *Exile* was a hangover from the end of the sixties.

Were the seventies a harder time to be inspired?

Well, judging from the records, perhaps they were. I mean, at the time I felt I was just carrying on, but . . . well, it's a long way from *Exile* to "Angie." I don't think that one would've gone on *Exile*. The Rolling Stones is just a straight-ahead rock & roll band.

Do you consider that a limitation?

Yes, it is limiting, but I *like* the limitation of that. That's fine.

For years, though, the Rolling Stones seemed to define what rock & roll could be at its best. You know, "The World's Greatest Rock & Roll Band" and all that.

    I never trumpeted us as such . . . though I did put up with it, I suppose.

    I mean, people have this obsession: They want you to be like you were in 1969. They want you to, because otherwise, their youth goes with you, you know? It's very selfish, but it's understandable.

the

legacy of

jim morrison

and

the doors

*n*early twenty-five years ago, in the middle of a season in which rock & roll was seeking to define itself as the binding force of a new youth community, the Doors became the houseband for an American apocalypse that wasn't even yet upon us. Indeed, the Los Angeles–based quartet's stunning and rousing debut LP, *The Doors,* flew in the face of rock's new emerging positivist ethos, and in effect helped form the basis for an argument that persists until the present day in popular music. Whereas groups like the Beatles or the many bands emerging from the Bay Area scene were earnestly touting a fusion of music, drugs, and idealism that they hoped would re-form—and redeem—a troubled age, the Doors had fashioned an album that looked at prospects of hedonism and violence, of revolt and chaos, and embraced those prospects unflinchingly. Clearly, the Doors—in particular the group's thin, darkly handsome lead singer, Jim Morrison—understood a truth about their age that many other pop artists did not understand: that these were dangerous times—and dangerous not only because youth culture was under fire for breaking away from established conventions and aspirations. On some level, Morrison realized that the danger was also internal, that the "love generation" was hardly without its own dark impulses. In fact, Morrison seemed to understand that any generation so bound on giving itself permission to go as far as it could was also giving itself a permission for destruction, and he seemed to gain both delight and license from that understanding.

Consequently, in those moments toward the end of the Doors' experimental Oedipal mini-opera, "The End," when Morrison sang about wanting to kill his father and fuck his mother, he managed to take a somewhat silly notion of outrage and make it sound convincing, even somehow *just*. More than the songs of Bob Dylan or the Rolling Stones, Morrison's lyrics were a recognition that an older generation had betrayed its children, and that this betrayal called for a bitter payback. Little wonder, then, that the Doors' music (in particular, "The End") became such a meaningful favorite among the American youth fighting in Vietnam, in a war where children had been sent to kill or die for an older generation's frightened ideals. Other groups were trying to prepare their audience for a world of hope and peace; the Doors, meanwhile, were making music for a ravenous and murderous time, and at the group's best, the effect was thoroughly scary, and thoroughly exhilarating.

Now, a generation later—in a time when, at home, anti-drug and anti-obscenity sentiments have reached a fever pitch, and when, abroad, the Doors' music is once again among the favored choices of young Americans fighting in the Gulf War—Jim Morrison seems more heroic to many pop fans than ever before. Indeed, a film like Oliver Stone's *The Doors*—which is the most ambitious, epic-minded movie yet produced about rock culture and its discontents—can even make it seem that the band, in a dark way, has won its argument with cultural history. But back in the midst of the late 1960s, it seemed rather different. To many observers, it appeared that the group had pretty much shot its vision on its first album. By the time of the Doors' second LP, *Strange Days* (October 1967), the music had lost much of its edginess—the sense of rapacity, of persistent momentum, that had made the previous album seem so undeniable—and in contrast to the atmosphere of aggression or dread that Morrison's earlier lyrics had made palpable, the new songs tended too often to the merely melodramatic ("Strange Days"), or to flat-out pretension ("Horse Latitudes"). It was as if a musical vision that, only a few months earlier, had seemed shockingly original and urgent had turned flatly morbid, even parodic.

In addition, Morrison himself was already deeply caught up in the patterns of drug and alcohol abuse and public misbehavior that would eventually prove so ruinous to him, his band, his friends, and his family. Some of this behavior, of course, was simply expected of the new breed of rock hero:

In the context of the late 1960s and its generational schisms, youth stars often made a point of flaunting their drug use, or of flouting mainstream or authoritarian morality. Sometimes, this impudence was merely showy or naive, though on certain other occasions—such as the December 1967 incident in which Morrison was arrested after publicly castigating police officers for their backstage brutality at a New Haven concert—these gestures of defiance helped embolden the rock audience's emerging political sensibility. More often than not, though, Morrison's unruliness wasn't so much a gesture of countercultural bravado as it was simply a sign of the singer's own raging hubris and out-of-control dissipation.

In other words, something far darker than artistic or political ambition fueled Jim Morrison's appetite for disruption, and in March 1969, at an infamous concert in Miami, this sad truth came across with disastrous results. In the current film version of this incident, Oliver Stone portrays the concert as part pageant and part travesty, and while it was perhaps a bit of both, most firsthand accounts have described the show as simply a pathetic, confusing mess. The Doors had been scheduled to perform at 10 P.M., but had been delayed nearly an hour due to a dispute with the show's promoters. By the time the group arrived onstage, Morrison was already inebriated, and continued to hold up the performance while he solicited the audience for something more to drink. A quarter-hour later, after the music started, Morrison would halt songs in mid-performance and wander about the stage, berating the audience to commit revolution and to love him. At one point during the evening, he pulled on the front of his weatherworn leather jeans and threatened to produce his penis for the crowd's perusal. (Oddly enough, though more than twenty years have passed, and more than ten thousand people witnessed Morrison's performance—including band members and police officers onstage—it has never been clearly determined whether Morrison actually succeeded in exposing himself that night.) Finally, toward the end of the show, Morrison hounded audience members into swarming onstage with him, and the concert ended in an easy version of the chaos to which the singer had long professed to aspire.

At the time, the event seemed more embarrassing than outrageous, but within days, the *Miami Herald* and some political-minded city and legal officials had inflated the pitiable debacle into a serious affront on Miami and the nation's moral welfare; in addition, Morrison himself was sized up as a foul embodiment of youth's supreme indecency. The Doors' nationwide schedule ground to an immediate halt, and in effect, the band's touring days were finished. Amid all the hoopla that would follow—the public debate, Miami's shameful trial for obscenity—almost nobody saw Morrison's gesture that evening for what it truly was: the act of a man who had lost faith in his art, himself, and his relation to the world around him. On that fateful evening in Miami, Jim Morrison no longer knew what his audience wanted from him, or what he wanted from himself for that matter, and so he offered up his most obvious totem of love and pride, as if it were the true source of his worth. The Doors' lead singer—who only two years before had been one of rock's smartest, scariest, and sexiest heroes—was now a heartrending alcoholic and clownish jerk. He needed help; he did not merit cheap veneration, and he certainly did not deserve the horrid, moralistic-minded brand of jailhouse punishment that the State of Florida hoped to impose on him.

Of course, Morrison never received—or at least never accepted—the help that might have saved him. By 1970, the Doors were a show-business enterprise with contracts and debts, and these obligations had been severely deepened by Morrison's Miami antics. To meet its obligations, the band would produce five albums over the next two years, including two of the group's most satisfying studio efforts, *Morrison Hotel* and *L.A. Woman:* surprisingly authoritative, blues-steeped works that showed Morrison settling into a new, lusty, dark-humored vocal and lyrical sensibility. But if Morrison had finally grown comfortable with the idea of rock & roll–for-its-own-sake, he also realized that he no longer had much of consequence he wanted to say in that medium—or at least nothing he cared to say in the context of the Doors.

In March 1971, Morrison took a leave of absence from the Doors, and along with his common-law wife, Pamela Courson, moved to Paris, ostensibly to distance himself from the physical and spiritual rigors of rock & roll, and to regenerate his vocation as a modern poet. Perhaps in time he might have come to a compassionate wisdom about what he and his generation had experienced in the last few years, as the idealism of the 1960s had finally given way to a deflating sense of fear and futility. (Certainly there were glimmers in Morrison's last few interviews that he had begun to acquire some valuable insight about the reasons and sources for his—and his culture's—bouts of excess.) As it turned out, Morrison simply continued to drink in a desolating way, and according to some witnesses, he sometimes lapsed into depression over his inability to reinvoke his poetic muse, taking instead to writing suicide notes.

Finally, at five in the morning on July 4, 1971, Pamela Courson found Morrison slumped in the bathtub of their Paris flat, a sweet, still grin on his face. At first, Courson thought he was playing a death-game with her. On this dark morning, though, Morrison was playing no game. His skin was cold to his wife's touch. Jim Morrison had died of heart failure, at age twenty-seven, smiling into the face of a slow-coming abyss that, long before, he had decided was the most beautiful and comforting certainty of his life.

INITIALLY, Morrison's death seemed to be the end for the Doors. In fact, the rock community accepted the news of his passing with a sad sense of logic. The year before, Jimi Hendrix and Janis Joplin had died as well, also of causes brought on by the use of alcohol or drugs. Now, Morrison's death—which had been more clearly foreseeable—made plain that young fatalities were likely to be one of the more frequent costs of rock heroism, that today's brightest prodigy might simply be tomorrow's next likely flameout. Though the surviving Doors—keyboardist Ray Manzarek, drummer John Densmore, and guitarist Robby Krieger—went on to make two trio albums under the band's name, they could never really rebound from Morrison's death. If, in some ways, Morrison had turned out to be the band's most troubling and limiting factor, he had also been the group's central claim to an identity or purpose, and without him, the Doors weren't even a notable name.

Today, though, over twenty years after Morrison's death, the Doors enjoy a renewed popularity that shows no signs of abating—a popularity that, in fact, might have proved far more elusive had Morrison survived and returned to the group. The roots for this renewal trace back to the mid- and late 1970s, and to the issues surrounding the advent of the punk movement. By 1976, many younger rock & roll fans and musicians began to feel that the pop world had lost touch with its sense of daring, that much of the music of the 1970s, and the work of the surviving mainstays of the 1960s, had grown too timid in content, and too obsessed with privilege and distance. As punk rose, it brought with it a reevaluation of rock history, and as a result, some of the tougher-minded bands of the late 1960s—such as the Doors, Velvet Underground, MC5, and the Stooges, all of whom had explored some decidedly difficult and often unpopular themes during their short-lived careers—enjoyed a new currency that transformed them into some of American rock's more enduring and pervasive influences.

The Doors' revival was also helped along by Francis Coppola's use of the band's music in his film, *Apocalypse Now*. Watching Coppola's repellently beautiful immolation of the Vietnamese jungles by napalm, accompanied onscreen by Jim Morrison intoning "The End," made vividly plain that the best of the Doors' music had, all along, been a brilliant and irrefutable soundtrack to one of the more notorious examples of modern-day hell. And finally, the Doors' comeback owes a great debt to *No One Here Gets Out Alive*,

Jerry Hopkins and Danny Sugarman's highly sensationalistic (and probably frighteningly accurate) account of Morrison's life and death. The book's excitable chief theme (a theme that has been appropriated and advanced by Oliver Stone in his film) is that "Jim Morrison was a god," a dark-tempered, visionary poet who was also a heroic example of the wisdom that can be found by living a life of relentless excesses.

In other words, Jim Morrison has gradually been rehabilitated into one of the more indelible, widely revered heroes of the 1960s, or of rock & roll history at large for that matter. In part, this has happened because several of the people involved in this curious reclamation have a stake in redeeming Morrison's legacy, and because they have found that there is still a considerable career to be made in perpetuating his and the Doors' history. But what is perhaps more interesting is to ask why Morrison's revival has played so well and so consistently with the modern rock audience of the last decade or so. In other words, what does a contemporary rock audience find in Morrison, or need from him, that cannot be found in the musicians of its own generation? After all, we are told repeatedly that this is a more conservative era, and that in particular, today's youth is far more conservative than the youth of the 1960s. If that's the case, why does such a large young audience continue to revere an artist that appeared to be so radically hedonistic (even nihilistic) in his outlook?

The truth is, Jim Morrison is an ideal radical hero for a conservative era. Though he may have lived a life of defiance and rebellion, it was not a defiance rooted in any clear ideology or political vision, unlike, for example, the brand of rebellion that John Lennon would come to aspire to. Morrison's defiance had deep personal sources—it derived from a childhood spent in a family with a militaristic and authoritarian disposition. As such, Morrison's mode of insurrection was hardly insignificant or without merit; indeed, it was often wielded as a badge of hard-won courage, and that courage is partly what today's audience recognizes and loves about him.

But Morrison's defiance also often took the form of outright disregard—an unconcern for how his impulses and temper could cause damage not only to uptight moralists, but to the people who loved and depended on him most. In short, Morrison committed his outrages and cultivated his hedonism in sometimes remarkably conscienceless ways, and unfortunately, this habit may also be part of what many rock fans admire or seek to emulate about him. In a time when some pop stars try to engage their audience in various humanitarian and political causes, and in a time when numerous role models and authority figures advise the young to make a virtue of modesty or abstinence, there are numerous fans who are unmoved by these admonitions. A few artists, such as Guns n' Roses [or, in 1997, Marilyn Manson], are seen to live out this bravado for today's defiant types, but none, of course, have lived it out quite as effectively as Jim Morrison, who was fond of telling his audience: "I don't know about you, but I intend to have *my* kicks before the whole fucking shithouse explodes." It isn't so much a radical message, since radicalism aims to change something beyond the domain of the self. In a sense, it's simply a dark extension of the philosophy of self-regard that became so indelibly identified with the Reagan-Bush era.

But the costs of this bravado can be sizable, and it would be nice if the custodians of Morrison and the Doors' history were more scrupulous about how they portray the nobility of his excesses or the fascination of his death. But then, the myth of a young poet and libertine who sought to test the bounds of cultural freedom and personal license; and who suffered the mis-understanding of not merely established American culture, but of family, friends, and rock culture as well; and who died because he just could not reach far enough or be loved deservedly enough, is probably too good, and too damn lucrative, for any biographer to resist romanticizing or exploiting.

After all, in some ways death is the perfect preserving element of Morri-son's legacy. It has the twofold advantage of having halted the singer's decline before he might have gone on to even worse behavior or art, and to a large degree it also helped absolve him for the failures of his last few years. It's almost as if, somewhere, somehow, a macabre deal were struck: If Morrison would simply have the good grace to die, then we would remember him as a young, fit, handsome poet; we would forgive him his acts of disregard and cruelty and drunkenness, and recall him less as a stumblebum sociopath and more as a probing mystic-visionary. Plus, there's a certain vicarious satisfac-tion to be found in his end. If you like, you can admire the spirit of someone who lived life and pursued death to the fullest, without having to emulate that commitment yourself. Which is to say, Morrison has saved his less nervy (and smarter) fans the trouble of their own willful self-negation.

And so Jim Morrison died, and then, with the help of former friends, band members, and biographers, pulled off the perfect comeback: the sort of comeback in which the singer and his band might never disappoint our renewed faith, because there would be no new music, no new art, no new statements to test their continued growth or our continuing perceptiveness. In short, it was a comeback in which Morrison would be eternally heroic, eternally loved, and eternally marketable.

Of course, it's probably a bit graceless to beat up too much on a dead man—especially one who already beat up on himself plenty during life. And so, let's allow Jim Morrison his posthumous victory: If, in some regards, he was perhaps just a bit too mean-spirited or selfish to be an easy hero of the

1960s, he has certainly proven to be in step with the temper of the last decade or so. Never mind that he threw away his greatest visions and potential in an endless swirl of drugs, alcohol, insecurity, and unkindness, and never mind that he is dead. Never mind, because in the end, death has been this rock & roll hero's most redeeming and most rewarding friend.

PART 3

remaking

the

territories

lou reed:

darkness

and love

*Lou Reed is the guy that gave dignity and poetry and rock
'n' roll to smack, speed, homosexuality, sadomasochism,
murder, misogyny, stumblebum passivity, and suicide, and
then proceeded to belie all his achievements and return to
the mire by turning the whole thing into a bad joke.*
          LESTER BANGS
          WRITING IN *SCREEM*

   *I met myself in a dream
   And I just want to tell you, everything was all right.*
          LOU REED
          "BEGINNING TO SEE THE LIGHT"

Seated in the dusky shadows of a San Francisco Chinatown bar, his face lit
by the glow of a trashy table lamp, Lou Reed looks like an artful compos-
ite of the mordant characters who stalk his songs. His thick, pale fingers
tremble a lot, and his sallow face, masked with a poised, distant expression,
looks worn. But behind that lurid veil lurks a sharp, fitful psyche, and with
several ounces of bourbon stoking its fire, it can be virulent.

   Lou has been ranting for almost an hour about his latest album, *Take
No Prisoners*, a crotchety, double live set hailed by some critics as his bravest
work yet, and by others as his silliest. He seems anxious for me to share his
conviction that it's the zenith of his recording career—something I can't

---

bring myself to do. Instead, I mention that the record might alienate even some of Reed's staunchest defenders. Instantly, his flickering brown eyes taper into bellicose slits. "Are you telling me," he snarls, "that you think *Take No Prisoners* is just another *Metal Machine Music?*"

Then, as quickly as he flared, Reed relaxes and flourishes a roguish smile. "It's funny," he says, "but whenever I ask anyone what they think of this record, they say, 'Well, I love it, but I'm a little worried about what *other* people will think.' Except one friend. He told me he thought it was very *manly*. That's admirable. It's like the military maxim the title comes from: 'Give no quarter, take no prisoners.' I wanted to make a record that wouldn't give an inch. If anything, it would push the world *back* just an inch or two. If *Metal Machine Music* was just a memo note, *Take No Prisoners* is the letter that should've gone with it.

"You may find this funny, but I think of it as a contemporary urban-blues album. After all, that's what I write—tales of the city. And if I dropped dead tomorrow, this is the record I'd choose for posterity. It's not only the smartest thing I've ever done, it's also as close to Lou Reed as you're probably going to get, for better or worse."

He has a point. *Take No Prisoners* is brutal, coarse, and indulgent—the kind of album that radio stations and record buyers love to ignore (it hasn't even nicked *Billboard*'s Top 200). Which is a shame, because it's also one of the funniest live albums ever recorded. The songs (a potpourri of Reed's best known, including "Sweet Jane" and "Walk on the Wild Side") serve merely as backdrops for Lou's dark-humored, Lenny Bruce–like monologues. At one point, responding to somebody in the audience who objects to one of his many ethnic slurs, Lou snaps, "So what's wrong with cheap, dirty jokes? Fuck you. I never said I was tasteful. I'm *not* tasteful."

But the record's real bounty is its formidable last side, featuring petrifying versions of "Coney Island Baby" and "Street Hassle"—the definitive accounts of Reed's classic pariah angel in search of glut and redemption. "Street Hassle," in particular, is the apotheosis of Lou's callous brand of rock & roll. The original recording, a three-part vignette laced beguilingly with a cello phrase that turns into a murky requiem on guitar, was Reed's most disturbing song since "Heroin." The new, live version of "Street Hassle" is an even more credible descent into the dark musings of a malignant psychology, littered with mercenary sex and heroin casualties, and narrated by a jaded junkie who undergoes a catharsis at the end.

Lou Reed doesn't just write about squalid characters, he allows them to leer and breathe in their own voices, and he colors familiar landscapes through their own eyes. In the process, Reed has created a body of music that comes as close to disclosing the parameters of human loss and recovery as we're likely to find. That qualifies him, in my opinion, as one of the few real heroes rock & roll has raised.

That is, if you're willing to allow your heroes a certain latitude for grimness. Long before the Velvet Underground, Lou Reed had begun preparing for a career as a hard-boiled outsider. When he was in high school, his mood swings and headlong dives into depression became so frequent that his parents committed him to electroshock therapy (an experience he later chronicled bitterly in a song called "Kill Your Sons"). Another time, during his student days at New York's Syracuse University, Reed reneged on his ROTC commitment by pointing an unloaded pistol at the head of his commanding officer.

After Syracuse (where, in his more stable moments, Reed studied poetry with Delmore Schwartz, a popular poet of the 1940s), Lou took a job as a songwriter and singer at Pickwick Records on Long Island. While there, he recorded mostly ersatz surf and Motown rock under a multitude of names, and met John Cale, a classically trained musician with avant-garde leanings. In 1965, Reed and Cale formed the Warlocks, with Sterling Morrison, an old Syracuse pal of Lou's, on guitar and Maureen Tucker on drums. The group was renamed the Falling Spikes and then the Velvet Underground, after the title of a porn paperback about sadomasochism.

In the context of the late-sixties hippie/Samaritan rock scene, the group seemed, to many observers, positively malignant. "I remember," says Reed, "reading descriptions of us as the 'fetid underbelly of urban existence.' All I wanted to do was write songs that somebody like me could relate to. I got off on the Beatles and all that stuff, but why not have a little something on the side for the kids in the back row? At the worst, we were like antedated realists. At the best, we just hit a little more home than some things."

In the case of the Velvet Underground's first album, nominally produced by Andy Warhol, that viewpoint was presented as a remarkably ripened and self-contained group persona. Songs like "I'm Waiting for the Man," "Run, Run, Run," and "Heroin" depict a leering, gritty vision of urban life that, until the Velvets, had rarely been alluded to—much less exalted—in popular music.

The Velvet Underground, of course, would go on to have a profound—probably incalculable—impact on modern popular music. Indeed, next to the Beatles, Bob Dylan, or the Rolling Stones, the Velvets were one of the most influential white rock forces of the 1960s. David Bowie, Mott the Hoople, the New York Dolls, Elliott Murphy, Roxy Music, Brian Eno, Patti Smith, the Sex Pistols, Television, Joy Division, Jim Carroll, R.E.M., and countless others would borrow from and extend the Velvet Underground's sound and vision, though none of them would ever fully match the original group's inventive depths and astonishing courage. The band's first three albums, *The Velvet Underground and Nico* (1967), *White Light/White Heat* (1968), and *The Velvet Underground* (1969) are works that stand strongly alongside *Revolver, Beggar's Banquet, Let It Bleed, Blonde on Blonde,* and *John Wesley Harding* as some of the most intelligent and illuminating music of the era.

But back in the milieu of the often skin-deep positivism and florid experimentalism of the late 1960s, the Velvet Underground's unswerving hardbitten temper, dissolute romanticism, and abrasive improvisations were, as Reed noted, viewed as "downer" elements, and the group itself was seen as a pack of sick party spoilers. I remember that several of my friends during that period—who shared my love for rock & roll—wouldn't stay in the same room when a Velvet Underground record hit the stereo. (One friend even scratched up the song "Heroin" because of what he termed its "counterrevolutionary nihilism.")

All together, the Velvets' catalog would sell something less than 50,000 copies during the time the band was together.

BY THE VELVETS' fourth album, 1970's *Loaded,* financial problems and lack of recognition prompted Reed to quit the band. He embarked on a solo career that became so spotty it seemed irreconcilable with the promise of his earlier work. After finally achieving commercial success in 1972 with "Walk on the Wild Side" (from *Transformer,* coproduced by David Bowie), Reed immediately began to test his audience's endurance. First he grilled them with the much-maligned *Berlin* narrative, then later with *Metal Machine Music.* In between, there were the hits, *Rock 'n' Roll Animal* and *Sally Can't Dance* (the latter actually went Top 10), records he now denounces as trivial, commercial contrivances.

Then, in 1976, after a brief, tempestuous marriage (the fodder for *Berlin*) and increasingly strained relationships with his manager and producer—brothers Dennis and Steve Katz—Reed rebounded. He disengaged himself from Dennis Katz, assembled a stoical, one-shot band, and recorded *Coney Island Baby,* his most personal set of songs since his days with the Velvets. Following that, he left RCA Records for Arista and last year delivered *Street Hassle*—a jolting statement of self-affirmation—and now is about to release *The Bells,* which he thinks will surpass *Take No Prisoners* and which features a few songs cowritten with Nils Lofgren. It would seem that Reed's gifts of vision and expression are fully revivified and newly honed to a lethal edge.

Sitting in the bar, as a last flush of rain washes away the daylight outside, I figure both of us have had enough to drink for me to ask about where those lost years went. As a way of broaching the subject, I quote a passage from *Rolling Stone*'s review of *Street Hassle*, in which Tom Carson describes Reed's decline as a degeneration into "a crude, death-trip clown." It sobers Reed right up. He smiles grimly and glances around the room. "That's not for me to comment on, is it? Obviously it's someone else's construction."

After a taut moment, he reconsiders. "Let me tell you a little story," he says. "It comes from a collection of personal prose that my friend, the late poet Delmore Schwartz, wrote, called *Vaudeville for a Princess*. In this one chapter he's talking about driving a car, and how as a youngster he had driven one as contemporary as he was; in other words, the year he was driving it was the year of the car's model. Subsequently, as he got older and fortune, perhaps, didn't smile upon him as he wished it would, the car he would drive was not at all of the same year as he was driving it, but it would be older—five, ten years older. Eventually, we get around to a time fifteen years later and he felt he was making progress because the car he was driving was only two years older than the year in which he was driving it. As a slight tangent, he makes mention not to mock him over this because he, too, has seen visions of glory and ticker-tape parades in New York City. Anyway, he's now at last out driving this car that's almost contemporary with his time, so he's obviously progressing. But he observes that nobody is with him to take note of the event, because he didn't have a license and his erratic driving reflected the fact that 'life, as I had come to know it, had made me nervous.'"

Lou pauses and smiles curtly. "Life, as I had come to know it, had made me nervous. I've probably had more of a chance to make an asshole out of myself than most people, and I realize that. But then not everybody gets a chance to live out their nightmares for the vicarious pleasures of the public."

*E*ARLIER IN OUR conversations, during the tour that spawned *Take No Prisoners*, Lou and I meet in the same bar. Instead of his usual playfully testy demeanor, he seems sullen, almost solitary. "This is one of those days," he says, taking a seat at a corner table, "where everything's going to go wrong."

At first Reed's mood is hard to place, since his shows of the night before had clearly been fervently fought successes. But then I recall that when he'd come out for his second show, he found his guitar out of tune and threw it angrily to the floor in the middle of the opening number, cracking its body. "I could've cried then," he says, "but I don't really care now. I use my moods. I get into one of these dark, melancholy things and I just milk it for everything I can. I know I'll be out of it soon and I won't be looking at things the same way. For every dark mood, I also have a euphoric opposite. I think they say that manic-depressives go as high as they go down, which isn't to say that I'm really depressive."

Since Lou in his dark moods, though, is probably Lou at his most reflective, I decide to ask him how this affects his songwriting. He's said in the past that he never writes from a personal point of view, that he has "nothing remotely in common with the Lou Reed character." Indeed, much of his work, especially *Berlin,* seems the product of a detached observer, with no stake in the outcome of his characters' lives and no moral interest in their choices. But *Coney Island Baby* and *Street Hassle* seem as revelatory and personal as anything in seventies music. Isn't the real Lou Reed in there someplace?

Lou sits quietly for several moments, studying a gold-plated lighter cupped in his hands. When he speaks, it's in a soft, murmuring voice. "There are some severe little tangent things in my songs that remove them from me, but, ah, yes, they're very personal. I guess the Lou Reed character is pretty close to the real Lou Reed, to the point, maybe, where there's really no heavy difference between the two, except maybe a piece of vinyl. I keep hedging my bet, instead of saying that's really me, but that *is* me, as much as you can get on record."

Lou signals the waitress over to order a double Johnnie Walker straight. He seems to be coming alive a bit to the idea of conversation, his eyes studying me as he talks. "I have songs about killing people, but Dostoevski killed people, too. In reality I might not do what a character in my songs would, if only because I'd be jailed. It goes back to when I began to write songs—I didn't see why the form should be looked upon as restrictive, although since then I've seen the resistance it can generate. But that's only if you lose your impetus.

"In my own writing, for instance, I'm very good at the glib remark that may not mean something if you examine it closely, but it still sounds great. It's like a person who can argue either side of a question with equal passion, but what do they really think? They might not think anything, so you might not get to know them."

Lou spots a copy of the *San Francisco Chronicle* on a nearby table and fetches it to show me a review of his concert the night before. He turns momentarily livid. The reviewer, Lou is quick to point out, spent most of his space denouncing the ticket price ($9.50 at the door) and Reed's take (reportedly $7,500 a night) before commenting on his "unmusical manner," "incoherent lyrics," and his spawning of "sick-rock."

I recall that the Velvet Underground received similar reviews when they played the West Coast. "When we left New York," says Lou, "we were *shocked* that we were such a big deal. For anyone who goes to movies or reads anything, why should we have been shocking? One reason, I guess, is that singing a rock & roll song is a very real thing; it's accessible on an immediate level, more so than a book or movie. People assume that what's on a record applies to the person singing it and they find that shocking, although they can pick up the newspaper and read things far more shocking.

"Maybe one of the reasons my stuff doesn't have mass appeal is that it *does* approach people on a personal level. It assumes a certain agreement of mores, or if not an agreement, then at least an awareness on the listener's part. But with somebody like this—"Lou slaps the review with the back of his hand—" it's just deemed incoherent and offensive from the top. *Unmusical manner,*" he spits. "What a great phrase to be used by such a poor writer. It's like saying Philip Marlowe was unsavory.

"Anyway, there wasn't anything like us at the time of the Velvet Underground. There still isn't. 'Heroin' is just as right on the nose now as it was ten years ago. Shocking? I suppose, but I always thought it was kind of romantic."

Romantic?

"Yes, because it's not really like that at all," he replies. "There's not that much strain in that world. I've had kids come up to me and say, 'You turned me on to junk because of that song.' Well, you can't concern yourself with being a parent for the world. People deserve the right to be what they're going to be, both in the positive and pejorative sense. I just wish they'd see that you can't evolve through someone else."

But one thing that disturbs people about Reed's music, I note, is its lack of what might be called a moral stance. Lou shrugs his nose in disdain. "It's simply professional detachment," he says. "I'm not spinning around in the caldron of it all with no viewpoint. There *is* a viewpoint, although it's mainly the view that that's the way things are. Take it or leave it. The thing that allows a lot of my characters to leave it is something that ends up negating them.

"Let me propose something to you. Take the guy who's singing in the second part of 'Street Hassle,' who's saying, 'Hey that's some bad shit that you came to our place with/But you ought to be a little more careful around those little girls. . . .' Now, he may come off as a little cruel, but let's say he's also the guy who's singing the last part about losing love. He's already lost the one for him. He's not unaware of those feelings, he's just handling the situation, that's all. And who would know better than the guy who lost somebody in a natural way? That's what my songs are all about: They're one-to-ones. I just let people eavesdrop on them. Like that line at the end of 'Street Hassle': 'Love has gone away/Took the rings right off my fingers/There's nothing left to say/But oh how I miss him, baby.' That person really exists. He *did* take the rings right off my fingers, and I do miss him."

Lou digs into the pocket of his jacket for his cigarettes. He lights one and gives me a level look. "They're not heterosexual concerns running through that song," he says. "I don't make a deal of it, but when I mention a pronoun, its gender is all-important. It's just that my gay people don't lisp. They're not any more affected than the straight world. They just *are*. That's important to me. I'm one of them and I'm right there, just like anybody else. It's not made anything other than what it is. But if you take me, you've got to take the whole thing."

I'm not sure what to say for the moment, so I sit there, returning his stare. I recall something he said the day before about Delmore Schwartz: "It must have been really incredible to have been good-looking, a poet, and be straight."

SEVERAL DAYS LATER, Lou is in Los Angeles for a series of shows at the Roxy. On the afternoon of his last show, I visit him at his Beverly Hills hotel and find him lying on the floor before the TV, watching a videotape of the previous night's performance. "Look at that guy," says Lou, pointing at himself on the screen. "He sure is shameless about occupying his own life." Lou Reed on the screen turns and looks over his shoulder and smiles at Lou Reed on the floor. Lou Reed on the floor smiles back.

On the screen a jagged tango pulse announces "Street Hassle." I've seen Lou do this song eight times, and each time something remarkable happened to his character—and to the audience. Although several of the people at those shows were hearing it for the first time, they nearly always sat in stunned silence. It was as if Lou were guiding them through a private and treacherous world, the world of Lou Reed's ethos. To miss this performance is to miss one of the greatest psychodramas in rock & roll.

Lou on the TV screen slicks his hair back now and begins declaiming to some unseen guest about how that guest has been too reckless with his dope, bringing his girlfriend to Lou's apartment and then fixing her up so carelessly that she overdoses on the spot. "I know this ain't no way to treat a guest," says Lou on the screen, "but why don't you grab your old lady by the feet and lay her out in the darkened street/And by tomorrow morning she's just another hit-and-run/You know, some people got no choice and they can never find a voice to talk with that they can call their own/So the first thing they see that allows them the right to be, they follow it/You know what it's called? *Bad luck.*"

"You know," says Lou on the floor, turning to me, "every time I'm doing that song, when it gets to that awful last line I never know just how it's going to come across. 'So the first thing they see that allows them the right to be, they follow it/You know what it's called?' And here comes that line and it should punch like a bullet: *Bad luck.* The point of view of the guy saying that is so *awful.* But it's so true. I only realize sometime afterward what Lou Reed's talking about. I just try to stay out of the way."

Lou is up on his feet now and decides he wants to ride into Hollywood to find an obscure patch cord for one of his tape decks. Outside, it's a damp, gray winter day in Los Angeles. "This is the kind of day where, if you were in the Village in New York," says Lou, "you might go down to some gay bar and see if you can make a new friend."

As we swing onto Santa Monica Boulevard, Lou injects the tape resting in my cassette player. "We're the poison in your human machine," roars Johnny Rotten. "We're the future—You-rrr future." Lou has a queasy look on his face. "Shakespeare had a phrase for that," he says. " 'Sound and fury signifying nothing.' I'm so tired of the theory of the noble savage. I'd like to hear punks who weren't at the mercy of their own rage and who could put together a coherent sentence. I mean, they can get away with 'Anarchy in the U.K.' and that bullshit, but it hasn't an eighth the heart or intelligence of something like Garland Jeffreys' 'Wild in the Streets.' "

We arrive at the stereo store, and Lou spends the next hour meticulously picking through accessory bins until he finds the cord he needs. Back in the car we talk a bit about the early Velvets albums. I ask Lou again why it was so hard for him, after he left the group, to maintain his creative momentum. He frames his reply carefully. "It was just an awful period. I had very little control over the records; they were really geared for the money. When I made *Coney Island Baby,* Ken Glancy, the president of RCA at the time, backed me to the hilt because he knew me. There were rumors that I couldn't stand tours because I was all fucked up on dope and my mind was going. I put out *Metal Machine Music* precisely to stop all of it. No matter what people may think of that record, it wasn't ill-advised at all. It did what it was supposed to do. But it was supposed to do a lot more. I mean, I really believed in it also. *That* could be ill-advised, I suppose, but I just think it's one of the most remarkable pieces of music ever done by anybody, anywhere. In time, it will prove itself."

What made *Coney Island Baby* such a statement of renewal?

"Because it was *my* record. I didn't have much time and I didn't have much money, but it was mine. There was just me and Rachel [Reed's male companion of the last several years and the raison d'être of *Street Hassle*] living at the fucking Gramercy Park Hotel on fifteen dollars a day, while the lawyers were trying to figure out what to do with me. Then, I got a call from Clive Davis [president of Arista Records] and he said, 'Hey, how ya doing? Haven't seen you for a while.' He *knew* how I was doing. He said, 'Why don't we have lunch?' I felt like saying, 'You mean you want to be seen with me in public?' If Clive could be seen with me, I had turned the corner. I grabbed Rachel and said, 'Do you know who just called?' I knew then that I'd won.

"It's just that turning that corner was really hard. When Ken Glancy backed me, that was step one; when Clive gave me a call, step two; and *Street Hassle* and *Take No Prisoners* are like step three. And I think they're all home runs. I'm a long-term player. Saying 'I'm a Coney Island baby' at the end of that song is like saying I haven't backed off an inch, and don't you forget it."

We arrive back at Lou's hotel and he invites me in to hear the difference the patch cord makes in his tape deck. Inside, two members of his sound crew are already waiting to take him to the afternoon's sound check, but Lou wants to play with his machines first. "It's funny," he says, sitting on the floor with his miniature speakers sprawled around him, "but maybe the most frightening thing that can be said about me is that I'm so damn *sane*. Maybe these aren't my devils at all that people are finding on these records—they're other people's. When I start writing about my own, then it could prove really interesting."

Maybe so, but I can't help recalling his earlier comment about what a master of the glib remark he is. I think Lou's been exposing plenty of his devils all along, and I think he knows it. On an earlier occasion, I'd told him his work sometimes reminded me of that of Diane Arbus, the late photographer known principally for her studies of desolate and deformed subjects. Lou recoiled instantly at the suggestion. "Her subject matter's grotesque," he said. "I don't consider mine grotesque. To show the inherent deformity in normally formed people is what I'm interested in, not in showing beauty in deformity."

By saying that, Lou seems to be saying he knows exactly what devils he's after, and that he won't pass them off on anyone as angels.

If Lou Reed has accomplished nothing else, that victory alone would be moral enough.

AFTER THE HARROWING scenarios of his 1978 masterwork, *Street Hassle,* Lou Reed began working to counteract his profligate image—or perhaps simply to reveal more of the real sensibility behind his songs. The first glimpses came in his 1979 album, *The Bells* (in some ways, his most resourceful work), during "Families"—a song about a son speaking to his hardened parents across a chasm of mutual heartbreak: "And no no no no no no, I still haven't got married," Reed sang in a pain-filled quaver, "And no no no, there's no grandson planned here for you. . . . And I don't think I'll come home much anymore." With *The Bells,* Lou Reed fulfilled—maybe even laid to rest—a longstanding ethos: one of grim choices and unsparing accountability. A song like "Families" sounded as if it used up the whole of Reed's emotional being. It didn't seem possible that either his art or his life could ever be the same again. In fact, they couldn't.

Reed moved deeper into the theme of familial fatalism—the fear, hate, and defeat that parents too often bequeath upon their children as their most lasting and bitter legacy—on the following year's album, *Growing Up in Public.* But *Growing Up in Public* was also an album about summoning up high-test courage: the courage to love, and along with it, the will to forgive everybody who—and everything that—ever cut short your chances in the first place. On *Growing Up,* Reed's material bridged the difficult chasm between moral narrative and unadulterated autobiography. In part, the new compositions were about Reed's decision to marry again—a decision that flabbergasted many of the people who'd pegged him as a middle-aged, intractable gay—but they were also seared recollections of the prime forces that almost fated him. In "My Old Man," he railed at the memory of a Karamazov-like father in a burst of near-patricidal rage: "And when he beat my mother/It made me so mad I could choke . . . /And can you believe what he said to me/He said, 'Lou, act like a man.' " And Reed *did* act like a man. He shattered the album's claustrophobic web of hatred and self-defeat—perhaps the most frightening he'd ever constructed, because it was also the most universal—by choosing to run the same risk at which his parents failed: the risk of the heart. "When you ask for somebody's heart," he sang in that album's most tender moment, "You must know that you're smart/Smart enough to care for it." It was hardly a detached lyric: On Valentine's Day, 1980, Reed married Sylvia Morales, and for a time, both his life and music seemed deepened by the union.

Indeed, several of the records that Reed made during that marriage—including *The Blue Mask, Legendary Hearts,* and *New Sensations*—were tough-willed statements of personal love as the only remaining act of defiance, and as such, they also worked as a reexamination of his earlier mores. In "Heavenly Arms," he made the act sound like nothing less than an urgent and vital good fight: "Lovers stand warned/Of the world's impending storm." But in such songs as "Legendary Hearts" and "Home of the Brave," Reed fully expressed the difficulty of trying to integrate the frustrations and limitations of his distant past and the reality of his fiery temperament with the knowledge that real love requires constant recommitment—demands, in fact, a daily renewal to a struggle of uphill faith. "The thing about love," he told me back during our 1979 and 1980 conversations, "is that it isn't logical. You don't necessarily love what's logical or good for you. Believe me, *I* know. At the same time, that's the beauty of love—when you're passionately caring for the welfare of somebody beyond yourself." Then he laughed. "Maybe what we're talking about is the touch of an angel's wing. And the possibility of transcendence."

In time, Reed's marriage to Morales ended, and as I write these words in 1997, it is reported that he has recently been quite happy with artist and singer Laurie Anderson (talk about a meeting of the minds). In the 1990s, Reed has continued to make strong, vital, and imaginative records—including *New York, Songs for Drella* (an elegy to Andy Warhol, co-written with former Velvets partner John Cale), *Magic and Loss,* and *Set the Twilight Reeling.* He also briefly re-formed the Velvet Underground in the early 1990s, making—oddly enough—for the only truly unaffecting music that remarkable group ever produced.

After all my years of listening to and loving popular music, I can say that—along with Bob Dylan—Lou Reed remains my favorite rock & roll artist; indeed, along with Dylan, he is probably the only artist who has grown and weathered so well, and whose lapses are even something to pore over, time and again, in wonder. If I had to pick my favorite lines he has ever written, they would be these: "It was good what we did yesterday/And I'd do it once again/The fact that you are married/Only proves you're my best friend/But it's truly, truly a sin" (from 1969's "Pale Blue Eyes"). Also, these: "With a daytime of sin and a nighttime of hell/Everybody's going to look for a bell to ring" (from 1979's "All through the Night"). It seems to me that in his best music—even in his darkest, most brokenhearted reveries—Lou Reed has always rung a bell, loud and clear, pealing a clarion call of hope that the glory of love, despite (or *because* of) our daytimes of sin and nighttimes of hell, might see us all through yet.

brothers:

the

allman brothers

band

S ome say there was a ghost. Some unkind spirit, the rumor went, had clambered up out of a dark legacy of death and bad news, and had attached itself to the Allman Brothers Band, like a mean dog trailing its quarry, until it had dragged the band down into the dust of its own dreams.

Maybe the group had attracted the spirit on one of those late nights more than a generation before, when various band members would gather in the Rose Hill Cemetery, not far from where the Allman Brothers lived in Macon, Georgia. The story is, they drank wine and whiskey there, smoked dope, took psychedelics, played and wrote dark, obsessive blues songs, and laid their Southern girlfriends across sleek tombstones on humid, heat-thick Southern nights, and made love to warm, twitching bodies that were laying only a few feet above other bodies, long prone and long cold. Maybe on one of those occasions, in some ungodly moment in which sex and hallucinations and blues all mixed and formed an unwitting invocation, an insatiable specter was raised, and decided to stay close to the troubled and vulnerable souls that had summoned it. Or maybe it was something even older and meaner that trailed the Allmans—something as old as the hellions and hellhounds that were said to haunt Southern rural crossroads on moonless nights.

Yes, some say there was a ghost. Some even say they witnessed that ghost—or at least, witnessed how palpable it was for those who had to live with the effects of its haunts. There are stories about late night reveries in the early 1970s, when the band's most famous member would sit in darkened hotel rooms, watching early morning TV, brooding. By this time, the Allman Brothers Band was the most successful pop group in America—in fact, the band had played for the largest audience ever assembled in the nation's history. But perhaps that success was never enough to stave off fears that there was yet more that this band was destined to lose.

In those postmidnight funks, the blond blues singer sat and watched TV, sometimes horror movies with the sound down. An empty chair was sometimes close by. To at least one visitor, the singer insisted that a spirit sat in that chair—and that he knew that spirit well. In fact, he said, he and the ghost were on a first-name basis. He and the ghost even shared the same last name.

WALK INTO A room to meet the surviving members of the original Allman Brothers Band, and you walk into the midst of a complex shared history. It is a spooky, gothic story of family ties—of both blood brotherhood and chosen brotherhood—and it is also a story of amazing prodigies, dogged by amazingly bad fortune. Indeed, the four men seated in this room—keyboardist Gregg Allman, guitarist Dickey Betts, and drummers Jai Jaimoe and Butch Trucks—are people who helped *make* history: They once personified what rock & roll and blues could achieve in those forms' grandest moments of musical imagination, and they also once played a significant role in the American South's social and political history. But like anybody who has made history that matters, the members of the Allman Brothers were also bruised by that history. They do not seem like men who are unduly arrogant or proud; rather, they seem like men who have learned that proud moments can later form the heart of indelibly painful memories.

It has been several years since these musicians have recorded together, but on this sultry afternoon in mid-spring, as they gather in the lounge at Miami's Criteria Studios, they are beginning the final work on *Seven Turns*—a record that they boldly claim is their most important and accomplished work since 1973's *Brothers and Sisters*. In many ways, this is an adventure they never thought they would share. In 1983, after a restive fourteen-year history, the Allman Brothers dissolved into the caprices of pop history. The band had broken up before—in the mid-1970s, on rancorous terms—but this time they quit because the pop world no longer wanted them. "We had

_____

been credited as being a flagship band," says Dickey Betts, pulling nervously at his mustache, his eyes taking a darting scan of the other faces in the room. "All of a sudden managers and record company people were telling us that we should no longer use terms like 'Southern Rock,' or that we couldn't wear hats or boots onstage, that it was embarrassing to a modern audience. We finally decided we couldn't meet the current trends—that if we tried, we were going to make fools out of ourselves playing disco music, and ruin any integrity we had left. Looking back, splitting up was the best thing we could have done. We would have ruined whatever pleasant images people had of us by trudging along."

The band members went separate ways. Allman and Betts toured with their own bands off and on, playing mainly clubs and small venues, and even teamed up for a tour or two. Butch Trucks went back to school, opened a recording studio in Tallahassee, raised his family, and involved himself in the difficult fight to stop record labeling in Florida. Jai Jaimoe packed a set of drums in his Toyota and spent years traveling around the South, playing in numerous jazz, R&B, and pop bands. Occasionally, the various ex-Allmans would come together for the odd jam or gig, but nobody spoke much about the collective dreams they had once shared. Clearly, the glory days were behind them, and there wasn't much point in talking them to death.

Then, toward the late 1980s, pop music began going through one of its periodic revisionist phases. Neo-blues artists like Stevie Ray Vaughan and Robert Cray began attracting a mass audience; plucky country singers like Lyle Lovett and k. d. lang had started attracting a broad spectrum of alternative and mainstream fans; and the long-suffering, brandy-voiced Bonnie Raitt enjoyed a major comeback with her surprisingly straightforward renditions of blues and R&B music. As a result, Dickey Betts received a call from Epic Records: Was he interested in making a Southern Rock LP? Betts thought Epic was joking, but nope—the label even wanted him to assemble a band with a twin-guitar frontline, and yes, if he really wanted, he could wear his cowboy hat onstage. Betts put together a solo act, and eventually he and Trucks received calls from Epic that led to an invitation to re-form the Allman Brothers. At first, both were wary—Gregg Allman's drug and alcohol problems remained legendary, and they weren't sure about touring or playing with him under those circumstances. But Betts, who had seen Allman often in recent years, said that Gregg was in good shape and better voice than ever, and that like the rest of them, he had missed the music they had made together. So Betts called Epic back and asked: For a Southern Rock band, how would the label like to have *the* Southern Rock group, the Allman Brothers Band? Epic was thrilled—until it was learned that the band planned to tour before recording.

"They were afraid we would *break up* again before we ever finished the tour," says Betts, laughing. Actually, touring was reportedly part of the deal the bandmembers had struck about Gregg Allman: Before entering a studio to work on new material, or before committing themselves to spending a few more years together, they wanted to see how Gregg would handle the road; in fact, they wanted to see how *everybody* would handle working together again. Mainly, they wanted to see if they could still play like the Allman Brothers, rather than as a once-removed imitation.

"It would have been pitiful to have put this band back together, just to be an embarrassment," says Betts. "I don't think we could have dealt with that. The trouble is, we'd already been compared to ourselves a lot, and not always in a good way."

As it turned out, the timing was good: Numerous other older acts—including the Rolling Stones, the Who, the Jefferson Airplane, Ringo Starr, and Paul McCartney were hitting the road in 1989 with largely retrospective tours, and PolyGram was also preparing a multidisc historical overview of the Allmans for imminent release. For the first time in nearly a decade, the Allmans had a context to work in. Betts and Allman recruited some new members—guitarist Warren Haynes, bassist Allen Woody, and keyboardist Johnny Neel—and the Allman Brothers Band was reborn. More important, they were once again a forceful live band, playing their hard-hitting brand of improvisational blues with the sort of vitality the band had not evinced since the early 1970s. "Once more, we were getting compared to ourselves," says Betts, "but this time in a positive way. The ideal, of course, would be to have all the original members of the band still alive and with us, but that can't be. But I'll say this: This is the first lineup we've had since Duane Allman and Berry Oakley were in the band that has the same spirit that we had in those days."

Butch Trucks—who can be the most paternal and also the saltiest-talking member of the band—puts it differently. "It feels like the Allman Brothers again," he says, "and it hasn't felt that way in a long, long time. I like it. It makes my sticker peck out."

Periodically, as Betts and Trucks talk, Gregg Allman tries to seem inter-ested in the conversation. He will lean forward, clasp his hands together, look like he has something to say . . . but he never voluntarily fields a single question. After a bit, he settles back into the sofa and simply looks as if he's in his own world. He seems to spend a lot of time inside himself, staring into some private, inviolable space. In the entire conversation, he will say only one complete sentence: "It's hard to live those ten or twenty years, and then try to start all over again with another band."

Abruptly, Gregg is on his feet, excusing himself. He is scheduled to begin final vocals today, and he is restless to get started. When asked if it's okay to watch him record at some point, he visibly freezes. "Um, Gregg won't let *anybody* in there when he's singing," says Betts, coming to Allman's rescue. "Vocals are real personal, you know. You're just standing there naked."

"Yeah, with your dick hanging out," says Trucks. After Gregg leaves, Trucks adds: "I've never seen anybody so nervous about letting others listen."

Recently, there had been some concern about Gregg's vocals. Reportedly, producer Tom Dowd—the owner of Criteria Studios, and the producer of the band's early classics, *At the Fillmore East* and *Eat A Peach*—was worried that he might not get workable complete performances from Allman, and would have to paste the final vocals together from earlier rough tracks. Nobody knows at the moment whether Gregg can sing as well as they are hoping he will sing—indeed, any Allmans reunion effort would fall flat without Gregg's trademark growly vocals—and nobody's sure how Gregg's current unease bodes for the band's upcoming summer tour.

"It's hard to be sober again after all these years," says Trucks, who went through a drying-out period of his own. "At a time like this, Gregg probably doesn't even know if he can talk to people, much less sing. But the thing is, he did it for too many years *not* to go for it now."

AROUND MIDNIGHT, a warm spring storm is dropping heavy sheets of rain all over north Miami. Drummer Jai Jaimoe (who was once known as Jai Johnny Johanson, but now prefers to be called simply Jaimoe) stands in the main hallway at Criteria Studios, unpacking a crate of new cymbals, caressing their nickel-plated gleam with obvious affection. He is wearing a pink, blue, and green knitted African cap; bright green baggy pants; and knee-length black T-shirt bearing the statement, "The objects under this shirt are smaller than they appear."

Down the hall, Gregg Allman is taking passes at his vocal on "Good Clean Fun," and from what one can hear, he is sounding more confident, more vibrant by the moment. A few feet away, Dickey Betts is strumming an acoustic guitar for some friends, singing "Seven Turns"—a haunting song he has written about the Allman Brothers' hard losses and renewed hopes. In the main lounge, Butch Trucks sits watching a golf tournament, trying to explain the Zen principal of the sport to his wife, who does not seem to be buying the idea. Various Allman wives and girlfriends—including Gregg's new wife, Danielle—sit around talking or reading true-crime books, and

Dickey and Gregg's dogs wander in and out of the action, sniffing empty food cartons and looking perplexedly at the downpour outside. Also drifting in and out are producer Tom Dowd—who wears a perpetually rumpled professorial manner—and the legendary Allmans roadie Red Dog, a notorious but charming womanizer, a terrific dirty-joke teller, and plainly the band's most devoted fan. It must seem a bit like old times here, only considerably more easygoing. "I missed playing with these people," Jaimoe will say at one point. "We had something together that I could never find with other bands."

Between storm bouts, Jaimoe suggests taking a walk across the parking lot to a nearby studio, where it will be possible to talk with less distraction. People in and around the Allmans will often joke about Jaimoe—they say that for over a generation, he has been perpetually reclusive, inscrutable, even spacey. But they also make awed references to the drummer's near-encyclopedic knowledge of jazz and rhythm & blues artists and styles, and certainly, nobody can imagine attempting a reunion at this time without his involvement. In fact, it is often joked that Jaimoe was *the* original member of the Allman Brothers—or at least that he was the one who had always been waiting for a band like the Allmans to come along. "All my life I had wanted to play in a jazz band," says Jaimoe, settling into a sofa in an empty, dimly lighted studio control booth. "Then I played with Duane Allman."

Like Allman, Jaimoe had harbored a special passion for Southern-based musical styles. By the mid-1960s, he had served as a regular session drummer at the Fame Studio in Muscle Shoals, Alabama—where some of the most renowned Southern soul music of the period was recorded—and he performed with numerous R&B and blues artists, including Percy Sledge, Otis Redding, Joe Tex, and Clifton Chenier. "I think I had been preparing to play in this band without really knowing *what* I was preparing for," says Jaimoe, shifting his weight on the sofa. "I think it was from playing with all those other musicians that I got all that fiery stuff that people hear in my playing."

In the course of his studio work, Jaimoe met the two people who would become among the principal driving forces behind the Allman Brothers Band: Duane Allman and a fledgling entrepreneur named Phil Walden. Walden was born and raised in Macon, Georgia, a middle-sized town that still relied on agriculture for much of its economy, and that still maintained much of its pre–Civil War architecture (General Sherman had considered the town too insignificant to plunder or ravage). In the 1950s, Walden had grown enamored of Memphis-style rock & roll and, in particular, black R&B of singers like Hank Ballard and the Five Royales, and by the mid-1960s he was managing numerous black stars, including Sam and Dave, Percy Sledge, Al

Green, Johnny Taylor, Joe Tex, Arthur Conley, and, most famously, Otis Redding.

Walden's affection for black music was anathema to many of Macon's leading businessmen and church officials. Walden didn't present himself as a civil rights activist, but he *did* bristle at provincial racism, and he refused to kowtow to local pressures. The South, he often told his critics, would have to change its attitudes, and what's more, the popularity of the new Southern soul was a harbinger of that change. "I think rhythm and blues had a hell of a lot to do with turning the region around on race relations," he would later tell an interviewer. "When people get together and listen to the same music, it makes hating kind of harder."

But Walden's involvement in R&B was cut suddenly and brutally short. In December 1967, Otis Redding—a few months after his triumphant appearance at the Monterey International Pop Festival, and on the verge of a long-anticipated mass breakthrough—was flying a small twin-engine plane from Cleveland to Madison, Wisconsin, when the plane went down in a Wisconsin lake, killing Redding and four members of his backup band, the Bar-Kays. Walden was known as a proud, ambitious, and clever man—even indomitable—but for him, Redding's death was more than the loss of a prize client, and more than the termination of one of the most brilliantly promising artistic careers of the period. It was also a devastating personal loss, and according to many of the people who knew him, Walden thereafter kept a greater emotional distance from his clients.

Duane Allman had also had his life and sensibility transformed by sudden death. In 1949, when Duane was three and his little brother Gregory was two, the Allman family was living in Nashville, Tennessee. That Christmas, the boys' father, an Army lieutenant, was on holiday leave from the Korean War. The day following Christmas, he picked up a hitchhiker, who robbed and murdered Duane and Gregg's father. The Allmans' mother, Geraldine, eventually enrolled her young children in a military academy in Lebanon, Tennessee, and then, in 1958, relocated the family in Daytona Beach, Florida. As young teens, the Allman brothers rarely talked about their father's death—they were too young to know him well—and in many ways, they were like other boys their age: Duane hated school, and quit in a hot temper several times, then spent his free time attending to his favorite possession, a Harley-Davidson 165. Gregg, meantime, stuck through school and was reportedly a fair student and athlete, though he regarded it as a thankless ordeal.

Early on, both Duane and Gregg found themselves drawn to music of loss and longing—particularly the high-lonesome wail of country music, and the haunted passions of urban and country blues. Gregg had been the first to leap in: He had listened to a neighbor playing old-timey country songs on an acoustic guitar, and at thirteen, Gregg worked a paper route and saved money to buy a guitar at the local Sears and Roebuck. While Gregg was slogging his way through school, Duane started playing his brother's guitar—and to his surprise and Gregg's initial annoyance, discovered that he had a gift for the instrument. Soon, Duane and Gregg each owned electric guitars, and Duane would hole up with his instrument for days, learning the music of blues archetype Robert Johnson and jazz guitarist Kenny Burrell. Around that time, Duane and Gregg saw a B. B. King show during a visit to Nashville, and Duane's mind was made up: He and his brother were going to form a blues band of their own; in fact, they were going to make music their life. Duane continued studying numerous guitarists, including King, Muddy Waters, Howlin' Wolf's Hubert Sumlin, Elmore James, and French jazz prodigy Django Reinhardt, as well as the emerging British rock guitarists—especially a young firebrand named Eric Clapton—and the guitarists who were playing for soul artists like James Brown and Jackie Wilson. Duane also began paying attention to saxophonists like John Coltrane, to hear how a soloist could build a melodic momentum that worked within a complex harmonic and rhythmic structure. Meantime, Gregg began favoring jazz organists like Jimmy Smith and Johnny Hammond, and developed a special passion for sophisticated blues and R&B vocalists like Bobby "Blue" Bland, Ray Charles, and Roy Milton.

But there was more to the brothers' quest than a mere attraction for music that took painful feelings and turned them into a joyful release. The Allmans—in particular, Duane—seemed intent on forming bands as an extension of family ideals, and they often invested these bands with the same qualities of love and anger, loyalty and rivalry, that they had practiced at home. In a way, this family idealism was simply a trend of the era: The 1960s were a time when rock bands were often viewed as metaphors for a self-willed brand of consonant community. But in the Allmans' case, the sources of this dream may have run especially deep. Their real-life family had been tumultuously shattered, and forming a band was a way of creating a fraternity they had never really known.

But the Allmans were also forming musical bonds in a time when the South was being forced to reexamine some of its cultural and racial traditions, and Duane and Gregg were unusually open to ideals of interaction and equality. To their mother's initial displeasure, the brothers preferred the music being played by local black talents, and in 1963, they helped form one of the area's first integrated bands, the House Rockers. It was a period of fierce feelings, but the Allmans, like Phil Walden, would not back off from a belief that their culture was starting to undergo radical and deeply needed social change.

In any event, Duane and Gregg went through a rapid succession of blues-oriented rock bands, including the Allman Joys, who toured the Southern teen circuit and recorded two albums' worth of material (including several Yardbirds and Cream covers). By 1967, the group had been overhauled into the Hour Glass and had relocated to Los Angeles, where they recorded two LPs for Liberty. Both were better than average cover bands, and they gave Duane a chance to hone his flair for accompaniment and improvisation, and also helped Gregg develop as a sultry organist and an unusually inventive modern blues composer. But none of these groups matched Duane's boundless ambitions, and in 1968, the bossy and restless guitarist quit the Hour Glass and accepted an invitation from Fame Studios' owner-operator Rick Hall to work as a sideman on an upcoming Wilson Pickett session. Duane left Gregg in L.A. to fulfill the Liberty contract, and in Muscle Shoals, Alabama, he played sessions with Pickett, Clarence Carter, King Curtis, Arthur Conley, and Ronnie Hawkins; in New York, he played with Aretha Franklin. By 1969, Duane Allman had gained a reputation as one of the most musically eloquent and soul-sensitive session guitarists in contemporary music.

It was in this time that Jai Johanny Johanson met Allman. "I had a friend who was doing session work with Wilson Pickett and Aretha Franklin," says Jaimoe. "He came home to Macon one day and told me, 'Jai, they got a white boy down in Alabama by the name of Duane "Skydog" Allman. He's a hippie with long, stringy hair,' he said, 'but you've *got* to hear him play.' I remember listening to the radio late one night in Macon—there wasn't anything else to do there; everything was closed up—and this Aretha Franklin thing, 'The Weight,' came on the radio, with this stand-out guitar solo, and I thought, 'That's got to be "Skydog" Allman, man.' I thought he was a cool guitarist, but he wasn't any Barney Kessel or Tal Farlow, and those were the only Caucasian cats that I heard who could really play the instrument."

A bit later, Jaimoe visited Muscle Shoals during a King Curtis session and sought out Allman. The two musicians became close friends, and between sessions, they would hang out in one of Fame's vacant studios, jamming for hours head-on. Then one day, another skinny, long-haired white boy—a bassist named Berry Oakley, whom Duane had met in Jacksonville, Florida—started joining on the jams. "Man," says Jaimoe, "when Berry joined us, that was some incredible shit. I remember that people like [bassist] David Hood, [pianist] Barry Beckett, and [drummer] Roger Hawkins [all among Muscle Shoals' most respected session players] would come into the room when we were playing, and we were trying to get them to join in. But *none* of them would pick up an instrument. We scared the shit out of them guys."

Somewhere around this time Allman attracted the attention of Phil Walden, who was in the process of forming his own label, Macon-based Capricorn Records, to be distributed by Atlantic. One day, Rick Hall played for Walden a new album he had just recorded with Wilson Pickett, including a cover of the Beatles's "Hey Jude." Walden was transfixed by the work of the guitarist on the session, and after traveling to Muscle Shoals, he eventually made a deal to manage Duane Allman. Walden thought he had found his Elvis Presley: a white musician who could play black, blues-based forms in a way that would connect with an entire new mass audience.

There had been talk of Allman, Jaimoe, and Oakley forming a trio based on the sparse but furious improvisational dynamics of the Jimi Hendrix Experience or Cream, but Walden encouraged Allman to seek his own mix of style and texture. Allman knew he wanted to work with Jaimoe and Oakley, but he had also been drawn to a few other musicians, including lead guitarist Dickey Betts (who had played with Oakley in a band called the Second Coming, and with whom Allman had played several twin-lead jams), and drummer Butch Trucks (with whom Gregg and Duane had played in Jacksonville). One day, these five musicians gathered at Trucks' home in Jacksonville, and began playing. It turned into a relentless jam that stretched for four hours and left everybody involved feeling electrified, even thunderstruck. When it was over, Duane stepped to the entrance of the room and spanned his arms across the doorway, forming a human blockade. "Anybody who isn't playing in my band is going to have to *fight* their way out of this room," he said.

Duane told Walden and Atlantic vice president Jerry Wexler—who had advanced Walden $75,000 to form Capricorn—that he wanted to bring his brother Gregg back from L.A. to sing in the newly formed group, but the company heads initially balked. Says Jaimoe: "I remember Duane saying, 'Man, Jerry and them, they don't want me to have my brother in the band. They don't want no two brothers in the band. It's always been trouble. I mean, me and my brother, we don't get along that much—I don't like him. You know how it is: Brothers don't like each other.' And then Duane would say, 'But Jaimoe, there ain't *no*body else that can sing like my brother. In fact, I can't think of another motherfucker who can sing in this band *except* my brother. That's who I really want.' "

In the end, Duane Allman got his way—and it proved to be a brilliant choice. Gregg Allman had been lonely in Southern California, had endured a troubled love affair and had even, he would later report, contemplated suicide. When Duane called him to join his new band, Gregg saw the invitation as deliverance from a grim reality. And what he brought with him would amount to one of the band's signature attractions: a powerfully erotic, poignant, and authoritative blues voice. When Gregg Allman sang a song like "Whipping Post," he did so in a voice that made you believe that the song's fear and pain and anger were the personal possessions of the singer—and that he had to reveal those dark emotions in order to get past the bitter truths he was singing about.

Phil Walden moved the band to Macon, and then put it on the road year-round. He and Duane didn't always see eye to eye on matters, weren't always close, but they agreed on one thing: The Allman Brothers Band was going to be both the best and biggest band in the country—or die trying.

ANOTHER DAY into the new sessions, Dickey Betts is seated on a worn sofa in the foyer at Criteria Studios. Down the hall, Gregg Allman is still working on his vocals, and it is apparent from his and Tom Dowd's improved moods that the work is going well.

Betts had stayed up late the night before, listening to a cassette of an Allman Brothers show from a 1970 venue at Ludlow Garage in Cincinnati. PolyGram's Bill Levenson (who compiled the 1989 Allmans retrospective, *Dreams*) had recently remastered the session for commercial release, and last night was the first time Betts had heard the performance in twenty years. "I knew if the quality was anywhere above being embarrassing, that it would be good," he says with a fast smile. Betts can seem the edgiest member of the group—he gets up and moves around while he talks, his eyes move constantly, and he is wary about how he phrases things—but behind that manner, he is amiable and honest, and he clearly possesses a remarkable breadth of intelligence. For many years now, he has been regarded as the real heart of the Allman Brothers Band, though he often tends to downplay his leadership role. Right now, he seems to enjoy talking about the revolutionary music the band began making in its early days. "If I recall," he says, "Ludlow was like a dungeon: a cement floor, with a low ceiling, kind of like a warehouse garage. Real funky. As I remember, it was recorded around the time of our first album, way before we started getting anywhere. We were still underground at that point. We had a private, almost cultlike following."

The Allman Brothers may have been relatively "underground" in 1970, but they had already developed their mix of bedrock aggression and highflown invention that would become their hallmark fusion. Like many bands of the time, the group was trying to summarize a wide range of rock, blues, and jazz traditions, and at the same time extend those traditions in new unanticipated directions. In contrast, though, to the Grateful Dead or Miles Davis (both of whom often played improvisatory blues in modal formats and freewheeling structure), the Allmans built tremendously sophisticated melodic formations that never lost sight of momentum or palpable eroticism. For one thing, the band was genuinely attuned to the emotional meanings of blues and the stylistic patterns of rock & roll—that is, group members not only found inspiration in the music of Muddy Waters, Howlin' Wolf, and Robert Johnson, they also understood how that music's spirit had been extended and transmogrified in the later music of Chuck Berry, James Brown, and other rock and soul pioneers. At the same time, the Allmans loved jazz, and had spent many hours marveling at not only the prowess of musicians like Davis, Coltrane, Charlie Parker, Eric Dolphy, and Roland Kirk, but at how these visionaries had taken the same primitive blues impulses that had thrilled and terrified Robert Johnson and Louis Armstrong and turned them into an elaborate art form, capable of the most intricate, spontaneous inventions. Plus, there was an exceptional confluence that resulted from the Allmans' collective talents. In its straightahead blues mode, the band could barnstorm and burn with a fervor that even such white blues trendsetters as John Mayall's Bluesbreakers, Cream, and the Rolling Stones were hard-pressed to match. And when the Allmans stretched their blues into full-scale, labyrinthine improvisations—in the largely instrumental "In Memory of Elizabeth Reed," "Whipping Post," and "Mountain Jam"—the band was simply matchless.

"Duane and Gregg were students of the urban blues," says Betts. "Their thing was like a real honest, truthful, chilling delivery of that music, whereas Oakley and I may have been influenced by the blues and were students of it, but we were more innovative. We would try to take a blues tune and, instead of respecting the sacredness of it, we would go *sideways* with it. But on our own, Berry and I were always missing something—a certain foundation—while Duane and Gregg didn't quite have the adventurous kind of thing. So when we all came together, we gave each other a new foundation."

It proved to be a unique amalgam, with Allman and Betts' twin-lead guitars often locking into frenzied and intricate melodic flights, and Jaimoe and Butch Trucks' double drumming forming a webwork of rhythm that both floated and pushed the drama of the guitars. The only other band in rock that attempted such an adventurous lineup was the Grateful Dead, though in the Dead's case, drummers Mickey Hart and Bill Kreutzmann's rhythms too often pulled apart and lost momentum, and guitarist Bob Weir was never quite inventive enough to engage Jerry Garcia's considerable skill.

Likelier prototypes were the double-saxophone and double-drum sextets and octets led by John Coltrane and Ornette Coleman in the mid-1960s, as well as the twin-guitar and guitar-fiddle lineups of numerous western-swing and country-western bands. "I was always real fond of the twin guitars that Roy Clark and Dave Lyle played in Wanda Jackson's band," says Betts. "But it wasn't that we consciously copied any of these sources. It was just that later we realized that people like Clark and Lyle, and Coltrane and Pharoah Sanders, had been pursuing the same idea many years before. For a rock & roll band, though, it was a pretty new adventure. I mean, one of the good things about the Allman Brothers, we listened to jazz and were influenced by it without ever pretending we were jazz players.

"But make no mistake: It was a matter of Duane being hip enough to see that potential and responding to it. He was absolutely in charge of that band. Had he missed that possibility or that chemistry, there would have been no Allman Brothers Band."

Betts also cites Berry Oakley as a key shaper of the Allmans' early sound. Certainly, Oakley was a singular bassist. Like such jazz hero-bassists as Oscar Pettiford, Jimmy Blanton, Ray Brown, or Scott LaFaro, Oakley had a profound melodic sense that combined fluently with a pulsing percussive touch; and like the Dead's Phil Lesh or Jefferson Airplane's Jack Cassady, he knew how to get under a band's action and lift and push its motions. "There were times," says Betts, "when Berry would be playing a line or phrase, and Duane would catch it, then jump on it and start playing harmony. Then maybe I'd lock into the melodic line that Duane was playing, and we would all three be off. That kind of thing was absolutely unheard of from a rock bassist. I mean, Berry would take over and *give us* the melody."

In fact, says Betts, it was Oakley who came up with the arrangement for "Whipping Post," the Allmans' most famous jam vehicle. "Oakley heard something in it that none of the rest of us heard—this *frightening* kind of thing. He sat up all night messing around and came back in the next day with a new opening in eleven/four time, and after that, ideas started flying from every direction. That sort of thing always happened with him."

By the end of 1970, the Allman Brothers had acquired a formidable reputation. They had recorded two critically praised LPs of blues-rock, interlaced with classical- and country-derived elements, and Duane had gained pop renown for his contributions to Eric Clapton's Derek and the Dominos project, *Layla and Other Assorted Love Songs.* But it was as a live unit that the band enjoyed its greatest repute, and in the year or so ahead, they would play somewhere around two hundred concerts. In part, to sustain their energy during the incessant and exhausting tours, and in part as a by-product of a time-old blues and jazz tradition (and a by-product of rock culture), the

Allmans used an increasingly wide range of drugs—at first, primarily marijuana and occasional psychedelics and, in time, cocaine and heroin. It was a habit that bought the band some short-term potency, maybe even inspiration, but it would also eventually cost them their fraternity. Looking back, Betts has misgivings about the whole experience, and its legacy. "The drugs that were being done back in the sixties and seventies," he says, "were a lot easier to have fun with and be open about, and to find acceptable, because they were drugs to enhance your awareness, instead of an escape into some blackness. I'm not saying those drugs had any redeeming qualities, but at least that was the idea that people had at the time: It was an effort to open the mind up and go even further.

"Today, though, the drugs are so damn deadly, so absolutely dangerous. There's nothing about them that's trying to enhance your awareness at all. The whole idea is to *kill* your awareness, to escape. It's just a perverted thing, and that's why I think that nowadays it's absolutely irresponsible and ignorant to sing in a positive way about doing drugs."

It was in this period that the Allman Brothers singlehandedly pioneered a style and demeanor that would become popularly known as Southern Rock: music that was aggressive yet could swing gracefully, played by musicians who were proud of their region and its musical legacies. Though later bands would reduce Southern Rock to a reactionary posture and a crude parody of machismo, the Allmans began the movement as a blast of musical and cultural innovation. In fact, their outlooks and music were emblematic of the American South's ongoing struggle for redefinition, and for its mounting desire to move away from its violently earned image as a region of fierce racism and intolerance. But while the South of the early 1970s was less like the land of fear and murder that had destroyed the lives of so many blacks and civil rights activists, Betts acknowledges that the territory could still live up to its vulgar notoriety. "There were times," he says, "when you would go out for breakfast after you finish playing a club and just have to accept the chances of getting in a damn fist fight with somebody. But what are you gonna do: sneak home? I mean, you'd just go out and somebody starts calling you some kind of faggot or something about your long hair. I guess we *were* shocking in those days, and some of those damn cowboys are pretty quick to show their feelings. Now half of them have hair as long as mine. Also, there were a few times in some real ignorant little towns where we'd have trouble going into a restaurant with Jaimoe." Betts pauses and shakes his head with remembered exasperation. "Those were isolated incidents, but they stick out in my mind. I was horrified at that kind of thing.

"But you know, things just changed tremendously in the seventies, at least in Florida, Georgia, North Carolina, and the other Southeastern states. The South just got new attitudes."

By the early 1970s, Macon—which had once been troubled by Phil Walden's championing of R&B music—regarded the Allmans as homegrown commercial and regional heroes. Indeed, nearly all the acts that Walden signed to Capricorn had strong Southern identities, and some observers believed it was Walden's aspiration to build a personal and political empire, based on the ideal that "the South Will Rise again." Betts, though, disavows this ambition. "We had *nothing* to do with that whole ideal, 'the South will rise again,' " he says. "That was somebody else's idea. The thing is, we *did* appreciate our culture, and a lot of people in the South were proud of the Allman Brothers, because we were typically and obviously Southern. That was part of our aura. But beyond that, I don't think we were part of what was changing the South. It was people like Jimmy Carter and Martin Luther King, Jr., and John Kennedy who helped affect Southern attitudes. We were just a good thing for some people to identify with, and obviously, we influenced the music from the South a great deal. A lot of musicians thought, 'Hey, they're speaking for or representing the way *I* feel'—and that was a cool thing."

It was a heady time. In 1971, the Allmans toured the country relentlessly, and in March they recorded two of their three performances at Bill Graham's Fillmore East in New York, for a two-record set, *At the Fillmore East*—still widely regarded as the finest live recording that rock & roll has ever produced. In its August 1971 review of the album, *Rolling Stone* described the Allmans as "one of the nicest things that ever happened to any of us," and as the band's popularity grew, the rock mainstream seemed finally ready to share this estimation. In concert, the Allmans earned every inch of their adulation. Night after night, Duane Allman would stand centerstage, and bouncing lightly on his heels, he would begin constructing meditative, rhapsodic solos that ended up going places that rock had never gone before. An unschooled musician, Allman thought in perfectly formed complete lines, that had all the grace and dynamics of a carefully considered composition. He was perhaps the most melodically inventive and expressive instrumentalist that rock would ever witness.

But on October 29, 1971, as the band was at its creative peak and was recording a new work that promised to be both a commercial and creative leap forward, bad news made its first fateful visit to the Allmans. That afternoon, Duane had visited the band's "Big House" in Macon to wish Berry Oakley's wife a happy birthday, then mounted his motorcycle to head back to his own home. Some have speculated that Duane was overtired from relentless touring and was less attentive to his driving than usual. In any event, in the early evening darkness of a Southern night, Duane swerved his bike to avoid a truck that had turned in front of him. His cycle skidded, pinning Allman underneath and dragging him fifty feet. Duane's girlfriend and Oakley's sister had been following in a car, and stayed with Duane until an ambulance arrived. After three hours of emergency surgery, he died at Macon Medical Center. He was twenty-four years old. Like the young deaths of Charlie Parker, Hank Williams, Patsy Cline, Buddy Holly, Sam Cooke, John Coltrane, Otis Redding, Jimi Hendrix, and Janis Joplin, the loss of Duane Allman was the loss of a tremendous musical promise. There would be bright days to come for the Allmans, but clearly, the band's creative center and emotional driving force had been extinguished.

"We *knew* what we had lost," says Betts. "We even thought seriously about not going out and playing anymore. Then we thought, 'Well, what can we do better? We'll just do it with the five of us.' We had already risen to great heights by that point. But Duane didn't experience the highest point—he didn't experience being accepted across the board." Betts pauses for a long moment, and his intense eyes seem to be reading distant memories. It's as if, after all these years, he can still sense deeply all the potential joy and invention that were obliterated on that day.

A few minutes later, Gregg Allman walks in, smiling. "We got it," he tells Betts, with obvious pleasure. Betts rushes off to the control booth, where Dowd plays back the finished vocal. After a few bars of Gregg singing with an uncommon ferocity about a man who just wants to feel some hard-earned pleasures before life cheats him again, Betts' face lights up in a proud and relieved grin. Later, in a private moment, Betts corners Allman in the hallway and slugs him affectionately in the shoulder. "That was some good work," he says. Gregg blushes and the two trade a look that speaks volumes. For all the disappointment they have shared, and all the anger that has passed between them, Dickey Betts and Gregg Allman are still brothers of the closest sort.

EARLY IN THE EVENING, as another storm seems to be closing in, Butch Trucks is conducting an impromptu tour of Criteria Studios. He is looking for some of Tom Dowd's most prized trophies—the gold records he earned for engineering and producing countless legendary acts, including James Brown and Aretha Franklin—when, in one of the older studios, he stumbles across an ebony-colored grand piano. "That's the 'Layla' piano," he says, referring to the instrument on which Jim Gordon played pop's most famous and rapturous coda. It is impossible to resist touching its still-shining white and black keys. It is not unlike touching something sacrosanct. Clearly, this is a room where essential modern cultural history was made—where American and British rock & roll met for its finest and most enduring collaboration.

Trucks settles into a nearby chair and begins to recount the story of the *Layla* sessions. Clapton had come to Miami to record with the Dominos (pianist Bobby Whitlock, drummer Jim Gordon, and bassist Carl Radle). Producer Tom Dowd, who had worked with the Allmans on *Idlewild South* and *At Fillmore East*, mentioned the visit to Duane Allman, a longtime Clapton fan, who asked if he could come by some night and watch the recording. During one of the Dominos rehearsals, Dowd relayed the request to Clapton, who replied, "Man, if you *ever* know where Duane Allman is playing, let me know." A couple of days later, the Allmans were playing Miami, and Dowd took the Dominos to the show. Later that night, back at Criteria, Duane and Eric started jamming, and Clapton invited Allman to play twin-lead on the sessions. Together, Clapton and Allman found an empathy they had never experienced with any other players, and that they would never match. They played probing, deeply felt interweaving melodic lines like two strangers earnestly striving to discover and match each other's depths—which turned out to be an ideal musical metaphor for the sense of romantic torment that Clapton wished to convey with *Layla*.

On another night, Trucks says, Clapton invited the Allmans in for an all-night jam with the Dominos. "I don't remember how good we were," says Trucks, "but it was fun. It sure would be great to hear that music again.

"After we finished that jam," he continues, "Eric and Duane were playing the song 'Layla' back for us, and all of a sudden Duane said, 'Let me try something.' And he put on his guitar and came up with that five-note pattern that actually announces the song—that signature phrase that just kind of set that song on fire." Trucks pauses and shakes his head. Perhaps he realizes that he is sharing a remarkable disclosure: The most revelatory riff of Eric Clapton's career was actually one of Duane Allman's inspired throwaway lines.

Trucks is surprised to learn that archivist Bill Levenson has recently dug up the Dominos-Allmans session and plans to edit and master it for release in a *Layla* retrospective package. Trucks seems intrigued at the prospects, but he also admits that perhaps some experiences are better left to memory. "I remember one night that was the epitome of this band," he says. "It was during the closing of Fillmore East, but it wasn't the closing night, which was the one we recorded for *Eat a Peach*. Instead, it was the night *before*. We went on for the late show, about 1 A.M., and played a normal three-and-a-half-hour set, and when we came back for the encore, the feeling we got from the crowd . . . it was something I'll never forget. I remember sitting there with tears, just really emotional, and then we started jamming, about four in the morning, and we quit about eight o'clock. It was just one jam that went on and on, one thing leading to another, and it was magic.

"All together, we ended up playing seven or eight hours, and when we finished playing, there was no applause. The place was packed, nobody had left, but not even one person clapped. They didn't need to. Somebody got up and opened the doors and the sun came in, and this New York crowd, they just got up and quietly walked out while we were all sitting up there onstage. My mouth's hanging open, and I remember Duane walking in front of me, just dragging his guitar behind him, his head down, shaking it, and he says, 'Goddamn, it's like leaving church.' To me, that's what music is all about. You *try* to reach that level. If you're lucky, you might get there once or twice. That night—maybe the greatest night of our life—*wasn't* recorded, and in an odd way, I'm glad."

Like Betts, Trucks says the loss of Duane Allman was insurmountable. "On just about any level you can think of, it was devastating. What kept us going was the bond that forms when you have to deal with that kind of grief. Also, we did it for his sake as much as ours. We had just gone too far, and hit so many new plateaus in what we were doing, to simply quit.

"The funny thing is, when Duane came back from King Curtis's funeral [the R&B saxophonist—one of Allman's favorite musicians—had been stabbed to death in New York in August 1971], he was thinking a lot about death, and he said many times, 'If anything ever happens to me, you guys better keep it going. Put me in a pine box, throw me in the river, and jam for two or three days.' We tried taking six months off after his death, but we were all just getting too crazy from it. There wasn't any other way to deal with it but to play again. But the hardest thing was just that he wasn't there, you know? This guy was *always* right there in front of me—all I did was look over and there he was—and he wasn't there anymore."

But the band paid hard costs for its determination. Gregg Allman would later say he began his long bouts of drug and alcohol addiction in the months after Duane's death. In addition, bassist Berry Oakley began having serious difficulties. In some ways, the mantle of leadership passed to Oakley, but according to many observers, he was too grief-stricken over Duane's death to accommodate the demands. Then, in November 1972, Oakley was riding his motorcycle through Macon when he lost control and slammed into a city bus. The accident occurred just three blocks from where Duane had been fatally injured, a year and two weeks earlier. Like Allman, Oakley was twenty-four. And like Allman, he was buried in Macon's Rose Hill Cemetery.

"As much as Duane, Berry was responsible for what this band had become," says Trucks. "But in some ways, you could see Berry's death coming. With Duane, man, it was just a shot out of the blue. But Berry . . . he just couldn't cope with Duane being gone, and he got very self-destructive. There were nights when you wouldn't even know if he would be capable of playing. More than once, he would just fall off the stage. By the time Berry died, it was almost a relief just to see the suffering end. It was devastating, but it was expected. We could see it coming.

"That might sound cold or whatever, but by then another direction was coming."

In some ways, it was a more fruitful direction. The Allmans had recruited a second keyboardist, Chuck Leavell, and after Oakley's death, they added a new bassist, Lamar Williams, who had played around Macon with Jaimoe years before. In 1973, the band released its long-anticipated fifth album, *Brothers and Sisters*; within weeks it went to number 1, and spawned the group's first Top 10 single, Dickey Betts' countrified "Ramblin' Man." At long last, the Allman Brothers Band had become the dominant success that Duane Allman and Phil Walden had dreamed it would become; indeed, as much as any other act, the Allmans defined the American mainstream in the decade's early years. At the same time, no central guiding vision or consensus had emerged to replace Duane's sensibility. In time, there were reports that Chuck Leavell wanted to lead the band on a more progressive, fusion-jazz-oriented course, but that Betts felt the group was drifting too far afield from its original blues and rock & roll roots. Also, a somewhat uneasy spirit of competition was developing between Betts and Gregg Allman. Both had released solo LPs and had formed their own bands (Allman's included Jaimoe, Williams, and Leavell), and gradually, Gregg was becoming the most identifiable celebrity in the group. In part, this was due to his stellar romance with (and turbulent marriage to) superstar Cher, as well as his by-then-widely-rumored drug appetites. But Gregg's fame was also based on something more morbid: He was a survivor in a band that seemed both brilliant and damned, and many watched him with a certain fatalistic curiosity.

"By this time the initial spark was gone," says Trucks. Outside, the flash storm is hitting hard. A raging rain slashes against the windows around the room. "We were getting a lot more predictable and were cashing in, and we did more and more of that as the years went on—to the point where it just finally got ridiculous, where even *we* could see it through our drunken stupor."

Even the band's biggest moment—when the Allmans appeared at Watkins Glen, New York, with the Grateful Dead and the Band, for an audience of 600,000: the largest crowd ever assembled in America—was a hollow and somewhat bitter experience. "We just gave the people what they expected," says Betts. "Also, it was not a time for making friends. I remember that Jerry Garcia came out onstage with us and took over. There was no *doubt* he was going to dominate: He'd step right on top of Dickey's playing. Then he made the mistake of playing 'Johnny B. Goode,' and Dickey just *fried* his ass, and we left." Trucks laughs at the memory, then looks saddened. "They never seemed to like us, the Grateful Dead, and they had been gods to us at one time. But everything was so on edge in those days, and like us, they were really in a certain eye of the storm. They were playing for huge audiences and were trying to sell lots of records and they had also lost a couple members of their band, so they were probably feeling a lot of the same doubts."

Trucks pauses and watches the rain for a moment. "The lifestyle we were going through," he says with open distaste. "It was just insane, fucking rock-star ridiculousness. Also, we had quit living together, which I think really had a lot to do with our demise. Everybody would get their own limousines and their own suites, and we'd see each other onstage, and that was it. And God, the cocaine was *pouring*. You would go backstage and there would be a line of thirty dealers waiting outside, and the roadies would go check it out. Whoever had the best coke, they could get in, and they would just keep it flowing all night. That right there probably has a lot to do with my negative feelings about the whole time. We were drifting further and further apart, until the last couple of years were just pure bullshit. Actually, to me they were just a blank. I was drunk twenty-four hours a day."

Then, almost simultaneously, the Allmans achieved their proudest success and their greatest downfall. By 1975, Phil Walden was taking a hand in Georgia politics. He had met and struck up a friendship with Governor Jimmy Carter a couple of years before, and Walden was among the first to know of Carter's plan to seek the presidency. In the fall of 1975, when Carter's campaign was almost bankrupt, Walden began organizing benefit concerts, featuring numerous Capricorn acts, including the Allman Brothers—Carter's favorite American band. In the end, with Walden's help and federal matching funds, Carter had raised over $800,000; without Walden and the Allmans' support, it is unlikely that Carter would have survived the expensive primary campaigns long enough to win the Democratic party's 1976 nomination.

But at the same time, the Allmans' cavalier attitude toward drug use caught up with the band. In early 1976, a federal narcotics force began investigating drug activities in Macon. In a short time, Gregg Allman found himself threatened with a grand jury indictment unless he testified against his personal road manager, Scooter Herring, who had been charged with dealing drugs. Allman complied, and Herring was sentenced to seventy-five years in prison; plus, there were fears that further indictments might be leveled against other figures in the Capricorn and Allman organizations. The band members were furious. Herring, they insisted, had saved Allman from drug overdoses on more than one occasion, and now Herring had been betrayed. They felt that Gregg had dishonored the group's sense of fraternity. "There is no way we can work with Gregg again ever," said Betts at the time—and his sentiment was reportedly shared by every other member of the band. In effect, Gregg Allman had killed off the Allman Brothers Band. The various members went on to other projects. Betts formed Great Southern; Leavell, Williams, and Jaimoe played in Sea Level; and Gregg moved to Los Angeles, where he recorded with Cher, and suffered a difficult marriage in exile.

It took a couple of years, but the wounds healed. Betts now says: "Six months later I read the court transcripts and said, 'Goddamn, this guy had his ass between a rock and hard place.' Actually, I think we had all been set up by a Republican administration that was trying to discredit Jimmy Carter through his connection with Phil Walden and us."

In the interim, the band members found they had missed playing together—that they couldn't achieve with other bands what they had found together, and couldn't win the success separately they had enjoyed collectively. In 1978, they regrouped; Leavell and Williams opted out for Sea Level, and the band added guitarist Dan Toler and bassist Rook Goldflies; and for a brief time, Bonnie Bramlett joined on vocals. The band made one successful record, *Enlightened Rogues,* but then quit Capricorn, filing suit against Walden for unpaid royalties. Shortly, Capricorn went bankrupt; Phil Walden's great Southern Rock empire had collapsed, bitterly. "Walden raped us financially," says Trucks. "He felt like he had done it all and we had nothing to do with it. His worst point was his arrogance: I think Phil has a hard time believing that musicians are on a social level with him. But there's really not much point in talking about Phil Walden."

The Allmans moved to Arista and made two misconceived records, *Reach for the Sky* and *Brothers of the Road,* but at decade's end, the great pop wars of disco and punk were raging, and there was no longer an embracing receptivity for Southern Rock. "If we had found an audience that was ready to listen," says Trucks, "we would have kept going. But the yuppies wanted to get as far away from sex, drugs, and rock & roll as they could get. Wanted to raise their families and pretend like it never happened. Our generation was denying its history. Well, all good things come to an end."

In 1982, the Allmans disbanded a second time. The group members occasionally toured in pairings, or collected for a jam, but they were playing music that seemed to have outlived its historical moment. And there were further bad ends: In 1979, Twiggs Lyndon—who was the Allmans' first road manager and favorite roadie; who had once stabbed to death a club manager because he tried to cheat the band; who had gone to prison and undergone tremendous remorse—was skydiving over a New York town named Duanesburg, and failed to pull his rip cord; he was dead before he hit the ground. In 1983, Lamar Williams died of cancer. The greatest American band of the 1970s was no more; it was itself merely another ghost in a memory-skein of ghosts, knitted together by the bonds of dark remembrances and lost dreams.

THERE REMAINS one subject that people in the Allman camp aren't always anxious to speak about, and that is the matter of Gregg Allman—the troubled singer who still bears the band's deepest debts and highest expectations. "It's almost unfair that we're called the Allman Brothers Band," says Trucks, "because people just zone in on that blond singer: the last Allman. It puts a lot more pressure on him than needs to be there. At the same time, he puts the pressure on himself. He's messed up plenty, and he knows it. He's doing everything he can to rectify it, but it's a heavy burden. And like anybody that has his problems, it's a day-to-day procedure, but we're all here with him.

"Anyway, one thing's for sure: You couldn't do the Allman Brothers without him. We've lost too many of us already."

Indeed, Gregg is at once the most problematic and essential member of the band. His drug, alcohol, and temperament problems have caused both him and the band famous grief, and he has suffered lapses recent enough to have made some people in and around the band wonder if this reunion can truly last. And yet, as Trucks notes, the group cannot do without him: Gregg Allman is more than the band's most visible namesake; he also has the band's voice. Dickey Betts, Johnny Neel, and Warren Haynes can write the blues, and along with Trucks and Jaimoe, they can still play it better than any other rock-based band in the world. But Gregg genuinely *sings* the blues. It is not an easy talent, nor can it be faked. Unfortunately, it is also a talent that, to be rendered at its most effective, has too often involved the physical, moral, emotional, and spiritual ruin of those who practice it. Living the blues may sound like the hoariest cliché in the rock world, but it is also true that really *living* the blues can cost you everything—and Gregg Allman has lived the blues, as much as any singer alive.

The trick is, getting Gregg to *talk* about the blues he has lived. Actually, the trick is getting Gregg to talk about much of anything. He doesn't open up much to outsiders, and he even seems reticent with the friends and musicians who have known him for a generation or more. In particular, though, he is wary with members of the press—and for fair reason: It must not have been much fun to find his marital and drug problems plastered across the front pages of sensationalist tabloids for years on end. Also, he has pretty much gone on record repeatedly and at great length about his brother's death (it almost drove him crazy), the Scooter Herring incident (it terrified and humiliated him), and his troubles with Cher (which confused and angered him), and chances are, he may not yet truly understand just *why* he has had so many recurring drug and alcohol problems. Or perhaps he understands perfectly well, and wouldn't dream of explaining it.

What *would* be interesting to know, however, is how Allman's relationship to music has sustained him—and whether its siren's call has hurt him more than it ever healed him. But in Miami, he isn't of the mind to talk. He stays busy finishing the vocals for *Seven Turns,* and he doesn't spend his voice on gratuitous conversation with anybody. And late at night—a time when, it has been suggested, Gregg may be more inclined to talk—Gregg is nowhere to be found.

One weekend a few weeks later, though, Gregg is playing a blues festival and civil rights benefit on Medgar Evers Day, in Jackson Mississippi. *Seven Turns* is now finished, and reportedly Gregg is as ready as he will ever be for an interview. Also, Gregg's personal manager, Dave Lorry, wants the singer to get used to playing some live shows before the Allmans' summer tour begins. Apparently, Gregg can still be nervous about performing live, and this anxiety is part of what has contributed to his difficulties with drugs and alcohol in the past. For his part, Gregg is playing the festival because two of his old blues friends, B. B. King and Bobby "Blue" Bland, are on the bill; in addition, Little Milton is scheduled to appear. Little Milton is Gregg Allman's favorite singer—a model for his own passionate style—but in a quarter-century of following blues, Allman has never seen Milton sing live, nor has he met him. He says he is looking forward to the chance, and is especially anxious to play a late night jam that will feature himself, King, Bland, and Milton.

The blues festival is being held in a big open-air metallic structure at a fairgrounds on the edge of town. Like Miami, Jackson is subject to sudden storms, and just before Gregg's van arrives at the site, a late spring torrent has turned the surrounding area to mud. Looking for a dry place for the interview, Dave Lorry talks Bobby Bland into accommodating some visitors on his homelike bus.

Seated in the bus's central room, with his wife Danielle nearby, Gregg isn't much more talkative than he was in Miami. It isn't that he's unfriendly, nor is he unintelligent; it's more like he's shy or wary or simply exhausted from twenty years of inquiries. He doesn't really have much to say about *Seven Turns* ("It's a good record; I'm proud of it"), or even about working with the Allmans again ("They're a fine band; I'm proud to work with them"). Even when he's talking, Gregg seems to be living someplace inside himself. He gets in and out of answers as quickly and simply as he can. Music is something he plays and sings, rather than talks about, and his life, he makes plain, is off limits. "The private facts of my life are just as private and painful as anybody's," he says in his most direct moment. "I don't enjoy going over that stuff all the time."

After a few minutes, Bland comes back to visit with Allman. It is a heartening experience to meet Bobby Bland, to watch and hear him speak. He is probably blues music's finest living singer—a vocalist as sensual and pain-filled as Frank Sinatra. In addition, he has a transfixing face: big, open, warm, impossibly beautiful and animated. It is a gracious face and he is a gracious man. If there were any justice, Bobby Bland's image would be celebrated on postage stamps, his bus would be full of Grammys, and he would have the pop audience he has always deserved.

When Bland takes a seat across from Gregg, Allman's entire manner changes. He relaxes visibly, puts his feet up on a nearby bench, sinks back into the sofa, and even allows himself a few unguarded smiles. Clearly, these two men like and respect each other. They start by talking about watching the Rolling Stones' recent live TV broadcast, but it is not Mick Jagger or Keith Richards or even guest guitarist Eric Clapton that they gossip about. What engaged their interest and humor was the appearance of quintessential boogie-bluesman John Lee Hooker onstage with the Stones and Clapton.

Allman laughs as he recalls the times he has seen Hooker on the blues circuit. "He always has these two big white women with him, both of 'em taller than he is," says Allman, smiling.

"Yeah," says Bland, "John Lee is crazy about them white women." His face opens up into a gentle leer, and he and Allman share a knowing laugh.

Bland regards Gregg warmly for a moment then says, "I just wanted to see you were okay. You know, taking care of yourself." He levels an inquiring look at Gregg.

Gregg Allman returns the look, and then blushes. "Yeah, man," he says, "B. B. King gave me the same once-over last night."

Bland smiles without embarrassment. "Well, we're just checking on you," he says with paternal warmth. "Letting you know we care."

For whatever their differences in age, temperament, or cultural and racial background, these two men are colleagues. Bland regards Allman as a fellow traveler on the inescapable blues road. He knows the life Allman has lived. He knows its hopes, and he knows its ends.

Bland also knows it's time to let his family come aboard the bus, and get out of the pouring rain. This means, for the moment, the interview is over—after maybe ten minutes. Gregg can't help looking a bit relieved. "We'll talk later," he says. "Right now I'd like to stay and talk with Bobby a little while."

Actually, as it turns out, the interview is over for good. Later, Allman simply disappears again. One moment, he and Danielle are seated at the side of the stage, watching Bland's elegant blues act, and then he is nowhere to be found. He will not be there when the evening's blues-superstar jam transpires, nor will he meet or hear his idol, Little Milton. When those events take place, Gregg is someplace else—maybe in a darkened motel room, watching TV, brooding.

But midway through the afternoon, he is true to his vocation, and takes the stage in Jackson, with the rudimentary blues band that backs Wolfman Jack. This isn't the Allman Brothers, but Gregg remains that band's spirit, and as he sits behind a Hammond organ, he sings Blind Willie McTell's "Statesboro Blues," Muddy Waters' "Trouble No More," and Sonny Boy Williamson's "One Way Out" not as if they were tired songs that he has sung for a generation, but as if they were bitter facts that he was just facing in his life. *This* is not the man who seemed skittish back in Miami, nor is he the relaxed crony who shared ribald laughs with Bobby Bland earlier. No, it is a different man altogether who sits on this stage, before maybe five hundred people, and closing his eyes tight and tilting his head back until his blond hair grazes his shoulders, sings as if his soul depended on it. *This* man is a blues singer—he sings the music as if it were his birthright, and as if it offers the only moments in which he can work out the mysteries of his life and his confusion. Gregg Allman shuts his eyes very, very tight, and sings like a man who understands that every time he sings, he is singing to ghosts. Maybe he's trying to make his peace with those ghosts, or maybe he's just trying to haunt them as much as they have haunted him.

keith jarrett's

keys to

the cosmos

*A*n itchy silence rules the backstage corridor of the Pasadena Civic
Auditorium—a silence just about as bearable as the hush that trails a
judge's gavel at sentencing. Keith Jarrett, thirty-three, a short, curly-headed
bundle of muscle, leans in a corner doorway rubbing the bridge of his
nose with both hands in a prayerlike motion. Just minutes before, he
finished playing the midway date of a worldwide solo piano concert tour,
a performance that should easily rank as one of the more florid and
sinewy displays of his career. But Jarrett seems heedless of the fact. He
has answered the few attempts at congratulations by the backstage party
with mutters and glares, and for the moment seems intent on a brooding
reverie.

After several strained moments, Jarrett coughs a sharp, private laugh
and scans his guests with an impish grin. "I never realized until now," he
says, resting his stare on me, "how vain and purposeless it would be to
attempt to describe what I just did on that stage. I mean, I'm not thinking
about the music I just played, I'm thinking about *talking* to you about the
music. Words are a poor substitute for experience, and in order for me to talk
about any of this at all, I'm going to have to play games with you." He pauses
to pet the bristly contour of his mustache. "I think it's totally appropriate
that we say nothing now."

With that, the itchy silence returns.

ALTHOUGH HE WOULD probably bridle at the suggestion, Keith Jarrett is to jazz what Jerry Brown is to California politics—a guileful and feisty enigma. Jarrett doesn't exactly brim with what might be termed straight talk, because, simply, he doesn't believe his designs to be comprehensible under the myopic lens of Western scrutiny.

Jarrett, who first won acclaim for his work in Charles Lloyd's and Miles Davis' early fusion ensembles, creates music that by all surface criteria is jazz: an improvised form of music rooted in swing rhythms and blues-derived scales. Yet his music also has a strong harmonic similarity to the work of such twentieth-century European composers as Debussy, Bartók, Schönberg, and Stockhausen, which writers and fans alike laud as a union of jazz technique and modern classical theory.

According to Jarrett, though, it's nothing of the sort. He asserts that his music is beyond categorization—devoid of will, purpose, influences, or even conscious methods, music that very nearly transcends human processes, and therefore, human considerations.

Jarrett has often said that when he takes his seat at the piano for a solo concert, he has no idea what his fingers will play, that his entire performance is in fact a "spontaneous composition." That places what he does outside the usual provinces of improvisation, which generally means extemporizing melodic lines on given themes, harmonic progressions, or modal settings. Jarrett theoretically constructs his theme and overall structure on the spot, which is hardly as unprecedented or superhuman as some of his supporters claim, but Jarrett pursues it more extensively than anyone else ever has. It is a risky undertaking, and Jarrett's concerts meander just as often as they enthrall.

In emphatic contrast to so many of his colleagues who rose to prominence in the last decade—particularly those who, like Jarrett, passed through Miles Davis' bands—Jarrett has proudly shunned fusion and funk in favor of strictly acoustic settings, including his solo campaign. Of the twenty-five albums or collections he has released in the last five years (comprising forty-three discs), five of those (or eighteen discs' worth) have been solo piano volumes, a staggering output for any artist, and all the more impressive when one considers how first-rate it's been.

The showstopper is Jarrett's latest release, the *Sun Bear Concerts,* a ten-record account of his 1976 solo tour of Japan assembled in a booklike slipcase with a suggested retail tag of seventy-five dollars. No one has ever before released a ten-record set of all new music, and it isn't likely that anyone ever will again—unless it's Jarrett. His previous solo volumes have sold well enough to border on gold—unusually good for jazz—but Warner Bros. (the distributors for Jarrett's German-based ECM label) worried about how to promote the bulky *Sun Bear*. Jarrett undertook a solo tour scheduled expressly to promote his monolith. Spanning New York to Tokyo, it has been his most extensive undertaking to date.

Releasing a ten-record set doesn't strike Jarrett as a particularly indulgent act, just as his oft-stated claim that no other composers or jazz artists have influenced his style doesn't strike him as a conceited or ill-founded boast. In fact, he avidly disavows the merit of most contemporary music other than his own (though he does profess a liking for Linda Ronstadt's pipes and an occasional Bob Dylan song), and *all* electronic music, he insists, is poisonous.

Underscoring Jarrett's grandiloquence is his temperament. On occasion he can be just plain arrogant. He's famous for halting concerts to scold late arrivals or berate photographers. Other times, he's stopped performing until the piano can be retuned to his standards. In short, Jarrett's music may spring, as he claims, from egoless sources, but his disposition, it would seem, is nothing less than the epitome of an artistic ego—proud and moody.

JARRETT AND I meet for the first time in New York, the day after his tour opened in mid-October 1978, with a concert at the Metropolitan Opera House (the only other soloist who has ever been invited to play the Met was Vladimir Horowitz). Although I've been in the city for four days, Jarrett has had no time for an interview, and when we finally meet, it is in the back seat of a limousine en route to LaGuardia Airport, where he is to leave for Chicago. As we speak, he strokes the handle of a tennis racket and peers through smoky sunglasses at New York's disappearing skyline.

"My time is fairly important," he says in a brittle, clipped cadence, "so I don't have much of it to spare. Just what did you want to ask?" There's nothing haughty about his manner, particularly, and nothing intimate. Indeed, it's about as bald and matter-of-fact as I've ever encountered.

I start by asking him how consciously or analytically he monitors the music as he's improvising it, how much his own ear dictates what an audience hears.

"The process is mysterious," he says evenly, removing his sunglasses and fixing his dark eyes on mine. "That's the best thing I can say about it."

"Surely there are decisions you make in that moment-to-moment process about what notes to play and not to play, and how long and how loud to play them?" I ask.

He shrugs a smile and half nods his head. "Since it's all improvised, every second may contain a hundred choices for me, and my first job is to know whether I'm making those choices mentally or not. Like, if my finger is about to play a note, I can't play it because I *want* to play it, and yet I can't *not* play it because I don't want to. It's a course of thought and no thought, decision and no decision."

WHEN JARRETT talks about the course of "decision and no decision," one gets the impression of a man knee-deep in an Oriental discipline, and, in fact, some critics have viewed his music as the proselytizing excesses of a yoga, Sufi, or Zen student. Jarrett does adhere to some kind of stoical code, but what it is, he won't say. The closest I can place it is Taoism, the Chinese religious and political movement based upon the ancient *Tao-te Ching*. The idea of Tao translates, roughly, as the "way" or "path," a driving power and rhythmic force in nature that is life's ordering principle. It informs and motivates man's spirit, and when one surrenders to its pulse, one grows in tune with the benign dictates of the universe, becoming a vehicle for its will.

Wherever Jarrett's notions of self-propelled music spring from, they've certainly come home to roost on the *Sun Bear Concerts*. Nowhere else in his collected works does music seem more effortless and splendid. From the opening phrase onward, it unfolds like an idyllic dream on the border of consciousness, and like the best of dreams—or narratives—you never want it to end. It is, to my mind, one of the few real self-contained epics in seventies music.

Jarrett's improvisations rarely rank as bona fide compositions because they're usually formless adventures, devoid of identifiable themes, movements, and resolutions. But this is also their strength. Instead of clearly delineated melodic trains, Jarrett focuses on a mood—most effectively in a minor key or mode—then traces it through interminable transitions that just skim the rim of a retainable melody. That he can do it as effectively with atonal structures as he can with blues or impressionist forms merely indicates the expanse of his imagination.

Probably the most striking feature of Jarrett's solo music is the degree of intimacy he has with his instrument, which adds an interesting hitch to his claim that music flows of its own will through his blank consciousness. More likely it is a process far less mystifying: Every time Jarrett places his fingers on the keys, he isn't just opening himself to the whims of a muse, he's summoning his variegated background as a pianist.

Jarrett, of French-Hungarian extraction, grew up in Allentown, Pennsylvania. A prodigy, by age fifteen he had consumed a classical repertoire ranging from Bach to Bartók and was attracted to jazz by the Ravel-influenced reveries of pianist Bill Evans. In the early sixties, Jarrett studied improvisation at Boston's Berklee College of Music, where he eventually was discharged for insubordination. He played support to almost any Boston and New York club act that would have him (including, most notably, Art Blakey), a practice he now lauds as the prime influence in his eclectic point of view.

By 1966, Jarrett had settled into Charles Lloyd's Quartet, who, with their cultivated hippie air and breakthrough shows at the Fillmore, were one of the earliest harbingers of fusion jazz. With them, Jarrett first began to attract an audience for his idiosyncratic flights, including a fondness for pummeling the piano's interior. His subsequent tenure with Miles Davis was weird and fitful, though he now says that the experience was as positive as he could hope for with electronic music: "It was music that was conceived for electronics. There was no other way of playing what Miles was coming up with."

In 1972, everything fell together for Jarrett. His own group—which included bassist Charlie Haden, saxophonist Dewey Redman (alumni of Ornette Coleman groups), and drummer Paul Motian—released two stunning albums: *Birth* (Atlantic) and *Expectations* (Columbia), showcasing one of the most protean and irrestrainable quartets of the seventies, featuring a fully ripe Jarrett hammering out complex blues and polytonal fugues with rock-derived fervor. Also that same year, he released his first solo album, *Facing You,* for a then-obscure, budding German label called ECM (Editions of Contemporary Music), prompting critic Robert Palmer to exult in these pages that, "When he plays alone, Jarrett pushes his creativity to its limits. . . . It is without a doubt the most creative and satisfying solo album of the past few years."

After that first solo effort, Keith's heart belonged to ECM—and solo recording. Although his quartet (which had moved to ABC/Impulse) continued to record prolifically—including in a one-year span, three of their finest albums, *Fort Yawuh, Death and the Flower,* and *Treasure Island*—they increasingly became a perfunctory, misshapen unit bound together by contractual commitments.

At ECM, the label's producer/mentor, Manfred Eicher, allowed Jarrett to record in any style he fancied, from the flawed *In the Light* (compositions for chamber ensembles) to the sublime three-record *Bremen-Lausanne.* With

Bremen-Lausanne and the subsequent *Köln Concert*, Jarrett found his niche, freely mixing gospel, impressionist, and atonal flights into a consonant whole.

While Eicher's production style is so meticulous and refined that it leaves most ECM artists sounding cold and prosaic, in Jarrett's case Eicher furnishes the canvas best suited to the artist's brush. Together, they make some of the most sterling ascetic music of the day. If Keith Jarrett has at last arrived, it hasn't been alone.

WHEN JARRETT and I meet again, it's on the far side of the continent, in the backstage corridor at the Pasadena Civic Auditorium. After the show and Jarrett's terse dictum about the futility of words, a small cluster of nervous admirers files into Jarrett's dressing room for autographs. Jarrett for the most part is cool but polite with the visitors, who seem to be seeking some meaningful banter or disclosure about the mystery behind his music. Jarrett appears to both relish and reject his role as sage, depending upon the questioner.

"How does it happen," asks a scraggly Scandinavian in stumbling English, "that you have so much energy in your hands?"

"How does it not happen that no one else does?" replies Keith with his imp's smile. A few moments later he abruptly turns aside another blushing devotee's jittery inquiry, saying, "I can't take people who are as serious and philosophical as you." In near tears, the kid turns and leaves.

The next morning, Keith and I hook up again in a limousine en route to the Los Angeles Airport, where Keith and manager Brian Carr are to catch a flight to Hawaii. Jarrett's cheeks and chin are marked by lines of exhaustion, pinching his face into a tight pucker. Grudgingly he acknowledges the transaction of an interview. That morning in the bustling airport bar we have a brief conversation:

"Several of the people backstage last night seemed to be trying to tell you that they find something beyond music in your concerts—some action or discipline that may be tied to a spiritual or philosophical level," I venture.

"I don't know what the words *philosophical* and *spiritual* mean. I know that what goes on while I'm playing could be translated into philosophy by anyone who wants to eliminate a lot of their being in the process, by converting it into a system of thought or discipline. I don't have the privilege of doing that. If I did, it would limit the music."

"Do you think your music conveys emotions to the audience?"

"Conveying an emotion would be music at its most gross use. Conveying the clarity of energy is music at its highest. Emotions are already so colored. . . . For example, the music might convey an emotion if I heard somebody click a camera. I'd then have a momentary feeling; I would have to explode. Now that wouldn't necessarily create music, but it *would* be an enema of sorts, you know, to rid myself of the moment that had just defiled what was happening.

"I'd like to say something here without you asking a question. I came to realize recently that I can't let go of the essence of what's happening to me, moment to moment, just for the sake of etiquette. That means I'm as committed to spontaneity now as I would be playing the piano onstage. Spontaneity tells me what should be happening at this exact second. So if your questions don't fit into that, it's an impossible subject to deal with. In a way, the concerts preserve my life outside of the music, and vice versa. And if I let either of them down, I'm sinning.

"The music is the reason I'm known at all. It created the interest in doing an interview with me. But because it was music that did, it means that I should adhere to the laws of music. I understand the process that you need to deal with, but I can no more help you with it than if *no* one was sitting in this chair. To me, you want to talk about subjects in which I have absolutely no concern."

"You have no concern if people choose to categorize your music as jazz?"

"Well, you're helping that. What I mean is, a lot of people won't read this because it's an article on jazz, and you're helping to reinforce that architecture. Now you're trying to reduce things that are of no concern into interesting questions and answers. I hope my music can't be understood within the context of your article. Why do you think it's so easy to forget what I play? Because what I do isn't about music. It's about an experience beyond sound."

"You also once said that your purpose is 'blowing people's conceptions of what music means.' "

"That was me in the role of an ego. I'm growing now, and making less of those doctrinaire statements."

"Does that mean that your feelings about electronic music might change in time, too?"

"No, because those aren't feelings, they're physiological facts. Just being in the same room with it is harmful, like smoking cigarettes. . . . But what you're doing is what the Western world would love to have continue forever, which is picking apart a world that doesn't deserve to be picked apart. If there's going to be a profile of me in your magazine, it's a profile you're

---

drawing from yourself, and you're getting answers from me because I'm not being myself enough to jump in the air, turn a cartwheel, and leave this room—which is what I feel like doing."

With that, Jarrett excuses himself to make a call to his wife in New Jersey before catching his flight. Our interview, I gather, is over.

"Look," says Brian Carr, who's been sitting by attentively the whole time, "you should come over to Hawaii for a couple of days. There, he'll have a chance to relax and talk with more ease. After all, you two should have more contact than this."

THREE DAYS LATER, standing in an open-air hotel lobby in rainy Lahaina, Maui, I tell myself that more contact with Keith Jarrett is the last thing I should have. I have been in the hotel for about an hour, trying to reach Brian Carr with no luck, so I decide instead to ring Jarrett's room and say hello. It's a mistake. Maybe I have interrupted some kind of cosmic process, but whatever, Jarrett is fit to be tied.

"I don't have a machine to protect me," he snaps. "I only have one person to act as a buffer between me and everyone else, and I don't feel like I should have to be disturbed by someone calling *me* instead of Brian. You're proving more and more that there's nothing to talk about—and that there's no meaning to the things that we talk about."

Does this mean, I ask myself, that I am *unknowledgeable? Unenlightened?* Then fine. I've followed this prima donna from New York to Hawaii and have only been able to get an hour's worth of conversation with him. I feel like packing my hopelessly limited Western point of view into my overnight bag, turning a cartwheel, and leaving this island, because that seems to be what the moment dictates. In fact, I'm about ready to do just that when I get a call in the hotel lobby from Carr, asking me to meet him in a bar in downtown Lahaina.

Carr has been something of a counselor to me in my dealings with Jarrett, and the combination of his suasion and two mai tais cools down my indignation considerably. I agree to stay and wait for the spirit of spontaneity to move Jarrett to a more colloquial frame of mind. Finally, as luck would have it, in the middle of *Kiss Meets the Phantom of the Park,* I get a call that Keith will see me now.

Jarrett, clad in a black Avedis Zildjian Cymbals T-shirt and jeans, greets me at the door of his penthouse with the same distracted air that he uses to greet his audiences. Without a word, he strolls over to the balcony, slides the glass partition open, then settles into an apricot-and-lime-tinted sofa. The moist air, washing in off the ocean waves a few yards away, seems to ease some of the tension in the room. Perched forward on the edge of his seat, Jarrett studies his thick, muscular fingers as they clinch one another in a vise grip.

"This interview has been hard for me," he says in a subdued tone, "because I don't feel like I'm able to shake the foundation of what words are supposed to do, which is the only way it could be *my* interview. I'm shaking foundations with music, so it only makes sense that I should be able to do that in other areas, too. The thing is, how can I express that there's no more to say—that all interviews are bullshit—and still allow you to do your job?"

He sinks back into the folds of the sofa, hooking his arms over its back like a bird in roost and occasionally fluttering a hand to underscore a point. "The solo thing I'm doing is growing more sensitive, and also more subject to destruction, so it has to be protected. There are things now that I can't be asked to do that maybe five years ago I would, not because I'm getting more eccentric or arrogant, but because the process requires more consciousness, more tuning. Everything gets fussier and purer. . . . You know, it's funny, but death hovers around quite a bit at a solo concert."

"Death?"

"Yes, the possibility that I might not live through a concert because of how vulnerable I am to anything that happens. It's like my ego isn't strong enough to protect me at those moments. Sometimes I feel as if I'm putting my finger on an electric line and leaving it there."

I recall something Brian Carr had said when we first met: "It's quite an ordeal Keith goes through to do these solo concerts. There's always the possibility in some people's minds that this just might be the night he can't play, the night he remains blank. I think that possibility seems just as real to him as anyone else."

Maybe, but I have a hunch that Keith's ego is a whole lot tougher—and more cunning—than he may admit. It probably shapes and informs his music to a greater, more artful degree than any trancelike communion with higher forces ever could. The detractive part of that ego is its haughty manner with the real world and its capacity for indulgence. But that's probably okay. Certainly there's no correlation between an artist's talent or vision and his temperament, because a lot of real bastards have made some damn transcendent art.

I don't have to live with Jarrett's bullying, insolent manner, but I'm more than happy to live with his music. As distasteful and pretentious as he can be, he has created a vital and durable body of recordings that is going to serve as consummate documents of solo improvisation for generations.

After a few minutes the conversation turns to the *Sun Bear Concerts*. Keith is interested in my reactions to the set and whether I think it can find an audience. "If there's anything I wish would sell for the right reason," he says, "it's that set. I was involved in a very searching period of time when we recorded that, and the music itself was almost a release for the search. I've been thinking—*Sun Bear* is the only thing I've recorded that runs the gamut of human emotion. I think that if you got to know it well enough, you'd find it all in there someplace."

"Just were did the name *Sun Bear* come from, anyway?"

For the first time in our conversations, Keith looks genuinely shy, almost humble. "It's a very light-hearted reason," he replies with a disarming smile. "While we were on that tour I went to a zoo, where I saw a Sun Bear, a small bear that looks real gentle, like a house pet, and doesn't exist anywhere but in Japan. The next day I had lunch with one of the Japanese recording engineers, and I asked him about the bear because I remembered its face—a real friendly little face. And he said, 'Yeah, it's a beautiful bear, but if you get close enough, it knocks you about three blocks down the street.'

"I just liked that whole idea of an animal that looked like it would be nice to get close to, but if you did, it would shock your very conception of life."

It's my guess that if it ever came to blows between Keith Jarrett and a Sun Bear, that little bear might have to reexamine a few conceptions of its own.

life & death

in the u.k.

the sex pistols, public image ltd.,

joy division, new order,

and the jesus and mary chain

johnny Rotten was one of the few terrific anti-heroes rock & roll has ever produced: a violent-voiced bantam of a boy who tried to make sense of popular culture by making that culture suffer the world outside—its moral horror, its self-impelled violation, its social homicide. His brief, rampaging tenure with the Sex Pistols—the definitional punk band of the late 1970s—had the effect of disrupting rock & roll's sound, style, and meaning, unlike any pop force before or since. Even seeing the band only once, as I did at San Francisco's Winterland in January 1978, brought home their consequence with an indelible jolt. That night, Rotten danced—waded, actually—through a mounting pile of debris: everything from shoes, coins, books, and umbrellas, all heaved his way by a tense, adulatory crowd. Draped in a veil of smoke and sweat, the scene resembled nothing so much as a rehearsal for Armageddon, and Rotten rummaged through it all like some misplaced jester. But when he sang—railing at the crowd, jeering the line, "There's no future, no future, no future for YOU!"—he was predatory and awesome. It was the most impressive moment in rock & roll I have ever witnessed.

The morning after the show, the other Sex Pistols and their manager, Malcolm McLaren, fired Rotten. McLaren, who conceived the group and purportedly engineered its rise and fall, charged that Warner Bros. (the Pistols' American label) had purposefully driven a wedge between Rotten and the rest of the band, and that Rotten himself—who had influenced punk ethos more than any other single figure—had turned into a glory-basking rock star. "What really happened," Rotten will tell me more than two years after the band's end, "is that the other Pistols [guitarist Steve Jones and drummer Paul Cook] wouldn't speak to me anymore. Malcolm flew them around in airplanes, while Sid [Vicious] and I traveled across America with roadies. You come here to see the fuckin' country, not fly over it." It is nearly 1 A.M., and as we talk we are seated in the bar at a Los Angeles Sunset Strip hotel, drinking rum and Cokes.

"If you really want to know, I think the Sex Pistols failed . . . *miserably*," Rotten says, spouting the last word with a thespian flourish. "Actually, it was a bit embarrassing. The other people in the band never understood what I was singing about."

IN CONTRAST TO Johnny Rotten, John Lydon—who rose from the ashes of Johnny Rotten and the Sex Pistols to form the experimentalist postpunk band Public Image Ltd.—impresses some erstwhile followers as just a plain antagonist: a tedious, ill-affected *artiste* who deserted his own dread visions for fear they might destroy him. In a way, that may be true. By dealing exclusively in abstract images and accidental sounds, Lydon no longer has to run the risk of caring—which means he no longer needs to run the risk of meaning. (Director Julien Temple—who made the Sex Pistols feature *The Great Rock 'n' Roll Swindle*, and would later film *Absolute Beginners*—once told me: "What John understands is that if people love you, they have control over you, because they can always say they *don't* love you and destroy you. But if they hate you, and you hate them in return, then you're freer.")

It's also true that Lydon rankles critics and punk diehards alike because he's repudiated his past. By his own admission, the music he has made with PIL aims to devastate classicist rock & roll—including punk rock—by blackening its themes and confounding its forms. It's as if, after distancing himself from the merciless primitivism of the Sex Pistols, Lydon found a fatal flaw in rock & roll itself—namely, that it imparted the illusion of order and transcendence—and decided to remake the genre. In creating PIL, Lydon announced that he wanted to form a group that was "anti-music of any kind. I'm tired of melody." To help him realize this end, Lydon recruited two friends—classically trained guitarist and pianist Keith Levene, who'd been a founding member of the Clash, and Jah Wobble, a novice bassist and reggae enthusiast. Lydon also saw all this new musical change as a chance to debunk the myth of Johnny Rotten. (Actually, he delights in interchanging the surnames: on PIL's album jackets he lists himself as John Lydon, though in conversation he generally refers to himself as Johnny Rotten.) "Malcolm and the press had a lot to do with fostering that *Rotten* image," Lydon says. "I chose to walk away from it because otherwise you have all these people out there waiting for you to kill yourself on their behalf.

"I mean, look what happened to Sid," he adds, referring to bassist Sid Vicious' arrest for the murder of his girlfriend, Nancy Spungen, and his subsequent 1979 death by heroin overdose. A plaintive look crosses Lydon's face, and he stares into his drink for a long moment. "Poor Sid. The only way he could live up to what he wanted everyone to believe about him was to die. That was tragic, but more for Sid than anyone else. He really bought his public image."

It is fitting then, that Lydon named his new group Public Image Ltd. ("The name," he says, "means just that: Our image *is* limited"), and that their debut single, "Public Image," was an indictment of the Pistols and McLaren. But the real focal point of the song, as well as the subsequent album, *Public Image*, was the musical content: amorphous structures and unbroken rhythms, paired with minimal melodies and Lydon's hoodoo vocals. The concept had its roots in the drone and modal experimentalism of the Velvet Underground, Brian Eno, avant-garde composer La Monte Young and the German group Can, while the actual sound mix resembled the prominent bass and deep-echo characteristic of reggae dub production. In actual effect, Lydon and PIL simply rerouted the Pistols' much vaunted anarchism, applying it to song structure, and in the process, authored the first major attempt to transmogrify rock parlance since Captain Beefheart's *Trout Mask Replica*.

The rock press, though, lambasted *Public Image. Rolling Stone* termed it "postnasal drip monotony," while England's *New Musical Express* dismissed it as a "Zen lesson in idolatry." (Warner Bros. declined to release the album in America, even though PIL rerecorded and remixed parts of it.) Basically, PIL agreed with the critics: "They all slagged it," says Keith Levene, "because it was self-indulgent, nonsimplistic, and non–rock & roll. Those are all *good points.* But that's the kind of music we intend to make. We don't want to be another Clash, making old-fashioned, twelve-bar rock & roll."

But in 1980, critical perspectives on PIL start to shift. In part, that's because the group has come to be seen as progenitors of the English postpunk movement, which at the time includes electronic, theorizing, doleful bands like Cabaret Voltaire, Joy Division, and many others. It's also because PIL's own music matured measurably. With *Second Edition* (originally released in November 1979 in Britain by Virgin Records, in limited edition as *Metal Box*—a set of three 12-inch forty-fives packaged in a film canister), Levene fashioned a mesmerizing, orchestral guitar and synthesizer mesh that embroiders and enwraps the dance beat–oriented rhythm section, while Lydon wrote some of his most forceful lyrics (particularly those to "Poptones," a deathly account of rape told from the victim's point of view, and "Swan Lake," a song about his mother's death).

"Now all the critics *love* us," Lydon says with a scornful smile. At 2 A.M. the waitress calls for last rounds. Lydon orders a double (I can't help but copy him), then he continues: "I don't trust all these people who praise us now. They're the same ones who waited until the Pistols were over before they accepted them. And I'm not sure the press appreciates at all that Public Image is more than just a band *I'm* in."

But, I note, when people open *Rolling Stone* and see a picture of Lydon only—since Keith Levene wouldn't be photographed—doesn't that help reinforce the notion that PIL is, indeed, Lydon's band?

His eyes flicker. "They can think what they fuckin' want," he snaps. "I gave up a long time ago bothering about people's opinions and impressions. If Keith don't want his picture taken, that's fine. It's a band decision, is it *not*? Just appreciate it for that."

*B*UT, OF COURSE, PIL *was* John Lydon's band—which would become inarguably plain with the band's next (and probably best) album, *Paris au Printemps*.

Paris au Printemps (recorded live in France in January 1980 though never released in the United States) is the album on which PIL's formlessness finally became formulated—which is to say that if they could reproduce their apparently inchoate, unpremeditated music letter-perfect live (and they could), then it wasn't really orderless or even all that experimental. Yet it was visceral. Guitarist Keith Levene, bassist Jah Wobble, and drummer Martin Atkins play momentously throughout, interweaving deliberate rhythms and backhanded melodies into a taut webwork of crosscurrent designs and motions. Lydon offers a stunning, protean vocal performance: by turns gleeful, derisive, virulent and, during "Chant" and "Careering," so terrifying—invoking images of mob rule one minute, murder the next—as to be almost unendurable.

But what we hear on *Paris au Printemps* is more than animated, frictional music: We hear the way that music can rub up against, even threaten, people who aren't ready for it. By the LP's second side, the crowd—a horde of recherché, loud-mouthed, self-conscious gothics—have had about all the cacophony they can handle. They want pogo beats, block chords, primal thrums—in short, the familiar punk mannerisms they know how to react to. Not getting these, they start to taunt Lydon, spitting jeers, demands, and audible gobs of phlegm at him. John Lydon returns the contempt, leaning lethally into his vocals, narrowing the distance between himself and the implied violence, turning the insensibility of the moment back into the faces of an audience he helped conceive but can no longer abide. "Shut up!" he barks at one point, his scorn echoing through the hall. "I'll walk off this fucking stage if you keep spitting . . . *Dog*!" Minutes later, at the close of "Poptones," that's exactly what he does, dropping his microphone on the saliva-soaked floor and stomping into the wings. In that moment, you can hear Lydon further remove himself from any conceivable culture or subculture that might contain him. He kisses off the whole oppressive orthodoxy of punk mindlessness, just as he once decried the manifest hopelessness of British society.

Little wonder that *Paris au Printemps* also depicts an end of sorts for PIL. Following the group's 1980 American tour, Martin Atkins (the finest drummer PIL's ever had; he made the music pounce where others made it loiter) left to form a puerile and comedic postpunk band, Brian Brain. Then, a few weeks later, Lydon, Levene, and hidden member Jeanette Lee (who handles much of PIL's business) parted company with Jah Wobble after he released two solo albums in quick succession, charging that the bassist had used PIL backing tracks without permission.

THE FLOWERS OF ROMANCE—released in 1981—sounds as if it were recorded to scorn a myriad of losses. Only Lydon, Levene, Lee, and, on a strictly work-for-hire basis, Atkins make the music this time, and it's probably the most brutal, frightening music Lydon has lent his voice to since "Anarchy in the U.K." (A bit *too* frightening for PIL's British-based label, Virgin, which initially balked at issuing the new LP, claiming it was arrantly noncommercial. Meanwhile, Warner Bros., which declined to release either the first PIL album or *Paris au Printemps* in America, grudgingly agreed to a small pressing.)

In contrast to the group's earlier records—on which Levene and Lydon piled thick, splayed layers of guitars and synthesizers on top of thunderous, bass-heavy rhythm tracks until chance melodies and imperative tempos seemed to take perverse shape and then pull apart again—*The Flowers of Romance* pares PIL music down to a minimalist, primordial-sounding mix of mostly vocals and percussion. In the first cut, "Four Enclosed Walls," Atkins' drum shot cracks the air like rifle fire, and Lydon answers it with a quavering howl. From there, the track turns into a fierce drum-and-vocal dialogue, with Atkins pounding out an aberrant martial pattern and Lydon ululating through the clatter, chanting an obscure, dreamlike conjuration about Western dread and Islamic vengeance.

Later, in "Under the House"—in which John Lydon and Martin Atkins carry their colloquy to a harrowing peak—Lydon can't seem to separate the nightmares from wakeful terror. Something's after him: maybe a cadaver, maybe a mercenary, maybe even a bad memory—it's hard to say exactly what. Specters of fear, death, and flight stack up so fast that words and meanings cease to matter much. All that counts is the way the singer gives in to the momentum of his tale, letting animistic horror possess and propel him, as if he might fend off doom with its own likeness.

Almost everything on *The Flowers of Romance* pulls back, shrinks into shielding self-interest. The title tune has already been described by certain critics as John Lydon's belated farewell to Sid Vicious (who, before joining the Sex Pistols, once belonged to a band called Flowers of Romance—named by none other than Johnny Rotten). And indeed, the song, with its disdainful references to failed friendships and its resigned air of parting, sounds like some sort of remembrance. But it could just as easily be about what the lyrics purport: a ruined romance that Lydon had no difficulty leaving. For that matter, the singer manages to denigrate or refuse so many possible alliances over the course of this LP—sexual commitment ("Track 8"), punk fandom ("Banging the Door"), and notions of musical accord in general—that sometimes the only ground he seems left with is the narrow path of his own hubris.

Suddenly, in the album's final compositions, "Go Back" and "Francis Massacre," the world closes in. "Go Back," which features Keith Levene's only flaring guitar part on the record, is a methodical, mocking sketch of life in Tory Britain, where the future has been banked on recycled mottos ("Improvements on the domestic front," gibes Lydon. "Have a cup of tea—good days ahead/Don't look back—good days ahead").

"Francis Massacre," on the other hand, is about a future sealed off forever. It's a scanty, discordant account of Francis Moran—a man presently serving a life sentence in Ireland's Mountjoy Prison for murder. Nobody—including Irish penal officials and Lydon's own representatives—cares to disclose any specifics about either Moran or his crime, and it's hard to tell from the lyrics alone (a yowling litany of "Go down for life/Go down for life") how Lydon feels. But the sheer desolating force of the music he and Levene make—a blaring, claustrophobic, rapacious tumult of atonal piano, metallic drums, and furious singing—seems to act out the passions of murder while simultaneously seeking to annihilate those passions, which (to me) seems as jolting a deed of protest as music can perform.

It's something like those incandescent moments in the Sex Pistols' "Bodies" or "Holidays in the Sun" when the singer sought to illuminate terror by embodying it. In "Francis Massacre," though, John Lydon means to turn the terror outward—to level it against a world that contains so much pain and so many nightmares that the most reaffirming recourse available is a brutal, racking cry of unwavering outrage.

THE MUSIC OF Joy Division—an art-minded English postpunk band that initially struck reviewers as a tuneful version of PIL—sets forth an even more indelible vision of gloom. In fact, it's a vision so steeped in deathly fixations that it proved fatal: on May 18, 1980, the group's lead singer and lyricist, Ian Curtis—a shy, reticent man who'd written some of the most powerfully authentic accounts of dissolution and despair since Lou Reed—hung himself at his home in Macclesfield, England, at the age of twenty-three. According to journalistic accounts, he'd been depressed over failed love. According to his songs, he'd looked upon the horror of mortal futility and understood the gravity of what he saw: "Heart and soul—one will burn."

In the United Kingdom, Curtis' suicide conferred Joy Division with mythical status. The band's second and last album, *Closer* (recorded just prior to Curtis' death and released shortly afterward by Factory), became one of the fastest-selling independent-label LPs in British history. By the end of 1980, it had topped several critics' and readers' polls as best album. More significant, an entire legion of Joy Division emulators—most notably Section Twenty-Five, Crispy Ambulance, Mass, Sort Sol and the Names (names *nobody* now remembers)—cropped up around England, each professing the same icy passion for sepulchral rhythms, minor-mode melodies, and mordant truths.

The danger in all of this grim-faced, wide-eyed hagiography, of course, is that it serves to idealize Curtis' death and ignores the fact that he contributed and submitted to the wretchedness he reviled by committing the act of self-murder. Why bother then with music so seemingly dead-end and depressing? Maybe because, in the midst of a movement overrun by studied nihilism and faddish despair, it's somehow affecting to hear someone whose conviction ranged beyond mere truisms. Maybe because Ian Curtis' descent into despair leaves us with a deeper feeling of our own frailty. Or maybe even because it's fascinating to hear a man's life and desire fading away, little by little, bit by bit. Yet none of that really says much about how obsessing Joy Division's music can be, how it can draw you into its desolate, chiaroscuro atmosphere and fearful, irretrievable circuits. Draw you in and threaten to leave you there.

ACTUALLY, JOY DIVISION didn't make all that much music. The group's earliest work—demo tapes recorded under the name Warsaw and a debut EP, *Ideal for Living* (some of which appeared in a later compilation)— was a worthy but hardly exceptional example of a band attempting to forge art-rock influences (mostly David Bowie, Brian Eno, and Roxy Music) and primitivist archetypes (some Sex Pistols, a little Who) into a frenetic counter-poise. By the time of their first LP, *Unknown Pleasures,* Joy Division had tempered their style, planishing it down to a doleful, deep-toned sound that often suggested an elaborate version of the Velvet Underground or an orderly Public Image Ltd. In its most pervading moments—in numbers like "Day of the Lords," "Insight," and "New Dawn Fades," with their disoriented melodies and punishing rhythms—it was music that could purvey Curtis' alienated and fatalistic sensibility. But it was also music that could rush and jump and push, and a composition like "Disorder"—or better still, the later single "Transmission," with its driving tempo and roiling guitars—seemed almost spirited enough to dispel the gloom it so doggedly invoked.

Yet Joy Division never really aspire toward transcendence. In fact, their most obsessive, most melodic piece of music, "Love Will Tear Us Apart," raises the possibility and then sadly shuts the door on it. A flurry of thrashing guitars and drums—crashing out the same insistent backbeat that impels the Clash's "Safe European Home"—launches the song, then surrenders to the plaint of a solitary synthesizer and Ian Curtis' frayed singing. "When routine bites hard," he murmurs, "And ambitions are low/And resentment rides high/But emotions won't grow . . . /Then love—love will tear us apart— again." By tune's end, Curtis has run out of will, but the music hasn't. Thick, surging synthesizer lines—mimicking the hook from Phil Spector's "Then He Kissed Me"—surround and batter the singer as he half talks, half croons the most critical verse of his career: "And there's a taste in my mouth/As desperation takes hold/Yeah, that something so good/Just can't function no more."

Closer seems resigned to fatality from the start. It descends, with a gravity and logic all its own, from the petrifying scenario of "Atrocity Exhibition" (a story borrowed from J. G. Ballard about a world that proffers degradation of the flesh as sport) to the raw, raging "Twenty Four Hours," in which Curtis allows himself a last, longing glance at the fading vista of existence: "Just for one moment/Thought I found my way/Destiny unfolded/ I watched it slip away."

But *Closer* doesn't stop there. Instead, it takes us through the numbing ritual of a funeral procession ("The Eternal") and then, in the mellifluent "Decades," into the very heart of paradise lost:

> We knocked on the doors of hell's darker chambers
> Pushed to the limits, we dragged ourselves in
> Watched from the wings as the scenes were replaying
> We saw ourselves now as we never have seen
> Portrayal of the trauma and degeneration
> The sorrows we suffered and never were free.

The unknown now appears known, maybe even comforting. "We're inside now, our hearts lost forever," sings Curtis in a voice as rueful as Frank Sinatra's. Somehow, it's the album's most beguiling moment.

In the end, *Closer* accedes to horror, settles into frozen straits of inviolable damnation. The music turns leaden, gray, and steady because it means to fulfill a vision of a world where suffering is unremitting and nothingness is quiescent. Joy Division's art is remarkably eloquent and effective, yet it lacks the jolting tone of revolt that PIL's work, even at its most indulgent, boasts: that desire to attack and disarm the world, to make it eat its own hopelessness. Ian Curtis died for reasons that are probably none of our business, but it would seem, at least in part, that he killed himself to slay that portion of the world that so hurt and appalled him. John Lydon lives because he's figured out a way (more than once) to knock off the world and live beyond it.

Guitarist Bernie Albrecht, bassist Peter Hooke, and drummer Stephen Morris (the three surviving members of Joy Division) have, with a guitarist named Gillian, formed a group called New Order. This band faces not only the task of living up to its own mythic past, but of getting by the pain of that past and the shadow of Ian Curtis. New Order's initial single, "Ceremony" (reportedly written while Curtis was still alive), says that they probably can. It's a transfixing, vehement, big-sounding piece of music, brimming with taut cross lines of blaring guitars and an indomitable, bottom-heavy rhythm section. Behind it all, mixed somewhere along with the hi-hat so that his singing sibilates in pulsing waves, Bernie Albrecht makes a chancy vocal debut, telling an impassioned tale about bitter memories, ineradicable losses, and unbeaten determination.

Ironically, these images of resolve and recovery seem to suggest the same conviction that Joy Division—who, after all, took their name from the euphemism used to describe the prostitute section of German concentration camps—intended to convey in the first place: that no horror, no matter how terrible, is unendurable. Maybe that sounds as joyless and morose as everything else about Joy Division's music, but it shouldn't. In this case, it's nothing less than a surpassing testament to the life force itself.

A FOLLOW-UP on PIL and New Order: I saw Public Image Ltd. on three occasions in the years surrounding the time I wrote the above stories (which was in 1980 and 1981). On each occasion, it became increasingly evident how hard—if not impossible—it would be for John Lydon to outdistance his past with the Sex Pistols. In truth, the audience simply wouldn't allow it.

At PIL's 1980 Los Angeles debut—at the city's downtown Olympic Auditorium—the band played terrifically and Lydon was plain transfixing, but the audience that assembled to celebrate the band's appearance, a crowd of thuggish-looking jar-head punks who eventually became dubbed the area's "hardcore" subculture, very nearly upstaged the show. It was the first time this audience had made its identity felt in such a large, collective, and forcible way. And though its members perhaps couldn't relate to the abstract rhythms and forms at the heart of PIL's music, they knew Johnny Rotten was still a punk icon, and that was cause enough to turn the whole show into one long skirmish.

Lydon would remain stuck with that same crowd of punk holdouts who didn't care much for his changing ideas of music, but instead exalted the event (or myth) of his personality. When PIL played at the Pasadena Civic Center in 1982, members of the audience attempted to overrun or command the stage, and some scaled the towering speakers only to leap back onto the crowd below. Seeing PIL with that audience was both a tiresome and reckless experience. I spoke with many fans who vowed they would never see the band again.

I felt the same way, though not because of the audience so much as simply that, as good as PIL were, all their aspirations to innovation had begun to seem as tired and dated as the old rock & roll styles they had once set out to subvert. But when they played the Hollywood Palladium in June 1983, the main draw (at least for me) was the news that Keith Levene (who had written much of PIL's best music but had become increasingly undisciplined in the studio, and was a boor to boot) had quit the group. This forced Lydon to see if he could still rise to the task of leading a band.

Of course, the punk contingent in the audience didn't care much about Lydon's personal growth: They merely wanted to thrash in the spectacle of his presence. And though Lydon's manner still proved fearsomely charismatic, he seemed in many ways a much changed performer. He chatted, joked, and flirted with the audience. (When one excitable girl jumped on-stage to give him a kiss, Lydon kissed her back, then gushed "Guess I must be a sex symbol!") At times, Lydon's easy manner had the effect of poking fun at his own myth ("How many Johnny Rottens have we got out there?" he inquired of the massed punks), but it was also meant to assure the audience, if not himself, that this new version of PIL still aimed to put music above mystique. And indeed, it turned out to be the most impressive performing version of PIL that I would see. Lydon had assembled an all new, tuxedo-clad group (he didn't mention their names) that not only did an exemplary job of replicating the former PIL's adventurous sound, but who added a new sense of sharpness and resiliency to it.

But as involving as the new PIL were, they still couldn't match the temerity of their audience. Throughout the group's near hour-long show, punk after punk would scrabble onstage from out of the pressed mass down front, and dance and flail around Lydon or try to pat his red-tufted head, until some beefy security hack would heft them off their feet and toss them over the heads of the audience. At times it would resemble a melee, but in truth it wasn't: It was a carefully orchestrated ritual (though the punks possessed a good deal more grace, and sometimes restraint, than the guards), and though the punks' behavior may have seemed an unnecessarily stupid, ruffian activity, it also made for a great spectator sport (probably a great participant sport too, if you prefer bowling from the ball's perspective).

But all the audience's excitement, and the pleasure that some of us took in PIL's musical growth, seemed secondary to one generous, surprising, and revealing gesture by Lydon at the show's end. "We're going to do an oldie for ya," he said in his familiar mocking tone, as the band returned for their first encore. "Sing along—you know the words." With that, PIL vaulted into a roaring version of the Sex Pistols greatest moment, "Anarchy in the U.K." It didn't have quite the startling, shearing effect that the Pistols' rendition of the song did at Winterland in 1978, in their final performance, but it was still damn exciting, and the audience responded by thrashing in near-religious fervor.

In 1996, Rotten made a career out of that moment. He and the original Sex Pistols—guitarist Steve Jones, drummer Paul Cook, and the band's first bassist, Glen Matlock—re-formed for a tour of Europe and America. In one way, it meant nothing, not even nostalgia, since they were simply playing their old songs again but without the context of daring and risk that they brought to every stage they mounted from 1976 to 1978. In another way, it meant a great deal: The late-1990s Sex Pistols showed they were still up to the job of assaulting rock & roll with as much venom and intelligence as anybody, and more important, their shows were reminders of what a damn fine, indelible, and *perfect* body of rock & roll songwriting (matchlessly inventive anthems) they wrought in their brief, world-changing season twenty years prior. For those few nights in 1996, John Lydon was undeniably Johnny Rotten again, and it seemed wonderfully possible that rock & roll might still be the fiercest, most frightening popular art on earth.

NEW ORDER'S STORY also continued—in fact, still continues. More or less.

At first it was obvious that the band couldn't immediately surmount the loss of Ian Curtis, who had pretty much shaped and dominated Joy Division's thematic image. Some fans, in fact, felt his presence was so overpowering that it held the band back onstage. But for all of Curtis' deadly excesses, he also had a clear-cut point of view: Curtis knew that damnation was what he stood for, and he didn't flinch from what that entailed.

By contrast, New Order didn't seem to have much of an idea of *what* they stood for, except outliving the grim shadow of their past. Just when an audience was finally eager to hear what this band had to say, they lost the personality who had made them notable in the first place. And while nobody in New Order seemed to want to imitate Curtis, nobody in the band seemed up to replacing him either.

In such early singles as "Everything's Gone Green," and their disappointing debut album, *Movement,* New Order didn't offer much more than a synthesized reworking of their once thick, surging sound. It was prettier and more disciplined than Joy Division's sound, to be sure, but also less exciting and involving. Whatever was being said about their new life—that of a band that had to live with an ineradicable loss—was never clear. The words, and even the vocals themselves—delivered by guitarist Bernie Albrecht—got lost in tricky mixes that reduced lyrics to a kind of atmospheric filler. As a result, *Movement* didn't matter as much as Joy Division's music or myth had. As the

U.K. scene shifted to a more rhythmic aesthetic, Joy Division's influence diminished, and with it, perhaps, New Order's best chance for preeminence.

And then in 1983, New Order rebounded with *Power, Corruption and Lies*—one of the most compelling albums of that year, and nearly the equal to their former achievements with Joy Division. Still, it was pretty much impossible to say what *Power, Corruption and Lies* was "about" in the way that one could say what Joy Division's music was about. If anything, New Order seemed to be a band *about* form. Their version of postpunk sound was a clean, taut, swirling lacework of interlocking guitar and synthesizer motifs, buttressed by a massive, uniform dance pulse—a sound that overshadowed the emotions and meanings within it, to the degree that sound became the sole medium and object of those emotions. This idea first came across in the group's wondrous 1982 single "Temptation," but it came into its own fully with *Power, Corruption and Lies*.

The collective elements of sound on that album (still New Order's best) *feel* as if they're about a great deal indeed. The sharp-edged arpeggiated guitar lines and swathed synthesizer webs on "Your Silent Face," "Leave Me Alone," and "Age of Consent" interweave over pulsating dance patterns as though the sound were meant to put across a vital meaning—yet as if that feeling and meaning were simply the expression of the sound itself. By comparison, the vocals aren't much more than a fine touch of emotional embellishment, putting forth some surprisingly axiomatic notions of romantic desperation as if it was finally time to acknowledge the truth of Ian Curtis' dissolution. Yet the words aren't what carry *Power, Corruption and Lies'* substance. Even the best vocals and lyrics on the album pale beside the eloquence of the guitars and synthesizers which surround and overwhelm them.

Power, Corruption and Lies was a synthesis of rhythm, texture, and emotion, existing for its own pleasure. In 1983, it sounded like rhapsodic, impassioned pop: music with a force of human heart that counted all the more for the hard truths it had to withstand to find its own confidence and soul. But New Order never really surpassed that moment. They went on to make several more albums, some rapturous-sounding, some forgettable, and none that ever helped make up for what they lost on that fatal day in May 1980.

WHAT WOULD HAVE happened if a group dared to resurrect or reinvent punk in Britain with the same mix of arrogance and vision that the

Sex Pistols once flourished? No doubt that group would have been condemned and resented as Johnny Rotten's band was—which is just what befell the most controversial and perhaps most important British band of the mid-1980s, a ragged-looking, glorious-sounding quartet called the Jesus and Mary Chain.

Like the Pistols, the Jesus and Mary Chain played music that was immediately a shock, music that demanded you come to terms with its perspective, if only to reject or fight it. The group's early singles, "Never Understand" and "Upside Down," pitted lovely tunes and dreamy vocals against screeching feedback and relentless pandemonium—a mix that, as one British writer put it, suggested a plausible teaming of the Beach Boys and Cleveland, Ohio's, late 1970s great avant-garde pre-punk band, Pere Ubu. This approach was both acclaimed and derided in England, where the Jesus and Mary Chain, much like the Sex Pistols, largely had to be seen to be heard. (The band's early concerts reportedly incited strong reactions—sometimes outright crowd convulsions—just like early punk.)

While the group's 1985 debut album, *Psychocandy*, didn't win over many detractors or break through the hegemony that ruled that period's British and American radio, the album nonetheless showed that the Jesus and Mary Chain's musical conceptions probably had both substance and mileage. The band's mix of mellifluence and noise held up beautifully over *Psychocandy*'s forty-minute-plus length. Every track on the album had a life and magnetism of its own, and they all sounded affecting, galvanizing, and inventive.

But for all the brave new territory *Psychocandy* staked out, at times it seemed to summarize or refashion pop-punk style instead of breaking with it. Between the album's wailing dissonance and lovely melodies, one could find allusions to many musical parents, not merely the Pistols (while the Jesus and Mary Chain caught that band's howling guitar sound, they preferred patient rhythms to galloping ones), but also hints of the Beatles (Jesus' "Just like Honey" took "Love Me Do" and fused it with "Helter Skelter"), elements of mid-1960s pop styles (imagine Motown as it might have sounded played by the Seeds and produced by Phil Spector), and, of course, strong echoes of such earlier trailblazers as the Velvet Underground and Joy Division.

Psychocandy proved among the finest, most provoking British albums of the mid-1980s. By balancing sweet melodies and raw cacophonies so powerfully, the Jesus and Mary Chain were saying that dreams and anguish, hope and fear, are necessary counterparts in both life and music. By asserting that obvious truth, the group reinvented (if only briefly) punk's original courage and vision, on the band's own terms.

Whereas punk drew a dividing line across rock & roll and demanded that you stand on one side or another, the Jesus and Mary Chain drew a line and then occupied it alone, turning that line into a scary and alluring union of two opposing worlds. Jesus and Mary Chain—like the Sex Pistols or Joy Division—pretty much ended up as one of the few that truly made good on the possibilities that their music raised. The band went on to make other terrific records—the mesmerizing *Darklands* (1987), as well as *Barbed Wire Kisses* (1988), *Automatic* (1989), *Honey's Dead* (1992), and *Stoned and Dethroned* (1994). None of them, though, would prove such a wailing judgment of what became of British punk and pop style as 1985's *Psychocandy*. All these years later, it is still a record that can thrill you—like the best and worst stolen orgasms of your life—or that can drive you into a bad, spooky corner of your mind and spirit, as if you just finally realized how mad, worthless, wonderful, and disarrayed life truly is, regardless of your best efforts to impose hope and design on to all its unbeatable final disorder.

the clash:

punk beginnings,

punk endings

f uck that shit," says Joe Strummer, the thuggish-looking lead singer of the Clash, addressing some exultant kids yelling "Happy New Year" at him from the teeming floor of the Lyceum. "You've got your *future* at stake. Face front! Take it!"

In sleepy London town, during the murky Christmas week of 1978, rock & roll is being presented as a war of class and aesthetics. At the crux of that battle is a volcanic series of four Clash concerts—including a benefit for Sid Vicious—coming swift on the heels of the group's second album, *Give 'Em Enough Rope*, which entered the British charts at number 2. Together with the Sex Pistols, the Clash helped spearhead the punk movement in Britain, along the way earning a designation as the most intellectual and political punk band. When the Pistols disbanded in early 1978, the rock press and punks alike looked to the Clash as the movement's central symbol and hope.

Yet, beyond the hyperbole and wrangle that helped create their radical myth, the Clash brandish a hearty reputation as a rock & roll band that, like the Rolling Stones or Bruce Springsteen, must be seen to be believed. Certainly no other band communicates kinetic, imperative anger as potently as the Clash. When Nicky "Topper" Headon's single-shot snare report opens "Safe European Home" (a song about Strummer and lead guitarist Mick Jones' ill-fated attempt to rub elbows with Rastafarians in the Jamaicans' backyard), all hell breaks loose, both on the Lyceum stage and floor.

Like the Sex Pistols, the Clash's live sound hinges on a massive, orchestral drum framework that buttresses the blustery guitar work of Jones, who with his tireless two-step knee kicks looks just like a Rockettes' version of Keith Richards. Shards of Mott the Hoople and the Who cut through the tumult, while Strummer's rhythm guitar and Paul Simonon's bass gnash at the beat underneath. And Strummer's vocals sound as dangerous as he looks. Screwing his face up into a broken-tooth yowl, he gleefully bludgeons words, then caresses them with a touching, R&B–inflected passion.

Maybe it's the gestalt of the event, or maybe it's just the sweaty leather-bound mass throbbing around me, but I think it's the most persuasive rock & roll show I've seen since I watched the Sex Pistols' final performance in San Francisco earlier in the same year.

I try to say as much to a reticent Joe Strummer after the show as we stand in a dingy backstage dressing room, which is brimming with a sweltering mix of fans, press, and roadies. Strummer, wearing smoky sunglasses and a nut-brown porkpie hat, resembles a roughhewn version of Michael Corleone. Measuring me with his wary, testy eyes, he mumbles an inaudible reply.

Across the room, Mick Jones and Paul Simonon have taken refuge in a corner, sharing a spliff. "You a Yank?" Jones asks me in a surprisingly delicate, lilting voice. "From 'ollywood? Evil place, innit? All laid back." According to the myth encasing this band, Jones, who writes nearly all of the Clash's music, is the band's real focal nerve, even though the austere Strummer writes the bulk of the lyrics. In the best Keith Richards tradition, the fans see Mick as a sensitive and vulnerable street waif, prone to dissipation as much as to idealism. Indeed, he looks as bemusedly wasted as anyone I've ever met. He's also among the gentler, more considerate people I've ever spent time with.

But the next evening, sitting in the same spot, Mick declines to be interviewed. "Lately, interviews make me feel 'orrible. It seems all I do is spend my time answering everyone's charges—charges that shouldn't have to be answered."

The Clash *have* been hit with a wide volley of charges, ranging from an English rock-press backlash aimed at what the critics see as reckless politics, to very real criminal charges against Headon and Simonon (for shooting valuable racing pigeons) and Jones (for alleged cocaine possession). But probably the most damaging salvo has come from their former manager, Bernard Rhodes, who, after he was fired, accused the band of betraying its punk ideals and slapped them with a potentially crippling lawsuit. Jones, in a recent interview, railed back. "We're still the only ones true to the original aims of punk," he said. "Those other bands should be destroyed."

THE CLASH FORMED as a result of Joe Strummer's frustrations and Jones' rock ideals. Both claimed to have been abandoned at early ages by their parents, and while Strummer (the son of a British diplomat) took to singing Woody Guthrie and Chuck Berry songs in London's subways for spare change during his late teens, Jones retreated into reading and playing Mott the Hoople, Dylan, Kinks, and Who records. In 1975, he left the art school he was attending and formed London SS, a band that, in its attempt to meld a raving blend of the New York Dolls, the Stooges, and Mott, became a legendary forerunner of the English punk scene.

Then, in early 1976, shortly after the Sex Pistols assailed London, Mick Jones ran into Strummer, who had been singing in a pub-circuit R&B band called the 101ers. "I don't like your band," Jones said, "but I like the way you sing." Strummer, anxious to join the punk brigade, cut his hair, quit the 101ers, and joined Jones, Simonon (also a member of London SS), guitarist Keith Levene (later a member of Public Image Ltd.) and drummer Terry Chimes (brilliantly renamed as Tory Crimes) to form the Clash in June of 1976. Eight months later, under the tutelage of Bernard Rhodes, the Clash signed with CBS Records for a reported $200,000.

Their first album, *The Clash* (originally unreleased in America; Epic, the group's label stateside, deemed it "too crude"), was archetypal, resplendent punk. While the Sex Pistols proffered a nihilistic image, the Clash took a militant stance that, in an eloquent, guttural way, vindicated punk's negativism. Harrowed rhythms and coarse vocals propelled a foray of songs aimed at the bleak political realities and social ennui of English life, making social realism—and unbridled disgust—key elements in punk aesthetics.

But even before the first album was released, the punk scene had dealt the Clash some unforeseen blows. The punks, egged on by a hysterical English press, began turning on each other, and drummer Chimes, weary of ducking bottles, spit, and the band's politics, quit. Months passed before the group settled on Nicky Headon (also a member of Mick Jones' London SS) as a replacement and returned to performing. By that time, their reputation had swelled to near-messianic proportions.

When it was time for a new album, CBS asked Blue Oyster Cult producer Sandy Pearlman to check out the Clash's shows. "By a miracle of God," says Pearlman, "they looked like they believed in what they were doing. They were playing for the thrill of affecting their audience's consciousness, both musically and politically. Rock & roll shouldn't be cute and adorable; it should be violent and anarchic. Based on that, I think they're the greatest rock & roll group around." Mick Jones balked at first at the idea of Pearlman as their producer, but Strummer's interest prevailed. It took six months to complete *Give 'Em Enough Rope,* and it was a stormy period for all concerned. ("We knew we had to watch Pearlman," says Nicky Headon. "He gets too good a sound.")

But nowhere near as stormy as the album. *Give 'Em Enough Rope* is rock & roll's *State of Siege*—with a dash of *Duck Soup* for comic relief. Instead of reworking the tried themes of bored youth and repressive society, Strummer and Jones tapped some of the deadliest currents around, from creeping fascism at home to Palestinian terrorism. The album surges with visions of civil strife, gunplay, backbiting, and lyrics that might've been spirited from the streets of Italy and Iran: "A system built by the sweat of the many/Creates assassins to kill off the few/Take any place and call it a courthouse/This is a place where no judge can stand." And the music—a whirl of typhonic guitars and drums—frames those conflicts grandly.

THE DAY AFTER the Clash's last Lyceum show, I meet Joe Strummer and Paul Simonon at the Tate Gallery, London's grand art museum. Simonon leads us on a knowledgeable tour of the gallery's treasures until we settle in a dim corner of the downstairs café for an interview.

We start by talking about the band's apparent position as de facto leaders of punk. Strummer stares into his muddy tea, uninterested in the idea of conversation, and lets Simonon take the questions. Probably the roughest-looking member of the group, with his skeletal face and disheveled hair, Simonon is disarmingly guileless and amiable. "Just because I'm up onstage," he says in rubbery English, "doesn't mean that I'm entitled to a different lifestyle than anyone else. I used to think so. I'd stay up all night, get pissed, party all the time. But you get cut off from the workaday people that way. I like to get up early, paint me flat, practice me bass. I see these geezers going off to work and I feel more like one of them."

But, I note, most of those same people wouldn't accept him. They're incensed and frightened by bands like the Clash.

Strummer stops stirring his tea and glowers around. "Good," he grunts. "I'm pleased."

This seems a fair time to raise the question of the band's recent bout with the British rock press. After *Give 'Em Enough Rope*, some of the band's staunchest defenders shifted gears, saying that the Clash's militancy is little more than a fashionable stance, and that their attitude toward terrorist violence is dangerously ambiguous. "One is never entirely sure just which side [the Clash] is supposed to be taking," wrote Nick Kent in *New Musical Express*. "The Clash use incidents . . . as fodder for songs without caring."

Strummer squints at me for a moment, his thoughtful mouth hemming his craggy teeth. "We're against fascism and racism," he says. "I figure that goes without saying. I'd like to think that we're subtle; that's what greatness is, innit? I can't stand all these people preaching, like Tom Robinson. He's just too direct."

But that ambiguity can be construed as encouraging violence.

"Our *music*'s violent," says Strummer. "We're not. If anything, songs like 'Guns on the Roof' and 'Last Gang in Town' are supposed to take the piss out of violence. It's just that sometimes you have to put yourself in the place of the guy with the machine gun. I couldn't go to his extreme, but at the same time it's no good ignoring what he's doing. We sing about the world that affects us. We're not just another wank rock group like Boston or Aerosmith. What fucking shit."

Yet, I ask, is having a record contract with one of the world's biggest companies compatible with radicalism?

"We've got loads of contradictions for you," says Strummer, shaking off his doldrums with a smirk. "We're trying to do something new; we're trying to be the greatest group in the world, and that also means the biggest. At the same time, we're trying to be radical—I mean, we never want to be *really* respectable—and maybe the two can't coexist, but we'll try. You know what helps us? We're totally suspicious of anyone who comes in contact with us. *Totally*. We aim to keep punk alive."

The conversation turns to the Clash's impending tour of America. "England's becoming claustrophobic for us," says Strummer. "Everything we do is scrutinized. I think touring America could be a new lease on life."

But the American rock scene—and especially radio—seems far removed from the world in flames that the Clash sing about. (While the Clash may top the English charts, they have yet to dent *Billboard*'s Top 200. "We admit we aren't likely to get a hit single this time around," says Bruce Harris of Epic's A&R department. "But *Give 'Em Enough Rope* has sold forty thousand copies and that's better than sixty percent of most new acts.") I ask if a failure to win Yankee hearts would set them back.

"Nah," says Strummer. "We've always got here. We haven't been to Europe much, and we haven't been to Japan or Australia, and we want to go behind the iron curtain." He pauses and shrugs his face in a taut grin. "There are a lot of other places where we could lose our lives."

THE NEXT TIME I meet the Clash, over three years later, is in fact in America—in the city of Los Angeles.

By way of greeting me, Joe Strummer points at the roughhewn crop of Mohawk hair that flares from the top of his head, his thumb cocked back like a pistol. "You know why I did this, don't you?" he asks, leaning forward, a conspiratorial smile shaping his lips. We're seated in a dressing room backstage at the Hollywood Palladium, where the Clash are midway through a five-date engagement—their first appearances in the area since the group's 1980 *London Calling* tour. Strummer and his bandmates—guitarist Mick Jones, bassist Paul Simonon, and drummer Terry Chimes (the latter, newly returned to the Clash's fold)—are about to hit the stage for the afternoon's peremptory soundcheck, but first Joe wants to share a little revelation about his newly acquired headdress.

"I did it," he says, "to try to force some confrontation this time around. I wanted people to react to it, to ask me just *what the hell* I'm on about. I thought it might stir up a little *friendly* conversation, if you know what I mean."

And has it? I ask.

Joe gets a look that's part disappointment, part bafflement. "No, not much. Maybe people find it a little too scary, you know, too *serious*. Over here, you Americans never seem to know how to take matters of style. It's like you view it as a threat, as rebellion. In England, style signifies, um . . . like identity. I would never equate something as simple as a radical haircut with a true act of rebellion."

"So, Joe, then what *is* true rebellion? Because cultural revolt seems to be the signal thing the Clash stand for in a lot of people's minds."

Strummer regards the question in silence for a few moments, then fixes me with a level stare. "Cultural revolt . . . I'm not sure that's it exactly. But I'll tell you what I've come to think *real* rebellion is: It's something more personal than that—it's *not giving up*. Rebellion is deciding to push ahead with it all for one more day. *That's* the toughest test of revolt—keeping yourself alive, as well as the cause."

PERSEVERANCE as revolt: The notion may seem a far cry from the brand of immediate, imperative, insurgent passion that made Joe Strummer's early exclamations seem so fearsome and world-wrecking—the youth-prole sentiments, stricken terrorist manifestos and iconoclast allegations that stoked incendiary rally calls like "1977," "Guns on the Roof," "White Riot," and "Safe European Home"—but at the same time, no other band in recent history has made stamina stand for as much as has the Clash.

Indeed, over the lightning distance of six years, four U.S. tours (and at least twice as many U.K. treks), and five album sets (comprised of eight LPs and a hundred songs), the Clash have managed to stake a larger claim on questions of cultural, political, and moral effect—place greater weight and liability on the purposes of rock & roll—than any other band since the Beatles, the Rolling Stones, or the Who. Probably the only other band that compares with them in terms of social and aesthetic force these last ten years is the Sex Pistols—and their design, it seems, was simply not just to raze popular culture, but also to level the world around it, themselves included. The Sex Pistols could never have made a second album, and chances are they always knew it—but then making records wasn't their long suit. For the Clash, making music is a way of making further possibilities of life, a way of withstanding inevitable defeats—a way of *"not giving up."*

Yet trying to live out revolt as daily ethos can be a steep act; for one thing, it means no doubling back. Since 1977, each new Clash release has sought to outdistance its predecessors in bold and irrevocable ways. *Give 'Em Enough Rope* (1978) magnified the band's musical force, while also broadening their sociopolitical focus, from the narrow obsessions of U.K. punk sedition to the fiery reality of the world outside—a world mired in tyranny and aflame in blood and mutiny. *London Calling,* at the close of the following year, carried revolt over to the means of style and the object of history—resulting in the band's most sharply crafted, popularly accessible effort to date. It also resulted in a resounding statement on how to live heroically and honorably in a world where such notions spell certain disillusionment and probable subjection ("Clampdown," "Death or Glory"). And then, in 1980, the group issued their uncompromising, bulky masterwork, *Sandinista!*—an opus that tried to expand the vernacular and sensibility of popular music by melding rock's form with remote cultural idioms—like reggae, gospel, Europop, American funk, and rap—and unflinching social realities; in other words, by mixing dread with innovation, for matchless effect. Overall, what has emerged is a body of work that has upped the ante on punk—forced it to reach outward, to risk compromise, to embrace conflict, even if it means conflict with punk's own narrow presentiments.

What also results, though, is a kind of self-imposed state of contradiction that can, on occasion, seem to undermine the group's grandest designs. After all, it's one thing to start out to upend rock convention, and quite another to end up proclaimed as "The World's *New* Greatest Rock & Roll Band." Yet the physical impact of the Clash's live shows, and the stimulative force of *London Calling*—incorporating, as it did, British symbols and symptoms as text, and American rock & roll as context—had just that effect: It made the Clash appear as the last great hope, if not preservers, of the very tradition they had set out to thwart.

Yet the Clash have also tainted some of their best gestures with a maddening flair for miscalculation and self-importance. *Sandinista!* falls under that charge for many critics and fans ("Imagine," one writer friend told me, "the audacity, the waste behind believing that *everything* you record deserves to be heard: who do these guys think they are—the Keith Jarretts of punk?"), though for my taste, it's the Clash's strongest, best enduring work, an unrepressed paradigm of creativity.

Less successful, I think, was last year's late spring series of concert events at Bond's Casino in New York (eighteen shows in fifteen days), that seemed to indicate on one level the Clash's startling naiveté about audience prejudices and business concerns, and on another, their inability to adopt *Sandinista!*'s range and depth to a live format. (In true scrupulous fashion, the Clash, along with friend and filmmaker Don Letts, documented the whole debacle in movie form: *The Clash on Broadway*, though it never received wide release.) More recently, there are the problems of *Combat Rock*— a heavy-handed, strident, guileful, muddled album about artistic despair and personal dissolution that derives *from* those conditions rather than aims to illuminate them—and, of course, Joe Strummer's widely reported defection—or "hiatus," as the group calls it—in the early part of 1982.

Not surprisingly, the Clash worked those setbacks to their favor. Strummer returned to the group after a month-long sabbatical in Paris (though by that time, virtually their entire U.K. tour had been blown out of the water), appearing stronger and more resolved than ever before. What's more, *Combat Rock* proved to be the band's most critically and commercially successful record in England since 1978's *Give 'Em Enough Rope* (not bad work for a band that had grown painfully, almost fatally, unfashionable in their own homeland).

Not even the loss of Topper Headon—the prodigious drummer who had reportedly held great influence on the band's recent musical progressivism, only to bail out five days before their current American tour for reasons that may never be publicly explained—not even that could disarm the Clash's resurging spirit. Manager Bernard Rhodes (also newly returned to the fold) and road organizer Kosmo Vinyl simply recruited original drummer Terry Chimes on a work-for-hire basis, and sequestered him, along with the group, for three days of relentless rehearsals. Forty-eight hours later, the Clash, the very same Clash that had recorded the group's resplendent 1977 debut album, were on tour once again in America—a bit battle-scarred, more than a little uncertain at moments, but playing with more mastery, unity, and momentum than they ever had before.

In fact, oddly enough, it's the hardcore potency of their current shows that may be the only thing to fault the Clash for this time around. From the opening edict of "London Calling" to the closing salvos of "Complete Control," "Clash City Rockers," and "Garageland," these are urgent, clamorous, throat-throttling shows—as if the band had just jumped out of *Black Market Clash* and onto a stage, replete with ferment and sweat. But in that, they're also surprisingly prudent affairs. Missing are all the adventurous touchstones from *Sandinista!*, or even the off-center filler pieces from *Combat Rock.* The lamentable "Know Your Rights" and "Should I Stay or Should I Go?" were the staples here, with occasional game stabs at "Rock the Casbah," "Car Jamming," or the beautiful, mournful "Straight to Hell."

And yet . . . and yet, though this is the Clash's unabashed greatest-hits concessional tour, these were also the most moving, powerful and meaningful shows I've ever seen from this band. To watch the Clash in their early English jaunts or their first couple of U.S. tours—with the group issuing "Safe European Home" and "Guns on the Roof" as life-threatening and world-saving calls to truth—was to watch a rock & roll band (the strongest since the Who; the most vaulting since the Rolling Stones) stake a larger claim on terror, revolution, and deliverance than any pop culture force before it (the Sex Pistols fell just short of the deliverance part—that is unless you equate deliverance with self-dissolution). But to watch the Clash in 1982—as they mount the pace of "Somebody Got Murdered," or seize the pulse of "Clampdown"—is to watch a band that has learned how costly it can be to try to live those claims, a band that's learned that to redefine the intent and weight of pop culture isn't enough: You have to make a new definition with every new gesture; you have to keep the designs behind those gestures sharp and unsparing; and you have to be willing to risk the refusal or flattening of those gestures, if not your own failure. Above all, it's to watch a band that's learned that they will probably lose far more than they'll ever win, that someday, if they really care enough, they'll probably lose it all.

"I'LL TELL YOU what makes these shows so strong," says Mick Jones, one late afternoon, over eggs and hash-browns at a popular Santa Monica Boulevard diner. "It's a celebration: We're out there celebrating that we *exist*—we made it this far, we made it another night."

Jones pauses for a few moments and pokes idly at his still unexplored breakfast. "Still, I wonder," he says. "Don't you think people just like it because they think they're getting the old Clash this time around—the Clash the way it should be? I bet that's what it is."

No, I answer, I think they like it because it seems like an explosive, unyielding show. Also, to be frank, because the band's never sounded more confident or better unified.

Mick ponders that for a moment as he watches the flutter and traffic of the boulevard. "I think we *are* playing pretty good . . . I feel all right about the shows, but I don't feel it's as much fun as it used to be somehow. We used to kind of *explode*. We play better now but for me personally . . .

"I'm in a place now where I'm working onstage in accompaniment to what Joe's doing with the words. My part of it is to hold it all together, help keep the rhythm section locked. Joe stops playing the guitar a lot, you know, and those are moments where the instrumentation could use a bit of embellishment, so me hands are going all the time. But also, I'm just not going over the top as much these days, leaping about and all that. I'm trying to control myself a bit more."

Yet, I point out, Jones has some of the most commanding rock & roll moments of the show—in particular, his galvanizing performance of "Somebody Got Murdered." Every time they perform that song, a large segment of the audience shouts along on the line: "I've been very hungry/But not enough to kill."

"The important thing about that song," says Jones, "is that it isn't any particular person who gets killed—it's just *any*body. It's funny, in some places we play, where people live in extreme poverty—like northern England—the audience seems to understand the line about *not killing* better. But in richer places, people understand the other part better, the part about 'Somebody's dead forever.' I think it's their way of saying that, even though they might have money, they understand they can still lose it all—not just the money, but their lives. But the audiences are more mixed here in L.A., aren't they?"

Jones starts to pick gradually at his breakfast, now that it's good and cold. "America," he says, a thin tone of distaste in his voice. "The people here never really took punk of our kind seriously—always treated it like some sort of bloody joke. It's a shame that a group like the Sex Pistols had to come out here to the land of promise just to burn out. Come out here and act out their gross end—that Sid and Nancy play. America screwed them up. That's what we've tried not to have happen to us, going the way of the Sex Pistols—getting swallowed up by America."

It's interesting I note, that almost all of the Clash's music since the first album has moved more and more away from strictly English topic matter and styles. *Sandinista!* seemed like a rampart of Third World concerns.

"Yeah, well it was," says Mick, "and that didn't particularly win a lot of hearts and minds at the record company. We knew it was going to be difficult, because we kept meeting resistance with the idea, but we were very stubborn and went straight ahead. *Sandinista!* is quite special to me. It wasn't, as some critics say, a conscious effort to do ourselves in. Originally we'd wanted to do a single a month, then put out a double album at the end of the year, like *London Calling.* But CBS wouldn't have that, so we thought, All right, three albums for the price of two it is. We probably could've gone without releasing another record for a year or so. I think people would've still been listening to it—there's enough there.

"*Combat Rock* is like the best of *Sandinista!*—a concise statement, even though it contains just as much diversification. There's an art to making one album as well as three, you know."

Yet *Combat Rock,* I note, seems shot through with the idea that death is an ever-present possibility. In fact, it almost seems a death-obsessed album, what with tracks like "Death Is a Star," "Ghetto Defendant," "Sean Flynn," "Straight to Hell". . . .

"All me favorite tracks," says Mick with a broad smile. "No, I know what you mean. A lot of critics are saying this album reflects our death fascination, or the group's own depression or confusion, but I don't think that's true. I think it's clear that we know exactly where we're at—we're not confused at all. The problem is, a lot of people equate depression with reality, so they find the record depressing. I think it just touches on what's real. I wouldn't say it's exactly optimistic, but I wouldn't call it pessimistic either."

But some critics, I tell him, have found the Clash's brand of political rhetoric and realism just as naive as that jaunty romanticism of the pop bands.

Mick takes a sip of his coffee and regards me with a bemused expression. "You mean like the *Village Voice* calling us 'naive,' and *Sandinista!* a 'pink elephant'? Well, we are, and it is. It doesn't particularly discourage us, that kind of talk. It's important we stick to getting our point across. Not just because people will try to discredit us, but because somebody has to counteract all the madness out there, like the bloody war fever that hit England over this Falklands fiasco. It's important that somebody's there to tell them that there aren't any winners where there aren't any real causes. It may appear that Maggie Thatcher's won for the time being, but not because she's made the British winners. Instead, she's made them victims, and they can't even see it.

"What's interesting," Jones continues, "is that the American critics don't seem to like *Combat Rock* much and the English do, whereas with *London Calling* and *Sandinista!*, it was just the opposite: Americans *loved* them and the British critics really got down on us. But I think what they like about *Combat Rock* is that it's one of the few things in English pop right now that bothers to be real. Most of the new pop doesn't try to engage reality at all—which isn't necessarily bad, because I like a lot of the new stuff too, like Human League. But sometimes you just have to get down to facing what the world's about—and that's not something all those party bands want to do.

"I don't know," says Mick, his voice soft and museful. "I mean, don't get me wrong, we have our share of fun too, but these days . . . it's just that all the parties seem so far away."

I ask him: Do you think your audience understands that? Some of the people I've seen at the band's shows—both the punk contingent, plus the mainstream crowd that have adopted them as the new Rolling Stones—seem to miss the Clash's point by a mile. Slam dancing, not to mention spitting on and pelting opening acts like Joe Ely and Grandmaster Flash, doesn't seem much different to me than any other mindless party ritual.

Mick bristles mildly. "They're not really assholes, are they? They just don't know how to act. I mean, at Bond's it wasn't actually racism. At first, we sat around backstage thinking, 'What jerks!' But when we made it clear that we were having a rough time with the idea of them adoring us but hating the opening acts, it seemed to stop. I think it was just initial overexcitement."

Still, aren't there times when you wonder just who your audience really is, and if you're really reaching them?

"All the time, all the time," says Jones. "For every example you get of people who you think are really into it, who have really got the message, you also run up against the people who are completely misinformed. We just do the best we can to contain those contradictions, and hope enough of our meaning rubs off here and there."

Mick glances at the wall clock. It's nearly time to head out to the afternoon's sound check. I pose one last question: "When Joe disappeared, did you think it might be the end of the Clash?"

Mick smiles wryly. "That Joe—what a bastard, eh? If he ever does that again . . . um, yeah, for about ten minutes I sat down and died. I thought the group might be ending, and I thought it was a shame, but I wasn't about to let it stop me from getting on with living.

"It was bad timing on Joe's part, but it was also an admirable thing. It's very difficult to put your own needs first like that, but the only problem is, once you start doing it, it's easier to do again. Still, it made us ask ourselves what we were going to do. It *certainly* made Topper ask himself what was happening with him. I even thought about getting into something else myself, but it will have to wait now.

"We all decided we could start over with this band—Joe, Paul, me—and now, some nights, it's almost like we're a new group out there onstage.

"We should change our name, don't you think? How about Clash Two?" Mick mulls the idea over a bit more, then bursts into a titter. "No, wait, I've got it: How about Clash *Now*?"

How *HAS* THE CLASH managed to hold together? After all, punk never offered itself as a breeding place for enduring comradeship.

Paul Simonon, the group's craggily handsome bass player (recently elected to *Playgirl*'s "The Year's Ten Best Looking Men" list), ponders that question as he picks his way through a bowl of guacamole and chips (all the band's members are vegetarians) shortly before leaving the hotel for that night's show.

"You're talking about things like corruption, disintegration, right?" he says in his thick Brixton accent. "I tell you what I've seen do it to other groups: drugs. I've been through all sorts of drugs; at one time I took them just for curiousity, and I *learned*—it's not worth it. It's like a carrot held in front of you, and it's the downfall of a lot of bands we've known.

"We just cut it out—we don't deal with that stuff anymore. I'd much rather use the money to go out and buy a record, or a present for me girlfriend, or phone me mum up from Australia."

Does Simonon feel comfortable sharing that anti-drug concern with the Clash's audience?

Simonon shrugs and gnaws another chip. "Sure. I don't see why not. I think that's part of what we're about, is testing our audience."

Does he ever worry, though, about leaving the audience behind—worry that the band might be growing in different directions?

"Well, I think it's this band's natural course to grow. When we did *London Calling* we got a lot of flak, but that was just a warm-up. I think the real turning point for us came when we recorded 'The Magnificent Seven'; it was the start of a whole new music for us. I thought, 'This is going to wake people up, especially the ones who keep expecting us to do the same old thing; maybe it'll even make them chuck the bloody album out the window.'

"But we knew that's what we wanted: to test the people who'd been listening to us. We didn't want to be dictated by anybody else's interests. That could've happened very easily after the first album, either way—we could've gone off in a more commercial style, because of what the record company people wanted, or gotten deadlocked into a hard punk thing, because of what the fans wanted. We didn't do either one, and I suspect that's hurt us as much as it's helped. We certainly had an easy formula that would've carried us for a while."

Does Simonon think the Clash still attracts much of a punk audience in America or England—the hardcore and Oi types?

"Yeah, a little, but by and large the music of those bands doesn't interest me. I've listened to it, but so much of it is just noise for its own sake. Plus the things they deal with, things like racism and getting drunk and slapping your girlfriend around the face—I don't have any use for supporting that kind of thing.

"You know, people ask me all the time if we're still *punk*, and I always say, 'Yeah, *we're* punk,' because punk meant not having to stick to anybody else's rules. Then you look around and see all these bands that are afraid to break the rules of what they think punk is. *We're* punk because we still have our own version of what it means. That's what it is: an attitude. And we'll stay punk as long as we can keep the blindfolds off."

I s IT TRUE THAT Bob Dylan was in the audience last night?" Joe Strummer asks, as we settle down at the bar at the Clash's hideaway hotel, a couple of hours after the next-to-last of their five-night engagements at the Hollywood Palladium. "Somebody told me that Sinatra came to one of the Bond's shows, but I thought that was a bit far-fetched. But Dylan. . . ."

I tell him that yes, Dylan did come out to see the Clash, and from all accounts, seemed to like what he saw.

Strummer just shakes his head, muttering in incredulity.

Would that have intimidated you, I ask, knowing that Dylan was out there?

"Well, yeah. I mean, somebody told us he was up in the balcony, watching us, but you always hear those kinds of rumors. But if I'd known it was true, I'm not sure how I would've felt. Playing for Dylan, you know, that's a bit like playing for . . . *God,* ain't it?" Strummer orders us a round of drinks—a Bloody Mary for himself; a rum and Coke for me—and continues his musings on Dylan.

"You know, me and Kosmo (Vinyl, the band's road manager and press liaison), we're the only real Dylan diehards around the Clash. In fact, when Kosmo came down to Paris to take me back to London after I'd split, we went out celebrating one night at a French bar, with me playing piano, pounding out Dylan songs, howling stuff like, '*When you're lost in Juarez/And it's summertime too . . .*'

"I realize it's almost a cliché to say it," he continues, "but we probably wouldn't have done the kind of music we have if it hadn't been for Bob Dylan. It's easy for all these cynics just to write him off, but they don't realize what he did—I mean, he spoke up, he showed that music could take on society, could actually make people want to save the world."

There are many of us, I say, who have put the Clash in that same league as Dylan, or for that matter, as the Rolling Stones. We see you as spokespersons, as idealists and heroes, as a band who are living out rock & roll's best possibilities. In fact, we've even called you, time and time again, the World's Greatest Rock & Roll Band. Did those kinds of claims ever confuse the band's purpose—after all, you'd set out to play havoc with rock & roll—or did they instead help you secure the kind of mass audience you now enjoy in America?

"No to both questions," says Strummer. "First of all, we never took that 'World's Greatest' crap seriously. That's just a laugh. What does it matter to be the greatest rock & roll band if radio won't even touch you? I mean, let's face it: We *don't* have the sort of mass audience in America that you mentioned, and it's because radio won't play our music. If you listen to the airwaves in this country, *we don't matter*—we haven't even made a dent, outside 'Train in Vain.'

"The last time I talked to you," he continues, "that time in London, just before our first tour here, I think I pissed off the idea that America might really matter to us. But now I understand just how important it is: You can reach more people here than anywhere else in the world, and I don't mean just record buyers. I mean reaching real *people,* making them wake up and see what's happening around them, making them want to go out and do something about it."

But does Strummer think that's what's really happening? What about all the time-warped punks who merely want to act out the surface images of revolt? Or that broader mainstream audience that's taken to the Clash as the new Rolling Stones, and want little more than the commodity of vicarious sedition, or bombastic euphoria, for their money? Aren't there times when Strummer looks out there and wonders who the band's audience actually *is* at this point, if their ideals are really the same as the Clash's?

"Every night we play," Strummer says, "I wonder who our audience is. But you have to figure you're reaching some of them. Maybe we're *only* entertaining most of them, but that's not really so bad when you think about it—look what it is that we entertain them with. I reckon each show we reach some new ones, *really* reach them. It's like fighting a big war with few victories, but each of those victories is better than none."

Joe tosses back the rest of his drink and signals for a fresh round. The liquor's starting to do its work. We're both feeling voluble. "Let me tell you," he continues, "if you can't find cause for hope, then go *get* some somewhere. I mean, I've had some bad times, dark moments when I came close to putting a pistol to my head and blowing my brains out, but . . ." Strummer lapses into a private silence, staring fixedly at the remains of the drink before him. "But screw that," he says after a few moments. "I think if you ain't got anything optimistic to say, then you should shut up—*final*. I mean, we ain't dead yet, for Christ's sake. I know nuclear doom is prophesied for the world, but I don't think you should give up fighting until the flesh burns off your face."

But *Combat Rock,* I note, sounds like the Clash's *least* optimistic record.

"*Combat Rock* ain't anything except some songs. Songs are meant to move people, and if they don't, they fail. Anyway, we took too long with that record, worried it too much."

Still, it does have sort of a gloomy, deathly outlook, I tell him. All those songs like "Death Is a Star," "Straight to Hell."

"I'll tell you why that record's so grim," says Strummer. "Those things just have to be faced, and we knew it was our time. Traditionally, that's not the way to sell records—by telling an audience to sober up, to face up. The audience wants to get high, enjoy themselves, not feel preached to. Fair enough, there ain't much hope in the world, I don't want to kill the fun but still . . ."

Strummer hesitates in thought for a few moments, then leans closer. "Music's supposed to be the life force of the new consciousness, talking from 1954 to present, right? But I think a lot of rock & roll stars have been responsible for taking that life force and turning it into a death force. What I hate about so much of that '60s and '70s stuff is that it dealt death as style, when it was pretending to deal it as *life*. To be cool, you had to be on the point of killing yourself.

"What I'm really talking about," he continues, "is drugs. I mean, I think drugs ain't happening, because if the music's going to move you, you don't need drugs. If I see a sharp-looking guy on a street corner, he's alive and he's making me feel more alive—he ain't dying—and that's the image I've decided the Clash has to stand for these days. I think we've blown it on the drug scene. It ain't happening, and I want to make it quite clear that nobody in the Clash thinks heroin or cocaine or any of that crap is cool.

"I just want to see things change," he continues, hitting a nice stride. "I don't want it to be like the '60s or '70s, where we saw our rock stars shambling about out of their minds, and we thought it was cool, even instructive. That was death-style, not life-style. Those guys made enough money to go into expensive clinics and get their blood changed—but what about the poor junkie on the street? He's been led into it by a bunch of rock stylists, and left to die with their style. I guess we each have to work it out in our own way—I had to work it out for myself—but the Clash have to take the responsibility to stand for something better than that.

"Like I say," Strummer continues, "I don't want to kill anybody's fun. But certainly there's a better way of having fun than slow suicide." Strummer takes a long sip at his drink, and an uneasy expression colors his face. "Suicide is something I know about. It's funny how when you feel really depressed, all your thoughts run in bad circles and you can't break them circles. They just keep running around themselves, and you can't think of one good thing, even though you try your hardest. But the next day it can all be different."

I'm not sure what to say, so I let the mood hang in the air, as palpable as the liquor. Finally, I ask if Joe's sudden disappearance to Paris was a way of working himself out of a depression.

"It sure was," he says quickly. "It's very depressing in England these days—at least it can get that way, it can get on top of you. But I had a personal reason for going to Paris: I just remembered how it was when I was a bum, how I'd once learned the truth from playing songs on the street corner. If I played good, I'd eat, and that direct connection between having something to eat and somewhere to stay and the music I played—I just remembered that.

"So I went to Paris and I only got recognized once, but I conned my way out of it. I'd grown a beard and looked a bit like Fidel Castro, so I simply told them I was my hero. I didn't want to be recognized."

While he was gone, I ask, was he worried it might mean the end of the Clash?

"I felt a bit quilty, but . . ." Joe pauses and looks toward the bartender for one more round. It's already well past closing hour, Strummer and I are the last customers in the bar, but the barkeep obliges. "I felt guilty," Strummer resumes, "but I was also excited, feeling I was bringing everything to a head. I just contrasted all those pressing business commitments with that idea that I used to be a bum—that's why I'd *started* to play music, because I was a bum—and I decided to blow, maybe just for a day or two.

"But once I was in Paris, I was excited by the feeling that I could just walk down the street, go in a bar and play pinball, or sit in a park by myself, unrecognized. It was a way of proving that I existed—that I really existed for once *for me.* This was one trip for me. We make a lot of trips, but that one was for me.

"I'll tell you this," Joe adds as a parting thought, "I really enjoyed *being* a bum again. I wish I could do it every day, really. But I can't disappear anymore. Time to face up to what we're on about."

And what is that?

"Well, if I wanted to sound naive, I guess I'd say it's something like trying to make a universal music for a world without governments. Or a better way of putting it is to say for a world under One World Government. All this nationalism, these border wars, they're going to erupt into the death of us."

It *does* sound a bit naive, given the state of things.

"Let me tell you," he says, "I'd rather talk to a naive person than a cynic. Sure, there are a lot of young naive people out there, but at least they can be moved, their ideals can be inspired. That's why, even though a lot of the critics have been very kind to us and love us, we never aim our music at them. We're writing for the young ones, the audience, because they carry the hope of the world a lot more than a few critics or cynics. Those young ones can go away from our show with a better idea of a better world. At least they haven't written it all off yet. Their ideals can still be inspired."

The liquor's run out and so have the bar's good graces. We gather our jackets and get ready to leave. "I know it sounds simple, says Strummer, but I *believe* in naivete. It's a good breeding idea for rebellion. It's a bit like believing in survival, you know—I mean, surviving is the toughest test, and we had to find out the hard way. *I* had to find that out. But in the end, I realized it's the only rebellion that counts—not giving up.

"It's like I said: We ain't dead yet, for fuck's sake. If you ain't got hope, you should get where there is some. There's as much hope for the world as you find for yourself."

punk:

twenty years

after

though none of us knew it at the time, when the Clash finished their *Combat Rock* tour in 1982, they were very near their own end. The band split in 1983, with Mick Jones going on to form Big Audio Dynamite (also known as B.A.D., which turned out to be an unfortunately clairvoyant nickname), and Strummer going on to something less than a solo career. Still, the Clash's trek had been glorious—they made a larger and more meaningful volume of great punk music than any band before or since (that is, unless you count Elvis Presley and Frank Sinatra as punks—which perhaps you should), and compared to most late 1970s punk acts, their seven-year career seemed downright protracted.

In the last twenty years, there was no single movement in popular (or in this case, semipopular, even *un*popular) music that I cared or argued more about than punk, no movement I tracked more closely. But to be a fan of punk was to resign oneself to many uneasy realities—including dealing with a great deal of derision. It also meant accepting that many of punk's best artists and best music would pass you by faster than a bullet-train. Remember the Au Pairs, the Vibrators, the Avengers, Magazine, X-Ray Spex, Wire, the Adverts, Young Marble Giants, Marine Girls, Liliput, the Raincoats, Kleenex, ESG, Gang of Four, the Germs, Y Pants, Penetration? If you do, you know they all made great music, and then they were gone almost before you knew it. It was as if a troop of ghosts had laid mines across the field of modern-day pop. If you were lucky, you stepped on those mines, and their explosion could be epiphanies that might change your life.

Though I wrote about punk more than any other theme since 1977 (especially during my years as pop music critic for the *Los Angeles Herald Examiner*), the subject receives only a limited amount of space in this present volume. In part, that's because there are other writers who have done wonderful and thoughtful jobs of delineating punk's history and meaning (see Jon Savage's *England's Dreaming* and Greil Marcus' *Lipstick Traces* and *ranters & crowd pleasers*—the latter published in the United Kingdom as *In the Fascist Bathroom*). It's also because there were ways in which I became disillusioned with how punk eventually was received, and how some of its best meanings were robbed. I remember a film from a few years back, *1991: The Year Punk Broke*. The title referred to the commercial and generational breakthrough represented by the success of Nirvana—which indeed was a wonderful (though for the band, horribly costly) event. But the truth is, anybody paying attention had heard that same claim—that punk had broken through, been accepted by a hidebound American audience—for at least a decade, ever since the Clash hit big with *London Calling* in 1979. It was heartening, of course, that music like the Clash's and Nirvana's reached many people, for these victories meant far more than commercial success; they also gave hope, voice, courage, and *fun* to many people whom the traditional pop world was reluctant to accommodate, or even to recognize. At the same time, I'm afraid that—at least in the mid-1980s—what many people meant when they claimed that punk (also known by the more generic, "acceptable" designation of "new wave") had broken through in America was that the music— and even parts of the punk movement itself—had finally been incorporated into a thriving commodity form. As far back as 1983, certain elements of punk style were already ubiquitous: quirky music, tough-posing fashions, and sharp, insouciant stances permeated much of American radio (on stations such as Los Angeles' trend-setting KROQ-FM) and television (the horrible *Square Pegs* series and, of course, MTV) and international film (*Diva*, *Star Struck*, *Liquid Sky*, and others), as if the whole creative expression of domestic pop culture suddenly had realigned itself. It was as if punk and postpunk had finally won the pop wars only to surrender its ideals.

Which is to say, it was as if nothing had changed: Yesterday's pop— which new wave set out to upend—was largely a music of relentless sameness, kneejerk sexism, and social unconcern. But new wave pop quickly became a music of exotic sameness, cloying sexiness, and, to some degree, social denial. There was nothing meaningful or revealing in the success of such glitz-and-sex acts as Berlin, Missing Persons, or Duran Duran, even though they blazoned a "new" sound that personified modern trends and attitudes.

What went wrong? How did a music of such unruly origins end up so trivial and diffused? It helps to remember that punk began as a genre born of attitude and circumstance: In the airlessness of British society and aridity of American rock music in the late '70s, outrage or desecration seemed the only animating, even rational, course—a way of staking distance from all the sameness of those scenes, and also affronting, provoking them. Sedition-minded acts like the Sex Pistols and Clash played their music as if the corruption of British values had *forced* the noise from them, while their early American counterparts—Talking Heads, Blondie, the Ramones, and Television—didn't comment on social forces so much as make new claims for the way vital modern music must sound. To the media, much of this brutal, apocalypse-informed modernism seemed merely silly or incomprehensible, while to radio—which stood to break or make punk with a large audience—the music and its style-makers loomed mainly as a loathsome, noncommercial force. What hits radio allowed—the B52s, Cars, Blondie, the Vapors, the Police—seemed elected mainly to quell the music's insurgency.

Maybe this was a reasonable action, because the best new wave, punk, and postpunk records were actively fierce, profane stuff. Consider the evidence: "Anarchy in the U.K." and "Bodies" (by the Sex Pistols), "White Riot" and "Guns on the Roof" (the Clash), *Crossing the Red Sea with the Adverts* (the Adverts), "Oh Bondage Up Yours!" (X-Ray Spex), "Don't Dictate" (Penetration), "At Home He's a Tourist" (Gang of Four), "Shot by Both Sides" (Magazine), *Fear of Music* (Talking Heads), "Discovering Japan" (Graham Parker), "She's Lost Control" (Joy Division), *Broken English* (Marianne Faithfull), "Ghost Town" (Specials), *Metal Box* (Public Image, Ltd.), *This Year's Model* (Elvis Costello).

All of these songs or albums were attempts to force popular culture—and a young, developing segment of pop at that—to accommodate visions of social horror, private dissolution, and plain old willful rancor. That they were among the most truthful and important music of their day was largely a missed fact; that they were virtually unheard outside of a community of (anti-) pop activists was certainly a disservice, though to radio's way of (non-) thinking, more a necessity than choice. This was music that meant to rend the pop world in half—and that's an ambition that radio (which has since divided the real world into unnecessary black and white factions) figured it could never survive.

But punk always had a built-in defeat factor, and that was basically the way the music would be enervated as it was adopted by a gradually larger audience. Many fans presumed that to adhere to new wave music and its fabricated fashions was to become *a part of* its culture. In fact, British art and social theorist Dick Hebdige devoted the better part of a book (*Subculture: The Meaning of Style*, Methuen, 1979) to the idea that this adherence to a

collective style gave British punks and mods a "genuinely expressive artifice"—a sense of "Otherness" that set them apart from the beliefs and values
of the dominant society. To a degree, this is true: To crop one's hair into a
bright-dyed, spiky cut, or dress in vivid vinyl colors, *is* to make a choice that
sets one apart in new social alignments. Of course, like the initial uniqueness
of long hair or short hair, it's a short-lived difference. One doesn't necessarily
become a punk by fashion and musical choices alone.

In America in the 1980s, the whole new wave shebang amounted to
even less than a change in weather—more like a change in flavor. That's
because in America, new wave was largely a music of surfaces and faddism—
a sound that became as increasingly self-conscious as a chic dance-floor pose.
What this meant was that the emerging dominant American new wave audience didn't necessarily share social or even aesthetic values in the same way
that the initial art-informed New York and street-bred London punks and
postpunk crowd did. Instead, the MTV and KROQ audiences—which were
smack dab in the middle of new wave's rise—simply shared a fondness for
the immediate look and feel of the music, without much driving concern
over the ideas or responsibilites implicit in their musical choices. (How else
might a thinking audience embrace, on the same bill, bands as diametrically
opposed as the Clash and Men at Work?)

What this also meant was that both punk music and its culture could
now contain as many political and aesthetic incongruities as the dominant
society around them.

IN THE EARLY and mid-1980s, if punk meant or proved anything vital in
America, then it was in Los Angeles, more than anywhere else. In the sprawling webwork of riches and dread that was Los Angeles in those days, few
people lived out their caprices more colorfully or more fiercely than the
punks—as if they were hell-bent on defacing the city's pacific gloss, or simply
underscoring its balled-up artistic and ethical climate. In a sense, punk in
California was always something of a paradox: The city's self-possessed styl-
ishness and cold-blooded opulence are so steady, so pervasive, that anyone
who attempts to assert rage or ugliness as aesthetic values can't help seeming
a bit misplaced, if not just plain pretentious. But there was an inescapable
rightness about what the punks were doing in Southern California: In a place
where one of the most widely held ambitions is leisure, and the most commonly respected product of art is prosperity, some of the few voices that
made much moral difference at all were the ones that blazoned hostility.

In any case, punk—as a digression in culture or community, more than an adventure in music or art—flourished in Los Angeles as it had in no other place outside of London. In fact, Los Angeles was the one place where punk has come closest to living up to its name—the one place where, as David Byrne noted, "you find punks who really are punks: mean as Hell, and not just the creators of an interesting persona." It was as if all the spike-haired, skin-headed, self-styled guttersnipes you saw haunting the streets and clubs in L.A. were devoted to carrying out what they perceived as punk's first and foremost possibilities: namely, artful nihilism and studied primitivism.

It's that fondness for the ignoble that helped give L.A. punk its nasty streak. In his essay about British punk in *The Rolling Stone Illustrated History of Rock & Roll*, Greil Marcus noted: "By far the most violent in appearance and rhetoric of any musical movement, punk was probably the least violent in fact—though by far the most violence was directed against it." Los Angeles was the place where the punks evened the score.

For the most part, L.A.'s punk violence was confined to a thuggish little ritual called, quite aptly, slam dancing: dancers gathered into kinetic clusters and collided off one another like pool balls caroming around a snookers table. To most observers, it resembled a microcosmic version of pandemonium. (The music for these melees—a rabid, samely version of early monorhythmic, nonmelodic punk, usually dispensed by Fear, Black Flag, the Circle Jerks—was both prompting and incidental: merely a relentless agitating soundtrack or backdrop for the real performers, the audience.)

Sometimes the dancing turned into communal violence. What might begin as a shoving or jeering match between some punks or punks and outsiders could turn hurriedly into a mob action, with half a dozen or so partisans leaping into the fracas, drubbing their hapless target into a bloodied, enraged wreck. Often, scrambles swept across the whole breadth of a club or ballroom floor, touching off eruptions of chaos like a chain-blaze in a dry timberland.

Some observers I know described these flare-ups as essentially the celebrative rites of a community defining itself; others charged that the media hyperbolized the whole scene. I don't think either of those claims is entirely true: Punk violence was far from being the most troubling form of violence in Los Angeles—a place where the police force was almost never censured for its shootings of citizens and suspects—but what went on in the clubs here wasn't anything particularly festive or transcendent. It was simply a demonstration of would-be miscreants trying to make a shared style out of accepted notions of alienation and despair.

So what is it about the promised land that inspired so much enmity among its children? Craig Lee (a late Los Angeles–based journalist who played drums and guitar for Catholic Discipline and the Alice Bag Band) did a nice succinct job of summing up the partisan's point of view in an article about surf punks for *L.A. Weekly:* "The English press has often snidely alluded to punk in L.A. being a farce, not like the London scene that grew from a revolt against a life of lower class drudgery. But facing a sterile, anonymous life in suburbia is as depressing to some kids as facing a life of dull labor and low wages is to the English punks."

I have my own view of the subject, which is simply that when you're trying to act out dreams of desperateness in a place where those dreams aren't intrinsic, then you just have to act a little harder and a little tougher. After all, it's a great kick, a great fancy of revolt, to feign hopelessness in a place just drowning with hope. When the passion and the moment faded, the punks could always kick back and settle into the subliminal, lulling rhythm of the city—and many of them did. That cadence of insensibility has been what's always kept time here: it even, in its own way, gave the punks their momentum, and eventually it outlasted them. Undoubtedly, that made some of the scene's detractors fairly happy. But for the rest of us, those few voices of outrage that startled this vast, unconcerned cityscape are something we miss terrifically.

ALONG THE WAY, the L.A. punk scene produced a handful of bands that were seen by some as great hopes—including X and the Go-Go's (I know it's hard to believe, but the Go-Go's really *were* a punk band once upon a time, until A&M Records signed them and fixed that problem for good). Of those two groups, clearly X was the more considerable (though vastly less popular) force. Indeed, X made definitional, high-reaching, great punk records (especially *Wild Gift* and *Under the Big Black Sun*) and also played definitional, high-reaching, great live shows. In concert, guitarist Billy Zoom, drummer Don Bonebrake, bassist John Doe, and vocalist Exene Cervenka took songs like "Sex and Dying in High Society," "Johnny Hit and Run Pauline," "The Once Over Twice," and "Your Phone's Off the Hook, but You're Not" and pushed them to their limit, as if they wanted to punish the structures of the songs in order to strengthen their meanings. At the same time, the group never abandoned its sense of essential unity. X was, after all, a band about community—for that matter, a band that asserted the ideal of family as a loving but practical-minded alternative to personal dissolution and fashionable nihilism—and for all the tension and frantic propulsion in their music, the individual elements of the sound hung together like firm, interconnected patterns.

But by 1985, X's sense of family—and perhaps a bit of their spirit—began to fray. John Doe and Exene Cervenka not only sang the best team vocals in punk's history, they had also been a real team—husband and wife. But then that marriage suffered a breakup, and though the pair's creative partnership remained intact, the romantic disunion took its emotional toll.

In most ways that count, the album that came from that rupture, *Ain't Love Grand,* was an album about how fiery love comes to rugged and embittered ends, and how, after the ruin, it can sometimes forge new bonds of esteem and comradeship. Of course, before one can arrive at any such understanding, one has to cut through the remembrances of romantic hell: all the charges and admissions of infidelity ("My Goodness" and "Little Honey"), all the mourning of a lost, ideal union ("All or Nothing" and "Watch the Sun Go Down"). At one point, in "Supercharged," Exene delivers a taunting account of the feverish and relentless sex she enjoys with a new lover, and John Doe sings along with her, like a grim witness to his own exclusion. One can't help but wonder, what must Doe have been thinking at such a moment?

Perhaps he was simply thinking that this is what one must do to get past the bad truths. After all, the band survived this rupture, and somehow emerged with one of its bravest works yet. It's as if, in the place of children, Doe and Cervenka spawned a certain artistry that demanded a continued fellowship; they worked and sang together not merely for the sake of their music, but because of the knowledge that they could make music this grand and fulfilling and revealing no place else but in this band, with each other. The two no longer shared the same home or same love, but they certainly shared the same harmonies—an affinity they could find only in each other—and that's worth whatever the cost of their continued alliance. Of course, this time it meant something far different for the two to sing together, and not surprisingly, they pulled off their most memorable performances in a trio of songs ("All or Nothing," "Watch the Sun Go Down," and "I'll Stand Up for You") where they stepped away from recriminations and faced the challenge of their abiding friendship and partnership. "When my friends put you down, I'll stand up for you," Doe sings to Exene in the album's most heartening and generous moment. "I'll stand up for you, and you'll stand up for me."

In their music and their forbearance, Doe and Cervenka asserted that some traditions should withstand the necessary negation that comes along with modern times and new values. X never made this claim more meaningfully than in *Ain't Love Grand.*

As for the Go-Go's—I have to admit, I had a hard time liking them. The band's first album, *Beauty and the Beat* (1981), was an eager though savvy attempt to meet commercial expectations of new wave diffusion, and their second *(Vacation,* 1982) was merely the obvious follow-up attempt at cranking out *more* surface-fun fare. But the third record, 1984's *Talk Show,* proved to be something more than their vindication—something closer to a self-directed work of vengeance, as if the group had something to make up for by upsetting their former pop refinement. In any event, some twist of thinking—or perhaps just the internal friction within the band during that season—occurred to make *Talk Show* a surprisingly hard-edged revelation. In fact, the record was so good it had the effect of splitting the group up—though not forever. When the band returned in 1994 with *Return to the Valley of the Go-Go's,* they sounded like they were playing just for the mere fun of it. Yet "mere fun" can also be its own deep truth—especially in Los Angeles. As Greil Marcus noted in *Mystery Train,* L.A. is a city where Nathanael West's and Raymond Chandler's dark version of urban realism are no more reflective of deep truths than Brian Wilson's fun-in-the-sun view of the city's ethical climate. Pop, as a medium of fun, and fun as a purpose of pop, is still an inevitable and necessary tradition in the L.A. scene.

LOS ANGELES in the 1980s also produced two other bands I'd like to comment on briefly. One is the Minutemen, a three-man outfit made up of guitarist D. Boon, bassist Mike Watt, and drummer Mike Hurley, who were part of the scene nearly since its inception. In the early 1980s, they released what were two of the most impelling of all American hardcore albums (and perhaps the most inventive punk-style recordings since the Clash's debut LP): *The Punch Line* and *What Makes a Man Start Fires.* They were politically and musically involving works, full of quick, hard thinking, and quicker, harder tempo changes.

The Minutemen were at once both the thinking listener's and thinking musician's hardcore band—which is to say they wrote and performed art-informed music from a singular and committed political point-of-view, and they played from a funk-derived punk perspective. Big, hard, fleet shards of bass guitar cut across the contending structure set up by the impetuous guitar lines and eruptive drum patterns, and in that vibrant webwork, surprising references—everything from Chuck Berry to Sly Stone, from Miles Davis to James "Blood" Ulmer—exposed themselves and took on new identities, and, in the process, new histories. Seeing them live, they made me feel I had finally seen Moby Dick onstage, and had finally understood why Ahab lost. Some things are too big to get over or around, and too irresistible to ignore.

On December 22, 1985, D. Boon was killed in an automobile accident, and the Minutemen necessarily came to an end. The loss was immense. In his quest with the Minutemen, Boon clearly worked more as a comrade in action—an equal—than as a lead figure. In fact, sometimes on record it was hard to sort out his particular songwriting style from that of Watts and Hurley, which may be a tribute to the sense of unity and functional democracy that the trio achieved—much like that achieved by groups as disparate as the Band and the Ornette Coleman Quartet. Onstage, though, Boon often seemed the more central and commanding figure in the Minutemen, and not merely because of his obvious physical bulk, nor because his vocals tended to sound a bit better humored and ironic than Watts'. Actually, what made him such a dominating performer was that he seemed to have some kind of imperative physical involvement with the music. I can recall shows in which he seemed to be wringing his guitar, pulling and twisting wondrous, complex clusters of notes from it, then reshaping them into new patterns to fit the vaulting rhythms being served up by Watts and Hurley.

D. Boon and the Minutemen left eleven albums and EPs and one epic-length cassette, comprising some of the most probing, resourceful, and continually surprising American music of the 1980s. Watt and Hurley went on to form fIREHOSE with guitarist and vocalist eD fROMOHIO, and in 1995, Mike Watt released a widely respected album, *Ball-Hog or Tugboat?*, featuring contributions by Eddie Vedder, Henry Rollins, Evan Dando, and members of Nirvana, Screaming Trees, Sonic Youth, Meat Puppets, and Soul Asylum.

PERHAPS MY FAVORITE 1980s L.A. punk group was the one that, at moments, also disappointed me the most: Dream Syndicate. In the early 1980s, I was working evenings in an L.A. record store, Westwood's Rhino, alongside a young, friendly guy named Steve Wynn. I learned that Wynn had formed a band, Dream Syndicate, and he invited me to catch their maiden appearance at a Valley spot, the Country Club. From their first moments onstage, I was in love. They had that ideal mix of reference sounds—part Bob Dylan, part Velvet Underground, part Neil Young, part John Fogerty—but they also had something all their own: a willingness to take their music anywhere it might go at any given moment, even if that moment resulted in chaos or decomposition. They also had spirit and humor. The audience that night—who'd gathered to see some no-account new-wave headliner or another—*hated* Dream Syndicate on the spot. They booed the band, pelted them with beer cups, spit on them, and demanded they GET OFF THE STAGE. Finally, Wynn said, "I've got some good news for you: This is our last song of the night," and for the first time in Dream Syndicate's set, the audience erupted in a cheer. "The bad news," he added, "is that it goes on for a *really* long time," and the audience groaned as one. And the song *did* go on for a long time—about twenty-five minutes. By the time it was over, there were only maybe five people left seated in the hall, myself among them.

Dream Syndicate's first full-length album, *Days of Wine and Roses*, was one of the best works of 1983—boisterous and reckless, and full of a weird and stirring beauty. That was when Dream Syndicate caught the ear of A&M Records (you remember them from the Go-Go's, right?), and suddenly something went terribly wrong. Some said it was outside pressures, some said it was internal problems, but whatever the cause, Dream Syndicate seemed to freeze up right before our eyes and ears. The group's A&M debut, *Medicine Show* (1984)—which had taken months to make and had cost a fortune— ended up sounding more drenched in attitude than meaning, and was utterly without the spark of spontaneity that had made their earlier music so riveting. Worse, the group's live shows, which had once seemed so chancy, degenerated into pat, heartless performances. What had begun as an inspired vision had turned simply into another guileful career, and it was hardly surprising when, a few months later, we learned that the group's leaders, Wynn and guitarist Karl Precoda, had parted ways.

But the best dreams die hard, so the tale moves on. In 1985, Dream Syndicate regrouped, with a new guitarist and producer, Paul Cutler. Their next album, *Out of the Grey*, was a bracing work of redemption. In particular, it seemed to be a record about what it means to lose one's way and to summon the will to find a new direction and start again. In such songs as "Dying Embers" and "Now I Ride Alone," Steve Wynn conjured bitter, dark remembrances of blown chances and bad choices, and while he clearly cared a great deal about the people who get swallowed up in such dissolution, he refused to surrender to the romance of it all. "Spit out the poison and get on with it," he sang at one point, even though he was singing about somebody whom he knew could never let go of his own decline or his own broken past. Maybe Dream Syndicate lost their crack at the big time, but they still had music to make, and Wynn sounded as if he intended to make it as honestly and compassionately as he knew how. Dream Syndicate broke up and regrouped more than once and Wynn went on to make two fine solo albums, *Kerosene Man* and *Dazzling Display*. But *Out of the Grey* was the best music Dream Syndicate ever made.

I wrote about Dream Syndicate often in my days at the *Herald Examiner*. One smog-bound, gray-brown winter day, I was driving to work, listening to KROQ—L.A.'s new wave station that played mainly cloying music. Then the D.J. said a few words that perked my interest. "We've been reading a lot about this L.A. band the Dream Syndicate," he said. "I haven't heard anything by them yet, but we believe in giving new bands a chance at KROQ, so here goes."

With that, "Halloween," from *The Days of Wine and Roses*, began blaring from my car speakers—its frictional, slow-moving-but-exciting sound unlike anything I'd yet heard on that station. It reminded me of the sense of daring that causes one to fall in love with rock & roll in the first place, that sense of inquiring emotion that can pin you like a bolt of recognition. There it all was: flashes of the Velvet Underground, Television, and white noise Rolling Stones, in the collision of guitars and the hard, uncompromising beat and . . . and . . . all of a sudden, it was *gone*. After only thirty seconds of rapturous cacophony, it disappeared with soundless abruptness.

The D.J. fumbled his way back on the air, his voice shaky with anger. "That's all I need to hear," he said. "I like to give new local bands a chance, but this is ridiculous. You won't be hearing more of that band on this station."

And indeed, I never did.

I told this story to Wynn one day during an interview, while we were seated at a hamburger stand on Santa Monica Boulevard. He looked wonderstruck, then just shook his head, laughing.

"God, that's wonderful," he said. "To think we could disturb somebody who's supposed to be as aware of 'new music' as these people are supposed to be . . ." He let the thought trail off into a bemused smile.

"At least we won't be overexposed," he said after a while, laughing once again.

BY THE LATE 1980s, L.A.'s punk scene no longer meant as much. As it developed, though, punk was something that was now all over the world—in fact, maybe it had always been in the air, in the history, in one form of voice or another, from Robert Johnson and Presley, to Jerry Lee Lewis and Sinatra. But without what punk accomplished in the late 1970s and in the early 1980s, American artists like R.E.M., L7, Pearl Jam, Nine Inch Nails, Marilyn Manson, or even (God help us) Alanis Morrisette, and U.K. acts like ABC, Human League, Oasis, Blur, Pulp, U2, Sinéad O'Connor, and the Prodigy, might never have happened or meant as much.

But as the 1990s began, the place where you could hear punk at its brightest and most exhilarating was in Seattle, Washington, especially in the music of a trio called Nirvana. But we will come to that story later.

van halen:

the endless party

*Our ancestry is firmly rooted in the animal world, and to
its subtle antique ways our hearts are pledged. Children of
all animal kind, we inherited many a social nicety as well
as the predator's way. . . .*

ROBERT ARDREY
FROM *AFRICAN GENESIS*

*It's like we always say: There's a little Van Halen in
everybody—all we're trying to do is bring it out.*
ALEX VAN HALEN

david Lee Roth makes quite a picture as he stands in front of his dressing-room mirror backstage at Detroit's Cobo Arena. Arching his hips lewdly and tugging at the waistband of his ruby-red spandex tights until the elastic crotch zone bulges like a gaudy Christmas stocking crammed with apples and bananas, Van Halen's lead singer preens and postures like a bestial champion of autoeroticism. Actually, this steamy display is a thoughtful gesture for the ladies who will crowd around the stage tonight—the idea being that when they look up and behold David, they also behold his Goliath.

After a quick check to make sure the view looks as mouthwatering from the rear as from the front, Roth swaggers over to where I'm sitting and plops down in a folding chair. "Hey, man," he says, tossing his woolly tresses back from his shoulders with a blasé flick of the head, "I want you to feel free to ask us anything you want, write about anything you see. Van Halen's got nothin' to hide. But," he adds, leaning closer and slipping deeper into his patented street patois, "let me forewarn you: What you've walked into here is a self-created fantasyland, where everything happens four times as much and four times as quick, like an around-the-calendar New Year's Eve.

"It's like, *anything* you desire you can find here—whatever your vice, whatever your sexual ideals. Whatever somebody else can't do in his nine-to-five job, *I* can do in rock & roll."

Tickled by his description of rock & roll privilege, Roth laughs lustily and bounds back to the mirror. "I guess what I'm saying, man, is that I'm *proud* of the way we live, not so much because of the records we sell or the money we make, but because of the party we're going to have afterward to celebrate all that."

ALL THINGS considered, Roth and the other members of Van Halen—bassist Michael Anthony, guitarist Eddie Van Halen, and his brother, drummer Alex Van Halen—have plenty to celebrate. Their most recent album, *Women and Children First,* vaulted into *Billboard*'s Top 10 only one week after its release. The band's previous LPs, *Van Halen* and *Van Halen II,* have reportedly sold more than 7 million copies worldwide. In addition, the pair of sold-out shows in Detroit—part of the 1980 Invasion tour, the group's most extensive and extravagant headline trek to date—denotes an even more crucial triumph of the marketplace: a fervid acceptance of Van Halen by America's heavy-metal heartland. The group is now one of the undisputed kingpins of hard rock, ranking alongside such venerable Visigoths as Led Zeppelin, Ted Nugent, and Aerosmith.

Van Halen, though, differs from the current crop of metal bands (such as Rush, the Scorpions, UFO, and Triumph) that have been enjoying a formidable resurgence in popularity. Their ignoble posturing is a welcome reprieve from the empty-headed pomposity of blowhards like Rush, and their music is concise, tuneful, and impelling.

Van Halen, however, isn't an example of resurgent heavy metal so much as the inevitable progeny of yesteryear's metal epoch. Roth blusters and blares onstage like a brazen, self-endeared crossbreed of Black Oak Arkansas' Jim Dandy Mangrum, Grand Funk Railroad's Mark Farner, and Zeppelin's Robert Plant. Eddie Van Halen, the group's musical conscience, plays guitar like some pyrotechnical, virtuosic offspring of Eric Clapton, Jeff Beck, and Jimmy Page. Altogether, Van Halen comes off as intuitively smart and scrupulously artless—perhaps the most satirical symbols of metal mythology since Nugent, or at least Cheap Trick.

But, like many of their heavy-metal brethren, they can also come off as a band of vulgarians. At the outset of this tour, at the University of Southern Colorado in Pueblo, group and crew members trashed a dining room, dressing room, and restroom after the caterers refused to remove some brown M&M's from a plate of candy. (Van Halen has a clause written into their performance contracts that prohibits the serving of brown M&M's backstage. When asked why, Alex Van Halen replied, "Why not?") The result of that little lark, according to one report, was $10,000 to $15,000 worth of damage and a ban on rock concerts in Pueblo for the forseeable future.

Instances like that one have prompted some critics to describe Roth as "vainglorious" and "brutish" and to view the band itself as a pack of lack-witted, carnal-minded musical barbarians—a common enough appraisal of heavy-metal groups. Sitting with Roth backstage, watching as he pulls on a pair of scarlet-plumed boots, I ask what he thinks of the critics' aspersions.

"You want to know if we're animals?" Roth says, gazing at his feathered footwear. "Let me put it this way: When I'm onstage, with the volume rippling my body like a glass of water, and thousands of people generating heat in my direction, there's no pause for thought. My basement faculties take over completely.

"Sure—it's animal. I mean, people might like to talk about art, but look where art *is:* It's in the fucking gutter, starving. Van Halen likes to keep things simple; none of this vague, symbolic shit. All we're doing is giving our daily lives melodies, beats, and titles—what we sing about is what we live."

WHEN DAVID LEE ROTH declares that the life Van Halen leads is the same as the one the band sings about, what he's saying is that it's a life brimming with easygoing sex and unabashed affluence. Like many of their comrades of the metal persuasion, Van Halen ballyhoos the time-honored ideal of ceaseless, remorseless, inebriated partying. In fact, in their capable hands, the party ideal becomes a hard and fast commitment: that no matter where Van Halen alights, a boisterous, full-blown saturnalia is bound to follow.

Tonight, the appointed place is the Cobo Arena, where nearly twelve thousand heavy-metal zealots—all with more than just a little latent Van Halen in them—have gathered to lend their voice to the party. And lend it they do. When Van Halen hits the stage, heralded by Eddie Van Halen's storming prelude to "Romeo's Delight," a thundering yowl of acclamation greets them from the floor. "Let me tell ya," says Roth from the lip of the stage, "when Detroit raises its voice, it's fucking *scary*."

Everything about this show—from the titanic, military-motif stage to the overhanging rainbow-spectrum light system (touted as the largest such setup ever taken on the road)—is designed to search out even the most narcotized kid in the furthest reaches of Cobo's three-tiered balcony and thump him in the chest, good and hard. The big thumper, of course, is the music, a sense-numbing blend of Alex' double-barreled drum bursts, Michael Anthony's hulking, palpable bass lines, and Eddie's fleet, blazing guitar.

Eddie, in particular, accounts for the bulk of the sound. He plays with unbridled strength, stacking up layers of leviathan chords, then cutting them down with volleys of staccato fireworks and glimmers of harmonic-phrased melodies. At certain moments, when Anthony's bass hammers out a steady rhythm-pulse, and Eddie's guitar and Alex' drums interknit into a cacophonous counterpoint, Van Halen's heady brand of heavy metal aspires to a near-orchestral scope (which is *not* to say near-classical).

Musical prowess aside, Van Halen concerts are mostly showcases for Roth and his gregarious talents. Roth wangles the crowd from overture to encore, cavorting throughout like a carnal gymnast and trotting out a bookful of born-to-raise-hell bromides. "Swear to God, I smelled *dope* when I walked in here tonight," he says solicitously at one point, then has a dutiful roadie haul out something resembling a joint for him to puff on. Later, while swigging from a half-empty Jack Daniel's bottle, Roth proclaims, "Tonight, I'm going to teach you how to drink for yourself; but when I come back next year, I'm going to teach you how to drink for *other* people."

After the concert, the party spirit extends backstage. As ZZ Top's "I'm Bad, I'm Nationwide" pours out of Roth's portable stereo, two young women climb up on a banquet table and cheerfully strip down to their boots and panties, to the rowdy delight of the men and the silence of the other women. Eddie Van Halen is hanging out at the rear of the room, wearily watching it all with unconcern. Brother Alex, however, and Michael Anthony move up close.

Alex thoughtfully produces a flashlight, which he uses to illuminate the dancer's pelvic motions. In return, the women spread their legs and rub themselves delightedly. Catching my eye from across the room, Roth comes over and gives me a fraternal slap on the shoulder. "Lost denizens of the night," he says, smiling at the women writhing on the table. "Man, I relate to them heavily."

Y̲OU'RE ONLY as good as your worst night, and I feel like I went through hell tonight."

It's the wee hours before dawn, and Eddie Van Halen is sitting on my hotel-room floor. When he showed up about half an hour ago, he seemed dragged out and depressed because he felt his guitar playing earlier in the evening had been haphazard and prosaic. Now, after a couple of glasses of straight bourbon, he appears ruminative. "I suppose what bothers me," he says, "is that often the kids don't even notice when I'm bad. I come offstage and get compliments up the ass. That's *so* frustrating."

Unlike Roth, twenty-three-year-old Eddie Van Halen seems strangely disquieted by mass adulation. "Just three years ago," he says, "I was fighting my way up front with the rest of the kids to see Aerosmith. Then a year later, we were *playing* with them. That boggled me to death. I mean, I knew I'd always play guitar, but I had no idea I'd be in the position I'm in now."

In a way, it might have been predicted. Born in Nijmegen, in the Netherlands, the sons of a jazz musician, Eddie and Alex Van Halen grew up studying counterpoint theory on piano and playing the music of Mozart, Beethoven, and Tchaikovsky. But after the family moved to Pasadena, California, in 1968, the two brothers grew enamored of American and British rock & roll.

While still teenagers, Eddie and Alex formed Mammoth, a heavy-metal-*cum*-party band that frequented Pasadena's wet T-shirt circuit. Alex still bristles when he recalls the bantering he and Eddie used to receive from friends for playing "primitive" music: "They used to call us 'musical prostitutes' because we were playing songs that had simple structures. But it's much harder to write a stable melody in a basic blues format than the stuff these progressive musicians come up with; they change chords and tempos more often than I change my underwear. Some people might call that technical proficiency, but I just call it jerking off."

Whatever lingering doubts the Van Halens may have had about their music's validity were dispelled for good after they hooked up with Roth, who was doing a blues troubadour act at Pasadena's Ice House. (One of the few things Roth *does* exercise restraint about is discussing his personal background, though he admits to growing up on a farm in Indiana and spending weekends at his Uncle Manny's Cafe Wha? in Greenwich Village before moving to Pasadena in the early seventies.)

"Dave was more entertainer than musician," says Eddie. "As a result, he had a better eye for the commercial thing. He was into short-format stuff because people's attention spans are only so long."

After Roth joined up, the Van Halens also enlisted rival Pasadena band-leader Michael Anthony to play bass, then elected to change Mammoth's name to Rat Salade. Roth persuaded the brothers that their surname might prove a more imposing title. "I didn't like the idea at first," says Eddie, "but now I have to admit it sounds powerful—like a German nuclear bomb."

Van Halen traversed the city's basin for almost four years, handling their own management and booking their own dates. Finally, following a successful series of self-produced concerts at Pasadena's Civic Auditorium and an extravagant demo session produced by Kiss bassist Gene Simmons, record labels began to express an interest in the group. One night in 1977, Warner Bros. producer Ted Templeman hauled the label's president, Mo Ostin, over to see the group at a near-empty Hollywood club. In effect, Van Halen signed with Warner Bros. that night.

"The guys in the band still don't know this," says Templeman, who has produced all three of Van Halen's LPs, "but I went down to see them the night before I brought Mo Ostin along, and they just floored me. David Roth came across as the most convincing thing I'd seen in a rock & roll theater since Jim Morrison, but mainly it was Eddie who impressed me.

"Of all the people I work with, besides Michael McDonald, Eddie Van Halen is a true virtuoso. I think he's the best guitar player alive, and I've listened extensively to George Benson, Django Reinhardt, Tal Farlow, Charlie Christian, Jim Hall, and Jimi Hendrix. Eddie can play thirty-second-note melodic lines with a complexity that rivals Bach, and I haven't heard *any-body* who can phrase like him since Charlie Parker. Believe me, Eddie is a killer."

Eddie, though, winces at any mention of praise. "I don't know shit about scales or music theory," he says, "and I don't want to be seen as the fastest guitar in town, ready and willing to gun down the competition. All I know is that rock & roll guitar, like blues guitar, should have melody, speed, and taste, but more important, it should have emotion. I just want my guitar playing to make people feel something: happy, sad, even horny."

Eddie smiles slightly, then pours himself a final glass of bourbon. "Actually, I hate people telling me how good I am. All that really says to me is that I have a lot of friends these days who aren't really friends. I mean, if we stopped selling records tomorrow, bye-bye friends and bye-bye compliments.

"I guess that doesn't *really* bother me—it's just that it's the one thing I never expected."

THE AFTERNOON of the second Cobo Arena show, Van Halen and a small entourage of security and promotion personnel pile into two limousines standing outside the Detroit Plaza Hotel. The band members are slated to make a round of radio interviews, but judging from their bedraggled faces, they would probably prefer using the time to make up for lost sleep.

Moods brighten measurably, though, when the band sees the bevy of fans—most of them female—waiting outside the first station. Roth and Alex fix in on a pair of silk-stockinged, milk-skinned twins and spirit them off to the radio booth. "Welcome to the top," chuckles Roth, snuggling between them, his large hands cuddling their backsides. "You've finally hit the big time." The twins float off to one of the booth's corners, where members of the entourage cajole them into displaying their bare breasts. The band, fully revivified now, settles down for the startled D.J.'s first question.

As it happens, he never gets to ask it. Van Halen quickly turns the proceedings into a chaotic, comic slingfest, tossing out more sexual innuendoes, ethnic slurs, and harmonized burps in two minutes than the Marx Brothers probably managed in their entire careers. "I'd like to present Al with the 'Most Incredible Performance Back at the Hotel Award' for last night," sniggers Roth. "It was definitely a *nine* on the sphincter scale." The band chortles knowingly, and the D.J. blanches.

To celebrate his award, Alex grabs an open beer bottle, jams it in his mouth, tilts his head back so the bottle stands fully upended, and drains its contents in two awe-inspiring gulps. Then he ejects the bottle with a thrust of his tongue and repeats the ritual with a new bottle. The twins squeal admiringly.

"Hey, I got an idea," says Roth, moving over to a picture window. Catching sight of him, the fans in the parking lot below emit a volley of whoops and whistles. Roth turns back to the anxious D.J.: "Why don't you play 'Everybody Wants Some!!' from the new album." As the sound of Alex's undulating jungle beat and Roth's Tarzan yodel booms out of the studio monitors, Roth pulls a chair over to the window and has one of the twins stand on it, her back to the kids in the parking lot.

When the song gets to its tawdry spoken passage, Roth lip-syncs the words and handles the twin like a prop: "I like the way the line runs up the back of the stockings," he mouths, hoisting the woman's skirt above her hips and tracing the seam on her left leg, from ankle to ass. Miming to the lyric, he tells the young woman to leave on her heels, turn a provocative pose, and show her legs from the side, up to her hip bone. The fans outside, including the females, greet every motion with clamorous, assenting hoots.

At the display's end, the grimacing D.J. swallows hard and tries to think of something to ask. After a few minutes, he says, "Uh, that reminds me. It was unbelievable at your show last night. The response was so enormous, you couldn't even hear yourself think."

Roth grins back triumphantly, then notes, "Would it be worth listening in the first place?"

ALEX VAN HALEN props himself on the edge of a dressing-room table and offers me a lenient smile. "Why *should* rock & roll be meaningful?" he asks in reply to a question about the seemingly slight themes of Van Halen's songs. "I mean, is *sex* . . ." He pauses, and a wistful smile curls his lips. "I was going to say, is sex meaningful, but I guess that's the whole point: If something feels good, then it's meaningful. And since our music is designed to make people feel good, it is meaningful."

Just then, the door swings wide and Roth struts in, pulling a tall, moon-eyed blond by the hand. "Go to another room," he directs us in a bearish voice. "Me and this lady got to talk."

Alex looks the woman up and down savoringly, then snickers. "Yeah, I bet you want to talk."

"There's an empty room across the hall," replies Roth, undaunted. "You guys can go over there." Then Roth spies my tape recorder and an inspired look crosses his face. "Okay, wait a minute. We'll give you an in-*depth* perspective of Van Halen." He turns back to the young woman. "What was your name again? Okay, look, darling, this guy is from a magazine and . . ."

The young woman sends a befuddled look in our direction and shakes her head. "You can't fool me. I know who that guy is. That's *Alex.*"

Alex laughs like a firecracker, and Roth looks embarrassed. "No, this guy *here*—he's from a magazine and is doing a story about us." Roth picks up the tape recorder and holds it up to the woman's face. "Just tell him what you think of us."

She looks even more confused. "You mean what I think of *Alex*?"

Alex erupts in laughter again, and Roth stares at the woman disgustedly. "No. *Not* Alex. Us. Tell the tape recorder what you think of *us.*"

"You want me to talk into this thing and say what I think about the band?"

"C'mon, babe, don't waste the man's time."

The young woman gives a shaky look, then takes the recorder. "Okay, here I am and they're asking me about Van Halen," she says with a quivery Midwestern accent. "What I think of Van Halen is that I enjoy the show very much, and they rock & roll definitely all the way. It's hard core, makes you want to move, makes you want to groove, makes you do anything you want to do. And for another thing," she adds, smiling broadly at Alex and Roth, "every *one* of the guys in this band knows how to get *down*—that's for *god*damn sure."

Roth pulls the recorder from her hand and gives it back to me with an uncertain smile. "I think maybe I just put my neck on the line."

Alex, still laughing hard, takes me by the elbow and steers me out of the room. "Can you believe," he says in a titillated whisper, "the mentality of some of these girls?"

W OMEN — SERVILE WOMEN, that is—are a matter of endless fascination to the members of Van Halen, as they are, indeed, to many male musicians. But during my stay with Van Halen, I've seen enough nude women and heard enough graphic, abasing morning-after anecdotes to fuel an article about porn-rock—or a diatribe against sexism. It doesn't seem, I tell Roth at one point, that Van Halen holds women in very high regard.

Roth looks surprised by the comment. "What are you talking about? I like women *very* much."

After pausing to hoot over his latest witticism, Roth continues: "I suppose you mean that rap earlier with the girl in the silk stockings? Well, *she* wore the stockings, I was merely complimenting her. That ain't sexist. What *you're* talking about is sexy feelings, and that's what Van Halen's striving to create. I mean, we don't have songs about *forcing* women to do anything. It takes two to tango, let us remember.

"As for me personally, I feel sexy a whole lot of the time. That's one of the reasons I'm in this job: to exercise my sexual fantasies. When I'm onstage, it's like doing it with twenty thousand of your closest friends. And that's a great relationship, because you never have to ask them, 'Did you come?' They'll let you know."

IN A SENSE, the intercourse that takes place between Van Halen and their audience may be more political than sexual. Whether the musicians accept it or not, Van Halen is a massive success because the band represents the real ideals of a massive audience. Or, to put it another way, the members of Van Halen may live the life they sing about, but they also sing about a life their audience reveres, even aspires to.

That idea comes across with resounding force at the group's second Cobo Arena show, where the howl of the crowd often rivals the squall of the band, until the two meet and meld in one deafening, indivisible roar. But the biggest clamor occurs when Roth sings the opening verse from Van Halen's current single, "And the Cradle Will Rock"—a smart and funny song about how the early 1980s heavy metal generation, like so many rock & roll upstarts that have preceded and will follow them, bewilder and frighten their elders. But it's also a song about how those elders fail to understand their own children, and how the young people's unrest amounts to a good deal "more than just an aggravation."

The crowd sings along from start to finish, in the process appropriating the song and raising it to anthemlike status.

A little later, as Roth rests backstage, I share my theory of heavy-metal political intercourse with him. He doesn't seem all that impressed.

"I don't speak for kids," he replies, "and I don't represent people. I'm simply one *of* the people. But I'll tell you this much: When that crowd out there tonight went nuts, they weren't going nuts because David Lee Roth is so cool, or because Van Halen is so hot. They went nuts because they were enjoying *themselves.*

"That's what we mean when we say there's a little Van Halen in all of us and we're just trying to bring it out. It's like something bursts inside of you, something that makes you not care what people around you are thinking. It makes you feel invincible—like, if a car hit you, nothin' would happen. It should make you feel like the Charge of the Light Brigade, even if you're just going to the bathroom. When you do that on a mass level, it becomes *hysterical,* not political. It expands to a large group of people not caring about conventions, just getting into the thrill of being themselves. That experience is about the audience, not us. All we do is provide the soundtrack."

Roth decides it's time to join the party in the outer room, but first he has a final comment to share about the audience: "When people ask how far I think I've come in this racket, I always say twelve feet—from the audience to the stage. And when this is all over—because you know how it goes in this business—I'm going back into that audience, and back to the streets."

One could pass that off as just another bit of bravado on Roth's part, but the statement says something vital and valid about Van Halen's appeal. Like some other rock writers I know, I used to entertain the fantasy that the heroism of punk would eclipse, even negate, the mindlessness of heavy metal.

But heavy metal, quite plainly, has remained the music of choice for most of America's young rock partisans, and Van Halen is a salient case in point why: They provide their audience with a heady, spectacular respite from the daily, drudging rhythms of common futility. That, plus an invitation to the party.

In the end, maybe that's no different—no better, no worse—than an offer of shelter from the storm.

PART 4

dreams

and

wars

bruce

springsteen's

america

On the night of November 5, 1980, Bruce Springsteen stood onstage in Tempe, Arizona, and began a fierce fight for the meaning of America. The previous day, the nation had turned a fateful corner: With a stunning majority, Ronald Reagan—who had campaigned to end the progressive dream in America—was elected president of the United States. It was hardly an unexpected victory. In the aftermath of Vietnam, Watergate, the hostage crisis in Iran, and an ongoing economic recession, America had developed serious doubts about its purpose and its future, and to many observers, Reagan seemed an inspiring and easy response to those hardships. But when all was said and done, the election felt stunning and brutal, a harbinger for the years of mean-spiritedness to come.

The singer was up late the night before, watching the election returns, and stayed in his hotel room the whole day, brooding over whether he should make a comment on the turn of events. Finally, onstage that night at Arizona State University, Springsteen stood silently for a moment, fingering his guitar nervously, and then told his audience: "I don't know what you guys think about what happened last night, but I think it was pretty frightening." Then he vaulted into an enraged version of his most defiant song, "Badlands."

On that occasion, "Badlands" stood for everything it had always stood for—a refusal to accept life's meanest fates or most painful limitations—but it also became something more: a warning about the spitefulness that was about to visit our land, as the social and political horizon turned dark and

---

frightening. "I want to spit in the face of these badlands," Springsteen sang with an unprecedented fury on that night, and it was perhaps in that instant that he reconceived his role in rock & roll.

In a way, his action foreshadowed the political activism and social controversy that would transform rock & roll during the 1980s. As the decade wore on, Springsteen would become one of the most outspoken figures in pop music, though that future probably wasn't what he had in mind when he vaulted into "Badlands" on that late autumn night. Instead, Springsteen was simply focusing on a question that, in one form or another, his music had been asking all along. In a way it was a simple and time-old question: Namely, what does it mean to be born an American?

WELL, WHAT DOES IT mean to be born in America? Does it mean being born to birthrights of freedom, opportunity, equity, and bounty? If so, then what does it mean that so many of the country's citizens never truly connect with or receive those blessings? And what does it mean that, in a land of such matchless vision and hope, the acrid realities of fear, repression, hatred, deprivation, racism, and sexism also hold sway? Does it mean, indeed, that we *are* living in badlands?

Questions of this sort—about America's nature and purpose, about the distance between its ideals and its truths—are, of course, as old as the nation itself, and finding revealing or liberating answers to those questions is a venture that has obsessed (and eluded) many of the country's worthiest artists, from Nathaniel Hawthorne to Norman Mailer, from D. W. Griffith to Francis Coppola. Rock & roll—an art form born of a provocative mix of American myths, impulses, and guilts—has also aimed, from time to time, to pursue those questions, to mixed effect. In the 1960s, in a period of intense generational division and political rancor, Bob Dylan and the Band explored the idea of America as a wounded family in works like *The Basement Tapes, John Wesley Harding,* and *The Band;* in the end, though, the artists shied from the subject, as if something about the American family's complex, troubled blood ties proved too formidable. Years later, Neil Young (like the Band's Robbie Robertson, a Canadian with a fixation on American myths) confronted the specter of forsworn history in works like *American Stars 'n' Bars, Hawks and Doves,* and *Freedom.* Yet, like too many artists or politicians who come face to face with how America has recanted its own best promises, Young finally didn't seem to know what to say about such losses. When all is said and done, it is chiefly pre-rock singers (most notably, Robert Johnson,

Hank Williams, Woody Guthrie, Charley Patton, and a few other early blues and country singers) and a handful of early rock & roll figures—Elvis Presley, Chuck Berry, Jerry Lee Lewis—who have come closest to personifying the meaning of America in their music. In particular, Presley (a seminal influence on Springsteen) tried to seize the nation's dream of fortune and make himself a symbol of it. But once Presley and those others had seized that dream, the dream found a way of undoing them—leading them to heartbreak, decline, death. American callings, American fates.

Bruce Springsteen followed his own version of the fleeting American Dream. He had grown up in the suburban town of Freehold, New Jersey, feeling estranged from his family and community, and his refusal to accept the limitations of that life fueled the songwriting in his early, largely autobiographical albums. Records like *Greetings from Asbury Park; The Wild, the Innocent and the E Street Shuffle;* and *Born to Run* were works about flight from dead-end small-town life and thankless familial obligations, and they accomplished for Springsteen the very dream that he was writing about: That is, those records lifted him from a life of mundane reality and delivered him to a place of bracing purpose. From the outset, Springsteen was heralded by critics as one of the brightest hopes in rock & roll—a consummate songwriter and live performer, who was as alluring and provoking as Presley, and as imaginative and expressive as Dylan. And Springsteen lived up to the hoopla: With his 1975 album *Born to Run,* Springsteen fashioned pop's most form-stretching and eventful major work since the Beatles' *Sgt. Pepper's Lonely Hearts Club Band.* But for all the praise and fame the album won him, it couldn't rid Springsteen of his fears of solitude, and it couldn't erase his memory of the lives of his family and friends. Consequently, his next work, *Darkness on the Edge of Town,* was a stark and often bitter reflection on how a person could win his dreams and yet still find himself dwelling in a dark and lonely place—a story of ambition and loss as ill-starred (and deeply American) as *Citizen Kane.*

With *The River,* released in 1980, Springsteen was still writing about characters straining against the restrictions of their world, but he was also starting to look at the social conditions that bred lives split between dilemmas of flight and ruin. In Springsteen's emerging mythos, people still had big hopes, but often settled for deluded loves and fated families, in which their hopes quickly turned ugly and caustic. In the album's haunting title song, the youthful narrator gets his girlfriend pregnant, and then enters a joyless marriage and a toilsome job in order to meet his obligations. Eventually, all the emotional and economic realities close in, and the singer's marriage turns into a living, grievous metaphor for lost idealism. "Now, all them things that seemed so important," sings Springsteen, in a rueful voice, "Well, mister, they vanished right into the air/Now I just act like I don't remember/Mary acts like she don't care." In *The River's* murky and desultory world—the world of post-Vietnam, post-industrial America—people long for fulfillment and connection, but often as not, they end up driving empty mean streets in after-midnight funks, fleeing from a painful nothingness into a more deadening nothingness. It's as if some dire force beyond their own temperaments was drawing them into inescapable ends.

The River was Springsteen's pivotal statement. Up to this point, Springsteen had told his tales in florid language, in musical settings that were occasionally operatic and showy. Now he was streamlining both the lyrics and the music into simpler, more colloquial structures, as if the realities he was trying to dissect were too bleak to bear up under his earlier expansiveness. *The River* was also the record with which Springsteen began wielding rock & roll less as a tool of personal mythology—that is, as a way of making or entering history for personal validation. Instead, he began using it as a means of *looking* at history, as a way of understanding how the lives of the people in his songs had been shaped by the conditions surrounding them, and by forces beyond their control.

This drive to comprehend history came to the fore during the singer's remarkable 1980–81 tour in support of *The River*. Springsteen had never viewed himself as a political-minded performer, but a series of events and influences—including the near-disaster at the Three Mile Island nuclear reactor, and his subsequent participation in the No Nukes benefit, at New York City's Madison Square Garden in September 1979—began to alter that perception. Springsteen had also read Joe Klein's biography of folk singer Woody Guthrie and was impressed with the way popular songs could work as a powerful and binding force for social consciousness and political action. In addition, he read Ron Kovic's harrowing personal account of the Vietnam War, *Born on the Fourth of July*. Inspired by the candor of Kovic's anguish—and by the bravery and dignity of numerous other Vietnam veterans he had met—Springsteen staged a benefit at the L.A. Sports Arena in August 1981, to raise funds and attention for the Vietnam Veterans of America (a group whose causes and rights the American Legion and Veterans of Foreign Wars had steadfastly refused to embrace). On one night of the Los Angeles engagement, Springsteen told his audience that he had recently read Henry Steele Commager and Allen Nevins' *Short History of the United States* and that he was profoundly affected by what he found in the book. A month earlier, speaking of the same book, he had told a New Jersey audience: "The idea [of America] was that there'd be a place for everybody, no matter where you came from . . . you could help make a life that had some decency and dignity to it. But like all ideals, that idea got real corrupted. . . . I didn't know what the government I lived under was doing. It's important to know . . . about the things around you." Now, onstage in Los Angeles, getting ready to sing Woody Guthrie's "This Land Is Your Land," Springsteen spoke in a soft, almost bashful voice, and told his largely well-off audience: "There's a lot in [the history of the United States] . . . that you're proud of, and then there's a lot of things in it that you're ashamed of. And that burden, that burden of shame, falls down. Falls down on everybody."

IN 1982, AFTER the tour ended, Springsteen was poised for the sort of massive breakthrough that people had been predicting for nearly a decade. *The River* had gone to the top of *Billboard*'s albums chart, and "Hungry Hearts" was a Top 10 single; it seemed that Springsteen was finally overcoming much of the popular backlash that had set in several years earlier, after numerous critics hailed him as rock & roll's imminent crown prince. But after the tour, the singer was unsure about what direction he wanted to take in his songwriting. He spent some time driving around the country, brooding, reading, thinking about the realities of his own emotional life and the social conditions around him, and then settled down and wrote a body of songs about his ruminations. On January 3, 1982, Springsteen sat in his home and recorded a four-track demo cassette of the new songs, accompanied for the most part only by his ghostly sounding acoustic guitar. He later presented the songs to producer Jon Landau and the E Street Band, but neither Landau nor the musicians could find the right way to flesh out the doleful, spare-sounding new material. Finally, at Landau's behest, Springsteen released the original demo versions of the songs as a solo effort, entitled *Nebraska*. It was a work like very few in pop music history: a politically piercing statement that was utterly free of a single instance of didactic sloganeering or ideological proclamation. Rather than preach to or berate his listeners, Springsteen created a vivid cast of characters—people who had been shattered by bad fortune, by limitations, by mounting debts and losses—and then he let those characters tell the stories of how their pain spilled over into despair and, sometimes, violence. In "Johnny 99," he told the story of a working man who is pressed beyond his resources and in desperation, commits robbery and impulsive murder. Johnny doesn't seek absolution for what he's done—he even requests his own execution, though more as an end than a payment—but he does earn our compassion. Just before sentence is passed, Johnny says: "Now judge I got debts no honest man could pay/The bank was holdin' my mortgage and they was takin' my house away/Now I ain't sayin' that makes me an innocent man/But it was more'n all this that put that gun in my hand." In "Highway Patrolman," Springsteen related the tale of an idealistic cop who allows his brother to escape the law, recognizing that the brother has already suffered pain from the country he once served.

There was a timeless, folkish feel to *Nebraska*'s music, but the themes and events it related were as dangerous and timely as the daily headlines of the 1980s—or of the 1990s, for that matter. It was a record about what can occur when normal people are forced to endure what cannot be endured. Springsteen's point was that, until we understood how these people arrived at their places of ruin, until we accepted our connection to those who had been hurt or excluded beyond repair, then America could not be free of such fates or such crimes. "The idea of America as a family is naive, maybe sentimental or simplistic," he told me in a 1987 interview, "but it's a good idea. And if people are sick and hurting and lost, I guess it falls on everybody to address those problems in some fashion. Because injustice, and the price of that injustice, falls on everyone's heads. The economic injustice falls on everybody's head and steals everyone's freedom. Your wife can't walk down the street at night. People keep guns in their homes. They live with a greater sense of apprehension, anxiety, and fear than they would in a more just and open society. It's not an accident, and it's not simply that there are 'bad' people out there. It's an inbred part of the way that we are all living: It's a product of what we have accepted, what we have acceded to. And whether we mean it or not, our silence has spoken for us in some fashion."

NEBRASKA ATTEMPTED TO make a substantial statement about the modern American sensibility in a stark and austere style that demanded close involvement. That is, the songs required that you settle into their mournful textures and racking tales and then apply the hard facts of their meaning to the social reality around you. In contrast to Springsteen's earlier bravado, there was nothing eager or indomitable about *Nebraska*. Instead, it was a record that worked at the opposite end of those conditions, a record about people walking the rim of desolation, who sometimes transform their despair into the irrevocable action of murder. It was not exulting or uplifting, and for that reason, it was a record that many listeners respected more than they "enjoyed." Certainly, it was not a record by which an artist might expand his audience in the fun-minded world of pop.

But with his next record, *Born in the U.S.A.*, in 1984, Springsteen set out to find what it might mean to bring his message to the largest possible audience. Like *Nebraska, Born in the U.S.A.* was about people who come to realize that life turns out harder, more hurtful, more close-fisted than they might have expected. But in contrast to *Nebraska*'s killers and losers, *Born in the U.S.A.*'s characters hold back the night as best they can, whether it's by singing, laughing, dancing, yearning, reminiscing, or entering into desperate love affairs. There was something celebratory about how these people faced their hardships. It's as if Springsteen were saying that life is made to endure and that we all make peace with private suffering and shared sorrow as best we can.

At the same time, a listener didn't have to dwell on these truths to appreciate the record. Indeed, Springsteen and Landau had designed the album with contemporary pop style in mind—which is to say, it had been designed with as much meticulous attention to its captivating and lively surfaces as to its deeper and darker meanings. Consequently, a track like "Dancing in the Dark"—perhaps the most pointed and personal song Springsteen has ever written about isolation—came off as a rousing dance tune that had the effect of working against isolation by pulling an audience together in a physical celebration. Similarly, "Cover Me," "Downbound Train," and "I'm on Fire"—songs about erotic fear and paralyzing loneliness—came off as sexy, intimate, and irresistible.

But it was the terrifying and commanding title song—about a Vietnam veteran who has lost his brother, his hope, and his faith in his country—that did the most to secure Springsteen's new image as pop hero and that also turned his fame into something complex and troubling. Scan the song for its lyrics alone, and you find a tale of outright devastation: a tale of an American whose birthrights have been torn from his grasp, and paid off with indelible memories of violence and ruin. But listen to the song merely for its fusillade of drums and its firestorm of guitar, or for the singer's roaring proclamation, "*BORN* in the U.S.A./I was *BORN* in the U.S.A.," and it's possible to hear it as a fierce patriotic assertion—especially in a political climate in which simpleminded patriotic fervor had attained a new and startling credibility. Watching Springsteen unfurl the song in concert—slamming it across with palpable rage as his audience waved flags of all sizes in response—it was possible to read the song in both directions at once. "Clearly the key to the enormous explosion of Bruce's popularity is the misunderstanding [of the song 'Born in the U.S.A']," wrote critic Greil Marcus during the peak of Springsteen's popularity. "He is a tribute to the fact that people hear what they want."

One listener who was quite happy to hear only what he wanted was syndicated conservative columnist George Will, who in the middle of the

1984 campaign that pitted Walter Mondale against Ronald Reagan attended a Springsteen show, and liked what he saw. In a September 14, 1984, column that was read by millions, Will commended Springsteen for his "elemental American values" and, predictably, heard the cry of "Born in the U.S.A." as an exultation rather than as pained fury. "I have not got a clue about Springsteen's politics, if any," Will wrote, "but flags get waved at his concerts while he sings about hard times. He is no whiner, and the recitation of closed factories and other problems always seem punctuated by a grand, cheerful affirmation: 'Born in the U.S.A.!' "

Apparently, Reagan's advisors gave a cursory listening to Springsteen's music and agreed with Will. A few days later, in a campaign stop in New Jersey, President Ronald Reagan declared: "America's future rests in a thousand dreams inside your hearts. It rests in the message of hope in songs of a man so many young Americans admire: New Jersey's Bruce Springsteen. And helping you make those dreams come true is what this job of mine is all about."

It was an amazing—even brain-boggling—assertion. Reagan's tribute to Springsteen seemed about as stupefying as if Lyndon Johnson, during the awful uproar over Vietnam, had cited Bob Dylan for his noble influence on America's youth politics, or as unnerving as if Richard Nixon, with his strong disregard for black social realities, had honored Sly Stone for the cutting commentary of his 1971 classic, *There's a Riot Goin' On*. Clearly, to anybody paying attention, the fierce, hard-bitten vision of America that Springsteen sang of in "Born in the U.S.A." was a far cry from the much-touted "new patriotism" that Reagan and many of his fellow conservatives claimed as their private dominion. And yet there was also something damnably brilliant in the way the president sought to attach his purposes to Springsteen's views. It was the art of political syllogism, taken to its most arrogant extreme. Reagan saw himself as a definitional emblem of America; Bruce Springsteen was a singer who, apparently, extolled America in his work; therefore, Springsteen must be exalting Reagan as well—which would imply that, if one valued the music of Springsteen, then one should value (and support) Reagan as well. Reagan was manipulating Springsteen's fame as an affirmation of his own ends.

The president's gambit left Springsteen with a knotty challenge: Could he afford to refute Reagan's praise without also alienating his newly acquired mass audience? Or should he use the occasion to challenge the beliefs of that audience—maybe, in the process, helping to reshape those beliefs? *Or* should he simply ignore the hubbub, and assume that his true fans understood his viewpoint?

A few nights later, Springsteen stood before a predominantly blue-collar audience in Pittsburgh and, following a rousing performance of "Atlantic City" (a song about American decay), decided to respond to the president's statement. "The president was mentioning my name the other day," he said with a bemused laugh, "and I kinda got to wondering what his favorite album might have been. I don't think it was the *Nebraska* album. I don't think it was this one." Springsteen then played a passionate, acoustic-backed version of "Johnny 99"—the song about a man who commits impulsive murder as a way of striking back against the meanness of the society around him—a song he wrote, along with other *Nebraska* tunes, in response to the malignant public and political atmosphere that had been fostered by Reagan's social policies.

Springsteen's comments were well-placed: *Was* this the America Ronald Reagan heard clearly when he claimed to listen to Springsteen's music? An America where dreams of well-being had increasingly become the province of the privileged, and in which jingoistic partisans determined the nation's health by a standard of self-advantage? When Reagan heard a song like "My Hometown," did he understand his own role in promoting the disenfranchisement the song described? If Reagan *truly* understood that the enlivening patriotism of "Born in the U.S.A." was a patriotism rooted in pain, discontent, and fury, perhaps he would have been either a better president or an angrier man. More likely, of course, he probably would have dismissed any such notions with his characteristic shrug of contempt—which is no doubt what he did when he finally heard of Springsteen's response.

But Reagan's attempt to co-opt Springsteen's message also had some positive side effects. For one thing, it made plain that Springsteen now commanded a large and vital audience of young Americans who cared deeply about their families, their futures, and their country, and that Springsteen spoke to—and perhaps *for*—that audience's values in ways that could not be ignored. The imbroglio also forced Springsteen to become more politically explicit and resourceful at his performances. After Pittsburgh, he began meeting with labor and civil rights activists in most of the cities that he played, and he made statements at his shows, asking his audience to lend their support to the work of such activists. He also spoke out more and more plainly about where he saw America headed, and how he thought rock & roll could play a part in effecting that destiny. One evening in Oakland, when introducing "This Land Is Your Land," he said: "If you talk to the steelworkers out there who have lost their jobs, I don't know if they'd believe this song is what we're about anymore. And maybe we're not. As we sit here, [this song's promise] is eroding every day. And with countries, as with people, it's easy to let the best of yourself slip away. Too many people today feel as if America has slipped away, and left them standing behind." Then he sang the best song written about America, in as passionate a voice as it had ever been sung.

But none of this action was enough. In November 1984, Ronald Reagan was reelected president by an even more stunning mandate than the first time. It seemed plausible that many (if not most) of the millions of fans of voting age who had made *Born in the U.S.A.* the year's biggest success had cast their votes for the man to whom Springsteen so obviously stood in opposition. Perhaps it nettled him, but Springsteen was finally facing the answer to the question he had been asking during the length of the decade: To be born in America, to be passionate about the nation's best ideals and to be concerned over the betrayal of those ideals, meant being part of a nation that would only believe about itself what it wanted to believe. It also meant that one still had to find a way to keep faith with the dream of that nation, despite the awful realities that take shape when that dream is denied.

IN 1984, AMERICA had not had enough of Ronald Reagan, or it would not have reelected him. It had also not had enough of Bruce Springsteen: After an international tour, he returned to the States a bigger, more popular artist than ever. It may seem like a contradiction that a nation can embrace two icons who differed so dramatically, but the truth is, Reagan and Springsteen shared an unusual bond: Each seemed to stand for America, and yet each also was largely misunderstood by his constituency. Reagan seemed to stand for the values of family and improved opportunity for the working class at the same time that he enacted policies that undermined those values. Springsteen seemed to stand for brazen patriotism when he believed in holding the government responsible for how it had corrupted the nation's best ideals and promises.

To his credit, Springsteen did his best to make his true values known. In the autumn of 1985, he embarked on the final leg of his *Born in the U.S.A.* tour, this time playing outdoor stadium-sized venues that held up to 100,000 spectators. Playing such vast settings was simply a way of keeping faith with the ambition he had settled on a year or two earlier: to see what it could mean to reach the biggest audience he could reach. It was also an attempt to speak seriously to as many of his fans as possible, to see if something like a genuine consensus could be forged from the ideals of a rock & roll community. And of course, the gesture also entailed a certain risk: If Springsteen's audience could not—or would not—accept him for what he truly stood for, then in the end, he could be reduced by that audience.

In some surprising respects, Springsteen's ambition succeeded. At the beginning of the stadium swing, many fans and critics worried that he would lose much of his force—and his gifts for intimacy and daring—by moving his music to such large stages. But if anything, Springsteen used the enlarged settings as an opportunity to rethink many of his musical arrangements, transforming the harder songs into something more fervid, more moving, more aggressive than before, and yet still putting across the more rueful songs from *The River* and *Nebraska* with an uncompromised sensitivity. If anything, he made the new shows count for more than the election-year shows, if only because he recognized that addressing a larger audience necessarily entailed some greater responsibilities. In Washington, D.C., on the opening night of the stadium shows, Springsteen told a story about a musician friend from his youth who was drafted and who, because he did not enjoy the privilege of a deferment, was sent to Vietnam and wound up missing in action. "If the time comes when there's another war, in some place like Central America," Springsteen told his audience of 56,000, "then you're going to be the ones called on to fight it, and you're going to have to decide for yourselves what that means. . . . But if you want to know where we're headed for [as a country], then someday take that long walk from the Lincoln Memorial to the Vietnam Veterans Memorial, where the names of all those dead men are written on the walls, and you'll see what the stakes are when you're born in the U.S.A. in 1985." By the last few nights of the tour, at the Los Angeles Memorial Coliseum, he had added Edwin Starr's 1970 hit "War" to the show, coming down hard on the line, "Induction, destruction/ Who wants to die—in a war?" There was something heartening about watching a man who gazed into his audience and who—in defiance of the country's political mood and perhaps even the beliefs of that audience—cared enough about them to hope they would not die in a futile or demoralizing military action.

But for all his intensified fervor, Springsteen was gracious at the end of the tour. At the end of "Dancing in the Dark," in that moment when he generally pulled a female fan from the audience to dance with, Springsteen brought out his new wife, Julianne Phillips, danced with her sweetly, then took her in his arms and gave her a long kiss. Maybe it was his way of saying that this new relationship was where he would live, now that his tour was ending; or perhaps that his marriage was a way of attempting to live up to the best ideals of his own music. Later, at evening's end, Springsteen stood before his band, his friends, and his audience and said: "This has been the greatest year of my life. I want to thank you for making me feel like the luckiest man in the world." Indeed, Springsteen had begun the tour as a mass cult figure; he was leaving it as a full-fledged pop hero—a voice of egalitarian conscience unlike any rock had yielded before, with a remarkable capacity for growth and endurance.

In short, Springsteen seemed to emerge from the tour occupying the center of rock & roll, in the way that Presley, or the Beatles and Dylan and the Rolling Stones had once commanded the center. And yet the truth was, in 1980s pop, there was no center left to occupy. Rock was a field of mutually exclusive options, divided along racial, stylistic, and ideological lines, and each option amounted to its own valid mainstream. In fact, by the decade's end, even the American and British fields of rock—which had dominated the pop world thoroughly for a quarter-century—were gradually losing their purism and dominance, as more and more young and adventurous musicians and fans began bringing African, Jamaican, Brazilian, Asian, and other musical forms into interaction with pop's various vernaculars. In modern pop, as in the modern globe, America no longer overwhelmed the international sensibility.

In any event, Springsteen seemed to step back from rock & roll's center at the same moment that he won it. In 1986, he assembled a multidisc package of some of his best performances from the previous ten years of live shows—a box set intended as a summation of his artistic growth and his range as a showman. In a sense, it was the most ambitious effort of his career, but also the least satisfying and least consequential. It didn't play with the sort of revelatory effect of his best shows or earlier albums, and it didn't captivate a mass audience in the same way either. Then, the following year, Springsteen released *Tunnel of Love*. Like *Nebraska*, the work with which he had begun the decade, *Tunnel of Love* was a more intimate, less epic statement than its predecessor—a heartbreaking but affirming suite of songs about the hard realities of romantic love. Maybe the record was intended to remind both Springsteen and his audience that what ultimately mattered was how one applied one's ideals to one's own world—or maybe the songs were simply about the concerns that obsessed Springsteen most at that time. In any event, *Tunnel of Love* was one of Springsteen's most affecting works, and it fit into his life with painfully ironic timing. A few months later, Springsteen separated from his wife of three years, Julianne Phillips, and was rumored to be seeing the backing vocalist in his band, Patti Scialfa. Eventually, Springsteen divorced Phillips and married Scialfa. In life, as in music, sometimes one's best hopes take unexpected, somewhat hurtful turns.

At the end of the decade, Springsteen was on tour again. Reluctant to continue playing oversized venues, he returned to the arena halls where he had done some of his most satisfying work in the years before, and restored a more human scale to his production. It was another election year, and while he still spoke out about issues from time to time, Springsteen seemed wary of being cast as merely a rock politician or statesman. Perhaps he realized that America's political choices just couldn't be affected very tellingly from a rock & roll stage, or maybe he was simply discouraged by what he saw around him. To be sure, there was plenty to be disheartened about: It was a season when Oliver North enjoyed status as a cultural hero, and when George Bush turned patriotism and flag-waving into brutal, vicious, and effective campaign issues. (Though one night in New Jersey, in a burst of inspiring temper, Springsteen went on record with an electoral choice of sorts. "Don't vote for that fucking Bush," he told his audience, "no matter what!")

At the same time, Springsteen remained committed to the idea of turning the rock & roll audience into an enlightened and active community. After the *Tunnel of Love* tour, he headlined Amnesty International's Human Rights Now! world tour in the fall of 1988. Along with Live Aid, the Amnesty tour was one of the most ambitious political campaigns in rock's history. And the fact that it could occur at all and could reach an audience that was both massive and ready was in some ways a testament to the sort of idealism for which Springsteen had fought throughout the 1980s.

WITH HIS FIRST records in the 1990s, Springsteen retreated further from his role as an icon and spokesperson, and attempted to redefine the scope of his songwriting. *Human Touch* and *Lucky Town* (the double offering from 1992), worked on smaller scales: They were dark and complex works about personal risks, and as such, they seemed to say much about the internal realities of Springsteen's own life, as he went from a highly publicized failed marriage to an apparently sounder second one, in which he became the father of three children. It was as if, in both his art and his life, Springsteen was attempting to say that to make your best hopes and ideals count for anything real, you have to bring them into your own home and heart, and see if you can live up to them.

Meantime, though, much changed about the larger family that Springsteen and the rest of us live in—that tormented home we still call America— and too little of it for the better. Back in the 1980s there was a vital argument to be waged about what it meant to be an American, and which visions and dreams best delineated our collective soul and destiny. In the 1990s, that argument hasn't been settled so much as it's been shunted to the side, or compromised between the maleficence of a Republican Congress and the artful ambitions of Bill Clinton's presidency. Some of our most valuable and necessary instruments of economic opportunity and social justice have been curtailed or ended—tools such as affirmative action, immigration rights, and welfare protection for children and families in poverty conditions—and our criminal justice system is imprisoning poor and young people at increasing rates (indeed, no other democracy in the world locks up as many of its citizens as America). The message is clear: No more help for people on the fringe, no more chances for the losers. These are pitiless times, and there have been too few voices in either our arts or our politics who dare to tell us that the America we are making will be a more perilous, bloodier place than we might ever have imagined.

The 1995 album *The Ghost of Tom Joad* was Bruce Springsteen's response to this state of affairs—you could even call it his return to arms. In any event, it was his first overtly social-minded statement since *Born in the U.S.A.*, eleven years earlier. *Joad* isn't an easy record to like immediately. Its music is often sorrowful and samely, its words soft-spoken, sometimes slurred. In addition, it creates an atmosphere as merciless in its own way as the world it talks about. That is, it is a record about people who do *not* abide life's ruins—a collection of dark tales about dark men who are cut off from the purposes of their own hearts and the prospects of their own lives. In this album, almost none of the characters get out with both their beings and spirits intact, and the few who do are usually left with only frightful and desolate prayers as their solace. "My Jesus," Springsteen intones at one song's end, "your gracious love and mercy/Tonight I'm sorry could not fill my heart/Like one good rifle/And the name of who I ought to kill." At the end of another song, a man prays: "When I die I don't want no part of heaven/I would not do heaven's work well/I pray the devil comes and takes me/To stand in the fiery furnaces of hell." Plaintive, bitter epiphanies like these are far removed from the sort of anthemic cries that once filled Springsteen's music, but then, these are times for lamentations, not anthems.

On the surface, *Tom Joad* bears obvious kinship to *Nebraska*. Like that album, *Joad*'s musical backings are largely acoustic, and its sense of language and storytelling owes much to the Depression-era sensibility of Guthrie and such authors as John Steinbeck, James M. Cain, John Fante, and Eric Knight (the author of *You Play the Black and the Red Comes Up*). The stories are told bluntly and sparsely, and the poetry is broken and colloquial, like the speech of a man telling the stories he feels compelled to tell, if only to try and be free of them. That's where the similarities end. In *Nebraska*, Springsteen wrote about people living their lives at the edges of hopelessness and suppression—people whose lives could turn dangerous and explode—and the music conveyed not just their melancholy but, at moments, also their escape into rage. In *Tom Joad*, there are few such escapes and almost no musical relief from the numbing circumstances of the characters' lives. You could almost say that the music gets caught in meandering motions, or drifts into circles that never break. The effect is brilliant and lovely—there's something almost lulling in the music's blend of acoustic arpeggios and moody keyboard textures, something that lures you into the melodies' dark dreaminess and loose mellifluence. But make no mistake: what you are being drawn into are scenarios of hell. American hell.

Many of *Tom Joad*'s characters are caught in this place, waiting for some event to make sense of their existence, or to explain to them their fates. You get the picture right at the start, in the broken cadences of the title track. A man sits by a campfire under a bridge, not far from endless railroad tracks. He is waiting on the ghost of Tom Joad, the hero of John Steinbeck's *The Grapes of Wrath*, who at the end of John Ford's 1940 film version of the novel, says: " 'Wherever there's somebody fightin' for a place to stand/Or decent job or a helpin' hand/Wherever somebody's strugglin' to be free/Look in their eyes . . . you'll see me.' " But such hopes of salvation in the mid-1990s aren't really much more palpable than ghosts, and the man sitting, praying by the fire, will wait a long time before his deliverance comes. In "Straight Time," an ex-con takes a job and marries, and tries to live the sanctioned life. But the world's judgments are never far off—even his wife watches him carefully with their children—and he waits for the time when he will slip back into the deadly breach that he sees as his destiny. In "Highway 29," a lonesome shoe clerk surrenders to a deadly sexual fever that leads him into an adventure of robbery and murder and ruin, and he realizes that it is *this*—this dead-ended flight of rage and self-obliteration—that his heart has always been headed for.

The most affecting stories on *Joad*, though, are the ones that Springsteen tells about a handful of undocumented immigrants, and their passage into Southern California's promised land. Some of these tales are drawn from real-life instances, as reported in the *Los Angeles Times*. In "The Line"—an achingly beautiful song, with a melody reminiscent of Bob Dylan's "Love Minus Zero/No Limit"—a border patrol cop falls in love with an immigrant woman, Louisa, and he helps her and her child and younger brother sneak into the States. But in a confrontation with another officer, he loses track of her, and never again finds her. In "Sinaloa Cowboys," two young brothers, Miguel and Louis, come from north Mexico to the San Joaquin Valley orchards to make money for their hungry families, and get involved in dangerous and illegal drug manufacturing. One night there is an explosion in the shack where they work; one brother is killed, and the other is left to bury him and tell their family. And in "Balboa Park," an undocumented teenage immigrant called Spider gets caught up working in San Diego as a sex hustler and drug smuggler, until one night, during a border patrol, he becomes victim of a hit-and-run. These people come to their fates quickly—much like that doomed planeload in Woody Guthrie's "Deportees"—one of the first songs that awakened Springsteen's political awareness. In one moment, these characters' "undocumented" lives are over, and the world takes no note of their passing or shot hopes.

People like Spider, Louisa, Miguel, and Louis are not people we hear much about in the popular music and literature of our time. In fact, they are the people that politicians like California governor Pete Wilson and Republican presidential candidate Pat Buchanan tell us are part of our national problem: folks who do not speak our language or share our birthrights. It is a testament to Bruce Springsteen's continuing vitality as one of our greatest writers that he has found the stories of these people—and the stories of the other characters caught in *Tom Joad*'s lower depths—worthy of being comprehended and told. By climbing into these people's hearts and minds, Springsteen has given voice to people who rarely have one in this culture—and that has always been one of rock & roll's most important virtues: giving voice to people who are typically denied expression in our other arts and media. In the midst of confusing and complex times, Bruce Springsteen has written more honestly, more intelligently, and more compassionately about America than any other writer of the last generation. As we move into the rough times and badlands that lie ahead, such acts might count for more than ever before.

the

problem of

michael jackson

In the 1980s, when I was pop music critic for the *Los Angeles Herald Examiner*, I wrote about Michael Jackson more than almost any other single pop figure of the time. I almost wish I hadn't. In the pages that follow, I'll try to trace and explain some of what it was that caught me about Jackson, and what it was that eventually left me feeling disillusioned and saddened about him.

THIS FIRST PIECE ran in the *Herald* on April 11, 1983. It appears here with only slight editing:

> Everywhere this last season I've heard this animating sound. It begins with taut, maddened, funk-infused guitar lines that scramble against the upsweeping curve of a string section in a heady depiction of emotional panic. Then a high-end, sensually imploring voice enters the fray and imposes elegance and resolution upon the panic: What does it mean, the singer seems to ask in a breathtaking voice, that he is the one who is appointed to dance alone, for our pleasure, and attention? The song is Michael Jackson's "Billie Jean," and it has suddenly, surely, become one of the most ubiquitous—and exciting—breakthrough singles in recent pop history.

Whenever a song becomes as madly popular as "Billie Jean," it can be fun to examine the reasons why: Is it simply the appeal of the music's exacting but impelling sound? The fine phrasing and tremulous emotion at play against one another in the singer's voice? The allure of the artist's personality or celebrity?

In the case of "Billie Jean," it is a bit of all of these things. Clearly, since a string of brilliant childhood triumphs with the Jackson 5 (the last great 1960s-style Motown group), the now-twenty-two-year-old Michael Jackson has long been one of soul *and* rock's most stirring singers. But it wasn't until 1979's *Off the Wall* that he stood out as a mature, stylish vocal force in his own right. For that reason, as much as for the memorable songwriting of Stevie Wonder, Paul McCartney, and Rod Temperton, or the ravishing production of Quincy Jones, the record proved one of the most consistently exuberant (and popular) black pop works of the last ten years.

It came as a surprise, then, that at first few listenings, Jackson's long-awaited follow-up, *Thriller*, seemed somewhat disappointing. Quincy Jones—whose elegant but edgy arrangements on *Off the Wall* exalted Jackson's evocative vocalizing in much the same manner Nelson Riddle's graceful, rousing work once enlivened Frank Sinatra—had taken to displaying both dominating and overprudent instincts in his recent work. As a result, he seemed to restrict Jackson on much of *Thriller* to a catchy but somewhat tame brand of dance-floor romanticism.

Indeed, the boldest sounding tracks on the album were the ones Jackson himself had the strongest hand in writing, producing, and arranging: "Wanna be Startin' Somethin'," "Beat It," and "Billie Jean." After hearing these songs find their natural life on radio, it became evident that they were something more than exceptional highlights. They were in fact the heart of the matter: a well-conceived body of passion, rhythm, and structure that defined the sensibility—if not the inner life—of the artist behind them.

These were instantly compelling songs about emotional and sexual claustrophobia, about hard-earned adulthood, and about a newfound brand of resolution that seeks to work as an arbiter between the artist's fears and the inescapable fact of his celebrity. "Wanna be Startin' Somethin' " had the sense of a vitalizing nightmare in its best lines. (Especially in the lines in which he describes himself as a sort of vegetable, being devoured for his fame and oddness.) "Billie Jean," meantime, exposed the ways in which the interaction between the artist's fame and the outside world might invoke soul-killing dishonor ("People always told me . . . be careful of what you do 'cause the lie becomes the truth," Jackson sings, possibly thinking of a debilitating paternity charge from a while back). And "Beat It," in many ways the album's toughest song, was pure anger: In its relentless depiction of violence as an enforced social style, it conveyed terror and invincibility almost as effectively as Grandmaster Flash and the Furious Five's "The Message."

But the ultimate excitement here is that "Billie Jean" is merely a first step. When Michael Jackson performed the show a couple of weeks ago at Motown's twenty-fifth anniversary bash (in what was one of his first public acts as a star outside and beyond the Jacksons), it was startlingly clear that he is not only one of the most thrilling live performers in pop music, but that he is perhaps more capable of inspiring an audience's physical and emotional imagination than any single pop artist since Elvis Presley—and I don't know anyone who came away from that occasion with a differing view.

There are simply times when you know you are hearing or seeing something extraordinarily fine and exciting, something that simply captures all the private hopes and dreams that you have ever wanted your favorite art form to aspire to, and that might unite and inflame a new audience. That time came for those of us who saw Jackson onstage that night, and now every time I hear "Billie Jean," I have a vivid image of one of rock & roll's brightest hopes. "Billie Jean" is the sound of a young man staking out his territory—a young man who is just starting to lay claim to his rightful pop legend.

FROM THERE, things went up—far up—and then far down. *Thriller* went on to place an unprecedented seven singles in *Billboard*'s Top 10, and also became the biggest-selling album in pop history (over 35 million copies, or something like that), and at the 1984 Grammy Awards Show, Michael Jackson captured eight awards, including Best Album and Best Record of the year. Then, a few months later, it was announced that Michael would be setting out on a nationwide tour with his brothers, the Jacksons. By that time, the massiveness of Jackson's fame was already starting to work against him—

and the controversies that started surrounding the Jacksons' Victory tour (as it was billed) only made matters far worse. For one thing, there were fears that Jackson's popularity would attract such large crowds that something horrible might result—something like the crowd rush that occurred at a 1979 Who show in Cincinnati, where eleven young people were trampled to death or smothered. Also, there were charges of greed: The Jacksons were charging as much as thirty dollars a ticket, and had also accepted the multimillion-dollar sponsorship of the Pepsi company.

The tour began in Kansas City, Missouri, in July 1984, and days before the group ever hit a stage, things had gone weird and awry. At times—what with the tireless histrionics of promoter Don King (who said that anybody who saw the Jacksons' show "will be a better person for years to come") and the manner in which local politicians and sports officials ingratiated themselves with the Jacksons' organization—it was easy to forget that this was primarily to be a musical event, featuring one of the more popular and captivating performing groups in pop's recent history.

Unfortunately, that fact seemed lost even on the Jacksons. When the group finally took the stage at Kansas City's Arrowhead stadium, amid curls of purple smoke and crimson laser beams, some of the reporters were eyeing the crowd for signs of the much-predicted hysteria. We never found them. Instead, what we saw was an overwhelmingly white, affluent-looking audience of forty-five thousand fans—largely parents and children—exhibiting a kind of polite exhilaration at the vision of Jackson going through his trademark, impossibly adept maneuvers. It was good, of course, that there was no mob hysteria (in fact, I doubt if there was so much as a scratch in the audience that night), but it also would have been nice had there been something of real excitement taking place onstage. But on this night, Michael and his brothers—Marlon, Jermaine, Tito, and Randy—didn't work as effectively as a cooperative unit as they did on their 1981 tour. For that matter, the best collaboration I saw that whole night came from a clique of about five black and white tots standing in the aisle near my seat, dancing in joyful abandon with one another, trading quick, sharp, fancy moves in a fun and funky exchange, mimicking the action they saw onstage (or rather, on the large screen *above* the stage). When I looked closer I realized they were all wearing the souvenir Michael-style sunglasses that were being sold at the arena, and then I realized that for these kids this was truly a transfixing dream that no amount of critical scrutiny might ever obscure or alter.

Well, good for them, because for some of the rest of us, the whole thing really wasn't that much fun. Much of the press that came to Kansas City wanted *something* to be critical of, and the Jacksons had unwittingly served that interest with the displays of apparent greed and incompetence that preceded the tour. Worse, they delivered a show that didn't work—a show that proved too susceptible to the allure of spectacle, as if an epic display of technology and stagecraft might also count as substance and excitement. Simply, the group was overwhelmed by its own trappings—forced into a position in which it attempted to connect with the audience through predictable displays of pyrotechnics and flashy mechanics rather than by force of their own performing matter. (The audience, it must be said, seemed to enjoy it all: Musical art and physical mastery be damned, give us the BOMB!) It was frustrating to watch a performer as resourceful as Michael Jackson succumb to such a grandiose and ultimately unimaginative interpretation of his art.

The problem was, Michael Jackson should never have done the 1984 tour in this way. He was unquestionably beyond the Jacksons by this time, and he seemed constrained in his role as a frontman for a group he truly no longer felt a part of. By all rights and reason, Michael should have been working a stage alone. After all, his best performances worked as public declarations of intensely private fears; that's the quality that gave his art whatever anxious depth it possessed at that time. The 1984 tour was to be Jackson's way of paying off—and breaking off—family ties, but what it would cost him, in a way, was that moment he had finally captured, after a lifetime of waiting.

A MONTH LATER I was in New York City to attend the New Music Seminar, during the same week in which the Jacksons were playing several dates at the city's Madison Square Garden. By this time, the skepticism and suspicion that had greeted the tour's start in Kansas City had turned into outright hostility in some quarters—most of it directed at Michael Jackson himself. On more than one occasion, when Jackson's name would be cited during panels at the New Music Seminar as somebody who had helped dispel some of the racial barriers in the 1980s pop scene, the notion was met with jeers.

This is what is called "backlash," and in the case of Michael Jackson it was not a simple or pretty matter. To be honest, some of the anger directed at Jackson had to do with the press's notion that somehow Michael and his brothers were simply the latest case of pop-cultural hype—a charge that was also frequently leveled at Elvis Presley and the Beatles in the early stages of their mass fame. Clearly, there is a big difference between what Michael Jackson represented to his audience (an instinctual physical and emotional savvy meant to turn personal fear into public celebration) and what Presley and the Beatles represented to theirs (good, old-fashioned youth-cultural disruption). Yet all these artists shared one thing: They bound together millions of otherwise dissimilar people in not just a quirk of shared taste, but also a forceful, heartfelt consensus that spoke to common dreams and era-rooted values. In 1984, it wasn't yet clear whether Jackson would go on to have the continuing momentum or epic sweep of Presley and the Beatles, but at the time I thought it likely that his mass popularity represented something more significant than the incidental mass appeal of such artists as Peter Frampton or the Bee Gees. Looking back, I think I was both right and wrong—and I'm not sure which likelihood today disturbs me more.

I remember a friend telling me, during that New York visit, "If Jackson had never gone out on this tour, I would still resent him, and so would other people. The awful thing is, Jackson consciously wanted the biggest audience in the world, but he didn't want to give them anything too revealing or risky."

This was true: Michael Jackson wanted it all, and got it. It is obvious, in retrospect, that *Thriller* was designed with mass crossover audiences in mind. Jackson put out "Billie Jean" for the dance crowd, "Beat It" for the white rockers, and then followed each crossover with crafty videos designed to enhance both his intense allure and his intense inaccessibility. But as a ploy, was that really such a bad thing? Was it, for that matter, any different than what Elvis Presley did with his hillbilly/blues/rock & roll crossover music, and what he accomplished in his Dorsey Brothers and Ed Sullivan TV appearances? In fact, wasn't Presley initially a song and dance act, somebody who captured the moment of a transition in pop culture, somebody who took his personal fearfulness and made a public passion out of it, and won intense mass affection as a result? Didn't Presley, too, set out to capture the biggest audience in the world—and isn't that still (at least for some people) one of the most evident dreams pop can aspire to? Why, then, did we need to condemn Michael Jackson for his popularity?

The truth is, by the mid-1980s, some music partisans just weren't terribly fond of the idea of Presley- or Beatles-sized popularity anymore (and that's even more the case in the late 1990s). That, plus the notion that Jackson didn't, for some, really fit the modern definition of a pop hero: He wasn't somebody with literary or sociopolitical aspirations or dreams of sexual revolution. But as another thoughtful friend pointed out to me, there was an even touchier problem about Jackson's success—one that made the temporary vexations of the Jacksons tour seem paltry. "What turned me off to him," this critic told me, "was his eagerness to trade his former black constituency for an overwhelmingly white audience. Plain and simple, he doesn't want a black identity anymore. He records with proven white stars like Paul McCartney and Mick Jagger, and he's allowed the tickets to be priced so high for this tour as to exclude the majority of working or young black fans in this country. Just look at the makeup of these audiences—*barely* ten percent black. But what really drove the nail into the coffin is that Jackson appeared at the White House with Ronald Reagan. That announced to everybody that he'd divorced himself from the concerns of the black audience at large."

I couldn't argue with that one. Certainly, it would have been better if Jackson had refused the invitation to the White House, in protest of the administration's anti-black policies. It would have been even nicer if he had openly repudiated Reagan. Still, many of our best pop stars have made some unworthy choices, including Elvis Presley and James Brown aligning themselves with Richard Nixon—and don't forget, Neil Young was once an outspoken fan of Reagan (though he reportedly later switched to Jesse Jackson—weird guy, that Neil). As fans, we can boycott or condemn our pop heroes for such lapses, or mourn their tastes in politics while marveling at their artistic sensibilities. I've been doing the latter with Frank Sinatra for more years than I care to count.

Interestingly enough, about the only person I heard defend Jackson during my New York visit was James Brown, and it almost cost him the affection of a fawning music business audience. The moment came at the New Music Seminar during the artists panel that featured Brown, among others. A member of the audience asked the panel what an artist's responsibility is to his fans, given the outrageous prices the Jacksons had imposed on their following. Brown agreed that the ticket price was unrealistic, regardless of the tour's supposed overhead costs, but went on to say that he didn't think it fair to expatriate Michael Jackson or his brothers on the basis of their bad business sense. "It's a mistake, let's hope it doesn't happen again, but believe me, these are good people. Give them another chance."

Cries of angry disagreement shot up from the floor. The mood in the room became riled, like that of a piqued political caucus. But Brown stood his ground. "You don't really know what Michael had to go through to make this tour happen. I won't stay here and let you attack somebody who isn't present to defend himself."

What Brown didn't mention is that he had reportedly declined Michael Jackson's invitation to sing with the group at Madison Square Garden because he privately felt the ticket prices would exclude any real soul audience. He could have scored big and easy points with the NMS crowd by divulging that, but it was a testament to his integrity, and to his respect for the difficulty of Michael Jackson's position with the press and public, that he kept his censure measured, and made his defense sound reasoned.

Of course, it would have been even better if Jackson had expressed more concern for the audience who sustained him during his singular rise to pop stardom. But like Presley before him, Michael Jackson was now in uncharted territory, and every move he made would either map out his redemption or his ruin.

THE JACKSON'S TOUR came to its close in early December 1984, with six sold-out performances at Los Angeles' Dodger Stadium. I almost skipped the whole thing. I was weary of all the arguments and vitriol surrounding Michael Jackson by this time, plus I'd already seen the show in Kansas City and Manhattan, and the experience hadn't been worth either trip. But on the tour's last night, I went. It was my job.

As it turned out, this was the only Victory tour show I saw that had a good dose of something that the other dates had lacked: namely, Michael Jackson's unbridled passion. Let me say it without apology: It was a hell of a thing to see.

Pass it off, if you like, as Jackson's possible sense of relief at leaving the long debacle behind, but from his wild, impossibly liquid-looking glides and romps during "Heartbreak Hotel" (still his best song), to the deep-felt improvisational gospel break at the end of the lovely Motown ballad, "I'll Be There," and the fleet-tongued, raw-toned scat-rap exchange he shared with Jermaine at the end of "Tell Me I'm Not Dreaming (Too Good to be True)," Michael accomplished as much as was likely possible that night—short of kicking his brothers offstage and setting Don King afire. At moments, he seemed so refreshingly lively and acute that it almost worked against him. What I mean is, watching Jackson at this peak is a bit like watching pornography—something so provoking it can rivet you and seem incomprehensible (maybe even unbearable) at the same time. Which means a little goes a long way, and a lot can seem plain numbing.

In any event, on that last night I thought: Maybe there's hope for the guy after all.

FOUR YEARS LATER I was on the Michael Jackson road again, writing coverage (this time for *Rolling Stone*) of the opening dates of his first solo tour. Jackson had a recent album to promote, *Bad*, and once again he was nominated for some key Grammy Awards. But in 1988, Jackson was up against some hard competition. Artists like U2 and Prince had fashioned some of the most ambitious and visionary music of their careers—music that reflected the state of pop and the world in enlivening ways. By contrast, Jackson's *Bad* seemed mainly a celebration of the mystique and celebrity of the artist himself.

More important, in 1988 there was suspicion among many critics and observers that Jackson's season as pop's favorite son may have passed. When Jackson arrived in New York to attend and perform at the Grammys and to give a series of concerts at Madison Square Garden, he was met with some bitter hints of this possibility. In the 1987 *Rolling Stone* Readers and Critics Poll, Jackson placed first in six of the readers' "worst of the year" categories (including "worst male singer"); in addition the 1987 Village Voice Critics Poll failed to mention Jackson's *Bad* in its selection of 1987's forty best albums. This was a startling turnaround from four years before, when Jackson and his work topped the same polls in both publications.

Plus, Jackson still possessed a knack for grand gestures that often seem overinflated. I remember one morning in a Manhattan disco, where Michael Jackson stood, smiling uneasily before a throng of reporters and photographers. The occasion was a large-scale press conference, convened by Jackson's tour sponsor, Pepsi, to commemorate a $600,000 contribution from the singer to the United Negro College Fund. But the philanthropy of the event was somewhat overshadowed by Pepsi's other purpose: namely to premiere Jackson's flashy new four-episode commercial for the soda company, which would make its TV debut the following night, during the broadcast of the Grammy Awards at Radio City Music Hall. All in all, it was an odd excuse for a press gathering, and Jackson looked uncomfortable with the stagy formality of the situation. Not surprisingly, he was willing to say little about the occasion, nor would he take any questions from the nearly five hundred journalists who were crowding the room. In short, like most Michael Jackson press conferences, the event proved little more than a grandiose photo opportunity—and yet it had all the drawing power of a significant political function. In a sense, it's easy to see why. It's as close to Michael Jackson as most members of the press will ever get, and though many reporters remain put off by the singer, they still find him fascinating and are quite happy to ogle at his transfixing, part beautiful, part grotesque countenance.

But why Jackson would find it necessary to endure an occasion like this is another story. According to one associate (who like most people around Jackson would prefer not to be quoted for attribution), high-profile media galas like this—or the following night's Grammy program—have a special significance for the singer.

"You have to keep in mind," the associate told me, "what happened to Michael during the 1980 Grammy Awards. His album *Off the Wall* had sold over 6 million copies. In effect, Michael was the biggest black artist America had ever produced. He fully expected to be nominated for the Album of the Year and Record of the Year awards, and he deserved to. But instead, he won only one award—best male R&B vocal.

"That experience hurt Michael, and it also taught him a lesson. You could be the biggest black entertainer in history, and yet to much of the music industry and media, you were an invisible man. That's why he aimed to make *Thriller* the biggest record of all time, and that's why he has aligned himself with Pepsi. Pepsi gave him the biggest commercial-endorsement contract that anybody has ever received, and to Michael, the more accomplishments to your name, the more people have to recognize you. That's what an event like this is all about. Michael still wants the world to acknowledge him."

THE NEXT NIGHT, as the Grammy show progresses, things go better and worse than expected. The good news is that Jackson turns in an inspired performance that also serves as a timely reminder of an almost forgotten truth about him: Namely, that whatever his eccentricities, Jackson acquired his fame primarily because of his remarkably intuitive talents as a singer and dancer—talents that are genuine and matchless and not the constructions of mere ambition or hype. Moreover, it is also plausible that in certain ways, Jackson's phenomenal talent may not be completely separable from his eccentricity. That is, the same private obsessions and fears and reveries that fuel his prowess as a dancer and songwriter and singer may also prompt his quirkiness, and perhaps without all that peculiarity he would be far less compelling to watch.

In a sense, Jackson's opening moments on the Grammy telecast—in which he delivers a slow-paced, Frank Sinatra–inspired reworking of "The Way You Make Me Feel"—are exemplary of his famed quirkiness. He seems self-conscious and strained pulling off the song's cartoonish notion of streetwise sexuality, and his overstated hip thrusts and crotch snatching come off as more forced than felt. And yet when the music revs up, all the artifice is instantly dispelled. Jackson seems suddenly confident and executes startling, robotic hip-and-torso thrusts alongside slow-motion, sliding mime moves that leave the audience gasping.

But it is in his next song, the social-minded, gospel-inflected "Man in the Mirror," that Jackson defines for himself some surprising new strengths.

It is a deceptively straightforward delivery, and yet its simplicity prompts Jackson to an increasingly emotional performance. By the song's middle, he isn't so much singing or interpreting as he is simply surrendering to the song. At one point—spurred on by the majestic vocal support of Andrae Crouch and the New Hope Baptist Church Choir—Jackson breaks into a complex, skip-walking dance step that carries him across the stage and back. He then crashes hard to his knees in a posture of glorious, testifying abandon, sobbing fervently as Crouch comes forward and dabs the sweat from his forehead, then helps him back to his feet.

It is a moment that reminds some viewers of James Brown's famous stage routine, but in truth, Jackson has taken the move from the same sources that Brown appropriated his from: archetypal gospel shouters like Claude Jeter and James Cleveland.

But a few minutes later, as Jackson takes his seat in the front row alongside producer Quincy Jones, his triumph comes to a fast, sobering end. As many observers expected, U2's album *The Joshua Tree* takes the Album of the Year Award, and before the evening is out, Jackson will also lose all the remaining awards that he is nominated for.

Perhaps Jackson's most telling response comes during an uproarious incident when Little Richard, presenting the Best New Artist Award, playfully castigates the academy for neglecting him throughout his career, stating, "You all ain't never gave me no Grammys, and I been singing for *years*. I am the *architect* of rock & roll." Jackson is among the first spectators to his feet, bouncing up and down and clapping hard.

Maybe it's only the hilarious spirit of the moment, but maybe it's something more. In a way, Jackson is Little Richard's vengeance. He is the brilliant, freakish black prodigy who would not tolerate being snubbed, and so he figured a way to win pop music's attention and acclaim. But as the late James Baldwin once wrote, "[Michael Jackson] will not swiftly be forgiven for having turned so many tables, for he damn sure grabbed the brass ring, and the man who broke the bank at Monte Carlo has nothing on Michael." On this night, Jackson may have learned the hard lesson behind Baldwin's words: What can be won big can also be taken away—and losing it is sometimes harder than never having had it in the first place.

JACKSON'S GRAMMY LOSS serves to raise expectations for his Madison Square Garden shows, which get under way the night following the Grammys with a benefit performance for the United Negro College Fund. Some of his supporters speculate that Jackson intends to use the concerts to redeem his reputation by putting on the most impressive and assertive shows of his career—and that is precisely what he does. In contrast to the tour's opening shows a week earlier in Kansas City, Missouri—where he had often seemed overwhelmed by glitzy and relentless staging—Jackson seems not merely involved and animated but often flat-out magnificent in his New York shows.

But it is during the two songs toward the show's end, "Billie Jean" and "Man in the Mirror," that Michael Jackson's greatest strengths—as well as his greatest problems—as a live performer are displayed. "Billie Jean," in fact, conveys both at once. When Jackson first performed the song in public— during his startling appearance on the 1983 "Motown 25" TV special—he was still close to its meanings, to the fear and anger that inspired the song. In addition, he was performing it as the first public declaration of his adult independence—as if not only his reputation depended on it but also his future. Now, though, with all its letter-perfect maneuvering and moonwalk-ing, "Billie Jean" seems less like a dance of passion than a physical litany of learned steps; less like an act of personal urgency than a crowd-pleasing gesture. Even so, "Billie Jean" is still a marvelous and bewitching thing to behold.

But as Jackson demonstrated the night before at the Grammys, his live version of "Man in the Mirror" is an act of living passion. In fact, it now seems a more personal and heartfelt song for Jackson than "Billie Jean." Back in 1983 the latter song seemed like his way of negotiating with the world—a way of attracting the world's curiosity in the same motion that he announced that he was afraid of being misinterpreted or used up by that world. But with "Man in the Mirror," a song about accepting social and political responsibil-ity, Jackson may be trying to integrate his way back into the world, or at least to embrace his place in it a bit more. It is hardly an easy peace that Jackson seeks. After all, at the end of the song he retreats back into his *real* world, a very private and isolated place. What's more, it may be that the world no longer loves or wants him as much as it once did. But after watching Jackson on nights like this, when his power and passion are so undeniable, the idea of his audience rejecting him amounts to a sad loss on everybody's part.

A FEW NIGHTS later, Michael Jackson sits on a dais between Liza Min-nelli and Elizabeth Taylor at the United Negro College Fund's annual benefit dinner. The dinner is being held to honor Jackson for the major contributions he had made to the UNCF in recent years, and consequently it is a full-fledged gala, attended by a legion of black educators and business people, as well as numerous celebrities, such as Whitney Houston, Spike Lee, and Christie Brinkley.

Like much of the rigmarole that surrounds Jackson, this event tends to cast the singer in superhuman terms. In speech after speech, adulators lionize Jackson embarrassingly, and even Ronald Reagan—who will later make history as the first president in a century to veto major civil-rights legislation—turns in an appearance, via video, apotheosizing the star's talents and humanitarianism and his merits as a model for the black race.

This is all fine, but in a way it has nothing to do with what *is* genuinely great about Michael Jackson: Namely, that he is at heart an absolutely terrific rock & roller, an astonishing singer whose vocalizing is both a consummation of R&B history as well as a fresh new start, and a matchless mover, who embodies the whole spectrum of black dance style from Cab Calloway to James Brown and then some. What's more, on his best nights, Jackson can combine these gifts in an electrifying, stunning way that can outdistance even the finest work of Bruce Springsteen or Prince—a way, in fact, that has only been equaled in rock history by Elvis Presley. Like Presley, Jackson is at his best when he reacts on troubled-yet-joyous impulses and makes a liberating, riveting public performance of them. And again like Presley, Jackson is a half-mad and extraordinary talent in a nation that both sanctifies him and hates him for his prowess—and either response spells a difficult artistic future.

Just how much pressure Jackson constantly faces as a result of his fame becomes plain in an incident at the UNCF benefit, during the lull when the dinner is served. No sooner have the speakers stopped speaking than literally hundreds of people—most of them sophisticated, intelligent people—begin streaming toward the table where Jackson is seated, hoping for an autograph, a photograph, maybe even a chance to talk. Immediately, a half dozen or so bodyguards and publicists line up in front of the singer, attempting, first politely and then adamantly, to turn people back to their tables. Finally, it is a stalemate. The people cannot get any closer to Jackson, but they will *not* turn away from him. They just stand facing him, staring, craning to get a view of his remarkable, enchanting, and disturbing face—a face that, at this moment, looks terribly frightened but is holding its place.

Jackson's face, of course, is probably his most famous and controversial aspect, and while some critics suspect he has reconstructed it to seem forever childlike, others charge that he has had cosmetic surgery so that he would appear "less black."

In his autobiography, *Moonwalk*, (Doubleday), Jackson explains:

You must remember that I had been a child star and when you grow up under that kind of scrutiny people don't want you to change, to get older and look different. When I first became well known, I had a lot of baby fat and a very round, chubby face. That roundness stayed with me until several years ago when I changed my diet and stopped eating beef, chicken, pork, and fish, as well as certain fattening foods. I just wanted to look better, live better, and be healthier. Gradually, as I lost weight, my face took on its present shape and the press started accusing me of surgically altering my appearance.

I'd like to set the record straight right now. I have never had my cheeks altered or my eyes altered. I have not had my lips thinned, nor have I had dermabrasion or a skin peel. All of these charges are ridiculous. If they were true, I would say so, but they aren't. I have had my nose altered twice and I recently added a cleft to my chin, but that is it. Period. I don't care what anyone else says—it's my face and I know.

In any event, it's a visage that disturbs many people, and earlier in the week one person who has been observing Jackson offered an explanation: "I think people find it upsetting, because they know they're looking at racism made flesh. They're looking at a tacit admission that to make it in a white world, you have to be white. It's an indictment. It's a face that says, 'You made me this way. I can't be really black if I want to be really famous.' And people don't want to look at that face, because they don't want to look at their own racism."

This may well be true, but if so, is that really what is on the minds of the people standing here staring at Jackson, most of whom are black? Are they staring at somebody who represents dark truths, or somebody who embodies a complex history of hopes and dreams made good or simply at somebody who is the biggest star of all stars? Maybe they are looking at all these things. At one point in the evening, the dinner's host, Ossie Davis, stares at Jackson for a long moment and then utters a line as illuminating and resonant as scripture. "God bless the child," he says, "that's got his own."

ONE LAST NEW YORK tale remains to be told.

It is in the hectic moments after the Grammy Awards show is over, and the blocks around Radio City Music Hall are jammed with celebrity watchers.

On the street behind the hall, a crowd of a couple hundred mostly black fans stand on the other side of a police barricade, hoping for a glimpse of a departing star or two. A huddled, cloaked figure darts out the backstage door and into a long white limousine, and the car begins to inch its way down Fifty-first Street. A small group of onlookers keep pace with the car, trying to peer into its darkened windows. "Hey," says somebody, "I think that's Michael Jackson in that car." Immediately, people in the crowd begin to call out to the car, "Hey, Mikey. . . . Mikey, is that you? Come out and talk to us, Mikey!"

After a few moments, the top of the limousine rolls back, and up pops Michael Jackson. The people in the crowd break into a wild cheer and start to surge forward, holding out their hands toward the star, but some policemen rush in and keep them away from the car. On the limousine's other side, a lone fan calls to Jackson and begins moving toward him. Jackson turns and smiles at the fan and holds out his hand. The fan, who is only a few feet away, reaches out to Jackson, but before the two can touch, the car speeds up. Jackson stands for a moment, looking at the face of the disappointed fan, then smiles a strangely forlorn smile, waves, and drops back into the limousine.

In moments, the white car turns the corner and is gone, and Michael Jackson is carried back to the inviolable world in which he lives.

WE ALL KNOW what happened next. Michael Jackson's world didn't stay inviolable. In 1993, he began the year by playing at a preinaugural gala for President Clinton, and a month later gave a lengthy TV interview to Oprah Winfrey, in which he tried to dispel the rumors about his eccentricities and the lightening of his skin (the latter, he said, was the result of a skin disease, vitiligo). Then in August, Jackson was hit with public charges that he had sexually abused an underage boy. The police raided Jackson's house, looking for evidence; his sister LaToya claimed that Michael often spent the night with young boys in his room; Jackson was forced to cancel a worldwide tour that was under way; and Pepsi ended its long relationship with the singer. In early 1994, lawyers for both Jackson and the boy's father announced that the matter had been settled out of court for an undisclosed sum. The criminal investigation was eventually dropped, and Jackson steadfastly maintained his innocence, despite the settlement that he had agreed to.

Whether the charges were true or not, Michael Jackson had fallen, from a very big height. In light of the rumors, his earlier peculiarity began to take on an even deeper creepiness for many people. Michael went on to marry, then divorce, Lisa Marie Presley, Elvis Presley's daughter. To some people, it seemed as if the Presley name had been just another big prize for Michael to claim for his own, in much the same way, a few years before, he had bought much of the Beatles' song catalog. Then, in 1997, Jackson had his own child; the event became the unfortunate subject matter of bad jokes and trash reporting. There was also speculation that Jackson had fathered a child of his own largely to offset his own strange image.

For my part, I don't know really what to say anymore about this troubled and troubling man. Reconsidering Michael Jackson has been the hardest part of assembling this volume for me, and several times I thought of leaving him out altogether. Still, I guess I should own up to what I once thought of him—that Michael Jackson was an artist of immense talents and possibilities—and I should also own up to what I think of him now: that he is a man of even *more* immense hubris and tragedy.

I'm not sure it was all his fault. He had an intensely strange, unkind, and horribly coerced childhood, and later, when he would finally win his dream, he would also win intense hatred for realizing that dream. As a result of both of these things, perhaps Michael Jackson had long been living in a no-win dimension. At the same time, he seemed unwilling to learn from his fall; he seemed unwilling to be seen as anything less than a demigod. He allowed statues to be built of himself, and he insisted that *his* had been the most injured innocence of all. Michael Jackson may yet again make music that is pleasurable to hear, but I don't think it can ever really matter again. He lives in—as critic Dave Marsh once pointed out—a trap, and while much of it is of his own doing, no doubt some of it is of our making as well. He is among the best proofs I've seen in my lifetime of William Carlos Williams' famous perception: "The pure products of America go crazy," and rock & roll's America has had few purer products than Michael Jackson.

Still, I'll never forget that night back in March 1983, when onstage in Pasadena, California, at the Motown anniversary show, Michael Jackson gave his first public performance, vaulting into that astonishingly graceful, electrifying version of "Billie Jean." Dancing, spinning, sending out impassioned, fierce glares at the overcome audience, Jackson did a powerful job of animating and mythologizing his own blend of mystery and sexuality. I'd never seen anything quite like it—maybe I never will again—even if so much of what followed after that night was simply Michael Jackson's moonwalk to his own ruin.

upstarts:

over & under

the wall, & into the

territory's center

SKIRMISH ONE: DISCO, POP'S INTERNAL WAR

*a*t the outset of the 1970s, rock & roll still prided itself on its aspirations to revolution. From rockabilly to glitter rock, it was music that not only articulated and vented the frustrations of cultural outsiders, but that also won those upstarts a station and voice that they might otherwise have been denied. But in the mid-1970s, a genuine revolution took place within the bounds of pop culture—and rock & roll *hated* it. The upheaval was called "disco," and it subverted not just rock's familiar notions of fun and form, but also its pretended ideals of community and meaning. It was a music that, without rhetoric or stridor, seized and transformed the pop mainstream and its long-unchallenged star systems, and it empowered cultural outlanders that rock & roll had snubbed or simply abandoned. In the process, disco became the biggest commercial pop genre of the 1970s—actually, the biggest pop music movement of all time—and in the end, its single-minded, booming beat proved to be the most resilient and enduring stylistic breakthrough of the last twenty years or so. In short, disco—the pop revolution that was quickly overthrown by an ungrateful pop world—figured out a way to outlast its own demise, a way to remain dominant, while feigning an ignoble death.

So how did this cultural rupture happen? How did disco become both one of the most popular and reviled mileposts in pop music's history?

To answer these questions, one has to look at the confluence of musical history and social longing that produced the disco explosion. Musically, disco was a logical outgrowth of how soul music had developed in the 1960s, and how it had adapted in order to survive in the early 1970s. From the terse protofunk of James Brown and the spare but accentuated dynamics of the Stax-Volt sound, disco derived its obsession with a simple but relentlessly driving beat; and from the pop savvy of Motown, as well as from the suave romanticism of such Philadelphia-based producers and writers as Thom Bell (who had defined the Spinners' sound) and the team of Kenny Gamble and Leon Huff (who worked with the O'Jays, the Intruders, Harold Melvin and the Blue Notes, and Teddy Pendergrass, among others), disco gained its undying passion for elegant, swooning, sexy surfaces that were their own irrefutable rewards. But disco was more than music as sound, or sound as style or artifice. It also aimed to reaffirm one of music's most time-worn purposes: namely, its power as a social unifier, as a means of bringing together an audience that shared a certain social perspective and that found meaning and pleasure in the ritual of public dancing. In this sense, disco had roots in traditions as urbane as Big Band and Swing music; as rowdy as blues-style juke joints and country-western honky-tonks; and as sexually irrepressible as early rock & roll and its cleaned-up public exposition, "American Bandstand."

More immediately, though, disco extended (in fact, *revived*) some of the most joyful ambitions of 1960s pop. In the early 1960s—before Motown or the Beatles—the media largely perceived pop music as little more than a medium of transient dance styles, like the Twist, Mashed Potato, and Hully Gully, that lived out their heady but brief vogues in crowded and intoxicating public venues, such as New York's Peppermint Lounge, and numerous other discotheques scattered across America and Europe. When the 1960s exploded with the British Invasion and soul, it became apparent that rock was more than an agency for dancing—though clearly, dancing was now more fun, more an assertion of generational identity and power, than ever before. But as rock became more ambitious, more "significant," it gradually abdicated the dance floor. Though it isn't often acknowledged, the San Francisco hippie community grew out of a dance movement: young people coming together in the city's ballrooms and clubs, to dance exhaustingly to the colorful psychedelia that was being invented by such community bands as the Jefferson Airplane and Grateful Dead; indeed, dancing, even more than drugs or sex, was how that scene first publicly realized its ideals of communal ecstasy. But within a season or two, the scene's followers were dancing a lot less.

Instead, they were now paying serious attention to the new music, to its lyrical pronouncements and aural constructions, and as often as not, they did so from a sitting posture. By the early 1970s, rock was something you *listened* to, and for whatever the numerous and undeniable virtues of such artists as the Eagles, Pink Floyd, the Allman Brothers, or even early David Bowie, there was little about their music that inspired a mass terpsichore. Dancing was something practiced by established stars like Mick Jagger—it was not something that an audience did. The star was empowered to *move*, while the audience was obliged to pay, to watch and listen, to revere.

Still, there were audiences for whom dancing was a vital social bond and an essential sensual act, though they were largely audiences that had been shut out by rock & roll's developing styles and pretensions. Certainly, for the early 1970s black audience—which had enjoyed something of an alliance with the rock mainstream in the mid-1960s—pop no longer offered much embrace, or much satisfaction. For the various Hispanic audiences, and for numerous other ethnic minorities, the reality was even more exclusionary: Pop accommodated ethnic styles in only the most vague or diluted sense, as in the pyrotechnic Latin rock of Santana. In addition, there was one other large audience that had been shut out of rock's concerns, and that was the gay underground—an audience for whom dancing proved an important assertion of identity and community. In 1973 and 1974, these audiences gradually (and perhaps a bit unwittingly) began to form an ever-expanding network—or at least they began influencing each other's musical preferences—as dance clubs sprang up around the East Coast and Europe, and as the D.J.s at these clubs began searching out some of the hippest dance-oriented black, Hispanic, and European pop to play for these audiences. As the trend grew, the D.J.s refined their style of programming: Usually cutting back and forth between two turntables, the D.J.s aimed to play a sequence of songs in such a manner that beats between the songs were consistent, each track blending into the following track, making for a steady, seamless flow, and for a mounting mood of physical frenzy among the dancers. Like the music of the 1960s, disco was supposed to be a celebration of community and ecstasy—only this time, the revelers who were celebrating these ideals were the same ones who had been forgotten or expatriated by the established rock world.

*T*HIS EMERGING DANCE movement turned out to be one of the most pivotal and radical developments in 1970s rock. In fact, it upended pop's common values and its known hierarchy. Whereas, for the vast majority of the post-Beatles audience, it was the artists and their statements that constituted rock's main pleasures and main worth, disco's partisans agreed on some new values. What mattered in disco's ethos wasn't the apotheosis of the artist, but the experience and involvement of the audience itself. Consequently, disco elected a new system of pop heroes. On the romantic side, the heroes were the dancers, who were acting out this new egalitarianism on the dance floor. On the practical side, the heroes were the people who knew how to shape and manipulate sound in order to construct moods and motivate an audience—the D.J.s and producers and arrangers who were the *real* auteurs of disco style and meaning.

In other words, in disco, the artists—the singers and instrumentalists—were an essential backdrop, but they weren't the focus of the action; disco fans didn't go to disco shows to watch disco stars. Indeed, what disco declared was that our pop stars *weren't* our representatives, but that we could (and should) be the stars in our own scenarios of pleasure and empowerment. To some pop fans and critics, this assertion—namely, that "everybody is a star"—seemed a bit trivial, even pathetic. But to the emerging disco audience, it amounted to nothing less than a vision of empowerment: It said that whatever the reality of your existence, you could refuse to be defined by menial conditions. You could put on your best clothes, go out in public, and act out your worthiness, as if you were entitled to all the acts and trappings of luxury that were flaunted by the dominant culture. In other words, you could appropriate those trappings. In *other* other words, strike a pose; there's nothing to it.

In time, disco's obsessions with dressiness would become elitist and defeating—especially once the scene's clubs began enforcing dress codes that simply affirmed the very ideals of affluence and privilege that the original disco audience had meant to usurp, rather than simply emulate. But in the early 1970s, disco's "everybody is a star" mentality was genuinely liberating: It had the effect of empowering (and even briefly unifying) an audience of gays, blacks, and ethnics that had, for too long, been disdained or displaced by a rock world that had become overwhelmingly white. This rising coalition of outsiders—pop's equivalent of a silent majority—was about to become the biggest audience in pop's history, though in a thoroughly unprecedented way. In fact, disco became a mass revolution at pretty much the same time that it remained an underground phenomenon. Because disco was a music played in clubs, a music without clearly identifiable central stars, a music that radio and pop media largely ignored at first, its massive popularity was almost invisible. Indeed, for a year or two, the disco world was a network of clubs, dancers, and music makers that didn't so much enter the pop mainstream as simply form an equally viable alternative to that mainstream, that could launch massive-selling hits without benefit of radio or media exposure. Without intending to, the disco world had seized and exercised its own power by the most effective means possible—by means of pure commerce—and this development would have a galvanic effect on the business and culture of popular music.

Of course, this meant that disco's genuine mainstream assimilation was inevitable, and that the music itself would be co-opted and marketed as a formula. Indeed, by 1974, disco had been codified. The beat ruled—it was a tightly uniform, booming 4/4 pulse, without patience for rhythmic shifts or improvisation. But within its rigid limitations, the structure allowed for a surprising amount of nuance and variation: It could be elegant, coy, and tuneful, as in Van McCoy's "The Hustle"; it could be taut and sweetly funky, as in Shirley and Company's "Shame, Shame, Shame"; it could be sexy and evocative, as in the Hues Corporation's "Rock the Boat" and George Mc-Crae's "Rock Your Baby"; it could be propulsive and soulful, as in Average White Band's "Pick Up the Pieces." The following year, disco even launched its first certified star: a former church and theatrical singer named Donna Summer, who began as merely another prop-singer (with the mock-orgasmic "Love to Love You Baby"), and would shortly become the form's most ambitious and enduring artist.

In the mid-1970s, disco fused with the public imagination in an incendiary mass moment. By this time, numerous artists—including Donna Summer, Labelle, K.C. and the Sunshine Band, Wild Cherry, and Silver Convention—had already scored Top 10 disco hits. But the genre's biggest milestone, of course, was the 1977 *Saturday Night Fever*—a film that gave a sympathetic and fairly accurate portrayal of how disco night life provided a transcendent identity for certain East Coast working-class ethnic youths. More significant than the film, though, was its soundtrack album. Featuring the music of the Bee Gees and the Trammps, among others, it rapidly sold over 25 million copies, and set a record as the biggest-selling record in pop history at that time.

Disco's triumph was complete, which of course, only signaled the movement's end. Actually, disco had been taken out of the hands of both its creators and its audience. *Saturday Night Fever*'s (and disco's) biggest stars were the Bee Gees—a group of British pop stars who had created a glossy adaptation of the form's style and popularity as a way of reviving their flagging careers. In addition, in the rush to exploit disco's hitmaking abilities, several other established pop stars—including the Rolling Stones, Paul Mc-Cartney, Elton John, the Eagles, and Rod Stewart—had also started accommodating their music to the disco style and its audience. Suddenly, disco's pulse was omnipresent: It dominated film scores, TV commercials, Top 40 radio, and almost every lounge and club where recorded music was played for a dancing audience. It wasn't just that the music was now pervasive; it also seemed bent on revising all known music history. Everything—from the hits of the Beatles to the dark beauty of Beethoven—became fair game for disco's pounding 4/4 formula, and the sameness of it all began to rub many people the wrong way.

As disco became the pop norm, a counterreaction set in—in swift and fierce terms. By 1978, rock fans were beginning to sport T-shirts emblazoned with hostile decrees—"Disco Sucks" and "Death to Disco." And then, in July 1979, a hard rock radio D.J. from Chicago's WLUP turned a baseball game at Comiskey Park into an anti-disco rally. As he incited the audience to chant "Disco sucks," the D.J. piled disco LPs into a wooden crate in center field—and exploded the crate. It was a supremely ugly moment, and its message was plain: The mainstream pop audience wasn't about to allow a coalition of blacks and gays to usurp rock's primacy. Indeed, it seemed hardly coincidental that, at a time when America was about to elect Ronald Reagan as president, and enter its most savage period of cultural denial, that disco's dream of an all-embracing audience would invite rabid antipathy. Instead of opening up the pop world to a new consensus, disco had made plain that rock was fast becoming a field of diverse, often mutually antagonistic factions.

So DISCO WAS ended. Even as the Village People—a gay goof that became tiring quickly—became, for a short time, the biggest-selling band in America, the pop industry and media were already in retreat from disco. By 1980, disco was clearly a dirty word. Record sales plummeted almost overnight, and numerous artists, producers, and executives—even entire record labels and radio stations—fell into an irreclaimable oblivion. Disco had been overthrown, in part by its own excesses, and in part by a rising ugly racist and anti-gay sensibility.

But in many ways, disco transmuted its style and survived ingeniously—or at the very least, it has had a considerable legacy. In fact, in the 1980s, its rhythmic principles were adopted by two divergent audiences: the new wave crowd, who—from the Tom Tom Club to Billy Idol to Depeche Mode—enjoyed some of their biggest commercial successes by adapting disco's dance structures to their own conceits; also, hip-hop and rap music based much of their linguistic and textural innovation on disco's foursquare rhythmic pulse. In addition, the success of many of the 1980s' biggest stars—

including Michael Jackson, Prince, and Madonna—would have been unthinkable without the breakthroughs that disco made in both style and audience appeal. It's also true, of course, that disco didn't necessarily make the pop world more tolerant.

In general, though, disco managed to restore to rock the principle of dancing as one of music's primary purposes and pleasures—and if anything, that truth is more dominant in the 1990s, in hip-hop, rave, and techno, than it was in the 1970s, at disco's height. Disco also reasserted a vital truth: that dancing could be an act of affirmation—that it could unite people, could redeem (or at least help vent) their pains and longings, and could even empower those who had been too long denied or forgotten. In the end, the question isn't why disco enjoyed such phenomenal success. The real question is, why didn't *more* of 1970s rock & roll stand for those same worthy values?

SKIRMISH TWO: ROCK & ROLL'S POLITICS

Does dedication to rock & roll entail any political commitments?

That was a question I raised in the pages of the *Los Angeles Herald Examiner* in September 1984, in the aftermath of Ronald Reagan's attempt to appropriate Bruce Springsteen's hard-bitten Americanism as a round-about endorsement of the president's addled social policies (see this book's earlier chapter). At the time I posed the question largely as a way of suggesting that to esteem the music of Springsteen and yet also support the reelection of President Reagan was (to my mind then and my mind now) to embrace a likely contradiction in ideals—that, in effect, the two interests simply wouldn't mix. (Springsteen, I believe, made the same point when, shortly after Reagan's action, he told a Philadelphia audience: "It's a long walk from a government that's supposed to represent all the people to where we are today.") Several readers agreed with my suggestion, though many others—all of whom, interestingly, professed strong fondness for both the singer and the president—did not. In fact, some bristled at the idea that a love for rock & roll was tantamount to any political view whatsoever.

In part, I bring this matter up because some of those letters forced me to do some thinking about my stand. But I also reinvoke it because, at the time I wrote this article (two weeks before the Ronald Reagan–Walter Mondale presidential election) we were about to select a president, and to be honest, I've never cast a vote for that office without somehow reflecting on what rock & roll has taught me about my country.

I don't say this lightly or jokingly. Just as there are people who believe that to follow certain religious convictions necessitates voting or acting in a specific political manner, I believe that to value rock's contribution to popular culture requires (or eventually produces) given sociopolitical creeds, including a commitment to racial equality and an opposition to illiberalism in general. But if, as some partisans insist, rock no longer speaks for the sociopolitical disposition of American youth—or worse, if the political disposition it speaks for is as ungenerous as post 1930s' Republicanism (meaning from 1940 to the year 2000, and probably beyond)—then maybe the rock movement has finally turned feckless and empty.

Is this true? Are we finally witnessing a humiliation of rock's traditional intractability? Has the musical tradition of Elvis Presley, Little Richard, Bob Dylan, Sly Stone, and Marvin Gaye finally grown to seem socially docile— even to the extent of enjoying conservative endorsement or co-option? Didn't we, during the punk revolt of the late 1970s, come through some great "new music" revolution—an insurrection designed to overthrow the staid, cautious, apolitical murk that had gripped the pop scene in the aftermath of the frenetic 1960s?

Well, yes and no. True, the Sex Pistols, the Clash, and Graham Parker carved a hard line across the face of rock complacency, except their distinctly British brand of sociopolitical passion seemed too threatening to the American rock sensibility of the late 1970s and early 1980s—that is, until U.S. record companies figured a way to sell the music for its increasingly refined surfaces, while disregarding its political foundations. Whatever true punk revolution there was, by the mid-1980s it would merely look cute, poppy, and clearly marketable—stuff that even young Republicans can (and *do*) embrace, and by embracing defuse, without acknowledging the music's real contents, meanings, or consequences.

While much of the best mid-1980s music (which in the case of such British bands as Eurythmics, Culture Club, and others mixed black rhythmic forms within a sleek pop outline) still advanced a liberal, pointedly antiracist point of view in the context of British society, in America it was originally interpreted by a force like MTV as fun-minded style, without social significance (of course, this was back in that cable network's pre-"Rock the Vote" period; "Rock the Vote" has turned out to be a smart and effective force, not to mention a nice redemption of the station's early political stupefaction). To be sure, many 1980s bands—from Husker Du and the Minutemen to Rank and File and Lone Justice—fashioned a new and virile brand of politically informed rock, but until 1984, radio and MTV pretty much shunned (and thus discouraged) such adventurous sounds and outlooks. In fact, with rare exceptions—most notably Bruce Springsteen's *Nebraska* and *Born in the U.S.A.*, and the odd funk or country single—precious little *overtly* social-minded American rock music won public favor in the early 1980s.

Of course, some folks would argue that to delight in rock and soul music was never exactly the same as staking out a political stand—that, by example, reveling in the early ground-breaking achievements of Elvis Presley, Little Richard, Jerry Lee Lewis, Chuck Berry, and Gene Vincent was to make an essentially *nonpolitical* choice based on generational diversion, not cultural insurrection. Even so, the choice had far-reaching political consequences: Rock & roll, remember, was vehemently and openly attacked in many U.S. cities as "nigger music." Presley, and others like him—whether they intended to or not—brought a previously (much feared, despised) audience and sensibility into America's wide-ranging predilections, and because of his actions, that "outsider" style (and its meanings) became publicly, massively integrated to an unprecedented extreme. This development, I believe, also helped play a role in the more significant advance of the civil rights cause.

By the mid-1960s, rock & roll was clearly politicized—but then so was everything else. The racial disquiet of the 1950s had given way to an impassioned and eventful civil rights struggle, while an emerging youth culture (defined in large part by the explosive sensibility of the Beatles) was quickly being turned to fodder for the self-realizing horror of U.S. involvement in Vietnam. Initially, it was such left-derived folk activists as Peter, Paul, & Mary; Joan Baez; and Bob Dylan who recognized not merely the bearing these issues might have on their predominately young (though not yet rock-oriented) audience, but also understood the moral and emotional influence that music might have on social problems. When Dylan crossed over to a pop context (a move initially interpreted by the folk crowd as a sellout), he simply updated Presley's implicit threat of brandishing rock & roll as a means of radicalizing—or at least disrupting—American mainstream entertainment.

More remarkable was the extent to which all this political music affected the *business* of music. While a company like MGM (under the direction of Republican hopeful Mike Curb) purged its roster of incendiary thinkers (like the Velvet Underground), other corporate structures (including CBS, Warner Bros., Atco/Atlantic, Decca/MCA and even the famously conservative RCA—the latter the home of Elvis Presley and the Jefferson Airplane) largely supported the activism of their artists as both good business and good ideals. (For example, consider this note from the inner-fold of Chicago's first album: "With this album, we dedicate ourselves, our futures and our energies to the people of the revolution. . . . And the revolution in all its forms." Was this simple-minded sedition or simply sound commercialism?)

Then, in the late 1970s, after the furor of Vietnam and Watergate had started to die down and when the battle over civil rights seemed to reach a certain (though only momentary stability), and after acts from such record companies as Elektra/Asylum and Capricorn had helped support the presidential campaigns of Jerry Brown and Jimmy Carter—both of whom professed a strong liking for rock—two upheavals occurred that dramatically altered the temper of American rock. The first was the punk revolt, a movement that began in the United States as an aesthetic insurrection yet was adopted and expanded in Britain (by such acts as the Sex Pistols and Clash) as fierce, radical-minded music, leveled in protest against the United Kingdom's emerging, reactionary, Margaret Thatcher–led mood. Consequently, the U.S. radio and record industries eschewed punk, looking on its grim tactics as tasteless and off-putting.

The other disturbance was more decisive. The bottom fell out of the overextended record business, cutting grandiose record sales in half and making simple survival seem more necessary than comfortable political ideals. In short, financial recovery became the first priority of the marketplace, which caused many music moguls (not to mention many musicians) to throw their support to Ronald Reagan, with his promise of restoring financial bounty to the corporate sector. It wasn't Reagan (of course) who saved the music industry's ass. Rather, it was that cleaned-up descendant of punk alluded to earlier—a largely dance-informed version of new wave—that did the trick. England's most radical cultural export of the mid-1980s became one of America's favorite urban trends. Who said, "This ain't no party/This ain't no disco"?

Where does this leave us? Has rock & roll come full circle, so that it is once more viewed as an art and entertainment form largely without political meaning? Or rather, in 1984, did American rock's political bias actually start shifting to the right—to jingoism, hawkishness, and regressive racial prejudices? Did the rock "vote"—the vote of those who see rock & roll as somehow central to their view of pop culture—go, in 1984, to Ronald Reagan, a man who as California's governor, once bandied the notion of engaging in a "blood bath" with America's young dissidents?

I would like to think not—I'd like to think that rock still speaks to our best mixed impulses of insurgence and compassion—but that may not be realistic. Rather, it may simply be that rock is too big for much aesthetic or ideological unanimity, that it is now as variegated as America's many regions and as disparate as the differences between the United States and the United Kingdom. It is also important that leftist fans like myself recognize that rightist rockers may well possess a redeeming genius, just as Frank Sinatra, Merle Haggard, Ray Charles, or even Neil Young made the misfortune of their politics seem secondary to the depth of their art. Maybe in the years ahead we will stop thinking of rock as a folk-art form that liberates its audience, and instead we'll start regarding it as something that reinforces sunshine nationalism and grasping opulence. After all, given rock & roll as a spawn of American myth and wide-eyed ambition, unkind possibilities were never far beneath the music's surface.

But there is another, better possibility, which has nothing to do with right or left, party or rhetoric: Namely, that rock & roll is no longer an answer so much as a big question mark pointed at each of us, asking us what we make of it, what bearing it has on our passions and dreams, and on our view of the world around us. After all, music has the ability to address our hearts personally—to reach me at the same moment it reaches you, no matter our political bonds or differences, despite the caprices of our government and of its self-serving leaders. If that stays true—if rock & roll continues to reach our hearts, and in doing so bids us to find purpose in its raw exhilaration—it will remain an inducement to freedom, and that is the best one could ever ask of any American-born dream or calling.

SKIRMISH THREE: OF SEX, VIOLENCE, PRINCE, MADONNA, SATAN, MURDER, METAL, AND THE NEW PARENTS

Does rock & roll threaten the morals of its most susceptible fans? Can it foment debauchery, cultural dissipation, sexism, even violence? These questions, in some form or another, have been the subject of repeated and passionately unresolved debates, stretching back as far as Elvis Presley's first unabashedly sexy nationwide TV appearance—an event many critics and moralists viewed as a shocking signal of the degeneracy of postwar America.

Over the years this charge and its refutation have become a fixed and venerable part of the rock tradition for virtually every American and British parent and child (or censor and libertine) who have felt the volatile fluctuations of pop culture, from the initial jolt of Presley to the purposeful nihilism of the Sex Pistols to the coy androgyny of Boy George. But the continual controversy has also become a rite of passage that has a way, years later, of making unseeming conservatives and old fogies out of yesterday's progressives. In the 1960s, many of us witnessed the moral pedagogy of parents and older siblings who had acted out the surface gestures of rebellion with Elvis but were angered by the social liberalism of the Beatles and the San Francisco bands and repelled by the sexual bravura of the Rolling Stones. By the same token, in the late 1970s, many of those former pop insurgents (the tiring "Big Chill" generation) resisted the punk mutiny, chafing at the knowledge of a younger crowd mocking their own once-daring but now enervated (or, more accurately, now abandoned) ideals.

I am both happy and sad to say that in 1985 things really aren't that much different [nor are they different in 1997, as I revise this piece]. I am happy because I believe it's every subsequent generation's inalienable right (if not obligation) to disturb or offend the status quo, and sad because it invariably seems that so many of yesteryear's iconoclasts, while they remain pious about their own periods of rebellion, end up disparaging the worth of any later upheavals or progressions. Sometimes it seems as if the children of '56, '67, or '77 feel they have a patent on legitimate pop revolt, that their discovery of the thrill of change or disruption was the last cultural discovery worth sanctioning. The truly confounding part of this is that, with the rapid turnover these days in pop styles and values, it doesn't take long for old-fogyism to creep in. For example, consider all the late-1970s punks who turn up their noses at anything that gives off even a whiff of techno-pop.

But the real subject here, of course, is the moral content of much of today's pop, which certainly seems to be rankling many folks. Among them is freelance journalist Kandy Stroud, who in a 1985 *Newsweek* "My Turn" column, called for the legislative censorship of "pornographic rock." Stroud (who professes to "being something of a rock freak," by which she means she enjoys performing aerobics to it) was incensed when she discovered her fifteen-year-old daughter listening to Prince's "Darling Nikki," with its glaring reference to a woman "masturbating with a magazine." After that, Stroud's newly awakened ears found filth all over the place—in Madonna cooing "Feels so good inside" in "Like a Virgin"; in Frankie Goes to Hollywood singing of gay sex in "Relax"; in Sheena Easton extolling arousal in (Prince's) "Sugar Walls." Claiming that all this music degrades and corrupts its listeners, and noting that most parents don't have the time or wherewithal to monitor what their children listen and dance to, Stroud proposed that the time has come for the public suppression of such songs—either by self-imposed restraints from the radio and record industry or by the enactment of local legislation.

Stroud finished her article with this thought: "Why can't musicians . . . ensure that America's own youth will be fed a diet of rock music that is not only good to dance to but healthy for their hearts and minds and souls as well?" Welcome to the new parents: rock fans who demand that the music adopt and stand for the prudish values that their generations were once free to reject.

Well, I guess Stroud's question is fair: Why can't rock stars produce music that is "healthy for hearts and minds and souls . . . ?" To my way of thinking, of course, rock musicians already *are* producing music that nurtures our souls and hearts, but here is the better answer to Stroud's question: Because they don't have to, *nor are they morally obliged to*. American and British artists are free to assume any perspective—even to exalt or to deride another person's beliefs. Remember "freedom of expression"? It extends even to rock & roll upstarts.

PART OF WHAT Stroud and so many others miss or overlook is that sex is among the causal impulses of rock & roll. (Of jazz too, for that matter; remember the old rumor that the word *jazz* was derived from "jism" or "jizz"?) It wasn't merely the bold, unmistakable thrust of the music's grinding rhythms (a trait inherited from the pulse of blues and R&B) or the often prurient text of the lyrics (the sort of salty stuff that got songs like "Work with Me Annie" and "Sixty Minute Man" banned in some places in the mid-1950s), but rather the way the music brought chance masses of people into potentially excitable contact. From Alan Freed's explosive live shows to the Rolling Stones' 1960s tours, sexual provocation, expression, and implicit interaction were the sustaining subtext of rock's popularity. What made this message so culturally eventful was that it forged inseparable facts out of youthful bravura and racial declaration. Of course, it was for this very feature (and for bringing undiluted black and hillbilly sounds into the pop mainstream) that many people regarded the rise of rock & roll as an ill omen: a sign of the coming of permissiveness and liberality in America. Fortunately, it was exactly that.

In the epoch since that initial eruption, everything and nothing have changed. Certainly rock & roll has consciously aspired to more overtly artistic and political (and even mystical) ambitions, just as art and politics (and yes, mysticism too) have aimed at more openly sexual concerns. Still, it is pop music that has done the most effective job of mixing and balancing these various elements—and of examining hard questions about how these matters relate in our daily lives.

In the music of Elvis Costello, for example, one finds an uncommonly deft examination of how some sexual-romantic interactions often resemble acts of social tyranny. Meantime, in the music of Bruce Springsteen, one finds accounts of erotic playfulness (such as "Pink Cadillac" and "Fire") juxtaposed alongside harrowing portrayals of how sexual fear can fuel debilitating isolation ("Dancing in the Dark," "Downbound Train," "I'm on Fire") and even sudden meanness ("You Can Look").

Of course, all this sexual obsessiveness is also a two-edged knife: What once worked as a personally and politically liberating influence in some ways turned back on itself, until the liberation itself seemed like nothing so much as a costly indulgence paid for by sexual typecasting. One has only to regard what happened to punk and new wave in the early and mid-1980s to witness this development at its most troubling. In its early stages, punk asserted itself as music that rejected the knee-jerk carnality of the pro forma 1970s rock attitude, and in time—in its brief postpunk incarnation, through such bands as Au Pairs, Gang of Four, Young Marble Giants, and Delta 5—the music went on to consider questions of political friction and sexual rapprochement. One could almost imagine it as a worthy version of a sex classified: Good beat seeks good idea, for healthful intercourse.

Then, almost overnight, as new wave and video pop joined resources to help rejuvenate the record industry, the notion of social-sexual progressivism began to fall off. Calculated, arty sex poses—from artists like Dale Bozzio, Teri Nunn, Duran Duran, or Adam Ant—seemed indivisible from sleek textures and throbbing beats. In its rush to find wide acceptance, the new music had been reduced to a token of sexual manipulation—transformed into an easy version of excitement that sold easy and obvious (though still fun) ideals of sensual experience.

This, then, became the quandary: How does a music that derives in part from sexual rhythm and style remain sexy without becoming a medium of exploitation or debasement? Is the sort of sexiness that was once advanced by Elvis Presley, Tina Turner, James Brown, Jimi Hendrix, Mick Jagger, David Bowie, and so many others still tenable or understandable in a time where anti-sexism and anti-pornography have become large causes? Does pop romance need to be *straitlaced* to prove positive? Are implicit or graphic portrayals of sexual relations in rock (or pop culture in general) necessarily oppressive? Are vivid testimonials to lust essentially sexist?

If you want to see just how twisted these questions can get, consider the widely popular (at least in the mid-1980s) music of Prince and Madonna— two ambitious Minnesota-raised pop stars who made indelible content out of a manifest sexual style. Prince's example might seem more substantial. He won his first bout of serious fame and acclaim with the 1980 album *Dirty Mind*, which presented unmistakable accounts of incest, infidelity, oral sex, and implicit bisexuality. At the same time, the record asserted Prince's lionizing of sex as a means of striking back at all the tireless advocates of discrimination, avarice, inequity, and war who had helped hem in the world that the artist came up in. By the time of *Controversy* (1981) and *1999* (1982), Prince was already striving to make political, racial, and religious sense of his concerns—and while his social-sexual musings were sometimes contradictory or plain arrogant, they were also just as often edifying, not to mention provoking.

Interestingly, up through *1999*, Prince's unabashed sexual interests were hailed by most pop critics for their spunk and intelligence. But with *Purple Rain*—the surprise success film of 1984 about a maverick pop prodigy who must overcome selfishness and brutality to find redemption and acceptance—Prince began meeting reproof. *Purple Rain*'s detractors saw the film's two male leads—Prince and the Time's Morris Day, both playing men who contemptuously exploited the women around them for sexual and career purposes—as glorified endorsements of sexism, and also saw the cartoon-style sexiness of the female characters as a damaging stereotype.

What these critics seemed to miss is that the sexism of the Prince and Day characters runs pretty true to form for much of the pop scene. That is, the Prince and Day characters are mildly likable, unctuous men who come to look on women as the prize of privilege, and not surprisingly, they attract mildly likable, willing women who have learned to wield sex as an entrée to the realm of privilege. But like any worthy dramatic portrayal, *Purple Rain* gave these characters more depth than simple villain and victim delineations. In Prince's case, the character he plays ("the Kid") is self-interested and ungenerous as the result of a brutal family environment; he hates his father for his violent tirades against the mother, but at the same time can't even bring himself to give a fair hearing to the music of the women in his band, or allow his girlfriend the room for a pop career of her own (in fact, he slugs her when she announces her plans). At the film's end, though, the Kid takes a small yet crucial step toward rejecting the brutality that trapped his parents, and the film puts forth a moving vision of redemption and equality as related ambitions.

But then Prince, um, climaxes the movie with an image of himself playing a guitar that literally ejaculates. Is this, as some critics insisted, an offensive image? (If so, what about Jimi Hendrix's masturbatory displays with *his* guitar?) To some people, sure, that sort of imagery *is* offensive. It was probably even more offensive to some when Prince further celebrated orgasms by making a Top 10 single out of "Erotic City"—the first massively popular song ever to place the word "fuck" right in the heart of mainstream radio. Maybe this is a tawdry achievement, but it's also an honest act of rejoicing. Prince may be a sensationalist and opportunist, but that doesn't preclude him from being a serious and worthy artist: He aims to assert that a celebration of sex isn't far removed from a celebration of life—which in the 1980s' climate of voguish avarice and nuclear dread, could seem pretty transcendent and affirmative.

Madonna, too, is a sensationalist. From the start, with her hungry leer and her bemusedly mercenary view of romance, Madonna outraged some pop-leftists who believe that such manifestations of sexiness further objectify the cultural image of women, thereby undercutting feminism at a poltically precarious moment. In other words, Madonna isn't what some folks call a "sister."

As a result, in perhaps an even more enticing way than Prince, Madonna had proven a great divider in modern pop. Either you like her (not a simple affair, since for many of us it involves an appreciation for irony and a belief that feminism and lustful sexiness can be reconciled), or you revile her. And to a surprising extreme, many of Madonna's detractors vilified her in dehumanizing ways—such as a 1985 *Village Voice* review that labeled her as "whorish," and numerous items in other magazines and newspapers that described her with the word *sleazy,* as if image and repertoire alone are enough to merit such a verdict. (Even record stores got into the act: Los Angeles' Tower Records on Sunset carried Madonna's "Like a Virgin" in its racks under the title "Like a Slug.") All this for a brazen belly button and an (at worst candid but more likely satiric) "boy-toy" image? If Madonna stands condemned under this sort of narrow-headed puritanism, I'm only glad that Eartha Kitt and Julie London got to make the best of their bedroom-and-furs bit before our current era of "enlightenment"—and I'm amazed that Tina Turner's wonderful raunch (both past and present) has gone unscathed.

It's also possible that Madonna's critics just haven't got a very good sense of humor, and also aren't willing to afford a young woman the right to a brazen sexuality in the same manner they allowed Prince. ("I thought about that," Madonna once told me. "He was certainly just as sexually provocative, if not more than I was. I wasn't talking about giving *head.*") Could the real message of these critics be that if a woman aspires to bold or cocky achievements, she must measure up to higher standards than her male counterparts? If that's so—if this is the way we truly care to measure and condemn Madonna's image—then is it really she who is guilty of the greater crime of sexism?

*B*ACK TO KANDY STROUD and her questions about rock's obligations. I admit, there are no easy answers to these concerns. If I were a parent like Stroud, there might be times when I also would worry about how my kids hear and assimilate some of pop culture's images. Perhaps the closest I ever came to this was in the late summer of 1985, when I received a package of releases from the Important and Combat labels, representing the music of new heavy metal bands from around America. Here was a collection of all the vile vogues that alarmists had warned us about during the years: songs like "Kill Again," "Necrophilia," "Deliver Us to Evil," and "A Lesson in Violence," about rape, carnage, suicide, and devil worship, from bands with such names as Venom, Impaler, Exodus, Savatage, and Abattoir (which means "slaughterhouse"), some packaged in album jackets sporting clear images of bloody and nauseating misogyny and campy cannibalism.

Even more troubling was the actual contents of the songs—none of that kid's stuff that Ozzy Osbourne served up, nor the phony posing of the death punk bands. This was the cry of the *real* punks. Consider this verse from an Exodus song: "Get in our way and we're going to take your life/Kick in your face and rape and murder your wife/Plunder your town, your homes they'll burn to the ground/You won't hear a sound until my knife's in your back." Most of the other records also brandished themes of murder, relentless hate, sacrifice, the abyss of life, the inferno (and morbid allure) of death, and an apocalypse that would cleanse the world of religion and virtue. In a word, yikes! Mean, where are *these* kids' moms and dads?

Obviously, not all these horrific proclamations were meant to be taken as the literal values of these bands, just a few (if any) stalk-and-slash flicks reflect the real world views of their writers and directors. Still, there are clearly some young rock fans who find a sense of valor and meaning in the fearful iconography of the more violent-minded brands of heavy metal—some who, as a matter of record, have even tied acts of murder to their obsession with the image and music of some bands. While this kind of behavior is, of course, damn rare, one can understand why many folks of all social and political persuasions feel uncomfortable knowing that some rock music actually exalts these sentiments.

So, what should one do? Make this music illegal, prohibit its sales to minors? (Don't worry about limiting airplay; it gets damn little.) Compose legislation that would allow victims to sue the bands that "cause" or "inspire" Satanist crime? And does one then penalize those who make similar-minded horror films?

Well, I hope not, and not simply because I regard freedom of expression as sacrosanct. These would be cosmetic solutions to serious symptoms, syndromes that don't so much create attitudes and cause damage as they reflect certain realities of society and subcultures from which they spring. It's too easy to blame Madonna, Prince, and half-witted devil rock bands for fomenting sexism, pornography, and violence, and it is too simple-minded to assume that by silencing these musicians' messages, one has eliminated any causes or problems, or even any real unpleasantness. Anyway, just because

I'm not crazy about the subjects that some of these bands sing about doesn't empower me to gag them. I can rail against them if I like or choose not to support their music, but if push comes to shove, and any of these pop stars are threatened with repression, well, I've been a rock fan too long not to side with the profligates and upstarts.

VERY SHORTLY AFTER I wrote the words above, push *did* come to shove—and it never stopped. Also, in the fall of 1985, an incident occurred that only made matters worse. Even if you had scripted it, it would be hard to come up with a timelier—or worse—turn of events.

For weeks, a Washington, D.C., group of powerfully connected "concerned citizens" (inspired in part by Kandy Stroud's *Newsweek* column), who called themselves the Parents Musical Resource Center (the PMRC—led by Tipper Gore, married then to Senator Al Gore, who is now the vice-president of the United States) had been raising a storm over the sexual and violent imagery of rock music and videos, with the aim of pressuring record companies and national broadcasters into a collective exercise of self-censorship. Pop had gotten out of hand, they claimed, and because much of its audience is young and presumably impressionable, that music possesses a startling potential (in fact, predilection) for corrupting the morals of its fans. Consequently, the PMRC wanted all pop music perused and rated ("X" for profane, "V" for violent, "O" for occult), plus they wanted the most provoking songs yanked off the airwaves—and if the music industry wouldn't cooperate, the PMRC warned, perhaps Congress would take the matter under control.

During the same period that this movement was gathering force, a killer was traversing Southern California—raping, bludgeoning, murdering people in their sleep, leaving a vast community angry and terrified. There were few reported clues to this person's identity or personality—except that at the scene of one crime he had left a hat emblazoned with the symbol AC/DC: the name of an Australian rock band that made hedonistic music with occasional menacing overtones. As it develops, the hat wasn't so much a clue as a foretoken of media hysteria. Following the arrest of Richard Ramirez, the man who was accused, tried, and convicted of the "Night Stalker" murders, reports came fast and hard that Ramirez had indeed been an AC/DC fan—and that he had been particularly affected ("obsessed" was how most reports put it) by a song called "Night Prowler," a horror-movie-type account of nocturnal crime. Unfortunately, this fact was made to carry more significance than was warranted: Los Angeles newspapers and newscasts carried features detailing the song's lyrics, as if they were searching this evidence for an explanation to the Stalker's horrible crimes. Some reports went further: "Could a song like this push somebody over the edge?" asked one TV reporter.

What was particularly galling about all this was the surprising misinformation spread in many of the reports. If anything, it was an example of the news media reading the surface of a medium—rock & roll—they have little understanding for. Thus AC/DC—an over-the-hill but respectably rousing heavy metal outfit—became a "Satanist" group because of such album titles as *Highway to Hell* and a photo depicting one member in showy devil's horns. The truth is, beyond a display of sinister bravado (a commonplace of heavy metal style), there isn't anything genuinely menacing or satanic in either the group's stance or repertoire, and reporters could have discovered that by doing more than cribbing each other's sensationalistic coverage, or by simply examining the band's work a little more carefully.

But perhaps the most asinine as well as damaging example of misrepresentation was the widely reported assertion that the group's initials stood for "Anti-Christ/Devil's Child" or, according to another source, "After Christ, the Devil Comes." Well, get ready, because here's the hard truth: AC/DC is an *electrical* term; the band's logo even includes an *electrical* volt; these guys play loud and powerful *electric* music—indeed, *electricity* is the lifeblood of heavy metal. AC/DC means high-voltage *electricity*—get it? The group has never hinted at any other possible interpretation—not even the obvious bisexual reference that the initials also sometimes stand for.

There are a number of bad side effects to this kind of reportage and speculation, including that it tends to simplify the real, complex, and more awful reasons a man like Richard Ramirez would commit such atrocities. But because I am a pop critic and a pop fan, I have a partisan interest in the matter: I think it bad-raps rock & roll, distorts its content and aims, makes it seem like a nefarious secret world with an unhealthy, maybe deadly effect. Obviously, as I noted earlier, there *is* some heavy metal rife with violent imagery and it's fair to question such work. But it is a great leap to divine that such music endorses or might actually inspire murder, and it is a terrible thing to suggest that AC/DC or any other group is responsible for the dementia of its fans. How many parents came away from all those news reports fearing heavy metal as much as they had feared the Stalker? It must have seemed to some as if a terrible evil was already within their homes.

This, of course, is the very message that the PMRC wanted America to believe at the time: that much rock has become a dangerous influence and should be more actively scanned by concerned parents and by the industries that profit from it. When questioned by the *Los Angeles Herald Examiner* about the Night Stalker case, a PMRC spokesman said: "It's a little early to say whether we'll be citing it, but we're certainly watching the case with interest."

NOT MUCH LATER, the PMRC pretty much got their way. After a series of congressional hearings, the record industry announced that it had reached a compromise agreement with the PMRC: Record companies would begin a voluntary labeling effort, as a way of warning parents that some records contained "offensive" content. The settlement pertained only to rock and black pop records and not to country music—which made a kind of perverse sense, given that Al Gore was the senator from Tennessee at the time, and was understandably sensitive to the temperament of the Nashville music industry. The stickers also would not be affixed to classical music—weird, considering just how much murder and betrayal you can find in the stories told in opera.

So, some new releases were stickered. In a way, little changed—at least at first. Some artists kept making "offensive" music, and some of that music sold in the millions. And rock & roll remained a force of controversy—a music that (as Ronald Reagan termed it) was about "violence and perversity." But rock & roll also remained music that is a call to freedom, a music about *not* shutting up, about not staying quietly in one's place, and about not having to accept the dominant social order's safe-minded morality. As Prince told *Rolling Stone:* "I wish people would understand that I always thought I was bad. I wouldn't have got into this business if I didn't think I was bad."

But this first step toward a ratings system wasn't enough for some people—and that brings us to the last skirmish of this present story, though certainly not the last one that rock & roll and other forms of popular music will ever have to endure or combat.

SKIRMISH FOUR: OF RAP, PORN, WITCHES, TRIALS, AND REFUSED FLAGS

Nineteen-ninety was another year when pop fans were forcibly reminded that rock & roll is, after all, *still* rock & roll: a disruptive art form, viewed with scorn by numerous cultural guardians and with outright animosity by many conservative moralists. Rock, of course, wasn't alone in this regard. A coalition of fundamentalists and lawmakers assailed a wide range of American artists and charged them with disseminating obscenity, subversion, and blasphemy. But no other art form was threatened as frequently and as rigorously as pop music—and in the end, this atmosphere of peril may have done more to renew rock's sense of purpose and courage than any event in years.

The first indication that 1990 was to be a contentious year came in March, when *Newsweek* ran a cover story entitled "The Rap Attitude." Though the main article was ostensibly a report on the rise of bigotry and sexism in popular music in the late 1980s—and though the story made brief mention of the disturbing racial attitudes of white rock & rollers like Guns n' Roses' Axl Rose—*Newsweek* saved its greatest disdain for rap: a music that, in the magazine's estimation, amounts to little more than a "streetwise music," rife with "ugly macho boasting about anyone who hangs out on a different block—cops, other races, women, and homosexuals." The article proved a remarkably misrepresentative view of a complex subject. While it is true that there are rap performers who deserve to be criticized for their misogyny and homophobia, it is also true that, by and large, rap addresses questions about race, community, self-determination, drug abuse, and the tragedy of violence in intelligent and probing ways, and that it does so with a degree of musical invention that no other popular form can match. *Newsweek*, though, ignored this larger picture, and settled for a surprisingly alarmist view of rap and its practitioners that dismissed both as a "repulsive" culture.

The *Newsweek* article was perhaps the most scathing indictment of rock-related culture by major media in over a generation, but it was only the opening salvo of a difficult season. That same month, one of America's most powerful religious patriarchs, Roman Catholic Archbishop John O'Connor, told a congregation at New York's Saint Patrick's Cathedral that he believed that rock music was "a help to the devil." O'Connor seemed to have heavy metal in mind when he claimed that certain kinds of rock could induce demonic possession and drive some listeners to suicide. It wasn't the first time such a charge had been leveled. Three times parents have attempted to sue singer Ozzy Osbourne for the purported influence of his song "Suicide Solution" on the deaths of their sons, and at the time that O'Connor made his remarks, a similar suit—charging the lethal use of subliminal messages—was being prepared in Reno, Nevada, against Judas Priest. These were grim charges—that rock & roll could enter the souls of the young; that it could deliver them to dark forces and darker ends—and suddenly they seemed to be granted both religious and legal plausibility.

The most dauntless of rock's foes was the Parents Music Resource Center (PMRC)—the powerful watchdog organization founded in 1985 by

Tipper Gore. Though the group claims that its primary aim is simply to make parents aware of the provocative themes and raw language that characterize much of today's rock, the PMRC has in fact courted both the media and lawmakers as it has relentlessly pressured record labels to impose rating systems on their artists. Indeed, the PMRC had been rumored to have privately aligned itself with ultraconservative outfits like the Eagle Forum and Missouri Project Rock, and together, these factions have been decisive in bringing about the rising view that rock has become a force for moral and social disorder, and that the music's themes and effects should be more closely monitored. As a result, the PMRC would become the most effective adversary that rock & roll has ever faced.

By early 1990, anti-rock sentiment had grown enough to fuel a full-fledged national movement calling for the labeling of controversial pop recordings. Under the aggressive crusading of such state representatives as Missouri's Jean Dixon and Pennsylvania's Ron Gamble, nearly twenty states were considering legislation that would require that any pop releases containing explicit language or describing or "advocating" certain sexual or violent behavior to be emblazoned with a bright warning sticker. The states differed a bit over which offensive subjects merited stickering (though Pennsylvania seemed to have the most representative list, running the gamut from "suicide," "incest," "murder," and "bestiality" to "sexual activity in a violent context" and "illegal use of drugs or alcohol," among other affronts). But nearly all the proposed bills agreed on one matter: If a record that featured any of the cited disturbing themes, or that featured explicit language, was sold *without* a warning sticker—or, in some cases, if a stickered recording was sold to a minor—the seller ran the risk of a fine or even of jail.

It was a mind-stopping development: Nearly half of the United States were considering measures that, if enacted, would subject one of the most popular (and one of the worthiest) art and entertainment forms of our time to state regulation. In addition, the proposed legislation would have the effect of stigmatizing some of the art form's most important works, simply because of the music's willingness to trade in the sort of language and themes that are commonplace in not only much of today's more relevant film and literature, but also in the course of modern everyday life. But then, for a zealot like Representative Jean Dixon—who admits she gained her perspective on modern rock from the PMRC, the Eagle Forum, and other similar partisan groups—stigmatizing rock-related music was perhaps precisely the point. "Rebellion is like witchcraft," said Dixon early in 1990, explaining her reprehension for the spirit of cultural and social insurrection that rock embodies for many of its fans. "That's what it is, it's like witchcraft."

And if history is any indicator, where one finds witchcraft and witches, then witch hunts and witch trials are likely not far behind.

*I*T IS UNLIKELY, of course, that any of the proposed legislation would have withstood ultimate constitutional scrutiny. Even so, the mainstream recording industry—which has a history of conciliatory stands when it comes to dealing with prolabeling forces—elected not to stand up for principle. In March, eager to ward off any further legislative action and anxious not to stir up public reaction, the Recording Industry Association of America (the RIAA, the alliance of major record companies, which had capitulated to the PMRC's pressures for "voluntary labeling" in 1986) announced that it was creating a uniform sticker for use by all record companies. The bold black-and-white label would carry the warning: PARENTAL ADVISORY: EXPLICIT LYRICS. What's more, the organization pledged to watch new pop releases more attentively, and to make certain that any recording which might merit such a label would not end up in record stores without one. A few weeks later the PMRC—joined by several state senators, representatives of the PTA, and the National Association of Recording Merchandisers (NARM, whose members include record retailers)—held a press conference in Washington, D.C., and announced that, in light of the RIAA's action, pending labeling legislation would now be dropped in thirteen states, with more likely to follow. Though both sides hoped to give the impression that a compromise had been struck, the conservative coalition had, in effect, won: The prolabeling forces had induced the recording industry to impose a stickering system, without having to resort to the legal process, and without having to face a constitutional test. And, according to Jean Dixon's spokesman, if the industry failed to live up to its promise to police new releases, "I guarantee you there will be legislation in fifty states next year." (Later, Dixon was to lose her bid for reelection in a Missouri primary.)

As it turns out, the threat was hardly necessary. Stickering followed with a vengeance, cropping up on numerous rap and heavy metal releases—sometimes without apparent reason and sometimes over the stated protests of the recording artists. In addition, some artists were apparently pressured to change explicit or potentially controversial words or phrases, or to drop entire songs. (In the case of the pointedly violent-minded debut album by the rap group the Geto Boys, Geffen Records chose to drop the entire work.) In the end, only one major label—Virgin Records—refused to sticker its artists, instead adorning its releases with the First Amendment. By contrast, only a few of the independent labels—where some of the most aggressive and explicit rap, metal, and punk music has been cultivated—chose to abide by the RIAA agreement.

But for one conservative moralist, a Coral Gables, Florida, lawyer named Jack Thompson, stickering was beside the point. Thompson—who, like Tipper Gore, describes himself as a long-standing rock fan—is a Christian Evangelical who fancies himself a Batman-style crusader against pornography and child abuse. At the beginning of 1990, Thompson received a transcript of the lyrics to *As Nasty as They Wanna Be,* by the 2 Live Crew, a black Miami group whose specialty is X-rated raps about male sexual prowess. Inflamed by the 2 Live Crew's graphic language and by what he regarded as the band's rapacious attitude toward women, Thompson launched a letter-faxing campaign to law-enforcement officials throughout Florida, urging them to take action against *As Nasty as They Wanna Be* as an "obscene" work. Thompson's arguments caught the attention of Florida governor Bob Martinez, who set into motion a series of actions that resulted in a federal judge officially declaring the album "obscene" in June—the first such ruling for a recorded work in American history. Two days later, record store owner Charles Freeman was arrested in Fort Lauderdale after he sold a copy of the album to an undercover police officer. Within the week, three members of the 2 Live Crew—including leader Luther "Luke" Campbell—were arrested for performing material from the album at an adults only concert at a Broward County club. Meantime, Jack Thompson vowed to keep up his campaign against *Nasty,* citing his skirmish with the 2 Live Crew as merely "an opening shot in a cultural civil war."

Thompson couldn't have been more correct. In what was undoubtedly rock & roll's most embattled year since the rise of Elvis Presley, nothing shocked the music community more than the Broward County arrests. It wasn't that music professionals particularly revered or respected the 2 Live Crew; indeed, the band had been publicly and forcefully criticized for its puerile sexist humor by numerous critics and fellow rappers. But Florida's heavyhanded response to the 2 Live Crew's relentless sex raps (which, though coarse, were also a good deal funnier and less mean-spirited than is generally admitted) amounted to a clear effort to abrogate an artist's rights to free speech—an action that, if successful, could endanger the rights of numerous other Americans in the oncoming censorship wars. Plus, there was another concern: Why had a black rap group been singled out for an obscenity prosecution—particularly in a county in which strip shows, adult reading material, and pornographic videos were readily accessible to consenting adults? "The subtext of this event," said Jon Landau, manager and producer of Bruce Springsteen, "invites the suspicion that there is a substantial racist component. This is selective prosecution at its most extreme. Therefore, until Luke's rights have been secured, discussion of the merits of his music is not really the point. The point is to make sure that we're all free to express ourselves whatever the point of view, however extreme."

As it turned out, much of the pop world shared Landau's view. By making the 2 Live Crew a central target in a potentially far-reaching cultural and political battle, Jack Thompson forced many in the music industry to recognize how much ground had been conceded to the anti-rock forces. In addition, Thompson also helped transform Luther Campbell into something of an unlikely *cause célèbre*. In late June, when Campbell sought permission from Bruce Springsteen to use the backing track of "Born in the U.S.A." for the 2 Live Crew's account of their troubles in Florida, Springsteen granted the use free of charge. The result, called "Banned in the U.S.A.," was the 2 Live Crew's most laudable moment—or at least the one instance in which the group aspired to something other than puerile scatology. In response, Thompson fired off a fax to Springsteen: "Dear Mr. Springsteen," he wrote, "I would suggest 'Raped in the U.S.A.' as your next album. . . . You're now harmful to the women and children who have bought your albums." Later, in a *Los Angeles Times* interview, Thompson added: "Bruce and Luther can go to hell together."

But the biggest drama was that of the trials. In October, a jury composed of five white women and one Hispanic man convicted store owner Charles Freeman of peddling obscenity; later that month, a different jury in the same Florida county acquitted Campbell and the other 2 Live Crew members of the obscenity charges. In essence, it was a split verdict—and nobody quite knew how to read its meaning. Meantime, in the year's other big rock trial, Judas Priest was acquitted in Reno on charges that subliminal messages in the band's music had led to the suicide of one youth and the attempted suicide of another—but the judge's ruling left many legal questions unresolved and made it plain to the music industry that heavy metal recordings would likely remain subject to legal actions in the future. In response to all this activity, MTV—once a cautiously apolitical entertainment forum, and now probably rock's most powerful media force—turned its annual awards show into an anti-censorship rally. In addition, with the help of artists like Madonna, the network launched a voter-registration drive, designed to mobilize the vote against pro-censorship crusader-politicians in upcoming elections.

In the end, none of these events settled the debate over rock's rights to free speech. Certainly, in the rough seasons ahead, there will be further calls for censorship. More arrests and more trials are also likely, and given the

---

rightward drift of America's federal courts, it is hard to say how these campaigns will play themselves out. Still, there is hope: The tide of cultural history suggests that, as troubling as the notion may be to some, freedom of expression is a right that ultimately will not be undone. At the same time, perhaps the most frightening lesson of the Reagan era is that sometimes the tide of cultural history can be reversed.

IF NOTHING ELSE, all the brouhaha over censorship served to remind many of us that rock still has the power to unsettle and to inflame. Of course, sometimes it chooses to provoke its critics by merely taunting them with surefire irritants like explicit sexual descriptions, or rants about violence or the devil—but then sometimes the most effective (and hilarious) response to haughty disapproval is simply to become more unconscionable. At its best, though, rock & roll is a good deal more than a mere affront or a subject for argument. It is, in fact, perhaps the sole art form that most regularly *forms* an argument. That is, rock & roll is itself a disagreement with established power—a refutation of authority's unearned influence.

Not surprisingly, some of the music that did the best job of both taunting *and* arguing in 1990 came from the two camps that experienced the greatest heat—heavy metal and rap. On the surface, these two genres might seem to have little in common, in terms either of audience or style. And yet both are derived from the structures of blues music, and by keeping that form's temper fresh, rap and metal have also done a tremendous amount to revivify rock's essential incendiary spirit. In addition, both rap and hard rock speak for and to the concerns of young and often disenfranchised audiences—working class and black youth, who are frequently viewed with fear and suspicion by much of the American mainstream—and it is this power to articulate and stir the passions of youthful outsiders that today scares so many people about rock & roll.

But it was rap that enjoyed more attention than any other pop genre in 1990, and for fair reason. Despite all the swipes directed at it, rap remained committed to holding forth on some of the most disturbing concerns of the day. Records like Public Enemy's *Fear of a Black Planet,* Above the Law's *Livin' Like Hustlers,* Kid Frost's *Hispanic Causing Panic,* Ice Cube's *AmeriKKKa's Most Wanted,* and the Geto Boys' debut album were works that offered tough and unflinching appraisals of a broad range of unpleasant topics—including gang violence, misogyny, racism, and drug dealing—and despite the naysayers who warned that this music amounted to "ugly macho boasting" and "obscenity," all of these albums enjoyed substantial sales. Is that cause for concern? Does it mean that the audience that buys rap records is an audience that likes this music because it espouses values of anger? Do people in that audience, in fact, take some of the songs on the Ice Cube, Geto Boys, Kid Frost, or Above the Law records as literal celebrations of misogyny or violence?

Obviously, few of the people who hear a musical account of a drive-by shooting lose their repulsion toward such acts in real life, much less feel any inclination to take part in such horror. Yet this isn't to deny that one shouldn't raise hard questions about the meaning and impact of some of this music. A record like *The Geto Boys* (which, remember, Geffen found so offensive, the label refused to release it) relates some truly unsettling tales about gang violence and homicidal rape, and does so from a first-person point of view that brings both the narrator and listener into the heart of modern urban horror. It may be among the most terrifying works that popular music has ever produced. Certainly, it is a record that one should take a good hard look at—indeed, any art that might seem to celebrate hatred and murder is art that should be scrutinized, and, when necessary, criticized. At the same time, that isn't really what *The Geto Boys* is about. Like Martin Scorsese, whose *GoodFellas* is deeply felt drama about contemporary gangster life, the Geto Boys and other rappers are reporting on a social reality—in the Geto Boys' case, one that they know firsthand—and at times such reportage can seem ugly and morally questionable. But whereas Scorsese's work is singled out as an artistic achievement, *The Geto Boys* is roundly condemned as brutal trash. Why? Is it because the Geto Boys are talking about conditions of violence *so* modern, *so* threatening, that we can't view any of it with distance? Or is it because, by telling their tales in the first person, rappers seem to commit themselves to the worst impulses of their scenarios?

There are no simple answers to these questions. All that is clear is that works like *The Geto Boys* are disturbing for good reason—they're *meant* to be disturbing—and it is to our peril and discredit when we fail to examine the conditions that have made such music possible, or necessary.

One other artist had a rough time of it in 1990, and that was Irish singer Sinéad O'Connor. The year began wonderfully for her, with a number 1 hit single, "Nothing Compares 2 U," and an equally high-ranking album, *I Do Not Want What I Haven't Got.* But during the summer, when O'Connor refused to allow the national anthem to be played at one of her performances in New Jersey, local and national media treated the event as major news. Overnight, there were calls for her to be deported back to the United Kingdom; radio stations announced they were boycotting her music; and she was vilified by other celebrities (including Frank Sinatra) and harassed in public.

Over and over, irate Americans asked the same question: What did O'Connor have against the national anthem? (The answer is easy, and fairly innocent: O'Connor is opposed to nationalism of any sort, and in fact refused to pose with an Irish flag for a photo session for *Rolling Stone* earlier in the year.) But there was another question that wasn't asked and perhaps should have been: Namely, in a year when rock was treated as subversion by so many American lawmakers and pundits, how could any principled rock & roller do anything but refuse any false tributes? Why should any performer be forced to pay tribute to a nation that is so reluctant to stand up for the rights of its own artists?

The incident was merely another reminder that these are dangerous times to advertise yourself as a malcontent in American pop culture. But it was also a reminder that rock's best and bravest heroes aren't about to back down when confronted by indignant authoritarians. Kicking against social repression and moral vapidity—that's an activity which, for well over thirty years now, rock & roll has managed to do better than virtually any other art or entertainment form. But at this juncture, the forces that would not only condemn but curtail or silence that impulse are formidable. If 1990 taught us anything, it is that if we value rock as a spirit of insolent liberty, then the time has come to form a bulwark against those who would gladly muzzle that spirit.

clash

of the titans:

heavy metal

enters the 1990s

*i*t looks like hell," says the security guard, gazing at the scene before him. "It's like hell just came popping up all over the place."

It is a hot spring night in 1991, in Dallas, Texas, at the open-air Starplex theater, where the Clash of the Titans—a bill featuring three of the leading exponents of speed-metal rock & roll, Megadeth, Anthrax, and Slayer—is playing its opening date of a two-month trek across America. Onstage, Megadeth is playing a loud-hard-fast set of songs about rage and apocalypse, but at the rear of the theater, on a large grassy slope, it looks like apocalypse may be happening for real. Up on that knoll, hundreds of heavy metal fans have started to build bonfires and dance and stomp around them in an almost tribal fashion. From a distance it almost looks as if the fans are tossing themselves in and out of the pyres, like one of Bosch or Bruegel's portrayals of the inferno brought to modern life.

"Man, I have *never* seen anything like that," says the security guard, shaking his head, still transfixed. "This is what we get for letting this heavy metal shit into this place. I tell you, the stuff is fucking *evil.*"

HEAVY METAL: Over the course of its history it has been accused of everything from musical low-mindedness and lousy politics to the spread of teenage suicide and suburban Satanism. It has also been blasted by federal legislators, local lawmakers, conservative (*and* liberal) moralists, concerned parents, and prominent religious figures, all of whom see the music as a corrupting influence on the young: a music that is capable of entering the souls of its listeners and delivering them to the darkest forces of evil.

But for all the scorn and dismissal that has been perpetually hurled its way, heavy metal is the only constant standard-bearer that rock & roll can claim. Whereas movements like rockabilly, psychedelia, disco, and even punk played out their active histories in a handful of years each, metal has proven consistently popular for over twenty years now. Plus, it has also served as a vital and reliable rite of passage for its audience—that is, it is music that articulates the frustrations, desires, and values of a youth population that has too often found itself without any other cultural advocate or voice. Indeed, metal often works as music for outcasts: kids who feel pressed or condemned by adult society, who feel despised or hopeless or angry, and who need to assert their own pride and bravado. Consequently, a music that many regard as a form without redemption is actually a music that can help powerless young people feel powerful—or at least feel like they've found a means to outrage or repel an increasingly coldhearted society.

In other words, metal persists. Though the music may remain a prime target for legislators and moralists—and though many critics are now claiming that guitar-driven rock & roll has lost its primacy in the world of popular music—heavy metal remains as audacious and defiant as ever. At present, in fact, it supports one of the most energetic and far-reaching alternative-culture scenes in all modern pop, a vast and complex international network of record labels, magazines, radio stations, nightclubs, newsletters, and leather-and-T-shirts shops. What's more, metal (in the early 1990s) is enjoying the widest spectrum of musical stylists it has ever seen, including the progressive hip-hop and punk-inflected rock & roll of Living Colour; Faith No More; and 24-7 Spyz; the classic bad-boy posturing of Guns n' Roses, the blues-derived majesty of the Black Crowes, the pretty-boy raunch of Poison and Warrant; the grungy grandeur of Pacific Northwest bands like Alice in Chains, Soundgarden, Screaming Trees, and Tad; and the avant-garde extremism of British grindcore bands like Napalm Death, Carcass, and Godflesh.

Yet when it comes to sheer disrepute or bravado, nothing in all pop—

except for some of the more notorious rap artists of the day—can compare with speed-metal or thrash-metal bands like Slayer, Megadeth, and Anthrax. Inspired as much by the brutal rhythms and bellicose stance of early 1980s hardcore punk as by heavy metal's own styles and obsessions, these bands are making some of the boldest music of our time, and, some critics would claim, also some of the most frightening. "When victory's a massacre," sings Slayer in a song from the group's latest album, *Seasons in the Abyss*, "When victory is survival/When this end is a slaughter/The final swing is not a drill/ It's how many people I can kill." It's a brutal decree, and though it's possible to read it as an indictment of the bloodshed that it describes, it's also possible to hear it as a celebration: a surrender to the exhilaration of the kill. Either way, it's one of those moments that serves notice that something in rock & roll's moral center is now shifting. An art form which has often striven to convince its audience that the world might yet be redeemed through action or opposition now seeks to tell us unflinchingly violent truths about the increasingly violent modern soul.

"Bands like us are writing a new book in rock & roll history," says Dave Mustaine, the lead singer and guitarist for Megadeth. "If Elvis Presley liberated the body and Bob Dylan released the mind, we're releasing whatever's left: all the stuff that people would rather overlook in a world that's gone mad. Actually, I prefer to think of us as modern troubadours who are spreading joy and harmony by saying 'shit, fuck, piss, kill,' and all the rest of it."

For THE BETTER PART of the last decade, Megadeth, Slayer, and Anthrax have been working in rock's margins, making extreme music for a fervid young audience that much of the pop world—including the heavy metal mainstream—would just as soon ignore. In fact, as far as much rock media is concerned, this whole scene may as well be invisible.

But the Clash of the Titans tour is an attempt to change all that, and to assert that these bands can attract a mass following that is a legitimate pop community in its own right. It's an ambitious venture, but also a risky one. Though the three co-headlining bands share a roughly similar style, they don't all share the same interests. Slayer, a Los Angeles–based band, plays rageful tunes about the horror of interminable warfare and unconscionable murder, while Megadeth—despite its smartly humored songs about drug abuse, ecological disaster, and impending apocalypse—is pretty much a band for guitar aficionados. Anthrax—a New York band—plays some of the most erudite and ambitious political rock of the day, with an eye toward helping the heavy metal audience understand the power and responsibility that lies within its own community. In short, there is as much separating these three bands (including profoundly different philosophies in politics and personal behavior) as there is uniting them (namely, a shared belief that metal is one of the most exciting, intelligent, and viable pop forms of the day).

Consequently, there is some concern about what might happen when the bands' various audiences mingle. Megadeth tends to draw a crowd of headbangers—long-haired young males who stand around bobbing their heads as a way of keeping time with the music's lickety-split rhythms—while Anthrax draws a crowd that likes to slam-dance and mosh: a style of dancing in which kids stomp around together, flailing and bouncing off each other at a furious pace. Slayer's audience, however, can sometimes seem flat-out violent. At Slayer shows in Los Angeles in recent years, the LAPD (always good for an overreaction) sent in riot squads and helicopters to deal with some rowdy fans outside the concert halls, and at an ill-famed show at New York's Felt Forum in 1988, the group's fans went wild, tearing seats apart and hurling them around the floor and getting into fights with security guards. The band's lead singer, Tom Araya, tried to calm the crowd down, but after a few songs the Forum's management ejected Slayer from the stage. "Thanks a lot, assholes," Araya told the crowd. "You fucked this up for yourselves."

For this tour—which will easily draw some of the biggest thrash or mosh crowds ever assembled in the States—the three bands have hired a special security overseer, Jerry Mele, who previously worked with Madonna, among others. Shortly before each show, Mele convenes a meeting of the hall's various security and management personnel. "Look," Mele tells the guards assembled at the Starplex amphitheater in Dallas, "I want you to treat these kids with respect. It may look like they're fighting or hurting each other out there, but it's their way of having fun. If they come over the barricade down front—and some of them will—don't hurt them and don't throw them out. Bring them over to me at the side of the stage. I'll have a talk with them and give them another chance. Believe me, if you do things this way, we won't have any serious trouble here." You can see the look of skepticism on the faces of these guards—big, muscular men, some who are accustomed to resolving rowdiness with force—but in the end they agree to Mele's requests.

The first test comes an hour later, when Slayer opens the Dallas show (the three bands will rotate the headline slot). There is nothing in all modern pop like the moment Slayer takes a stage. The whole place rises to its feet as the band slams into "Hell Awaits" at a ludicrous breakneck pace, and hundreds of kids press their way to the front of the stage, where they proceed to throw themselves into each other, moshing and slamming with a furious intensity. At first the security force looks a bit edgy—it is not always an enviable position to be staked out between Slayer and its fans—but in a short time their patience and gentleness with the fans pays off. Nobody shoves or punches anybody, and the few times that any guards see a kid who looks like he's trying to hurt other dancers in the mosh pit, Mele makes his way into the crowd and drags the offender out himself. Later, when Anthrax makes its appearance, the slamming is even more congenial—though in large part that's because Anthrax's music, in contrast to Slayer's, is more concerned with questions of community than with the thrills of violence. When Anthrax plays, even young women find the mosh pit a fun place to hang out—which is rarely the case during a Slayer set.

But then, just before Megadeth is set to perform, the fires on the hill begin: eerie-looking eruptions of flame, surrounded by stomping circles of kids, all pushing and shoving to dance as close to the flares as possible.

When you venture up close, though, the fire-dancing doesn't seem particularly threatening or licentious. In fact, there appears to be a rather strict social order at work in constructing the event. First, one or two kids strip off their T-shirts and set them ablaze, waving them over their heads like fiery flags until they attract the attention of other fans. It's almost as if they are setting the fires as a way of drawing each other in closer, as a way of finding other sympathetic souls in a dark landscape. After a bit, the kids toss the burning rags into a heap and toss in paper cups and other inflammable scraps until they have something like a watchfire going. Meantime, a growing circle of dancers begins to tramp around the fire in a mosh rhythm, picking up speed and attracting new members as it spreads outward. The only time the scene ever gets scary is when security guards charge up the hill, pushing the kids aside and extinguishing the fires with chemical sprays. The resulting smoke is harsh and burns the eyes, causing the kids to turn and run, sometimes knocking each other down in the process. Invariably, though, the fires start up again, and the circle of wildly stomping dancers reconvenes.

It's as if the conflagrations taking place on the hill were an enactment of the defiance and rage that the music onstage has been proclaiming all day long. At the end of Megadeth's set, Dave Mustaine sings the Sex Pistols' "Anarchy in the U.K."—the song that first announced that rock & roll could accommodate the vision of a world in ruin. By the time he gets to the song's incendiary closing verse—"I want to be anarchy, you know what I mean?/ 'Cause I want to be an anarchist/Again I'm *pissed*/DESTROY!"—the hill has erupted in small bonfires from top to bottom, as if the fans are acting out the song's incitements as fast as Mustaine can proclaim them.

In the end, not much real damage is done. In the morning there will be a few square feet of torched grass and some predictable local media outrage. But for some of the kids gathered here, a genuine power struggle took place tonight—the first one that many of them have ever won.

THE NEXT DAY'S show in Lubbock, Texas, proves to be something of a letdown. The turnout is one of the smallest that the tour will see—a little over two thousand fans show up in an arena that can hold over twice that many—but a bigger problem seems to be the sound. The members of each of the bands come off the stage complaining that they could not hear themselves playing, and that the mix in the sound monitors had been messy and dim. In particular, Megadeth's Dave Mustaine is coldly furious. At the end of the evening, he stands in the backstage area and tells his tour manager that he wants the sound man suspended from the board for the following evening. It is plain that the tour manager will not find this an easy request to accommodate, though it's also plain that Mustaine—who has a formidable reputation for being arrogant and headstrong—isn't about to give ground.

It's only two days into this trip, but already Dave Mustaine is beginning to wear on the nerves of some of the others involved in the tour, particularly Slayer. A former heavy drug user and drinker, Mustaine these days is scrupulously clean and healthy. As a result, he insists on keeping himself at a distance from the members of Slayer, who still enjoy drinking and acting up. In a *Los Angeles Times* article that appeared at the outset of the tour, Mustaine told an interviewer that he had been embarrassed by Slayer's behavior during their recent European tour together. "There were times where it was detrimental to my sanity," he said. "When we travel and we're stuck on the same plane, and they're completely inebriated, swearing at the top of their lungs and belching and guzzling. . . . I felt like I wanted to crawl off into the bathroom of the plane and die. . . . I have more respect for their luggage than their behavior." Needless to say, these comments haven't gone over well, nor has Mustaine's insistence that Megadeth stay in different hotels than Slayer and that the band's two dressing rooms are located as far apart as possible.

But there is also another side to Dave Mustaine, and it can be surprisingly affecting. A few minutes after his tantrum about the sound problem, the thin, blond Mustaine sits on the band's bus in the parking lot of the Lubbock Coliseum and talks quietly about all the years and friendship that were lost to his drug abuse. In moments like this, there is nothing in Mustaine's manner that is arrogant or taxing. Instead, he comes across as somebody who is smart, conscience-stricken, and deeply sad—as if he has endured a long nightmare and is just now coming to terms with how he managed to inflict so much damage on himself and others over the years.

In some ways, Mustaine's long bouts of self-abuse were probably an extension of the ruin he had felt as a child. When he was seven, his parents divorced, leaving Mustaine and his sisters and mother living in poverty in the suburbs of Southern California. By his early teens, his mother was absent much of the time, and Mustaine spent the next few years residing with his sisters and their families. One day, when he was fifteen, says Mustaine, one of his brothers-in-law punched him in the face when he found him listening to Judas Priest's *Sad Wings of Destiny*. "I decided right then," says Mustaine, "that I was going to play this music. That would be my revenge."

In the early 1980s, after playing in a series of pop and metal cover bands, Mustaine hooked up with Lars Ulrich and James Hetfield, from Norwalk, California. Together, they formed Metallica—a band that, within a few years, would become the most important heavy metal ensemble since Led Zeppelin. It was Metallica, in fact, that codified speed-metal as a music derived from the rhythmic brutality of hardcore punk and the yowling melodic drive of early-1980s British denim-and-leather metal bands like Motorhead and Iron Maiden. But for all its gifts, the group was also beset with serious personality conflicts. Mustaine and the others fought frequently—sometimes about drug use, sometimes about leadership of the band—and in time, the tension became unbearable. "One day," says Mustaine, "they woke me up and said, 'Uh, look, you're out of the band.' And I said, 'What, no warning? No second chance?' And they said, 'No, you're out.'

"To this day," continues Mustaine, "I have a hard time seeing those guys. Something inside me feels like saying, 'You know, you guys are really fucked for firing me. You didn't give me a chance—and I really miss you; I miss playing with you.' And while they're responsible for their own success, I don't think they ever would have developed the way they did if I hadn't come into the picture. I was a key part of that band."

Back in Los Angeles, Mustaine settled deeper into his drug use and thought for a time about quitting music altogether. But in 1984, after he met Dave Ellefson, a bassist who had just moved to California from rural Minnesota, Mustaine decided to take another stab at band life, and formed Megadeth. "I thought of this band as not just the return of Dave Mustaine," he says, "but also my revenge. I thought, 'This is the music I want to play: a jazz-oriented, progressive music that's going to alter heavy metal as we understand it.'" Mustaine proved good to his promise. Though Megadeth shared Metallica's passion for hard-and-fast riffs, the best tracks on albums like *Peace Sells . . . But Who's Buying* and *So Far, So Good, So What!* demonstrated a melodic and textural versatility that no other band in metal has matched.

But Megadeth has also seen its share of problems—including numerous band firings, as well as Mustaine's worsening drug problem. "One of the earlier members in the band," he says, "finally got me into heroin. He had told me it was like being back in the womb, and, I mean, I was a slut. Pussy was my favorite thing in the world and for me to be fully *inside* a pussy was the fantasy of a lifetime, and that's what heroin was like to me. I became like a dope-seeking missile, and after a while I was losing my mind. I got to the point where I just *could not play* anymore. I knew that I was going to die if I didn't get sober, and even that wasn't enough to make me stop. I would have done anything for coke or heroin. I would have even gone into prostitution."

One morning in early 1990, while driving home in a drug-and-alcohol stupor, Mustaine was pulled over by the police. He had heroin, cocaine, speed, and liquor in his blood system, and he also had some of those same substances in his car. He was arrested, and a short while later he was given a choice: Get clean—and *stay* clean—or go to jail. It turned out to be the impetus Mustaine needed. Within a few weeks he had joined a twelve-step addiction recovery program, and has stayed clean since. "In fact, tonight," he says, seated aboard the bus in Lubbock, "is my birthday: A year ago today was the last time I used any drugs. And you know what? Now a lot of my dreams are coming true. In the last year I got married, we put together our best version of Megadeth yet, and we also finished our best record, *Rust in Peace*. I think it all has to do with the fact that now I pray and meditate a lot. I don't sit at home by the phone waiting for some fucking creep to come over with powder."

Mustaine glances at the clock on the wall. It is now past 1 A.M. The bus should already be on its way to the next stop, but everybody's waiting for a final band member to arrive. When somebody suggests that the musician is out having sex with a young woman that had been seen backstage, Mustaine turns momentarily livid. The woman, says Mustaine, is a recently recovered addict, and he won't tolerate anybody in his band using her. As it turns out, the rumor is false—the person in question had barely even met the woman—and a few moments later when the woman shows up to say goodbye to everybody, Mustaine and bassist Ellefson (who is also a recovered addict) spend several minutes talking with her and encouraging her to keep up her sobriety.

"A lot of things have changed for me," Mustaine will say later. "I think I now have a more genuine concern for others—though I'm still not strong enough to be around people who are drinking or using drugs. Also, I don't have the same kind of interest I once had in the occult. I think it's simply that now I know that there *is* a God, and, uh, it's not me."

THE NEXT DAY—when the Titans tour appears in San Antonio—is a Sunday, and one of the local newspapers bears a story on its front page under the headline: "Face to Face with a Devil." It is a flimsy story of a woman who was reportedly exorcised of a demon by a local priest, but it is covered as if it is major news, and it also serves as a reminder that these Texas cities that this tour has been visiting the last few days are strongholds for conservative religious values. On the surface, towns like these might seem unlikely places to harbor a substantial heavy metal audience. (In fact, a few years back, San Antonio's city officials considered banning heavy metal concerts within the city, but instead settled for an ordinance restricting kids under the age of fourteen from attending "obscene performances.") But as Donna Gaines points out in *Teenage Wasteland* (probably the best book written about contemporary youth culture), conservative communities tend not only to breed a fair amount of repressed anger and fear, they also tend to breed conservative fears—like fears of the devil and rock & roll. And, if you're young and have had to live with these sort of values too long, what could be better as a way of rubbing against the local ethos than subscribing to the symbology and values of heavy metal?

You can see signs of the local youths' appetite for offense as the crowd begins to arrive at San Antonio's Sunken Gardens amphitheater. Most of the fans here are young, and many of them are wearing black T-shirts emblazoned with the names of their favorite metal bands (besides this show's headliners, big favorites include Metallica, Iron Maiden, Judas Priest, and Danzig). These shirts are rife with horror-derived imagery, including depictions of rotting ghouls, greenish skulls, and apocalyptic demons. The iconography may sound gruesome, and yet when you're confronted with an endless variety of these shirts in mass quantity, there's actually something mesmerizing—even lovely—about it all. Plus, it's simply a kick to draw the attention or disapproval of others by wearing these shirts. It's a way of boasting your toughness and your proud status as an outcast. Conservative moralists can fume all they like about the question of what art is tolerated inside our museums, but they're missing an important point: The canvas has shifted in this culture, and it is kids like the ones who are gathered here in San Antonio who are bearing the defiant new art on their chests. And the best part is, there is no way this art can be shut down or deprived of its funds. It has already spilled over into the streets, and into our homes.

At 7:00 P.M., Slayer takes the stage in San Antonio, and begins to slam across its fierce music. There is a dense and pummeling quality to the band's sound—the bass rumbles, the drums explode at a rat-a-tat-tat clip and the guitars blare and yowl in unison—but it's all played with a remarkable precision and deftness. Meantime, the audience that is jammed up close to the stage erupts in frenzy, with some kids slamming and bounding hard against each other while others clamber atop one another so they can dive over the barricade. This goes on and on until even the band can't take its eyes off the action. On a night such as this, there isn't anything in all rock & roll like a Slayer show. Watching the melee and hearing the fulmination of the music, you feel like you're seeing a live band as exciting as the Sex Pistols.

At the same time, this is a band that deals with some fairly unsettling subject matter. When Slayer first emerged in the mid-1980s—chasing hard after the punk-metal coalition that had been made possible by bands like Black Flag, Metallica, and Venom—the group's repertoire (written at the time by guitarists Kerry King and Jeff Hanneman) was heavy with songs about Satan and hell. But in recent years, under the influence of bassist and vocalist Tom Araya—who is now the band's chief lyricist—the emphasis has shifted. Araya—whose family fled Chile during a time of political unrest and who has lived around some of the rougher sections of Los Angeles and witnessed the effects of gang warfare—decided the band should write more about the human and social horror of the modern world, and over the course of the band's last three albums, he has developed a special affection for topics like political oppression, modern warfare, gang killings, and serial murders. Perhaps the band's most chilling song is "Dead Skin Mask," told from the point of view of Ed Gein, the famous mass murderer who killed numerous children and adults and flayed them, and who later served as the inspiration for such works as *Psycho, Texas Chainsaw Massacre,* and *The Silence of the Lambs.* In "Dead Skin Mask," Araya enters into Gein's heart and mind, and tells the story of his crimes from inside that dark and awful place.

"I know that a song like that," says Araya, "where I'm writing it as if I *am* the person who is doing the killing, freaks people out. They say, 'How could you sit there and think that way?' Well, it isn't hard at all. In fact, it's very easy. I sit there and I ask myself, 'Now how would it feel if I really wanted to kill somebody?' And I know: I'd feel an exhilaration. I'd feel awesome.

"See, when I wrote 'Dead Skin Mask,' I had just read this book called *Deviant,* about Ed Gein. As I read it I was trying to understand this guy— why he did what he did, and how he got that way. The fact that he could seriously skin these people and preserve their body parts . . . I mean, this guy had noses and ears. He had garter belts made from female body parts. This guy was fucking *out* there. Can you imagine doing that and thinking that it's okay, and not really knowing the difference between right and wrong? That's just fucking amazing, to do things like that with no heart at all. And then I came across another book about this guy named Albert Fish, who a long time ago murdered all these little boys and then ate their penises. He said he tried eating their testicles, but he found them too chewy."

As he speaks, Araya's face gradually lights up, until by the time he gets to the part about chewy testicles, he is smiling delightedly. After a moment or two, he catches what he's doing and blushes. "You know," he says, "I can sit here and talk about mutilation with a smile on my face and laugh because of the things these people do, but I *do* know the difference between wrong and right. I mean, I sit and think about murder, and sometimes I think it would be real easy to do. And then I write the stuff, and for me it works as kind of a release. I figure, well, I've thought about it, I know what it would feel like— and that's good enough for me."

LISTENING TO Tom Araya talk about the titillations of murder can be as unnerving as listening to Slayer's music—in fact, even more so. At least with Slayer's music it's possible to make a case that, by presenting horror in such unflinching and unromantic detail, some of the band's boldest songs actually work as critiques of violence and evil. But after talking to Araya, you have to wonder if some of the songs aren't precisely what they sound like: namely, celebrations of the ruin of life.

Actually, either interpretation—critique or celebration—seems fine by Slayer, who is probably more adept than any other band at depicting terrible realities without giving any indication of how the band views the moral dimensions of those realities. But by completely sidestepping any moral reaction, it's possible that Slayer has misjudged just how deep the horror runs in the stories it has chosen to tell. Killers like Ed Gein or Albert Fish may be fascinating to read or talk about, or to see portrayed on the screen, but the truth is, real human lives were tortured and destroyed at their hands, and the horror and misery didn't end there: The surviving families and friends of both the victims and the killers had to live the rest of their lives with the effects of those crimes, and with the knowledge of all the hopes that were forever transformed and sealed off in the seasons of their bloodshed. *This* is the sort of horror that never knows an end—the sort that lasts beyond death or fiction or art—and it may be a greater evil than Araya and his band are prepared to comprehend or address.

At the same time, for all his creepy interests, there's really nothing unpleasant or evil-seeming about Araya himself. In fact, he comes across as a basically funny, courteous, and sweet-tempered guy who has a deep affection for his family and his fans, and who only becomes really unpleasant when he witnesses a security guard roughing up some exuberant fan. In short, Araya is a bit like many of the rest of us: On one hand he can be fascinated by the depictions of evil in a true-crime book or a piece of fiction like *The Silence of the Lambs,* but when the real violence spills over into his own world, he is genuinely repelled.

And sometimes that violence can spill over in unexpected ways. For example, during the recent Persian Gulf War, Slayer received several letters from troops stationed on the front line, some of whom stated they were anxious to kill the Iraqis ("the fucking ragheads," as one soldier fan put it) and thanked Slayer for providing them with the morale to do so. Closer to home, Geraldo Rivera presented a show a year or so ago called "Kids Who Kill." It featured a panel with five adolescents, all of whom had killed either other kids or family members, and all of whom cited a passion for thrash or speed-metal bands—particularly Slayer. To some critics, incidents like these might suggest that Slayer's art is a dangerous one, that it works as an endorsement of violence or might even help embolden it. Well, perhaps. But at the same time, what would it be like if the music of Slayer *didn't* exist? If the band disappeared or were silenced, would that absence diminish the frequency of murder? Would it have had any impact on the killings committed by the children on Geraldo Rivera's show?

Jeff Hanneman, one of Slayer's lead guitarists (and the author of "Angel of Death"—the song that got the band thrown off CBS Records), doesn't think so. "Obviously," he says, "a lot of our fans *do* identify with evil—or at least they think they do. But the truth is, when you come across one of the most hardcore Slayer fans—one of these guys going *Sa-tan! Sa-tan! Sa-tan!*— and you say, 'Now calm down, dude; do you really believe in Satan?' he might go, *'Yes!* Sa-*tan!'* And then you go, 'No, no—do you *really* believe in Satan?' he'll go, 'Uh, well, no, not really.' You know, to him it's cool because it's evil, and evil is rebellion.

"I mean, these are just normal kids—at least normal by today's standards," Hanneman continues. "You have to remember, this society has changed a lot, and some of these kids are coming from some pretty rough family realities and some pretty hopeless conditions. This music is a way of reacting against all that. They go to a show, thrash around for a few hours, and then they go home and hopefully they've worked some stuff out of their systems. Whereas when they listen to something like Mötley Crüe, with some song about a hot girl . . . well, they can relate to that, but they've got this anger inside that they need to get out and Mötley Crüe doesn't help them do that.

"Basically, I think we're doing a positive thing," says Hanneman. "But if some kid goes overboard, I can't take responsibility for that. I mean, we all have an inborn capacity for violence, but most of us know where to stop. If somebody goes over that line, then their boundary is obviously gone, but that has more to do with how they grew up than with our music. Sometimes we're a little bit over the borderline about killing and stuff like that, but it isn't like we're out there giving them knives, saying, 'Here, cut your throat. Hurt somebody.' That isn't what we're doing."

Rick Rubin, who has produced Slayer since the mid-1980s, has his own view of the band's impact on its listeners. "There's no question," he says, "that a lot of really troubled people like this band. You can see them some nights at the show: kids who are living with boredom and stress every day of their lives, kids who really have no ambition and nothing to live for. And I think that these kids recognize that the people in this band are troubled spirits as well. There's a kinship there. All these people—both the band and its audience—have these feelings in common. Slayer exists because people feel this way—because some kids kill, or want to kill. But Slayer is simply a reflection of that condition, not the cause, and you shouldn't blame a mirror for what it reflects. If you don't like what Slayer represents, then change the world, and make it a better place. Do that, and bands like Slayer won't exist."

TO A CASUAL listener, most speed-metal bands might seem rather interchangeable. After all, most of them tend to boast predictably dire names (some of the more memorable current ones include Morbid Angel, Suicidal Tendencies, Atrocity, Entombed, Carcass, Coroner, Repulsion, Dismember, Deathcore, Abomination, Hellbastard, Napalm Death, Pungent Stench, Death Strike, and, uh, Defecation), and nearly all of them trade in predictably dire topics like, you know, death, the devil, and damnation. What's more, they all feature guitarists who blast out grinding sheets of rhythm and noise, and vocalists who yell or growl impossibly wordy descriptions of perdition at impossibly breakneck clips.

But these are simply the givens of the genre—the shared traits that give any pop style its claim to singularity or separateness. Within the kingdom of speed-metal, each band is singular unto itself, but there is probably none that is more inspiriting than Anthrax. Like Slayer or any other number of bands, Anthrax often deals with questions of rage and despair. But in contrast to these other bands, Anthrax wants to know where those dark feelings come from, and how they affect the lives of the people in the group's audience. If speed-metal can lay claim to its own Clash or Who—a band that tries to make sense of its audience's moment in history and how that moment can be transformed into the basis for community—then clearly, that band is Anthrax.

In part, Anthrax's commitment to the ideals of community owes as much to the band's interest in punk as to its roots in metal. Like most of the other musicians on this tour, the members of Anthrax first developed their passion for heavy metal in the middle and late 1970s, when artists like Kiss, Ted Nugent, Black Sabbath, and AC/DC were defining the frontier of rock & roll bravado. But in 1976, all that changed. Punk groups like New York's the Ramones and England's Sex Pistols took heavy metal's style and stripped it of its excesses—its overreliance on flashy lead guitars and pretty-boy cock-rock—and transformed it into something that was at once both more primitive and more radical. Indeed, punk bands drew new stylistic, generational, and political lines across the breadth of rock & roll, and they declared that if you did not stand on punk's side of the line, then you did not stand anywhere that counted. As a result, the punk and metal factions didn't get along very well, despite a common interest in passionate, guitar-and-drums-driven rock & roll.

But Scott Ian, who was a heavy metal fan attending high school in Jamaica, Queens, New York, when punk was at its peak, couldn't see the reason for all the division and antipathy. "To me," he says, "Iron Maiden was every bit as underground—and every bit as valid—as the Ramones or Sex Pistols."

In 1981, when Ian and a couple of other friends co-founded Anthrax, he envisioned the group as drawing from metal's style but punk's spirit. At first not much came of the idea; others in the group were happy to stick with metal's familiar styles and fans. But on Sundays, when the band wasn't playing or rehearsing, Ian and Anthrax drummer Charlie Benante started hanging out at Manhattan's legendary punk club, CBGBs, and making friends with members of the local hardcore scene. For a brief while, they even formed a side band—the legendary Stormtroopers of Death, regarded by many as a key punk-metal crossover group. In time, many of the hardcore kids started coming to Anthrax's shows, and they brought with them some of their scene's more colorful rites—like stage-diving and slam-dancing. The mingling of the two audiences made for some tense alliances at first; punks thought the metalheads had wretched fashion sense and bad politics, and the headbangers didn't dig the punks' violence. But by the mid-1980s, the punk scene had lost most of its stylistic inventiveness and some of its cultural clout, and the emerging thrash and speed-metal bands simply appropriated punk's rhythmic intensity and its radical zeal as well.

These days, Anthrax can pretty much be exactly what it wants to be—a heavy metal band with a punk-informed conscience. Over the course of the group's last four albums, Anthrax has become increasingly politically savvy and activist-minded, yielding some of the smartest songs about the social and emotional conditions of modern-day youth culture that rock & roll has produced in the last decade. But sometimes the band's progressivism hasn't set well with parts of its audience. In 1989, when the members of Anthrax appeared on the cover of heavy metal magazine *RIP* with their friends in Living Colour, a black metal band, the magazine received some ugly responses from several readers. Angered by the incident, and by the killing of black youth Yusef Hawkins in New York's Bensonhurst area, Ian wrote "Keep It in the Family" and "H8Red," a pair of scathing songs about race hatred that appeared on *Persistence of Time*.

Says Ian: "I think there's a pretty good percentage of our audience—you know, white middle-to-lower-class kids—that hates black music and probably hates blacks as well. *Why* they hate blacks, they probably don't know; it's a prejudice that they've never questioned. I'm exposed to it all the time. People see me wearing a Public Enemy T-shirt, and they ask me, 'Why do you like that nigger music?' I can't really talk to somebody like that, you know? I don't care if they've bought every one of our albums, I'm just not going to waste my time talking to somebody like that, and I'm certainly not going to condone their attitude just because they're an Anthrax fan. They can like us or not, but I still think they're an asshole."

Ian pauses for a moment and shakes his head. "I wish there were a way to reach those people," he says after a bit. "Maybe for some of them the music *does* make a difference. Maybe they can hear a song like 'H8Red' and understand that it's a song about being hated just because of the way you look—whether it's because you have long hair or you're a skinhead or you're black.

"I mean, I think for a lot of our fans who are into this music things aren't easy. Some of them are working jobs they can't stand, and they aren't sure who to blame for their lives, and so some of them end up getting drunk all the time or turning to drugs. I think what we try to say to them is: 'Hey, we've all gone through some of the same shit, but, you know, you can find a place in your life where you can make it. You know, you may hate your parents and hate your job and hate your life, but it's *your* life, and you just got to fucking do what you got to do to make yourself and your world better.'

I think if Anthrax has any message, that's it: Make yourself and your world better."

A short while later, Scott Ian and the other members of Anthrax—singer Joe Belladonna, drummer Charlie Benante, bassist Frank Bello, and guitarist Dan Spitz—are onstage in Houston, spreading that message the best way they know how: by playing brilliant and enlivening rock & roll. It's debatable, of course, whether the audience completely understands or agrees with what the band is saying in its music; maybe for many of those here the sheer visceral impact of the band's performances is the only real meaning that matters. Still, there is something heartening about watching Joe Belladonna deliver a song like "Keep It in the Family"—which admonishes the band's fans not to fall into the easy traps of their parents' legacies of racism—and witnessing the audience flailing and thrashing to the words, as if this were a declaration worth raising a ruckus over.

A little later, though, when the band gets around to "Antisocial," there's no question that everybody knows what is being talked about. On record, the song is a rousing attack on a man who uses law and order and wealth to beat down the people he doesn't understand. But in concert, it becomes something else. "You're anti, you're anti*social,*" yowls the band, pointing its fingers at the audience, and the audience stands up on its chairs and roars back the same line—"You're anti, you're anti*social*"—pointing back at the band. Finally the band and the audience are yelling the same refrain to each other at the same moment, over and over, until the voices rise into the thousands. In that moment, both the crowd and the band are taking a term that has been used for years as a method of branding young people as outcasts and they turn that epithet into both a mutual accusation and a mutual affirmation. They are telling one another that they know exactly how the world views them, and that they are proud to be known by those terms. In that moment, Anthrax and its audience are forging a bond of community that, quite likely, they rarely find outside the society of heavy metal music. It is a way of saying: "We are here for each other. Whatever the rest of the world might say about us, we are here for each other."

In the world that heavy metal and its fans are consigned to live in, that isn't such a bad promise.

PART 5

lone

voices

randy newman:

songs of

the promised

land

*Coming over the pass, you can see the whole valley spread
below. On a clear morning, when it lies broad and colored
under a white sky, with the mountains standing far back
on either side, you can imagine it's the promised land.*

ROSS MACDONALD
THE WYCHERLY WOMAN

*t*rouble in Paradise, Randy Newman's first pop album since 1979's *Born
Again*, is perhaps the most forceful, full-formed statement about life in Los
Angeles that popular music has yet produced. In it, Newman regards the
city's infamous frivolity and relentless, pacific gloss with humor, affection,
fury, and bite—and he affirms them as worthy images (and even worthier
ends) for a city with an incurable fixation on surface appearances. Newman
also acknowledges that beneath such surfaces (and perhaps because of the
broken confidence and swift hatred that those surfaces can also breed—
particularly for those buried under those surfaces) there lurks an inevitable
undertow of disillusionment and fear. Disillusionment that can turn quick
fun into quicker meanness, especially when arrogance and indulgence become common ways to attain pleasure.

Trouble in Paradise is only partly about Los Angeles, but it's those parts that give the record such resonance and depth. And by and large, it's the city's sheen and exuberance that compels Newman here. In the surging, boastful, "I Love L.A.," Newman barrels along in a sleek convertible, a "big nasty redhead" beside him, and calls out the names of the city's most familiar symbols of opportunity and escape. In a rousing, challenging voice he shouts: "Century Boulevard!" And a boisterous chorus roars back: "We love it!" "Victory Boulevard!" "We *love* it!" "Santa Monica Boulevard!" "We LOVE it!" "Sixth Street!" "WE LOVE IT!"

Some critics regard "I Love L.A." as an ironic pose rather than a heartfelt anthem, as if what Newman says in the song is that this city is all quick surfaces and images. Well, he *is* saying that, but if you think he says it with cynicism or disdain, think again. Newman means what he purports here: He *does* love L.A.—in no small part because it's the place he calls his home, but also because he's fascinated by its knack for promoting veneer as its own distinction. Which isn't to say Newman is oblivious to the empty-headedness the city cultivates. In "My Life Is Good," an obnoxious *nouveau riche* songwriter declares to his son's schoolteacher that wealth and position guarantee a claim to license and the servitude of others; by song's end, Newman has deflated the haughtiness and sense of privilege that many in this city brandish as unassailable rights. At the same time, Newman isn't so sure that the shallowness L.A. fosters belies its claim as the last American prom-ised land. After all, a promised land is as good as a land of last hope. And when last hopes are gone, what often emerges is a place whose people are resentful of its culture and of one another, and who verge on ethical (not to mention aesthetic) desperation. The displacement born of this desperation is what has always made L.A. such an alluring place to write about—and an increasingly risky place to live.

Newman's advocacy of L.A. is an interesting position for anyone to stake out in early-1980s pop music. Since the pop explosion of the 1960s (when Phil Spector, the Beach Boys, Lou Adler, and the Byrds created ver-sions of L.A. sound that set new standards in rock fun and studio art), and throughout the 1970s (when such artists as the Eagles and Jackson Browne forced those conceptions of fun to accommodate a new, heavily idealized ethos), Los Angeles has stood for a measured, bright-toned sound, espousing certain romanticized truths. The city's music has also depended upon mass popularity (meaning accessibility) to assure its validity.

But in the late 1970s and early 1980s, L.A. became the setting for a revealing conflict of pop styles. Though the Eagles, Fleetwood Mac, Toto, and other well-bred L.A. acts continued to command a mass audience, a sharp-tempered and persistent underground movement also rose, spawning bands like X, the Germs, the Go-Go's, Black Flag, and Fear—all of whom sought to give as much definition to the sound and ideals of modern L.A. as any of the bands that came before them. There's a part of me that would like to think Newman's *Trouble in Paradise* is a record that's smart and expansive enough to contain both versions of L.A. (Warren Zevon's records, too, might be seen as working this trick, though Zevon perhaps too strongly represents personal concerns as an exemplar of cultural style.) Certainly at its best, Randy Newman's lyricism is as acerbic as that of, say, X, and obviously a lot wittier and more adept at parody than the tiresome punk burlesque of Fear.

Even the best and brightest of today's punk-derived artists could learn an invaluable lesson from the way Newman wields point of view, and the way he inhabits and animates a song. The character in "There's a Party at My House," who winds up what began as an innocent saturnalia with an implied vision of rape (maybe even sportive sex murder), isn't repugnant merely because of his dangerous impulses, but because he speaks to us in a way that can arouse our own desire to join the party. As a result, the song is more powerful than the anti-misogynist rock of Gang of Four, or for that matter, the *pro*-misogynist rock of Fear.

Yet what clearly separates Newman from the punks isn't so much his idea of intelligence or viewpoint as it is his particular allegiance to sound. To be sure, *Paradise* is, in places, an assaultive, even bombastic record—in fact, Newman's *most* physical sounding rock & roll since "Gone Dead Train" on 1970's *Performance* soundtrack. But it is also a meticulously crafted, professionally realized work—a work that asserts precision and control as clear-cut aesthetic choices. "I Love L.A." may roar and careen like a fine, fast, heady ride down the Imperial Highway, but there isn't a reckless turn or offhand moment on the whole track, or anywhere else on the album.

In effect, Newman's attention to artifice amounts to something of a recasting of his former sound. Though elaborate arrangements often graced the music of *12 Songs*, *Sail Away*, and *Good Old Boys*, they almost never determined the actual form or temper of Newman's Tin Pan Alley– and blues-infused songwriting. But on *Paradise*, the arrangements—the very outward show and force of some of the songs—are often as much a part of the songs' meanings as the characters and wordplay that make up their textual detail. This may be Newman's way of saying that he stands for (and stands *up* for) that exacting refinement which so many critics identify with the L.A. sound. Newman has as much as said so in recent interviews: The good values, he asserts, are not the guileful intelligence that a songwriter like Elvis Costello employs, or the social-minded bravura of the Clash, but rather the stylish dourness of Don Henley and the fastidious musicianship of Toto. To underscore his point, Newman rounded up several Los Angeles signature performers (including Henley, Rickie Lee Jones, Christine McVie, and Linda Ronstadt) as a way or reaffirming that, at its best, the L.A. sound was always more the result of shared community than cliquishness.

Which all means that Newman's championing of that sound is much like his backhanded advocacy of L.A. as a culture of veneer: Either one can accept the city (and its music) for its surfaces, or one can accept it for the variety of truths those surfaces conceal, even nurture.

In some ways, this is where *Paradise* achieves its greatest literary effect. Both the sound and the meaning of its songs contain a vision of fun that does not end in mere fun, and a darker vision which is too complex to give in to rote notions of L.A. as a vast, sprawling network of desperation. According to Newman, desperation alone isn't any more notable as a version of truth than fun is. In a sense, such recent L.A. bands as the Go-Go's and X approach a similar conclusion, though from differing angles. Each band represents a contrary truth about this city—quick fun, or desperate action. But neither can fully convey the idea that to find the truth of this city, you must first penetrate those poses of fun and trouble and examine the way the search for fun (and the inability to capture it for very long) creates trouble and despair. (Neither do X or the Go-Go's reveal enough about how trouble can enrich the idea of fun, or at least make its invention necessary.)

So what does Randy Newman say when cruising down the fabled mean streets that have fed the dark ruminations of Raymond Chandler, James M. Cain, F. Scott Fitzgerald, Nathanael West, Charles Bukowski, and Joan Didion? He says: "Roll down the window/Put down the top/Crank up the Beach Boys, baby/Don't let the music stop."

Trouble in Paradise so often weaves fun with darkness and gentleness with meanness that they begin to seem interchangeable, and *then* they seem inseparable. It tells us that hard truths wouldn't matter much—wouldn't be endurable—without the chance to hit the highway, where the wind can cleanse us of thoughts and the radio can fill the gaps in our feeling the way it fills the shiny, dirty sky around us.

It's the way we've learned to ride out hell, in the City of Angels.

al green:

sensuality

in the service

of the lord

When Al Green takes a stage, both miracle and mystery attend his arrival. Miracle, because the man sings heartfelt, revealing praises to his idea of God, in a wonder-working voice. Mystery, because the man has willfully—pointedly—abdicated the massive pop audience he could so easily command (and still actively merits) at the same time he has raised his performing talents to new pinnacles. Quite simply, when we witness Green, we are witnessing our greatest living soul singer—witnessing him stare down the vista of a self-willed, commercially barren future, smiling at the promise of boundless riches at the end.

But whether Green commands a substantial audience is beside the point, at least in his own mind. At L.A.'s Greek Theater one night in August 1983, where he played to a perhaps half-capacity crowd, he dismissed the importance of popular acclaim, exhorting the crowd, "Clap your hands and give the praise to *God.*" That's a fittingly deferential gesture for a performing Christian (though I can hardly picture Bob Dylan or Jerry Lee Lewis offering similar directives), but the piety of it is also beside the point. This is a knotty issue, but it's only fair to offer my own prejudices up front: I enjoy many religious performers (not only gospel vocalists, but also sufferin' rockers like Van Morrison and Pete Townshend) for much the same reason I can enjoy angry eccentrics like Bob Dylan and Johnny Rotten: because the conceit of their conviction manages to fuel their jeering conception of modern life as a loathsome hellhole, and because that conviction gives order and purpose to the unruly limits of their pain. It doesn't matter, in terms of their art, whether their beliefs amount to "truth" or not; it suffices that theirs is a self-sustaining vision that informs and shapes their regeneration.

In the same respect, the fact that Al Green promotes God as the *raison d'être* of his art doesn't particularly secure or sanctify Green's music. It's fine, I suppose, to limit music's purpose to a celebration of God, but music as a way of canvassing for salvation—which is what much of modern gospel is—is an inevitably self-advancing notion. Or at least it's self-centered more than purely great-hearted or altruistic: The supplicant is concerned with proclaiming himself as a model for deliverance by virtue of personal faith and received grace, which is a lot like the sexual boasting Green *used* to sing about, but not at all like true outgoing, reciprocal romance. Somehow, I always thought there was as much integrity in Albert Camus' affirmation, in *The Rebel*, of those religious insurrectionists (or resisters) who reject the certainty of salvation for themselves because of its elitist, nonegalitarian conditions. Of course, the day I hear a pop (or gospel) song about *that* view, I'll figure real miracles are afoot. It's just that a hardbitten look at real life seems a bit more demanding than a blithe contemplation of a distant afterlife; real life is where spiritual hope is tested and tempered—and remeasured.

In any event, Al Green clearly feels that today's pop world is anathema to the purposes of his music, and given his talents, I wouldn't slight his current repertoire. "The Lord taught me how to sing," Green explained to his audience at the Greek, "but I rewarded him by singing 'Love and Happiness' and 'Let's Stay Together.' " The audience roared hungrily at the mention of the songs. "And people ask me, 'Why can't you still sing "Call Me" or "For the Good Times." ' Well, Jesus brought me through all that—He brought me through 'How Can You Mend a Broken Heart' and 'I'm Still in Love with You.' Good songs, good times, but I want you to know I found the *Rock* . . . ," and with that, Green moved into a beautiful rendering of "Amazing Grace," and it seemed just as well that something *had* brought him through all his previous greatness, because his new greatness is so sweetly convincing.

Ah, but what greatness it once was. Green, who possesses as well-mannered a drawl as R&B has ever yielded, was pretty much *the* classy singles artist of the 1970s, producing an even more consistent string of high-art hits than Stevie Wonder or Elton John. Between 1971 and 1976, he slotted thirteen Top 40 singles, including the aforementioned "Love and Happiness," "Let's Stay Together," "Call Me (Come Back Home)," and "I'm Still in Love with You," as well as "Sha-La-La (Makes Me Happy)," and "L-O-V-E (Love)." Produced by Willie Mitchell for Memphis' Hi Records, Green's records were exemplary post-Stax soul: sparse, bass-driven arrangements covered and colored by Green's breathy, high, fragile crooning. They were records that also bespoke unfathomable reserves of casual, elegant sexiness, and Green's image as a ladies' man was further enhanced by a swoony, physically stirring live act in which his lithe yet unrestrained presence gave new depth to sexual euphoria.

Apparently, the image also carried over to his personal life. In 1974, a woman who loved Green and had tried to fasten him to a promise of marriage, grew wild at his rejection. Embittered, she reportedly attempted to wound him with scalding grits before killing herself. Green's career fell into quick disarray, and he never recorded another major hit after the incident. When he recouped in 1977, producing himself for the first time, Green seemed still pulled by some of the same old urges, but also reanimated by a new spiritual awareness. "It's *you* that I want but it's *Him* that I need," he sang in one of his finest songs, "Belle" (from *The Belle Album*), and it sounded as if Green were firmly trying to shut out the hope of pop heroism for good. Whatever conflict remained, Green resolved it fairly quickly: All of his albums since that date—including *Truth 'n' Time, Higher Plane, The Lord Will Make a Way, Precious Lord,* and *I'll Rise Again*—have been gospel affairs, sometimes transfixing, sometimes miscast, but never less than masterly sung.

Perhaps gospel is Green's way of making up for the implicit excesses of his previous sex style, but that sexiness—that revelry in loss of inhibition, that surrender to sensual movement—is still very much a part of Green's live act. At the end of a lovely and rousing version of "People Get Ready," he tossed off his beige, double-breasted jacket and prowled the stage like a fierce, balletic wolf, as ravenous and alluring as his former carnal self had ever seemed. And just as jolting, too: When, early in the show, he stripped off his black bow-tie, one woman to my left, who had been shouting "Hallelujah" only moments earlier, suddenly shrieked, "Take it *all* off, *Al!*" Revelations indeed.

But Green didn't seem entirely comfortable with this response. During one point when he attempted to venture into the audience and was rushed by women trying to plant fervent kisses on his face, he fairly begged, "Shake my *hand,* please!" Religious fervor is as much a way of covering for past fears as it is a way of expressing necessary worship, and in those moments, Green looked like a haunted, fearful man.

But the fear and the correlated joy he has found in his supplication has made of Green a better singer and greater artist. That last trait is what is central here, for what is truly transcendent about Green isn't the spirituality of his songs so much as the uplifting art he brings to bear upon his religion, for Green is still the most dazzling soul singer around—only now he takes the calling literally. Indeed, he's as riveting a live vocalist as Frank Sinatra or Dylan. His reading of Curtis Mayfield's "People Get Ready" was the ideal example: He curled around the song's imperative spirit with an impossible effortlessness, imbuing his pinched, high breathiness with the same old tested sensual elegance.

It was a lot like hearing religion, and also a lot like hearing sex, but nothing like the playful manner in which Marvin Gaye or Prince might mix the two extremes. Green has been through the fire of the latter, and the fiery balm of the former, and he sees nothing light or trendily shocking in juxtaposing the two. But I doubt that I'll hear anything more sensually pleasing than that vocal on "People Get Ready"—a physical expression of spiritual longing that made me feel good all over, and also made me feel sort of transported. I could listen to Al Green from here to Judgment Day and it would seem like salvation to me. Or at least close enough for this hell on earth.

jerry lee lewis:

the killer

Look, we've only got one life to live. We don't have the
promise of the next breath. I know what I am. I'm a
rompin', stompin', piano-playin' sonofabitch. A mean
sonofabitch. But a great sonofabitch. A good person. Never
hurt nobody unless they got in my way. I got a mean
streak. . . . I gotta lay it open sometimes.

JERRY LEE LEWIS, 1977

Jerry Lee Lewis—the Louisiana-born, wild-haired piano player—had as
much assaultive impact on rock & roll culture as any artist prior to the Sex
Pistols: He lived out rock & roll's sexual and impulsive audacity with such
hauteur and flamboyance as to be deemed a perilous talent in the late-1950s.
For that distinction—as well as for the startling depth and display of his
talent—there are many rock & roll chroniclers who regard Lewis as the
exemplary performer of his era: more unrepressed than Elvis Presley, more
forcible than Chuck Berry, more insolent than Little Richard.

Of course, it is not only for his musical swagger that Lewis seemed
preeminent, but also for the manner in which he has consistently embodied—that is, lived out—the promise of rock & roll's threat. Rock & roll is
mean and corrupting music, he has said many times, and to perform that
music, Lewis has forsaken many hopes and a few beliefs. Indeed, he lives and
speaks as a man who has lost his soul—and knows exactly what that loss
means. For this act, existentialists would have named him a rebel, though his
friends and fans simply call him the Killer.

It is a tough moniker, but Lewis has been tempered by the times. In
mid-1958—at the peak of a career that looked to overtake Presley's—he

married Myra Gail Brown, his thirteen-year-old third cousin (it was his third marriage), and the resulting scandal reduced him to a career of secondary concert dates and record deals that he never quite overcame. In subsequent years, Lewis would bury two sons, lose Myra and other wives to divorce, hatred, and death, and lose his property and wealth to tax liens filed by the U.S. government. Over the years, it became increasingly difficult to tell where Jerry Lee-the-victim ended and Jerry Lee-the-culprit began. The man who was once a preacher began assaulting his wives and lovers with a fearful savor, and in 1976, in a drunken incident on his forty-first birthday, he shot two bullets into the chest of his bassist, Butch Owens (Lewis was charged with a misdemeanor: firing a gun within city limits). In 1981, he entered a Memphis hospital in enfeebled shape and had most of his stomach removed—the result of years of steady consumption of liquor and drugs.

But the most serious discredit to the Lewis legend was detailed in an article that appeared in the March 1, 1984, issue of *Rolling Stone*, "The Mysterious Death of Mrs. Jerry Lee Lewis." Written by Richard Ben Cramer (a reporter for *The Philadelphia Inquirer*, and the recipient of a Pulitzer prize for journalism), the article seems a scrupulous account of Lewis' two-and-a-half-month marriage to twenty-five-year-old Shawn Michelle Stephens and the mystifying events surrounding her August 23, 1983, death: the bruises and blood on her body, the scratchlike wounds on Lewis' forearm, the permeation of fresh, small bloodstains around Lewis' Mississippi home, and the superficial police investigations and coroner's reports that followed. Though it was eventually concluded that Shawn had died as the result of an overdose of methadone and that there was "no indication of foul play," Cramer uncovers much overlooked (and withheld) evidence, including clear indications that there had been some sort of fight at the Lewis house the night of the young woman's death. The article raises disturbing questions about Lewis' accountability in the demise of his fifth wife, and though Cramer doesn't accuse the rock performer of murder, he certainly indicates that the matter merited a more careful inquiry.

But it isn't my purpose here to recount the *Rolling Stone* article, and certainly not to draw conclusions about Jerry Lee Lewis' culpability. From my understanding of Cramer's reportage, it may no longer be possible to reach any incontestable conclusions on the matter. If I were to be callous about it, I might add that Lewis' guilt may be beside the point: Jerry Lee clearly has developed a reputation as some kind of archetypal modern American "outside the law" (as one writer put it), living out tragedy, violence, and dissolution as the fruits of a self-willed fall from grace. That's a fairly romantic conception, and for my interest, it raises another, equally troubling question: Do we (meaning his fans and chroniclers) really care much about whether Lewis has brutalized his wives, or in fact contributed to Shawn Stephens' death? Or does the possibility somehow further his antiheroic standing? Or as one friend put it, if we thought Lewis *had* killed his wife, would we still buy his music, attend his shows? Would we disown our conviction in the importance of his earlier work?

These are questions that each of us can answer only for ourselves and I must admit I'm not sure what my own answers might reveal. Like many other pop writers, I have often celebrated the angry, violent impulses of rock & roll, because, in part, such impulses seem born of a hard-earned moral courage, though also, I should admit, because the angry, violent side of rock can be fun. (If you doubt me, listen to the Who or the Sex Pistols, or see *The Wild One, Rebel Without a Cause, The Blackboard Jungle, The Harder They Come, Quadrophenia,* or *High School Confidential*—the latter featuring Jerry Lee Lewis on the title song.)

But it is also true that fans and critics have often romanticized rock & roll's violent side to a distorted degree—until a roughhouse aesthetic and mean-eyed stance seem to take on matchless and inevitable value. By example, the hardened, menacing posture of punk was so widely reported and lionized that violence appeared as a genuine and off-putting trait of the movement, though in fact it was always more stylized than it was necessary or actual. Of course, that didn't stop some punks from living up to an acquired style: When Sid Vicious was arrested for the murder of his girlfriend Nancy Spungen in 1978, and then died by heroin overdose later, to many punk followers those deaths had the ring of idyllic, inescapable pop history about them. And yet the critics and fans who venerated "punk violence," and who memorialized Vicious' pathetic end, didn't have to live with the consequences of his life. It was as if the rise and fall of the Sex Pistols, Spungen's murder, and Vicious' death were all part of a merciless pageant lived out for our dark enjoyment.

But then that's the immutable allure of violence: It makes for great entertainment, great mystique, and as a fan of hard-boiled crime novels (the best of which inquire after the impulse to murder), I am hardly one to moralize. The problem develops when an art form's stylized violence becomes so idealized to its critics and audience that its real-life performances seem some sort of enactment of bravado. Or worse, when we begin regarding real-life victims as less consequential than the music or mystique of their victimizers.

How all this relates to the troubles of Jerry Lee Lewis is a tricky question. Certainly, to read Nick Tosches' fine biography of Lewis, *Hellfire,* or Myra Lewis' equally adept account of her marriage to the pianist, *Great Balls of Fire,* is to come face-to-face with the heart-affecting story of a wild, mean, and unequaled pop star—a man robbed of his shot at rock glory and so irrecoverably confounded in spirit that his ambition, intelligence, wit and pride prompted him to turn his back on redemption. "I'm draggin' the audience to hell with me," Jerry Lee is famous for saying, and while that may seem a darkly alluring statement, it implies awful possibilities: A man who is no longer fearful of death, but feels certain only of damnation, may no longer fear the consequence nor the conceit of any deeds. If that is so, Jerry Lee Lewis may be telling us enough about himself to inspire our distance.

miles davis:

the lion

in winter

*f*ace-to-face, Miles Davis seems much like the Miles Davis one might expect him to be: That is, he has the manners and bearing of the legendary Dark Prince of post-bop, one of the last great icons and agitators of jazz. He greets me at the door of his multilevel Malibu guest house, leads me into the lower den strewn with his many-colored erotic-expressionist ink paintings, and graciously offers me some of the homemade gumbo simmering on the stove. But quick as a blink (and it is startling how fast this abiding fifty-nine-year-old man can will moods and wits), the amiability can disappear. At one point he asks me what I think of a particular track on his soon-to-be-released *You're Under Arrest,* and I tell him I haven't heard the track because it isn't on the advance copy of the album that I received. Davis' eyes flicker behind his tinted, thick glasses and his notorious wrath flares. "Shit, you're trying to talk to me about my *music* and you don't even give a *listen* to my music?" I go out to my car, fetch the advance tape that Columbia Records had sent me, and hand it over to Davis. He studies the tape and sees that, indeed, the track under discussion had been omitted—which only makes him angrier.

"Man, they fucked up the way you're supposed to hear this transition," he says in his raw, irascible voice, then pulls out his own master cassette of the album, slaps it into the Nakamichi mounted into the wall, and keeps the music rolling throughout the visit. Occasionally he will call attention to specific passages—pointing out the album's constant counterplay between the forcible rhythms and hot textures of the band arrangements and the cool, playful, mellifluent, often introspective tone of his trumpet lines. As he talks, the man himself seems much like his music—fiery, then lulling, then impossibly complex, indefinable. His dark, dignified features may seem drawn these days, but they also ripple with the creases of experience, and the wear of myth.

Still, as impressive or disarming as Davis' bearing and temper may seem, for some reason there's nothing that inspires awe so much as when, during an idle point in our conversation, he picks up the trumpet that has been resting nearby, places it in his lap, and begins stroking it, in an offhand way. This particular horn is princely looking—black, with curled, gold gilt that spells MILES around its edge, and a weatherworn mute nuzzled into its flared bell. It just may be the single most famous, best played instrument in all America. And at that moment when he raises it to his lips, breathes gently into its looped tube as he fingers its valves, filling his corner of the room with a tone so subdued it seems almost private—well, the distinctions between Davis and his instrument blur. It is, in fact, a powerful but unconscious gesture that fuses the man's legend with his art. It is also an instant that drives home the fact that one is in the presence of perhaps the most important living musical hero in America—the essential (and solitary) link between the music of Charlie Parker and Jimi Hendrix, John Coltrane and Michael Jackson.

Indeed, since his first recordings with Parker, Dizzy Gillespie, Bud Powell, and Max Roach in the late 1940s, Miles Davis has been involved in and has nurtured more diverse jazz forms (from be-bop to cool to neo-bop, from modal reveries to electric atonalism) than any other figure in the music's history—and has also connected those traditions to rock and funk style and pop aspiration with bold, controversial, and liberating effect. Of course, in many fans' and critics' eyes, it was Davis' plunge into electronic texture, his mix of open-ended melodic improvisation and hard-edged, R&B-derived tempos, that spawned the dread specter of fusion jazz in the 1970s. In the end, the movement itself proved merely crass and formulaic, and perhaps also broke jazz history in two, inspiring a generation of technique-obsessed instrumentalists who proved unable to advance Davis' original vision. The style even seemed to enclose the trumpeter himself: Whereas early, groundbreaking excursions like *In a Silent Way, Bitches Brew,* and *Jack Johnson* had been seen as imaginative and unforgettable tone poems, later flurries like *Agharta, Pangaea,* and *Dark Magus* were seen as furious, pain-ridden, self-destroying exercises—work so forbidding, chaotic, and frustrating, some critics charged that they had been designed to keep an audience at bay (though for me, their fitful, disturbed brilliance places them among my favorite Miles Davis recordings).

Those records were also his final spurt of recording for years. Beset with crippling health problems (including leg injuries and a bone erosion in his hip that has left him slightly stooped), Davis retired into a six-year period of reclusion rumored to be so dark and narcotic, many insiders were convinced that he would never reemerge. When he did—in 1981 with *Man with the Horn*—several ungracious critics bemoaned his seeming unwillingness to once again move jazz in new directions, and even proclaimed that he had lost much of his tone and phrasing. Yet every subsequent wo:k (the live and good-humored *We Want Miles*, the blues-steeped *Star People*, and the protean *Decoy*) has drawn the intriguing portrait of a resourceful artist who is making his way through resurgent and autumnal periods in the same motion—a man who, for the moment, is more a musician than a harbinger; who has discovered that he can unite and reconcile classical repertoire, blues sensibility, and modern texture with a naked and deep-felt expressiveness. True, Davis may not be speaking in the intriguing harmonic and melodic parlance that James Blood Ulmer or Ronald Shannon Jackson have coined, nor playing in the inspiring blend of traditionalism and avant-gardism that Julius Hemphill, David Murray, Henry Threadgill, and Hamiet Bluiett pursue, but he can still set loose with a straight-ahead yet visionary brand of musical oratory that is simply matchless and, as well, delightfully sly.

But if much of what Davis has recorded since his return has sounded like a man looking to regain his voice—plus looking to find a fulfilling context in which to apply his regained strength—the 1985 *You're Under Arrest* is the place where this artist again makes a stand, one as vital to his own aesthetic as the stands he took with *Kind of Blue* and *Bitches Brew*. It's likely, of course, that with its lovingly straightforward and exacting covers of pop material by Michael Jackson ("Human Nature"), Cyndi Lauper ("Time After Time"), and D-Train ("Something on Your Mind"), the album will strike many jazz diehards as a disheartening commercial surrender. But that would be a depthless reading of what is actually a stirring and complicated work: perhaps Davis' most cohesive comment in twenty years on the balance between song form and improvisation, between tone and melodic statement, between cool and hot style, as well as his most exhaustingly worked-over music since his landmark orchestral sessions with Gil Evans in the 1950s. It is also simply a beautifully played album: Davis wrings the heart out of "Time After Time" with consummate grace, then turns around and blares into "You're Under Arrest" (the opening version of which features Sting in a cameo vocal) with the same cutting force that he once brought to *Jack Johnson*.

Asked whether he is concerned how this record may affect his already precarious standing with jazz purists, Davis appears to ignore the question, preferring instead to concentrate on the bowl of steaming gumbo before him. We are seated on the sofa in his den—the only spot of furniture not occupied with the trumpeter's paintings or scholarly tomes on modern art. "I don't put out records just to satisfy jazz buffs," he rasps after a while. He nods toward the TV set that is mounted above us. "These sounds coming out on television—these commercials and some of the music on MTV: That stuff sounds better than the jazz artists I'm hearing lately. These young guys, too many of them are so unsure of their own sound that somehow pop music scares them. They miss the point that *that's* where a lot of the real innovation—in both songs and rhythms—is coming from.

"Anyway, why should some jazz fan be upset that I recorded 'Time After Time'? It's nothing different than what I've always done. I mean, they liked it when I did 'Porgy and Bess,' when I did 'Green Dolphin Street,' when I did 'Bye-bye Blackbird,' when I did 'My Funny Valentine'—pop songs, all of them. They also liked it when I did *Bitches Brew* and *Jack Johnson*. Now why can't they like a record that puts all that together, hmm? The point is, if you keep repeating the old styles, then there's no advancement—nothing happens. Jazz has always drawn on pop songs; it's no different with today's pop, as far as drawing on it for interpretation."

Still, I note, in the jazz-rock fury of fifteen years earlier, nobody expected to hear Davis ever play a straight-ahead ballad again—particularly with such restrained tone and without melodic variation. What persuaded him to render Lauper's hit in such a plain-spoken fashion?

Davis' features soften and his scowl transforms into a faint smile. "Oh man, if I hear a melody I like, I don't care who plays it. I get that thing up here"—he taps the area between his throat and heart—"that thing you get when you see something you like." He laughs wickedly. "You know, some art work, a girl, cocaine. . . . Anyway, I got that when I first heard it, because she had the *sound* for the meaning of the ballad.

"But you have to treat the song the way it should be interpreted: your way and hers. I just love how Cyndi Lauper sings it. I mean, that woman is the only person who can sing that song right—the only one who really knows what it means. The song is part of her—it's written for her heart, for her height, for the way she looks, the way she smells. She has imparted her voice and soul to it, and brought something kind of sanctified and churchly to it. Why distract from its meaning by messing around with a lot of variations and stuff?

"So I don't do nothing to it: It's just the sound of my tone and the notes of that song, but they seem to work together in their own right. Still, when I like something, I try to give it to you my own way." Davis pauses and his eyes grin. "Give it to you with a little *black* on it. Now, when I play it live, everybody seems to like it that way. I also think people know when they like a melody: A song like this gets people in a mass groove, like a tribe."

Miles says he would talk more but he has a rehearsal to catch. Before we break off, he speaks briefly about his planned next album: a live retrospective of his career, recorded with a twenty-piece orchestra, rhythm section, and guitarist John McLaughlin, at his acceptance of the Soning Award in Copenhagen—an honor bestowed previously only on Leonard Bernstein, Isaac Stern, and Igor Stravinsky. We also discuss that this will be his last album for Columbia on this contract, and he allows that he is thinking about switching labels. "Man, they never know what to do with me. You know, they'd rather lean toward Wynton Marsalis or somebody like that. Well, let 'em. I'll tell ya, *I'm* not the one who's afraid of trying something different."

Which, of course, is an understatement. If Davis no longer seems to prompt jazz styles or sire new dynasties, it is also clear he no longer needs to. Instead, he has learned to move comfortably between jazz and funk, pop and blues, to assert gentle introspection with the same eloquence and savvy with which he expresses his casual melodic fervor—almost as if he were saying that it is the breadth of expression at this late stage in his career that best defines how he cares to be seen. In other words, maybe jazz's most mutable and enduring legend simply wants to be accepted now as a player and not a leader—a man who can imbue modern styles with a venerable, unadorned technique. True, that may make him too irreverent for jazz and too seasoned for pop, but mostly it marks him as an American original who, at fifty-nine, is still too young to be denied his vision.

feargal sharkey:

songs

of hearts

and thieves

a Good Heart," written by Los Angeles' Maria McKee, of Lone Justice almost-fame, and sung by the U.K.'s Feargal Sharkey, was played repeatedly on U.S. radio in the spring of 1986 (in England, in fact, it became a number 1 hit), and for fair reason. "A Good Heart" is an irresistibly crafted dance track about romantic search that communicates a great surface of good-natured hope, and a great depth of petrified fear. The song is also the opening track for the eponymous solo debut album by Sharkey (once the lead vocalist for Northern Ireland's most promising late-1970s pop-punk band, the Undertones), and with the singer's wavery voice intoning the heartening chorus, "A Good Heart" opens the album in the manner of a tremulous invocation: "I know that a real love is quite a price/And a good heart these days is hard to find. . . . /So please be gentle with this heart of mine."

But if "A Good Heart" is a lover's prayer, the song that immediately follows it, "You Little Thief" (written by Tom Petty's keyboardist, Benmont Tench), is as bitter a curse as I've ever heard in pop—a magnificent statement of pain so wrathful, so intense, so true, chances are you will never hear it on radio. "You little *THIEF*," rails Sharkey, "you let me *love* you/You saw me

STUMBLING, you saw me FALL/You left me broken/Shattered and blEEEding/ But there's no hard feelings/There's no feelings/At ALL."

Of course, that last claim isn't exactly true: There's so much lyrical and musical temper in this song, and in Sharkey's vocal delivery of it, that it is almost too overpowering to hear. Instantly, you are reminded of the most deep-felt moments in the music of Rod Stewart and Bryan Ferry—two singers who, like Sharkey, once sang so forcefully, so nakedly, that they could redeem *any* conceit or frivolity—and instantly you realize just how inadequately their best music compares to what this Irish aspirant manages to achieve here, by only half-trying. In part, that's because Sharkey isn't weighed down by any of the self-defeating irony or preening hubris that have always been part and parcel of Stewart's and Ferry's acts. Instead, Sharkey just sings as if the art of these songs resides in the meaning of their words, and not in the histrionics of the performer. The result is one of the most genuinely emotive, intoxicating vocal triumphs of 1986.

marianne faithfull:

trouble

in mind

i have never heard blues sung in the manner of "Trouble in Mind," the performance that opens the soundtrack to the 1986 movie of the same name. It is more like a painting of the blues—or some kind of stripped-down study of the music's elements—than a true enactment of the form. And yet it's as definitive an example of what blues might do in these modern times as you'd hope to find.

The song opens with an ethereal, harplike synthesizer sweep—not much more than an exercise in texture—played by arranger Mark Isham. Then Isham dresses up the moment a little: some muted trumpet (suggestive of Miles Davis' on *In a Silent Way*), a few moody piano arpeggios—all the elements weaving together at a snail's pace, congealing into a cool-to-the-touch, high-tech consonance. Then a voice enters, stating its lament as directly, as simply, as brokenly as possible: "Trouble in MIND, that's true/I have AL-MOST lost my mind/Life ain't worth livin'/*Some*times I feel like dyin'." The voice belongs to Marianne Faithfull, and she imparts immediately, in her frayed matter-of-fact manner, that she understands firsthand the experience behind the words: She lifts the song from blues cliché to blues apotheosis. What is remarkable, though, is how she does this without indulging for a moment in the sort of growly vocalese that many singers pass off for feeling. In fact, Faithfull does it simply by adhering to a literal, unembellished reading of blues melody. But behind that artlessness, the song's meanings inform her tone—they even inform the silences between notes—and that tone alone nails the listener, holding one's ear to an extraordinary performance. Not much more happens in the song, but not much more needs to. The directness of the vocal and the stillness of the arrangement virtually sound like a portrait of emotional inertia—and of course, that's the way they're supposed to sound.

Before *Trouble in Mind*'s soundtrack ends, there is one more unforgettable moment: Faithfull and Isham's rendition of Kris Kristofferson's "The Hawk (El Gavilan)." At the outset, a lone synthesizer delineates a melodic motif, a trumpet dips between the spaces of the strain, and Faithfull takes on the lyric in the same unvarnished manner as the earlier song. "Got to make your own rules, child," she sings, "Got to break your own chains/The dreams that possess you/Can blossom and bless you/Or run you insane." The textures move a bit more here, and there's a more gradual undertow to the arrangement—an undertow as gentle and sure as the momentum that carries life to death. Couple the music's steady, calm flow with the lyric's images of loss and flight and yearning, and you have a performance that manages to sound both resigned and unyielding at once. Which is to say, Kristofferson-Isham-Faithfull's "The Hawk" may be pretty-faced, high-tech pop, but at the recording's heart, it is a spawn of the blues. Its resonance is beyond trend: It is ageless.

stan ridgway's

wrong people

*A*s leader of the Wall of Voodoo, Stan Ridgway was nearly despicable: He didn't so much reduce hard-boiled cynicism to a cliché as he reduced it to a sneering inflection—which might have been a kick if the attacks hadn't all been delivered in a slurring monotone. In other words, Wall of Voodoo's gambit was a mean-minded, dead-ended one, and apparently even Ridgway realized this, for just as the band reached an audience large enough worth insulting, the singer "fired himself" from the enterprise. The joke, it seems, was up.

Maybe so, but the hard work had just begun. In 1986, two years after checking out, Stan Ridgway checked back in with *The Big Heat* (I.R.S.), and damn if it wasn't among the best L.A.-founded albums of that year. Perhaps what made *The Big Heat* work so well is that, instead of viewing his characters from the outside and laughing at their uneasiness and their seeming dispensability, Ridgway now crawled inside their skin—and discovered that it's actually kind of an intriguing place to be, a place that lends itself to hauntingly, rollickingly effective storytelling. In any event, instead of sneering, Ridgway now shudders a bit as he relates the accounts of people in flight—people running from or chasing after murder and deception, people who seem horrified and enthralled by their own admissions, people who have been forgotten but sure won't leave life that way. They are, in fact, California characters like those in the works of James M. Cain and Jim Thompson (mean and damned), or of Kim Nunn, Robert Siodmak, or Fritz Lang (rugged and redeemed). Either way, they are people you give a full hearing to—and as a result, *The Big Heat* also demands no less than a full hearing.

In *The Big Heat*, the wrong people—hateful, bored, lost, hurting, dangerous people—not only are given a voice, but, here and there, are given a shot at victory. Somehow, it's an exhilarating victory. "You gotta watch the ones who keep their hands clean," sings Stan Ridgway in the title song. On *The Big Heat*, the artist gets his hands dirtier than ever. Hence, he's maybe, just maybe, worth our trust. One thing's for certain: There are few artists who can be so scary and unaffected at the same time as Stan Ridgway.

sinéad o'connor's

songs of

experience

"Can we shut out the lights?" asks Sinéad O'Connor, in a soft voice.

It is a cold and blustery late February 1990 night in the center of London, and O'Connor—a twenty-three-year-old, bantam-sized Irish-born woman, with round, doleful eyes and a quarter-inch crewcut—is perched on a stool in a BBC Radio sound studio, holding an acoustic guitar, and looking a little uneasy. She has come here to perform some songs from her newly released second album, *I Do Not Want What I Haven't Got*. And for reasons of her own, she feels like singing these songs in the dark tonight. After the lights dim, the room falls quiet, and O'Connor begins strumming the hushed opening chords to "The Last Day of Our Acquaintance"—the account of a young woman who has been brought to the edge of her deepest-held hopes and dreams, and then deserted by the one person she needed and trusted most. It is one of O'Connor's most powerful and affecting songs, and for good reason: Not so long ago, she more or less endured the experience that she is singing about, and it transformed her life.

Tonight, she seems to be singing the song as if she were composing its painful recollections and caustic indictments on the spot. In a voice that veers between hesitation and accusation, O'Connor sings with a biting precision about the moment she realized that the man she loved and trusted no longer cared for her need or faith in him—it was in the instant that she recognized he would no longer hold on to her hand as a plane would lift off—and she rues all the abandonment and betrayal that her expectation has left her with. And then, just when the music should surge into the crashing chords and snarling yowls that frame the song's bitter kiss-off, O'Connor halts the performance abruptly, and for several long seconds, there is only silence from the dark booth. "I need to practice that one a bit," she says finally, in a shaky tone. "I need to calm down."

A minute later O'Connor resumes the song, and this time she leans harder into the performance. It is an exceptional thing to witness. Somewhere in that darkened booth, a young woman with an almost supernatural voice—a voice that can convey rage, longing, shock, and sorrow, all in the same breath—is both chasing down, and being chased by, some difficult private memories, and it seems less like a pop performance than an act of necessary release. It is also a timeless ritual: Pop and jazz and blues singers have been sitting in darkened recording booths turning private pains into public divulgence for generations now. But many of the best of those singers—from Billie Holiday to John Lennon—were, in one way or another, ravaged by that darkness. If Sinéad O'Connor has her way, she is going to howl at that darkness until there are no more bitter truths that it can hold.

MAYBE IT'S HER startling looks that first catch you—that soft black bristle that barely covers her naked head or those soulful hazel eyes that can fix you with a stare that is hungry, vulnerable, and piercing in the same instant. Sooner or later, though, it is Sinéad O'Connor's voice—and its harsh beauty—that you will have to reckon with. According to her father, it is a voice that she inherited from her mother, a passionate and often troubled woman. According to Nigel Grainge, the president of her record company, it is a voice that bears the lineage of her strife-torn and heartbroken homeland, Ireland. "We're talking soul singing, like Van Morrison," he says. "That is, *real* soul singing." O'Connor herself says she never really thought much about where her voice emerged from. Like her heart and memory, it was just another sign of deep familial pain.

Whatever its origins, O'Connor's voice is a remarkable and forceful instrument, and it has quickly established her as one of the most estimable new pop artists to emerge in years. This is a heartening development, though also—given the sort of music that O'Connor makes—a completely unlikely one. On the basis of her 1987 debut work, *The Lion and the Cobra*—a brilliant album about sexual fury and spiritual passion—O'Connor seemed fated for a career like that of Van Morrison, Lou Reed, Leonard Cohen, or many of rock's other great truth-tellers: namely, a career of essential artistry, on the border of mainstream affection. But with her current work, *I Do Not Want What I Haven't Got,* Sinéad O'Connor has achieved both widespread success and flat-out greatness. Furious and lovely, *I Do Not Want What I Haven't Got* is the work of a young woman who has had to weather some hard and haunting losses, and who sets out to rebuild her faith. By the album's end, she has won a certain measure of hard-earned peace, but only by venting some racking pain, and by leveling an excoriating rage at those who have betrayed her. In an era when even many of the best pop albums are increasingly subservient to the dominance of style and beat, Sinéad O'Connor has fashioned a full-length work that takes uncommon thematic risks, and that makes style entirely subservient to emotional expression. Like Bob Dylan's *Blood on the Tracks* and John Lennon's *Plastic Ono Band,* O'Connor's *I Do Not Want What I Haven't Got* is an intensely introspective work that is so affecting and farsighted, it seems capable of defining the mood or experience of an entire audience.

Which is exactly what it appears to be doing. In the United Kingdon, where it was released in late February 1990, the album bulleted to the top of the charts in its first week of release. In America, *I Do Not Want What I Haven't Got* vaulted to number 1 on Billboard's Top 100 album chart within a month of its release—an almost unprecedented feat for a relatively unknown female artist. Apparently, there is something in O'Connor's fierce and rapturous music that is touching a public nerve, though the singer herself believes that it is the video version of the album's first single—a deep-blue cover of Prince's "Nothing Compares 2 U"—that has paved the way for the album's success. Indeed, "Nothing Compares 2 U" is a gripping performance: For five minutes, O'Connor holds the camera—and therefore the viewer—with a heartsick gaze, and tries to make sense of how she lost the one love that she could never afford to lose. One instant she tosses out sass, the next, utter desolation, until by the song's end, the singer's grief has become too much for her, and she cries a solitary tear of inconsolable loss.

"I didn't intend for that moment to happen," says O'Connor, "but when it did, I thought, 'I should let this happen.' I think it shocks people. Some people, I know, really hate it—maybe because it's so honest, or maybe because they're embarrassed by displays of emotions.

"But I think I'm probably living proof of the danger of *not* expressing your feelings. For years I *couldn't* express how I felt. I think that's how music helped me. I also think that's why it's the most powerful medium: because it expresses for other people feelings that they can't express, but that need to be expressed. If you *don't* express those feelings—whether they're aggressive or loving or whatever—they will fucking blow you up one day."

SPEND MUCH TIME around O'Connor, and you'll find that she's a lot like her music—that is, she is smart and complex, and she can effortlessly tap into deep wells of sadness and anger. But as often as not, she can also prove sweet and goofy, and can seem truly bewildered by the rituals and expectations that accompany fame. For example, the day after her performance at BBC Radio, during the photo session for this story, O'Connor takes the occasion as an opportunity for listening to some homemade tapes of reggae oldies and recent hip-hop faves like Queen Latifah and N.W.A. (Hip-hop, says O'Connor, is the one pop form that she feels has the closest spiritual kinship to her own music.) In between shots, O'Connor dances around and shares giggle fits and hilarious private asides with her longtime friend, personal assistant, and constant companion Ciara O'Flanaghan. Sometimes, right before striking a serious pose, Sinéad will roll her eyes and crack up, as if she's both tickled and embarrassed by the notion of her own celebrity.

At other times, the realities of O'Connor's fame can prove less amusing. The afternoon following the photo shoot, O'Connor is walking down a hallway at the offices of her London record company, wearing dark sunglasses and a black leather jacket. She has the hood of a white jersey pulled over her head, and seems deep in thought as she walks along, staring down at her feet. At first, she doesn't respond to hearing her name called. It turns out that she has just finished reading a blistering article about her in the latest issue of the pop music newsweekly *New Musical Express*, and it has left her near tears.

In England, O'Connor has become something of a controversial figure with both the music and mainstream press. When she arrived on the scene, she was given to uttering often acerbic views about politics, the music business, and sex—and came across, in *NME*'s estimation, as "the female Johnny Rotten of the '80s, an angst-ridden young woman who shocked established society with her looks and views."

Recently, O'Connor has done her best to undo this image, though the British press has been reluctant to let her outdistance or make amends for her past, and *NME* in particular still regards her as [an] *l'enfant terrible*. In this morning's article, the newspaper takes several of the more controversial statements that O'Connor made a couple of years ago on a range of topics— including her views about U2, the Irish political situation, and her former manager, Fachtna O'Ceallaigh—and contrasts them with her recent statements on the same subjects. It's a scathing and intentionally mean-witted piece of journalism, and at the article's end, writer Eugene Masterson asks:

"Does a leopard change its spots so quickly or is Sinéad a chameleon who changes her views to suit her moods?" *NME*'s implication couldn't be clearer: O'Connor is a fickle opportunist and manipulator, who has abandoned her forthrightness at the first blush of success.

"When the press looked at me," she says, "they saw a woman with a shaved head and a pair of Doc Marten boots, and they assumed that I was aggressive and strong and tough. The truth is, I'm not really *any* of those things." As she talks, O'Connor is tucked into the backseat of a taxi, en route to her home in the Golder's Green area of North London. She stares out the window as the car makes its way through the rain-drenched maze of British urban sprawl, and she talks in a low but intense voice. "Just because I'm a woman that speaks my mind about things and doesn't behave like some stupid blond bimbo, doesn't mean that I'm aggressive. It really hurts me when people think that—when they make me out to be some sort of nasty person, when all I want to do is be a *good* person. It can hurt so much that I feel like crying."

O'Connor pauses and pulls absently at the hint of forelock at the front of her hair. "They don't care that if they say, 'Sinéad O'Connor's a complete bastard,' I'm going to sit up all night and think, 'I *am* a complete bastard.' And when I'm walking down the street, I'll be thinking, 'Everyone's looking at me, thinking what a *complete bastard* I am.' Obviously, if they listened to any of my music—to a song like 'The Last Day of Our Acquaintance'—they would realize that I couldn't possibly be as secure and strong as they would expect me to be. Obviously there's a lot of insecurity in there.

"But they don't care about what a person has been through."

A FEW MINUTES later, O'Connor arrives at her home in North London. It is a medium-sized, two-story cottage-style house, nestled into a side street of similar residences, just a stone's throw from an ancient-looking graveyard. "I *like* dead people," says O'Connor, when asked if she ever minds the proximity. "I find it comforting to have them close by."

Inside, O'Connor's home is strewn with careworn toys and a few stray strands of Christmas lights, left over from the holidays. In the smallish living room, she turns on some heat, takes off her leather jacket, grabs some cigarettes and a lighter from beside a portable cassette boom box—the house's main stereo—and settles down in the corner of a weather-beaten sofa. A gray cat patiently watches O'Connor's moves, and then leaps onto the sofa and curls into a contented ball beside the singer. There is nothing in this scene of domestic modesty that would tell you that you are visiting in the home of what one critic has called "the decade's first new superstar," and apparently, O'Connor likes it that way.

"I *never* think of myself as Sinéad O'Connor, *rock star,*" she says with a bashful smile. She picks a Silk Cut cigarette from her pack and lights it, and thinks quietly for a moment. "The truth is," she continues, "music doesn't really play a huge part in my life. I know it seems that way at the moment, because I'm just putting an album out, and of course, that means a lot to me. But the most important part of my life *isn't* the album: It's the experiences that are written about in the album. To me, these records are like a chronological listing of every phase I've been through in my life. They're simply an accumulation of everything I've experienced. And it's those experiences—not the music—that have made me happy or pissed me off."

For O'Connor, many of her experiences have been harsh from the start. She was born the third of four children to John and Marie O'Connor, a young Catholic couple living in the Glenageary section of Dublin, Ireland. John, an engineer, and Marie, a former dressmaker, had married young, and by the time Sinéad came along, the relationship had already turned sour. It was a tense, sometimes brutal home life, and the violence was occasionally carried over to the children—particularly the two daughters with whom Marie had a strained relationship. "A child always thinks that it's *their* fault that these things happen," says Sinéad. "I was extremely fucked up about that for a long time. Between the family situation and the Catholicism, I developed a real capacity for guilt."

One thing the family shared good feelings about was music. Marie O'Connor had sung Gilbert and Sullivan operettas in her youth, and she encouraged her children to explore their vocal talents. "Sinéad, in particular, had a good musical ear," says John O'Connor. "The first time she cut a record, I had her out for a walk one Saturday, up in the Dublin mountains, and I had a business Dictaphone along. It was never meant for singing, but Sinéad sang so pretty and nice this one time that I kept it on the tape. It's interesting to hear how true Sinéad's voice was, even at that stage. She could hit a note on the head and hold it for fifteen seconds or so—just like she can today."

To Sinéad, though, singing was more a release than a pleasure. "I remember when I was very young," she says, "I'd go out for walks and I'd sort of be making little songs up. I think I was just so fucked up that I wanted to make noises or something—like shout and scream about the whole thing. I suppose that's how it started. It wasn't that I wanted to be a singer: It was just that I could actually *express* the pain that I felt with my voice, because I didn't have the facilities to express it in any other way. It was just all bubbling up in there and it had to come out."

In 1975, when Sinéad was eight, John and Marie O'Connor separated (divorce was not allowed by Irish laws). For the first few years, Sinéad lived mostly with her mother. Though Marie was "*extremely* strict," Sinéad felt sorry for her, and also felt guilty for preferring the protection and freedom that her father's home offered. By the time she was thirteen, O'Connor found life with Marie too grim and repressive, and she settled into her father's. "I think I took everything out on him," she says. "I'd just come out of years of being severely abused. Suddenly I had all this freedom, and I didn't know what to do with it."

Sinéad began cutting classes, sometimes spending entire school weeks holed up in Dublin's bowling alleys, playing video games. She also began stealing—first lifting money from her father, then from strangers, then eventually shoplifting clothes, perfume, and shoes from local shops. "Any book that you read on child psychology," says Sinéad, "will tell you that you can't take a child who's been in a violent or psychologically intense situation for years and expect it to be able to cope with normal life. I wasn't *used* to life being normal. I was used to it being melodramatic and awful."

Eventually, Sinéad got caught shoplifting—in fact, she got caught a few times. By this time, John O'Connor had tired of working as an engineer and had taken up the practice of law—and he understood that his daughter might be headed for serious legal trouble. "She had good bloody reason to be unhappy with her home life," he says, "though maybe it's my own feeling of guilt, my failure to do what was right for the kids at the time, that is speaking here. Anyway, Sinéad never did anything seriously wrong—she wasn't a sex fiend or a dope fiend. But after she got caught nicking a pair of shoes in a shop in downtown Dublin, there was a fear that she was getting wayward."

In the early eighties, Sinéad's father sent her to Sion Hill in Blackrock—a school for girls with behavioral problems, run by Dominican nuns—and then to a succession of boarding schools that included Mayfield College in Drumcondra, and Newtown School in Waterford. "I sent her to these places," he says, "because I couldn't handle the problem any other way. She was resentful, but she also knew that she needed help. And she *did* go through a tremendous change pattern while she was in Waterford. That kid came out of that school and she never looked back insofar as moral integrity is concerned. She's now absolutely and fiercely honest, and she wasn't when she went into that school."

For Sinéad, though, it was a hard stretch. "Being sent off," she says, "just refueled the whole thing about being a bad person. Also, I had few friends at these schools. I didn't know how to tell people, 'I'm not nasty and horrible and unfriendly. I'm just fucked up.' I'd been through a whole lot of shit that they could never understand in a million years, these people from fucking great happy families. They had no understanding of what life was like for other people. So, I didn't enjoy it at all. I was extremely withdrawn and slouched over. I thought I was mental."

It was during her tenure in the boarding schools that Sinéad moved closer to music, spending evenings in her room, playing guitar and gradually writing some of the songs that would end up on *The Lion and the Cobra*. In 1982, a teacher at Mayfield asked the fifteen-year-old O'Connor to sing at her wedding. O'Connor sang Barbra Streisand's "Evergreen," and her full-throated delivery caught the ear of Paul Byrne, the bride's brother, who was also the drummer for In Tua Nua, an Irish band with ties to U2. The two struck up a friendship, and later, O'Connor co-wrote In Tua Nua's first single, "Take My Hand." For a time, there was talk of her touring with the band, but her father insisted she stay in school. However, Sinéad's brush with recording had enlivened her, and with another friend, Jeremy Maber, she began singing in a folk duo around Waterford's coffeehouses and pubs, where she became known for haunting and unusual originals like "Never Get Old" and "Drink before the War," and for her forceful covers of Bob Dylan songs, like "Simple Twist of Fate" and "One More Cup of Coffee."

"Whatever depth and intensity was inside me," says O'Connor, "it was coming out in my music. I didn't know whether it was mystical or religious or what, but it was as if I was pulling a big rope out of the middle of me—a rope that had been there since before I was born."

By the next year, O'Connor had decided it was time to leave school and become a professional singer, but her father refused. "And then," he says, "she made the most determined statement she ever made about a professional career in music: She simply walked out of the school, saying nothing to anyone, and disappeared. She was only sixteen, and I was up a wall. I didn't know *where* she was. When she came home, it was plain that she had made up her mind. So we sent her to the College of Music in Dublin. She had this big booming voice, and I was hoping that she would get some classical education in singing so as not to damage the vocal cords. She also studied piano. She's *not* a naive composer. She knows where she is in music."

Then, in early 1985, Marie O'Connor was killed in a car wreck. It had been almost two years since Sinéad had seen her mother, and at the time of the death, their relationship was unreconciled. "I was completely and utterly destroyed," she says. "I felt that we had never really *had* a relationship. But looking back, I know that my mother knew I loved her very much, and I know that she loved me. More than anything, I just felt sorry for her. Her life had been such misery, and as a result, *our* lives had been misery. It just must have been hell for her. She had lost her career when she got married, she'd had baby after baby, and I don't think she ever had time in all those years to figure herself out, like I've had since leaving Ireland.

"More than anything, I think she is the reason why I sing."

By 1985, GALVANIZED by the international success of Irish heroes U2, Dublin had become something of a hotbed for aspiring rock and folk acts. In the early part of the year, Nigel Grainge and Chris Hill, the director and manager of London's Ensign Records (and early supporters of Ireland's Thin Lizzy and Boomtown Rats), paid a visit to Dublin, auditioning area bands at a local rehearsal studio. Nothing much caught their attention until the last group on their list—Ton Ton Macoute, who had acquired some acclaim for their new lead singer.

"At first," says Chris Hill, "they looked like another godawful pub rock band. Then Sinéad walked in. She had thick black hair and she was *so* pretty, though she wasn't made up to look pretty. I mean, she looked scruffy, dressed in a baggy jersey, and staring at the floor. Then she sang. The songs were dreadful, but her voice was incredible. It ranged from this kind of pure little folk voice to a banshee wail, like something from the depths of somewhere. Yet she was *so* self-conscious. If she could have crawled into the corner and sang with her back to us, she would have. We thought, 'This girl's got a *remarkable* voice. Pity it's such a dreadful band with no songs.' At the end, Nigel said to her, 'What you're doing now isn't right for us, but if you feel you hit on something, get in touch.' The usual thing."

Six weeks later, back in London, Nigel Grainge got a letter from Sinéad. "Dear Nigel," she wrote, "I've left the band. I'm writing my own songs. You *did* say you would be interested in recording some demos of my stuff, so when I finish the songs, will you do it?" Grainge had made no such promise, but he was impressed by O'Connor's sly ambition and sent her an airplane ticket. Two weeks later, when O'Connor arrived, Grainge had forgotten about her impending visit. Flustered, he called Karl Wallinger, who had just left the Waterboys to form World Party, and asked him to help the young Irish singer through her demos. That night, when Grainge visited the session, Wallinger met him at the door with a smile. "I think you're gonna get a real surprise here," he told Grainge. As Grainge walked in, O'Connor was in the middle of taping her last song, "Troy"—a mesmeric account of sexual need and romantic betrayal. Grainge was riveted. "We *never* sign anybody," he says. "We're as choosy as can be." But on the basis of the demos with Wallinger, Grainge signed Sinéad O'Connor to Ensign. "Her performances," he says, "were absolutely devastating."

Within days, news of O'Connor's signing spread through the Dublin scene. According to some sources, U2's Bono was so impressed by the demos that he offered to help Sinéad find a better deal with a bigger label. O'Connor insisted on sticking with Ensign, though she later agreed to collaborate with the Edge on "Heroine," a song for the guitarist's 1986 soundtrack LP, *Captive.*

Shortly, O'Connor had moved to London and started work on the material for her first album. It should have been a heady time, but at first O'Connor found it isolating. "She was clearly very lonely," says Grainge. "She spent a lot of time hanging around the office, making tea, and answering phones. Our big charge was to play her records. The first time we ever heard her, we said, 'You sound like Grace Slick.' She said, 'Grace *who?*' Another time, I asked, 'How much Aretha Franklin have you ever heard?' And she said, 'I don't know—who's Aretha Franklin?' "

"To get someone that early in their development was remarkable," says Chris Hill. "I asked her once, 'Where do you think you fit in musically?' And she said, 'Well, somewhere between Kate Bush and Madonna. I'm not sure where.' And we thought, '*That* covers every fucking angle, right?' "

O'Connor was writing music and developing at a surprising pace—and the sense of change began to show in her appearance. "She was always playing with her hair," says Grainge. "One minute she had a Mohican. That was on for a couple of weeks, and then it all went—she walked in, and she had shaved herself bald. We thought, 'Well, *there's* a statement.' " Over the next few years, O'Connor's bare scalp would strike various journalists as provocative, frightening, ugly, gorgeous, sexy, and shocking—and would also help make her one of the most unforgettable new faces in all pop.

During this period, O'Connor met two other people who were to figure prominently in her life. The first was John Reynolds, former drummer with British trash-pop band Transvision Vamp. Reynolds started dating O'Connor after joining her studio band, and a month later, Sinéad was pregnant. "I was the only one that felt completely sure and delighted about the idea of me having a baby," she says. "I could understand John's reluctance. Suddenly his whole life was flashing before him. But then there was the record company. They thought I was jeopardizing my career. *My* attitude was that if I had been a man, and my wife or girlfriend was pregnant, they wouldn't be telling me that I couldn't have it.

"I was very upset, and very hurt. How could I choose between my career or a child? They're both as important as each other. It wasn't a

Catholicism thing—I had nothing against abortion. In fact, I was actually in the hospital bed about to have an abortion, and then I left. It wasn't *me* that wanted to have the abortion. *I* wanted the baby—and I decided to have it."

The other person that Sinéad met in this time was Fachtna O'Ceallaigh—an Irish patriot who had managed Boomtown Rats and Bananarama, and who also headed U2's fledgling label for homegrown Irish bands, Mother Records. To the consternation of Nigel Grainge, O'Connor wanted O'Ceallaigh for her manager. "I opposed the connection," says Grainge. "I knew Fachtna from many years before, when the Boomtown Rats were on Ensign. Fachtna gets very emotionally involved with his acts, to such a degree that some people would call it irrational. He can be very inspiring, but he can also be infuriating when he doesn't get his way. I told Sinéad: 'I *don't* want to work with Fachtna, and I don't want him to be your manager.' Which was the absolute wrong thing to say. It was like a father telling a child, 'You can't do this.' She came back to me and said, 'Fachtna O'Ceallaigh is my manager. Get on with it.' And Fachtna became very closely involved with Sinéad. I mean, he was her mentor for a serious period of time."

In the fall of 1986, O'Connor had begun to work with producer Mick Glossop on the first album, but the sessions soon fizzled. "The tracks sounded like a cabaret rock version of these wonderful songs," says Grainge (O'Connor herself once described the failed sessions as "all fucking Irish ethereal and mystical"). Adds Chris Hill: "She was a young girl of nineteen years, who was pregnant and frightened that if she fucked up, she was gonna lose her record deal, and be told to go back to Ireland."

A few weeks later, Grainge proposed a solution. "I kept thinking about what she had done with the demos," he says, "how great they had felt. So I said, 'Go in with a decent engineer, Sinéad, and produce it yourself. *You* know what these songs are about, and how they should sound.' About that time Fachtna came heavily into the situation. His style of management is to completely divide the artist from the record company, and from that stage, she stopped coming into the record company."

In April 1987, at age twenty, seven months pregnant and with almost no studio expertise, O'Connor took over the production of her maiden album. Two months later, she had finished a record that all parties were thrilled by, and two weeks after that, she gave birth to her son, Jake Reynolds. In theory, it should have been a triumphal time. *The Lion and the Cobra* was a terrific album full of deep-felt songs about desire, damnation, and courage, and O'Connor produced and arranged it all in a style that spanned folk music, orchestral rock, and bass-heavy dance pop.

But within months, O'Connor found herself embroiled in feuds and controversies. In early 1988, U2 dismissed Fachtna O'Ceallaigh from his position as manager of Mother Records, citing "incompatible tempera-ments" (in addition, O'Ceallaigh had once told a reporter, "I literally despise the music U2 makes"). Later, in an interview with Britain's *i-D* magazine, O'Connor made some disparaging remarks about U2's "bombastic" music, and found herself reproached by the band's associates. Before long, angry feelings and bitter statements had escalated on both sides, fueled by the sensationalistic-minded U.K. music press (in particular, *NME* milked the schism for a spate of cover stories). At one point, O'Connor was quoted as saying: "I have no respect for Bono and no affiliation with his music or ideas. . . . I know he's faking that sincerity." Another time, in a bit less gracious mood, she told *Melody Maker*, "[U2] take themselves so fuckin' seriously. [Bono's] just a stupid turd."

O'Connor has attempted to make amends for the affair, but a certain rancor still lingers. "I felt ostracized and punished over that whole thing," she says. "But I also felt guilty because I knew at the back of my mind that some of the things I was saying were *not* said for myself. I expressed anger with U2 because the band had hurt Fachtna, who was a friend of mine. I was wrong to do that, because, really, Fachtna should fight his own battles. I had been hateful toward somebody I had no right to be hateful toward. U2 hadn't really done anything shitty to me. But I also learned that U2 was a popular and powerful band, and that the British and Irish music establishment would *not* allow you to be critical of them."

O'Connor's comments about the IRA—the outlawed political move-ment that seeks a united Ireland and opposes Britain's dominance of the country, and has committed numerous killings and bombings to achieve its aims—were considered even more controversial. On one occasion, O'Connor was quoted as saying: "I support the IRA. . . . I don't like the violence but I do understand it, it's necessary even though it's terrible." In the British press—with whom the IRA are extremely unpopular—these comments were construed as an endorsement of terrorist violence.

O'Connor has long since disavowed any support of the IRA or its methods, but the issue continues to plague her. "I was involved in very complex relationships during that time," she says now, "and I was influenced by the people I was hanging around with. I wanted their approval, and I was expressing things in order to get that approval, without realizing that that's what I was doing. I should not have condoned the use of violence by anyone. I *don't* believe that it's right for either side involved in the war to kill people. I also don't think for a second that the British government has any right to be in Ireland. But as I say, I was condoning violence to impress the people I was involved with, and I should not have done that."

The period following *The Lion and the Cobra* was also rough for more personal reasons. Shortly after Jake's birth, O'Connor and John Reynolds separated for a time. Then, following O'Connor's appearance at the 1988 Grammy Awards, she returned to London, and to the surprise of many friends and associates, married Reynolds. "I was in a lot of pain during that time," she says, "but it wasn't due to John. It was the fact that I was with somebody else who was fucking me up."

It is now late in the afternoon, and the light in the living room has grown dim. O'Connor gets up, turns on a lamp, then settles back into the sofa, lighting a cigarette. "Around the time I got married," she continues, "I had been physically ill for a long time. I'd been going to doctors, and nobody could figure out what was wrong. Then, for a whole summer, I saw a woman who's like a spiritual healer and a dietitian, and I started doing yoga with her. That process gave me a chance to get my act together mentally, and to begin to see that I was involved with people who were bringing out negative things in me.

"I realized that I had no control over myself—that other people were in control of me, that I was expressing opinions that were other people's, that practically everything I was doing was to please other people. So I decided I had to assume control over myself in every aspect, and that meant I had to sever some relationships that were very, very difficult to sever. I had to summon the strength to be able to say 'bye-bye' to people that I had previously thought I couldn't function without. Now, I feel like I'm sitting at the helm where I'm supposed to be sitting. Now, I'm the captain of my own ship."

One of the relationships—perhaps the primary one—that O'Connor severed at this time was with Fachtna O'Ceallaigh. According to John O'Connor, "Fachtna came too close to seeing Sinéad as a possession. Management should be an arm's-length affair; there's a relationship that has to be kept scrupulously in its place. The manager's first duty is that their client's career should be maximized, and they should not let their personal feelings enter into it at all—whether they're political feelings or emotional feelings."

In December of 1989, Sinéad O'Connor dismissed O'Ceallaigh as her manager (she was subsequently represented by Steve Fargnoli, former co-manager of Prince). Neither party is inclined to discuss the details of the separation, though O'Connor says: "Fachtna had given me a sense of my rights as an artist. He instilled in me the idea that if it wasn't for people like me, the record industry would not exist—which is true. And he instilled in me the idea that I must have control over what goes on regarding how my image and work are presented. Most important, he was instrumental in showing me that I should be honest and true, and not compromise myself."

But according to Chris Hill, O'Ceallaigh's contribution went beyond that. "He did two important things: He helped her discover a part of herself—that is, her sense of purpose and worth—but he also badly fucked her up. And the two things together are what made Sinéad O'Connor what she is."

For his part, O'Ceallaigh says simply, "What is important to me is what Sinéad says. She is the one who knows exactly what occurred over the three-year period that I managed her. And even more important than that, her reaction means everything to me because she has always been and will always continue to be, as long as I'm alive, a best friend of mine. Everything else—whether it's success or fame or whatever, all the things that attend success—it's all basically rubbish. I never thought of Sinéad as a person or object who made records. I thought of her as a human being and a friend."

Following the firing of O'Ceallaigh, O'Connor holed up in a garage studio with sound engineer Chris Birkett, and in a surprisingly short time had finished writing and self-producing the tracks for *I Do Not Want What I Haven't Got*—in effect, a collection of hard-hitting and heartrending songs about the circumstances of her recent life. Says O'Connor: "It is simply a record about a twenty-three-year-old human being and her experiences, and what she makes of those experiences and of herself. Some of the experiences are angry and some are hurtful. I write about whatever it is I happen to be going through at the time, and so if something awful was happening to me, that's what I wrote about."

Around the end of 1989, O'Connor called Nigel Grainge and Chris Hill. She had been trying to rebuild relations with the pair, and felt the time had come to play them the rough mixes for *I Do Not Want What I Haven't Got*. "After we first heard it," says Hill, "we were shell-shocked. I mean, it's so *personal,* we couldn't even make a judgment about it, and we couldn't think in terms of whether it was a hit record. It is *intense.* I know she thinks it's a happy record, but it doesn't convey happiness—it conveys trauma. Because of our reaction, she thought we didn't like it, and she said, 'It's not for men to like; it's a woman's statement.' But Nigel and I had both been through divorces. You listen to some little girl singing 'The Last Day of Our Acquaintance,' and you *know* what it's about. We've *been* there."

Says O'Connor: "Nigel told me, 'You can't put that out; it's too personal.' I said, 'People that like me, like me *because* of that. That's what I do.'"

Now, though, as O'Connor sits in her living room discussing the record, it seems evident that *I Do Not Want What I Haven't Got* is going to be more than anyone imagined. "If you think about the kind of songs I write," she says, "it's strange that they would be commercial. I mean, they're *so* personal. I think about why I wrote a song like 'Last Day of Our Acquaintance,' and then I think about millions of people buying and listening to it. . . . It's really weird."

There is a noise—actually, an ear-splitting scream—at the living-room door, and in a moment, O'Connor's two-and-a-half-year-old son, Jake, bounds in, all smiles and whoops. He is blond-haired and red-cheeked, and has the same deep eyes as his mother, but he turns shy when he sees a stranger sitting in the room. He is followed by his father, drummer John Reynolds, a tall, gracious man, who is home from rehearsals with his own band, Max. John and Sinéad have some family business to discuss—Sinéad's brother Joseph has just signed a contract for his first novel, and John and Sinéad are wondering where to take him and her father for a family celebration next evening. Finally, they settle on a local transvestite club—where a drag queen is reportedly delivering an impression of Sinéad singing "Nothing Compares 2 U," replete with tear—and then John and Jake take off to begin dinner. Before going, Jake emits one last glorious yelp. "He's mad, that child," says O'Connor, shaking her head and smiling. "I feel like he really wanted to be born—he's such a happy kid."

She falls quiet for a few moments, pulling at her forelock. "A couple of years ago," she says, "I was having a hard time as far as my personal life was concerned, and that mattered much more to me than whether my record was doing well, or anything like that. But at the moment, I'm very happy. I have a lovely husband, a lovely son, and everything's going wonderfully.

"Really, I don't know what more I could want—except to know myself a bit better. But then, that's what I'm trying to do when I write songs."

A MONTH LATER, Sinéad O'Connor stands before a twenty-three-piece orchestra in London's elegant Whitehall Banqueting House, dressed in a lime-green low-cut dress, singing a lush and sweet version of Cole Porter's "You Do Something to Me." The occasion is a press conference to announce *Red Hot & Blue*, an upcoming double album and television special that will feature pop artists like O'Connor, U2, David Byrne, Fine Young Cannibals, and Neneh Cherry, interpreting the music of Cole Porter. More important, the project will benefit AIDS charities, as well as disseminate information about the disease and its prevention. O'Connor is the press conference's surprise guest, and it is plain from her performance of this Tin Pan Alley chestnut just what an exemplary singer she is. She rocks gently to the song's steady but tricky groove, and in those moments when the lyric calls for a subtle roar, she pulls her mouth back from the microphone in the manner of a seasoned jazz vocalist.

After her performance, O'Connor bounds down the backstairs to a waiting car and heads across town to a full day of rehearsals for her own show. In the last few weeks, O'Connor's world has exploded all over again, though this time in a beneficent fashion. "Nothing Compares 2 U" has become a huge international hit—the biggest record of the year, so far—and earlier in the week, *I Do Not Want What I Haven't Got* stormed into *Billboard*'s Top 10. In a few days, O'Connor will begin a lengthy world tour, and in preparation for it, her life has become filled up with appurtenances—like personal beepers, portable cellular phones, and the nice new blue car in which she is being driven around. All these attachments are designed to make things easier and more efficient, but in other ways, they also amount to signs of pressure and obligation. Plus, there are the demands of real life itself: O'Connor's son, Jake, has had a bad cold in the last week, and O'Connor has been staying up nights with him, then showing up at rehearsals, too tired to sing. In the last couple of days, friends have convinced her that she should get some rest, so now she and Ciara O'Flanaghan are sleeping at a local Holiday Inn, while O'Connor's husband spends nights with Jake. This morning, O'Connor is in great spirits, though there are times, she admits, when the recent rush of events is exhausting. "It's like my life is changing," she says at one point during the day. "It's like it will never be normal again."

Later in the afternoon, at her rehearsal, the pressures of the week begin to catch up with O'Connor. She has been in fine voice all day, singing powerful versions of "The Emperor's New Clothes," "3 Babies," "Jump in the River," and "Jerusalem," among others, but when she begins to work her way meticulously through "Nothing Compares 2 U," she becomes concerned that she is singing out of pitch. She stops the song repeatedly to ask Ciara and others if they think her voice is turning "croaky." Despite everyone's reassurances, O'Connor is convinced that she is singing badly, and eventually halts the rehearsal. On her way back to the hotel, she is almost inconsolable. She is worried that she may be losing her voice just as the tour starts, and that she is going to fail the people who are depending on her. For the moment, she seems in a funk as deep as the one that followed *NME*'s last reprimand.

Back at the Holiday Inn, she lights some candles, turns off the lights, and settles into a chair. She has changed into a T-shirt and jeans and is now barefoot. "I know I'm capable of singing better," she says, rubbing nervously at her throat, "so I get a bit pissed off at myself. Mainly, things are great right now, though there are times when I'm more stressed. I mean, it's a bit of a shock to the system. Every week something brilliant seems to happen, and I'm on the phone screeching."

A couple of minutes later the phone rings. O'Connor answers it, exchanges some pleasantries—and then begins to screech at an ear-splitting level. "You're joking!" she yells. "I don't *believe* you. Fucking *amazing*." She lets out another scream and begins jumping up and down on her bed. "How the *fuck* did you find out?" It turns out that it is a friend of O'Connor's, calling to tell her that "Nothing Compares 2 U" has just become the number 1 single in America, after only a few weeks in release. In addition, it appears likely that *I Do Not Want What I Haven't Got* will top the album charts the following week. "I can't believe it," squeals O'Connor. "I better go and phone my father. Actually, I'll phone you back. I've got to get control over myself."

A few seconds later, the phone rings again. It is her assistant, Ciara, telling O'Connor that her manager, Steve Fargnoli, is in the bar downstairs and wants to congratulate her. O'Connor bolts out of the door for the elevator, bouncing up and down in the hallway barefoot, exclaiming: "Number *one!* In *America!*" For the next couple of hours, O'Connor is a model of exultation and childlike glee, ordering Singapore Slings two at a time, calling her father in Ireland on the cellular phone (when Ciara points out that it's an expensive call, O'Connor says, "I know, but when you're number *one* in *America*—" then breaks into a blush, laughing). "From now on," she tells her friends in the bar, lifting her drink and tilting her nose in a mock high-society manner, "we are to refer to me as '*M'lady.*'"

Later, though, back in her hotel room, when asked what it means to her to have a number 1 single in America, O'Connor greets the question seriously. "I don't feel like it's *me*, almost. It's like a big fantasy. All the time you grow up, watching 'Top of the Pops' or being interested in music, you always wonder what it would be like.

"I mean, I'm very excited and very grateful that it's happened, but it really doesn't change what I said before. I don't want to be a rock star, I don't want to be treated like one, and I don't want any of the associations that go with it. I just want to be treated like an ordinary person, and I want people to remember that the most important things in my life are *not* making records and going around the world on tour. The most important thing is my family, and my spiritual beliefs. If I didn't have those things, I wouldn't be inspired to do anything."

O'Connor pauses, and then blushes. "I just remembered something," she says. "My publicist tells me that once I told her I wanted to be as big as Madonna. It surprises me that I said that. I was young, foolish, I suppose. Well, I'm a very different person now."

O'Connor seems utterly sincere and assured in her comments, but earlier, Chris Hill had said something trenchant about her capacity for success: "I think she has a fire in her to be the biggest. In fact, she once told me, 'I'm gonna be the biggest star there's ever been.' And I think she certainly likes the fame. But I also think that there's a point where she won't give any more than she needs to, and where she'll say, 'Fuck it, I'm not doing any more than *this;* the rest of my life is mine.' She could actually do that next week. She could turn around and say, 'This is as big as I want to be; beyond here I don't like it.'

"But at the moment," Hill continued, "there is a more important question that confronts Sinéad: Does her art always have to come from pain? And it *is* an important question. I mean, David Bowie hasn't made a fucking record worth thruppence in the last ten years, and the reason is, he's happy. It's also the reason why Keith Richards actually makes better records than Mick Jagger, because Keith is relatively fucked up, compared to Mick Jagger.

"With Sinéad, we won't know for years, because she's still a child compared to these others. She will still go through extremes of happiness and unhappiness in the next few years, unless she is in control of the unhappiness so much that she never again has to suffer from it. And I pray to God she'll be able to make great records when she's happy—not for our sake, because all we have to do is sell them. It's for her sake. No one should be sentenced to the unhappiness of a Van Gogh just because that's the only way they can work."

Watching O'Connor, as she calls friends and relatives and, with a sweet mix of shyness and pride, tells them that her single has gone to number 1, the last thing anyone would wish on her would be more hurt—even if it *would* make for more records as meaningful and captivating as *I Do Not Want What I Haven't Got.* Indeed, if the depths of the heart and mind can be determined by how one deals with unforgettable losses, or unattainable longings, then O'Connor has paid for her depths. She has learned some bitter truths—that life and love will break your heart, that success and fame are at best fleeting victories, and that no matter what blessings she finds in adulthood, nothing can undo the scars of past experiences, or undo their memories. And though she has found a way to accept those truths, she has also found a way to rage back at them.

Still, there are moments when O'Connor can be talking about all the newfound peace in her life, and a tortured look will suddenly cross her face. Maybe in those moments she fears the happiness as much as she ever dreaded the hurts—because few things hurt more than realizing that, sooner or later, happiness goes the way of all evanescent dreams. Or maybe it's a fear that what Chris Hill and others say is right: that maybe pain *is* the source of her art, and that she may have little choice but to serve that particular muse. In moments like that, sitting in crowded rooms with all the lights on, Sinéad

O'Connor may not be all that distant from an all-too-familiar darkness, though maybe now it's been internalized into a more manageable or companionable place.

Whatever the sources of that look, O'Connor wears it with a brave face. "Every experience I've had," she says, "is a good experience, even the bad ones. An understanding of sorrow and pain is an important thing to have, because if nothing else, it also gives you an appreciation for happiness. People who've been brought up happy and normal often don't have an understanding of what life might be like for other people. Whereas people who have had an unhappy life *have* that understanding. In the kind of work that I do, it's important to understand pain and what life is like for other people—and I never take that knowledge for granted.

"I realize," she says, offering a shy smile, "that I'm in a very lucky position, and maybe something I pass along in my songs might be able to help somebody else. But that couldn't happen if I didn't have the experiences I've had."

david baerwald's

songs

of secrets

and sins

*d*avid baerwald sits at an upright piano in the den of his mother's home in Los Angeles' well-heeled Brentwood district, and plays a private recital of a song called "Secret Silken World." It is a darkly humorous and unsettling song about a man who is lured into a world of power and sex and seduction—it is, in fact, about the bond that exists between the seducer and those whom he seduces. Some of Baerwald's friends—including Joni Mitchell—were so disturbed by the song's mix of damnation and glee that they persuaded Baerwald to leave the tune off his fine 1990 album, *Bedtime Stories*. Still, Baerwald takes a certain pleasure from regaling the occasional visitor with the song in its full, uncensored form. "The seats of his car were like velvet skin," Baerwald sings, glancing over his shoulder with a smile. "They made me think about all those places I've been/They made me understand violence . . . and sin. . . . /He said, 'Things would go better if you would be my friend/You don't have to like me but I can be a means to an end. . . . / It's a secret silken world/Of sex and submission/Of money and violence and acts of contrition/Where your enemies succumb/And the ladies all listen. . . .' "

At song's end, Baerwald studies his thin hands resting on the keyboard, then laughs. "You know what I think after singing something like that?" he asks. He strides over to the far side of the den, gesturing at something that hangs on a wall around the corner. It is a hand-tinted picture of Baerwald himself, at about age fifteen. His hair is browner and his face is fuller than now, with none of the lines, scars, and sunken pockets that currently make up his hawklike visage. It's a smiling and sweet face that looks out from the picture, but there is something lopsided and sly in its smile, not unlike the smile with which Baerwald now regards the photo. "Look at that face," he says, gazing at his former self. "Whatever happened to that kid? He looks so innocent—at least compared to this snaggle-toothed guy, singing about sex and violence."

Baerwald studies the picture for a moment longer, his thoughts seemingly far away. "What happened to that kid?" he says one more time, with a mirthless laugh.

IN ONE WAY there's an easy answer to that question: What happened to David Baerwald was that he became an uncommonly literate and seasoned songwriter. That is, he took the experiences and perspectives of a life lived hard, and fashioned them into a part-hard-boiled, part-empathetic lyrical sensibility that—in his songs with the much-acclaimed L.A. duo, David + David, as well as his own solo work—rivals the best musings of such similar-minded Southern California pop artisans as Warren Zevon, Randy Newman, and Donald Fagen. But whereas Zevon and Newman typically write in fictional modes, there is something deeply personal about Baerwald's scenarios. It's as if the voice singing about those who are living existences of ruin and longing has also known that existence himself.

The catch is, while Baerwald likes to joke about his own dissipated image, he isn't overly fond of disclosing the details of what shaped that sensibility. Indeed, Baerwald can prove a bit of a perplexity: He can speak endlessly and compellingly about a wide range of matters—from his favorite American authors (which include Raymond Chandler, Paul Bowles, Raymond Carver, and Andre Dubus) to his political passions (which lean toward unsentimental leftism), and he can tell hilarious off-the-record tales about some of his more famous acquaintances. But for all his obvious intelligence and wit, there is an unequivocal streetwise quality about Baerwald—an edginess that comes across in flash-quick moments, when a dark glare can cross his face, as a warning against delving too deeply into certain private concerns.

In other moments, Baerwald can turn resolutely vague. For example, a few minutes later, as he sits on the veranda of his mother's home, he seems both nonplused and cagey when the question is put to him directly: What *did* become of the young innocent-looking kid in that class photo? What is it about his past that turned him into such a keen profiler of bad-news souls?

Baerwald regards the question quietly for several long seconds, staring at the sharp points of his faded brown boots. "Um . . . I guess I gained perspective," he says, beginning softly, "and, uh, strength and, uh, knowledge. And I think I lost unquestioning good faith and innocence and, uh, you know, the youthful optimism that is untempered by facts. I'm not sure that those are terrible things to lose. But what I'm *really* upset about," he adds, pausing and fixing his visitor with an utterly sincere look, "is my complexion." Baerwald beams a quick, roguish smile, then lets out a loud laugh that echoes off the nearby hills.

Over the next hour or two, a slightly more detailed answer emerges. Baerwald was born in 1960 in Oxford, Ohio. His father was a respected political-science professor and his mother taught English and music. When Baerwald was five, his father accepted a position as Dean of Students at an English university in Japan, and moved the family to just outside Tokyo. Baerwald is sketchy about what the family life was like. There were two older sisters—both were musical prodigies, and both went through long unhappy periods—and his parents' marriage, he indicates, was strained and would eventually come apart. "They were an odd pairing," Baerwald says. "My father's a very austere, aristocratic German intellectual, and my mother's a warm midwestern woman from a family of farmers. I'm still pretty close to my mother [now a psychologist], and I have a very, uh, *cordial* relationship with my father. The two of us are definitely cut from the same cloth, which can be a bit distressing to admit."

It was a tumultuous time to be living abroad. America was involved in Vietnam, and there were riots and military actions at the university where Baerwald's parents taught. As a young American, Baerwald shared sympathies with those who protested the war, but he was also drawn to some less peaceful ideals. "I got interested in the way the Japanese cultural aesthetic can combine serenity with sudden violence," he says. "It's a trait I find I have an affinity toward, that warrior-poet ideal." In time, Baerwald found he had an even stronger affinity for the rock & roll revolution that was taking place back in America and in Britain—especially the music of the Beatles, the Rolling Stones, Jimi Hendrix, and the Band. To his parents' distaste, Baerwald began playing his own rock & roll, and shortly began writing some politically acerbic songs.

When he was twelve, the family moved to the Brentwood district around UCLA, but Baerwald found Los Angeles' air of cultural languor disorienting. "I mean, this neighborhood," he says, gesturing at the sprawling hills around him. It is a seductive landscape, brimming with beautiful homes tucked into rolling hills of affluence and privilege. "It just seemed kind of unreal, especially after coming out of a very vibrant scene. It's like, what's *really* going on here? You see nice houses, and nice people in nice cars with nice clothes, and you can't believe it's as idyllic as it looks.

"Anyway," Baerwald continues, "I started getting ejected from my junior high and high schools. I had a terrible temper, and I felt that the educational system existed solely to kill thinking. Coming from my background, there was nothing of interest to me in school. I'd already read and understood the religious symbolism of *The Scarlet Letter* at eight, and I wasn't going to get anything more from it at age fourteen. So I became a problem student. It started out with a war because I refused to wear shoes. And it deteriorated from that to, uh, violence." Baerwald pauses and smiles grimly. "It would be fair to say my teenage years were filled with violent explorations. Which I still draw on."

Somewhere along the line, Baerwald fell into trouble with the law, and ended up on probation. When this subject comes up, the singer leans forward with a dour look on his face and makes an admonishing gesture. "I will *not* go into the details of this," he says flatly. "Suffice to say that I survived it. And let me make one thing clear: It was *not* drugs that endangered me. I never had a drug problem, or anything on that level. It was *people*, you know? People were dangerous to me; drugs weren't."

Baerwald realizes he has tensed up, and leans back in his chair, offering an appeasing chuckle. "I'm going to do everything I can *not* to talk about that stuff, because it would end up becoming a focus. It's just something I went through, and it's over." He pauses. His eyes flicker warily behind his sunglasses, and for the moment, his thoughts seem to scan distant memories. "The people I knew then . . . ," he says after a bit, "the experiences I was involved in, the things I did . . ." He lets out a long sigh. "Those are things that I will probably continue using as details or colors for the characters in my songs for as long as I write." Baerwald fixes his visitor with a level gaze and crosses his arms over his chest. This subject, he signals, is closed.

In general, the late 1970s was a restive time for Baerwald. He recorded with one L.A. punk band, the Spastics, then spent three years playing bass, singing lead, and writing for another, the Sensible Shoes. "There was a part of me that knew that world was not a place I belonged," he says. "It seemed to me that punk had just become a cartoon of itself, and I didn't want to be in any more nightclubs. That life was too stupid and pathetic."

IN 1984, BAERWALD began collaborating with an old acquaintance, David Ricketts, a musician of serious training who had played in the Philadelphia club scene in the 1970s, and who had moved to L.A. in hopes of writing film scores. The two Davids were markedly different people— Baerwald held bedrock musical values, Ricketts was more attuned to jazz and progressive musical forms; Baerwald was impulsive and moody, Ricketts, methodical and introspective—but somehow the combination worked. "We just plugged into each other at exactly the right time," says Baerwald. "I remember the first thing we wrote was an abrasive punkish piece, and the second song was this sweet piano-and-string ballad. We did both in the same day, and we looked at each other and said: 'There's no limit to what we can do.' It felt like an incredible freeing up. Basically, I backed off from the music part, and Ricketts had no lyrical input or sense of what the lyrics were. So it was extremely easy to work together."

Almost immediately, Baerwald began to focus on songs about desperate dreamers, wounded lovers, and corrupt visionaries. "I could sense that I had a good well to draw from," he says, "that I had been living in a story-oriented environment. Also, I was formulating my experiences of the past, and I felt I had a lot to say about it all. I remember driving down Sunset with David, saying, 'Let's write the archetypal record about L.A. as metaphor.' I *actually* said that to him. It seemed like a fertile starting point for making records. So we approached it as if it were a first novel, setting the groundwork for everything else to come. The idea was to provide a cast of characters that would give us a deep *oeuvre* to work in."

In 1985, Baerwald and Ricketts signed a deal with A&M Records as David + David, and shortly teamed up with critic and producer Davitt Sigerson. Within a few sessions, the crew had fashioned *Boomtown*, a work that took a significant step toward realizing Baerwald's highfalutin literary ambitions. Indeed, like the L.A. literature of Raymond Chandler, John Fante, Diane Johnson, and James Ellroy, Baerwald was writing stores about the hopeful and the hopeless interconnecting in a desperate and morally polluted cityscape. Some of these characters come to the city with excited, even virtuous dreams of love, luxury, and salvation. Others—like the chronic, pathetic wife-beater of "Ain't So Easy" or the drifters and grifters of "Swallowed by the Cracks"—have darker needs, like uncaring sex and obliterating drugs, and as their own mean dreams fail, they take the innocent and loving down with them. Says producer Davitt Sigerson: "Baerwald wrote about some typically romanticized rock & roll characters—the down-and-outers—in a way that was unmawkish and that seemed to capture those people. And the musical settings that Ricketts came up with did a great job of cinematizing those stories. We always had this picture of the music as a beautiful setting with people losing their grip on life in the middle of it."

Indeed, *Boomtown* was something of an anomaly in L.A.'s mid-1980s rock scene. Like Dream Syndicate, Green on Red, Concrete Blonde, the Minutemen, X, the Blasters, and other local bands, David + David were serving up abrasive truths, though in a musical manner that was more conventionally accessible, and that sensibility, with its Steely Dan–derived blend of pop melodies and jazz rhythms, was well suited to the mainstream aesthetic. This approach earned the pair some scabrous dismissal from the scene's more rigid postpunk ideologues, but it also won David + David a fast-rising Top 40 single ("Welcome to the Boomtown"), and some fervent critical praise.

Within a season, though, David + David began to pull apart. "We got a lot of attention quickly," says Baerwald. "*Too* quickly. We began by pursuing this thing as a hobby, and six months later found ourselves doing an Italian TV show between two dog acts. When things happen that fast—when you're touring constantly, cooped up in hotel rooms under pressure, answering the same press questions over and over—you start drinking more. When you start drinking, you get more hostile and start picking at the things the other person says and does. It had always been something of a volatile relationship, though mainly in a pleasant way. Now, it was volatile in an unpleasant way."

In addition, the follow-up to *Boomtown* had to be delayed. Ricketts had become involved with folk singer Toni Childs, and started to arrange and produce her debut effort for A&M. Baerwald found Childs' posthippie mysticism a bit cloying and humorless, and when he couldn't resist poking fun at her manner, it led to tensions all around. Meantime, Baerwald was writing prolifically on his own, but A&M discouraged a solo venture so soon.

It was quickly turning into one of those bitter scenarios from Baerwald's songs: A pair of dreamers link up in a town of high hopes, only to crisscross one another and lose their dream in the process. In 1988, David + David entered the studio to record their long overdue second LP, but the strain was too much. "On the first LP," says Sigerson, "it was the fact that they barely fit that made it all brilliant. By the time of the second one, Ricketts had more of a sense of his career from having worked with Toni Childs, but Baerwald, who is explosive to begin with, had had a cork jammed in him for a year and a half. It was clear that he was growing as a writer—he had developed a better eye for characters—but it was hard for the two of them to be in a room together. Ricketts would try to get the keyboard sound right, and Baerwald—the K-mart Charlie Bukowski, who can get stuck in the schtick of his characters—would say, '*Fuck* the sound; let's do the *song*.' But when you say fuck the keyboard sound, you're also kind of saying, 'Fuck *you* and what you do'—or at least that's how Ricketts heard it. In the end, the vibe was more than the process could bear.

"You know," Sigerson continues, "Baerwald's kind of like a cocker pup. He's charming and delightful, but he's inclined to pee on your leg. If you treasure cocker pups, it's great. If you have a problem about getting your leg peed on, it can be an upsetting experience."

Baerwald concurs with Sigerson's assessment. "I never saw Ricketts as a sensitive guy," he says, "as somebody whom I could hurt. And so I said and did things that were hurtful, and in time I realized Ricketts was an open, bleeding wound. He felt his music as deeply as I felt mine. And the truth is, what a lot of people liked about David + David was not 'David Baerwald's streetwise, world-weary personification of the gritty realities of modern life' but rather the fact that the music *sounded* good, and Ricketts is the one who deserves credit for that."

Baerwald pauses to light up a cigarette. He looks suddenly weary and a little doleful. "When people think of David + David," he says, "the word *innocence* doesn't come to mind. But we *were* very innocent: We were doing our music because it felt good. And then it got taken out of our hands. It was corrupted very quickly, and we didn't have the emotional wherewithal to resist it. The record business is geared for fame bullshit and iconization bullshit.

"I guess it was over long before we realized it."

BAERWALD MADE UP for the disintegration of David + David with some hard living. He moved around L.A. a lot, moved through a few love affairs, and started running with a faster, flashier crowd—including several pop stars and actors, including Sean Penn, with whom Baerwald roomed for a time, and with whom he wrote an as-yet-unproduced screenplay loosely based on *Boomtown*'s themes and characters. In some ways, it was a heady time, though much of it amounted to frenzied behavior—not unlike the lives led by the characters of his songs. "That world of stardom and luxury," he says. "It can be a snobbish, vulgar, secret, sickened world."

As Baerwald speaks, it is a few days after our first meeting, and he is seated on a worn sofa in his living room, in the bottom part of the wooded duplex he occupies in Topanga Canyon. The place is a bit of a mess—strewn with clothes and bedding, and filled with guitars, exotic stringed instruments, and recording equipment. The dwelling has a makeshift feel about it, as if the person who lives here clearly lives on his own, and hasn't yet found a place he would describe as home.

"A big part of me dug that whole scene," says Baerwald about his fast-and-hard Hollywood life. "I was like a guy who's addicted to gambling or something: He knows what he's doing is stupid and ugly and wrong, but he keeps on doing it. Then you wake up one morning and find that you're not anything, that you lost perspective on what it is that you do. I could say, 'Hey, I'm doing research for my writing'—that I was actually carving something horrible out of my heart or psyche—which on a certain level was true. But as a person, I wasn't okay at all. I was a schmuck. I was twenty-six and I had a chip on my shoulder about a lot of things, and validation from some strata of society meant a lot to me at that moment."

Perhaps it was simply his mood, but Baerwald began to see his own dissolution reflected in the world around him. In 1988, he was living close by the Chinese Theater, in Hollywood. By day, it is a tourist district. By night, it is a tense, restless community of runaways, young prostitutes, bikers, skinheads, drug dealers, and occasional gang members: all those castoffs bred—and then discarded and condemned—by a society that is unwilling to examine the causes of its own ruin. Baerwald already knew what life on the fringe was like—he had lived it at times, and had chronicled it in *Boomtown*. Now, he wanted to see how the deterioration looked from a different vantage. At the prompting of Sean Penn, who had been acting in Dennis Hopper's *Colours*, about L.A.'s gang life, Baerwald began hanging out with cops, and interviewed them about the death and futility they faced every day.

"It was really a disturbing experience," he says, "and it entered into my life. I would look at these acts of degradation that these cops saw all the time, and I'd ask myself: 'How different am *I* from that?' You start realizing your own wicked soul, you know?"

Baerwald gets up, moves around restlessly for a few moments, then finally grabs a beer from the refrigerator and settles back into the sofa. "I started seeing all these connections," he says, unscrewing the cap on the beer bottle and taking a sip. "Connections between gangs and drugs and cops and the government, and I began thinking about what it meant to live in a free society. I just started thinking very dark thoughts about our civilization and everything we were doing, and I got a feeling of total impotence in the face of such insanity and such stupid violence.

"I saw I was as much a criminal as anybody," Baerwald continues, "because I was a part of the media, and I'd had this long fascination with violence. And I understood better how violence breeds violence and becomes a chain that never stops. The danger of the kind of environment we live in is that our own failures can breed a desire for violence—or at least we start using that as an excuse for our violence. But if you start thinking in social terms, you can get very bitter and very mad. Real community is a hard thing to achieve in our lives, much less our society. That's why I began writing so many love songs, because I didn't want merely to preach about these things. I wanted to relate them to the specifics of my own life."

From this mix of personal disappointment and social disenchantment came a new body of songs. In June 1989, Baerwald did some initial solo sessions with producer Steve Berlin (of Los Lobos), then a few months later, hooked up with bassist and producer Larry Klein (married at the time to Joni Mitchell). In many ways, the resulting album, *Bedtime Stories*, is superior to *Boomtown*: It is a musically affecting work, rife with finely observed vignettes about a city and nation disintegrating from denial, and it is a record brimming with haunting portrayals of people trying to make love work, despite the pain of their pasts and the hopelessness of their futures.

In the album's first single, "All for You," a hopeful man brings his young beautiful wife to L.A. He works hard to support her—so hard, she feels abandoned by him, and takes to bed with another man who seems more understanding. Along the way, the husband gets involved in illegal activities; he loses his wife and his hope; she loses her lover; and the lover—who had been a friend of the husband—loses some of his honor. There are no heroes in the tale, and no villains. Just real people, trying to find love and connection and meaning. And the adulterer, the lover who helped end his friend's marriage, was Baerwald.

"I'm trying to be more honest and intimate and specific about individuals this time," he says, "in the hopes that those individuals will illuminate a larger whole. The idea was that I wanted these characters to emerge with something intact—their humanity, or compassion, or sensitivity. Just *surviving*, in and of itself, isn't necessarily a heroic act. It's easy to survive if you're a killer—especially if what you've killed is something inside yourself. It's easy to live if you're dead. But surviving with your humanity intact, I think, is *always* heroic."

Across the room, the phone rings. Baerwald's machine picks up the call, and the caller—whoever he is—plays a wild Hendrix-like guitar solo, then hangs up. Baerwald shakes his head bemused. "Sounds like Ricketts to me," he says.

The two Davids are still good friends, still get drunk together, but there is clearly a distance between them now. "There's something about that relationship that just won't quit," says Baerwald. "Ricketts was like a terrific big brother, but I had to find out what I could do on my own, and I'm just *now* finding that out."

Baerwald takes another sip of beer and begins to explain that one of the harder-hitting songs on *Bedtime Stories,* "Dance," was written about the experience he had shared with Ricketts in the music industry. "I adapted 'Dance,'" he says, "from a Paul Bowles short story. It's about a naive language student who goes to Morocco to find a tribe that speaks this dialogue he's studying. He goes to the chieftain and says, 'I am a seeker of knowledge.' And the chieftain says, 'Oh, *are* you?' And the tribe grabs the student and they tear his clothes off and they castrate him, and blind him, and cut his tongue out. They feed him hallucinogenic drugs and they pierce his flesh with needles and dangle bells from him. And they make him *dance* for their entertainment."

Baerwald finishes his beer, and laughs uproariously at the story he has just told. "That story," he says, "reminded me of my experience with the record business. I came into this scene, and I said, 'I just want to learn to make music.' And these guys said, 'All right, fine. But you've got to dance, you know.'

"'But I don't know *how* to dance,' I said. And they said, 'Well, you will.'"

frank sinatra:

singing

in the dark

*f*rank Sinatra is one of pop music's most abiding prodigies—and also one of its most troubling icons. At the peak of his craft (during the 1950s and 1960s, when he recorded the definitional ballad and swing sessions that are documented so ambitiously on the 1990 packages *Frank Sinatra: The Capitol Years* and *Frank Sinatra: The Reprise Collection*), Sinatra raised the art of romantic singing to a new height, treating each song as if it were the inevitable expression of a personal experience, as if there were no separating the singer from the emotion or meaning of the songs he sang, and therefore, no separating the listener from the experience of a singular and compelling pop voice. But for all the grace of his talent, there is also a considerable darkness about Sinatra: a desperate hunger for the validation that comes from love and power, and a ruinous anger for anything that challenges or thwarts that validation. In many ways, that fierce need for love or vindication is the guiding force behind the best moments of Sinatra's career. Indeed, *The Capitol Years* and *The Reprise Collection* are the life testaments of a man who has learned to cling to one truth above all others: namely, that one could never win love so surely that one could stop imagining the pain of its loss.

It is a lesson that Sinatra learned early, and at great cost. In the 1940s, following his emergence from the Harry James and Tommy Dorsey big bands, Sinatra had been pop's biggest star: a romantic balladeer whose sexy, yearning voice had made him Columbia Records' biggest-selling recording artist. But then, toward the decade's end, Sinatra fell from grace—fast and hard. In part, the decline simply had to do with shifting musical tastes: In the exuberance of the postwar period, a new audience wanted more effervescence and more soul than Sinatra seemed capable of. In addition, Sinatra shocked many of his remaining supporters by abandoning his wife and family to pursue a steamy public affair with actress Ava Gardner (whom he married in 1950). By the early 1950s, Sinatra's relationship with both Columbia Records and his wife had turned stormy, and in the seasons that followed, the singer lost everything—including his record and film contracts, his marriage with Gardner, and, perhaps most devastatingly of all, he even lost his voice during a public performance. After that, no record company would take a chance on Sinatra, and he was back to the club circuit, playing to sparse audiences, and trying to regain the voice and confidence that had once come so readily.

Finally, in 1953, Capitol Records agreed to risk a one-year contract with Sinatra—if the artist was willing to forfeit his advance and pay all his own studio costs. It was a humiliating offer, but Sinatra took it—and in the process, turned his life around. With his first few sessions for the label, Sinatra surprised both critics and former fans by flaunting a new voice that seemed to carry more depth, more worldly weight and rhythmic invention than the half-fragile tone that he had brandished in the 1940s. And then, with his first full-fledged LP—*In the Wee Small Hours,* a deep-blue, after-hours ballad collection, conducted by Nat King Cole's up-and-coming arranger, Nelson Riddle—Sinatra staked out the vocal sensibility that would become the hallmark of his mature style, and that would establish him as the most gifted interpretive vocalist to emerge in pop or jazz since Billie Holiday. On the surface, Sinatra's new style seemed almost more colloquial than musical. That is, he took supremely mellifluent material like the title track and sang it as if it were a hushed yet vital communication: a rueful confession shared with an understanding friend over a late-night shot of whiskey, or more likely, a painful rumination that the singer needed to proclaim to himself in order to work his way free of a bitter memory. In other words, Sinatra was now singing songs of romantic despair as if he were living inside the experience of those songs, and as if each tune's lyrics were his and his alone to sing. "It was Ava who did that, who taught him how to sing a torch song," Nelson Riddle later told biographer Kitty Kelley. "That's how he learned. She was the greatest love of his life, and he lost her."

In effect, Sinatra's tenure at Capitol—along with the credibility he gained as an actor from his Oscar-winning performance in *From Here to Eternity*—proved to be the redemption of his career. Over the next ten years, he would record twenty-plus top-selling LPs for the label, alternating between sexy, uptempo, big band–style dance affairs and brooding ruminations on romantic despair and sexual betrayal, and he would also become one of the most consistently popular Top 40 singles artists of the decade. It was one of the richest and most successful growth periods that any pop artist has ever managed, and *The Capitol Years* aims to pay tribute to it by picking seventy-five of the artist's most sublime and most obvious musical milestones, and cataloging them in roughly chronological order. At its best, this three-CD set stands as a definitive summary of not merely Sinatra's most revealing vocal performances, but also a smart compendium of some of the best songwriting of the pre-rock era, by enduring songsmiths and lyricists like Cole Porter, Harold Arlen, Johnny Mercer, Richard Rodgers, Lorenz Hart, and George and Ira Gershwin, among others. But by abridging such a broad range of Sinatra's work, *The Capitol Years* also tends to make short shrift of the carefully constructed arcs of mood that made the singer's 1950s albums so innovative—and in Sinatra's art, dwelling on a mood until that mood can give up no other revelations is half the art.

By contrast, the anthology approach fares better on *The Reprise Collection,* largely because the set makes a surprisingly effective case for a diverse body of work that has often been viewed as fairly negligible. Sinatra started Reprise Records in 1960 as a vanity enterprise (and as an imprimatur of his hard-won eminence in the entertainment world), and some of his best work for the label—such as his collaborations with the Count Basie Orchestra and Quincy Jones, and the *September of My Years* project with composer-arranger Gordon Jenkins—stuck to the mold of the big band and saloon-song theme albums that he had popularized at Capitol. But by the mid-1960s, adventurous artists like the Beatles and Bob Dylan were transforming the pop mainstream, in effect killing off the generations-old Tin Pan Alley aesthetic that had provided singers like Sinatra with their repertoire. Sinatra had never much liked rock & roll (though he enjoyed a couple of hits in the style during the 1950s, which unfortunately haven't been reissued), but he was shrewd and vain enough to want to match the challenge of the new pop sensibility. Some of his efforts in this regard—like the shamelessly self-mythologizing "My Way," and the wooden, sappy "Something Stupid" (with his daughter Nancy)—are among his most lamentable recordings, though tracks like the roaring, soulful "That's Life" (with its savvy nod to Ray Charles), and the lilting bossa nova collaborations with Brazilian guitarist-composer Antonio Carlos Jobim, are not only fine testaments to Sinatra's self-willed resiliency, but are also blissful examples of the undervalued side of 1960s pop.

If *The Reprise Collection* falls short, it is in covering Sinatra's latter-day singing career, following his reemergence from a brief retirement in the early 1970s. Admittedly, this is the singer's most problematic period. After his return in 1973, Sinatra's voice had changed again, settling into a gruffer, brandytone inflection, and sometimes suffering from a shakiness in pitch and a shortness of breath. Indeed, with the exception of some of his work on the 1979 *Trilogy*, Sinatra never again found a recording voice as virile and affecting as the one that had carried him through the 1950s and 1960s.

And yet, in his live performances in the late 1970s and in the 1980s (a part of his career that has never been documented on record, and that is not included in *The Reprise Collection*), Sinatra often has been stunning, putting across big band rave-ups like "I've Got You Under My Skin," "I've Got the World on a String," and "You Make Me Feel So Young" with a surprising force and agility, and rendering his much-loved saloon soliloquies with a matchless sense of depth and grace. In fact, there is something especially poignant in seeing the aging Sinatra perched on a stool centerstage, ruminating over the lost love of Rodger and Hart's "The Gal That Got Away," or the lost youth of Gordon Jenkins' "This Is All I Ask." In such moments, Sinatra knows enough to surrender to his age, to sing the songs in the voice of an old man, stripped of all conceits and most hopes. Then, likely as not, he'll turn around and undercut his own best graceful moments by launching into one of his infamous diatribes against those who don't share his views or passions, such as the time in 1990 when he harangued Sinéad O'Connor for her anti-national anthem stance. All a fan can do at such moments is wince, and wait for the singer's next miraculous vocal epiphany—and sooner or later, those waits have usually paid off.

At age seventy-five [in 1990, when I wrote this piece], Frank Sinatra remains indomitable. Night after night, he stands onstage and sings songs about love and longing, about hope and despair, and each time he does, he communicates the emotional truths of those songs to a mass of strangers as if that mass were a handful of understanding intimates. Chances are, he is not doing this merely for the money; long ago, Frank Sinatra became rich enough to live in any world he wanted to build for himself. Instead, maybe he does it simply because somehow singing these songs enriches him, helps him realize a depth and compassion that does not come quite so easily in the realities of his daily private life. Or maybe singing has simply become his most reliable companion—the best way of forestalling the darkness and aloneness that long ago he came to loathe, and yet could not resist. In any event, in 1991, Sinatra still sings, and will likely continue to do so until he is physically unable to continue. In an interview from over a quarter-century ago, he may have uttered his own best defense: "Having lived a life of violent emotional contradictions," he said, "I have an overacute capacity for sadness as well as elation. . . . Whatever else has been said about me is unimportant. When I sing, I believe. . . ."

And when Sinatra stops singing—when he stops believing—we will lose a giant. We will lose a measurement of this century.

endings

dark shadows:

hank williams,

nick drake,

phil ochs

*t*hree "popular music" artists long dead—Hank Williams, Nick Drake, and Phil Ochs—all had new collections in record stores in the same week in August 1986. If this coincidence seems at all curious, or even a bit morbid, then consider what other traits these singers have in common:

Hank Williams was a restive country-western singer and songwriter who, in both his work and life, seemed perpetually torn between visions of heaven and sin, hope and fear, love and death. Somewhere along his celebrated route, dread gained the upper hand and the singer fell into drink, pills, and a bitter malaise. On January 1, 1953, at age twenty-nine, Hank Williams died in the back seat of a car, en route to a performance in Charleston, West Virginia. He was the victim of a deadly mix of drugs, alcohol, and hard living. All indications were, Williams had seen the end coming for some time. He even addressed it in a song called "The Angel of Death": "The lights all grow dim and dark shadows creep."

Roughly twenty years later in England, a frail-seeming folk singer named Nick Drake took an equally consuming look at notions of loss. Drake wrote haunting songs full of tenderness and resignation, beauty and despair—until, apparently, he could no longer find the words to convey the panicky depths of his experience. On a late November morning in 1974,

Drake was found dead at his parents' home in Birmingham, England, the casualty of an overdose of antidepressant medication and, according to the coroner, a suicide.

By contrast, Phil Ochs—a folk singer who had served as both an early champion and contemporary of Bob Dylan—had spent the better part of *his* career writing songs of angry hope and fierce humor, songs that seethed with idiosyncratic dreams of a better and more ethical culture. At the same time, some of Ochs' most memorable work also radiated with affecting, firsthand images of anguish and madness, until by the mid-1970s—after his vocal chords had been severely damaged by a mugging attack in Africa and his career had all but collapsed in disillusion—the agony became insufferable. In April 1976, Phil Ochs hanged himself at his sister's home in Far Rockaway, New York, and pop music lost one of its most conscientious and compassionate voices.

Hank Williams, Nick Drake, and Phil Ochs were all men who knew torment on an intimate and enduring basis—knew it so well that it robbed them of any practical will to escape its devastation. It is hard to say whether their music served to deepen or assuage their agony (certainly, in Ochs' and Drake's cases, the lack of a caring audience at times aggravated their depression, while for Williams, success seemed only to hasten dissolution), but one thing is plain: Their songs did not mask the reality of the men behind them. If anything, the quality of longing and desolation that characterized much of Williams', Ochs', and Drake's most indelible work seemed inseparable from the frightful realities of longing and desolation that eventually weighed down each man's life.

What is especially intriguing about the 1986 posthumous releases of these artists is that each project, to varying degrees, provides a telling—even definitive—overview of each singer's sensibility. That is, these works not only offer a glimpse of the artists' journey from inspiration to desperation, but more important, also provide heartening examples of how the singers sought to resist—or at least temper—their hopelessness.

In the case, however, of Nick Drake's *Fruit Tree* (a four-disc set on Hannibal made up of Drake's three late-1960s and early-1970s Island albums plus another disc of largely unissued material), this quality of resistance may seem a bit elusive at first hearing. After all, Drake began his career (with the 1968 *Five Leaves Left*) in what seemed a moody, perhaps even disconsolate frame of mind—singing songs about fleeting desire and lasting solitude in a smoky, almost affectless tone—and abandoned his vocation four years later with what is among the darkest works in modern folk history, *Pink Moon*. By that time, Drake had stripped his music of its innovative jazz and classical trimmings, until all that remained were his guitar and a mesmerizing, almost frozen-sounding voice that seemed to emanate from within a place of impenetrable solitude.

Yet for all its melancholy, there is surprisingly little in the actual sound and feel of Drake's music that is dispiriting or unpleasant. In fact, what is perhaps the most alluring and uplifting aspect of Drake's work is a certain hard-earned passion for aural beauty: There are moments in the singer's first two albums, *Five Leaves Left* and *Bryter Layter*—with their chamberlike mix of piano, vibraphone, harpsichord, viola, and strings—that come as close as anything in modern pop to matching the effect of Bill Evans' or Ravel's brooding music, and there are moments in Drake's final recordings that are as primordial and transfixing as Robert Johnson's best deep-dark blues. In short, there is something bracing about Drake's music despite all the painful experience that formed it.

By comparison, Hank Williams' music may seem far more soulful, but it was no less fundamentally heartsick—or at least that's the portrait that emerges from two 1986 eye-opening retrospectives that fill in important gaps in the singer's story. The first set, *I'm So Lonesome I Could Cry,* is the fourth volume in an ambitious series from PolyGram gathers all of Williams' late-1940s and early-1950s studio recordings in chronological order, including numerous invaluable outtakes and demo tracks—among them, versions of several songs never released before. As impressive as this series is (remarkably, it is the first attempt to assemble such a complete and well-documented library of the singer's studio works—though a ten-LP 1981 Japanese set was a big step in the right direction), the *other* new Williams' set, *The First Recordings* (Country Music Foundation), is perhaps even more priceless. Here, available for the first time, are the seminal demo sessions that the young songsmith recorded for Acuff-Rose in 1946, and at the very least they reveal that from the outset Williams was an immensely effective folk singer. That is, not only could he convey the spirit and meaning of his material with just voice and guitar, but in fact such a spare approach often reinforced that essential "lonesomeness" that always resided deep in the heart of his music. More important, though, Williams was already traveling the road between faith and dejection—and modern music would never be the same as a result of that brave and hurtful journey.

Similarly, Phil Ochs also made a difficult migration—and one would be hard-pressed to find a work that better illuminates that journey's brilliance and tragedy than *A Toast to Those Who Are Gone,* a compilation of previously unreleased songs assembled by Ochs' brother, archivist Michael Ochs, for Rhino Records. Apparently, nearly all of the fourteen songs presented here were recorded early on in Ochs' career—probably during 1964–65—and yet, like Williams' *The First Recordings,* this seminal material staked out virtually all the thematic ground that would concern the singer throughout his career. What emerges is a portrait of a man who loved his country fiercely and fearlessly, who could not silently abide the way in which its hardest-won ideals were being corrupted by slaughterous hate-mongers and truthless presidents. Eventually, according to some, there was a part of Ochs that grew sad and manic and that enabled him to take his life. However, listening to this music—which is among the singer's best—one hears only the inspiring expression of a man who wanted to live very, very much, and who wanted his country to realize its grandest promises. Perhaps as he saw all that became lost, both in his own reality and in the nation's, he could not sanely withstand such pain.

Listening to these records, one is forced to consider an unpleasant question: What is there, finally, to celebrate about men who lost their faith and ended their lives? Certainly there is nothing to extol about willful or semi-willful suicides, but there is nevertheless much to learn from them. For example, in heeding the work of Hank Williams, Nick Drake, and Phil Ochs, one learns a great deal about dignity and the limits of courage: These were men who held out against the dark as forcefully as possible and, in doing so, created music that might help improve and sustain the world they eventually left behind. Maybe, by examining their losses—and by appreciating the hard-fought beauty that they created despite their anguish—we can gain enough perspective or compassion to understand how lives might come undone, and therefore how we might help them (or ourselves) hold together. After all, if Williams or Drake or Ochs were still here, chances are it would be a better world for many people—including you and me.

IN THE EARLY 1980s, a young Canadian director named David Acomba made a film called, *Hank Williams: The Show He Never Gave.* It's among the best—certainly among the most unforgettable—music films I have ever seen. It uses pop music as a means of contemplating (even entering) imminent death, and in the process resolving, explaining, and perhaps redeeming the drama of one man's public life and sorrowful end. Shot in Canada, *The Show He Never Gave* opens its story on New Year's Eve, 1952, Hank Williams' final few hours on earth. A night-blue Cadillac is traveling on a lonely, snowy road. In the back seat, the lean grim figure of Hank Williams (played by a Woody Guthrie–influenced Canadian folk singer, Sneezy Waters) stirs fitfully. On the radio one of Williams' pedal-steel-laden hits is playing. Leaning forward, he abruptly snaps it off.

Williams begins to rue the loneliness of the night. "I wish I didn't have to be playing that big concert arena . . . tomorrow night," he mutters to himself. "*Tonight's* the night I should be playing . . . one of those little roadside bars we're goin' by right now." He gazes out at the blue darkness as if he were looking at a long-desired woman.

Moments later, Williams' ruminations become reality: We see him pulling up to a jam-packed honky-tonk, his five-piece band finishing the strains of "My Bucket's Got a Hole in It," a crowd of old rubes and young rowdies in semi-religious awe of this country kingpin. With self-conscious meekness, Williams takes the small stage and begins to play his exhilarating and broken-hearted minstrel songs—"Half as Much," "Hey Good Lookin'," "Cold, Cold Heart," "I Can't Help It If I'm Still in Love with You," "Kaw-Liga," "Lovesick Blues," "Your Cheatin' Heart," among others. He also talks to the audience self-deprecatingly about his alcoholism, muses over his separation from his first wife, worries that the audience at this little wayside stop may reject him. Indeed, the one injunction that every important voice in the film—devil or keeper—tells him is, "Give 'em a good show." Williams looks paralyzed at the mere suggestion.

Not much else happens. There are brief bouts of flirtation, camaraderie, and self-destructiveness backstage, some more icy self-reflections in the back seat of the Cadillac. And yet it becomes apparent that we are witnessing a man struggling to account for himself—his hurts, his hopes, his soul, his terror, his deviltry—in the measure of this handful of unpolished songs.

And that's just what happens. When in mid-show Williams begins to reminisce about his first wife, Audrey, and then moves into an unaccompanied reading of his haunting folk ballad, "Alone and Forsaken," the movie provides an emotional wallop that we never quite forget. From that point on, the crowd in the barroom watches Williams more heedfully, more perplexedly, as they gradually become aware that they are privy to the confessions of a man with a heart so irreparably broken that he may never get out of this world with his soul intact.

By the end, we have come as close to a reckoning with dissolution, death, and judgment as film—or pop music—has ever brought us. "It might seem funny that a man who's lived the kind of life I have is talking about heaven when he should be talking about hell," Williams tells his audience before moving into a desperately passionate version of his gospel classic, "I Saw the Light." Moments later, in the lonely, fading reality of the Cadillac's back seat, Williams admits to himself: "Only there *ain't* no light. I tried, Lord knows how hard I tried, to believe. And some mornings I wake up and it's almost there." The moment is more frightening and desolate than might be imagined.

As good as *Hank Williams: The Show He Never Gave* is, I'm afraid you might have to look damn hard to find it. Acuff-Rose, the Nashville publishing firm that owns the rights to Williams' extensive songbook, withheld permission for the filmmakers to use Williams' songs, thus in effect barring the film's U.S. release. Acuff-Roses's response was a little hard to fathom. After all, Williams' excesses were not merely pop legend—they were a matter of record. Roy Acuff himself was a member of the country gentleman Nashville establishment that expelled Williams from the Grand Ole Opry because of his drinking, drug use, intoxicated performances, and occasional gunplay.

Maybe Acuff came to regret Nashville's staidness so deeply that he preferred to see its history go unpublicized, or maybe he never quite forgave Williams for refusing to keep his demons private and thus marring the smooth façade of Nashville's decorum. In 1983, Wesley Rose of Acuff-Rose told me: "What I didn't appreciate about the film—because Hank was a personal friend—is the part where they show someone give him the needle. I never saw Hank take a needle. It isn't what you call expert criticism; it's what I call personal criticism. [The filmmakers] stressed the weakness of the man, rather than the greatness that rose from his work."

To my mind, *Hank Williams: The Show He Never Gave* did just the opposite: It got as close to the artist's greatness as any biographical or fictional work might. The only thing that gets closer is the frightened yet lucid soul of Williams' own songs. "The lights all grow dim and dark shadows creep." *The Show He Never Gave* takes us right into those shadows—and maybe that's not an easy thing to forgive.

tim hardin:

lost along

the way

*First time I got off on smack I said, out loud, "Why can't I
feel like this all the time?" So I proceeded to feel like that all
the time.*

TIM HARDIN,
WET MAGAZINE INTERVIEW, 1980

*t*o while away the time on their way to a gig in Cleveland, Paul Simon and
fellow band members in *One Trick Pony* play a game whose object it is to
name the most dead rock stars. Tim Hardin comes up, and an argument
ensues. One guy insists the drug-plagued 1960s folk-rock hero is alive in
Woodstock. A bet is placed: Twenty dollars says he OD'ed.

Life, as Oscar Wilde pointed out, imitates art. Less than six months after
the film's release, the Tim Hardin joke turned sour. Its point, however,
remains true: So many rock stars have died that one can hardly keep track of
them. Hardin pursued an infamously brutal and reckless manner of existence. Most people who loved the man, or revered his work, had steeled
themselves long ago for his end.

For the record, Hardin wrote some of the most indelible, affecting, and
frequently recorded love songs of the 1960s. Musicians who knew him in
Greenwich Village during that time considered him to be one of the best.
John Sebastian, formerly of the Lovin' Spoonful, played harmonica on Hardin's early Verve Forecast albums *(Tim Hardin I* and *Tim Hardin II)*. "Timmy

was breaking new ground," he recalls. "Probably everybody in the Village during that period stole something from his songs—which isn't exactly singular since we were all stealing from each other, anyway. But Timmy's talent *was* singular; he dared to go, both musically and emotionally, where most of us feared to go, and there was plenty to learn from the way he melded rock & roll and blues and jazz into a style all his own."

During a two-year span in the mid-1960s, Hardin wrote the bulk of the songs that secured his reputation, including "Misty Roses," "If I Were a Carpenter," "Reason to Believe," and "Lady Came from Baltimore," the latter a frank, self-indicting account of his romance with actress Susan Moore (who later became his wife). And although his own roughhewn readings of his songs never enjoyed much chart success, he still sang them better than anybody else, in a stray, harrowed voice, redolent of his chief vocal idols, Billie Holiday and Hank Williams. By 1970, Hardin's career had run aground. Beset by marital wrangles, managerial suits, and narcotic funks, he eventually fled to England, where he recorded one wholly unmemorable album, *Tim Hardin 9* (1973), and gradually receded into the dark custody of his own legend.

In 1980, he was back in Eugene, Oregon—his hometown—for a while, seemingly intent on a fresh start. Michael Dilley, a studio owner and former high school buddy of Hardin's, believed it was a serious effort. Hardin had gone off heroin in favor of beer and was in a good mood. "Occasionally, though, it was like he forgot what he was doing. He'd come into the studio, sit down at the piano, and come out with something absolutely gorgeous, and then it would hang there sometimes, like an unfinished sentence."

On the warm evening of December 29, 1980, responding to a tip from an anonymous caller, police found Tim Hardin's body lying on the floor of his small, austere Hollywood apartment. He was dead, at age thirty-nine. Just a few nights earlier he had finished work on the basic tracks for his first album in seven years. The centerpiece of the collection, a ballad called "Unforgiven," is one of the most haunting, lovingly crafted works of his career. It goes like this: "As long as I am unforgiven/As far as I am pushed away/As much as life seems less than living/I still try."

dennis wilson:

the

lone surfer

*R*ock & roll has had such a pervasive social influence because, in the postwar era of popular culture, it sometimes worked as the equivalent of a familial bond. Indeed, its principal rise—in the mid-1950s, following the advent of Elvis Presley—occurred during a period when family bonds and values were being strained, sometimes severed, by postnuclear conditions of generational freedom. Consequently, for millions of unrestrained young Americans, the connections they shared through Presley were often more genuine than the ties they found at home. The irony behind this, of course, was that rock & roll sprang from the Southern region, where strong family ties still mattered (though not always for the better).

By contrast, the Wilsons were a California family, subject to those same mid-1950s permutations, but distinct in their placement in a still largely undefined land, where both Western civilization and popular culture ran to their ends. Like many other Westerners, Murry Wilson regarded California as something of a promised land, rife with opportunity; like many other young people, his children experienced that opportunity as a boundless scenario of instant surface fun: sex, nature, cars, and even quick religious incentive. Underneath those surfaces resided something far more debilitating—including the reality of the Wilsons' home life, where Murry was reportedly an often cruel and brutal man. But in the fast exuberance of the early 1960s, few pop lovers were yet admitting to the depths—good, bad, or otherwise—under the surfaces.

In 1961, along with cousin Mike Love and neighbor Al Jardine, Brian, Dennis, and Carl Wilson began making music as the Beach Boys—a real family, acting out California dreams and rock & roll ambitions, advised and managed by father Murry Wilson. Brian wrote the songs—quick, brilliant anthems of youthful transcendence and romance, whirligigs of contrapuntal rock—but it was younger brother Dennis (the band's early drummer and later harmony singer) who provided Brian's songs with a model: He was the sole group member who took up the regional pastime of surfing, and he was also the family's most indulgent exemplar of hedonism (which reportedly led to much trouble between Dennis and his iron-handed father). Still, with Brian's talent and Dennis's unconstraint, the Beach Boys defined a new California pop ethos, and under the tutelage of Murry (who died in the early 1970s), the group became a pop force very nearly the equal of the Beatles.

But rock & roll, like any family affair (or family substitute), can be painfully capricious, and when the fun-and-sun style of that period gave way to a more high-flown late-1960s hedonism, the Beach Boys' run was, in a way, over. The group toyed for a while with the idea of a topical name change, and also flirted with psychedelia and mysticism (in fact, "Good Vibrations" is possibly the best psychedelic single by any group in that period). Challenged by the times, and by the Beatles' exceptional creative growth, the Beach Boys settled into a period of increasingly experimental albums—*Pet Sounds* (one of pop's finest and most intricate works), *Wild Honey, Smiley Smile,* and *Friends*—but none of them sold like their earlier work (with the exception of *Pet Sounds,* which barely hit the Top 10), and the public never again bought the group's contemporary recordings. Aside from a quirk hit in 1976 with "Rock and Roll Music," the Beach Boys never had a real hit after "Heroes and Villains" in 1967. (Four years after this article was written, the Beach Boys again had a number 1 single, 1988's silly and lamentable "Kokomo.")

Pushed aside, the group's members gave in to the dark side of Californian ambitions. Brian, beset by personal and drug problems, became a shadowy, receding presence in the band (replaced onstage by Glen Campbell, then Bruce Johnston). Meanwhile, Dennis fell into a fairly freewheeling lifestyle, including a surprisingly effective acting job in the 1971 film *Two-Lane Blacktop* (with James Taylor), and a brief association with Charles Manson (Manson co-wrote "Never Learn Not to Love," on the *20/20* album, though the group later purchased the rights). Despite these lapses, the band still made enterprising, often wonderful work—*Sunflower, Surf's Up, Holland*—but these records remained unloved by a new California audience that preferred the Doors and Buffalo Springfield. In time, of course, the group made its peace with the public: The political and artistic ambitions of the late 1960s subsided, and the Beach Boys were popularly accepted as a nostalgia act: a "reminder" of more "innocent" years. After that, they were largely consigned to living out their history according to past glories, despite occasional attempts to make new music.

When Dennis Wilson drowned on the evening of December 28, 1983—the victim of a diving accident—there was much talk about his ill-famed indulgences over the years. There was also much made of how the family and group—rarely inseparable but also rarely unified—had fallen into bitter bickering (the band, in fact, came close to disintegrating several times, and Dennis and Mike Love had such an abrasive relationship that they obtained restraining orders against one another). In the group's last tour, Dennis Wilson didn't even appear for several dates, purportedly for reasons of family friction and drinking problems.

There wasn't, however, much said about just how well this group had lived up to its artistry during their long period of public neglect (they were an inestimably better, more resourceful band than, say, the Doors), nor did many reports point out how the Beach Boys had managed to take all the disenchantment of their best late-1960s work and continuously parlayed it into creative resolve. Dennis Wilson was perhaps the most volatile member of the band, but he was also its most archetypal: He embodied the public's ideal of the band's myth, and he understood how the flipside of that myth was probably an inevitable turn of events. In the years since the late-1960s, Dennis—like the rest of the band—had come to live out his celebrityhood as a novelty star: as a reminder of a past long used and reclaimed merely to satisfy an audience's whims. If he drank or sulked a bit more as a result of swallowing that knowledge, I wouldn't want to begrudge him. Perhaps even more than his brother Brian, Dennis Wilson exemplified the band's real ethos, and when he fell into that deep, irretrievable chill last Wednesday, so did a part of the band's best history.

m a r v i n   g a y e :

t r o u b l e d

s o u l

*M*ore than any other artist of the pop generation, Marvin Gaye rose to the emotional promise, stylistic challenge, and cultural possibility of modern soul. In fact, he was often cited as the man who singlehandedly modernized Motown: a sensual-voiced man full of spiritual longings (and spiritual confusion) whose landmark 1971 album *What's Going On* commented forcefully yet eloquently on matters like civil rights and Vietnam—subjects that many R&B artists, up until that time, had sidestepped.

Though that eventful record was in some ways the apex of Gaye's career (he would never again return to themes of social passion), Marvin remained a resourceful performer up through the time of the last work released in his lifetime, 1982's *Midnight Love* (Columbia). Watching him command the stage at 1983's Motown Anniversary TV special, or seeing him graciously accept his first Grammy Award a few weeks later, it felt as if we were witnessing the rejuvenation of a once-troubled man, who learned to transform his dread into artistic courage, even grace. Hearing the news of his violent and improbable end—shot to death on April 1, 1984, by his minister father—it seemed likely that rugged emotions and rampageous fears were never far from the singer's closest thoughts, after all. According to David Ritz's 1985 biography of Gaye, *Divided Soul*, Gaye remained deeply troubled and ungovernable toward his life's end—indeed, a doomed and restless man marked by fear, debt, sexual violence, religious guilt, jealousy, and, ultimately, a self-loathing so active it almost purposely created the circumstances of his own murder. The facts presented in *Divided Soul* weren't pretty: Gaye abused cocaine to a degree of madness; he often struck and ridiculed the women in his life; he claimed to envision a violent death; and he even took a crack at suicide during his last weeks. On the surface, Gaye's art seemed passionate yet well proportioned; behind that surface, in the man's life and heart, it was all turmoil and craziness.

But then Gaye always understood the tense play between fear and rapture uncommonly well, and at times that knowledge overwhelmed his music. In part, the worldly-spiritual insight was a product of the singer's upbringing. Back during the period when his father, Marvin Gaye, Sr., was an active apostolic minister in Washington, D.C., Gaye grew up singing in an evangelical gospel choir, though he also spent much of his youth privately listening to the more secular forms of be-bop, doo-wop, big band jazz, and R&B. Both the spiritual and early influences left an indelible impression on the singer, and following a term in the air force, he returned to Washington and began singing in street-corner R&B groups, melding the passion of gospel with themes of ever-suffering worldly romance (which, in that period, was a refined metaphor for sex).

In 1957, Gaye formed his own vocal group, the Marquees—a polished harmony troupe—and with the support of Bo Diddley, the group recorded for the Okeh label. In 1958, Harvey Fuqua enlisted the group as his backing ensemble in the Moonglows, who recorded for Chess. In the early 1960s, while playing a club in Detroit, Gaye's breathy, silken tenor caught the interest of local entrepreneur Berry Gordy, Jr., who signed him to his then-struggling Tamla-Motown label. Shortly after, Gaye married Gordy's sister, Anna, and began working for Motown, primarily as a quick-witted, propulsive drummer (his bop-derived rhythmic drive can be heard on the early singles of Smokey Robinson and the Miracles, among others).

In 1962, Gaye scored his first Motown hit, "Stubborn Kind of Fellow," and throughout the decade recorded the most extraordinary body of Motown singles—all rife with a definitionally sexy-cool brand of vocalizing and a sharp, blues-tempered backbeat. Working with every substantial Motown producer of the period (including Smokey Robinson, Norman Whitfield, and the Holland-Dozier-Holland team), Gaye yielded a vital body of dance hits and sex-minded ballads that still remain as popular and indelible as the finest work of his prime songwriting competitors of the period, the Beatles. Gaye's best-known hits from the epoch included "Hitch Hike," "Baby Don't You Do It," "Can I Get a Witness," "I'll be Doggone," "How Sweet It Is to Be Loved by You," "Ain't That Peculiar," and his most successful 1960s recording, "I

Heard It Through the Grapevine." In addition, he advanced a romantic duet style with label-mates Mary Wells ("Once Upon a Time" and "What's the Matter with You"), and in the 1970s, with Diana Ross.

But Gaye's finest duet work—perhaps the most passionate singing of his career—was with Tammi Terrell, with whom he recorded such late-1960s standards as "Ain't No Mountain High Enough," "Your Precious Love," "Ain't Nothing Like the Real Thing," and "You're All I Need to Get By." In 1967, Terrell—who had developed a brain tumor—collapsed into Gaye's arms during a concert performance. Three years later she died, and Gaye, reportedly shattered, began rethinking the importance of a pop career. As a result of Terrell's death, he remained an infrequent and reluctant live performer until his 1983 tour (the final tour of his life).

When Gaye reemerged, it was in 1971 with the self-written, self-produced politically thematic *What's Going On.* The record not only forced soul music to deal with the unpopular realities of a hardened sociopolitical scene (though Sly Stone had also started to do the same in his music), but was also among the first albums to establish a soul-pop star as a major artist of his own design. The effect was seismic: Within months Stevie Wonder was fighting (successfully) for the same brand of creative autonomy that Gaye had achieved with Motown's factory-minded structure, while such other venerable R&B artists as the Temptations and Curtis Mayfield began recording social-minded soul-rock that had been inspired and in no small part made possible by Gaye's breakthrough achievement.

But Gaye refused to remain adherent to that one aesthetic-political epiphany, and in many ways that made for a varied but also wildly unsettled late career. In 1973, he turned his attention to purely erotic matters with *Let's Get It On,* which introduced a manner of sexual explicitness to mainstream pop that, for such inheritors as Prince, certainly had tremendous impact. In the meantime, Gaye's stormy marriage to Anna Gordy was coming to a rough end, and the divorce settlement (which caused Gaye to file for bankruptcy and eventually leave the United States for asylum in Belgium) was the subject of his most personal work, the two-record *Here, My Dear,* which the singer released to satisfy his overdue alimony payments (though his ex-wife later considered suing him over the record's contents). In 1981, Gaye released his final Motown work, *In Our Lifetime,* a haphazard but oddly compelling meditation on love—and a tortured, hell-fire vision of death.

By all accounts, Gaye was a despairing man during this period (by his own admission, he once attempted suicide by overdose of cocaine), and when he left Motown for Columbia in 1982, even his staunchest admirers surmised that his prime work was behind him. But *Midnight Love* (1982) was not merely an elegant, stylistic rebound, it was also the most hopeful and celebratory work of his career. Gaye wrote, arranged, produced, and performed all the music himself, and though on the surface *Midnight Love* seemed merely a reprisal of the sex themes and rhythms of *Let's Get It On*, the singer clearly pursued physical and spiritual notions of fulfillment on the album as if they were mutually inseparable ends. Gaye seemed to regard sex as a way of renewing will and spirit after debilitating emotional setbacks, and as an interesting if somewhat puzzling way of asserting his religious desires. "Apparently beyond sex is God . . ." he told Mitchell Fink in a 1983 *Los Angeles Herald Examiner* interview. "So one has to have one's fill before one finds God."

It is not likely that Gaye found his fill before his sudden, grievous death, nor is it likely that he was even close to peace of mind or to his God's grace. Just the same, his fans were not ready to witness the end of such an ingenious and alluring sensibility. Gaye's 1983 tour of America seemed to promise something more than a wildly enjoyable comeback: It seemed an act of brave reclamation—Gaye's way of reasserting his musical preeminence, and making sense of all those counterpoised notions of joy and anger, pain and ecstasy, that made up the character of his singing and writing for over two decades.

He was a major artist of our passage from pop innocence to social unrest, and he was just beginning to illuminate a new, even more complex, sensual temperament. Perhaps, as biographer David Ritz suggests, Gaye wanted nothing more than a way out of the madness and pain of his life— but perhaps he may have found that way in kinder terms, had his life not been blasted from him by his father. To our everlasting loss, we must live with what now seems—along with Sam Cooke's terribly foreshortened brilliance—the most hurtful of soul music's unfinished promises. But if anything can blunt such pain, it is the wonderful and transcendent legacy of Marvin Gaye's music itself. Though it was his friend Smokey Robinson, and not Gaye, who sang "I gotta dance to keep from crying," it is in such times as Gaye's murder that those words assert their deepest meanings.

no simple highway:

the story

of jerry garcia

& the grateful dead

There is a road, no simple highway
Between the dawn and the dark of night
And if you go, no one may follow
That path is for your steps alone
FROM ''RIPPLE,''
ROBERT HUNTER AND JERRY GARCIA

*h*e was the unlikeliest of pop stars, and the most reticent of cultural icons.

Onstage, he wore plain clothes—usually a sacklike T-shirt and loose jeans, to fit his heavy frame—and he rarely spoke to the audience that watched his every move. Even his guitar lines—complex, lovely, rhapsodic, but never flashy—as well as his strained, weatherworn vocal style had a subdued, colloquial quality about them. Offstage, he kept to family and friends, and when he sat to talk with interviewers about his remarkable music, he often did so in sly-witted, self-deprecating ways. "I feel like I'm stumbling along," he said once, "and a lot of people are watching me or stumbling along with me or allowing me to stumble for them." It was as if Jerry Garcia—who, as the lead guitarist and singer of the Grateful Dead, lived at the center of one of popular culture's most extraordinary epic adventures—was bemused by the circumstances of his own renown.

And yet, when he died on August 9, 1995, a week after his fifty-third birthday, at a rehabilitation clinic in Forest Knolls, California, the news of his death set off immense waves of emotional reaction. Politicians, newscasters, poets, and artists eulogized the late guitarist throughout the day and night; fans of all ages gathered spontaneously in parks around the nation; and in the streets of San Francisco's Haight-Ashbury—the neighborhood where the Grateful Dead lived at the height of the hippie epoch—mourners assembled by the thousands, singing songs, building makeshift altars, consoling one another, and jamming the streets for blocks around. Across town, at San Francisco City Hall, a tie-dyed flag was flown on the middle flagpole, and the surrounding flags were lowered to half mast. It was a fitting gesture from a civic government that had once feared the movement that the Grateful Dead represented, and that now acknowledged the band's pilgrimage across the last thirty years to be one of the most notable chapters in the city's modern history.

Chances are Garcia himself would have been embarrassed, maybe even repelled, by all the commotion. He wasn't much given to mythologizing his own reputation. In some of his closing words in his last interview in *Rolling Stone*, in 1993, he said: "I'm hoping to leave a clean field—nothing, not a thing. I'm hoping they burn it all with me. . . . I'd rather have my immortality here while I'm alive. I don't care if it lasts beyond me at all. I'd just as soon it didn't."

Garcia's fans and friends, of course, feel differently. "I think that Garcia was a real avatar," says John Perry Barlow, who knew the late guitarist since 1967, and has co-written many of the Grateful Dead's songs with Bob Weir. "Jerry was one of those manifestations of the energy of his times, one of those people who ends up making the history books. He wrapped up in himself a whole set of characteristics and qualities that was very appropriate to a certain cultural vector in the latter part of the twentieth century: freedom from judgment, playfulness of intellect, complete improvisation, anti-authoritarianism, self-indulgence, and aesthetic development. I mean, he was, truly extraordinary. And he never really saw it himself, or could feel it himself. He could only see its effect on other people, which baffled and dismayed him.

"It made me sad to see that, because I wanted him to be able to appreciate, in some detached way, his own marvel. There was nothing that

Garcia liked better than something that was really diverting, and interesting, and lively and fascinating. You know, anything that he would refer to as a 'fat trip,' which was his term for that sort of thing. And he wasn't really able to appreciate himself, which was a pity, because, believe me, Jerry was the fattest trip of all. About the most he would say for himself was that he was a competent musician. But he would say *that*. I remember one time he started experimenting with MIDI—he was using all these MIDI sampled trumpet sounds. And he started playing that on his guitar, and he sounded like Miles Davis, only better. I went up to him, the first time I ever heard him do it, and I said: 'You could have been a great, fucking trumpet player.' And he looked at me and said: 'I *am* a great fucking trumpet player.' So, he knew."

JEROME JOHN GARCIA was born in 1942, in San Francisco's Mission District. His father, a Spanish immigrant named Jose "Joe" Garcia, had been a jazz clarinetist and Dixieland band leader in the 1930s, and he named his new son after his favorite Broadway composer, Jerome Kern. In the spring of 1948, while on a fishing trip, Jerry saw his father swept to his death in a California river. "I never saw him play with his band," Garcia told *Rolling Stone* in 1991, "but I remember him playing me to sleep at night. I just barely remember the sound of it."

After his father's death, Garcia spent a few years living with his mother's parents, in one of San Francisco's working-class districts. His grandmother had the habit of listening to Nashville's Grand Ole Opry radio broadcasts on Saturday nights, and it was in those hours, Garcia would later say, that he developed his fondness for country music forms—particularly the deft, blues-inflected mandolin playing and mournful, high-lonesome vocal style of bluegrass's principal founder, Bill Monroe. When Garcia was ten, his mother, Ruth, brought him to live with her at a sailor's hotel and bar that she ran near the city's waterfront. He spent much of his childhood there, listening to the boozy, fanciful stories that the hotel's old tenants told, or sitting alone, reading Disney and horror comics, and poring through science-fiction novels.

When Garcia was fifteen, his older brother, Tiff—the same brother who, a few years earlier, had accidentally lopped off Jerry's right-hand middle finger while the two were chopping wood—introduced him to early rock & roll and rhythm & blues music. Garcia was quickly drawn to the music's funky rhythms and roughhewed textures, but what captivated him most was the lead-guitar sounds—especially the bluesy mellifluence of players like T-Bone Walker and Chuck Berry. It was otherworldly-sounding music, he later said, unlike anything he had heard before. Garcia decided he wanted to learn how to make those same sounds. He went to his mother and proclaimed that he wanted an electric guitar for his upcoming birthday. "Actually," he later said, "she got me an *accordion,* and I went nuts. *Aggghhh, no, no, no!* I railed and raved, and she finally turned it in, and I got a pawn-shop electric guitar and an amplifier. I was just beside myself with joy."

During this same period, the Beat scene was in full swing in the Bay Area, and it held great sway at the North Beach arts school where Garcia took some courses, and at the city's coffeehouses, where he heard poets like Lawrence Ferlinghetti and Kenneth Rexroth read their venturesome works. "I was a high-school kid and a wanna-be beatnik!" he said in 1993. "Rock & roll at that time was *not* respectable. I mean, beatniks didn't like rock & roll. . . . Rock & roll wasn't cool, but I *loved* rock & roll. I used to have these fantasies about 'I want rock & roll to be like *respectable* music.' I wanted it to be like *art.* . . . I used to try to think of ways to make that work. I wanted to do something that fit in with the art institute, that kind of self-conscious art—'art' as opposed to 'popular culture.' Back then, they didn't even talk about popular culture—I mean, rock & roll was so *not legit,* you know? It was completely out of the picture. I don't know what they thought it was, like white-trash music or kids' music."

By the early 1960s, Garcia was living in Palo Alto, hanging out and playing in the folk music clubs around Stanford University. He was also working part time at Dana Morgan's Music Store, where he met several of the musicians that would eventually dominate the San Francisco music scene. In 1963, Garcia formed a jug band, Mother McCree's Uptown Jug Champions. Its line-up included a young folk guitarist named Bob Weir and a blues aficionado, Ron McKernan, known to his friends as "Pigpen" for his often unkempt appearance. The group played a mix of blues, country, and folk, and Pigpen became the front man, singing Jimmy Reed and Lightnin' Hopkins tunes.

Then, in February 1964, the Beatles made their historic appearance on the "Ed Sullivan Show," and virtually overnight youth culture was imbued with a new spirit and sense of identity. Garcia understood the group's promise after seeing their first film, *A Hard Day's Night!* For the first time since Elvis Presley—and the first time for an audience that had largely rejected contemporary rock & roll as seeming too trivial and inconsequential—pop music could be seen to hold bold, significant, and thoroughly exhilarating possibilities that even the ultra-serious, socially aware folk scene could not offer. This became even more apparent a year later, when Bob Dylan—who had been the folk scene's reigning hero—played an assailing set of his defiant new electric music at the Newport Folk Festival. As a result, the folky purism of Mother McCree's all-acoustic format began to seem rather limited and uninteresting to Garcia and many of the other band members, and before long, the ensemble was transformed into an electric unit, the Warlocks. A couple of the jug band members dropped out, and two new musicians joined: Bill Kreutzmann, who worked at Dana Morgan's Music Store, on drums, and on bass, a classically trained musician named Phil Lesh, who, like Garcia, had been radicalized by the music of the Beatles and Bob Dylan. "We had big ideas," Garcia told *Rolling Stone* in 1993. "I mean, as far as we were concerned, we were going to be the next Beatles or something—we were on a trip, definitely. We had enough of that kind of crazy faith in ourselves. . . . The first time we played in public, we had a huge crowd of people from the local high school, and they went fuckin' *nuts!* The next time we played, it was packed to the rafters. It was a pizza place. We said, 'Hey, can we play in here on Wednesday night? We won't bother anybody. Just let us set up in the corner.' It was *pandemonium,* immediately."

It was around this time that Garcia and some of the group's other members also began an experimentation with drugs that would forever transform the nature of the band's story. Certainly, this wasn't the first time drugs had been used in music for artistic inspiration, or had found their way into an American cultural movement. Many jazz and blues artists (not to mention several country-western players) had been using marijuana and various narcotics to intensify their music-making for several decades, and in the '50s the Beats had extolled marijuana as an assertion of their noncon-formism. But the drugs that began cropping up in the youth and music scenes in the mid-1960s were of a much different, more exotic, sort. Veterans Hospital near Stanford University had been the site of government-sanc-tioned experiments with LSD—a drug that induced hallucinations in those who ingested it, and that, for many, also inspired something remarkably close to the patterns of religious experience. Among those who had taken the drug at Veterans Hospital were Robert Hunter, a folk singer and poet who would later become Garcia's songwriting partner, and Ken Kesey, author of *One Flew Over the Cuckoo's Nest* and *Sometimes a Great Notion.* Kesey had been working on an idea about group LSD experiments, and had started a make-shift gang of artists and rogues, called the Merry Pranksters, dedicated to this adventure. Kesey's crew included a large number of intellectual dropouts like himself and eccentric rebels like Neal Cassady (the inspiration for Dean Moriarty in Jack Kerouac's *On the Road*) and Carolyn Adams (later known as Mountain Girl, who eventually married Garcia and had two children with him).

The Pranksters had been holding parties at a house in the nearby town of La Honda, to see what would happen when people took LSD in a situation where there were no regulations or predetermined situations. At Kesey's invitation, the Grateful Dead—as the Warlocks were now called—became the house band for these collective drug experiments, known as the Acid Tests. The Dead would play for hours as the Pranksters filmed the goings-on—everything from freak-outs to religious revelations to group sex. The Acid Tests were meant to be acts of cultural, spiritual, and psychic revolt, and their importance to the development of the Grateful Dead cannot be overestimated. The Dead's music, Garcia later said, "had a real sense of proportion to the event"—which is to say that sometimes the group's playing would seem to overshadow the event, and at other times, it would function as commentary or backdrop to the action of the event itself. Either way, the band did not see itself as the star of the party; if there were stars, they were formed from the union of the music and musicians with the audience and the spirit and shape of what was happening, from moment to moment—which meant that there was a blur between the performers, the event, and the audience.

Consequently, the Acid Tests became the model for what would shortly become known as the "Grateful Dead trip." In the years that followed, the Dead would never really forsake the philosophy of the Acid Tests. Right until the end, the band would encourage its audience to be involved with both the music and the sense of kinship that came from and fueled the music. Plus, more than any other band of the era, the Grateful Dead succeeded in making music that seemed to emanate from the hallucinogenic experience—music like 1969's *Aoxomoxoa*, which managed to prove both chilling and heartening in the same moments. In the process, the Dead made music that epitomized psychedelia at its brainiest and brawniest, and also helped make possible the sort of fusion of jazz structure and blues sensibility that would later help shape bands like the Allman Brothers.

"I wouldn't want to say this music was written on acid," says Robert Hunter, who penned some of the album's lyrics. "Over the years, I've denied it had any influence that way. But as I get older, I begin to understand that we were reporting on what we saw and experienced—like the layers below layers which became real to me. I would say that *Aoxomoxoa* was a report on what it's like to be up—or down—there in those layers. I guess it is, I'll be honest about it. Looking back and judging, those were pretty weird times. We were very, very far out."

By 1966, THE SPIRIT of the Acid Tests was spilling over into the streets and clubs of San Francisco—and well beyond. A new community of largely young people, many sharing similar ideals about drugs, music, politics, and sex, had taken root in the city's Haight-Ashbury district, a run-down but picturesque section of the city adjacent to Golden Gate Park, where Garcia and the Grateful Dead now shared a house. In addition, a thriving club and dance-hall scene—dominated by Chet Helms' Avalon Ballroom and Bill Graham's Fillmore—had sprung up around the city, drawing the notice of the media, police, and various political forces. In part, all the public scrutiny and judgment would eventually make life in the Haight difficult and risky. But there was also a certain boon that came from all the new publicity: The music and ethos of the San Francisco scene had begun to draw the interest of East Coast and British musicians and were starting to affect the thinking of artists like the Beatles and Bob Dylan—the same artists who, only a year or two before, had exerted such a major influence on groups like the Grateful Dead. For that matter, San Francisco bands were having an impact on not just pop and fashion styles, but also on social mores and even the political dialogue of the times. Several other bands, of course, participated in the creation of this scene, and some, including Jefferson Airplane, Quicksilver Messenger Service, and Janis Joplin with Big Brother and the Holding Company, would make music as inventive and memorable as the Dead's. In addition, nobody should underrate concert promoter Bill Graham's importance to the adventure; he was an often acerbic character, but he would emerge as an invaluable and scrupulous caretaker of the community that he served.

Still, it was the Grateful Dead that became known as the "people's band"—the band that cared about the following that it played to, and that often staged benefits or free shows for the common good. And long after the Haight's moment had passed, it would be the Grateful Dead—and the Dead alone among the original San Francisco bands—who would still exemplify the ideals of camaraderie and compassion that most other '60s-bred groups long relinquished, and that many subsequent rock artists repudiated in favor of more corrosive ideals.

The San Francisco scene was remarkable while it lasted, but it couldn't endure forever. Because of its reputation as a youth haven, the Haight was soon overrun with runaways, and the sort of health and shelter problems that a community of mainly white middle-class expatriates had never had to face before. In addition, the widespread use of LSD was turning out to be a little less ideal than some folks had imagined: There were nights when so many young people seemed to be on bad trips, the emergency rooms of local hospitals could not accommodate them all. By the middle of 1967, a season still referred to as the Summer of Love, the Haight had started to turn ugly. There were bad drugs on the streets, there were rapes and murders, and there was a surfeit of starry-eyed newcomers who had arrived in the neighborhood without any means of support, and were expecting the scene to feed and nurture them. Garcia and the Dead had seen the trouble coming and tried to prompt the city to prepare for it. "You could feed large numbers of people," Garcia later said, "but only so large. You could feed one thousand but not twenty thousand. We were unable to convince the San Francisco officials of what was going to happen. We said there would be more people in the city than the city could hold." Not long after, the Dead left the Haight for individual residences in Marin County, north of San Francisco.

By 1970, the idealism surrounding the Bay Area music scene—and much of the counterculture—had largely evaporated. The drug scene had turned creepy and risky; much of the peace movement had given way to violent rhetoric; and the quixotic dream of a Woodstock generation, bound together by the virtues of love and music, had been irreparably damaged, first by the Manson Family murders, in the summer of 1969, and then, a few months later, by a tragic and brutal event at the Altamont Speedway, just outside San Francisco. The occasion was a free concert featuring the Rolling Stones. Following either the example or the suggestion of the Grateful Dead (there is still disagreement on this), the Stones hired the Hell's Angels as a security force. It proved to be a day of horrific violence. The Angels battered numerous people, usually for little reason, and in the evening, as the Stones performed, the bikers stabbed a young black man to death in front of the stage. "It was completely unexpected," Garcia later said. "And that was the hard part—the hard lesson there—that you can have good people and good energy and work on a project and really want it to happen right and still have it all weird. It's the thing of knowing less than you should have. Youthful folly."

The record the band followed with, *Workingman's Dead,* was the Dead's response to that period. The record was a statement about the changing and badly frayed sense of community in both America and its counterculture, and as such, it was a work by, and about, a group of men being tested and pressured—at a time when they could have easily pulled apart from all the madness and stress and disappointment. The music reflected that struggle— particularly in songs like "Uncle John's Band"—a parable about America that was also the band's confession of how it nearly fell apart—and "New Speedway Boogie," about Altamont. "One way or another, this darkness has got to give," Garcia sang in the latter song, in a voice full of fear, fragility, and hard-earned courage. *Workingman's Dead*—and the record that followed it, *American Beauty*—made plain how the Grateful Dead found the heart and courage and talent to stick together, and to make something new and meaningful from their association. "Making the record became like going to a job," Garcia said. "It was something we had to do, and it was also something we did to keep our minds off some of these problems, even if the music is about those problems."

As a result, *Workingman's Dead* and *American Beauty* were records that explored the idea of how one could forge meaningful values in disillusioning times. Says Robert Hunter: "When the Jefferson Airplane came up with that idea, 'Up against the wall,' I was up against them. It may have been true, but look at the results: blood in the streets. It seems the Airplane was feeling the power of their ability to send the troops into the field, and I wanted to stand back from the grenades and knives and blood in the street. Stand way back. There's a better way. There has to be education, and the education has to come from the poets and musicians, because it has to touch the heart rather than the intellect, it has to get in there deeply. That was a decision. That was a conscious decision."

Sometimes, adds Hunter, it was difficult to hold on to that conviction. "When *American Beauty* came out," he says, "there was a photograph due to go on the back which showed the band with pistols. They were getting into guns at the time, going over to Mickey's ranch, target shooting. It wasn't anything revolutionary; they were just enjoying shooting pistols. For example, we got a gold record and went and shot it up.

"I saw that photo and that was one of the few times that I ever really asserted myself with the band and said, 'No—no picture of a band with guns on the back cover.' These were incendiary and revolutionary times, and I did not want this band to be making that statement. I wanted us to counter the rising violence of that time. I knew that we had a tool to do it, and we just didn't dare go the other way. Us and the Airplane: We could have been the final match that lit the fuse, and we went real consciously the other way."

In addition, with their countryish lilt and bluesy impulses, *Workingman's Dead* and *American Beauty* were attempts to return to the musical sources that had fueled the band's passions in the first place. "*Workingman's Dead* was our first true studio album," Garcia told me in 1987, "insofar as we went in there to say, 'These are the limitations of the studio for us as performers; let's play inside those limitations.' That is, we decided to play more or less straight-ahead songs and not get hung up with effects and weirdness. For me, the models were music that I'd liked before that was basically simply constructed but terribly effective—like the old Buck Owens records from Bakersfield. Those records were basic rock & roll: nice, raw, simple, straight-ahead music, with good vocals and substantial instrumentation, but nothing flashy. *Workingman's Dead* was our attempt to say, 'We can play this kind of music—we can play music that's heartland music. It's something we do as well as we do anything.' "

In a conversation I had with Robert Hunter in 1989, he revealed something else that he thought had affected Garcia's singing in that period, and made it so affecting. "It wasn't only because of the gathering awareness of what we were doing," he said, "but Jerry's mother had died in an automobile accident while we were recording *American Beauty*, and there's a lot of heartbreak on that record, especially on 'Brokedown Palace,' which is, I think, his release at that time. The pathos in Jerry's voice on those songs, I think, has a lot to do with that experience. When the pathos is there, I've always thought Jerry is the best. The man can get inside some of those lines and turn them inside out, and he makes those songs entirely his. There is no emotion more appealing than the bittersweet when it's truly, truly spoken."

WITH *Workingman's Dead* and *American Beauty*, the Grateful Dead hit a creative peak and turned an important corner. For one thing, the two records sold better than anything the group had issued before, and as a result, the band was able to begin working its way free of many of the crushing debts it had accrued. More important, the Dead now had a body of fine new songs to perform onstage for its rapidly expanding audience. With the next album, a double live set, *Grateful Dead* (originally entitled *Skullfuck*, until Warner Bros., balked), the band issued an invitation to its fans: "Send us your name and address and we'll keep you informed." It was the sort of standard fan club pitch that countless pop acts had indulged in before, but what it set in motion for the Dead would prove unprecedented: the biggest sustained fan reaction in pop music history. (According to *The New Yorker*, there were 110,000 Deadheads on the band's mailing list in 1995.) Clearly, the group had a devoted and far-flung following that, more than anything else, simply wanted to see the Grateful Dead live. One of the aphorisms of the time was: "There's nothing like a Grateful Dead show," and though that adage sometimes backfired in unintended ways—such as those occasions when the band turned in a protracted, meandering, and largely out-of-tune performance—often as not, the claim was justified. On those nights when the group was *on*, propelled by the double drumming of Bill Kreutzmann and Mickey Hart, and the dizzying melodic communion of Garcia and Weir's guitar's and Lesh's bass, the Grateful Dead's verve and imagination proved matchless.

It was this dedication to live performance, and a penchant for near-incessant touring, that formed the groundwork for the Grateful Dead's extraordinary success for a period of more than twenty years. Even a costly failed attempt at starting the band's own autonomous recording label in the early 1970s, plus the deaths of three consecutive keyboardists—Pigpen McKernan, of alcohol-induced cirrhosis of the liver, in 1973; Keith Godcheaux, in a fatal car accident in 1980, a year after leaving the band; and Brent Mydland, of a morphine and cocaine overdose in 1990—never really deterred the Dead's momentum as a live act. By the summer of 1987, when the group enjoyed its first and only Top 10 single ("Touch of Grey") and album *(In the Dark)*, the commercial breakthrough was almost beside-the-fact in any objective assessment of the band's stature. The Grateful Dead had been the top concert draw in America for several years, and they rarely played to less than near-full capacities. In some years during the 1980s, in fact, the band often played to collective nationwide audiences of more than a million (sometimes twice that amount), and while it would be difficult to calculate with any absolute certainty, there is a good likelihood that the Grateful Dead played before more people over the years than any other performing act in history. But the nature of the band's success went well beyond big numbers and high finances: From the late 1960s to the mid-1990s, the Grateful Dead enjoyed a union with its audience that was unrivaled and unshakable. Indeed, the Dead and its followers formed the only self-sustained, ongoing fellowship that pop music has ever produced—a commonwealth that lasted more than a quarter-century.

At the same time, Jerry Garcia and the other members of the Grateful Dead paid a considerable price for their singular accomplishment. By largely forswearing studio recordings after the 1970s (the band released only two collections of all new music in the period from 1980 to 1995), and by never returning to the sort of songwriting impetus that made works like *Workingman's Dead* and *American Beauty* so notable, the Dead lost the interest of much of the mainstream and cutting-edge pop audiences of the last two decades. To the band's fans, the Dead's magic lay in their live extravaganzas, where the group's improvisational bents melded with their audience's willful devotion, to achieve the sort of bouts of musical-communal ecstasy that few other rock & roll performers ever manged to equal. As a result, for many years, the Dead tended to play out their career, and make their meanings, almost entirely in the live moment, in the process attracting a mass-cult audience for whom the group functioned as the only ongoing force to keep faith with the dreams of collective utopia popularized in the 1960s. To the group's detractors, though, the Grateful Dead often appeared as little more than a 1960s relic, a band frozen in the sensibility of exhausted ideals, playing to a gullible cult audience that, like the group itself, was out of touch with the changing temper of the times. Or as one critic put it, the Grateful Dead was a group of "nostalgia mongerers . . . offering facile reminiscences to an audience with no memory of its own."

Garcia and the other members of the Dead heard this sort of criticism plenty over the years, and it had to have cut deep into their pride. "It's mortifying to think of yourself as a 'nostalgia' act when you've never quit playing," said Robert Hunter. "For years and years we drew an audience of nineteen- or twenty-year old kids. Can you have a nostalgia for a time you didn't live in? I think some of our music appeals to some sort of idealism in people, and hopefully it's universal enough to make those songs continue to exist over the years."

Perhaps the general pop world's disregard and outright ridicule took a certain toll on the spirits of the various band members. In any event, something began to wear on Jerry Garcia in the mid-1980s, and whatever it was, it never really let up on him. By 1984, rumors were making the rounds among the Deadheads—who just may be the best networked community on the planet—that Garcia's guitar playing had lost much of its wit and edge, that his singing had grown lackadaisical and that, in fact, he was suffering from drug problems. The rumors proved true. Garcia had been using cocaine and heroin for several years—in fact, had developed a serious addiction—and according to some observers, his use had started to affect the spirit and unity of the band itself. "He go so trashed out," said the Dead's sound engineer, Dan Healy, "that he just wasn't really playing. Having him not give a shit—that was devastating."

Watching from his home in Wyoming, Garcia's friend John Barlow thought he was witnessing the probable end of the Grateful Dead. "I was very afraid that Garcia was going to die. In fact, I'd reached a point where I'd just figured it was a matter of time before I'd turn on my radio and there, on the hour, I'd hear, 'Jerry Garcia, famous in the sixties, has died.' I didn't even allow myself to think it wasn't possible. That's a pretty morbid way to look at something. When you've got one person that is absolutely critical, and you don't think he's going to make it, then you start to disengage emotionally, and I had. For a while, I couldn't see where it was all headed. I mean, I could see the people in the audience getting off, but I couldn't see any of us getting off enough to make it worthwhile.

"And it wasn't just Garcia," Barlow says. "There were a lot of things that were wrong. I don't want to tell any tales out of school, but I think our adherents have a more than slightly idealistic notion of what goes on inside the Grateful Dead, and just how enlightened we all are.

"What happened with Garcia was not unique."

IT WAS NOT LONG after this time that I had my only lengthy conversation with Jerry Garcia. It was during a period of high activity and high risks for the Grateful Dead. The band was putting the finishing touches on its first album of new songs in several years, *In the Dark*, which, in turn, would launch the band's only Top 10 single, "Touch of Grey," a touching song about aging, decline, rebirth, and recommitment. At the same time, the Dead were beginning rehearsals with Bob Dylan for a nationwide tour that would make for a series of performances that were, at times, disorderly at best, and other times, full of surprising ferocity.

Garcia and I met on an uncommonly warm evening in the spring of 1987, in the band's San Rafael recording studio. When our conversation began, we had just finished viewing a video documentary about the band called *So Far*, which was shot nearly two years before. *So Far* is an adventurous and impressive work that, in its grandest moments, attests to the much-touted spirit of community that the Dead shared with their audience. Yet certain passages of the hour-long production seemed to be rough viewing on this night for Garcia, who looked rather heavy and fatigued during the project's taping. At the time *So Far* was made, Garcia was deeply entangled in the drug problem that, before much longer, would not only imperil his own health but also threaten the stability of the band itself.

That fact lends a certain affecting tension to the better performances in *So Far*—in particular, the group's doleful reading of "Uncle John's Band." The song—with its country-style sing-along about people pulling together into a brave community in frightening times—had long been among the band's signature tunes, yet in *So Far*, the Dead render it as if they were aiming to test its meanings anew. In the video, Garcia and rhythm guitarist Bob Weir face off in a dimly lighted concert hall, working their way through the lyrics with an air of frayed fraternity, as if this might be their last chance to make good on the music's promise of hard-earned kinship. "When life looks like easy street, there is danger at your door," they sing to each other, and from the look that passes between them in that moment, it's impossible to tell whether they are about to pull together or come apart.

It is a raggedy but utterly remarkable performance, and on the occasion of our meeting, it seems to leave Garcia a bit uneasy. "There were so many people who cared about me," he tells me, "and I was just fucking around. . . . Drug use is kind of a cul-de-sac: It's one of those places you turn with your problems, and pretty soon, all your problems have simply become that one problem. Then it's just you and drugs."

It is now late in the evening. The other band members have all gone home, and only a couple of assistants linger in a nearby room, making arrangements for the next day's rehearsals with Dylan. Garcia looks tired on this night—it has been a long day, and the next one promises to be a longer one—but as he sips at a rum and Coke and begins to talk about the rough history of the previous years, his voice sounds surprisingly youthful.

"There was something I needed or thought I needed from drugs," he says directly. "Drugs are like trade-offs in a way—they can be, at any rate. There was something there for me. I don't know what it was exactly. Maybe it was the thing of being able to distance myself a little from the world. But there was something there I needed for a while, and it wasn't an entirely negative experience. . . . But after a while, it was just the drugs running me, and that's an intolerable situation.

"I was never an overdose kind of junkie. I've never enjoyed the extremes of getting high. I never used to like to sit around and smoke freebase until I was wired out of my mind, know what I mean? For me, it was the thing of just getting pleasantly comfortable and grooving at that level. But of course, that level doesn't stay the same. It requires larger and larger amounts of drugs. So after a few years of that, pretty soon you've taken a lot of fucking drugs and not experiencing much. It's a black hole. I went down that black hole, really. Luckily, my friends pulled me out. Without them, I don't think I ever would have had the strength to do it myself."

In fact, says Garcia, it was the Grateful Dead who made the first move to resolve his drug problem. "Classically," he says, "the band has had a laissez-faire attitude in terms of what anybody wants to do. If somebody wants to drink or take drugs, as long as it doesn't seriously affect everybody else or affect the music, we can sort of let it go. We've all had our excursions. Just before I got busted, everybody came over to my house and said, 'Hey, Garcia, you got to cool it; you're starting to scare us.' "

According to some sources, the request that the Grateful Dead made of Garcia on that day in January of 1985 was actually a bit more adamant. The band reportedly told Garcia that he was killing himself and that while they could not force him to choose between death and life, they could insist that he choose between drugs and the band. If he chose drugs, the band might try to continue without him, or it might simply dissolve. Either way, the members wanted Garcia to understand they loved him, but they also wanted him to choose his allegiance.

"Garcia was the captain of his own ship," Bob Weir says of that period, "and if he was going to check out, that was up to him. But you know, if somebody looks real off course, we might take it upon ourselves to bump up against him and try to push him a little more in a right direction."

Perhaps, in that confrontation, Garcia was reminded of something he had once said about the Grateful Dead's original singer, Pigpen, in 1972, after it had been disclosed that Pigpen had severely damaged his liver from drinking. "He survived it," Garcia told *Rolling Stone,* "and now he's got the option of being a juicer or not being a juicer. To be a juicer means to die, so now he's being able to choose whether to live or die. And if I know Pigpen, he'll choose to live." The following year, Pigpen was found dead. According to most reports, he had never really returned to drinking but had simply suffered too much damage to continue living.

In any event, Garcia reportedly made a decision: He promised the band he would quit drugs and would seek rehabilitative treatment within a few days. As it developed, he never got the chance. On January 18, 1985, while parked in his BMW in Golden Gate Park, Garcia was spotted by a policeman who noticed the lapsed registration on the vehicle. As the policeman approached the car, he reportedly smelled a strong burning odor and noticed Garcia trying to hide something between the driver and passenger seats. The policeman asked Garcia to get out of the car, and when Garcia did, the policeman saw an open briefcase on the passenger seat, full of twenty-three packets of "brown and white substances."

Garcia was arrested on suspicion of possessing cocaine and heroin, and about a month later, a municipal-court judge agreed to let the guitarist enter a Marin County drug-diversion program.

Looking back at the experience, Garcia was almost thankful. "I'm the sort of person," he says, "that will just keep going along until something stops me. For me and drugs, the bust helped. It reminded me how vulnerable you are when you're drug dependent. It caught my attention. It was like 'Oh, right: illegal.' And of all the things I don't want to do, spending time in jail is one of those things I least want to do. It was as if this was telling me it was time to start doing something different. It took me about a year to finally get off drugs completely after the bust, but it was something that needed to happen."

Garcia pauses to light a cigarette, then studies its burning end thoughtfully. "I can't speak for other people," he says after a few moments, "and I certainly don't have advice to give about drugs one way or another. I think it's purely a personal matter. I haven't changed in that regard. . . . It was one of those things where the pain it cost my friends, the worry that I put people through, was out of proportion to whatever it was I thought I needed from drugs. For me, it became a dead end."

Following Garcia's drug treatment, the band resumed a full-time touring schedule that included several 1986 summer dates with Bob Dylan and Tom Petty and the Heartbreakers. "I felt better after cleaning up, oddly enough, until that tour," Garcia says. "And then, I didn't realize it, but I was dehydrated and tired. That was all I felt, really. I didn't feel any pain. I didn't feel sick. I just felt tired. Then when we got back from that tour, I was just *really* tired. One day, I couldn't move anymore, so I sat down. A week later, I woke up in a hospital, and I didn't know what had happened. It was really weird."

Actually, it was worse that that: Though he had never been previously diagnosed as having diabetes, when Garcia sat down at his San Rafael home on that July evening in 1986, he slipped into a diabetic coma that lasted five days and nearly claimed his life. "I must say, my experience never suggested to me that I was anywhere near death," says Garcia. "For me, it had just been this weird experience of being shut off. Later on, I found out how scary it was for everybody, and then I started to realize how serious it had all been. The doctors said I was so dehydrated, my blood was like mud.

"It was another one of those things to grab my attention. It was like my physical being saying, 'Hey, you're going to have to put in some time here if you want to keep on living.'" As he talks, Garcia still seems startled by this realization. "Actually," he says, "it was a thought that had never entered my mind. I'd been lucky enough to have an exceptionally rugged constitution, but just the thing of getting older, and basically having a life of benign neglect, had caught up with me. And possibly the experience of quitting drugs may have put my body through a lot of quick changes."

At first, though, there were no guarantees that Garcia would be able to live as effectively as before. There were fears that he might suffer memory lapses and that his muscular coordination might never again be sharp enough for him to play guitar. "When I was in the hospital," he says, "all I could think was 'God, just give me a chance to do stuff—give me a chance to go back to being productive and playing music and doing the stuff I love to do.' And one of the first things I did—once I started to be able to make coherent sentences—was to get a guitar in there to see if I could play. But when I started playing, I thought, 'Oh, man, this is going to take a long time and a lot of patience.'"

After his release from the hospital, Garcia began spending afternoons with an old friend, Bay Area jazz and rhythm & blues keyboardist Merl Saunders, trying to rebuild his musical deftness. "I said, 'God, I can't do this,' " says Garcia. "Merl was very encouraging. He would run me through these tunes that had sophisticated harmonic changes, so I had to think. It was like learning music again, in a way. Slowly, I started to gain some confidence, and pretty soon, it all started coming back. It was about a three-month process, I would say, before I felt like 'Okay, now I'm ready to go out and play.' The first few gigs were sort of shaky, but . . ." Garcia's voice turns thick, and he looks away for a moment. "Ah, shit," he says, "it was incredible. There wasn't a dry eye in the house. It was great. It was just great. I was so happy to play."

Garcia smiles and shakes his head. "I am not a believer in the invisible," he says, "but I got such an incredible outpouring. The mail I got in the hospital was so soulful. All the Deadheads—it was kind of like brotherly, sisterly, motherly, fatherly advice from people. Every conceivable kind of healing vibe was just pouring into that place. I mean, the doctors did what they could to keep me alive, but as far as knowing what was wrong with me and knowing how to fix it—it's not something medicine knows how to do. And after I'd left, the doctors were saying my recovery was incredible. They couldn't believe it.

"I really feel that the fans put life into me . . . and that feeling reinforced a lot of things. It was like 'Okay, I've been away for a while, folks, but I'm back.' It's that kind of thing. It's just great to be involved in something that doesn't hurt anybody. If it provides some uplift and some comfort in people's lives, it's just that much nicer. So I'm ready for anything now."

IN THE YEARS following that 1987 conversation with Garcia, the Grateful Dead went on to enjoy the greatest commercial successes of their career. More important, though, was the symbiosis that developed between the band and its audience—a reciprocity likely unequaled in pop history. At the heart of this connection was the Dead themselves and their self-built business organization—the latter which did a largely independent, in-house job of handling the booking and staging of the band's near-incessant tours, and which also bypassed conventional ticket-sales systems as much as possible, by selling roughly fifty percent of the band's tickets through a company-run mail-order department. This model of an autonomous cooperative helped spawn what was perhaps the largest genuine alternative communion in all of rock: a sprawling coalition of fans, entrepreneurs, and homegrown media that surrounded the band, and that promoted the group as the center for a worldwide community of idealists—and that community thrived largely without the involvement or support of the established music industry or music press.

But any meaningful example of cooperative community isn't without its problems, and by the early 1990s, the Deadhead scene was increasingly beset by serious dilemmas. As far back as the mid-1980s, some of the group's more reckless and unfaithworthy fans—particularly the ones who gathered in parking lots outside the band's shows, begging for free tickets, sometimes selling various drugs, and often disrupting the peace and security of nearby neighborhoods—had grown so prevalent that several concert halls, local police departments, and city councils were forced to pronounce the Dead and their audience as unwelcome visitors. The Dead often tried to dissuade this sort of behavior among its followers, but it wasn't until the summer of 1995—following some serious bottle-throwing and gate-crashings that re-sulted in riot incidents—that the situation reached a crisis level and provoked a severe response from the band. The Dead issued an edict, in the form of fliers, demanding that fans without tickets stay away from the show sites, and advising that any further violent mass actions might result in the band canceling future tours. "A few more scenes like Sunday night," the band wrote, "and we'll quite simply be unable to play. . . . And when you hear somebody say 'Fuck you, we'll do what we want,' remember something. That applies to us, too." In response, Garcia received a death threat that was taken seriously by not only the band and its entourage, but by law enforcement officials as well. After events such as these, according to some observers in the Dead's camp, Garcia and the band had seriously started to question whether many of the people they were playing to truly made up the sort of commu-nity they wanted to sustain.

But there was something even more serious at hand. Garcia's health continued to be a problem in the years after his 1986 coma, and according to some accounts, so did his appetite for drugs. He collapsed from exhaustion in 1992, resulting in the Dead canceling many of the performances on their tour. After his 1993 recovery, Garcia dedicated himself to a regimen of diet and exercise. At first, the pledge seemed to work: He shed over sixty pounds from his former three hundred–pound weight, and he often appeared re-newed and better focused onstage. There were other positive changes at work: He had become a father again in recent years and was attempting to spend more time as a parent, and in 1994, he entered into his third marriage, with filmmaker Deborah Koons. Plus, to the pleasure of numerous Deadheads, he had recently written several of his best new songs in years with his longtime friend Robert Hunter, in preparation for a new Grateful Dead album.

These were all brave efforts for a man past fifty with considerable health problems and a troubled drug history. In the end, though, they weren't enough to carry him farther. In mid-July 1995, he checked into the Betty Ford Center in Rancho Mirage, for one more go at overcoming his heroin use. According to one report, he wanted to be clean when he gave away his oldest daughter, Heather, at her upcoming wedding. He checked out several days later, so he could spend his fifty-third birthday on August 1, with family and friends. A week later he went into a different clinic, Serenity Knolls in Marin County. He was already clean, most sources report; he just wanted to be in sound shape. This time, Jerry Garcia did not walk out and return to the loving fraternity of his band, his fans, and his family. At 4 A.M., Wednesday, August 9, 1995, he was found unconscious by a clinic counselor. In his sleep, it seems, he had suffered a fatal heart attack. According to his wife, he died with a smile on his face.

JERRY GARCIA and the Grateful Dead were so active for so long and were so heartening for the audience that loved them, that it seems somewhat astonishing to realize that the band's adventure is now over. Of course, anybody paying attention—anybody aware of the ups and downs in Garcia's well-being—might have seen it coming. Still, endings are always tough things to be braced for.

"He was like the boy who cried wolf," says John Barlow. "He'd come so close so many times that I think people gradually stopped taking the possibility as seriously as they otherwise would have. Or maybe we felt so certain that this would happen someday that we had managed—as a group—to go into a kind of collective denial about it. I mean, I looked at this event so many times, and shrank back from it in fear so many times, that I erected a new callous against it each time I did so. Now that I'm here at the thing itself, I hardly know what to think of it. Every deposition of every imagined version of it is now standing in the way of being able to understand and appreciate the real thing.

"But this is a very large death," says Barlow. "There are a lot of levels on which to be affected here, all the way from the fact that I'm going to miss terribly the opportunity to spend time in conversation with one of the smartest and most playful minds I've ever run up against, to the fact that there will never truly be another Grateful Dead concert. I never thought of myself as a Deadhead exactly, but that's been a pretty fundamental part of my life—of all our lives—for the past thirty years."

It is, indeed, a considerable passing. To see the Grateful Dead onstage was to see a band that clearly understood the meaning of playing together from the perspective of the long haul. Interestingly, that's something we've seen fairly little of in rock & roll, since rock is an art form, the most valuable and essential pleasures of which—including inspiration, meaning, and concord—are founded in the knowledge that such moments cannot hold forever. The Grateful Dead, like any great rock & roll band, lived up to that ideal, but they also shattered it, or at least bent it to their own purposes. At their best, they were a band capable of surprising both themselves and their audience, while at the same time playing as if they had spent their whole lives learning to make music as a way of talking to one another, and as if music were the language of their sodality, and therefore their history. No doubt it was. What the Grateful Dead understood, probably better than any other band in pop music history, was that nobody in the group could succeed as well, or mean as much, outside the context of the entire group, and that the group itself could not succeed without its individuals. It was a band that needed all its members playing and thinking together to keep things inspiring. Just as important, it was a band that realized that it also needed its audience to keep things significant—indeed, it would probably be fair to say that, for the last twenty years, the Dead's audience informed the group's worth as much as their music did.

In the hours after I learned of Garcia's death, I went online to the WELL, the Bay Area computer conference system that has thrived in no small part due to its large contingent of Deadheads. I wanted to see how the fans were doing, and what they were saying, in the recognition of their loss. For the most part—at least in those first hours that I scanned the messages—what I found were well-meaning, blithe comments, people sending each other "beams" (which are like positive extrasensory wishes) and fantasies of group hugs. They were the sort of sentiments that many people I know would gag at, and I must admit, they proved too maudlin for my own sensibility. Still, one of the things I had to recognize about the Deadheads years ago was that this was a group of people for whom good cheer wasn't just a shared disposition but also an act of conscious dissent: a protest against the anger and malice that seems to characterize so much of our social and artistic temper these days. The Deadheads may sometimes seem like naïfs, but I'm not convinced their vision of community is such an undesirable thing. After all, there are worse visions around. Consider, for example, the vision of our recent Republican Congress, which would scourge any community of the misfit or helpless.

In any event, for my tastes I saw far too little attention paid—by both the Deadheads and the media—to just how much darkness there was that made its way into Garcia and the Dead's music, and how strong and interesting that darkness was. For that matter, there was always a good deal more darkness in the whole sixties adventure than many people have been comfortable acknowledging—and I don't mean simply all the drug casualties, political ruin, and violence of the period. There was also a willingness to explore risky psychic terrain, a realization that your best hopes could also cost you some terrible losses, and I think that those possibilities were realized in the Dead's music and history as meaningfully as they were anywhere.

In fact, the darkness crept in early in the Dead's saga. It could be found in the insinuation of the band's name—which many fans in the early San Francisco scene cited as being too creepy and disturbing as a moniker for a rock group. It could also be found deep down in much of the band's best music—in the strange layers and swirls that made parts of *Aoxomoxoa* such a vivid and frightening aural portrayal of the psychedelic experience, and in the meditations about death and damage that the band turned into hard-boiled anthems of hope on *Workingman's Dead*. And of course, there was also all the darkness in the band's history that ended up bringing so many of its members to their deaths.

Not all darkness is negative. In fact, sometimes wonderful and kind things can come from it, and if there's one thing that was apparent to everybody about Jerry Garcia, it was that he was a good-humored man with generous instincts. But there was much more to him than that, and it wasn't always apparent on the surface. In a conversation I had several years ago with Robert Hunter about Garcia, Hunter told me: "Garcia is a cheery and resilient man, but I always felt that under his warmth and friendliness there was a deep well of despair—or at least a recognition that at the heart of the world, there may be more darkness, despair, and absurdity than any sane and compassionate heart could stand."

In his last interview with *Rolling Stone*, in 1993, Garcia had this to say about his own dark side: "I definitely have a component in my personality which is not exactly self-destructive, but it's certainly ornery. It's like . . . 'Try to get healthy'—'Fuck you, man. . . .' I don't know what it comes from. I've always clung to it, see, because I felt it's part of what makes me *me*. Being anarchic, having that anarchist streak, serves me on other levels—artistically, certainly. So I don't want to eliminate that aspect of my personality. But I see that on some levels it's working against me.

"They're gifts, some of these aspects of your personality. They're helpful and useful and powerful, but they also have this other side. They're indiscriminate. They don't make judgments."

Garcia, of course, made his own choices, and whatever they may have cost him, I would argue that in some ways they were still brave, worthy choices. Maybe they were even essential to the wondrous creations of his life's work. His achievements, in fact, were enormous. He helped inspire and nurture a community that, in some form or another, survived for thirty years, and that may even outlast his death; he co-wrote a fine collection of songs about America's myths, pleasures, and troubles; and, as the Grateful Dead's most familiar and endearing member, he accomplished something that no other rock star has ever accomplished: He attracted an active following that only grew larger in size and devotion with each passing decade, from the 1960s to the 1990s. You would have to look to the careers of people like Louis Armstrong, Duke Ellington, Count Basie, Miles Davis, or Charles Mingus to find the equivalent of Garcia's musical longevity and growth in the history of American band leaders.

Most important, though, he was a man who remained true to ideals and perceptions that many of the rest of us long ago found easy to discard— and maybe in the end that is a bigger part of our loss at this point than the death of Garcia himself.

My favorite Grateful Dead song of the last decade or so is "Black Muddy River," written by Garcia and Hunter. It's a song about living one's life in spite of all the heartbreak and devastation that life can bring, and in its most affecting verse, Garcia sang: "When it seems like the night will last forever/And there's nothing left to do but count the years/When the strings of my heart begin to sever/Stones fall from my eyes instead of tears/I will walk alone by the black muddy river/Dream me a dream of my own/I will walk alone by the black muddy river . . . and sing me a song of my own."

Those were among the last words Garcia sang at the Grateful Dead's final show, at Chicago's Soldier Field, in early July. Not bad, as far as farewells go, and not bad, either, for a summing up of a life lived with much grace and heart. It is a good thing, I believe, that we lived in the same time as this man did, and it is not likely that we shall see charms or skills so transcendent, and so sustained, again.

NOT EVERYONE, of course, would agree. As I noted earlier, Jerry Garcia's death was met with a massive and spontaneous outpouring of grief and praise, but all this respect for a hippie-derived popular hero also rankled a fair amount of social and political critics. In the *Washington Post*, liberal critic Colman McCarthy wrote: "The media's iconic excesses matched the self-indulgence of Garcia's brand of hedonism. This was someone who in the

1960s fueled himself on LSD and touted the drug for others. . . . As memories fade, that decade [the 1960s] needs to be linked with people, events, and ideas on higher levels than an unkempt druggie musician. . . . Rock bands and the Woodstock mud holes to which they drew their aimless fans were marginal to the genuine challenges to the culture of that time." Writing in the August 21 issue of *Newsweek,* columnist George Will shared a similar disdain, from the haughty conservative point of view: "The portion of popular culture that constantly sentimentalizes the Sixties also panders to the arrested development of the Sixties generation which is no longer young but wishes it were and seeks derivative vitality."

There were other voices of derision from other quarters as well. Several times in the days following Garcia's death, I received comments—either in conversation or by e-mail—from rock fans who couldn't fathom the bereavement they were witnessing. "What's all this about?" one friend wrote me. "It isn't like Jerry Garcia was John Lennon." Another said: "Maybe now all these Deadheads will be forced to get a life. God knows it's way past time." This last from somebody who, only a year and a half before, had been terribly hurt by the suicide of Nirvana's Kurt Cobain.

These sorts of sentiments were hardly uncommon, and they say much about how we have come to judge the worth and relevance of the people that we call our pop heroes. Because Garcia and the Grateful Dead had not been seen to participate in the ongoing flux of pop-music culture—because they chose to record few albums of newly written material, were not prominent on radio, MTV, or in the mainstream press, and because they elected to play largely for their own partisan following—many rock fans, critics, and casual observers had come to see them as a band whose time and importance had long faded: a "dinosaur" band. In a way, this sort of displacement of yesterday's rock heroes and values can be a healthy and revivifying thing—as we saw in the punk revolt of the late 1970s—plus it's simply the inevitable order of pop culture evolution. It is good to remind previous generations and their artists that they hardly hold a franchise on legitimate modes of rebellion or invention, and it is also good for each new era or movement to determine its own heroes, styles, and concerns and not be forced to grow only in the fading light of days gone by.

At the same time, much about the anti-1960s sentiment—particularly when manifest in the pop world—is unfortunate, unthinking, and, at best, plainly hypocritical. For one thing, it plays into the hands of critics like William Bennett, Newt Gingrich, and William F. Buckley (who also wrote a column denouncing Garcia's influence)—pundits with too much unchallenged voice in today's media, who are attempting to assert the monolithic view that the progressive risks and experiments of the 1960s have amounted to the undoing of our culture: that the whole period was a shameful mistake that must now be undone and never allowed to come to pass again. Regardless of the excesses and lapses of that time, we should remember that in the 1960s, many of our best cultural iconoclasts made some brave, smart, outrageous, and wonderful moves that had the effect of spreading a spirit of courage and defiance not just among the youth of one generation, but that also helped serve as an even greater impetus for many of the brave activists of the last decade or more. After all, it was hardly an accident that the soundtrack of choice at Tiananmen Square, in Berlin as the Wall came down, and in the streets of Czechoslovakia as communism fell, was the soundtrack of 1960s American rock & roll.

In particular, the 1960s rock revolutionists—including Jerry Garcia and the Grateful Dead—expanded the possibilities of what music might sound like, what it might say, and how it might matter in our lives and our society. These are notable and noble victories, and several of the best post-'60s rock-related movements, such as punk, rap, techno, and the many various dance schools, have exploited the promises born in those times, and have thrived greatly from them.

All these considerations aside, though, what made Garcia's lingering presence so valuable—and what made his death so consequential—was precisely the meaning that he and the Grateful Dead held for a *modern* audience. Indeed, for the Dead's fans, the band was not simply another popular phenomenon that spoke for any one certain moment, nor merely a band that achieved a temporary place of fame and commodity in the ongoing chronicle of pop music. To the group's believers, the Dead were something much bigger and more lasting, as well as something virtually unique in postwar musical history: a band that functioned as an ongoing, binding central point in a large-scale alternative music scene that viewed music as a crucial means of expressing a vision of a better, more hopeful and open-minded society.

To tell you the truth, the Dead's audience was frequently the part of the Dead's shows that I liked the best. For me, the band's music had lost much of its best edge and momentum many years before, which isn't to say they still weren't a protean or considerable ensemble; certainly I saw passages in various shows that were simply extraordinary. For all their musical imperfections, one sin the Grateful Dead never committed was to perform their own music with too much staidness or reverence. Rather, the Dead always played their best songs as if those compositions were still fair game for transmogrification, and as if running a collective risk—the risk of either fleeting transcendence or comic ruin—was the only way the band's members could imagine making it through life.

Still, it was the Dead's following, and its yearning for something that might unify and uplift it, that I became particularly attached to. I saw that crowd (with the band, of course) at speedways and in open fields, in stadiums and arenas, but for some reason, the setting I remember best was at New York City's Madison Square Garden. It was the early autumn of 1988, and the Dead were playing a nine-night stand at the arena—the biggest series of concerts ever presented in New York's history up to that time, and as it turned out, also the biggest American pop event (and money-grosser) of 1988. Yet even so, this fact was not acknowledged in what little local press the concerts received—just another sign of the massive disregard that the Grateful Dead suffered from most mainstream media, until the day of Jerry Garcia's death.

A giant inflatable rubber replica of King Kong, outfitted in a huge tie-dyed T-shirt, loomed above Seventh Avenue. Below it, thousands of young Deadheads—many also wearing tie-dyes—roamed the streets around the Garden, some looking for tickets for the various shows, some looking to buy or sell drugs, shirts, necklaces, and knicknacks. Most of them seemed to be circling the block simply to check one another out. There was nothing surly or competitive or hostile about this congregation. Indeed, it was so nonaggressive that many of the hundreds of policemen who had been assigned to cover the event seemed plain bored by their task. If anything, these kids just seemed to be milling in order to assure one another that they were all part of the same moment, the same conviction.

The inside of the hall was no less colorful or joyful. Several thousand young people lined the various foyers and corridors of the Garden, pirouetting to the band's genial rhythms, swirling their long hair and flowing dresses, twisting their hands and arms in elaborate gestures. One young woman— about fifteen, I'd say, dressed in a sweeping, black gossamer gown, her face adorned with multihued sparkles and tiny iridescent mirror discs—stopped me as I walked past one group of dancers. "Hey, mister," she said. "Did anybody ever tell you you have beautiful eyes? I mean, you know, for an old guy?"

In every Dead show I saw, there was always a moment when it became plain that the audience's participation in these gatherings—and its sanction of the band—was as much the purpose of the shows as was the musical performances. As often as not, I found that moment in the band's reading of the Buddy Holly hit, "Not Fade Away." There came a point toward the song's end when the guitars, bass, drums, and keyboards would drop out of the sound, and there was only the band and the audience shouting those old and timeless lyrics: "Love is love and not fade away/Love is love and not fade away."

"Not fade away," the crowd would shout to the band.

"Not fade away," the band shouted back.

"NOT FADE AWAY!" the crowd yowled, leaning forward as one.

It would go on like that, the two bodies of this misfit community singing hard to one another, bound up in the promise that as long as one was there, the other would always hold a hope.

Now that promise is gone, and along with it perhaps one of the last meaningful dreams of rock & roll community as well. In the seasons since Jerry Garcia's death, I have thought many times about that young woman in the flowing black gown who smiled, touched my face, and danced away into the darkness of the hallway, moving to the Dead's rhythms. And I have wondered: For whom will she dance now? Who will stir her hopes? I don't know, but I know this: We are poorer for having lost such dreamers.

tupac shakur:

easy target

i don't know whether to mourn Tupac Shakur or to rail against all the terrible forces—including the artist's own self-destructive temperament—that have resulted in such a wasteful, unjustifiable end. I do know this, though: Whatever its causes, the murder of Shakur, at age twenty-four, has robbed us of one of the most talented and compelling voices of recent years. He embodied just as much for his audience as Kurt Cobain did for his. That is, Tupac Shakur spoke to and for many who had grown up within (and maybe never quite left) hard realities—realities that mainstream culture and media are loathe to understand or respect—and his death has left his fans feeling a doubly-sharp pain: the loss of a much-esteemed signifier, and the loss of a future volume of work that, no doubt, would have proved both brilliant and provocative.

Certainly, Shakur was among the most ingenious and lyrical of the present generation of rappers, often pitting his dark-toned staccato-yet-elastic cadences against lulling and clever musical backdrops, for an effect as memorable for its melodic contours as for its rhythmic verve. In addition, his four albums—*2Pacalypse Now, Strictly 4 My N.I.G.G.A.Z. . . . , Me Against the World,* and *All Eyez on* Me (a fifth album, *Don Killuminati: The 7 Day Theory,* was released under the name Makaveli late in 1996)—ran the full range of rap's thematic and emotional breadth. In the first two albums alone, you could find moments of uncommon tenderness and compassion (the feminine-sympathetic portrayals in "Brenda's Got a Baby" and "Keep Ya Head Up"), astute political and social observation ("Trapped," "Soulja's Story," and "I Don't Give a Fuck"), and also declarations of fierce black-against-black anger and brutality (the thug-life anthems "Last Wordz" and

"5 Deadly Venomz"). What made this disconcerting mix especially notable was how credible it all seemed. Shakur could sing in respectful praise and defense of women then turn around and deliver a harangue about "bitches" and "ho's"—or could boast of his gangster prowess one moment, then condemn the same doomed mentality in another track—and you never doubted that he felt and meant every word he declaimed. Does that make him sound like a confused man? Yes—to say the least. But Shakur was also a man willing to own up to and examine his many contradictory inclinations, and I suspect that quality, more than any other, is what made him such a vital and empathetic voice for so many of his fans.

Shakur was also a clearly gifted actor (his first performance, as an adolescent, was in a stage production of *A Raisin in the Sun*)—though he wasn't especially well served by such mediocre young-blacks-coming-of-age films as *Poetic Justice* and *Above the Rim*. The 1992 *Juice* (his first film) wasn't much better, though it contains Shakur's best performance to date (two films, *Gridlock'd* and *Gang Related*, were released in 1997). In *Juice*, Shakur played Bishop—a young man anxious to break out of the dead-end confinements of his community, and who settles on an armed robbery as the means of proving his stature, his "juice." Once Bishop has a gun in his hand, everything about his character, his life, his fate, changes. He shoots anything that obstructs him—including some lifelong friends. He kills simply to kill, as if by doing so he will eventually shoot through the one thing that hurts him the most: his own troubled heart. "I *am* crazy," he tells a character at one point. "But you know what else? I don't give a fuck." Shakur speaks the line with such sure and frightening coldness, it is impossible to know whether he informed it with his own experience, or whether he was simply uncovering a disturbing but liberating personal ethos.

But it was with his two final recordings—*Me Against the World* and *All Eyez on Me*—that Shakur achieved what was probably his best realized and most enduring work. The two albums are like major statements about violence, social realism, self-willed fate and unappeasable pain, made by two different, almost opposing sensibilities. Or they could be read as the combined, sequential statements of one man's growth—except in Shakur's case, it appears that the growth moved from hard-earned enlightenment to hard-bitten virulence. *Me Against the World* (recorded after he was shot in a 1994 robbery and during his imprisonment for sexually abusing a woman) was the eloquent moment when Shakur paused to examine all the trouble and violence in his life, and measured not only his own complicity in that trouble but how such actions spilled into, and poisoned, the world around him.

In *All Eyez on Me*, released a year later on Death Row Records, Shakur gave way to almost all the darkness he had ever known—and did so brilliantly. Indeed, *Eyez* is one of the most melodically and texturally inventive albums that rap has ever produced—and also one of the most furious. Tracks like "California Love" and "Can't C Me" are rife with sheer beauty and exuberance, and even some of the more dangerous or brooding songs ("Heartz of Men," "2 of Amerikaz Most Wanted," "Life Goes On," "Only God Can Judge Me," "Got My Mind Made Up") boast gorgeous surfaces over their pure hearts of stone. In both albums, in song after song, Shakur came up against the same terrible realization: He could see his death bearing down on top of him, but he didn't know how to step out of its unrelenting way. So he stood there, waiting, and while he waited, he made one of rap's few full-length masterpieces.

The hardest-hitting, most eventful song of the *Eyez* project—and possibly of Shakur's career—appears as an extra cut on the "California Love" single: a track called "Hit 'Em Up." According to many in the rap community, the song is an attack aimed (mainly) at Sean "Puffy" Combs' Bad Boy label, (specifically) at recording artist Biggie Smalls (the Notorious B.I.G.). In the last couple of years, these figures had become arch rivals of Marion "Suge" Knight, owner and co-founder of Death Row Records, and Shakur indicated that he suspected they were involved in his 1994 shooting. As a result, "Hit 'Em Up" was much more than just a song—it was Shakur's salvo of revenge and warning. "I fucked your bitch, you fat motherfucker," he says, addressing Biggie Smalls as the track opens, referring to a rumor about B.I.G.'s wife and Shakur. But that boast is trite compared to what follows: "Who shot me?" he barks. "But you punks didn't finish. Now you're about to feel the wrath of the menace, nigga." A minute later, Shakur steps up his rage: "You want to fuck with us, you little young ass motherfuckers . . . ?" he rails. "You better *back* the fuck up or you get *smacked* the fuck up. . . . We ain't singin', we bringin' drama. . . . We gonna kill ALL you motherfuckers. . . . Fuck Biggie, fuck Bad Boy . . . and if you want to be down with Bad Boy, then fuck you too. . . . Die *slow* motherfucker. . . . You think you mob, nigga? *We* the motherfucking mob. . . . You niggas mad because our staff got *guns* in their motherfucking belts. . . . We bad boy killers/We kill 'em."

I have never heard anything remotely like Tupac Shakur's breathless performance on this track in all my years of listening to pop music. It contains a remarkable amount of rage and aggression—enough to make anything in punk seem flaccid by comparison. Indeed, "Hit 'Em Up" truly crosses the line from art and metaphor to real-life jeopardy. On one level, you might think Shakur was telling his enemies: We will kill you competitively, commercially. But listen to the stunning last thirty seconds of the track. It's as if Shakur were saying: Here I am—your enemy, and your target. Come and get me, or watch me get you first. (In a horrible echo of Shakur's own end, the Notorious B.I.G. was also gunned down a few months later, on the streets of Los Angeles.)

So: A MAN SINGS about death and killing, and then the man is killed. There is a great temptation for many to view one event as the result of the other. And in Tupac Shakur's case, there's some grounds for this assessment: He did more than sing about violence; he also participated in a fair amount of it. As Shakur himself once said, in words that *Time* magazine appropriated for their headline covering his murder: WHAT GOES 'ROUND COMES 'ROUND. Still, I think it would be a great disservice to dismiss Shakur's work and life with any quick and glib headline summations. It's like burying the man without hearing him.

I suspect also that Shakur's death will be cited as justification for yet another campaign against hardcore rap and troublesome lyrics. By this point, it's become one of the perennial causes of the last decade. In 1989, the FBI got into the act by contacting Priority Records to note the bureau's official distaste for the groundbreaking group N.W.A.'s unyielding, in-your-face song, "Fuck tha Police." In 1990, *Newsweek* ran a cover story titled "Rap Rage, Yo!," calling rap a "streetwise music," rife with "ugly macho boasting," and three years later the magazine reiterated its disdain with a Snoop Doggy Dog cover posting the question: WHEN IS RAP 2 VIOLENT? In 1992, conservative interest groups and riled police associations pressured Warner Bros. Records to delete "Cop Killer" from Ice-T's *Body Count* album (subsequently, Warner's separated itself from Ice-T). And in 1995, moralist activists William Bennett and C. DeLores Tucker succeeded in pressuring Warner's to break the label's ties with Interscope Records, due to Interscope's support of a handful of hardcore rap artists—including Tupac Shakur. You can almost hear Bennett and Tucker preparing their next line of argument: "Look what has come from the depraved world of rap: real-life murder on the streets! It's time to stop the madness." It isn't altogether unlikely that such a campaign might have some effect—at least on wary major labels. Already, according to reports in various newspapers and trade magazines, some record executives are questioning whether any further associations with rap and its bad image will be worth the political heat that labels will have to face.

It is true, of course, that certain figures in the rap community have taken their inflammatory rhetoric and violent posturing to an insane, genuinely deadly level. It is also saddening and horrible to witness such lethal rivalry between so many young men with such innovative talents—especially when these artists and producers share the sort of common social perspective that should bring them together. Death Row and Bad Boy could have a true and positive impact on black America's political abilities—but that can't happen if the companies seek merely to increase their own standing by tearing away at perceived-enemy black opponents. From such actions, no meaningful or valuable victories are to be had.

At the same time, there's nothing meaningful or valuable to be gained by censuring hardcore rap—or at least that course would offer no real solutions to the very real problems that much of the best (and worst) rap signifies. For that matter, it would only undermine much of rap's considerable contribution to popular culture. Rap began as a means of black self-expression in the early 1980s, and as it matured into the wide-ranging art form of hip-hop, it also became a vital means of black achievement and invention. In the process, rap began to report on and reveal many social realities and attitudes that most other arts and media consistently ignored—that is, rap gave voice and presence to truths that almost no other form of art or reportage was willing to accommodate. Works like N.W.A.'s "Fuck tha Police" and *Niggaz4Life* may have seemed shocking to some observers, but N.W.A. didn't invent the resentment and abuse that they sang about. Nor did Ice-T, Ice Cube, or the Geto Boys invent the ghetto-rooted gang warfare and drive-by shootings that they sometimes rapped about. These conditions and dispositions existed long before rap won popular appeal (also long before the explosive L.A. riots of 1992), and if hardcore rap were to disappear tomorrow, that state of affairs would still exist.

What disturbed so many about rap—what it is actually deemed guilty for—is how vividly and believably it gave force to the circumstances that the music's lyrics and voices illuminated. It wasn't pleasant to hear about murderous rage and sexist debasement—to many, in fact, it came across as actual threat. As one journalist-author friend told me when I recommended that he hear Snoop Doggy Dog's *Doggystyle:* "I don't buy records from people who want to kill me." Interestingly, such music fans didn't seem to brandish the same scrupulous distaste when rock groups like the Rolling Stones, the Sex Pistols, the Clash, and several others also sang about murder, violence, rage, and cultural havoc.

Tupac Shakur, like many other rappers, intoned about a world that he either lived in or witnessed—in Shakur's case, in fact, there was a good deal less distance between lyrics and life than is the case with most pop music figures. Sometimes, Shakur saw clearly the causes for his pain and anger and aspired to rise above being doomed by that delimitation; sometimes, he succumbed to his worst predilections. And far too often he participated in actions that only spread the ruin: He was involved in at least two shootings, numerous vicious physical confrontations, several rancid verbal assaults, and was convicted and served time for sexual abuse. In the end, perhaps Shakur's worst failing was to see too many black men and women with backgrounds similar to his as his real and mortal enemies.

But listen to Tupac Shakur before you put his life away. You will hear the story of a man who grew up feeling as if he didn't fit into any of the worlds around him—feeling that he had been pushed out from not only the white world, but also the black neighborhoods that he grew up in. You will also hear the man's clear intelligence and genius: his gifts for sharp, smart, funny perceptions, and for lyrical and musical proficiency and elegance. And, of course, you will hear some downright ugly stuff—threats, rants, curses, and admitted memories that would be too much for many hearts to bear. Mainly, though, you hear the tortured soul-searching of a man who grew up with and endured so much pain, rancor, and loss that he could never truly overcome it all, could never turn his troubled heart rightside up, despite all his gifts and all the acceptance he eventually received.

In case anybody wants to dismiss this man's reality too readily, consider this: We are experiencing a time when many of our leaders are telling us that we are vulnerable to people who live in another America—an America made up of those who are fearsome, irresponsible, lazy, or just plain bad; an America that needs to be taught hard lessons. And so we have elected to teach these others their hard lesson. In the years immediately ahead, as a result of recent political actions, something like a million kids will be pushed into conditions of poverty and all that will come with it—including some of the horrible recourses left to them. Imagine how many Tupac Shakurs will emerge from this adventure—all those smart kids, who despite whatever talents they'll possess, will not be able to overcome the awfulness of their youths, and who will end up with blood on their hands or chest, or both.

Indeed, what goes 'round comes 'round. The America we are making for others is ultimately the America we will make for ourselves. It will not be on the other side of town. It will be right outside our front doors.

ella fitzgerald:

grace over pain

*t*ime and again, in the days following Ella Fitzgerald's death in mid-June, at age seventy-eight, you heard the same assessment of what made her art great and what made it endure: She was among America's most prized jazz and pop vocalists because, unlike so many of her notable contemporaries, she sang in a voice that did not confess pain—indeed, she did not allow the emotional realities of her life to infuse or consume her craft. On the surface, this is an easy judgement to offer, and certainly not a disparaging one. It is true that Fitzgerald did not live a life that made the headlines, unlike Billie Holiday and Frank Sinatra, whose legends and whose art seemed carried along by rhythms born of darkness and despair. It is also true that, whereas Holiday found a personal release in the expression of other writers' material, and Sinatra understood the emotional fiber of a lyric better than any other vocalist of the century, Fitzgerald seemed virtually to purge personal considerations from her singing in favor of exalting the purity of melodic composition itself. She was often called an instrumentalist who *sang*—whose entire attention was given to form, tone, mellifluence, and a brilliant ability to improvise on how those elements mixed with a song's cadence and a band's beat. Listening to Ella, many fans got caught up in the pure joy of her ingenuity and balance, and because those things were such a wonder to hear, it did not appear that anguish might be a part of what had shaped her creativity.

Still, there was real pain—possibly even horror—in Ella Fitzgerald's early life, and it almost certainly played a decisive part in fashioning her artistry. She was born in Newport News, Virginia, in 1917, the child of a common-law marriage. She never knew her father—he left the family while she was an infant—and her mother died when Ella was a young teenager. That was when her true troubles began. According to a 1996 *New York Times* article by Nina Bernstein, Fitzgerald was abused by her stepfather following her mother's death, and at age fifteen, was taken in by an aunt in Harlem. There, Ella scavenged the neighborhood for money, running numbers for a time and helping street prostitutes avoid police searches. Eventually, she was caught by authorities and ended up in an orphanage, the New York State Training School for Girls, where, according to Bernstein's reportage, Fitzgerald—like many of the other young girls crowded into the school's decaying cottages and dark basements—was likely subject to frequent beatings by male staff members, and endured other tortures as well. According to at least one source, Fitzgerald never forgot her hatred of that experience.

But Ella also found a way to transcend—or at least to dream of transcending—some of that torment: She developed a love of pop singing and show dancing, and aspired to dance professionally in one of Harlem's many nightclubs. In 1934, she went onstage as a dancer at an amateur contest at the Apollo Theater, but when her moment in the spotlight came, she froze—too frightened to dance. Instead, she opened her mouth and sang—a rendition of Connee Boswell's "The Object of My Affection"—and she won first prize.

After that, Ella caught the attention of saxophonist Benny Carter, who had played with bandleaders Fletcher Henderson and Chick Webb. Carter pestered a reluctant Webb to give the ungainly-looking young singer a try, and after Ella won the favor of the bandleader's audiences, he arranged for her parole from the Hudson orphanage, into his custody. Fitzgerald became Webb's star attraction and co-wrote the band's biggest hit, "A-Tisket, A-Tasket." When Webb died in 1939, Ella became the band's leader for a time, and further developed her elegant swing sensibility and her remarkably lucid talent as a balladeer. In 1942, she went solo, and as jazz music changed over the years—from the fluid rhythms of swing to the complex melodic and rhythmic permutations of bop—so did Fitzgerald's style. She was one of the first singers to take the innovations of alto saxophonist Charlie Parker and trumpeter Dizzy Gillespie and apply their bebop methods to vocal improvisation. She developed a wild, gliding style of melodic extemporization and phonetic phrasing that became known as "scat" singing, and next to Billie Holiday, it established her as the most influential and admired vocalist in jazz.

It wasn't until the mid-1950s, though, that Fitzgerald began to make a major contribution to the recorded body of popular music. For several years, jazz producer Norman Granz had featured Ella in his Jazz at the Philharmonic productions—an annual tour series that featured such instrumentalists as Illinois Jacquet, Lester Young, Coleman Hawkins, and Charlie Parker playing in freewheeling improvisational jamborees. Granz came to believe that Ella's considerable prowess had been largely wasted on trite, novelty-minded material in her lengthy tenure at Decca. To offset that mistake, he set out, in 1956, on what was considered by many (including the singer herself) as a risky venture: He would pair Fitzgerald with the great songs of America's finest Tin Pan Alley, Broadway musical, and jazz composers—including Cole Porter, Irving Berlin, George and Ira Gershwin, Jerome Kern, Harold Arlen, Richard Rodgers and Lorenz Hart, Johnny Mercer, and Duke Ellington—in effect creating a massive recorded encyclopedia of American popular song. The results proved not only popular and groundbreaking (along with Sinatra's Capitol albums from this same period, the Granz-Fitzgerald recordings helped define the conceptual possibilities in the new long-player album format), but also historic in the best sense. There have been numerous other great composers of American popular music and there have been many other great interpreters of that work. But nobody outside of Fitzgerald and Granz ever set out to define an entire era's musical spirit, and managed to do so with such an epic effect. Forty years later, the series still stands as a matchless and indispensable achievement.

Ella would go on to make several other fine albums for Granz on Verve and his subsequent Pablo label, and would also join in memorable collaborations with Louis Armstrong (her most consistent vocal partner), and Frank Sinatra and Count Basie. But after the *Songbooks*—as before them—she was esteemed primarily for her prowess as a live artist. I had the pleasure of seeing Fitzgerald in concert a few times during the mid-1980s—a period in which her voice was widely regarded to be in decline, though I've often been drawn to aging singers; it is both instructive and poignant to hear how an older vocalist reconciles earned emotional wisdom with losses in tonal range and breath control. To my ears, Ella, really didn't have much to compensate for; she was, in fact, probably the most vibrant jazz vocalist I've ever watched. She could steer through such larks as "Sweet Georgia Brown" with a matchless, careening wit, wielding her springy swing sense, cheery phrasing, classical tonality, and gospel-inflected soulfulness with a dizzying aptitude. In addition, her frequent duets with her longtime bop-based guitarist partner, Joe Pass, on Duke Ellington songs—such as "Satin Doll," in which Ella wove a minor-key scat fugue around Pass' major-key harmonic patterns—were spellbinding and joyful. Clearly, she had been around this same territory many times before; she knew every melodic twist and turn with the certainty that a driver brings to his favorite homeward route. And yet, like a driver who couldn't resist kicking new life into familiar curves, she brought an impulsiveness to the material that transformed their performances into a thrilling ride for anybody within range.

In her later years, Fitzgerald was beset by increasingly debilitating physical problems—including eye cataracts, heart trouble, and diabetes. She kept performing until 1992, when the diabetes became incapacitating. In the following year, the condition led to the amputation of both her legs below the knee. After that, Ella stayed close to her home. She never sang again in public, but there was really no need. For over half a century, she expressed remarkable ideals of invention and beauty through her singing, but her voice wasn't just a pleasure to hear: It was also an amazing work of personal redemption. It is true that Ella sang in tones filled with joy, but her joy was not a simple thing—it was a joy born from her self-willed refusal to succumb to all the limitation and degradation that her childhood had known. Ella Fitzgerald's victories were all her own, and the rest of us—anybody who ever loved her or her voice—can only hope that someday, somehow, we are once again lucky enough to witness such glorious and hard-won grace in popular music.

timothy leary:

the death

of the

most dangerous man

*I*t is a late afternoon toward the end of spring, 1996. I am seated with
several other people on the floor of a bedroom in a ranch house, high up
in the hills of Benedict Canyon. Through the plate glass doors on one side of
the room, you can see the day's light starting to fade, and a breeze soughs
through the trees and bushes in the house's back yard. On the bed before
us lies a gaunt, aged man, covered in a red blanket, sleeping a restive
sleep.

We have all gathered into this room for the same purpose: We are here
to watch this man as he takes sleep's journey to death. It is not the sort of
thing that many of us have done before.

The man who is dying is Dr. Timothy Leary—one of the most controversial and influential psychologists of the last forty years, and a guiding
iconic figure of the countercultural tumult of the 1960s and 1970s. It was
Leary who, as a young promising clinical researcher, helped develop the
theory of transactional analysis—effectively changing the doctor-patient relationship in modern psychology—and it was Leary, who only a few years
later, conducted a provocative series of psychedelic experiments at Harvard

University that helped pave the way for an era of cultural and psychosocial upheaval.

But nothing Leary has done in the years since has stirred as much reaction as how he has been preparing for his death. A year and a half ago, Leary learned that he had fatal prostate cancer—and he promptly did the one thing almost nobody does in such a situation: He celebrated the news. Leary announced to family, friends, and media that he intended to explore the consciousness of dying the same way he once explored the alternative realities afforded by drugs: with daring and with humor. As time went along, though Leary's proclamations became more audacious. At one point he suggested that when the efforts of maintaining his life no longer seemed worth it, he might take one last psychedelic, drink a suicide cocktail, and have the whole affair televised on his World Wide Web site. Then, following his death, a crew of cryonics technicians would come in and freeze his body, later removing and preserving his brain. Needless to say, these sort of hints have attracted a fair amount of media interest and have also stirred disdain and criticism from various quarters—even from a few right-to-death advocates who felt Leary wasn't taking dying somberly enough. "They'd have me suffer in silence," he once told me, "so I can save them the pain."

But when all is said and done, Leary is *not* dying outrageously. Rather, he is dying quietly and bravely, surrounded by people he loves and who love him.

Even as he is dying, though, he is still Timothy Leary, and he still has something to say.

Around 6:30 in the evening he wakes, blinks, wincing momentarily in pain. He looks around him, seeing familiar people, including his stepson, Zachary Leary, and his former wife, Rosemary, who once helped him escape a California state prison and flee the United States. He winks at Rosemary, then—looking at the rest of his visitors—says: "Why?"

He smiles, tilts his head, then says: "Why *not*?"

A couple of people in the room laugh and repeat the phrase back to him.

It goes on like that for a few minutes, Leary saying "Why not?" over and over, in different inflections, sometimes funny, sometimes sad. At one point he says, *"Esperando"*—Spanish for: "Waiting." A few moments later, after another litany of "why nots," he will say, "Where's the proof?" And still later: "Go now."

He looks back to Rosemary and mouths: "I love you," and she mouths the same back to him. Finally, barely above a whisper, he says "Why?" twice more, then drifts back into his heavy sleep.

I FIRST MET Timothy Leary only a few weeks before his death. I approached him nervously.

Like many of the people I knew who came of age in the 1960s, I had been influenced by Leary's spirit and by his teachings. As a result I had taken psychedelics—mainly mescaline and LSD—with the idea that I might see visions that would change my life, and once or twice, I guess that's what happened. I remember one night I went looking for God (a required acid activity at some point or another) and came back realizing that God was indeed dead—or that at least if God was a divine power that might judge and condemn us for our frailties and desires and madnesses, then he was dead in my own heart and conscience. Exit God. Hasn't been seen since.

Another time, I took acid not long after a brother of mine had died following surgery (I know: not such a good idea), and I plunged into what was called (appropriately, I decided) a bad trip. That night I saw the death of my lineage—the deaths of my ancestors, the deaths of my parents and brothers, the deaths of the children I had not yet had (and still have not had), and, of course, the death of myself. I sat in a dark-red oversized chair that night and watched death move before me and in and out of my being, and I gripped tight to the arms of that chair until the morning came. It was the only sunrise I have ever been happy to see. I was not the same for days after. Maybe I was not ever the same again.

That was 1971, and it was the last time I took acid. It wasn't that I didn't like the psychedelic experience—I loved it and had much wonderful fun with it over the years. It's just that I didn't fancy the idea of running into death any more than necessary.

And so when I went to see Leary the first time, I wasn't sure what I was getting into. I was fascinated by his history and had things I wanted to ask him, but there was this problem: The man was dying, and that meant getting close to death.

You could say I was unprepared for what I found. Death had already been welcomed into Timothy Leary's house, and it was being teased relentlessly, even joyfully. The place, in fact, was full of life. About a dozen staff members and friends, most of them in their twenties—were in and out of the house constantly. Some of them—a crew called Retina Logic—were busy working in the garage on Leary's web site. It was a cause that was close to Leary's heart: He planned to have all his writings and various memoirs stored on it in perpetuity, and he was thinking of maybe even dying there, on an Internet telecast. Other house regulars, such as Trudy Truelove and Vicki

Marshall, were busy making Leary's schedule for him, slating him for a steady stream of interviews, visits with friends, dinner parties, and rock & roll concerts. Clearly, death did not hold the upper hand in this house—at least not yet.

As I waited for Leary in his front room—full of brightly colored art pieces—I noticed a contraption in the corner alongside his large glass patio doors. It was the cryonics coffin he was supposed to be placed in at the hour of his death. His blood would later be drained and replaced with antifreeze compounds, so that his brain might be preserved. It might have been a creepy thing to stumble across, except it was actually sort of comical. Somebody had draped it with Christmas lights and plastic toys, and a Yoda mask had been placed on the coffin's head pillow.

Leary entered the room seated in his motorized wheelchair. He was pretty adept with the thing, able to make sharp, quick turns and wiggle his way in and out of tight spots, though sometimes he would collide head-on with his big, beautiful golden retriever, Bo, who's blind as a bat. Bo wandered Leary's house and yard constantly, bumping into tables, doors, people, trees—a sweet, majestic Zen-style guard dog.

I learned quickly that it was almost impossible to conduct anything resembling a linear interview with Leary. It had nothing to do with his temperament. I found him always cheerful, funny, and eager to talk. But he was easily distracted. He'd break off suddenly to focus on whatever was happening around him or to gaze appreciatively at the short skirts that one or two of the women around him wore. "I'm senile," he told me on that first visit, "and I make it work for me." Some of the distraction, I suspect, was the by-product of the steady stream of pain-killers and euphorics that he availed himself of—including morphine patches, marijuana biscuits, Dilaudid tablets, glasses of wine, and balloons of nitrous oxide, his seeming favorite. I was glad he had the stuff. In those moments when I saw him doubled over, cringing in pain, I could only imagine how much worse it might have been without his calmatives.

Other days, I found him completely lucid and focused. One afternoon we were talking about, well, death. I had been telling him about my last acid trip. He winked at me and laughed. "But of course," he said. "Everybody says it's a dying, *death* experience. If you don't die, you didn't get your money's worth from your dealer. Dying was built right into it. Why do you think we were using the Tibetan Book of the Dead as our guiding text?"

I understood then that I was talking with a man who had already died many times over his years. It's like he said: that was one of acid's core truths. It could take you into all kinds of deaths—deaths of ego, deaths of misconceptions—and you could then walk back alive. More or less.

I asked him what he thought real death would be like.

He reached over to his nitrous tank, filled a large black balloon, and sat quietly for a few moments. "I don't think of it," he said, looking a little surprised at his own answer. "I mean, yes, every now and then, I go: 'Shit!' You know, every now and then. The other night I was looking around and I thought, 'Good God, my friends here—their lives have been changed by this. The *enormity* of it.' But I just take it as the natural thing to do."

He took a sip from his balloon, and seemed to be looking off into his own thoughts. "It's true that I've been looking forward to it for a long time," he said. "The two minutes between body death and brain death, the two to thirteen minutes there while your brain is still alive—*that's* the territory. That's the unexplored area that fascinates me. So I'm kind of looking forward to that."

Leary stopped talking for a moment, clenching at his stomach, his face crumpled in pain. After several seconds, he gained his breath and returned to his balloon.

"The worst that can happen," he said, his voice husky from the nitrous, "is that nothing happens, and at least that's, um, interesting. I'll just go, 'Oh, shit! Back to the Tibetan score card!' But yes, it's an experiment that I've been looking forward to for a long, long time. After all, it's the ultimate mystery."

TIMOTHY LEARY was fond of pointing out that the probable date of his conception was January 17, 1920: the day after the start of Prohibition—the official beginning of America's troubled attempts to regulate intoxicants and mind-altering substances in this century. Born in Springfield, Massachusetts, on October 22, 1920, Leary was the only child of his Irish-American parents. His father, Timothy—also known as Tote—had been an officer at West Point and later became a fairly successful dentist who spent most of his earnings on alcohol. In 1934, when Timothy was thirteen, Tote got severely drunk one night and abandoned his family. Timothy would not see him again for twenty-three years. In the most recent (and best) of his autobiographies, *Flashbacks* (1983, Tarcher/Putnam), Leary wrote: "I have always felt warmth and respect for this distant male-man who special-delivered me. During the thirteen years we lived together he never stunted me with expectations." But his father also served as a "model of the loner," and for all his charming and gregarious ways, Leary would have trouble in his life maintaining intimate relations with family members—a problem that would not disappear until his last several years.

By contrast, Leary's mother, Abigail, was a beautiful but dour woman who was often disappointed by what she saw as her son's laxity and recklessness. In her own way, though, she also served as a model. In *Flashbacks,* Leary wrote: "I determined to seek women who were exactly the opposite to Abigail in temperament. Since then, I have always sought the wildest, funniest, most high-fashion, big-city girl in town."

For years, Leary seemed prone to the wayward life that his mother feared so much. He studied at Holy Cross College, West Point, and the University of Alabama and had serious problems at each establishment (in fact, he was more or less driven out of West Point for his role in a drunken spree), though he finally received a bachelor's degree during his Army service in World War II. Then his life seemed to take a turn. In 1944, while working as a clinical psychologist in Butler, Pennsylvania, Leary fell in love with and married a woman named Marianne. After the war, the couple moved to California's Bay Area, and had two children, Susan and Jack. It was at this point that Leary's career began to show some promise. In 1950, he earned a doctorate in psychology from the University of California at Berkeley, and over the next several years, along with a friend and fellow psychologist, Frank Barron, Leary conducted some research that yielded a remarkable discovery. He and Barron were interested in proving just how effective psychotherapy was. Instead, by testing a wide range of subjects over an extensive period they learned that one third of the patients who received therapy got better, one third got worse, and one third stayed the same. In essence, Leary and Barron proved that psychotherapy—at least in its conventional applications—couldn't really be proven to work. Leary wanted to discover what *would* work—what methods might provide people with a genuine healing moment or growth experience. He began exploring the idea of group therapy as a possible viable solution, and he also started developing a theory of existential-transactional analysis that was later popularized in psychiatrist Eric Berne's *Games People Play.*

By the mid-1950s, Leary was teaching at Berkeley and had been appointed director of Psychological Research at the Kaiser Foundation in Oakland. He had also produced a book, *The Interpersonal Diagnosis of Personality,* which would enjoy wide-ranging praise and influence. But behind all the outward success, Leary's life was headed for a cataclysm. After the birth of Susan, in 1947, Timothy's wife, Marianne, went through a bad bout of postpartem depression, and became increasingly withdrawn from the world and, according to Timothy, from her husband and family. As time went along, both Marianne and Timothy began drinking heavily and fighting regularly. The source of their arguments was often the same: For two years, Leary had been conducting an affair with a friend's wife at a rented apart-

ment on Berkeley's Telegraph Avenue. The affair, combined with the drinking, the quarreling, and Marianne's depression, became increasingly painful
for her.

On a Saturday morning in October 1955—on Timothy Leary's thirty-
fifth birthday—he awoke to find himself alone in bed. He stumbled around
the house, groggy from a hangover, calling Marianne's name. A few minutes
later he found her inside the family's car, in a closed garage, with the motor
running and exhaust clouding around her. She was already cold to the touch:
Leary called to his startled children, who were standing in the driveway, to
run to the nearby firehouse for help, but it was too late. Marianne had
withdrawn for the last time.

Leary's hair turned gray within a short time.

"He took a lot of the blame on himself," says Frank Barron, his research
partner at the time. "After that, Tim was looking for things that would be
more transformative, that would go deeper than therapy. He was looking,
more or less, for answers."

By the end of the 1950s, Leary had quit his posts at Berkeley and the
Kaiser Foundation, and moved with his two children to the southern coast of
Spain. Though he was working on a new manuscript, *The Existential Transaction*, he was, by his own description, in a "black depression," and felt at a loss
about both his past and his future. In January 1959, in Torremolinos, he later
wrote that he went through his first thorough breakdown and breakthrough.
One afternoon, he suddenly fell into a strange feverish illness. His face grew
so swollen with water blisters that his eyelids were forced shut and encrusted
with a dried pus. Over the next few days, the disease got worse: His hands
became paralyzed and he couldn't walk. One night, he sat awake for hours in
the darkness of his hotel room, and after a while, he began to smell his own
decay. In his book *High Priest*, he described it as his first death: "I slowly let
every tie to my old life slip away. My career, my ambitions, my home. My
identity. The guilts. The wants.

"With a sudden snap, all the ropes of my social life were gone. I
was a thirty-eight-year-old male animal with two cubs. High, completely
free."

The next morning, the illness had abated. Timothy Leary was about to
be reborn.

IN THE SPRING of 1959, Leary was living with his children in Florence,
Italy, when Frank Barron, his old friend, paid a visit. Barron brought with

him two bits of information. First, during a recent research trip to Mexico, he had located some of the rare "sacred mushrooms" that had been alleged to provide hallucinations and visions to ancient Aztec priests, and the holy men of various Indian tribes in Latin America. Back at his home in Berkeley, Barron had eaten the mushrooms—and had a full-blown, William Blake–quality mystical experience. He thought that perhaps these mushrooms might be the elusive means to psychological metamorphosis that he and Leary had been seeking for years. Leary was put off by his friend's story, and, as he later wrote, "warned him against the possibility of losing his scientific credibility if he babbled this way among our colleagues."

Barron's other news was more mundane but of greater appeal to Leary: The director of the Harvard Center for Personality Research, Professor David McClelland, was on sabbatical in Florence and would probably be willing to interview Leary for a teaching post. Leary visited McClelland the next day and explained his emerging theories of existential psychology. McClelland listened and read Leary's manuscript on the subject, then said: "What you're suggesting . . . is a drastic change in the role of the scientist, teacher, and therapist. Instead of processing subjects, students, and patients by uniform and recognized standards, we should take an egalitarian or information-exchange approach. Is that it?" Leary said, yes, that's what he had in mind. McClelland hired him on the spot. "There's no question," he said, "that what you're advocating is going to be the future of American psychology. You're spelling out front-line tactics. You're just what we need to shake things up at Harvard."

Leary began his career at the Harvard Center for Personality Research in early 1960. That summer, he took his children on vacation to Cuernavaca, Mexico. Life, for the first time in several years, felt rewarding. Things were good at Harvard. Leary was enjoying his research and teachings, and was also enjoying the esteem of his colleagues. One day, an anthropologist friend stopped by the villa where Leary was staying. The friend—like Barron—had been seeking the region's legendary sacred mushrooms, and asked if Leary would be willing to try some. Leary was reminded of Barron's statement—that perhaps mushrooms could be the key to the sort of psychological trans-formation they had been searching for—and his curiosity got the better of him. A week later, he found himself staring into a bowl of ugly, foul-smelling black mushrooms. Reluctantly, he chewed on one, washed back its terrible taste with some beer, and waited for the much-touted visions to come. They came, hard and beautiful—and in the next few hours, Leary's life changed powerfully and irrevocably. "I gave way to delight, as mystics have for centu-ries. . . ." he wrote in *Flashbacks*. "Mystics come back raving about higher levels of perception where one sees realities a hundred times more beautiful and meaningful than the reassuringly familiar scripts of normal life. . . . We discover abruptly that we have been programmed all these years, that everything we accept as reality is just social fabrication."

Leary decided that mushrooms could be the tool to reprogram the brain. If used under the right kind of supervision, he thought, they could free an individual from painful self-conceptions and stultifying social archetypes, and might prove the means to the transformation of human personality and behavior, for as far as individuals were willing to go. It took some work, but Leary persuaded Harvard to allow him to order a supply of psilocybin—the synthesized equivalent of the active ingredient in the magic mushrooms—from the Swiss firm Sandoz Pharmaceuticals. Leary also joined forces with Barron, who had been invited by McClelland to spend a year teaching at Harvard, to help him devise and administer what would become known as the "Harvard Drug Research Program." In that strange and unlikely moment in educational and psychological history, the seeds of a movement were born that would transfigure not just Leary's life, but the social dynamics of modern America for years and years to come.

LEARY, OF COURSE, was not the first psychologist or modern philosopher to explore the potential effect of psychedelics—which is the term that had been given to thought-altering hallucinogenic drugs. The respected British author Aldous Huxley had already written two volumes on the subject, *The Doors of Perception* and *Heaven and Hell,* and other philosophers and psychiatrists, including Gerald Heard, Sidney Cohen, and Oscar Janiger (the latter's Los Angeles practice included such renown patients as Cary Grant and Anais Nin) had been working toward various modes of psychedelic therapy and had achieved some notable results in treating conditions such as neurosis and alcoholism. More notoriously, the CIA and the U.S. Army Chemical Corps had conducted covert research using powerful hallucinogens with the aim of brainwashing foreign and domestic enemies or driving them insane. But three factors set Leary's work apart. One was the incorporation of his transactional analysis theories into the overall experimental model: Therapists would not administer drugs to patients and then sit by and note their reactions but would, in fact, engage in the drug state along with the subjects. Another element was Leary's implementation of an environmental condition that became known as "set and setting": If you prepared the drug taker with the proper mindset and provided reassuring surroundings, then you increased the likelihood that the person might achieve a significant opportunity for a healthy psychological reorganization. But the final component that set Leary apart from all other psychedelic researchers was simply Leary himself—his intense charisma, confidence, passion, anger, and indomitability. He was a man set ablaze by his calling—and though that fieriness would sometimes lead him into a kind of living purgatory, it also emblazoned him as a real force in modern history.

For the first two years, things went well with Leary's Harvard experiments. Along with Barron and other researchers, Leary administered varying doses of psilocybin to several dozen subjects, including graduate students. He also gave the drug to prisoners and divinity students, with noteworthy results: The prisoners' recidivism rate was cut dramatically, and the divinity students, for the first time in their lives, had what they described as true spiritual experiences. In addition, Leary made two important contacts outside the university: Aldous Huxley and poet Allen Ginsberg (the latter had given the Beat literary movement its most exciting moment with his revolutionary poem "Howl"). With Huxley, Leary probed into the metaphysical fine points of the psilocybin mind state and debated whether psychedelics should remain the property of a small, select group of poets, artists, philosophers, and doctors, who would take the insights they learned from the drug and use them for the benefit of humanity and psychology. With Ginsberg, though, Leary settled the debate. Like Huxley, Ginsberg was convinced that it was indeed a keen idea to share the drug with writers and artists—and in fact arranged for Leary to do so with Robert Lowell, William Burroughs, Thelonious Monk, and Jack Kerouac, among others. But Ginsberg also believed in what became known as "the egalitarian ideal": If psychedelics had any real hope of enriching humankind, then they should be shared with more than just an aristocracy of intellectuals and aesthetes. Leary came to agree—fervently. Psychedelics, he believed, could be a way of empowering people to inquire into and transmute their own minds, and he suspected that probably the people who were most open to such an experience, who could benefit from it the most, were the young.

In the fall of 1961, Frank Barron returned to his job at Berkeley, and Leary found a new chief ally: a good-humored and ambitious assistant professor named Richard Alpert, who had a penchant for fine clothes, valuable antiques, and high living. From the beginning, Alpert and Leary shared a special bond. "I had never met a mind like Tim's," says Alpert. "He was like a breath of fresh air because he was raising questions from philosophical points of view. I was absolutely charmed by that. And there was a way in which our kind of symbiosis worked—our chemistry of the Jewish and the Irish, or the responsible, grounded, solid person and the wild, creative spirit. I thought that I was at Harvard by shrewd politicking rather than by intellect, therefore

I didn't expect anything creative to come out of me. And then I found that Timothy was freeing me from a whole set of values."

But for some others at Harvard, it seemed as though Tim might be freeing up just a few too many values. Some professors began to complain that Leary and Alpert's drug project was attracting too many graduate students, therefore detracting from the potential of other research agendas. Beyond that, some found the whole thing too unsavory—the very idea of giving students drugs that apparently took them out of reality, under the auspices of the university. Also, McClelland was growing uncomfortable with what was seen as the increasingly "religious" overtones of the enterprise. Leary, Alpert, and others began touting once obscure Eastern sacred texts, such as the Tibetan Book of the Dead, the Bhagavad-Gita, and Zen Buddhist scripture. What was Leary doing, McClelland wanted to know, advancing the values of societies that had been backward for hundreds of years?

At the insistence of several professors, McClelland scheduled an open meeting in the spring of 1962 to debate the merits of continuing the drug project. The day before the event, McClelland called Alpert into his office. " 'Dick, we can't save Timothy,' " Alpert recalls McClelland saying. " 'He's too outrageous. But we can save you. So just shut up at tomorrow's meeting.' " Alpert gave McClelland's advice some thought. "Being a Harvard professor," he says, "gives you a lot of keys to the kingdom, to play the way you want to play. Society is honoring you with that role."

The meeting turned out to be more like a prosecution session than a discussion. Two professors in particular, Herbert Kellman and Brendan Maher, tore into Leary with a vitriol rarely seen at Harvard meetings. They insisted that if he was to continue his project, he would have to surrender the drugs to the university's control and only administer them in the environment of a mental hospital. To Leary, it would mean retreating to the medical standard of the doctor as authority and the subject as lab rat—the same model that Leary had sworn to bring down. "Timothy was blown away by all the vehemence and vindictiveness," Alpert says. "He was, for once, speechless. At the end there was a silence in the room. And at that moment, I stood up and said, 'I would like to answer on behalf of our project.' I looked at Dave McClelland, and Dave just shrugged, and that was the beginning of the process that would result in our end at Harvard."

In 1963, in a move that made front-page news across the nation, Timothy Leary was "relieved" of his teaching duties and Richard Alpert was dismissed for having shared psilocybin with an undergraduate. (At the time Alpert and Leary were reported to be the only professors to be fired from the university in this century.) "I remember being at that press conference," says

Alpert, "surrounded by people who saw me as a loser, but in my heart, I knew we'd won."

Leary also wasn't distressed at the idea that his Harvard career was finished. He had, in fact, found a new passion. In the spring of 1962, a British philosophy student named Michael Hollingshead paid a visit to Leary and had brought with him an ominous gift. Hollingshead—who died a few years ago—is perhaps the shadiest, most mysterious figure in Leary's entire story. Alpert describes him as "a scoundrel—manipulative and immoral," and others have characterized him in even darker terms. But it was Hollingshead who first brought a jar of powdered sugar laced with LSD—an intensely psychedelic solution (in fact, the most potent chemical ever developed) whose psychoactive properties had been accidentally discovered in the 1940s by a Swiss scientist, Dr. Albert Hoffman—into Leary's home, and taunted Tim by ridiculing psilocybin as "just pretty colors," compared to the extraordinary power of LSD. Leary resisted the bait at first, as he had with the magic mushrooms, but one weekend he finally caved in. "It took about a half hour to hit," he later wrote. "And it came suddenly and irresistibly. Tumbling and spinning, down soft fibrous avenues of light that were emitted from some central point. Merged with its pulsing ray I could look out and see the entire cosmic drama. Past and future . . . My previous psychedelic sessions had opened up sensory awareness, pushed consciousness out to the membranes. . . . But LSD was something different. It was the most shattering experience of my life."

Hollingshead would come and go in Leary's life, sometimes valued, often reviled. But Hollingshead's gift, the LSD . . . that was a gift that stayed.

DESPITE THEIR FALL from Harvard, Leary and Alpert intended to continue their research into psychedelics, now focused primarily on the far more potent drug, LSD. They tried setting up a research community in Mexico, but the bad publicity of their troubles in the States resulted in their expulsion from that country. They made other attempts in a sequence of Caribbean islands and countries, with the same results. Then, in the fall of 1963, a friend and benefactor, Peggy Hitchcock, helped provide them with a sixty-four-room mansion that sat on a sprawling estate two hours up the Hudson River from Manhattan—a place called Millbrook. From 1963 to early 1967, Millbrook would serve as a philosophic-hedonistic retreat for the curious, the hip, and the defiant. Jazz musicians lived there, poets, authors, and painters visited, journalists scouted the halls; and actors and actresses flocked to the weekend parties. Some came for visions, some for the hope of an orgy, some to illuminate the voids in their souls. All of them left with an experience they never forgot.

This was a time of immense change in America's cultural and political terrain. It was, on one hand, an epoch of great dread and violence: the bloody civil rights battles, the assassination of President John F. Kennedy, and the rising anger over the war in Vietnam made it plain that America had quickly become a place of high risks. At the same time, youth culture was beginning to create for itself a sense of identity and empowerment that was unprecedented. The new music coming from Bob Dylan, the Beatles, the Motown and Southern soul artists, and San Francisco bands like the Grateful Dead and Jefferson Airplane only deepened the idea that an emerging generation was trying to live by its own rules and integrity, and was feeling increasingly cut off from the conventions and privileges of the dominant mainstream culture. More and more, drugs were becoming a part of youth's sense of empowerment—a means of staking out a consciousness apart from that of the "straight world," a way of participating in private, forbidden experiences.

It was during this time of strange possibilities (and the *fear* of strange possibilities) that LSD began to become the subject of a frenzied social concern. Despite the best efforts of such qualified experts as Frank Barron and Oscar Janiger, LSD was seen as a major threat to the nation's young, and therefore to America's future. Newspaper and television reports were full of sensationalistic accounts of kids trying to fly off buildings or ending up in emergency rooms, howling at the horrors of their own newly found psychoses. The level of hysteria drove Leary nuts. "[B]ooze casualties were epidemic," he wrote in *Flashbacks*, "so the jaded press paid no attention to the misadventures of one drunk. Their attitude was different with psychedelic drugs. Only one out of every thousand LSD users reported a negative experience, yet the press dug up a thousand lurid stories of bark-eating Princeton grads."

Nevertheless, for some in the psychiatric community, Leary had become part of the problem. By the nature of his flamboyance and his disdain for the medical model, they felt he had singlehandedly given psychedelics a bad name, and that he was endangering the chance for further valid research. "It was easy," says Frank Barron, "for Tim to say, 'There are people who are going to have psychoses under these circumstances; if they have that within them they should let it out.' These are brave words, but Tim and I had plush training in psychology. We had personal analysis. We were well prepared. But if you have an adolescent in the middle of an identity crisis and you give him

LSD, he can be really shaken. And I think that's where some of the more serious casualties occurred."

Indeed, Leary became indelibly identified with what *Time* magazine termed the "LSD Epidemic," and he was under fire from several quarters. When he appeared before the 1966 Senate hearings on LSD, he was held up to sustained ridicule by Senator Ted Kennedy. It was then, Leary realized, that—before much longer—LSD would be declared illegal and its users would be criminalized. At the same time, things in his personal life were going through momentous change. In late 1964, he married Nena von Schelbrugge. By the time the couple returned from their honeymoon a few months later, both the marriage and Millbrook were in trouble. Leary felt that Alpert had let the place get out of hand. The two friends argued over various grievances—including Leary's apparent discomfort with Alpert's homosexuality—and Alpert ended up cast out from Millbrook and, for a time, from Leary's life. (Alpert went on to change his name to Baba Ram Dass and became one of America's most respected teachers of Eastern disciplines. In time, the rift between him and Leary healed, but they were never again the fast partners they'd once been.)

Then, in the summer of 1965, Leary became close to a woman named Rosemary Woodruff, whom he eventually married in late 1967. The romance with Rosemary would prove to be perhaps the most meaningful of Leary's life, but it would also prove to be the one most beset by difficulties. During the week following Christmas 1965, Tim and Rosemary shut down Millbrook for the season and set out, along with Leary's children, in a station wagon, bound for a Mexico vacation. The couple had thoughts of changing their lives: Rosemary had hopes that perhaps they would have a child of their own, and Timothy entertained notions of returning to his studies and writings. At the Mexican border, however, they were denied entrance, and as they attempted to reenter America near Laredo, they were ordered out of the car. They were searched and a matron found a silver box with marijuana in Susan Leary's possession; she was then eighteen. Leary didn't hesitate. "I'll take responsibility for the marijuana," he said. The consequences of that moment reverberated through Leary's life for years. He was arrested for violating the marijuana laws in one of the most conservative jurisdictions in the nation. When his lawyer advised him to repent before the judge, Leary said he didn't know what the word meant. Eventually, he was given a thirty-year sentence and a $30,000 fine—the longest sentence ever imposed for possession of marijuana. Susan got five years. In 1969, the U.S. Supreme Court overturned the conviction because Leary had been tried under antiquated tax-violation laws. The Laredo prosecutor simply retried Leary for illegal possession and sentenced him to ten years.

Timothy Leary quickly became a national symbol for both sides of the drug-law dispute, and he did his best to rise to the occasion with wit and grace, but also with a certain recklessness. While free during his appeal of the Laredo conviction, he gave lectures and interviews around the country about drugs. He was invited as an honored guest to the Gathering of the Tribes festival, in San Francisco's Golden Gate Park, and he and Rosemary sang and clapped along at John Lennon and Yoko Ono's recording session for "Give Peace a Chance." He also recorded his own album of chants with Jimi Hendrix, Buddy Miles, Stephen Stills, and John Sebastian as sidemen. It all made for heady days and high nights, but it also made Leary the most obvious target for the country's rising mood of anger about drugs. President Richard Nixon told the American people that Timothy Leary was "the most dangerous man alive," and the directive couldn't be more plain: Both Leary and his philosophies should be brought down.

And, more or less, that's what happened. Back in New York, a local assistant district attorney named G. Gordon Liddy organized a raid on Millbrook. The charges were soon dismissed, but another raid followed—and those charges stuck. The raids had the desired effect of finishing Millbrook for good. Leary moved Rosemary and his family to Laguna Beach, California, but the day after Christmas 1968, he was arrested again for marijuana possession, this time along with Rosemary and his son Jack. (Leary always claimed that the joints had been planted by the arresting officer.) At the trial in January 1970, Rosemary and Jack were given probation, but Timothy was found guilty and sentenced to ten years. But this time the judge did something unexpected and rather extraordinary: Declaring Leary a menace to society and angrily waving a recent *Playboy* interview with the ex–Harvard professor, the judge ordered Leary to jail immediately, without an appeal bond.

Leary was forty-nine years old, and his future appeared certain. He was going to spend the rest of his life in jail for the possession of a small amount of marijuana that—even in the furor of the 1960s—rarely netted most offenders more than a six-month sentence.

U PON ENTERING the California State Prison at Chino, Leary was administered an intelligence test, to determine where he should be placed within the state's prison strata. The test happened to be based on psychological standards that Leary himself had largely authored during his groundbreaking work in the 1950s. He knew how to make it work for him. He marked all the answers that, in his own words, would make him seem "normal, nonimpulsive, docile, conforming." As a result, he was transferred to California Men's Colony–West at San Luis Obispo—a minimum-security prison.

On the evening of September 12, 1970, following a carefully mapped plan that depended on exact timing, Leary methodically made his way from his cellblock along a complex maze of twists and turns into a prison yard that was regularly swept by a spotlight. Dodging the light, he crossed the yard to a tree, climbed it, and then dropped down to a roof top covering one of the prison's corridors. He crept along until he came to a cable that stretched to a telephone pole outside the walls of the jail. Wrapping his arms and legs around the cable, he began to shimmy its length until, only a third of the way across, he stopped, exhausted, gasping for breath, barely able to keep his grasp. A patrol car passed underneath him. "I wanted Errol Flynn and out came Harold Lloyd," he wrote in *Flashbacks*. "I felt very alone. . . . There was no fear—only a nagging embarrassment. Such an undignified way to die, nailed like a sloth on a branch!" Then, some hidden reserves of strength and desire kicked in, and Leary grappled his way to the outside pole and descended to freedom. A couple of miles up the road, he was met by a car driven by sympathetic activists in the radical underground—members of the Weathermen, Leary later implied—and in a few days, he was out of the state, then out of the country.

A few weeks later, Timothy and Rosemary surfaced in Algiers, Algeria, where they had been offered asylum and protection by Eldridge Cleaver and other members of the Black Panther Party. Cleaver and his fellow Panthers had fled the United States after a 1968 shoot-out with policemen in Oakland and had been recognized by the socialist-Islamic Algerians as the American government-in-exile. At first Leary was excited at the idea of setting up a radical coalition abroad with Cleaver, but he soon found Algiers a grim, prudish town with little tolerance for culture or fun. The Learys also soon ran into trouble with Cleaver. Writing in *Rolling Stone* in the spring of 1971, Cleaver declared that it had become necessary for the Panthers to place Timothy and Rosemary Leary under house arrest in Algiers, claiming that Leary had become a danger to himself and to his hosts with his uncurbed appetite for LSD. Such drug use, Cleaver stated, would have no positive purpose in trying to bring about true revolutionary change—and what's more, he thought it had damaged Leary's once brilliant mind. "To all those who look to Dr. Leary for inspiration or even leadership," Cleaver wrote, "we want to say that your god is dead because his mind has been blown by acid."

Leary, for his part, claimed that Cleaver simply wanted to flex some muscle, and to demonstrate to his guests what it was like to live under oppression and bondage.

Looking back at the episode, Rosemary still feels a great sadness that the experiment between Leary and the Panthers failed. "That's always haunted me," she says, "the idea that we had the possibility for some kinship. I think Eldridge and the others wanted us to recognize the experiences that had brought them there, and how different it was from the experiences that they thought had brought *us* there. I mean, we were all exiles, but Tim and I were exiles from a different kind of America. They recognized that we weren't going to be killed in any confrontation with the law. The Black Panthers, though, *had* been killed. They'd been wiped out, slaughtered. We were so naive, so stupid. At the same time, we were frightened. Eldridge was very dictatorial. He kept me away from the women and the children, and then the Panthers threatened us and kept us in a dirty room in an ugly place for three days. So what were we to do?"

The only thing they could do: flee. Next stop: Geneva, Switzerland, where they enjoyed a short respite until the Swiss arrested Leary after the U.S. government filed extradition papers. Leary was in the Lausanne prison for six weeks—"the best prison in the world," he once told me, "like a class hotel"—until the Swiss, following the petitions of Allen Ginsberg and others, refused the Nixon administration's requests for deportation. By this time, though, all the years of harassment, fear, flight, and incarceration, plus the lost opportunities for any stable and real family life of their own, had taken a toll on Rosemary, and she decided to part with Leary. "I think I just had to consider that fate was really intervening in our lives, playing a role," she says, "and that we weren't going to have this prosaic family life. I had always felt it was my job to protect Tim—that seemed to be the role that I played. But Tim . . . he was Sisyphus: He was the mythic hero chained to the rock, and he was always going to be pushing that rock. He seemed to thrive on notoriety. He'd become a celebrity during those years, and that carries its own weight with it. It's not the lifestyle *I* would have chosen. I'd always wanted the quiet life, and with Tim, there simply wasn't the possibility for it.

"Did I regret having chosen Tim to love? I don't think so. He was always the most interesting person. Everyone else seemed boring, by comparison. Of course, by the time I wanted boredom, it was too late."

By late 1972, Leary had become a man without a country, and without recourse. The United States was exerting sizable pressure on foreign governments not to harbor the former professor—indeed, an Orange County D.A. announced he had indicted Leary on nineteen counts of drug trafficking, branding him as the head of the largest drug-smuggling enterprise in the world—and though the Swiss would still not extradite him, they would also not extend him asylum. Accompanied by his new girlfriend, Joanna Harcourt-Smith, Leary fled to Afghanistan, but he was arrested at the Kabul airport by an American embassy attaché and turned over to U.S. Drug Enforcement agents. He was brought back to Orange County, tried for escape, and sentenced to five years, in addition to his two previous ten-year sentences. He was also facing eleven counts from the second Millbrook bust and nineteen conspiracy counts related to his indictment as the head of a drug-smuggling outfit.

The U.S. government had succeeded in its campaign. LSD had been declared illegal and its most influential researcher and proponent had been pursued across the world, arrested, brought home, and put behind bars once again—bigger bars this time, in fact. The psychedelic movement had been shut down in a brutal way, and for decades after, Timothy Leary would be vilified for the inquiring and defiant spirit that he had helped set loose upon the 1960s. Looking back on the collapse of that experiment, writer Robert Anton Wilson, a longtime friend of Leary's and author of *The Illuminatus Trilogy*, says: "A lot of psychologists I've known over the years agreed with Leary—they acknowledged in private that LSD was an incredibly valuable tool for analyzing and effecting positive personality change in people. But these same psychologists backed off gradually as the heat from the government increased, until they all became as silent as moonlight on a tombstone. And Tim was still out there with his angry Irish temper, denouncing the government and fighting on alone.

"I don't want to discount that there are people whose lives have been destroyed by drugs," Wilson continues, "but are they the results of Timothy Leary's research, or the result of government policies? Leary's research was shut down and the media stopped quoting him a long time ago. Most people don't even understand what Leary's opinions were, or what it was he was trying to communicate. By contrast, the government's policies have been carried out for thirty years, and now we have a major drug disaster in this country. Nobody, of course, thinks it's the government's fault—they think it's Leary's for trying to prevent it, for trying to have scientific controls over the thing.

"He deserves a better legacy than that."

IN 1975, SOME nasty and frightening reports began to circulate about Timothy Leary. According to stories that appeared in *Rolling Stone* and other publications, Leary was talking to the FBI and was willing to give them information about radical activists and drug principals he had known, in exchange for his freedom. There was also a claim that he had written a letter to Rosemary—still in the underground—pleading with her to contact and cooperate with federal agents. Rosemary never answered the letter.

The rumors were hard to confirm—Leary was being moved from prison to prison on a regular basis by the FBI, and few friends saw or communicated with him for roughly a year—but even the idea had a chill effect on many of Leary's former compatriots. Allen Ginsberg, Ram Dass, Jerry Rubin, and Leary's own son, Jack, held a press conference denouncing Leary for collaborating and asserting that his testimony shouldn't be trusted by the courts.

The full truth about this matter has never been easy to uncover. In *Flashbacks*, Leary wrote that essentially he led the FBI on a wild goose chase and that nobody was imprisoned because of his statements—though he admitted that he had made declarations about certain people to a grand jury. "I think Tim played a very dangerous game with the FBI," says Robert Anton Wilson, "but as far as I know, nobody did go to prison." Says Rosemary: "Years later, I showed Tim a letter he had written me, urging me to turn myself in and lauding the minions of the law as being good, decent people. He said he didn't remember writing it. I think the truth is, he couldn't deal with it."

In any event, Leary was released from the California prison system in 1976, his reputation pretty much in tatters. Many of his old friends would no longer speak to him. "There was no question he was no longer the Tim I'd known before," says Frank Barron. "Prison doesn't improve anybody very much, and he'd suffered for it. His sense of invulnerability was gone. But he was determined to come back into the public and to reassert his mission."

Gradually, Leary rehabilitated his image. Shortly after his release, he separated from Joanna Harcourt-Smith, whom some thought had been an unfortunate influence in the whole FBI matter. He settled into Los Angeles and became a regular at Hollywood parties. In 1978, he married his fourth wife, Barbara Chase, and took her young son, Zachary, as his own. Though Timothy and Barbara would divorce fifteen years later, he would stay close to Zachary. It seemed that with Zachary, Leary found the sort of relationship that he had not been able to achieve with his son Jack—who stopped talking to Leary in 1975 and who only briefly saw him again two months before his death.

"It was a time for him to do it again," says Zachary, "and see if the whole domesticity of having a family was something really applicable to his life, and he found that it was. He was happy about that, because the sadness of his earlier family had been so great. So I think it was great for him, in his late fifties and sixties, to be a father again with a little kid, taking me to the ballparks and playing sports in the back yard. Young people—that's really what kept him going, that's what kept his theories alive. And I think that the biggest moral ground that he covered for me was communication: 'Never try and shut anything down,' he told me. I'm only starting to realize now the magnitude of the environment that I was lucky enough to grow up in. I really do consider Tim my father."

Leary went on to other interests. Primarily he became a champion of computer and communications technology, and was among the first to declare that these new developments—particularly the rapidly growing Internet—had the same sort of potential to empower creativity on a mass level and to threaten authority structures as psychedelics had once had in the 1960s.

In time, the old friends came back. Ginsberg, Ram Dass, and others made peace with the man with whom they had once shared such phenomenal adventures. "When people ask me why it is I treasure and respect Timothy," says Ram Dass, "I say it's because he taught me how to play with life rather than be played *upon* by life. That's the closest I've gotten to stating what it feels like. Timothy plays with life. People are offended by that because they think it doesn't give life its due respect. But I think it's quite a liberating thing."

In 1990, the newfound equanimity of Timothy Leary's life was shattered. His daughter, Susan Leary Martino, forty-two, had been arrested in Los Angeles for firing a bullet into her boyfriend's head as he slept. Twice she was ruled mentally unfit to stand trial. Then one morning she was found dead in her jail cell. She had tied a shoelace around her neck and hanged herself.

Some people close to Leary believe that Susan had never been the same since the Laredo arrest and trial—that she held herself to blame for her father's subsequent troubles, and that, like her mother, she had grown depressed and withdrawn over the years. Others claim that Susan had always loved her father powerfully, and that all the years and events that kept him from her—the arrests, the flights, all the many girlfriends and wives—ate away at her. Regardless of the causes, Susan's suicide hit Leary hard—a blow that many of those close to him feel he never really recovered from. "I don't think he could push that one away so easily," says Ram Dass. "I remember speaking with him on the phone and feeling a surprising vulnerability in Tim that I wasn't used to hearing."

The news of Susan's death also came as a terrible blow to Rosemary, who had been living on the East Coast under an assumed name, still a fugitive. "I'd been angry with him for a long time," she says, "but I'd been having dreams about them prior to her death, about Susan and Tim and myself in some bucolic setting with streams running and the three of us very happy. Which wasn't the case when the three of us were together. I was the wicked stepmother for most of our married life. So I knew I was being taught something, or told something, about Tim and Susan, and about my heart. And then, when she died, it was so *hard*. And I knew how hard it would be for him."

Rosemary, who hadn't spoken with Timothy or anybody close to him since 1972, called Ram Dass, who put her in touch with Tim. "We met in Golden Gate Park," she says. "It was a great romantic meeting. When I left him in Switzerland, we were quarreling, so to meet him and find that our love was still there—the love that we had for one another—was just incredible. It validated so much for me to know that about him and about myself, and to have given up the anger and the hurt that I had felt. The emotion involved in all that just opened the way for me to love Tim again."

Leary put Rosemary in touch with a lawyer and helped her resolve her fugitive status. "It was extremely easy," she says. "I had lived such a remarkable and paranoid life for so long, never sure who to trust or what to say. It was liberating to be free of all that. I just got my California driver's license with my name on it."

Rosemary began to see Tim often. She was impressed, she said, by how open his heart now seemed. But she also saw other changes. "I could tell he wasn't feeling wonderful. He'd always had an amazing constitution; I'd never known him to be ill, even with a cold." And then, around Christmas 1994, after a strenuous lecture tour, Leary was felled by a bout of pneumonia. "It was his first taste of mortality in terms of his body," says Rosemary, "and I think it was devastating for him to find himself so ill, and then not bounce back from it."

It turned out to be more than pneumonia. The doctors had determined that Leary had contracted prostate cancer, and it was inoperable. With the right treatment, they might be able to keep him alive for a year or two. Leary later told reporters he was "exhilarated" by the news. This would be the start of his greatest adventure—a conscious and loving journey into death. He called his friends—Rosemary, Ram Dass, Ken Kesey, Allen Ginsberg, and many others—and shared with them his excitement. "That's just the epitome of his personality," says his stepson Zach. "I guess it made perfect sense that he would feel that way about it. But when he was first disclosing it, I was much sadder than he was. I said, 'God, how could you *feel* like that?' But to him it was just another card in the hand—the death card. And now I have to say I've learned so much from him in these last few months."

Indeed, it seems the knowledge of his death brought out a gentle and transcendent quality in Timothy Leary. "He's more emotionally available now," says Ram Dass, "which is remarkable, because he's never handled his emotions at all. I mean, he's always been a very friendly person—fun and vibrant and stimulating, and all that—but deep emotions have been delicate to play with historically with Timothy. He's lived more on the surface of events and things rather than the slower, deeper rhythms of emotions. The last few times I saw him he was very much there, and that thrilled me. When we would look into each other's eyes, he was looking at me about death. We never said words about it, we never acknowledged it other than doing it, but it gave me the conviction that he isn't afraid of death. He knows he's going after one of the darkest secrets of the society, and it's humbled him in an interesting way."

There's also something about Leary's awareness of death's imminence that heightened his sense of play. In the last few months, there was nonstop activity around his home, and much of it was geared to fun stuff—dinners, outings to midnight rock & roll shows, around the clock visits by well-wishers and friends. "Silly silliness is being performed as a high art here," he told me one afternoon, with utter joy.

A good example of Leary's latter-day high art silliness is an event that became known as "Wheelchair Day." One day Leary decided to round up as many wheelchairs as possible, load his staff and friends into them, and hold wheelchair races on Sunset Strip, then wheel into the House of Blues, for a luncheon, designed on the model of DaVinci's *The Last Supper*. After the event, Leary was riding back to his house in the rented convertible of his friend, Internet rights activist and former Grateful Dead lyricist John Perry Barlow, with two of the young women from his staff, Trudy Truelove and Camella Grace, in the back seat. The radio was blasting as they headed west on Sunset, and Trudy and Camella were sitting on the car's trunk, goofing and making dancing gestures. Leary looked at Barlow, smiled, and shouted: "Life is good!" That was when Barlow glanced into his rear-view mirror and saw the flashing red and yellow lights of a Beverly Hills police car—and realized that the car he was driving was perhaps not entirely free of illegal substances. Shit, he thought to himself, Tim Leary's last bust.

Barlow rolled down his window and said to the officer: "I know what we were doing was wrong. But you see, my friend here is dying, and we're trying to show him a good time." Barlow later told me he'd never forget the look that Tim gave the policeman: "Caught in the act of dying like he had his hand in the cookie jar."

The officer smiled back at Leary, then turned to Trudy and Camella. "I'd be lying if I didn't say that looks like fun," he said, "but just because *he's* dying doesn't mean you should. Now get down in the seat and buckle up and I'll let you go."

When they pulled back into traffic, Leary turned to Barlow, laughed, and said: "What a fucking gift *that* was!"

NOT EVERYBODY, though, was enamored of the gallows humor of Leary and his troop.

On the night of the wheelchair-race caper, I arrived at Leary's to find an ambulance outside his house, being loaded with his cryonics coffin. It turned out that a short time before, a team from CryoCare—the outfit that was to undertake the freezing and preservation of Leary's brain upon his death— had come in to remove all their equipment.

For some time, a tension had been building up between the CryoCare representatives and Leary's crew. CryoCare felt that Leary and his staff had shown disrespect for their equipment by decorating it with lights and toys, and also believed that some people at the house had been trying to keep CryoCare's technicians away from Leary. More important, CryoCare's Mike Darwin had grown alarmed about Leary's pronouncements about his plan to commit suicide live (so to speak) on the World Wide web. Darwin did not feel that his organization (whose brochure bears the motto, MANY ARE COLD, BUT FEW ARE FROZEN) could afford to be involved in what he termed a potential crime scene, or that they should leave their equipment in a house were illegal drugs may be present or used.

For their part, the Leary folks had become increasingly put off by what they regarded as CryoCare's ghoulish interest in obtaining the head of Timothy Leary. The problem was only exacerbated when they learned that a CryoCare official who would be involved with the decapitation and freezing process, Charles Platt, had an assignment to write about the operation for

Wired magazine. (Platt had also been sending serial e-mail to various parties, expressing his disdain for the Leary staff and his impatience with Leary for not dying as soon as had been expected. "What insane will to live," he wrote in one letter.)

In any event, CryoCare's actions left Leary with a decision to make: He could either sign on quickly with another cryonics outfit, or he could accept that his death would be final—that his brain would not be preserved for some indeterminate future attempt at reamination. In the end, he decided against cryonics. "I have no real great desire to do it," he told me. "I just felt it was my duty to futurism and the process of smart dying."

Leary's decision was not a small thing for him. He once told me that he did not believe that anything human survived beyond death, and that if we possess a soul, then the soul is our mind, and the brain is the soul's home. By forgoing cryonics, Timothy Leary decided that even if he could, he would not return. His immortality, instead, would be his work and his legend, and it was his hope that those things would find an ongoing life on the World Wide web site that had become his most prized dream in his final season.

IT IS NOT LONG after this that the end came. One afternoon I had to drop something by Tim's place and we had a brief conversation. He was in the best spirits and most cogent form I'd seen him in. He told me touching stories about his relationship with John Lennon and Yoko Ono (about how Lennon had written "Come Together" for Tim when Leary was thinking about running for Governor of California, but then thought twice about it and kept it for the Beatles) and about how he had tried to warn Yoko that New York's Dakota was too risky a place—too exposed, too accessible—for a man like Lennon to live. "I wish I'd been wrong about that one," he said, looking at the large photo above his bed of himself and Rosemary with Lennon and Ono during the recording of "Give Peace a Chance." I left that day looking forward to visiting and talking with him some more.

A few days later I received a call from Zachary. "It looks like Tim is going today. You should come up soon if you want to say goodbye."

Zach later told me: "Tim just decided he couldn't live in that body any more and he wanted to get out. The key moment for him was when he went to take a shower last week and he stopped and looked at himself in the mirror, naked. That was all he needed to know. He was very clear and lucid and he looked at his body and saw it was pathetic and it was below his quality of life." That night, Leary called Zach and the house staff around him at the table and said: "Can you go on without me?"

"It was like he was asking for our permission," said Zach.

The morning that Zach called me, Tim had got out of bed and climbed into his motorized wheelchair and rode all over his ranch house. He stopped in the back yard where he sat drinking a cup of coffee, looking at the flowers that were coming to bloom in his garden. Then he said, "I'm tired. I'm going to take a nap," and wheeled back into his bedroom. A short while later his nurse summoned Zach and told him he should notify anybody who might want to see him one last time.

I sat for about an hour with several other people that afternoon and watched Leary as he slept. Occasionally he woke, smiled, took sips on the ice that the nurse gave him, and once or twice tried to say something. At one point, he opened his eyes wide and said: "Flash!"

Later, around 9 P.M., I made another visit to his bedroom. The only illumination in the room was a string of Christmas lights, on the wall above Leary's bed. Zach sat close, holding his stepfather's hand. Tim opened his eyes briefly at one point, looked at Zach, smiled, and said softly, "Beautiful."

It was the last thing Timothy Leary said.

A FEW HOURS later, around 2:30 A.M., I received another call, telling me that Tim had died at 12:45. I headed back to his house.

The lights were still dim in his bedroom. On a nearby chair sat Trudy Truelove, staring at Tim. "I've decided to stay with him until they remove him. I've decided to be his guardian."

Tim was laid on his back, dressed in white, the red blanket turned down. His mouth was wide open, frozen in his last exhaled breath. It looked as if he was calling out silently. Somebody had placed a large orange flower in his hand, its petals reaching up to his face.

Soon, the room filled with several people. We stood there for a long time in silence, until we were told that it was time to say our goodbyes. The mortuary people had come to claim Tim's corpse.

One by one, the people in the room approached Tim, some touching and kissing him, others whispering last words. When it was my turn, I went up to the bed and looked down at him. I hadn't been able to tell before, from the darkness in the room, but his eyes were wide open, and when you looked into them, it was as if they were looking back into you. I bent over, gave him my kiss, and then turned and left the room.

ONE NIGHT NOT LONG before Leary's death, I took LSD for the first time in twenty-five years. I guess I'd just grown curious after spending so much time around Tim, but I felt I also owed it to myself. I'd left psychedelics on bad terms, and that had never felt right. It was time, once again, to see what they held for me, what might be revealed after so many years.

I lay on my bed in the dark, listening to Bach's *Goldberg Variations*, and once more, death came to visit. I saw what seemed thousands of faces. They were all in agony, and then they died, and were swimming in straits of beauty and grace. Their suffering, I saw, was inevitable. And so was their dying. And so was their release. Once more I saw death move around and through me, and this time I did not try to hide from it. I laid there and cried, and somehow I felt a great comfort in what I'd seen.

I thought about this experience as I sat in Leary's bedroom at three in the morning and studied him in his death. As I implied earlier, I'd always been terrified of death—even to be near it. When I visited the funeral homes to see my father, my mother, my brother, lying in their coffins, I took short glances and got away quickly. I never touched my loved ones as they lay dead. I don't think I could have.

Sitting with Leary, I realized something had changed—and maybe it had been a gift on his part. His greatest achievement, I believe, was to ask the people he knew to face the darkest part of themselves, and to be willing to be there with them—to interact with them, to guide them—when they reached that place. I can't say whether he ever faced the darkest parts within himself in that same way—maybe it never really happened until that last day and night. And if that was the time, I'm glad there were good people there for him.

Being around Leary had taught me what nothing else had: that encountering death did not always have to be an experience of freezing horror. In those last hours, Timothy Leary could still be a good therapist.

I looked at Tim lying there in his death, his eyes hollow, the skin on his face already sinking, and I was reminded of something Rosemary once told me. It was a story about one of the last times she saw Leary before he fell ill. "I'd gone to New Mexico with him," she said. "He was lecturing there. He'd gone to the bar to pick up some drinks, and I was standing out of the light.

And just the way the light hit him in the bar, and illuminated the planes of his face—he was so beautiful. And it was the old face. I mean, the one from years ago. I don't know why. It was just the way the lighting hit him. Beautiful bones."

I sat there in the dark, looking at Tim, thinking of Rosemary's words. Beautiful bones, I thought. Even in death, beautiful bones.

allen ginsberg:

for the fucking

and the dying

*f*or many of us, Allen Ginsberg's death came with such suddenness, it proved to be a mind-stopping jolt—like learning that a guiding star had just been torn from the night sky and hurled to some unreachable void. Perhaps those final days seemed like a rush to darkness for the seventy-year-old poet as well—though it was no secret that Ginsberg had been suffering from liver disease during the last few years. Always a man of candor, he admitted to the pains and losses of aging in poems and interviews over the last decade. For that matter, it seems that Allen Ginsberg had been contemplating the meanings that come from death's inevitability for nearly the entirety of his writing career. In 1959, in "Kaddish," his narrative poem about his mother's decline and death, Ginsberg said to his mother's memory: "Death let you out, Death had the Mercy, you're done with your century. . . ." And in 1992, he wrote of himself:

> *Sleepless I stay up &*
> > *think about my Death*
> *—certainly it's nearer. . . .*
> *If I don't get some rest I'll die faster*

As it turned out, it was only seven days before his death that Ginsberg learned his illness had turned worse—that it was now inoperable liver cancer. Hearing the news, Ginsberg returned to his apartment in New York's East

Village and proceeded to do what he had always done: He sat down and wrote a body of poems about the experiences of his life—in this case, about the imminence of his end. One of these poems—a long, hilarious, and heart-affecting piece called "Death & Fame"—ran in *The New Yorker* the week following his demise. In the poem, Ginsberg envisioned hundreds of friends, admirers, and lovers gathered at his "big funeral," and he hoped that among the eulogies, someone would testify: "He gave great head."

In those last few days, Ginsberg also talked to friends—his lifetime compeer, author William Burroughs; his lover of several decades, Peter Orlovsky; poet Gregory Corso; among others—and he wrote a letter to President Bill Clinton (to be sent via George Stephanopoulus, another Ginsberg friend), demanding, in jest, some sort of medal of recognition. At one point during his last week, he listened to a recording of "C. C. Rider" by 1920s blues vocalist Ma Rainey—the first voice Ginsberg said he remembered hearing as a child. He sang along with it, according to one report, then vomited and said: "Gee, I've never done that before." By Friday, he had slipped into a coma. Surrounded by a few close friends, Ginsberg died early Saturday morning, April 5, 1997.

A quiet closing to a mighty life. Not since the 1977 death of Elvis Presley and the 1980 murder of John Lennon has a certain segment of popular culture had to come to terms with the realization of such an epochal ending. Allen Ginsberg not only made history—by writing poems that jarred America's consciousness and by ensuring that the 1950s Beat movement would be remembered as a considerable literary force—but he also lived through and embodied some of the most remarkable cultural mutations of the last half-century. As much as Presley, as much as the Beatles, Bob Dylan, or the Sex Pistols, Allen Ginsberg helped set loose something wonderful, risky, and unyielding in the psyche and dreams of our times. Perhaps only Martin Luther King, Jr.'s brave and costly quest had a more genuinely liberating impact upon the realities of modern history, upon the freeing up of people and voices that much of established society wanted kept on the margins. Just as Dylan would later change what popular songs could say and do, Ginsberg changed what poetry might accomplish: how it could speak, what it would articulate, and who it would speak to and for. Ginsberg's words—his performances of his words and how he carried their meanings into his life and actions—gave poetry a political and cultural relevance it had not known since the Transcendentalists of the 1840s (Ralph Waldo Emerson and Henry Thoreau, among them) or since the shocking publication of Walt Whitman's 1855 classic, *Leaves of Grass*. Indeed, in Ginsberg's hands, poetry proved to be something a great deal more than a vocation or the province of refined wordsmiths and critics. Ginsberg transformed his gift for language into a mission—"trying to save and heal the spirit of America," as he wrote in the introduction to fellow poet Anne Waldman's *The Beat Book*. In the process, he not only influenced subsequent writers like Bob Dylan, John Lennon, Lou Reed, Patti Smith, and Jim Carroll, but Ginsberg's effect could also be found in Norman Mailer's *Advertisements for Myself*, in the writings and deeds of Czechoslovakian president Vaclav Havel, in the lives and exploits of 1960s insurrectionists like Timothy Leary, Tom Hayden, and Abbie Hoffman. One can also hear Ginsberg's effect on such current artists as Sonic Youth, Beck, U2, and several of our finer hip-hop poets.

Ginsberg was also, of course, simply a man—at turns generous and competitive, self-aware yet self-aggrandizing, old in his wisdom, juvenile in his tastes and affections, and relentlessly promiscuous though deeply faithful. More than anything, though, Ginsberg was someone who once summoned the bravery to speak hidden truths and about unspeakable things, and some people took consolation and courage from his example. That example—that insistence that he would not simply *shut up*, and that one should not accept delimited values or experiences—is perhaps Ginsberg's greatest gift to us. Today, there are many other artists who have carried on in that tradition— from Dylan, Smith, and Reed to Coolio, Beck, and numerous others—and so in that way, Ginsberg's death does not rob us of unfulfilled possibilities, as happened in the horrid deaths of Kurt Cobain, Tupac Shakur, and the Notorious B.I.G. That's because Ginsberg's entire life was a process of opening himself (and us) up to possibilities. Still, Ginsberg's loss remains enormous. There is no question: We have seen a giant pass from our times. It is only fitting to look back on what he did for us and for our land.

ALLEN GINSBERG was born in 1926, the son of politically radical Russian-born Jewish parents who were also aesthetic progressives (Allen's older brother, Eugene, was named after labor organizer Eugene V. Debs; Ginsberg also recalled that the music of Ma Rainey, Beethoven, and Bessie Smith filled the family's home in Paterson, New Jersey). Allen's father, Louis, was a published and respected poet. Louis and Allen would have many arguments over the years regarding poetry's language and structure, though in his father's last few years, the two men often shared stages together, exchanging poems and genuine respect and affection.

But it was Ginsberg's mother, Naomi, who proved in many ways to have a more profound and haunting effect on her son's life, mentality, and writing. By 1919, she had already experienced an episode of schizophrenia.

She recovered for a while and returned to her life as an activist and mother, but when Allen was three, Naomi experienced an intense relapse. She committed herself to a sanitarium, and for much of the rest of her life, she moved from one psychiatric institution to another. During the times she returned home, she would often declaim frightened fantasies about a pact between her husband, Hitler, Mussolini, and President Roosevelt, all involved in an attempt to seize control of her mind. Also, she took to walking around the house nude. Allen—who was kept home from school to take care of his mother on her bad days—would sit reading, trying to ignore Naomi's nakedness and ravings.

Growing up witnessing painful madness and missing the attendance of a loving mother had an enormous impact on Ginsberg. For one thing, it taught him a certain way of preparing for and dealing with hard realities. In Jerry Aronson's film *The Life and Times of Allen Ginsberg,* Ginsberg stated: "I've had almost like this screen built, so I could hear people dying and get on with it. . . . I could survive without tears in a sense, so that the tears would come out in a poem later, rather than in an immediate breakup of my world. My world already was broken up long ago."

Naomi's problems—and her absence from the home—also brought out a neediness and uncertainty that stayed with Ginsberg in many ways his entire life, and that affected how, as a child, he made connections between erotic incentives and emotional fulfillment. Ginsberg often related how, during the lonely nights when his mother was away, he would cuddle up against his father, Louis, Allen rubbing his erect penis against the back of his father's leg while Louis tried to sleep and ignore the activity. Finally, Naomi's mental problems also made Ginsberg both more afraid of his own possible madness and also more sympathetic about the troubles of others—and it left him with a fear of shadows and ghosts and as a person prone to seeing visions. By the time he was eleven, Allen was already writing about these matters in his early journals, and he discovered something that gave him a certain comfort and strength: Words, unlike so much that surrounded him as a child, were something he could have dominion over, something that could express his thoughts, something he could take pride in.

But for all the loneliness and fearfulness that characterized his childhood family life, Ginsberg also inherited his parents' clear intelligence and much of their political compassion. By the time he was sixteen, he was also coming to the realization that he was attracted to men sexually; in particular, he worshipped a high school classmate who left Paterson for Columbia University in New York City. In 1943, Ginsberg received a scholarship from the Young Men's Hebrew Association of Paterson, and he promptly headed for Columbia.

Ginsberg arrived at the university planning to study to become a labor lawyer, but two differing intellectual milieus changed that course. The first was Columbia's formidable English studies department, which then included Pulitzer prize-winning poet Mark Van Doren and Lionel Trilling; Ginsberg became enamored of these men as mentors and soon changed his major to literature. Over the course of the next year or so, Ginsberg also met another group of men—some of them fellow Columbia students, closer to his own age—and it was this fraternity that turned his life around and that would function as a sort of secondary family for much of the rest of his life. Among these men were William S. Burroughs, Lucien Carr, and a football star with literary aspirations named Jack Kerouac. The bond that developed between them transformed not only their own destinies, but also those of future generations. In particular, Ginsberg and Kerouac seemed to share a special connection. Both were haunted by their childhoods—Kerouac had an older brother, Gerard, who had died young, and Kerouac's mother used to hold Jack as a child and tell him, *"You* should have died, not Gerard." But the most important thing these men shared was a sense that, in the mid-1940s, there were great secrets lurking at America's heart, that there were still rich and daring ways of exploring the nation's arts and soul—and that there was a great adventure and transcendence to be found by doing so. Indeed, America *was* about to change dramatically, but the significance of that change wouldn't be fully understood or reckoned with for another twenty years. In 1945, the nation emerged victorious from the horrors of World War II and would enter a long era of new prosperity and opportunity; the new American life, many politicians and critics declared, was now the world standard of the *good* life. But all this came at unexpected psychic costs: The knowledge of the possibility of nuclear devastation changed all the possibilities of the future. Plus, for all the nation's victories abroad, there were still many battles unwaged at home—including the delicate question of minority rights. Ginsberg, Kerouac, Burroughs, and the rest of their crowd were beginning to be drawn to some decidedly different ideals and hopes. They heard the music of bebop alto saxophonist Charlie Parker and pianist Thelonious Monk, they tasted the visions of marijuana and Benzedrine, they prowled the reality of Times Square. A new world—a world still largely underground—was being born, and they had keen eyes and a keen need for it.

The friendship that developed among them was complex, sometimes tense, sometimes loving, but what held it together for so long was a shared desire to inquire—in matters of the mind, of aesthetics, and of the senses. In time, this group became the nexus for a literary and artistic community known as the Beat Generation—the first countercultural movement that would have a major impact on America's popular culture. But all this was still years away, for before Beat became a movement or style, it was simply the way these men chose to live their lives, to examine their own experiences and their view of things both internal—like the spirit—and external, like the night and music and sex. Sometimes these men related to each other sexually (Ginsberg later told stories of he and Kerouac jacking each other off after a night of drinking; years later, Ginsberg also had an affair with Burroughs). Mainly, the group would spend nights consuming alcohol and mild drugs (though Burroughs soon turned to heroin), staying up until dawn, talking about the poetry, visions, and madness of Blake, Whitman, Rimbaud, Dostoyevsky, Céline, Genet, and Baudelaire; about how language might learn from jazz; about what was truly holy and what was truly allowed in one's life. Along the way, the group derived a certain ethos and aesthetic that they called the New Vision: It relied on stretching one's experiences, finding truths in distorted realities, in sexual pursuits, finding spirituality in the lower depths of life, and most important in making a commitment to an extemporized manner of living, writing, talking, and risking. Somewhere during this time another friend of the group, a bisexual junkie prostitute, Herbert Huncke, referred to them as "beat," meaning *beat down, wasted*. Kerouac saw in the word another possibility: *beatific*. In time, the term went both ways: Beat came to stand for the idea that to discover one's true self and the self's liberation, you first had to descend into some of the most secret, used up, and bereft parts of your heart, soul, body, and consciousness. Consequently, Beat became hard-boiled and loving at the same time, erotic and spiritual. Later, Ginsberg would write Kerouac: "I can't believe that between us . . . we have the nucleus of a totally new historically important generation."

But the budding movement also could lead to costly excesses. In August 1944, Lucien Carr stabbed to death a friend of his, David Kammerer, after a night of drinking and arguing. Carr was a beautiful young man, and Kammerer, who had been obsessed with him, had relentlessly pursued and pushed Carr. After the stabbing, Carr went directly to Burroughs' apartment and admitted what he had done. Burroughs advised Carr to turn himself in to the police. Carr then went and awakened Kerouac and repeated his confession. Kerouac helped Carr get rid of the knife. In a few days, Carr turned himself in to the police, and Burroughs and Kerouac were arrested as accessories after the fact. Ginsberg as well was castigated for being part of such a dangerous crowd. In truth, though, Ginsberg felt that in some way the group's "libertine" attitudes had helped make the tragedy possible—and that understanding made Allen much more careful, in years to come, about any excesses that might lead to violence. Eventually, Carr was sent to prison (he served two years), and for a short time, the old crowd dispersed. A few months later, Ginsberg was found in his Columbia dormitory in bed with

Kerouac; for that infraction—and for having written offensive graffiti in the dust of a windowsill—Allen was suspended from the university for a year. Things went up and down for the group for a few years. People drifted in and out of New York, and then in 1949, Ginsberg got involved in the life of Herbert Huncke, drug addict and thief. That association resulted later in Ginsberg's arrest and his being committed to the Columbia Psychiatric Institute—a turn of events that would in time have great effect on his poetry writing.

Prior to that, though, in late 1946, a new figure showed up in the Beat circle—and his involvement with the crowd had a seismic impact on both Ginsberg and Kerouac. Neal Cassady was a sharp-featured, handsome, fast-talking, brilliant natural prodigy. He didn't so much write (in fact, he wrote very little), but he did live his life as if it were a novel. He drove across America relentlessly, loved to masturbate frequently each day, and also fucked a good number of the beautiful women (and some of the men) he met along the way. He became involved with Carolyn Robinson, and the couple eventually settled down in Denver for a time. Kerouac was taken by Cassady's intense, fast-clip language—like a spoken version of bebop—and with Cassady's willingness to go as far as he could with the sensual experience and sensory rush of life. Ginsberg was impressed by the same traits, but he was also entranced by Cassady's beauty. One night, following a party, Ginsberg and Cassady found themselves sharing the same bed. Ginsberg was scared of his own desires, he later admitted, but Cassady put his arm around Allen and pulled him close, in a gentle motion. It was the first time in his life that Ginsberg felt truly loved, and it was also his first passionate sexual experience.

Ginsberg fell in love with Cassady, and his pursuit of that love—and the intensity of how wrong it all went—proved a key episode in leading to his development as an artist. Cassady, in the meantime, started to discourage the attraction. Ginsberg was undaunted and followed Neal to Colorado. Though he and Neal still had occasional sex, he knew it meant little to Cassady. He returned to New York, devastated, and later went on to fall into trouble with Huncke.

*B*y THE EARLY 1950s, Ginsberg had gone through severe pain over his loss of Cassady and had also gone through psychiatric treatment. He didn't know what he wanted to do with his life, and was working in an advertising agency in Manhattan. One day, discussing this matter, Ginsberg's therapist asked him what he *really* wanted to do with his life. Ginsberg replied: Quit his job and write poetry. The therapist said: "Well, why don't you?" Then, in 1954, the old crowd started to reassemble in the San Francisco Bay Area. The Cassadys had moved to San Jose, and Kerouac settled in for a visit. In San Francisco itself, a poetry movement was beginning to burgeon, inspired in part by the success of local poets Kenneth Rexroth and Lawrence Ferlinghetti—the latter who had just opened the nation's first all-paperback bookstore, City Lights, and who had started to publish local poets. Allen headed for San Jose. He was thinking about poetry, but he was also still thinking about Neal. One afternoon, Carolyn walked into her home to see Neal and Allen in bed, Ginsberg sucking Cassady's penis. She ordered Ginsberg from their home, drove him to San Francisco, gave him $20, and left him there.

It was the best thing that ever happened to Ginsberg. He soon fell in with the poet crowd in San Francisco's North Beach area, and he met a man that he would stay involved with for decades, Peter Orlovsky. All the hopes and visions that had formed years before in New York were starting to come to fruition for some of the old crowd—especially for Kerouac, who had finished two novels, and for Ginsberg, who was ready for something to break loose in his poetry. One afternoon in August 1955, Ginsberg sat down at a typewriter in his tiny apartment and attempted to write a poem for his own ear, but also a poem that would catch the free-flowing style that he had seen Kerouac hit upon in his own recent writing. Ginsberg wrote the whole day, thinking about many things: his lost loves, his found loves, the discarded people of America, the discarded promises of America, the fear that was just behind him, the fear that lay ahead for all.

Two months later, in October, Ginsberg—with help from Kenneth Rexroth—organized a poetry reading, to be given at a cooperative art gallery, the Six Gallery, to showcase a handful of the scene's poets. Six poets read that evening—including Gary Snyder, Michael McClure, and Philip Lamantia—to a crowd of maybe fifty to one hundred people, with Kerouac sitting on the gallery's floor, drinking and tapping out rhythms on a wine jug, urging "Go! Go!" to the cadences of the poets' words. Ginsberg was the last to read, and as he began "Howl"—the poem he had written in one sitting two months earlier—the crowd was transfixed from the first lines:

> I saw the best minds of my generation destroyed by madness, starving
> hysterical naked
> dragging themselves through the negro streets at dawn looking for an
> angry fix,
> angelheaded hipsters burning for the ancient heavenly connection to the
> starry dynamo in the machinery of the night.

Ginsberg went on to describe the fearsome evil that he saw America becoming—"Moloch whose blood is running money! Moloch whose fingers are ten armies!"—and when he finished, the crowd exploded in applause. "All of a sudden," Rexroth later said, "Ginsberg read this thing that he had been keeping to himself all this while, and it just blew things up completely. Things would never be quite the same again."

"Howl" was one of the most incandescent events in post-World War II literary history or popular culture, and its arrival later ensured the Beats their place on the map of modern time. Also, because "Howl" was a poem that had such force when read aloud by Ginsberg, it marked a return of poetry to the art of vocalization. But most important, "Howl" was the first major American work of the era that spoke for the outcasts, for the mad and the lost, and about what would soon happen in the nation's soul. In the context of those times, in the midst of a frightened new patriotism that was being defined by fears of socialism and communism and a desperate need to believe in the assurance of the family structure and traditional mores, "Howl" battered at the heart of the American ideal of civilization. It was a heroic work, on many levels. America was hardly prepared to admit that homosexuality might be anything other than a form of madness; for a poet—for anybody—to declare pride or pleasure to be queer was to run a monumental risk. To talk about—to cherish those who "let themselves be fucked in the ass by saintly motorcyclists, and screamed with joy"—was no small matter. In effect, it meant aligning oneself with madness, with inexpressible values. To find grace and worthy companionship and celebration in the company of junkies, prostitutes, and black jazz revolutionaries only pushed the ante more. Something opened up in America's culture and in its future the day that Ginsberg gave utterance to these thoughts with "Howl." The following year, working from quite different quarters, Elvis Presley in his own way helped push the gates open as well. "We liked Elvis," poet Gregory Corso later said of the night he and Kerouac watched Presley on "The Ed Sullivan Show." We identified with the sexual wiggling of his body."

"Howl" and Presley. Nothing would ever be the same after that. America's libido, America's likelihood, had been ripped wide open.

THIS ISN'T TO SAY that "Howl" was immediately or widely read or praised. Quite the contrary: The reaction of some people was that "Howl" should *never* be widely read. In 1957, Lawrence Ferlinghetti (who published the first editions of "Howl") and a City Lights Bookstore employee were arrested for knowingly selling obscenity and put on trial. The prosecutor was a Bay Area district attorney, Ralph McIntosh, bent on closing down porn shops and prohibiting the sale of magazines with nudity. The ACLU, Grove Press, *Evergreen Review,* and poet Kenneth Patchen, among others, offered their support to Ferlinghetti, Ginsberg, and "Howl." Among those testifying on behalf of the poem's serious merits were Rexroth and author Walter Van Tilburg Clark. In his final argument, McIntosh asked Judge Clayton W. Horn: "Your Honor, how far are we going to license the use of filthy, vulgar, obscene, and disgusting language? How far can we go?"

Horn ruled that "Howl" was not lacking in social relevance and therefore could not be ruled obscene. In delivering his decision, Horn also offered what may be the single best succinct review that "Howl" received: "The first part of 'Howl' presents a picture of a nightmare world, the second part is an indictment of those elements in modern society destructive of the best qualities of human nature; such elements are predominantly identified as materialism, conformity, and mechanization leading toward war. The third part presents a picture of an individual who is a specific representation of what the author conceives as a general condition. . . . 'Footnote to "Howl" ' seems to be a declamation that everything in the world is holy, including parts of the body by name. It ends in a plea for holy living."

Though Ginsberg was vindicated and suddenly famous, he was determined not to arrive as the Beats' sole writer-hero. Over the years, he helped Jack Kerouac in his long quest to publish *On the Road*—a book about Kerouac's adventures with Neal Cassady (who was called Dean Moriarty in the published text)—which had been turned down by numerous major publishers since 1951. The book was finally published by Viking, in 1957, as a result of Ginsberg's efforts, and went on to both good commercial and critical reception, and is now recognized as a milestone novel in modern literature. Ginsberg also championed the cause of William S. Burroughs—a much tougher sell, because Burroughs was a drug user who wrote radical prose (such as *Junky*), and because he had killed his wife in a shooting accident in Mexico in 1951. Ginsberg understood that his old friend felt a tremendous guilt and Ginsberg also believed Burroughs might never redeem himself unless he could concentrate his soul and mind on his writing. Ginsberg later helped Burroughs assemble the final draft of *Naked Lunch* and worked tirelessly until the book was published in the United States. (Which resulted in *Naked Lunch*'s own obscenity trial and another ruling that the book could not be held to be called obscene.)

The Beats were—at least for a brief time—a force in American arts and letters, but there remained many who were incensed by their words and beliefs. In 1960, FBI Director J. Edgar Hoover stood before the Republican

Convention and declared that "Beatniks" were among America's major menaces. In addition, Norman Podhoretz—an old classmate of Ginsberg's at Columbia and by 1958 the editor of *Commentary* magazine—asserted that the Beats were an affront to the nation's central ideals. By the end of the decade, the Beats had been sidelined, declared a silly aberration by moralist critics on both the right and left. But despite all the resistance and disdain, Ginsberg continued to grow and thrive as a poet—and to remain undaunted. At the conclusion of one of his most defiant works, "America," he wrote: "America I'm putting my queer shoulder to the wheel."

Then, in 1959, after a night of taking Benzedrine, listening to the rhythm & blues of Ray Charles, and walking New York's streets, Ginsberg sat down to write "Kaddish." It was his tribute to his mother, Naomi, whose mental pain had grown so horrifying that, in the late 1950s, Ginsberg signed papers allowing doctors to perform a lobotomy on her. Ginsberg never truly got over the guilt of that decision, and he would never enjoy the union and relationship with his mother that he'd longed for his entire life. In 1956, Allen sent Naomi a published copy of "Howl." Naomi died shortly thereafter. A few days after learning of her death, he received her last letter: "I received your poetry," she wrote. "I'd like to send it to Louis for criticism. . . . As for myself, I still have the wire on my head. The doctors know about it. They are cutting the flesh and bone. . . . I do wish you were back east so I could see you. . . . I wish I were out of here and home at the same time you were young; then I would be young."

In "Kaddish," Ginsberg remembered everything about his mother— tender things, scary things, the amazing perceptions that sometimes blazed through her madness—and with enormous love and compassion, he finally found her place in his heart (and recognized his in hers) and let her go to her death. It was most likely Ginsberg's finest moment as a poet, and it is impossible to hear any of his readings of that work and not be moved by how profoundly "Kaddish" measures just how much that people, families, and nations can lose as their hopes and fates unwind.

For the next three decades, Allen Ginsberg would remain an important artist and active force. Indeed, more than any other figure from the Beat era, he made the transition from the styles and concerns of the 1950s to those of the decades that followed. Jack Kerouac died in 1968, after living an embittered and alcoholic final few years at his mother's home in New Jersey (his mother hated Ginsberg and came between the two men's friendship whenever possible). Neal Cassady went on to become a popular figure in San Francisco's mid- and late-1960s Haight-Ashbury scene; he became the driver for Ken Kesey and the Merry Pranksters' legendary cross-country bus trek, and he also became a driver and companion to the Grateful Dead. But perhaps Cassady pushed his spirited self a bit hard. One day in 1968, after leaving a wedding in a small Mexican town, Cassady collapsed while walking alongside some railroad tracks. He died the next day, just short of his forty-second birthday.

Ginsberg not only survived, but kept pace with the spirit and needs of the times, with the permutations of youth culture; also, he kept faith with the humane and impassioned ideals that had made "Howl" so powerful in the first place. In 1964, he became friendly with the Beatles and Bob Dylan. Ginsberg's and the Beats' work already had meaning and effect for these artists. Dylan recalled that after reading Kerouac and Ginsberg, he realized that there were people like himself somewhere in the land—and indeed, when the singer made his startling transition to the electric, free-association style of music found in *Highway 61 Revisited* and *Blonde on Blonde* (and again later with *Blood on the Tracks*), Dylan was taking the language, cadences, and imagery of the Beats and applying it to a new form. The impact of this melding on 1960s music—like the effect of Ginsberg's "Howl" on the 1950s—was colossal. (In fact, one of the early proposed cover photos for *Blonde on Blonde* showed Dylan standing with Ginsberg and poet-playwright Michael McClure.) In addition, John Lennon had read the Beats in his years as an art student in Liverpool and changed his spelling of the group's name, Beetles, to Beatles, in part as tribute to the spirit of that inspired artistry. Dylan and the Beatles changed not just a specific art form—that is, rock & roll—but also transformed the perceptions and aspirations of youth and popular culture at large. But without the earlier work of Ginsberg and Kerouac, it is possible that these 1960s artists might not have hit upon quite the same path of creativity—or at least might not have been able to work in the same atmosphere of permission and invention.

Ginsberg also became increasingly involved and influential in the political concerns of the 1960s and thereafter—though he did so in a way that made plain his own conviction in a politics of nonviolence and joy, rather than of destruction and hatred. In some ways, in fact, the 1960s culture of the hippies and radicals amounted to the realization of what the Beats began to envision and prophesy in the late 1940s (interestingly, "hippie" was a term first coined by the Beats, meaning "half-hip," and the phrase "flower power" was first verbalized by Allen Ginsberg). In the summer of 1968, Ginsberg helped organize Chicago's Festival of Life (along with the Yippies, Abbie Hoffman, Jerry Rubin, Tom Hayden, and members of the Black Panthers), in protest to the Democratic Party's promotion of the Vietnam War and as a rebuke to Hubert Humphrey's capitulation to the party's hawkish elements. But when the events of those few days turned suddenly brutal and bloody— with policemen clubbing young people, old people, anything in their path, and demonstrators tossing bricks at, and taunting, the already enraged cops—Ginsberg turned sickened and horrified. On one occasion, as police raged through a crowd bashing protesters, a policeman came upon Ginsberg, seated in the lotus position, softly chanting. The policeman raised his club to crash it down on Ginsberg's head. The poet looked up at the officer, smiled, and said: "Go in peace, brother." The cop lowered his club. "Fucking hippie," he declared, then moved on. In 1970, when several of the key Chicago activists—known as the Chicago Seven, including Tom Hayden, Abbie Hoffman, Jerry Rubin, and Bobby Seale—were brought up on federal charges of conspiring to riot, defense attorney William Kunstler called Ginsberg to the witness stand. At Kunstler's request, Ginsberg recited parts of "Howl." When he reached the poem's climax—"Moloch the vast stone of war! Moloch the stunned governments!"—he turned in his chair and pointed at the judge who had been so hostile to the defendants, Julius Hoffman (ironically, the same judge who years earlier declared *Naked Lunch* not obscene).

In addition, Ginsberg became a key player in the 1960s argument over psychedelic drugs, such as LSD. He had, of course, taken several drugs in his days with the Beats, and already had some psychedelic experience. But in the early 1960s, Ginsberg heard about a Harvard professor, Dr. Timothy Leary, who was conducting authorized research at the university, and was sharing the drug psilocybin with his project's volunteers. Ginsberg contacted Leary and arranged for a visit to experiment with the drug. Leary and Ginsberg struck up an immediate friendship and had considerable influence on each other's thinking. Ginsberg believed strongly (in contrast to most of Leary's cohorts) that it was a good idea to move psychedelics from the domain of a small elitist group and share them with artists, writers, poets, and musicians—and as a result, hallucinogenic drugs and their visions made inroads into the arts, and later helped transmute the aesthetics and ideals of late twentieth century music, literature, painting, film and video. Ginsberg also convinced Leary that psychedelics could be a way of enabling people to examine and transform their own minds, and that it would be the young who would prove most receptive to such possibilities.

Ginsberg later forswore psychedelics, but his friendship with Leary continued off and on for more than thirty-five years. During the last few weeks of Leary's life, in the spring of 1996, the two men spoke often. Leary knew that Ginsberg had planned a trip to Los Angeles, in July, to attend an art show featuring Burroughs' work. Though Leary's health was daily diminishing as his body succumbed to prostate cancer, he hoped to live until Ginsberg's visit and made the date the last mark on his calendar. Leary would die without seeing his friend one last time. But in the hours preceding his death, Ginsberg's Buddhist teacher, Gelek Rinpoche, managed to reach Leary, uttering a final prayer for his passage into death.

GINSBERG STAYED active in politics, arts, and popular and renegade culture for the remainder of his life. In the mid-1970s, he toured with Bob Dylan and his Rolling Thunder Revue, singing and reading poetry. A few years later, he released his own sets of songs and collaborations with such artists as Dylan and the Clash—and it proved as exhilarating as his best poetry had a generation earlier. Throughout the 1970s, 1980s, and 1990s, Ginsberg befriended and encouraged many other poets, punk, and rap artists.

Of course, as time went along, the role of the renegade has grown more acceptable, more assimilated to some degree in mainstream culture. What was shocking in the 1950s was less shocking in the 1970s; what was disruptive in the 1970s was commonplace and profitable by the 1990s. Ginsberg understood this inevitable progression of how radical works and impulses are first resisted, then gradually diffused, and in his own way he had fun with that fact and mocked it a bit. He took to wearing suits and ties as he grew older— in part, it gave his pronouncements more authority, more respectability for some critics, but the other thing was: Ginsberg looked *great* in suits and ties. But for all his venerability and respectability, there was a part of Ginsberg that would never be domesticated much less silenced. In 1979, the National Arts Club awarded him a gold medal for literary merit. At the awards dinner, according to Burroughs' biographer Ted Morgan, Ginsberg bemusedly read a poem called "Cocksucker Blues," to the genuine consternation of his audience. He also remained a relentless supporter of author Burroughs. In the late 1970s, after his own 1973 induction into the rarefied ranks of the American Academy and Institute of Arts and Letters, Ginsberg began a campaign to have Burroughs inducted as well. Ginsberg met with a great deal of refusal— Burroughs was *not* a writer that several of the other fine authors wanted in their company—but the poet persisted. It took six years, but Ginsberg won Burroughs' entry into the institute, in 1983. Also, Ginsberg remained a fierce advocate of free speech. In recent years, he even took up a defense of NAMBLA—an organization dedicated to lowering the age of consensual sex between men and boys. Ginsberg's involvement with the outfit outraged many of his long-standing admirers, but Ginsberg would not be cowed. "It's a free speech issue," he said repeatedly, pointing out that to stifle the ability to discuss such a matter in a free society was perhaps its own kind of outrage. Also, apparently, he stayed as sexually active as he could. In "Death & Fame" in *The New Yorker,* Ginsberg boasted about the many men he had seduced throughout his lifetime, and he detailed what it was he liked about his sexual intimacy with these partners. But for all that Ginsberg did or attempted to do, to this day "Howl" still cannot be played over America's airwaves during the day, due to the efforts of Jesse Helms and the Federal Communications Commission.

AND SO HE IS gone. In the days since Ginsberg's death I have seen and heard countless tributes to his grace, power, skills, and generosity—but I have also seen and heard just as many disparaging remarks: what a shoddy writer he was; what a failure the legacy of his Beat Generation and the 1960s generation turned out to be; what an old lecher the guy was. Perhaps all this vitriol isn't such a bad thing. Maybe it's another tribute of sorts: Allen Ginsberg never lost his ability to rub certain nerves the wrong way when it came to matters about propriety, aesthetics, morality, and politics.

But I also know this: Allen Ginsberg *won*—against the formidable odds of his own madness-scarred childhood, against all his soul-crippling doubts of self, against all those stern, bristling, authoritarian forces that looked at this man and saw only a bearded radical faggot that they could not abide. Ginsberg won in a very simple yet irrefutable way: He raised his voice. He looked at the horror that was crawling out from the American subconscious of the 1950s—the same horror that would later allow the nation to sacrifice so many of its children in the 1960s to a vile and pointless military action— and he called that demon by its name: "Moloch!" He looked at the crazed and the despairing, those people hurting for a fix, for a fuck of love, for the obliteration of intoxicated visions, and he saw in them something to adore and kiss, something to be treasured and learned from. And Ginsberg looked at himself, and for all his hard-earned pride, lust, vanity, and audacity, he would not shut up even in the face of his own vulnerability. In one of his best poems, 1992's "After Lalon," Ginsberg wrote:

> *I had my chance and lost it,*
> *many chances & didn't*
>   *take them seriously enuf.*

Oh yes I was impressed, almost
   went mad with fear
I'd lose the immortal chance,
   One lost it.
Allen Ginsberg warns you
   dont follow my path
   to extinction

In an evening, long ago—an evening caught between two Americas, the America of the past and the America that was to follow, an afternoon where America was truly found, realized, and celebrated—a nervous, scared young homosexual Jewish man stood before a crowd, and he raised his voice. He said things that nobody had ever said before in quite the same terms to a crowd in this nation—filthy things, beautiful things—and when he was finished, he had become a braver man. He had, in fact, in that hour, transformed himself into the most eventful American poet of the century. When Lawrence Ferlinghetti—who was in the room that night and who brought "Howl" to the world—heard that his old friend was dying, he wrote the following: "A great poet is dying/But his voice won't die/His voice is on the land."

Ginsberg's voice will never leave us. Its truths and purposes will echo across our future as a clarion call of courage for the misfits, the fucked up, the fucking, and the dying. And we—all of us, whether we understand it or not—are better for it.

Good-bye, Allen Ginsberg. Thank you for illuminating our history—thank you for the gentle yet fierce slow-burning flame you ignited on that afternoon so long ago. Thank you for what you brought to our times, our nerve, and our lives.

Go in peace, brother. Your graceful, heavy, loving heart has earned it.

kurt cobain's

road from nowhere:

walking

the streets

of aberdeen

*I*t is early on a rainy Saturday night in Aberdeen, Washington, and nearly everybody in this small tavern off the main drag is already drunk. Aaron Burckhard is considerably less drunk than most—he's only on his third beer—though, in truth, he has fair reason to be drinking. It has been just a little over a week since the body of his old friend, Nirvana's Kurt Cobain, was found in Seattle, the victim of a suicide, and Burckhard is still reeling from the news.

Burckhard, who was Nirvana's first drummer, had not seen or spoken with Cobain in some time. Though the two of them had their share of disagreements—which came to a head when Kurt fired Aaron for being too hungover to show up for a rehearsal—Burckhard still had friendly feelings for his old bandmate, and for what he had seen Nirvana accomplish. "Kurt was the coolest person I knew, and still is," says Burckhard, staring straight into his beer glass. "I loved him."

Burckhard, who is now thirty, begins to tell how he heard the news of Cobain's death on the radio—how he began shaking so violently that he had to lay his five-month-old daughter down on the sofa next to him so that he would not drop her in his grief—when a guy in a jeans jacket comes reeling through the tavern door and stumbles across the room, toppling tables on his way. He staggers to the bar, orders a beer, and then sees Burckhard and edges our way. He begins telling Aaron about a mutual friend who recently began shooting heroin again, until Aaron, visibly pissed, cuts him off. "That's just *fucked*, man. That guy just got clean. Why would he start using again?"

The other man shrugs and sips from his beer. "You're right, that shit's bad. But then, hell, I'm strung out on it right now myself." The guy in the jeans jacket grips his beer and lurches to the other side of the tavern.

Burckhard shakes his head, then turns back to me. "Man, that is *so* fucked. There's been an epidemic of that shit around here lately."

He sits quietly for a few moments, until his thoughts return to Cobain. "You know," he says, "I never really understood why Kurt was so *down* on this town. I mean, everybody talks about what a depressed place it is to live, but I don't see what there is to *hate* about it. Except, maybe . . ." Burckhard pauses and glances around him—at the people staring with hard and angry looks into their beer glasses; at the woman who is talking in a loud and obnoxious voice and slapping ridiculously hard at the hands of her stymied boyfriend, who is mumbling incoherently to himself; at the junkie in the jeans jacket, who is talking quietly to a man in a cowboy hat over in the corner; at the bartender who is glowering at everybody who orders a drink. "Yeah," says Burckhard, "I don't know what there is to hate about this place. Except for, you know, the people who live here."

And then Aaron laughs and returns to his beer.

ABERDEEN IS A hard-hit lumber town, located midway up the Washington coast, and nestled at the deepest cut-point of a seaport called Gray's Harbor. The town is about three miles long and a mile wide, and it is flanked on its northern and eastern borders by a ridge of steep hills, where the richer folks—who have run the local sawmills—have traditionally lived, in lovely and ornate Victorian-style homes. Below those hills is a poorer part of town called "the flats," and it is here that Kurt Cobain grew up. His mother, Wendy O'Conner, still lives there, in a small, greenish house, with a tidy yard and drawn curtains. It is one of the better homes in the area. Many of the nearby houses are marred by faded paint and worn roofs, and the necessary neglect that is the result of indigence.

Stand in the heart of the flats—or in Aberdeen's nearby downtown area, where empty industrial structures stand like haunted shells—and the frequent fog that pours off the rich folks' hill can feel like something that might bog you down here forever. Move to the other end of town, where the main drag, Wishkah Boulevard, looks out toward the Chehalis River and Pacific Ocean, and you feel like you're staring at the end of the world—that if you kept walking or driving, you would simply drop off the last edge of America.

This is the town that Kurt Cobain could never repudiate enough. It was here that he was scorned and beat upon by both those who should have loved him, and by those who hardly knew him but recognized his otherness and wanted to batter him for it. It was here, no doubt, where Cobain first learned how to hate life.

YOU WOULDN'T know it now, but Aberdeen was once a hopping place, supported by thriving lumber companies and dozens of the West Coast's most popular whorehouses. But the prostitution was killed off decades ago, and the lumber boom started coming to a halt a few years back, as the economy fell and the land was depleted. These days, there is widespread concern that the northwestern logging industry can never fully recover, and as a result, that a town like Aberdeen is marked for a slow and ugly death.

To make matters worse, in the days following Kurt Cobain's suicide, Aberdeen became an object of national scrutiny and fast judgment. In large part, that's because Cobain had been outspoken in his dislike for his hometown—describing it essentially as a place of redneck biases and low intelligence. That disdain has influenced the media's recent depiction of the city as a dismal, hopeless place, in which those with an artistic sensibility—particularly the young—are regarded with disapproval or outright hostility. It's as if the town were being held in part accountable for Cobain's ruin—which is not an entirely unfathomable consideration. When you are confronted with the tragic loss of a suicide, you can't help sorting backward through the dead person's life, looking for those crucial episodes of dissolution that would lead him to such an awful finish. Look far enough in Kurt Cobain's life, and you inevitably end up back in Aberdeen—the homeland that he hated and fled. Maybe there was something damaging and ineradicable that he bore from this place, and that he could not shirk or annihilate until those last few moments, in that apartment above the garage of his Seattle home.

Certainly, there are some grim truths about the town that cannot be ignored. In April 1991, Aberdeen's local newspaper, the *Daily World*, ran an article chronicling the relatively high death rate in the region—especially in its suicide index. It is difficult to measure these things with any definitive accuracy, but Aberdeen's suicide rate would appear to average out to something like 27 people per 100,000—which is roughly twice the national suicide rate (though bear in mind that the town's population itself is something less than 17,000). Mix this news with high rates of alcohol and drug usage, as well as a high incidence of unemployment and domestic violence and a median household income of about $23,000, and you emerge with the not-so-surprising conclusion that Aberdeen can be an unusually depressing town to call your home.

One doesn't have to look much beyond Cobain's own family's history to see evidence of this truth. In July 1979, one of Cobain's great-uncles, Burle Cobain, committed suicide by way of a self-inflicted gunshot to his abdomen. Five years later, Burle's brother Kenneth also committed suicide. There are rumors that other relatives and ancestors may have committed suicide in previous years—making for the legend that Courtney Love has referred to as the Cobain curse.

It is hard to know what impact, if any, the suicides of his great-uncles and others may have had on Cobain—whether he mourned these deaths, or in fact saw in them the glimmer of a dark promise: a surefire prescription for release, come the day that any further days of pain or torment would be unbearable. In any case, there was something clearly kindred in the manner in which the young artist chose to end his life, as well as something horribly ironic. For all the ways that Kurt Cobain reviled what he saw as this area's redneck mentality, in the end he chose for himself the same sad style of death that others in his family and hometown had opted for: a gun to his head, obliterating his very identity, ruining the part of him that made him knowable to the outside world. As one friend, who had known him when he lived here, put it: "I hate to say it, but it was the perfect Aberdonian death."

THERE IS LITTLE doubt that Kurt Cobain did not have an easy time of life in this town. He was born in nearby Hoquiam in 1967, the first child of Wendy Cobain and her auto mechanic husband, Donald. The family moved to Aberdeen when Kurt was six months old, and by all accounts, he was a happy and bright child—an outgoing, friendly boy who, by the second grade, was already regarded as possessing a natural artistic talent. Then, in 1975, when Kurt was eight, Don and Wendy divorced, and the bitter separation and its aftermath were devastating to the child. Instead of the sense of family and security that he had known previously, Kurt now knew division, acrimony, and aloneness, and apparently some light in him began to shut off. He grew progressively introverted, and to others, he seemed full of shame about what had become of his family. In the years that followed, Cobain was passed back and forth between his mother's home in Aberdeen and his father's in nearby Montesano. It was in this period that the young Kurt became sullen and resentful, and when his moods became too much for either parent, he was sent along to the homes of other relatives in the region—some of whom also found him a hard kid to reach. (There are rumors that Cobain may have suffered physical abuse and exposure to drug abuse during this time, but nobody in the family was available to confirm or deny these reports.)

In short, the young Kurt Cobain was a misfit—it was the role handed to him, and he had the intelligence to know what to do with it. Like many youthful misfits, he found a bracing refuge in the world of rock & roll. In part, the music probably offered him a sense of connection that was missing elsewhere in his life—the reaffirming thrill of participating in something that might speak for or embrace him. But rock & roll also offered him something more: a chance for transcendence or personal victory that nothing else in his life or community could offer. Like many kids before him, and many to come, Kurt Cobain sat in his room and learned to play powerful chords and dirty leads on cheap guitars, and felt the amazing uplift and purpose that came from such activity; he held music closer to him than his family or home, and for a time, it probably came as close to saving him as anything could. In the process, he found a new identity as a nascent punk in a town where, to this day, punks are still regarded as either eccentrics or trash.

The punishments that he suffered for his metamorphosis were many, and are now legend. There are numerous stories that make the rounds in Aberdeen about how Cobain got beat up for simply looking and walking differently than other kids, or got his face smashed for befriending a high school student who was openly gay, or got used as a punching bag by jocks who loathed him for what they saw as his otherness. Hearing accounts like these, you have to marvel at Cobain's courage, and even at his heroism. It's a wonder he made it as far as he did without wanting to kill the world for what it had inflicted on him for so many and long seasons.

THOUGH COBAIN IS now Aberdeen's most famous native son, and though many people recall him from his time here, there's something about his presence here that proves shadowy and inscrutable to the locals. Lamont Shillinger, who heads Aberdeen High School's English department, saw as much of Cobain as most people outside his family. For nearly a year, during the time he played music with the teacher's sons, Eric and Steve, Kurt slept on Shillinger's front-room sofa, and in those moments when Cobain's stomach erupted in the burning pain that tormented him off and on for years, Shillinger would head out to the local Safeway and retrieve some Pepto-Bismol or antacids to try to relieve the pain. But for all the time he spent with the family, Kurt remains a mystery to them. "I would not claim," says Lamont Shillinger, "that I knew him well either. I don't think my sons knew him well. In fact, even to this day, I suspect there are very few people that really knew Kurt well—even the people around him or the people he was near to. I think the closest he ever came to expressing what was inside was in his artwork, in his poetry, and in his music. But as far as personal back and forth, I seriously doubt that he was ever that close to anybody."

Another Aberdeen High teacher, Bob Hunter, affirms Shillinger's view. Hunter, who is part of the school's Art department, began teaching Cobain during his freshman year, and worked with him for three years, until 1985, when Cobain quit school. Though the two of them had a good relationship, Hunter can recall few revealing remarks from his student. "I really believe in the idea of aura," says Hunter, "and around Kurt there was an aura of: 'Back off—get out of my face,' that type of thing. But at the same time I was intrigued by what I saw Kurt doing. I wanted to know where he was getting the ideas he was coming up with for his drawings. You could detect the anger—it was evident even then."

Hunter lost track of Cobain for a while after Kurt dropped out of school, until he had Cobain's younger sister, Kim, in one of his classes. From time to time, Kim would bring tapes of her brother's work to the teacher and keep him informed of his former student's progress. Says Hunter: "Even if Kim had never come back and said that Kurt was really making it as a musician, I would have kept wondering about him. I've taught thousands of students now, but he would have been up there in my thoughts as one of the preeminent people that I hold in high esteem as artists. Later, after I heard the contents of his suicide note, I was surprised at the part where he said he didn't have the passion anymore. From what I had seen, I would have thought the ideas would always be there for him. I mean, he could have just gone back to being a visual artist and he would have remained brilliant."

IN TIME, Cobain got out of Aberdeen alive—at least for a while. In 1987, he formed the first version of the band that would eventually become Nirvana, with fellow Aberdonians Krist Novoselic on bass and Aaron Burckhard on drums. A few months later, Cobain and Novoselic moved to Olympia, and eventually Burckhard was left behind. Nirvana played around Olympia, Tacoma, and Seattle, and recorded the band's first album, *Bleach*, for Sub Pop in 1988. The group plowed through a couple more drummers before settling on Dave Grohl and recording its groundbreaking major label debut, *Nevermind*, for Geffen in 1991. With *Nevermind*, Cobain forced the pop world to accommodate the long-resisted punk aesthetic at both its harshest and smartest, and did so at a time when many pundits had declared that rock & roll was effectively finished as either a mainstream cultural or commercial force. It was a remarkable achievement for a band from the hinterlands of Aberdeen, and the whole migration—from disrepute on Washington's coast to worldwide fame and pop apotheosis—had been pulled off in an amazingly short period of time. Back at home, many of the kids and fans who had shared Cobain's perspective were heartened by his band's accomplishment.

But when Cobain turned up the victim of his own hand in Seattle on April 8, 1994, those same kids' pride and hope took a hard blow. "After the suicide," says Brandon Baker, a fifteen-year-old freshman at Aberdeen High, "all these jocks were coming up to us and saying stuff like: 'Your buddy's dead. What are you going to do *now*?' Or: 'Hey, I've got Nirvana tickets for sale; they're half off.' "

Baker is standing with a few of his friends in an alcove across the street from the high school, where some of the misfit students occasionally gather to seek refuge from their more conventional colleagues. The group is discussing what it's like to be seen as grunge kids in the reality of post–Nirvana Aberdeen. Baker continues: "I realize that Kurt Cobain had a few more problems than we might, but him doing this, it kind of cheated us in a way. We figured if someone like him could make it out of a place like this . . . it was like he might have paved the way for the rest of us. But now, we don't want people to think that we're using his path as our guideline. It's like you're almost scared to do *anything* now. People around here view us as freaks. They see us walking together in a mall and they think we're a bunch of hoodlums, just looking for trouble. They'll throw us off the premises just for being together. I don't know—it's sad how adults will classify you sometimes."

The talk turns to the subject of the summer's upcoming Lollapalooza tour. In the last few days, Aberdeen's *Daily World*'s headlines have been given to coverage of a major local wrangle: the Lollapalooza tour organizers have proposed using nearby Hoquiam as the site for their Washington show, in part as a tribute to all that Cobain and Nirvana did for alternative music and for the region. Many residents in the area, though, are incensed over the idea.

They are worried about the undesirable elements and possible drug traffic that might be attracted by such an event, and even though the stopover would bring a big boon to the badly ailing local economy, there is considerable resistance to letting such a show happen in this area.

"You would think," says Jesse Eby, a seventeen-year-old junior, "that they would let us have this one thing—that the city council would realize we might appreciate or respect them more if they let something like this show come here. It would be such a good thing for the kids around here."

"Yeah," says Rebecca Sartwell, a freshman with lovely streaks of magenta throughout her blond hair. "I mean, can't we just have *one* cool thing to do, just one day out of the year? I mean, besides go to Denny's and drink coffee?"

Everybody falls silent for a few moments, until Sartwell speaks up again. "I don't know how to explain this," she says, "but all I want is *out*. Maybe I'll move to Olympia or Portland or someplace, but when I get there I don't intend to say, 'Hey, I'm from *Aberdeen*,' because then everybody's going to assume I'm an alcoholic, manic-depressive hick. It's bad enough having to live here. I don't want to take the reputation of the place with me when I leave."

Everybody nods in agreement with Rebecca's words.

NOT FAR FROM the place where Kurt Cobain's mother lives is a short span known as the North Aberdeen Bridge. It reaches across the narrow Wishkah River, leading into the part of town called North Aberdeen. In the winter of 1985, during a time when he had no place to live, Kurt Cobain used to spend his afternoons at the local library and his nights sleeping on a friend's sofa, or on the porch deck of his mother's house. Sometimes, though, he slept under the North Aberdeen Bridge, in a space up the sloping bank of the bridge's south side, just feet below the overhead pavement. I climbed under that bridge during my last rainy afternoon in Aberdeen, to take a look around. There's a hollow cleared into the brownish-red soil, close to the concrete buttresses, and it is here that Cobain slept. Indeed, there are more signs of him in this one place than in any other spot in Aberdeen, outside of his mother's home. The columns and cylinders are covered by his spray-painted graffiti, bearing the names of bands like Black Flag and the Meat Puppets, and slogans like FUCK and STOP VANDALISM.

I sit down in the hollow of the dirt for a few minutes and stare out at the Wishkah River. From here, its water doesn't appear to flow. Rather, it just seems to stand there, stagnant and green. I hear a clatter behind me and I turn around. A rat? The wind? I sit there and I think what it would be like to hear that sound in the dead of a cold night, with only a small fire at best to illuminate the dark. I try to imagine what it was like to be a boy in this town and turn to this bridge as your haven. Who knows: Maybe the nights Cobain spent here were fun, drunken nights, or at least times of safety, when he was out of the reach of the town that had already harmed him many times. But in the end I have to lapse into my own prejudices: It seems horrible that this was the kindest sanctuary a boy could find on a winter night in his own hometown.

I get up to leave and my eye catches something scrawled on a rail overhead. It is hard to make out, but the writing looks much like the examples of Cobain's penmanship that I have seen recently in books and news articles. The scrawl reads: WELL, I MUST BE OFF. IT'S TIME FOR THE FOOL TO GET OUT.

Maybe it is indeed Cobain's writing, or maybe it's the script of another local kid who came to realize the same thing Cobain realized: To save yourself from a dark fate, you have to remove yourself from dark places. Sometimes, though, you might not remove yourself soon enough, and when that happens, the darkness leaves with you. It visits you not just in your worst moments, but also in your best ones, dimming the light that those occasions have to offer. It visits you and it tells you that *this* is where you are from—that no matter how far you run or how hard you reach for release, the darkness, sooner or later, will claim you.

You can learn a lot of bad things when you are made to sleep under a bridge in your homeland, and some of those things can stay with you until the day you die.

Oh I do believe
If you don't like things, you leave
For some place you never been before
LOU REED
"I FOUND A REASON"

acknowledgments

I have been writing about popular music since 1974—that is, for twenty-three years. Not really that long of a period, but long enough to have racked up a few debts that I would like to acknowledge.

The first folks to thank, of course, are those artists who were willing to spend time with me, enduring yet another interview in their careers of being grilled and analyzed. I'm even grateful for the time spent with Keith Jarrett—in part, because it gave me the opportunity to hear him play solo on several occasions (always a rewarding experience), plus it gave me a good excuse to sound off a bit about an artist's hubris. I've talked to ruder people than Jarrett (well, maybe), but none whose haughtiness and discourtesy were offset with such a contradictory depth and beauty in their music making. Today, his jazz recordings remain worth seeking and hearing (though when I want to hear interpretations of Bach's *Goldberg Variations*, I'll take Rosalyn Tureck or Tatiana Nikolaeva any day), and if hubris is what it takes to fuel Jarrett's genius, then long may he play. Certainly he's not the first artist to be guilty of that particular sin.

In my youth—my teenage and early adult years in Portland, Oregon—I shared many long nights, experiences, and conversations either rooted in or abetted by music with the following people: Annette Cantrell, Don White-head, Shannon Riske, Jon Shoemaker, the late Tim Bowen, Michael Sugg, Linda Eklund, Debby Levin, and Byron Laursen. I also owe a great obligation to Shen Shellenberger (Hey, Grandma!), for recommending me as a music writer for my first critical assignment. Maybe I would have fallen on this path anyway (I suspect so), but Shen gave me the nudge—a nudge that became one of the best realizations of my life. Also during my Portland years, I worked with and learned much from Mark Christiansen, Andrea Wilson, Michael Adelsheim, James Kiehle, Tom Modica, Bennett Stein, and Stephanie Oliver.

The bulk of my journalism (or at least the bulk that has been seen outside of the Los Angeles area) has been written for *Rolling Stone*. I have never worked with better editors or collaborators, and among the people who helped me grow as a writer in the last generation at that magazine are: Ben Fong-Torres, Dave Marsh, Jann Wenner, Peter Herbst, Harriet Fier, Barbara Downey, Sarah Lazin, Chris Hodenfield, James Henke, Susan Murcko, Paul Nelson, Bob Wallace, Peggy Bellas, Delores Zeibarth, Cameron Crowe, Fred Schruers, Sid Holt, Bob Love, Tobias Perse, Barbara O'Dair, and Sheila Rogers (the latter person also helped enormously in many other ways and was of great inspiration during the time I worked on *Shot in the Heart*). I'd also like to thank Sue Sawyer, Holly Vincent, and Elaine Schock. None of them worked at *Rolling Stone*, but they were all fine people to share music and time with during the late 1970s and early 1980s, as I was adjusting to life in Los Angeles.

In the early 1980s, I wrote on a few occasions for the *Los Angeles Times*, under the good guidance of Robert Hilburn and Richard Cromlin, and with the advice and friendship of Kristine McKenna. In 1981, I became the music editor at *L.A. Weekly*, and in 1982, I became the pop music critic at the *Los Angeles Herald Examiner*. At the former, my thanks go to Jay Levin, Phil Tracy, the late Craig Lee, Greg Burk, Michael Ventura, Bill Bentley, Steve Erickson, and Ewa Wojciak (who will get thanked many times, for many things, though she can never be thanked enough). At the *Herald*, my first nod goes to Managing Editor Mary Ann Dolan, who gave me the job, and my second goes to Stan Cloud, who encouraged me to broaden my subject matter. I had my best music discussions at the *Herald* with Paul Wilner, Miles Beller, Mitchell Fink, David Chute, Rip Rense, Elvis Mitchell, Robert Lloyd, and (again) Chris Hodenfield, and I enjoyed a special comradeship with Jane Birnbaum. Also, during the mid- and late-1980s, I learned a lot about life and music from Erin Gilmore, Jennifer Lobianco, Steve and Mary Pond, and David Gans, and all those friendships remain of immense value to me.

In the early and mid-1990s, I had some of the best critical (and personal) discussions of my life with six extraordinary writers, Karen Essex, Helen Knode, Virginia Campbell, Emily White, Alice Joanou, and Stacy Horn. And during the time this book was being prepared, I shared afternoons and evenings of discussions with Tobias Perse, Bob Love, Rodd McLeod, Robert Greenwald, Edna Gunderson, Bruce Kalberg, Howard ("Two Eyes Open!") Rudnick, Suzi Gardner, Cilista Eberle, Heidi Snellman, Stanley and Suzanne Sobolewski, Dalia Chandoha, Nicholes Hill, my editor Betsy Lerner and my agent Richard Pine. Whether they know it or not, they all helped shape various thoughts that appear in this book's revisions. I'd also like to thank Holly Tooker and Scott Murphy for helping me find and organize some of my earlier writings that I'd thought were lost forever, and I'd like to thank Isaiah Wilner and David Imperiale for helping me obtain permissions for the lyrics herein. My biggest thanks, though, goes to Ewa Wojciak, who helped me assemble and reassemble old articles and who put up with the moods and obsessions of a surly writer and bad boyfriend.

Reading through these writings made me consider the question of influence—that is, who are the people whose writing in some way affected my thoughts or styles the most? I think I can honestly name only four, though I doubt if their influence in my own text would be apparent to anybody other than myself. They are: hardboiled crime novelists James M. Cain and Ross Macdonald, and music critics and historians Greil Marcus and Paul Nelson (none of whom, of course, should be cited as influences for any of my own lapses, twisted logic or prolix). I should probably also throw in my three all-time favorite fiction writers, Edgar Allan Poe, Fyodor Dostoyevsky and Philip K. Dick, if only because I've never read any other writers with a better understanding of the madnesses of mind and heart—an understanding that helped make such madnesses comprehensible, even bearable.

But my greatest debt is to the people whose music I have loved—the people whose music enriched my life and gave me pleasure and sometimes courage. Some of those are the artists I have written about in this volume. But there are many others that I have listened to and written about over the years who didn't find their way into these pages, and I'd like to acknowledge just a few of them: ABC, King Sunny Ade, Terry Allen, Laurie Anderson, the Animals, Aphex Twin, Archers of Loaf, Louis Armstrong, Artful Dodger, Babes in Toyland, Mildred Bailey, Count Basie, Bobby Bland, Carla Bley, Blue Cheer, Connie Boswell, David Bowie, Clifford Brown, James Brown, Tim Buckley, T-Bone Burnett, the Buzzcocks, the Byrds, Jackie Cain and Roy Kral, John Cale, Betty Carter, Sarah Carter, Rosanne Cash, Alex Chilton, June Christy, Gene Clarke, Jimmy Cliff, Patsy Cline, George Clinton, the Coasters, Leonard Cohen, Ornette Coleman, Bootsy Collins, John Coltrane, Chris Connor, Crazy Horse, Robert Cray, Cream, Julie Cruise, Ice Cube, Jack DeJohnette, Sandy Denny, the Dixie Cups, Donovan, the Dwarves, Duke Ellington, Booker Ervin, Bill Evans, the Everly Brothers, Tal Farlow, the Fastbacks, the Five Blind Boys of Alabama, John Fogerty, Helen Forrest, David Forman, Aretha Franklin, Jeffrey Fredericks and the Clamtones, the Bobby Fuller Four, Lefty Frizzell, Judy Garland, Jimmie Dale Gilmore, Goldie, Grandmaster Flash, Guided by Voices, Woody Guthrie, Charlie Haden, Merle Haggard, Butch Hancock, Herbie Hancock, Jimi Hendrix, Z.Z. Hill, Hole, Billie Holiday, Buddy Holly, John Lee Hooker, Howlin' Wolf, the Human League, Helen Humes, Alberta Hunter, Ian Hunter, Michael Hurley, Hüsker Dü, Wanda Jackson, the Jacobites, the Jam, Tommy James and the Shondells, Jane's Addiction, Jefferson Airplane, David Johansen and the New

454

acknowledgments

York Dolls, Linton Kwesi Johnson, Robert Johnson, George Jones, King Pleasure, the Kinks, Fela Kuti, Led Zeppelin, Peggy Lee, Little Feat, Lotte Lenya, Abbey Lincoln, Nils Lofgren, Jackie Lomax, Julie London, the Louvin Brothers, L7, Loretta Lynn, Carmen McRae, Maria McKee, Delbert McClinton, the Mamas and the Papas, Thomas Mapfumo, Bob Marley, Dean Martin, Johnny Mathis, MC5, John Mellencamp, Mabel Mercer, Helen Merrill, Charles Mingus, Joni Mitchell, Moby, Moby Grape, the Modern Lovers, Bill Monroe, Van Morrison, Ella Mae Morse, Mudhoney, Elliott Murphy, David Murray, Nas, Oliver Nelson, Ricky Nelson, Tracy Nelson, Willie Nelson, Nine Inch Nails, the Notorious B.I.G., Helen O'Connell, Carla Olsen and the Textones, Yoko Ono, Orb, Orbital, Charlie Parker, Van Dyke Parks, Gram Parsons, Dolly Parton, Pavement, Art Pepper, Carl Perkins, Oscar Pettiford, Tom Petty, the Platters, the Pogues, Iggy Pop and the Stooges, Bud Powell, the Pretenders, the Raincoats, the Ramones, the Raspberries, Marty Robbins, Smokey Robinson, Roxy Music, Savage Rose, Jimmy Scott, Judee Sill, Percy Sledge, Son House, Sonic Youth, Jeri Southern, Dusty Springfield, Kay Starr, Gary Stewart, Sly Stone, Sun Ra, the Supremes, Talking Heads, Art Tatum, Cecil Taylor, the Temptations, Thelonious Monster, Richard and Linda Thompson, Johnny Thunders, Ernest Tubb, Sarah Vaughan, Loudon Wainwright III, Tom Waits, Dinah Washington, Muddy Waters, Kitty Wells, the Who, Lucinda Williams, Tony Williams, Victoria Williams, Jackie Wilson, Womack and Womack, O. V. Wright, Tammy Wynette, the Yardbirds, Neil Young, Young Marble Giants, Frank Zappa, and Warren Zevon.

I could go on and on—I'm sure you get the idea—but two more names merit special mention: my family's patron saint, Johnny Cash, and Sam Cooke, whose 1963 *Night Beat* is one of the best soul and blues albums of all time. It's a record made for the 3 A.M. of your soul, and it's the record that gave me the idea and inspiration for this book title.

To anybody I missed or forgot, my apologies.

By the way, I'm not done yet with Bob Dylan and Frank Sinatra. There will be more to say about both, some place down the night road.

publication

credits

"Elvis Presley's Leap for Freedom" appeared originally in part in the *Los Angeles Herald Examiner* in 1984 and 1985, and parts are new.

"Beatles Then, Beatles Now" appeared originally in the *Los Angeles Herald Examiner* in 1984, in *Rolling Stone* in 1990, and much of it is previously unpublished.

"Subterranean: Bob Dylan's Passages" is assembled from pieces written for *Musical Notes* in 1976, for the *Los Angeles Herald Examiner* in the mid-1980s, from *Rolling Stone* in 1986 and 1991, and much of it is previously unpublished.

"The Rolling Stones' Journey into Fear" is assembled from pieces that appeared in the *L.A. Weekly* in 1981, in the *Los Angeles Herald Examiner* in 1983 and 1984, and in *Rolling Stone* in 1987.

"The Legacy of Jim Morrison and the Doors" appeared in *Rolling Stone,* April 4, 1991.

"Lou Reed: Darkness and Love" is assembled from writings that appeared in *Rolling Stone* in 1979 and 1980, and from numerous *Los Angeles Herald Examiner* articles in the mid-1980s, plus some of it is newly written.

"Brothers: The Allman Brothers Band" appeared in *Rolling Stone* in shorter form, October 18, 1990.

"Keith Jarrett's Keys to the Cosmos" ran in *Rolling Stone,* January 25, 1979.

"Life and Death in the U.K.: The Sex Pistols, Public Image Ltd., Joy Division, New Order, and the Jesus and Mary Chain" is from pieces published in *Rolling Stone* in 1980 and 1981, in the *Los Angeles Herald Examiner* in the mid-1980s, and parts of it are newly written.

"The Clash: Punk Beginnings, Punk Endings" is assembled from pieces that ran in *Rolling Stone* in 1979, and in the *L.A. Weekly* and *Musician* in 1982.

"Punk: Twenty Years After" is assembled from various mid-1980s *Los Angeles Herald Examiner* articles, a 1982 *Musician* story, and from new writing as well.

"Van Halen: The Endless Party" appeared in *Rolling Stone*, September 4, 1980.

"Bruce Springsteen's America" is from pieces that appeared in *Rolling Stone* in 1990 and 1995, in the *Los Angeles Herald Examiner* in the mid-1980s, and some of it is new as well.

"The Problem of Michael Jackson" is from various articles written for the *Los Angeles Herald Examiner* in the mid-1980s, for *Rolling Stone* in 1988, plus parts of it are new.

"Upstarts: Over and Under the Wall, and into the Territory's Center (Thoughts on Politics, Sex, Violence, Dancing, Rap, Hooligans, and Censors)" is from numerous mid-1980s *Los Angeles Herald Examiner* articles, from pieces published in *Rolling Stone* in 1987 and 1990, and parts are newly written.

"Clash of the Titans: Heavy Metal Enters the 1990s" appeared in shorter form in *Rolling Stone*, July 11, 1991.

"Randy Newman: Songs of the Promised Land" appeared in the *Los Angeles Herald Examiner*, January 23, 1983.

"Al Green: Sensuality in the Service of the Lord" is from the *Los Angeles Herald Examiner*, August 26, 1983.

"Jerry Lee Lewis: The Killer" appeared in the *Los Angeles Herald Examiner*, February 21, 1984.

"Miles Davis: The Lion in Winter" appeared in the *Los Angeles Herald Examiner*, August 26, 1983.

"Feargal Sharkey: Songs of Hearts and Thieves" is part of a longer article that appeared in the *Los Angeles Herald Examiner*, April 18, 1986.

"Marianne Faithfull: Trouble in Mind" is from a longer piece that ran in the *Los Angeles Herald Examiner*, April 25, 1986.

"Stan Ridgway's Wrong People" is from a longer piece that ran in the *Los Angeles Herald Examiner*, July 11, 1986.

"Sinéad O'Connor's Songs of Experience" appeared in shorter form in *Rolling Stone*, June 14, 1990.

"David Baerwald's Songs of Secrets and Sins" ran at a slightly shorter length in *Rolling Stone*, September 6, 1990.

"Frank Sinatra: Singing in the Dark" is from *Rolling Stone*, January 24, 1991.

"Dark Shadows: Hank Williams, Nick Drake, Phil Ochs" is from articles that ran in the *Los Angeles Herald Examiner* in 1983 and 1986, and parts are new.

"Tim Hardin: Lost Along the Way" originally appeared in *New West*, February 1981.

"Dennis Wilson: The Lone Surfer" ran in the *Los Angeles Herald Examiner* on January 2, 1984.

"Marvin Gaye: Troubled Soul" is from 1984 and 1985 articles in the *Los Angeles Herald Examiner*, and parts of it are new.

"No Simple Highway: The Story of Jerry Garcia and the Grateful Dead" is from articles that appeared in *Rolling Stone* in 1987 and 1995, and much of it has never been published before.

"Tupac Shakur: Easy Target" appeared in *Rolling Stone*, October 31, 1996.

"Ella Fitzgerald: Grace Over Pain" appeared in *Rolling Stone*, August 8, 1996.

"Timothy Leary: The Death of the Most Dangerous Man" appeared in slightly shorter form in *Rolling Stone*, July 11, 1996.

"Kurt Cobain's Road from Nowhere: Walking the Streets of Aberdeen" appeared at a somewhat shorter length in *Rolling Stone*, June 2, 1994.

"Allen Ginsberg: For the Fucking and the Dying" appeared in a slightly shorter version in *Rolling Stone*, May 29, 1997.

permissions